New Learning S

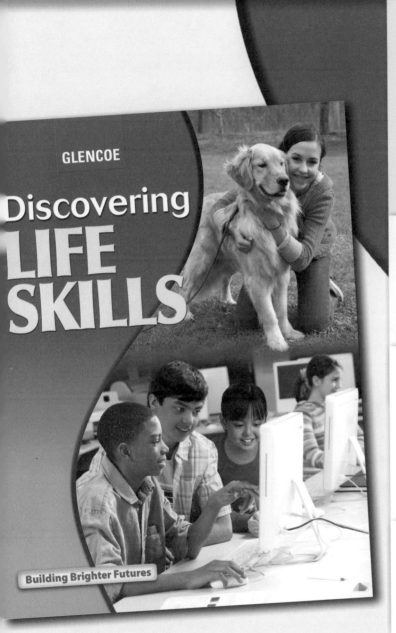

GLENCOE

Discovering
LIFE
SKILLS

Building Brighter Futures

New Rigor with Academic Integration

- National Academic Standards
- Academic Vocabulary
- Reading Guides
- Writing Tips and Activities
- Math and Science You Can Use Activities
- Standardized Test Practice

Relevance with Real-World Connections

- Financial Literacy
- Discover International Topics
- Discovering Careers

Build Relationships with Project-Based Learning

- Interpersonal and Collaborative Skills Support FCCLA
- Hands-On Labs
- How To Activities
- Life Skills Projects

Technology Resources

- Lesson Planner Plus™ CD
- *ExamView® Assessment Suite* CD
- *PresentationPlus!*™ PowerPoint Presentations CD

Online Learning Center

- Online Student Edition
- Graphic Organizers
- Evaluation Rubrics
- English Glossary/Spanish Glosario
- Additional Activities and Resources

 Log on to the *Discovering Life Skills* Online Learning Center at **glencoe.com**

Discovering
LIFE SKILLS

Glencoe

Printed in the United States of America.

Send all inquiries to:
Glencoe/McGraw-Hill
21600 Oxnard Street, Suite 500
Woodland Hills, CA 91367

ISBN: 978-0-07-888468-9   (Student Edition)
MHID: 0-07-888468-3   (Student Edition)
ISBN: 978-0-07-888469-6   (Teacher Annotated Edition)
MHID: 0-07-888469-1   (Teacher Annotated Edition)

1 2 3 4 5 6 7 8 9   079   11 10 09 08

Teacher Manual Table of Contents

Connect Students to the Real World

Unit Opener: Create a Relevant Framework

Discovering Life Skills contains 10 units that are organized into 23 chapters. Every unit begins with a list of the chapters in the unit, a description of the thematic project students will be asked to complete at the end of the unit, a journal exercise, and a photo to explore.

Thematic Project Preview At the end of the unit, students will be assigned a thematic project based on the unit's contents. This preview allows them to think about how the information they are learning in the unit will apply to the project.

UNIT
2
Take Charge of Your Life

Chapter 4
Communicate With Others

Chapter 5
Citizenship and Leadership

Chapter 6
Goals and Decision Making

Unit Preview

This unit is about being in control of your own life. In this unit, you will learn about:

- Using verbal and nonverbal skills to communicate efficiently.
- Recognizing the causes of conflict.
- The duties of being a responsible citizen.
- The importance of leadership skills.
- Why setting goals is essential.
- Making smart decisions.

Explore the Photo
Achieving a goal can be a very fulfilling experience. *What are some of the things you should think about when setting goals?*

72   Unit 2   Take Charge of Your Life

Life Skills Project Preview

Your Point of View
When you are done studying this unit, you will complete a project in which you will:

✓ Discover an issue in your community that you care about.

✓ Interview someone who holds an elected office.

✓ Share your opinion on the issue with your class.

The prewriting activity below will help you get started.

My Journal

Prewriting Activity
Research Newspaper Stories

Find and read stories in your local newspaper about local issues that you care about. Cut out these stories for your journal, and write a summary of the article beside each one.

- What are the facts and issues discussed in each article?

- What are the different opinions about each issue? There are often two sides to an issue. If this is the case, summarize the opinion of each side.

73

Explore the Photo By examining the photo at the beginning of the unit, students will begin to think about the topics covered in the unit. It visually guides the student with an engaging question to help interpret the meaning.

My Journal Students are asked to keep a personal journal. The suggested topics will help prepare your students for the project at the end of the unit.

# of Discovering Life Skills

Life Skills Project: Putting It All Together

This end-of-unit project provides an opportunity for students to apply what they learned in the unit to both academic and everyday situations. As students complete each project, they will make decisions, conduct research, connect to their communities, and develop a report. My Journal refers students back to their journal entries to see if their thoughts have changed.

Project Assignment This summarizes the steps students need to take to develop and complete the thematic project.

Project Checklist This at-a-glance checklist allows students to effectively manage their time and resources when planning and implementing their project.

Step-by-Step Instructions There are five steps in each thematic project. Each step explains how to successfully complete a phase of the project.

Self Evaluation Have students go to the Discovering Life Skills Online Learning Center through glencoe.com to download a rubric that they can use to evaluate their final projects.

Academic Skills The Standards tell students how the information and skills they will learn in the project apply to English Language Arts.

Chapter Opener: Promote Conceptual Understanding

Each chapter begins with a photo to explore, a preview of the main ideas in each chapter, and a writing activity that will get students thinking about what they will learn in the chapter.

Main Ideas Read this list to the class to preview the content your students will learn.

Explore the Photo By examining the photo at the beginning of the chapter, students will begin to think about the main topics covered in the chapter.

Chapter 6

Goals and Decision Making

Section 6.1

Goals

Main Idea You can accomplish your goals when you are focused and positive. Learn to set short-term and long-term goals to achieve success.

Section 6.2

Decisions

Main Idea You make decisions every day. Decisions can be big or small. Making responsible decisions now can have a positive impact on your future.

Explore the Photo
Throughout your life, you will set goals and make decisions along the way. *What goals did you set for yourself this week?*

Writing Activity

Autobiography

Who Are You? An autobiography is a story about who you are. Writing about yourself may seem like an easy thing to do. However, it can be challenging to write about yourself because there is so much to tell. To write your autobiography, focus your ideas into three areas: your personality, your hobbies and activities, and your job goals.

Writing Tips To write a strong autobiography, follow these steps:

1. Write an introduction that states your name and what you will write about.
2. Write three short paragraphs with details about each of the three areas.
3. Write a conclusion that ties the paragraphs together.

114   Unit 2   Take Charge of Your Life

115

Writing Activity The writing activity presents real-life writing assignments relevant to the chapter's main topics.

Chapter Review: Assess Student Comprehension

The chapter closer helps your students review what they learned in the chapter and apply their learning to both their academic and real-world knowledge.

Chapter Summary Students will find the most important concepts and ideas from the chapter.

Vocabulary Review Students can make sure they understand the content and academic vocabulary, and the chapter's key concepts.

Real-World Skills and Applications Help students apply what they have learned in the chapter to situations that they might encounter every day.

Active Learning and Net Connection Give students the opportunity to test what they learned in the chapter, and to conduct online research to expand their knowledge.

Critical Thinking If students can respond to the Critical Thinking tasks, then you will know that they understood the most important ideas in the chapter.

Academic Skills Students can use their English language arts, science, social studies, and mathematics skills to solve chapter-related problems.

Standardized Test Practice Use this section to see how students might do on standardized test questions.

Reading Guide: Enable Successful Learning

To strengthen students' reading success, each section of *Discovering Life Skills* begins with a Reading Guide to preview section content.

Graphic Organizer A visual tool will help students organize and remember new content. You and your students can download printable graphic organizers from the *Discovering Life Skills* Online Learning Center through glencoe.com.

Before You Read Students can make a quick comprehension self-check prior to beginning each section.

Read to Learn By reading the Key Concepts and Main Ideas, students will know what they can expect to learn in each section.

Vocabulary Students can check the Content and Academic Vocabulary lists for words they are not familiar with, and look them up in the glossary in the back of the book before and during reading.

Academic Standards Students can see which academic standards are integrated into the content of each section.

Section **7.1** Plan Your Career

Before You Read   Reading Guide

Check for Understanding If you have questions as you are reading, that means you are checking your understanding of the material. To get the most out of the text, try to answer those questions.

Read to Learn

Key Concepts
- ✓ **Describe** how to create a career plan.
- ✓ **Recognize** the importance of researching careers.

Main Idea
It is important to research and plan your career path.

Content Vocabulary
- ○ aptitude
- ○ portfolio
- ○ job shadowing
- ○ apprentice
- ○ networking
- ○ mentor

Academic Vocabulary
- ■ modify
- ■ reveal

Graphic Organizer
As you read, identify six factors to review when researching a career. Use a graphic organizer like the one shown to help you organize your information.

Job Research
1.
2.
3.
4.
5.
6.

Graphic Organizer Go to this book's Online Learning Center at glencoe.com to print this graphic organizer.

Academic Standards

English Language Arts
NCTE 5 Use different writing process elements to communicate effectively.

Science
NSES G Students should develop understanding of science as a human endeavor.

Social Studies
NCSS V G Individuals, Groups, and Instructions Analyze the extent to which groups and institutions meet individual needs and promote the common good in contemporary and historical settings.

NCTE *National Council of Teachers of English*
NCTM *National Council of Teachers of Mathematics*
NSES *National Science Education Standards*
NCSS *National Council for the Social Studies*

"**W**hat do you want to be when you grow up?" You have probably heard that question before. Have you really thought about your answer? Perhaps you are interested in becoming a gourmet chef or an astronaut. You have many choices. Whether you choose to be an attorney or a musician, it is not too soon to start thinking about the career you might want to have one day.

138   Unit 3   Make Your Career Plan

Section Review: Check Comprehension

After You Read features at the end of each section allow you to test the student's understanding of the content before the end of the chapter. The Key Concept questions are directly related to the main topics of each section.

The Internet

You can also learn about careers through the Internet. You can go online to get ideas, find out what jobs are available, and research specific job requirements. When you are ready, you can submit your résumé online. You will learn more about résumés in the next chapter.

Ask your parents, librarian, or teacher to help you:

- Search *The Occupational Outlook Handbook* or the *Dictionary of Occupational Titles.*
- Find job postings and job descriptions.
- Post a résumé.
- Locate professional organizations.
- Register with online employment agencies.

Find a Mentor Think about a person you admire and respect who has talents and skills you would like to learn. *How can a mentor help you with your career goals?*

Section 7.1 After You Read

Review What You Have Learned
1. **List** the factors you should consider when you think about career options.
2. **Explain** why it is important to network.

Practice Academic Skills

English Language Arts
3. Should a person ever choose a career that does not match his or her interests? Why or why not? Explain your answer in a short speech.

NCTE 5 Use different writing process elements to communicate effectively.

Social Studies
4. Locate professional organizations for a career that you are considering. What kinds of benefits do they offer for their members? Write a summary of how the organization could help you prepare for your career.

NCSS V G Analyze the extent to which groups and institutions meet individual needs and promote the common good in contemporary and historical settings.

Check Your Answers Check your answers at this book's Online Learning Center at

144 Unit 3 Make Your Career Plan

Review Students can organize and process their understanding of the key concepts found in each section.

Practice Connect the section's content to academic skills with these English language arts and social studies activities.

Check Your Answers Students can go online and check their answers to ensure comprehension.

Reading and Visuals: Help Students Study Effectively

Reading strategies are offered before, during, and after each section to help enrich students' reading skills. In addition to the Reading Guide and After You Read, there are a variety of strategies located throughout each section to ensure successful learning.

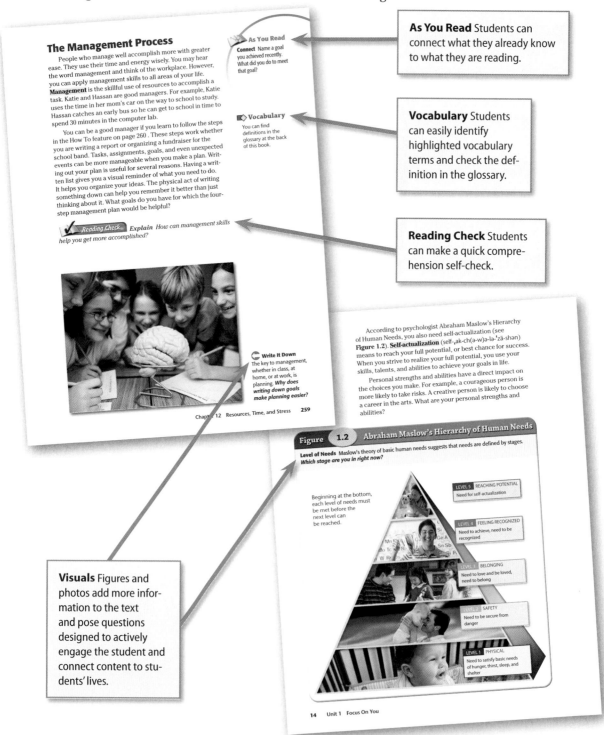

The Management Process

People who manage well accomplish more with greater ease. They use their time and energy wisely. You may hear the word management and think of the workplace. However, you can apply management skills to all areas of your life. **Management** is the skillful use of resources to accomplish a task. Katie and Hassan are good managers. For example, Katie uses the time in her mom's car on the way to school to study. Hassan catches an early bus so he can get to school in time to spend 30 minutes in the computer lab.

You can be a good manager if you learn to follow the steps in the How To feature on page 260 . These steps work whether you are writing a report or organizing a fundraiser for the school band. Tasks, assignments, goals, and even unexpected events can be more manageable when you make a plan. Writing out your plan is useful for several reasons. Having a written list gives you a visual reminder of what you need to do. It helps you organize your ideas. The physical act of writing something down can help you remember it better than just thinking about it. What goals do you have for which the four-step management plan would be helpful?

Reading Check *Explain* How can management skills help you get more accomplished?

As You Read

Connect Name a goal you achieved recently. What did you do to meet that goal?

Vocabulary

You can find definitions in the glossary at the back of this book.

Write It Down
The key to management, whether in class, at home, or at work, is planning. *Why does writing down goals make planning easier?*

Chapter 12 Resources, Time, and Stress   259

As You Read Students can connect what they already know to what they are reading.

Vocabulary Students can easily identify highlighted vocabulary terms and check the definition in the glossary.

Reading Check Students can make a quick comprehension self-check.

According to psychologist Abraham Maslow's Hierarchy of Human Needs, you also need self-actualization (see **Figure 1.2**). **Self-actualization** (self-,ak-ch(ə-w)ə-lə-'zā-shən) means to reach your full potential, or best chance for success. When you strive to realize your full potential, you use your skills, talents, and abilities to achieve your goals in life.

Personal strengths and abilities have a direct impact on the choices you make. For example, a courageous person is more likely to take risks. A creative person is likely to choose a career in the arts. What are your personal strengths and abilities?

Figure 1.2 Abraham Maslow's Hierarchy of Human Needs

Level of Needs Maslow's theory of basic human needs suggests that needs are defined by stages. *Which stage are you in right now?*

Beginning at the bottom, each level of needs must be met before the next level can be reached.

LEVEL 5 REACHING POTENTIAL
Need for self-actualization

LEVEL 4 FEELING RECOGNIZED
Need to achieve, need to be recognized

LEVEL 3 BELONGING
Need to love and be loved, need to belong

LEVEL 2 SAFETY
Need to be secure from danger

LEVEL 1 PHYSICAL
Need to satisfy basic needs of hunger, thirst, sleep, and shelter

14   Unit 1 Focus On You

Visuals Figures and photos add more information to the text and pose questions designed to actively engage the student and connect content to students' lives.

Features: Integrate Academics

Each section contains academic features that use students' mathematics and science skills to connect to the chapter content.

Math You Can Use Help students connect the information in each section with mathematic concepts they have learned or are learning. Each math concept is described for them, and a starting hint is given to help them solve each problem.

Math Handbook Students who need more assistance can visit the Math Handbook at the end of the book for a more detailed explanation.

Science You Can Use Help students connect the information in the chapter with the science content they have learned or are learning.

MATH YOU CAN USE

Teamwork

Deenie has formed a team with her classmates to design a garden for the school library. They must determine how much fencing they need to enclose the garden. The garden is in the shape of a triangle. The sides measure 6 yards, 8 yards, and 10 yards. How much fencing is needed to enclose the garden?

Math Concept **Finding Perimeter** The perimeter of any polygon (a closed shape with 3 or more sides) is calculated by adding the length of all of the polygon's sides.

Starting Hint The fencing will run along the perimeter of the garden. Calculate the perimeter by adding the 3 side lengths: 6 yards + 8 yards + 10 yards.

 For more math help, go to the Math Appendix located at the back of this book.

NCTM Measurement Apply appropriate techniques, tools, and formulas to determine measurements.

SCIENCE YOU CAN USE

Observe Child Behavior

To complete a scientific investigation or experiment, you collect data. Scientists collect data as numbers and descriptions, and then organize the data in different ways. Use your science skills to research the way different children react to the same activity.

Procedure Go to a park or children's play area to observe children at play. Select three individual children of the same age to observe. Record your observations in a chart like the one below. Examples are filled in for you.

Activity	Child 1	Child 2	Child 3
Slide	afraid to use it	used slide over and over	got to the top and changed her mind
Sandbox	played with pail and shovel	not interested	only wanted to use it when he was alone

Analysis What patterns do you notice in the data? What conclusions can you draw about the way children play?

NSES Content Standard A Develop abilities necessary to do scientific inquiry, understandings and scientific inquiry.

Financial Literacy

Working to Meet Goals

Toni set a long-term goal for herself to rent an apartment. She is comparing rent costs to help make her decision. She found a one-bedroom apartment downtown that rents for $600. She found a one-bedroom apartment in the suburbs that rents for 75% of the cost of the downtown apartment. What is the rent of the apartment in the suburbs?

Math Concept **Multiplying by Percents** To determine the cost of the apartment in the suburbs, multiply the cost of the apartment in the downtown area by 75%.

Starting Hint: To multiply by a percent, you must change the percent to a decimal. To do this, move the decimal point two places to the left. In this problem, 75% becomes .75, which you will multiply by $600.

NCTM Number and Operation Understand numbers, ways of representing numbers, relationships among numbers, and number systems.

 For math help, go to the Math Appendix at the back of the book.

Financial Literacy Help students learn the basics of personal finance by connecting the information with real life scenarios. A math concept is described in each feature.

Features: Develop Your Life Skills

Every unit includes a variety of practical, real-world features that students can apply to every-day life and to their school activities. They will learn skills and strategies that will be useful for the remainder of their school years, and well into the future as they prepare for further education, employment, and living on their own.

Presentation Skills

Rehearse Practice your speech before you present it to the class. Practice in front a mirror, or with a friend who will give you constructive feedback.

Time Management

Update Your Schedule Look at your schedule each morning. Add any tasks you did not complete the day before, and add new tasks.

Succeed in School These tips and ideas for achieving academic success can be applied to every class your students take, from now until they graduate. These useful tips serve as reminders that success in school goes beyond studying for tests and reading assignments.

Character Counts Your students are entering a new phase in their lives. They are learning that their actions have an impact on others, and they are getting ready to take on new responsibilities.

Safety Check

Online Communication

Technology has changed the way we talk to our friends. It can be fast, easy, and fun to talk online through e-mail, instant messages, blogs, and social networking sites. However, it also can be dangerous. Even if you think your messages are private, it is still possible for others to access your information. Use these tips to stay safe online:

- Do not post your real name, phone number, home address, or school name.
- Do not open e-mail from a source you do not know.
- Only accept messages from people you know and trust.

Protect Yourself Safety is more than just first aid. Students also need to learn that there are steps they can take to stay safe online, in food and sewing labs, and when they baby sit.

Character Counts

Compromise

Yanett and Deenie are twins. Each sister has her own bedroom, and they share a bathroom. Both girls are neat and take care of their rooms, but they have different ideas about how to clean and organize the bathroom. Yanett thinks it is faster and easier to clean when the supplies are kept on the counter. If she does not see them, she forgets that she needs to clean. Deenie thinks it looks messy to have the supplies out in the open. To her, leaving supplies out is the same as not making a bed. Though Yanett and Deenie get along most of the time, the bathroom cleaning situation it bothering them, and it is bothering other members of the family who have to listen to them argue.

You Make the Call

Who is right? Who is wrong? Is there only one efficient way to clean a shared space? Write a paragraph explaining what Yanett and Deenie should do before their situation gets worse.

The Right Thing To Do These real-life scenarios ask students, "What would you do?" Students will read about common problems teens experience with friends and family, then recommend solution.

Features: Develop Your Life Skills (continued)

Hands-On Lab Students will have opportunities in every unit to put their new skills and knowledge to work with hands-on activities.

Step-by-Step Processes Each lab includes easy-to-follow instructions for gathering materials and putting the plan into action.

How To Each unit includes a full-page How To feature to expand on the information in the unit.

Hands-On LAB

Be an Entrepreneur

In this activity you will imagine that you are an entrepreneur starting a new business. Before you begin, read through the entire Hands-On Lab assignment. Write down any questions that you have about the assignment. Reread the text or ask your teacher for help if you need it.

Supplies
✓ Calculator
✓ Computer with Internet access (optional)
✓ Paper and colored pens

Develop Your Plan
■ Choose a business such as babysitting, dog walking, or lawn mowing.
■ Find out what other teens would charge for the same jobs, or what clients would be willing to pay.
■ Gather supplies to create flyers, posters, and business cards to advertise your business.
■ If possible, access a computer graphics program to plan an imaginary Web page.

Implement Your Plan
■ Use graphics to create a fun and colorful flyer.
■ Create business cards with your name, contact information, and a brief list of your services.
■ Design an imaginary Web page to advertise your business.

■ Figure out how many hours you can spend on your business and what you will charge for your services.
■ Calculate the costs of maintaining your business, such as additional flyers and business cards, transportation, and Web site maintenance.
■ Multiply the hours you can work by your hourly rate. Subtract the costs to find your profit.

Evaluate Your Results
What did you learn about starting a business? Is there anything you would change if you could do it again? Do you think you would enjoy being your own boss? Write one or more paragraphs to explain your answer.

Projects and Activities Go to this book's Online Learning Center through glencoe.com for more projects and activities.

How To... Say "NO"

You will be faced with many choices and situations. Some are about choosing the way you behave toward others. Some are about reacting to how others behave toward you. Some situations will make you feel uncomfortable or put you in danger. Remember to say "NO" in these situations.

Tobacco, Alcohol, and Other Drugs True friends will not ask their friends to do things they do not want to do. You know what is right and wrong. Do not offer tobacco, alcohol, or drugs to anyone. Refuse any offers of these things from others. Stand up to peer pressure. Say "NO."

Shoplifting Shoplifting is stealing, and the penalties can have a long-term impact on your life.

Gangs Joining a gang can be very dangerous. You may be asked to do illegal things for the sake of other gang members.

Bullying Never try to bully anyone, and do not allow yourself to be bullied. Bullies should not be allowed to hassle anyone. Get an adult to help if you are being bullied or if you see someone else being bullied.

Guns You know that guns are not toys and are dangerous. Never try to bring a gun to school. If someone wants to show you a gun at school, just walk away. Report the situation immediately to an adult.

Evaluation After students complete the lab, they can use this evaluation exercise to check their results and analyze what they learned.

Tips for Success Students will learn a variety of useful skills, from changing a baby's diaper to choosing an exercise routine.

Introduce Students to Career Options

At the end of every chapter, students will find a Discovering Careers feature which focuses on careers related to the chapter content.

Discovering Careers Encourage your students to explore careers in a wide variety of industries and fields.

Discovering Careers

Focus on Careers in Emergency Response ▼

Do you work well under pressure? Are you able to make quick decisions? Do you want to help people in crisis? If you answered yes to any of those questions, you might want to consider a future in an emergency response career. The following chart explores several careers in the emergency response field.

Job Title	Job Description
Firefighter	Protect life and property from fires. Often the first emergency responders at traffic accidents. Firefighters are often required to treat injuries as well as fight fires.
Police Officer	Investigates complaints, maintains order, helps individuals, and identifies criminal offenders. Makes quick decisions in emergency situations.
Emergency Room Nurse	Cares for patients in various states of illness or injury. Helps decide which patients are in the most need of immediate care.
9-1-1 Operator	Answers calls from people in distress. Consults detailed manual to provide quick and often life-saving instructions to callers. Coordinates with fire, ambulance, and police services as needed.
Emergency Medical Technician (EMT)	Responds to emergency situations. Makes split-second decisions about patient care. Administers health care for accidents, injuries, and illness.

Career Activities These activities help students connect with their families and their community to help them start thinking about their future careers.

Career Activities ▼

At School
1. Select three of the careers listed. Research the education, training, and work experience required for each career. Write a summary of your results.

At Home
2. Create an emergency plan with your family in case of fire or other crisis. Make a map of your home with a planned escape route, and agree with you family on a specific place to meet.

At Work
3. Make a list of at least five jobs that require strong decision-making skills. Next to each job listed, write an example of a decision that might need to be made on the job.

In the Community
4. Contact and interview someone in your community who works in an emergency response career. Ask this person to describe what his or her typical work day is like. Share what you learned with your class.

Learn More Online ⓐ glencoe.com

Career Investigations Go to this book's Online Learning Center for activities and worksheets to help you explore careers.

128   Unit 2   Take Charge of Your Lif

Check Out More Careers Have students go online to find more information about careers at this book's Online Learning Center at glencoe.com.

Features: Connect to the Community

Community Connections
These features are sprinkled throughout the book to encourage your students to get involved.

COMMUNITY CONNECTIONS

Donate Sometimes you have clothes that are clean and in good repair, but you simply do not wear them any longer. Donate these clothes to a thrift shop or a charitable organization to help families and individuals in need.

How to Help Each feature highlights a volunteer opportunity related to the chapter or unit content. Students will learn how they can contribute to their community.

Global Connections Help students discover what they have in common with people all over the world. Their community is not just where they live and go to school – it is the whole world.

Vocabulary Each feature introduces students to a new international term or concept.

Discover International...

Currency

Guatemalan Quetzal

The quetzal is the currency, or money, of Guatemala. It is named after the national bird of Guatemala, the "Resplendent Quetzal." It is divided into 100 centavos, much like a United States dollar is divided into 100 cents. The Mayans, who are the native people of Guatemala, used the long tail feathers of the male quetzal bird as currency in ancient times. Today, both the United States dollar and the Guatemalan quetzal carry value for making purchases in Guatemala. The image of the quetzal bird appears on Guatemalan paper currency and on some coins, and it carries historical importance for the people of Guatemala.

quetzal |ket-|säl 1. a Central American bird with brilliant green and red feathers. The male quetzal has very long, streaming tail feathers. 2. the main unit of Guatemalan currency.

NCSS I D Compare and analyze societal patterns for preserving and transmitting culture while adapting to environmental or social change.

Choose Proven Teaching Solutions

Annotations: Point-of-Use Answers

Point-of use annotations within each chapter provide caption and feature answers and helpful teaching tips right as you need them.

Babysitting Responsibilities

When you babysit, you are totally responsible for the safety and well-being of the children in your care. If you do your job well, you will gain valuable experience and earn money. You will also have an opportunity to play with children and teach them new things.

Before you begin looking for a babysitting job, you should take a course in first aid through a local hospital, a community center, or the American Red Cross. You could also volunteer as a parent's helper. This is someone who cares for an infant or a young child under a parent's supervision. Parents looking for babysitters will appreciate, or be thankful for, someone who has taken steps to prepare for the serious job of babysitter.

When parents ask you to babysit, find out the following information before you accept the job:

- the number of children and their ages
- the time you should arrive
- how long the parents plan to be gone
- the rate of pay you will receive

If everything about the job sounds good to you, check with your parents to make sure that the job meets with their approval. After you accept the job, write down the date, time, and place. Give your parents the telephone number at the home where you will be babysitting. If possible, you should also give your parents the cell phone numbers of the parents for whom you are babysitting.

As You Read
Connect Think about your favorite babysitter. Why was he or she your favorite?

As You Read Answer Answers will vary but may include that the sitter was fun, caring, liked to play, took good care of children.

Photo Caption Answer You can practice your skills while the parents supervise. They can help you learn, and if you make mistakes they can teach you the correct things to do. You can gain experience without full responsibility for children until you are ready.

Succeed in School Tell students that even though it can be tempting to do homework in bed, it can lead to irregular sleep patterns, which have been linked to academic and behavioral problems.

Parent's Helper Volunteer to be a parent's helper to gain childcare experience. *How can this prepare you for babysitting jobs?*

SUCCEED IN SCHOOL!

Study Skills
Be Comfortable Find a good table and chair or desk for studying. If you are comfortable, you are more likely to focus and study longer.

Chapter 10 Child Care Basics 215

As You Read Answer The answer provides you with an opportunity to discuss the chapter topic with students to help boost reading comprehension.

Visuals The answers to the questions for photos and figures provide you with an opportunity to discuss important topics in the chapter and reinforce content. Answers also provide additional information on real-life topics.

In return for the rights you enjoy, you have responsibilities to your community. You are required to obey laws and rules. Communities benefit when everyone plays a positive role.

The way you handle your responsibilities as a citizen is called **citizenship**. One of those responsibilities is to give back to the community. Volunteer work can be a valuable experience. When you **volunteer**, you give your time and energy without pay to help others. Volunteering is a good way to demonstrate your citizenship skills. Working with others who share your concerns can be a good way to make friends. As a volunteer, you may come into contact with people you may not meet otherwise. These people may be hungry, homeless, or lonely. Helping people can make you a more compassionate, or caring, person. It can be very satisfying to know that something you do helps someone else.

There are many ways you can volunteer your talents and skills:

- Read to people in a hospital or nursing home.
- Volunteer for an organization that records reading materials for people with visual impairments.
- Join efforts to clean up parks and recreation areas.
- Offer to take care of pets when your neighbors go on vacation.
- Pick up litter and put it in the proper place.
- Return lost items to the lost-and-found department or to the rightful owner.

Whether you demonstrate your citizenship skills alone or in a group, being a good citizen can give you a sense of belonging. You can also develop work experience and skills that you can apply to future jobs. What other ways can you think of to show your citizenship skills?

MATH YOU CAN USE

Teamwork
Deenie has formed a team with her classmates to design a garden for the school library. They must determine how much fencing they need to enclose the garden. The garden is in the shape of a triangle. The sides measure 6 yards, 8 yards, and 10 yards. How much fencing is needed to enclose the garden?

Math Concept Finding Perimeter The perimeter of any polygon (a closed shape with 3 or more sides) is calculated by adding the length of all of the polygon's sides.

Starting Hint The fencing will run along the perimeter of the garden. Calculate the perimeter by adding the 3 side lengths: 6 yards + 8 yards + 10 yards.

Math For more math help, go to the Math Appendix located at the back of this book.

NCTM Measurement Apply appropriate techniques, tools, and formulas to determine measurements.

Math You Can Use Feature Answer The team needs 24 yards of fencing to enclose the garden. (6 + 8 + 10 = 24 yards)

Reading Check Answer A citizen is a member of a community such as a city, state, or country.

Reading Check Define *What is a citizen?*

98 Unit 2 Take Charge of Your Life

Feature Answers A variety of features helps you teach important concepts related to the chapter content. Feature answers provide an opportunity for you to further discuss the concepts in real-world settings.

Reading Check Answer Reading Checks help your students review information they have just read. Point-of-use annotation answers allow you to review these important points with them.

for Effective Results

Planning Guides: The Right Resources

Introduce and review each chapter in ways best suited to your students' individual needs.

Print Ancillaries Find additional activities, study guides, and test preparation strategies in the Student Activity Workbook. Answers are provided in the Student Activity Workbook Teacher Annotated Edition.

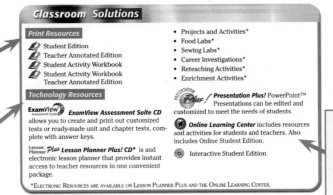

Classroom Solutions

Print Resources
- Student Edition
- Teacher Annotated Edition
- Student Activity Workbook
- Student Activity Workbook Teacher Annotated Edition

Technology Resources

ExamView *ExamView Assessment Suite CD* allows you to create and print out customized tests or ready-made unit and chapter tests, complete with answer keys.

Lesson Planner *Plus Lesson Planner Plus! CD** is and electronic lesson planner that provides instant access to teacher resources in one convenient package.

- Projects and Activities*
- Food Labs*
- Sewing Labs*
- Career Investigations*
- Reteaching Activities*
- Enrichment Activities*

Presentation Plus! PowerPoint™ Presentations can be edited and customized to meet the needs of students.

Online Learning Center includes resources and activities for students and teachers. Also includes Online Student Edition.

Interactive Student Edition

*ELECTRONIC RESOURCES ARE AVAILABLE ON LESSON PLANNER PLUS AND THE ONLINE LEARNING CENTER.

Technology Ancillaries Have the flexibility you need to create individualized learning plans for your students.

Online Ancillaries Encourage your students to get more information online at this book's Online Learning Center at glencoe.com.

Differentiated Instruction: Teaching Plans for All Students

The teaching strategies that appear throughout this teacher edition have been identified by various icons. The letters identify the different types of strategies or activities. The ability levels give you an idea of their suitability for students of varying learning styles. The ELL icon identifies ways in which you can include English Language Learners into classroom discussions.

KEY TO LETTERS

D Develop Concepts activities use various strategies to help you gauge and plan for students' concept development.

R Reading Strategy activities help you teach reading skills and vocabulary.

U Universal Access activities provide strategies to reach all types of learners in the classroom.

S Skill Practice provides leveled instruction to reach students at all ability levels.

W Writing Activity provides independent and guided writing practice to help students understand the text.

C Critical Thinking strategies help students apply and extend what they have learned.

KEY TO ABILITY LEVELS

L1 Strategies should be within the ability range of all students.

L2 Strategies are for average to above-average students or for small groups.

L3 Strategies are designed for students able and willing to work independently.

ENGLISH LANGUAGE LEARNER

ELL Strategies are for students who are learning the English language.

Teacher Manual Lesson Plans: Plan for Classroom Success

These teaching suggestions and ideas are offered to help you motivate and involve your students. They can assist you in reaching students of all levels of ability and backgrounds and make the course more rewarding for both you and your students.

Using the Six-Step Teaching Plan

Discovering Life Skills makes full and effective use of a mastery approach in six steps: focus, teach, assess, reteach, assess, and close. This widely accepted instructional method provides you with a consistent framework that makes it easy for you to teach the material.

Focus A Bell Ringer Activity begins the lesson, then pre-teaching activities such as Before You Read, Develop Concepts, and Graphic Organizer Answers assure that all students have the same background and preparation.

Teach This section provides suggestions for discussion, reading activities, and guided and independent skills practice.

Assess Review questions enable you to evaluate your students' needs.

Reteach Different activities are provided to reinforce lesson content. Questions are designed to help your students reinforce key concepts or apply and extend what they have learned.

Assess Re-evaluate student comprehension with varied assessments.

Close A Culminating Activity helps students make the connection between what they read and its meaning and application to the real world.

Teacher Manual Answer Keys: Evaluate Students' Progress

Find detailed answers to the Chapter Review and Applications questions. Suggestions for discussion points are also included for each chapter.

Vocabulary Review Review the Content and Academic Vocabulary with your students.

Key Concepts/Critical Thinking Answers Boost students' understanding of the chapter material and encourage further discussion.

Real-World Skills and Applications Answers Help students explore real-life situations using the skills they have learned from the chapter.

Standardized Test Practice Answer Encourage good test-taking habits in your students for success on standardized tests.

Chapter 18 Answer Key

Words You Learned
1. Students should write complete sentences using each vocabulary term correctly.

Review Key Concepts
2. Fabric preparation helps you to avoid mistakes, save time in the long run, and ensures that you have the right type of fabric for your project.
3. Fabric preparation includes laundering the fabric to preshrink it, pressing it to remove wrinkles, and checking the grain matching selvages and folding on the bias.
4. Stitch straight seams, stitch curved seams, turn corners, add seam finishes, make darts, gather fabric, ease fabric, make casings, make facings, sew on buttons and snaps.
5. A serger is a machine that sews, trims, and finishes a seam in one step.

Critical Thinking
6. Some fabrics need to be preshrunk and pressed, others do not. Cleaning instructions vary and can be found on the bolt of the fabric. Different fabrics, such as knits, silks, and sheers, require different sewing techniques.
7. The garment may not fit properly, errors may be made in cutting or measuring, materials can be wasted.
8. Sergers are high-speed machines that can save time and handle fabrics that are more difficult to work with, such as stretchy knits or slippery silks. Sergers keep edges from raveling on all fabrics. Unlike sergers, sewing machines can sew a single line of locked stiches. Sewing machines can create buttonholes, insert zippers, and some can do embroidery.
9. Answers will vary depending on students' experiences and opinions, but should demonstrate that the student understands both techniques and can clearly explain why one is more challenging than the other.

Real-World Skills and Applications
10. Evan should prepare his fabric and pattern. He should launder fabric according to instructions on the bolt, press if needed, and check the grain. He should read the pattern guides, measure and adjust the pattern as needed, and pin the pattern according to the layout. Then he can cut the pieces and begin sewing.

11. Answers will vary but may include that the first practical sewing machine was patented in 1846 by Elias Howe in Massachusetts, based on designs by European inventors. Manufacturers used the first sewing machines. Students might mention that in 1851, Isaac Merritt Singer, a machinist from Boston, Massachusetts, introduced the first and most successful sewing machine created for home use.

Financial Literacy
12. Answers will vary depending on students' clothing selection and shopping choices.

Active Learning
13. Students should present a completed pillowcase.
14. Reports will vary but should include details about historical clothing features, and who wore the clothing and why.

Net Connection
15. Examples will vary but should include details about teen clothing styles from today, 10 years ago, and 100 years ago.

Academic Skills
16. Flyers will vary. Sample flyer: To encourage boys to join as well as girls, flyer advertises vests, cargo pants, backpacks, pajamas, shorts, carpentry aprons, and duffel bags. Date, time, location, and what to bring are included. Flyer is creative, relevant, and appealing to both genders. Advantages to joining the club are to meet people, learn more sewing techniques, share ideas, and to have fun!
17. Answers will vary depending on students' opinions, but hypotheses should be stated clearly, and students should list facts that support the statement.
18. Each will spend an average of 240 minutes on the project.

Standardized Test Practice
19. c

Utilize Time-Saving Print

Print Resources

Help Students Succeed with the Student Activity Workbook

The Student Activity Workbook with Academic Integration includes a variety of worksheets and activities, correlated to each chapter in the text.

- Note-Taking
- Academics
  - English Language Arts
  - Mathematics
  - Science
  - Social Studies
- Study Skills
- Test-Preparation
- Test-Taking
- Content Vocabulary
- Academic Vocabulary

These worksheets and activities will help reinforce the chapter content, increasing your students' comprehension. The Student Activity Workbook offers students a chance to apply what they have learned and to use their critical thinking skills.

The Teacher Annotated Edition of the Student Activity Workbook includes cyan annotated answers to all of the student activities.

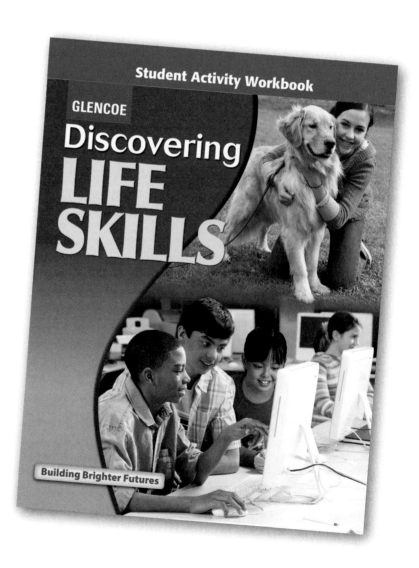

Student Activity Workbook

GLENCOE

Discovering LIFE SKILLS

Building Brighter Futures

and Technology Resources

Technology Solutions

Lesson Planner Plus

Lesson Planner Plus gives you instant access to a variety of useful program resources in one easy-to-use CD. The software provides a calendar format that allows you to plan lessons, manage daily activities, access textbook materials, and use Internet resources.

The Lesson Planner Plus program contains built-in lesson plans that can be customized to meet your individual classroom needs. It also includes links to printable program resources.

Printable Program Resources

Teacher Materials
- Student Activity Workbook TAE
- Answer Keys
- Performance Rubrics
- Correlations to national standards

Student Materials
- Lesson Summaries with Key Terms and Academic Vocabulary
- Graphic Organizers
- Food Labs
- Sewing Labs
- Career Investigations
- Unit Life Skills Project Self-Assessment Rubrics
- Enrichment Activities
- Reteaching Activities

Glencoe
Lesson Planner Plus
with **Teacher Resources**

Software Support Hotline
1-800-437-3715 or
epgtech@mcgraw-hill.com

Windows/Macintosh
Version 1.8

ISBN: 978-0-07-888474-0
MHID: 0-07-888474-8
03/09

Glencoe

- **Interactive Lesson Planner**
- **Student Activity Workbook TAE**
- **Blackline Masters**

1 2 3 4 5 6 7 8 9 10

Discovering Life Skills

180 Day Version

The McGraw-Hill Companies
Glencoe

Copyright © by The McGraw-Hill Companies, Inc. All rights reserved.

Program Resources

ExamView® Assessment Suite

Streamline assessment from start to finish with the *ExamView®* CD. This easy-to-use software allows teachers to customize and create unique tests to conduct quizzes, chapter tests, unit tests, midterm exams, or final exams. The *ExamView® Assessment Suite* works across platforms, on the Web, and across a local area network. If offers teachers a comprehensive solution that allows them to create, administer, and score tests. The test banks, which are organized by unit and chapter, use a variety of question types to improve assessment.

Use the *ExamView Assessment Suite* to:
- Create a paper test in fewer than five minutes.
- Print multiple versions of the same test.
- Create your own questions.
- Develop tests using state and national standards.
- Prepare online tests, study guides, and worksheets.
- Upload tests to WebCT and Blackboard.

Use the *ExamView Test Manager* to:
- Create a class roster.
- Automatically score a paper test using a scanner.
- Administer and score an online test.
- Prepare a variety of useful class and student reports.

Presentation Plus! PowerPoint® Presentations

The *Discovering Life Skills Presentation Plus!* CD provides visually motivating presentations that are helpful to both students and teachers. The presentations target key concepts by highlighting important text, providing graphic organizers, and utilizing visuals from the textbook.

How Teachers Can Use Presentation Plus!

The *Presentation Plus!* PowerPoint presentations are excellent teaching aids that present dynamic lessons for every section in *Discovering Life Skills.* The PowerPoint presentations can be edited and customized to meet the needs of individual students. It also includes chapter assessment presentations that can be used with TurningPoint® student response systems. Teachers can use *Presentation Plus!* PowerPoint presentations in the following ways:

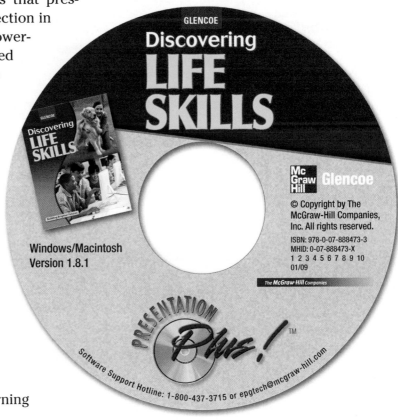

- To preview important concepts at the beginning of a new chapter or lesson
- To provide differentiated instruction for visual learners
- To create a customized learning experience for students

How Students Can Use *Presentation Plus!*

The *Presentation Plus!* PowerPoint presentations provide a visual overview of key concepts and vocabulary. The presentations are excellent study aids. Students can use *Presentation Plus!* PowerPoint presentations in the following ways:

- To preview important concepts, key terms, and skills that covered in a chapter before reading
- To review and reinforce difficult concepts after reading
- To prepare for quizzes and tests

Program Resources

How to Access the Online Learning Center

The Online Learning Center provides access to a wide variety of teacher resources. Follow these steps to access the textbook resources at the Discovering Life Skills Online Learning Center. The Online Learning Center is password protected.

Step 1
Go to glencoe.com.

Step 2
Select **your state** from the pull-down menu.

Step 3
Select **Teacher**

Step 4
Select **Family and Consumer Sciences.**

Step 5
Click **ENTER.**

Step 6
Click **Discovering Life Skills.**

Online Student Edition

The Online Student Edition is an interactive version of the textbook that can be accessed from the Online Learning Center. This version of the textbook is as easy to read and search. It offers the same content as the printed text, as well as multimedia-enhanced content.

Step 7
Click **Teacher Center** to access a wide variety of classroom resources.

Glencoe FACS Classroom Solutions™ e-Newsletter

Subscribe to Glencoe's free e-newsletter and receive the latest information about strategies, trends, and technology in family and consumer sciences. Subscribe through this book's Online Learning Center at **glencoe.com**.

Online Professional Development

Professional Development for Excellence in Teaching

Perkins IV has placed more emphasis than ever on providing a quality professional development for Career and Technology educators. The legislation mandates that the focus of professional development be the integration and reinforcement of academic competencies in order to improve student achievement. Specifically, Perkins requires measurements of students' academic success.

Glencoe and Professional Development

To support educators in their efforts to meet new professional development requirements, Glencoe now offers a new resource, Glencoe's Online Professional Development for Integrating Academics. This program offers a suite of online products designed to help teachers become more effective in teaching in reinforcing academic skills. The focus of this program is on instructional strategies that can help educators integrate challenging academic content seamlessly into their technical curriculum. These teaching strategies zero in on:

- Math
- Reading
- English Language Arts
- Differentiated Instruction
- English Language Learners Instruction

Glencoe's Online Professional Development for Integrating Academics

1. Professional Development Accredited Online Courses (academic credit available through Adams University)
2. Professional Development Web Site
3. Video Workshops
4. Mini-Clip Video Library
5. McGraw-Hill experienced consultants

For further pricing and ordering information, go to **mcgraw-hill-pd-online.com**.

for Integrating Academics

Professional Development in the Glencoe 6-Step Teaching Plan

Selected online mini-clips have been integrated into this Teacher Edition's 6-step teaching plan in order to support academic instruction. These mini-clips are free and accessible online from the *Discovering Life Skills* Online Learning Center through **glencoe.com**.

The Professional Development Mini Clip Video Library offers you instructional support for Reading, English Language Learners, and Math.

Integrate teaching strategies in your lesson plans. Mini-clip videos have been selected and matched to chapter content to help you integrate academics into your planning.

Teach **Discovering Life Skills**

Scope and Sequence

These charts provide an overview of the academic standards covered in *Discovering Life Skills*.

National Council of Teachers of English Standards for English Language Arts	
NCTE 1 Students read a wide range of print and nonprint texts to build an understanding of texts, of themselves, and of the cultures of the United States and the world; to acquire new information; to respond to the needs and demands of society and the workplace; and for personal fulfillment. Among these texts are fiction and nonfiction, classic and contemporary works.	6, 18, 30, 40, 52, 59, 76, 83, 96, 103, 116, 122, 138, 145, 158, 168, 184, 193, 208, 214, 234, 241, 258, 265, 282, 292, 304, 310, 326, 333, 346, 354, 361, 372, 379, 392, 399, 420, 429, 444, 452, 468, 474, 488, 497, 510, 517
NCTE 2 Students read a wide range of literature from many periods in many genres to build an understanding of the many dimensions (e.g., philosophical, ethical, aesthetic) of human experience	127
NCTE 3 Students apply a wide range of strategies to comprehend, interpret, evaluate, and appreciate texts. They draw on their prior experience, their interactions with other readers and writers, their knowledge of word meaning and of other texts, their word identification strategies, and their understanding of textual features (e.g., sound-letter correspondence, sentence structure, context, graphics).	23, 205, 240, 415
NCTE 4 Students adjust their use of spoken, written, and visual language (e.g., conventions, style, vocabulary) to communicate effectively with a variety of audiences and for different purposes.	17, 49, 109, 144, 179, 192, 201, 223, 229, 251, 271, 301, 319, 343, 398, 409, 450, 461, 463, 503
NCTE 5 Students employ a wide range of strategies as they write and use different writing process elements appropriately to communicate with different audiences for a variety of purposes.	89, 161, 229, 263, 339, 353, 365, 367, 413, 457, 473, 485, 497, 516
NCTE 6 Students apply knowledge of language structure, language conventions (e.g., spelling and punctuation), media techniques, figurative language, and genre to create, critique, and discuss print and non-print texts.	70, 132, 178, 228, 276, 320, 366, 414, 462, 528
NCTE 7 Students conduct research on issues and interests by generating ideas and questions, and by posing problems. They gather, evaluate, and synthesize data from a variety of sources (e.g., print and nonprint texts, artifacts, people) to communicate their discoveries in ways that suit their purpose and audience.	39, 58, 82, 277, 297, 308, 367, 385
NCTE 8 Students use a variety of technological and informational resources (e.g., libraries, databases, computer networks, video) to gather and synthesize information and to create and communicate knowledge.	65, 71, 102, 151, 155, 179, 213, 291, 376, 428, 437, 441, 481, 527
NCTE 9 Students develop an understanding of and respect for diversity in language use, patterns, and dialects across cultures, ethnic groups, geographic regions, and social roles.	186, 382, 500, 529
NCTE 10 Students whose first language is not English make use of their first language to develop competency in the English language arts and to develop understanding of content across the curriculum. All English Language Learner activities in the TAE Lesson Plan pages.	All English Language Learner activities in TAE Lesson Plan pages

and Academics at the Same Time

National Council of Teachers of English Standards for English Language Arts (cont.)	
NCTE 11 Students participate as knowledgeable, reflective, creative, and critical members of a variety of literacy communities.	68, 92, 204
NCTE 12 Students use spoken, written, and visual language to accomplish their own purpose (e.g., for learning, enjoyment, persuasion, and the exchange of information).	27, 45, 69, 93, 113, 116, 121, 173, 275, 315, 321, 332, 389, 463, 507, 523

National Council of Teachers of Mathematics Standards for Grades 9-12	
Numbers and Operations Understand numbers, ways of representing numbers, relationships among numbers, and number systems.	54, 120, 227, 261, 314, 319, 343, 422, 501
Numbers and Operations Understand meanings of operations and how they relate to one another.	172, 177, 255, 275, 360, 365, 527
Number and Operations Compute fluently and make reasonable estimates.	81, 188, 205, 277, 389, 407, 507
Algebra Understand patterns, relations, and functions.	93, 413, 447, 461
Algebra Represent and analyze mathematical situations and structures using algebraic symbols.	93, 330, 413, 461
Geometry Use visualization, spatial reasoning, and geometric modeling to solve problems.	415, 485
Measurement Understand measurable attributes of objects and the units, systems, and processes of measurement.	27, 131, 374, 155, 470, 529
Measurement Apply appropriate techniques, tools, and formulas to determine measurements	98, 295, 321
Data Analysis and Probability Formulate questions that can be addressed with data and collect, organize, and display relevant data to answer them.	49
Data Analysis and Probability Select and use appropriate statistical methods to analyze data.	148
Data Analysis and Probability Understand and apply basic concepts and probability.	318, 513
Problem Solving Apply and adapt a variety of appropriate strategies to solve problems.	441, 447
Problem Solving Solve problems that arise in mathematics and in other contexts.	11, 36, 69, 236, 217
Problem Solving Build new mathematical knowledge through problem solving.	113, 301
Problem Solving Understand the meanings of operations and how they relate to one another.	397

Standards are listed with permission of the National Council of Teachers of Mathematics (NCTM). NCTM does not endorse the content or validity of these alignments.

Academic Scope and Sequence

National Science Education Standards	
Content Standard A Students should develop abilities necessary to do scientific inquiry, understandings about scientific inquiry..	27, 93, 200, 266, 365, 384, 413, 435, 490
Content Standard B Students should develop an understanding of the structure of atoms, structure and properties of matter, chemical reactions, motions and forces, conservation of energy and increase in disorder, and interactions of energy and matter.	161, 476, 507
Content Standard F Students should develop understanding of personal and community health; population growth; natural resources; environmental quality; natural and human-induced hazards; science and technology in local, national, and global challenges.	64, 69, 205, 211, 275, 301, 305, 455
Content Standard G Students should develop understanding of science as a human endeavor, nature of scientific knowledge, historical perspectives.	142, 155, 239, 461

National Council for the Social Studies Standards	
NCSS I A Culture Analyze and explain the ways groups, societies, and cultures address human needs and concerns.	80, 213, 353, 398, 409
NCSS I B Culture Predict how data and experiences may be interpreted by people from diverse cultural perspectives and frames of reference.	23, 89, 339
NCSS I C Culture Apply an understanding of culture as an integrated whole that explains the functions and interactions of language, literature, the arts, traditions, beliefs and values, and behavior patterns.	343, 428, 441
NCSS I E Culture Demonstrate the value of cultural diversity, as well as cohesion, within and across groups.	245, 338, 527
NCSS II C Time, Continuity, and Change Identify and describe significant historical periods and patterns of change within and across cultures, such as the development of ancient cultures and civilizations, the rise of nation-states, and social, economic, and political revolutions.	116, 121
NCSS II F Time, Continuity, and Change Apply ideas, theories, and modes of historical inquiry to analyze historical and contemporary developments, and to inform and evaluate actions concerning public policy issues.	127
NCSS III B Time, Continuity, and Change Create, interpret, use, and synthesize information from various representations of the earth, such as maps, globes, and photographs.	49, 516
NCSS III G Time, Continuity, and Change Describe and compare how people create places that reflect culture, human needs, government policy, and current values and ideals as they design and build specialized buildings, neighborhoods, shopping centers, urban centers, industrial parks, and the like.	296
NCSS III J Time, Continuity, and Change Analyze and evaluate social and economic effects of environmental changes and crises resulting from phenomena such as floods, storms, and drought.	437
NCSS IV B People, Places, and Environments Identify, describe, and express appreciation for the influence of various historical and contemporary cultures on an individual's daily life.	45, 332, 485, 497, 503
NCSS IV C People, Places, and Environments Describe the ways family, religion, gender, ethnicity, nationality, socioeconomic status, and other group and cultural influences contribute to the development of a sense of self.	17, 192, 271

National Council for the Social Studies Standards (continued)	
NCSS IV D People, Places, and Environments Apply concepts, methods, and theories about the study of human growth and development, such as physical endowment, learning, motivation, behavior, perception, and personality.	201, 450
NCSS IV F People, Places, and Environments Analyze the role of perceptions, attitudes, values, and beliefs in the development of personal identity.	71, 167, 319, 361
NCSS IV I People, Places, and Environments Examine factors that contribute to and damage one's mental health and analyze issues related to mental health and behavioral disorders in contemporary society.	457
NCSS V B Individuals, Groups, and Institutions Analyze group and institutional influences on people, events, and elements of culture in both historical and contemporary settings.	223, 297
NCSS V D Individuals, Groups, and Institutions Identify and analyze examples of tensions between expressions of individuality and efforts used to promote social conformity by groups and institutions.	65, 151
NCSS V F Individuals, Groups, and Institutions Evaluate the role of institutions in furthering both continuity and change.	38, 308
NCSS V G Individuals, Groups, and Institutions Analyze the extent to which groups and institutions meet individual needs and promote the common good in contemporary and historical settings.	144, 315, 473
NCSS VI A Power, Authority, and Governance Examine persistent issues involving the rights, roles, and status of the individual in relation to the general welfare.	173, 251
NCSS VI G Power, Authority, and Governance Evaluate the role of technology in communications, transportation, information-processing, weapons development, or other areas as it contributes to or helps resolve conflicts.	82
NCSS VI J Power, Authority, and Governance Prepare a public policy paper and present and defend it before an appropriate forum in school or community.	133
NCSS VIII A Science, Technology, and Society Identify and describe both current and historical examples of the interaction and interdependence of science, technology, and society in a variety of cultural settings.	481, 523
NCSS VIII B Science, Technology, and Society Make judgments about how science and technology have transformed the physical world and human society and our understanding of time, space, place, and human-environment interactions.	240, 291
NCSS VIII C Science, Technology, and Society Analyze how science and technology influence the core values, beliefs, and attitudes of society, and how core values, beliefs, and attitudes of society shape scientific and technological change.	227
NCSS IX D Global Connections Analyze the causes, consequences, and possible solutions to persistent, contemporary, and emerging global issues, such as health, security, resource allocation, economic development, and environmental quality.	109
NCSS X B Civic Ideas and Practices Identify, analyze, interpret, and evaluate sources and examples of citizens' rights and responsibilities.	102
NCSS X C Civic Ideas and Practices Locate, access, analyze, organize, synthesize, evaluate, and apply information about selected public issues—identifying, describing, and evaluating multiple points of view.	113
NCSS X D Civic Ideas and Practices Practice forms of civic discussion and participation consistent with the ideals of citizens in a democratic republic.	133

Integrate Discovering Life Skills

The following Chart shows how *Discovering Life Skills* meets the NASAFACS standards or the following areas of study

Area of Study 1.0 Career, Community and Life Connections Integrate multiple life roles and responsibilities in family, work, and community settings.	
1.1 Analyze strategies to manage multiple roles and responsibilities (individual, family, career, community, and global).	8, 10, 41, 117-118, 120, 139-144
1.2 Demonstrate transferable and employability skills in school, community and workplace settings.	24, 46, 66, 90, 104-105, 107-109, 110, 128, 146-148, 152, 159-167, 169, 172-174, 202, 224, 252, 272, 316, 438, 458
1.3 Evaluate the reciprocal effects of individual and family participation in community activities.	2, 97-98,102
Area of Study 2.0 Consumer and Family Resources Evaluate management practices related to the human, economic, and environmental resources.	
2.1 Demonstrate management of individual and family resources such as food, clothing, shelter, health care, recreation, transportation, time, and human capital.	13-15, 31-35, 259-263, 265-268
2.3 Analyze policies that support consumer rights and responsibilities.	246
2.4 Evaluate the effects of technology on individual and family resources.	144, 150, 237-239, 243
2.5 Analyze relationships between the economic system and consumer actions.	13-15
Area of Study 3.0 Consumer Services Integrate knowledge, skills, and practices needed for a career in consumer service.	
3.1 Analyze career paths within consumer service industries.	106, 140, 149, 151
3.3 Analyze factors in developing a long-term financial management plan.	250-251
3.4 Analyze resource consumption for conservation and waste management practices	305-308, 310, 312-315
Area of Study 6.0 Family Evaluate the significance of family and its effects on the well-being of individuals and society.	
6.1 Analyze the effects of family as a system on individuals and society.	8, 31-33, 35, 36, 38-39, 41-45, 188
6.2 Evaluate the effects of diverse perspectives, needs, and characteristics of individuals and families.	8, 32, 44, 55, 101, 170, 245, 296, 382, 500
Area of Study 7.0 Family and Community Services Synthesize knowledge, skills, and practices required for careers in family and community services.	
7.1 Analyze career paths within family and community services.	106, 110, 143, 149, 151
7.4 Evaluate conditions affecting individuals and families with a variety of disadvantaging conditions.	191-192, 197
7.5 Evaluate services for individuals and families with a variety of disadvantaging conditions.	44
Area of Study 8.0 Food Production and Services Integrate knowledge, skills, and practices required for careers in food production and services.	
8.1 Analyze career paths within the food production and food services industries.	482, 504, 524
8.2 Demonstrate food safety and sanitation procedures.	469-473

Area of Study 11.0 Housing, Interiors and Furnishings Integrate knowledge, skills, and practices required for careers in housing, interiors, and furnishings.

11.1 Analyze career paths within the housing, interiors, and furnishings industry.	298
11.2 Evaluate housing design concepts in relation to available resources and options.	293-295

Area of Study 12.0 Human Development Analyze factors that influence human growth & development.

12.1 Analyze principles of human growth and development across the life span.	16, 187, 194-197, 199-201
12.2 Analyze conditions that influence human growth and development.	7-8, 14

Area of Study 13.0 Interpersonal Relationships Demonstrate respectful and caring relationships in the family, workplace and community.

13.1 Analyze functions and expectations of various types of relationships.	9, 37, 41, 53, 54, 56-58, 60
13.2 Analyze personal needs and characteristics and their effects on interpersonal relationships.	11, 13, 54
13.3 Demonstrate communication skills that contribute to positive relationships.	9, 61, 77-82, 150, 163
13.4 Evaluate effective conflict prevention and management techniques.	60-62, 64-65, 81-82, 84-89, 123-127, 187
13.5 Demonstrate teamwork and leadership skills in the family, workplace, and community.	11, 15, 35-36, 104-105, 107-109, 170-171

Area of Study 14.0 Nutrition and Wellness Demonstrate nutrition and wellness practices that enhance individual and family well-being.

14.1 Analyze factors that influence nutrition and wellness practices across the life span.	421-428, 432-436
14.2 Evaluate the nutritional needs of individuals and families in relation to health and wellness across the life span.	19, 421, 453-456, 494-495, 513, 515
14.3 Evaluate various dietary guidelines in planning to meet nutrition and wellness needs.	430-432
14.4 Evaluate factors that affect food safety from production through consumption.	469-473

Area of Study 15.0 Parenting Evaluate the effects of parenting roles and responsibilities on strengthening the well-being of individuals and families.

15.1 Analyze roles and responsibilities of parenting.	185-188
15.2 Evaluate parenting practices that maximize human growth and development.	33, 34, 190-192

Area of Study 16.0 Textiles, Fashion, and Apparel Integrate knowledge, skills, and practices required for careers in textiles and apparels.

16.1 Analyze career paths within textile apparel and design industries.	340, 362, 386, 410
16.2 Evaluate fiber and textile products and materials.	347-349, 357-361, 382
16.3 Demonstrate fashion, apparel, and textile design skills.	338-339, 349, 373
16.4 Demonstrate skills needed to produce, alter, or repair fashion, apparel, and textile products.	347-348, 374-376, 394-398, 401-404, 406

Pacing Guide

Make Your Teaching Flexible

90-Day Pacing Guide

18-Week Course		
	Traditional Schedule	**Block Schedule**
Week	Student Edition	Student Edition
1	Ch. 1	Ch. 1
2	Ch. 2, Ch. 3 (Sect. 3.1)	Ch. 2
3	Ch. 3 (Sect. 3.2); Unit 1 Thematic Project	Ch. 3; Unit 1 Thematic Project
4	Ch. 4, 5	Ch. 4, 5
5	Ch. 6; Unit 2 Thematic Project	Ch. 6; Unit 2 Thematic Project
6	Ch. 7, 8; Unit 3 Thematic Project	Ch. 7
7	Ch. 9, 10; Unit 4 Thematic Project	Ch 8, Unit 3 Thematic Project
8	Ch. 11	Ch. 9, 10
9	Ch. 12; Unit 5 Thematic Project	Unit 4 Thematic Project
10	Ch. 13, 14	Ch. 11, 12; Unit 5 Thematic Project
11	Unit 6 Thematic Project, Ch. 15	Ch. 13, 14
12	Ch. 16, 17	Unit 6 Thematic Project
13	Ch. 18, Unit 8 Thematic Project	Ch. 15, 16
14	Ch. 19, 20	Unit 7 Thematic Project
15	Unit 9 Thematic Project	Ch. 17, 18; Unit 8 Thematic Project
16	Ch. 21	Ch. 19, 20; Unit 9 Thematic Project
17	Ch. 22, Ch. 23	Ch. 21, 22
18	Unit 10 Thematic Project	Ch. 23; Unit 10 Thematic Project

Additional activities for each chapter can be found in the *Student Activity Workbook, Presentation Plus!* PowerPoint® Presentation CD-ROM, and *ExamView*® *Assessment Suite* CD-ROM.

Pacing Guide

and **Adaptable** to **Any Schedule**

180-Day Pacing Guide

36-Week Course		
	Traditional Schedule	Block Schedule
Week	Student Edition	Student Edition
1	Ch. 1 (Sect. 1.1)	Ch. 1 (Sect. 1.1)
2	Ch. 1 (Sect. 1.2)	Ch. 1 (Sect. 1.2)
3	Ch. 2	Ch. 2 (Sect. 2.1)
4	Unit 1 Thematic Project	Ch. 2 (Sect. 2.2)
5	Ch. 3 (Sect. 3.1)	Unit 1 Thematic Project
6	Ch. 3 (Sect 3.2)	Ch. 3 (Sect. 3.1)
7	Ch. 4	Ch. 3 (Sect 3.2)
9	Unit 2 Thematic Project	Ch. 4 (Sect. 4.1)
10	Ch. 5 (Sect. 5.1)	Ch. 4 (Sect. 4.2)
11	Ch. 5 (Sect. 5.2)	Unit 2 Thematic Project
12	Ch. 6	Ch. 5 (Sect. 5.1)
13	Unit 3 Thematic Project	Ch. 5 (Sect. 5.2)
14	Ch. 7 (Sect. 7.1)	Ch. 6
15	Ch. 7 (Sect. 7.2), 8	Unit 3 Thematic Project
16	Ch. 9	Ch. 7
17	Ch. 10	Ch. 8
18	Unit 4 Thematic Project	Ch. 9
19	Ch. 11	Ch. 10
20	Ch. 12	Unit 4 Thematic Project
21	Unit 5 Thematic Project	Ch. 11, 12
22	Ch. 13	Unit 5 Thematic Project
23	Ch. 14	Ch. 13, 14
24	Unit 6 Thematic Project	Unit 6 Thematic Project
25	Ch. 15	Ch. 15
26	Ch. 16	Ch. 16
27	Unit 7 Thematic Project	Unit 7 Thematic Project
28	Ch. 17	Ch. 17
29	Ch. 18	Ch. 18
30	Unit 8 Thematic Project	Unit 8 Thematic Project
31	Ch. 19	Ch. 19
32	Ch. 20	Ch. 20
33	Unit 9 Thematic Project	Unit 9 Thematic Project
34	Ch. 21	Ch. 21
35	Ch. 22, 23	Ch. 22, 23
36	Unit 10 Thematic Project	Unit 10 Thematic Project

Raise the Bar and *Help* Students Clear It

Academic Integration

Academic skills are crucial for success both inside and outside the classroom. In addition to traditional academic skills, your students will need communication skills, interpersonal skills, and strong technology skills in order to succeed in the real world. Basic skills will support your students in completing the tasks that their jobs and lives will demand.

The No Child Left Behind Act

The No Child Left Behind Act of 2001 emphasizes student achievement in basic academic subjects. It introduces strict accountability measures for schools in the form of standardized testing. Traditionally, core academic subjects have been defined as language arts, science, and mathematics. No Child Left Behind names the following academic subjects:

- English
- Reading/Language Arts
- Mathematics
- Science
- World Languages
- Civics and Government
- Economics
- Art
- History
- Geography

The Importance of Integrating Academics

In a recent survey of high school graduates—many of whom had gone directly to work rather than into postsecondary education—more than half the respondents said their high schools should have placed more emphasis on basic academic skills.

Unfortunately, these students—like so many others—were not able to recognize the relevance of their course work while they were in high school. By explicitly integrating academic skills into the family and consumer sciences curriculum, you can make students aware of the connections between schoolwork and the real world.

Integrated learning offers the following additional benefits to students:

- It provides real-world learning and thus establishes patterns of lifelong learning.
- It improves the academic achievement of all students—including those who will begin their careers directly after high school, those who will go on to postsecondary education or training, and those who will obtain four-year college degrees and beyond.
- It helps students make realistic plans for their own careers and education.

Academics in the Family and Consumer Sciences Curriculum

Integrate academic skills into the classroom as a regular part of your classroom activities. For example, by having students read class assignments and texts, write letters and reports, give presentations, and perform mathematics exercises, you are helping them improve their academic skills. Make expectations clear. For example, if you ask your students to prepare a written report, explain that grammar, spelling, and presentation will be evaluated along with subject content. These are skills that students will need for success in school and at work.

To integrate academics into your course, you must incorporate principles from other subjects in a way that students can understand either on a concrete level or in metaphoric terms. This type of teaching will help those students who learn best when they are exposed to a variety of examples.

Efficient Instruction to **All Students**

Accountability

A consequence of the No Child Left Behind Act, and the reauthorization of the Perkins Act through 2012, is that more states require testing for high school graduation. Accountability measures new to the Perkins reauthorization bill include:

- Academic proficiency as measured by the state criteria developed under NCLB;
- Graduation rates, also as defined by NCLB;
- Number of students to continue to postsecondary education;
- Number of students to complete state or industry certification or licensure; and
- Student achievement on assignments aligned with industry standards.

Connection to Relevance

With the mandatory requirements for proven test scores and graduation numbers, how can we assure that our students are learning? Most educators agree it is by connecting the relevance of education to life.

The Association for Career and Technical Education past-president Bob Scarborough says the Perkins reauthorization "ensures we are providing all students with an education that will help them succeed in the workplace and in life." William Daggett writes in *Achieving Academic Excellence through Rigor and Relevance*:

> What is important is that students enter the global economy with the ability to apply what they learned in school to a variety of ever-changing situations that they may not have been able to foresee before graduating.

The Rigor/Relevance Framework, developed at the International Center for Leadership in Education, illustrates leveled learning processes that enable students to perform high-level thinking. The learning process defines student performance in four sequential categories: acquisition, application, assimilation and adaptation.

As educators, our goal is to teach students to adapt their acquired knowledge and skills in complex ways to any situations, known and unknown. As educators, we are committed to provide the connectivity between classroom learning and real-world application.

Applications

Studies show that students understand and retain knowledge when they experience or apply it to relevant situations. The *Discovering Life Skills* program is dedicated to meet the challenge. Every chapter in *Discovering Life Skills* is filled with ways to engage students in experiential learning and applying their knowledge to their lives.

Features designed to help students find the relevance in content include:

- Unit Thematic Project (featuring skills self-assessment, and connection to the community)
- Community Connections
- Character Counts
- Discover International…
- Hands-On Lab and How To…
- Science You Can Use and Math You Can Use
- Discover Careers
- Chapter Review & Applications, including Real-World Skills and Applications and Academic Skills

The content and teaching strategies in *Discovering Life Skills* are designed to help applied learning students acclimate into the real world and to prepare them for making good nutrition and wellness choices throughout life.

Designing Instruction for a Diverse Classroom

The Diverse Classroom

No two students enter a classroom with identical abilities, backgrounds, experiences, and learning preferences, yet they are all expected to master the curricular objectives. Teachers face the enormous challenge of designing instruction to better meet the diverse learning needs of students.

Universal Access and Universal Design

Universal access and universal design, as well as differentiated instruction, provide a framework for professional educators to address the challenges and opportunities of a diverse classroom.

Universal Access

Universal Access (UA) means that all people have an equal opportunity to access information, products, and services. Universal access, from an educational perspective, means that all students have an equal opportunity to education. This means access to high-quality curriculum and instruction regardless of learning diversities. UA may involve the use of specialized technology and environments.

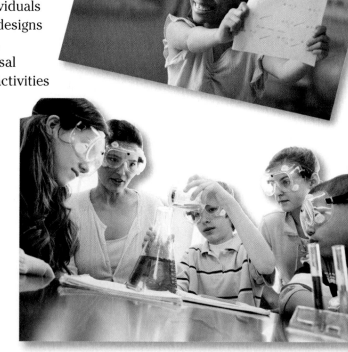

Universal Design

Universal Design (UD) has a foundation in architecture. UD originally focused on accessibility issues for individuals with disabilities. Current UD philosophy focuses on designs that support all individuals, not just individuals with disabilities. From an educational perspective, universal design makes instructional facilities, materials, and activities available so that all learners can achieve success. The key instructional element associated with UD is variety:

- A variety of teaching methods to deliver the content
- A variety of ways for students to interact with teachers and other students
- A variety of ways students can demonstrate their learning
- A variety of ways to assess and evaluate student learning

Differentiated Instruction

Differentiated Instruction (DI) is a planned, deliberate, sequential, and systematic instructional technique designed to maximize the learning and achievement of all students in the classroom. Because of the diversity in student learning abilities and preferences, instruction needs to be equally diverse. By recognizing and positively responding to diverse student backgrounds, languages, abilities, and learning preferences, teachers are better able to deliver instruction that creates opportunities for improved student learning, and success within the framework of universal design.

Five Key Steps for Delivering Differentiated Instruction

1. *Know your students' learning profiles.*

A student's learning profile may include information about learning disabilities, English language ability, learning preferences, customs, needs, interests, and background. To gather student learning profiles, record student inventories, take note of conversations, make observations, and connect with other education specialists. Use the Universal Access activities and suggestions found in *Discovering Life Skills* to craft lessons to suit your students' needs.

2. *Use a variety of instructional methods.*

Differentiated instruction varies the way that learning expectations are delivered to the students. *Discovering Life Skills* offers suggestions for modifying instructional delivery to include problem-solving activities, writing, models, demonstrations, and graphic organizers.

3. *Provide ample opportunities for student/teacher and student/student interactions.*

The varied use of small group, partner, and whole-class instruction provides a differentiated approach that can be used to support many needs, such as language skills, review, enrichment, or acceleration. Modify the independence of the activities in *Discovering Life Skills* using group and partner activity suggestions throughout the book, Interpersonal and Collaborative Activities in the chapter reviews, and Guided Practice activities in the Teacher Annotated Edition Lesson Plans.

4. *Allow students to demonstrate their learning with a variety of product options.*

Students should be given the opportunity to demonstrate their learning in diverse ways. For example, some students who struggle with writing may prefer to demonstrate their learning orally (speech, skit, audio recording), visually (model, exhibit, poster, drawing), or through media applications (video, PowerPoint®, music). Use the Hands-On Labs, Technology Applications, Active Learning activities, and other creative activities throughout *Discovering Life Skills* as models for alternative product options.

5. *Use varied methods to assess and evaluate student learning.*

Student assessments should be varied and frequent. They should be formal (graded, such as a test or product) and informal (non-graded, such as observations or group questioning for progress monitoring). Self-assessments allow the students to judge their own progress. Assessments should also include a range of low- to high-level thinking and responding skills in both traditional and authentic assessment formats. Use the Self-Evaluation Rubrics, quizzes, critical thinking assignments, and discussion questions in *Discovering Life Skills* to assess and evaluate student learning.

Delivering Instruction to Reach All Students

Differentiated Instruction for English Language Learners

Differentiated instruction is important in virtually all classrooms. It is critical in language-diverse classrooms, where many learning activities can be and should be modified and differentiated. Before determining what level of differentiation is needed for your English language learners (ELL), ask yourself two questions:

1. Which language proficiency level best describes my English language learners?

Many schools, districts, and/or states typically place their ELL students in one of several language proficiency levels. Each level offers suggested activity verbs that support student learning. The use of verb taxonomies for differentiating both the process and product of learning can be helpful to students. Use the verbs most appropriate for the students' proficiencies, as identified below:

Language Proficiency Levels

Beginning/Early Intermediate These students typically read English at 0–2.5 grade level. They may be able to write short simple paragraphs and identify main ideas and story characters. **Activity Verbs:** tell, point, circle, underline, name, draw, change, describe, and discuss.

Intermediate These students read English at 2.6–3.5 grade level and can often write paragraphs and identify "wh" questions (who, what, when, where, and why). **Activity Verbs:** apply, show, classify, modify, explain, solve, and demonstrate.

Early Advanced These students are near proficient. They read at 3.6–5.5 grade level and may be fluent in oral English. They often need help with academic and written English. **Activity Verbs:** analyze, compare, contrast, criticize, examine, create, predict, design, manage, and prepare.

2. Is some degree of activity modification necessary to assure achievement and success?

Some activities may not need modification for ELL students, but many will. There are three common ways to modify an activity:

- *Modify the Language Rigor.*
  Change the activity verb to better align with the student's language proficiency.

- *Modify the Independence Rigor.*
  Change the students' degree of independence to align with his/her needed support. For example, an activity that directs the students to complete a task "independently" could be changed to "with a partner."

- *Provide Product Options.*
  Allow students to demonstrate their learning in multiple ways by asking them to write a report or poem; draw; orally explain; or create a game, poster, commercial, video, presentation, song, or cartoon. Students may also teach a lesson, build a model, construct a diagram, or conduct an experiment.

Prior to any activity modification, confirm that all associated vocabulary is clearly understood by all students. Whenever possible, activity modification should be supported by graphic organizers, such as T-charts, webs, sequence, hierarchical, cluster, vocabulary, and data charts.

Sample Activity Modified for ELL Students

W Writing Strategy

Make a List Ask students to create a list of questions to ask when evaluating an advertisement. Have them create a worksheet that they can fill out when looking at an advertisement that contains their questions and space to answer them.

Modified for Beginner/Early Intermediate Students
ELL Writing Strategy

As a class, ask students to think of questions to ask when evaluating an advertisement. Write each question on the board. Give the class an advertisement to evaluate. Walk students through each question as a class. Write their answers on the board.

Modified for Intermediate Students
ELL Writing Strategy

In small groups, have students list four questions to ask when evaluating an advertisement. Have students answer each question orally to their group as they evaluate an advertisement.

Modified for Early Advanced Students
ELL Writing Strategy

In pairs, have students list four questions to ask when evaluating an advertisement. Have them create a worksheet listing questions they can answer in writing when looking at an advertisement.

Reading Skills Handbook

Empower Your Students with Reading Skills

How Can I Motivate My Students to Read?

As a teacher, your role is to help students make personal connections in order to answer the question, "Why do I need to learn this?" Emphasize that reading is not only a necessity for work and for life; it can also bring enjoyment and enlightenment.

Ask your students, "What role does reading play in your life?" You can open this discussion by modeling examples: I love historical biographies; I read menus and order meals in Spanish; I read magazines and access the Internet to stay up to date on my favorite sports teams.

Improving or Fine-Tuning Reading Skills Will Help Your Students:

- ◆ Improve grades
- ◆ Read faster and more efficiently
- ◆ Improve their study skills
- ◆ Remember more information accurately
- ◆ Improve their writing

The Reading Process

Good reading skills build on one another, overlap, and spiral in much the same way that a winding staircase goes around and around while leading readers to a higher place. The Reading Skills Handbook is designed to help your students find and use the tools to use before, during, and after reading.

Reading Strategies

- ◆ Identify, understand, and learn new words
- ◆ Understand why you read
- ◆ Take a quick look at the whole text
- ◆ Try to predict what you are about to read
- ◆ Take breaks during reading and ask questions about the text
- ◆ Take notes
- ◆ Keep thinking about what will come next
- ◆ Summarize

Vocabulary Development

Word identification and vocabulary skills are the building blocks of reading and writing. By learning to use a variety of strategies to build word skills and vocabulary, your students will become stronger readers.

Use Context to Determine Meaning

The best way for your students to expand and extend vocabulary is to read widely, listen carefully, and participate in a rich variety of discussions. When reading independently, students can often figure out the meanings of new words by looking at their context, or the other words and sentences that surround them.

They Will Use in the Real World

Predict a Possible Meaning

Another way to determine the meaning of a word is to take the word apart. If a reader understands the meaning of the **base,** or **root,** part of a word, and knows the meanings of key syllables added either to the beginning or end of the base word, it becomes easy to figure out what the word means.

Word Origins Since Latin, Greek, and Anglo-Saxon roots are the basis for much of our English vocabulary, having some background in one of these languages can be a useful vocabulary tool. For example, astronomy comes from the Greek root *astro*, which means relating to the stars. *Stellar* also has a meaning referring to stars, but its origin is Latin. Knowing root words in other languages can help readers determine meanings, derivations, and spellings in English.

Prefixes and Suffixes A prefix is a word part that can be added to the beginning of a word. For example, the prefix *semi* means half or partial, so *semicircle* means half a circle. A suffix is a word part that can be added to the end of a word. Adding a suffix often changes a word from one part of speech to another.

Using Dictionaries A dictionary provides the meaning or meanings of a word. Look at the sample dictionary entry in the student edition Reading Skills Handbook to see what other information it provides.

Thesauruses and Specialized Reference Books A thesaurus provides synonyms and often antonyms. It is a useful tool to use to expand vocabulary. Remind students to check the exact definition of the listed words in a dictionary before using a thesaurus. Specialized dictionaries such the *Barron's Dictionary of Business Terms or Black's Law Dictionary* list terms and expressions not commonly included in a general dictionary.

Glossaries Many textbooks and technical works contain condensed dictionaries that provide an alphabetical listing of words used throughout the text and their specific definitions.

Recognize Word Meanings Across Subjects Words often have different meanings when used for different purposes. The word *product* may mean one thing in math and another in science. For example:

Math After you multiply the two numbers, explain how you arrived at the **product.**

Science One **product** of photosynthesis is oxygen.

Economics The Gross National **Product** is the total dollar value of goods and services produced by a nation.

How Can I Help My Students Understand What They Read?

Reading comprehension means understanding—deriving meaning from—what has been read. Using a variety of strategies can help improve comprehension and make reading more interesting and more fun.

Read for a Reason

To get the greatest benefit from reading, teach students to **establish a purpose for their reading.** In school, some of the reasons for reading are to:
- learn and understand new information
- find specific information
- review before a test
- complete an assignment
- prepare (research) before you write

As reading skills improve, you will notice that your students apply different strategies to fit the different purposes for reading. For example, a person reading for entertainment may read quickly, but reading to gather information or follow directions might require reading more slowly, taking notes, constructing a graphic organizer, or rereading sections of text.

Draw on Personal Background

Drawing on personal background, or activating prior knowledge, helps students connect their culture and experiences to their reading. Before introducing a new topic, you may want to encourage students to ask:
- What have I heard or read about this topic?
- Do I have any personal experience relating to this topic?

You can also set common background knowledge with discussion before reading. For example, to prepare students to read the novel *A Farewell to Arms*, you might lead a discussion about these common background themes:
- World War I
- Italy (You might ask a student to show the location of Italy on a map)
- Other Ernest Hemingway titles
- The Nobel Prize in literature

Having this historical background will help to set the scene for students as they read.

Using a KWL Chart A KWL chart is a good device for organizing information gathered before, during, and after reading. In the first column, students list what they already know, then list what they want to know in the middle column. They use the third column to review and assess what they learned. You or your students can add more columns to record places where they found information and places where they can look for more information.

K (What I already know)	W (What I want to know)	L (What I have learned)

Adjust Your Reading Speed Reading speed is a key factor in how well students understand what they read. Reading speed can vary depending on the purpose for reading.

Scanning means running one's eyes quickly over the material to look for words or phrases. Readers scan to find a specific piece of information.

Skimming means reading a passage quickly to find its main idea or get an overview. Skim a passage as a preview to determine what the material is about.

Reading for detail involves careful reading while paying attention to text structure and monitoring understanding. Readers read for detail to learn concepts, follow complicated directions, or prepare to analyze a text.

Techniques to Help Students Understand and Remember What They Read

Preview

Previewing strategies help students begin at a visual level, then drill down to evaluate, predict, draw conclusions, and use contextual clues about what they will read.

Predict

Previewing Strategies

◆ Read the title, headings, and subheadings of the selection.

◆ Look at the illustrations and notice how the text is organized.

◆ Skim the selection. Take a glance at the whole thing.

◆ Decide what the main idea might be.

◆ Predict what a selection will be about.

As students read, they take educated guesses about story events and outcomes. They make predictions before and during reading. This helps them focus their attention on the text and that focus improves understanding.

Determine the Main Idea

When students look for the main idea, they are looking for the most important statement in a text. Depending on what kind of text they read, the main idea can be located at the very beginning (news stories in a newspaper or a magazine) or at the end (scientific research document).

Encourage students to ask these questions to determine the main idea:

• What is each sentence about?

• Is there one sentence that is more important than all the others?

• What idea do the details support or point out?

Keep track of the text's structure (see below). Looking at headers and content structure will give students important clues about the main idea.

Taking Notes

Cornell Note-Taking System There are many methods for note taking. The **Cornell Note-Taking System** is a well-known method that can help students organize what they read. To the right is a note-taking activity based on the Cornell Note-Taking System.

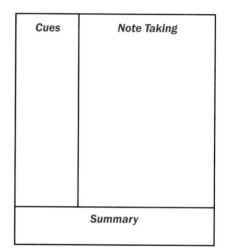

Graphic Organizers Using a graphic organizer to retell content in a visual representation will help students remember and retain content. Encourage students to make charts or diagrams to organize what they have read. Some good examples are:

Venn Diagrams: A Venn diagram is a good way to organize information in a compare-and-contrast text structure. The outer portions of the circles show how two characters, ideas, or items contrast, or are different, and the overlapping part compares two things, or shows how they are similar.

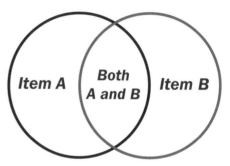

Flow Charts: Students can a track sequence of events or cause and effect on a flow chart. Demonstrate how to arrange ideas or events in their logical, sequential order. Then, draw arrows between ideas to indicate how one idea or event flows into another.

Go to glencoe.com for more information about note taking and additional study tools.

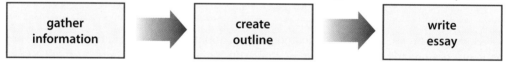

Visualize

Encourage students to try to form a mental picture of scenes, characters, and events as they read. This technique helps them to use the details and descriptions the author gives readers. If students can **visualize** what they read, they will become more interested and will remember the information better.

Question

Tell students to ask questions about the text while they read. Encourage them to ask about the importance of the sentences they read, how the sentences relate to one another, whether they understand what they just read, and what they think is going to come next.

Clarify

Encourage students to try these techniques when they do not understand meaning (through questioning):

> **What to Do When You Do Not Understand**
>
> ◆ Reread confusing parts of the text.
> ◆ Diagram (chart) relationships between chunks of text, ideas, and sentences.
> ◆ Look up unfamiliar words.
> ◆ Talk through the text as if explaining it to someone else.
> ◆ Read the passage once more.

Review

Make sure students take time to stop and review what they have read. Use note-taking outlines or other graphic organizers, charts, or visual aids.

Monitor Comprehension

Teach students to continue to check their understanding using the following two strategies:

Summarize Pause and state the main ideas of the text and the key supporting details. Try to answer the following questions: Who? What? When? Where? Why? How?

Paraphrase Pause, close the book, and try to retell what they have just read using their own words. It helps students to retell, or paraphrase reading into their own words.

Understanding Text Structure

Good writers do not just put together sentences and paragraphs; they organize their writing with a specific purpose in mind. That organization is called text structure. When students understand and follow the structure of a text, it is easier to remember the information they read. There are many ways text may be structured. Each type of structure usually makes use of some specific words. Teach students to watch for these **signal words.** They will help them follow the text's organization. (Remind them to use these techniques as they write.)

Comparison and Contrast

This structure shows similarities and differences between people, things, and ideas. This is often used to demonstrate that things that seem alike are really different, or vice versa.

Signal words: similarly, more, less, on the one hand/on the other hand, in contrast, but, however

Cause and Effect

Writers use the cause-and-effect structure to explore the reasons for something happening and to examine the results or consequences of events.

Signal words: so, because, as a result, therefore, for the following reasons

Problem and Solution

When writers organize text around the question "How?", they state a problem and suggest solutions.

Signal words: how, help, problem, obstruction, overcome, difficulty, need, attempt, have to, must

Sequence

Sequencing tells readers in which order to consider thoughts or facts. Examples of sequencing are:

Chronological order refers to the order in which events take place.

Signal words: first, next, then, finally

Spatial order describes the organization of things in space (to describe the placement of objects in a room, for example).

Signal words: above, below, behind, next to

Order of importance lists things or thoughts from the most important to the least important (or the other way around).

Signal words: principal, central, main, important, fundamental

Thinking About Reading

It is important for students to think about what they are reading to get the most information from a text, to understand the consequences of what the text says, to remember the content, and to form their own opinions about what they read.

Interpret

Interpreting involves asking, "What is the writer really saying?" and then using what students already know to answer the question.

Infer

Writers do not always state exactly everything they want readers to understand. They sometimes imply certain information by providing clues and details. To infer involves using reasoning and experience to develop the idea, based on what an author implies, or suggests. What is most important when drawing inferences is to be sure that readers have accurately based their guesses on supporting details from the text. If students cannot point to a place in the selection to help back up an inference, encourage them to rethink that guess.

Draw Conclusions

A conclusion is a general statement a reader can make and explain using reasoning or supporting details from a text.

Analyze

To understand persuasive nonfiction (a text that lists facts and opinions to arrive at a conclusion), readers must analyze statements and examples to see if they support the main idea. To understand an informational text, students need to keep track of how the ideas are organized to find the main points.

Hint: Have students use graphic organizers and note-taking charts.

Distinguish Between Facts and Opinions

This is one of the most important reading skills students can learn. A fact is a statement that can be proven. An opinion is what the writer believes. A writer may support opinions with facts, but an opinion cannot be proven. For example:

Fact: California produces fruit and other agricultural products.

Opinion: California produces the best fruit and agricultural products.

Evaluate

Remind students that to rely on accurate information, they will need to consider who wrote it and why. Where did the writer get information? Is the information one-sided? Can readers verify the information?

Reading for Research

To guide students in reading actively to research a topic, encourage them to follow these directions:

- Generate an interesting, relevant, and researchable question.
- Categorize that information.
- Evaluate the information.
- Organize information in a new way for a specific audience.
- Draw conclusions about the original research question.

Link Academic Vocabulary

What Is Academic English?
by Robin Scarcella, Ph.D.

Academic English is the language commonly used in business and education. It is the language used in academics, business, and courts of law. It is the type of English used in professional books, including textbooks, and it contains specific linguistic features that are associated with all disciplines. Proficiency in reading and using academic English is strongly related to long-term success in all parts of life.

What Is Academic Vocabulary?

By the time they complete elementary school, students should acquire the knowledge they will need to understand academic vocabulary. For example, in academic texts, a full 8% of the words are academic words. A basic 2,000-word vocabulary of high-frequency words makes up 87% of the words. Three percent are technical words that vary depending on the discipline. The remaining 2% are low-frequency words.

Why Should Students Learn Academic Vocabulary?

English language learners who have mastered a basic 2,000-word vocabulary are ready to acquire the majority of general words found in their texts and on standardized tests.

Knowledge of academic words, combined with continued acquisition of general words, can significantly boost an English learner's comprehension level of academic texts. English learners who learn and practice these words before they graduate from high school are likely to master academic material with more confidence and speed. They waste less time and effort in guessing words than those students who know only the basic 2,000 words that characterize general conversation.

Academic Vocabulary and Academic English in the Family and Consumer Sciences Classroom

Teachers can provide their students with rich samples of academic vocabulary and help students understand the academic English of their text. To develop academic English, students must have already acquired a large amount of basic proficiency in the grammar of everyday English.

to Career & Real-World Content

Academic English should be taught within contexts that make sense. Academic English arises not only from a knowledge of linguistic code and cognition but also from social practices in which academic English is used to accomplish communicative goals. The acquisition of academic vocabulary and grammar is necessary to advance the development of academic English.

Tips for Teaching Academic Vocabulary:

- **Expose Students to Academic Vocabulary**—Students learn academic vocabulary through use and in reading content. You do not need to call attention to all academic words students are learning because they will acquire them subconsciously.

- **Do Not Correct Students' Mistakes When Using Academic Vocabulary**—All vocabulary understanding and spelling errors are developmental and will disappear once the student reads more.

- **Help Students Decode the Words Themselves**—Once students learn the alphabet, they should be able to decode words. Decoding each word they do not recognize will help them more than trying to focus on sentence structure. Once they can recognize words, they can read authentic texts.

- **Do Not Ignore the English Learner in This Process**—These students can learn academic vocabulary before they are completely fluent in spoken English.

- **Helping Students Build Academic Vocabulary Leads to Broader Learning**—Students who have mastered the basic academic vocabulary are ready to continue acquiring words from the rest of the vocabulary groups. Use the Internet to find lists of appropriate vocabulary words.

Guidelines for Teaching Academic Vocabulary

There are a number of guidelines that teachers can follow when teaching academic English and vocabulary:

1. Use direct and planned instruction.
2. Employ models that have increasingly difficult language.
3. Focus attention on form by pointing out linguistic features of words.
4. Provide practice opportunities.
5. Motivate student interest and self-confidence.
6. Provide instructional feedback.
7. Use assessment tools on a regular basis.

Generate the Best Performance

Assessment

In response to the growing demand for accountability in the classroom, educators must use multiple assessment measures to accurately gauge student performance. In addition to quizzes, tests, essay exams, and standardized tests, assessment today incorporates a variety of performance-based measurements and portfolio opportunities.

Performance assessment activities provide hands-on approaches to learning concepts. Through activities, students are able to actually experience these concepts rather than just reading and listening about them. These types of activities also help students become aware of diverse audiences for their work. Performance assessment tasks are based on what is most essential in the curriculum and what is interesting to the student.

from *Your* Students

Performance-Based Assessments

One good way to present a performance assessment is in the form of an open-ended question.

- **Journals**—Students write from their own perspective on topics that affect their lives.
- **Letters**—Students write a letter from themselves to friends and family, or another audience.
- **Position Paper or Editorial**—Students explain a controversial issue and present their own opinions and recommendations, supported with strong evidence and convincing reasons.
- **Newspaper**—Students write stories from the perspective of a reporter. This could also involve the writing of editorials or letters to the editor.
- **Biographies and Autobiographies**—Students write about leaders either from the third person point of view (biography) or from the first person (autobiography).
- **Creative Stories**—Students integrate family and consumer sciences topics into a piece of fiction.
- **Poems and Songs**—Students follow the conventions of a particular type of song or poem as they tell about a topic or event.
- **Research Reports**—Students synthesize information from a variety of sources into a well-developed research report.

Oral Presentations

Oral presentations allow students to demonstrate their academic and topical literacy in front of an audience. Oral presentations are often group efforts, although this need not be the case.

- **Simulations**—Students hold simulations of actual events, such as a role play in a specific scenario.
- **Debates**—Students debate two or more sides of a policy or issue.
- **Interview**—Students conduct a mock journalism interview or job interview.
- **Oral Reports**—Students present the results of research efforts in a lively oral report. This report may be accompanied by visuals.
- **Skits and Plays**—Students use specific events or topics as the basis for a play or skit.

Visual Presentations

Visual presentations allow students to demonstrate their understanding in a variety of visual formats. Visual presentations can be either group or individual projects.

- **Model**—Students make a model to demonstrate or represent a particular process.
- **Museum Exhibit**—Students create a rich display of materials around a topic. Typical displays might include models, illustrations, photographs, videos, writings, and presentation software.

- **Graph or Chart**—Students analyze and represent data in a line graph, bar graph, table, or other chart format.
- **Drawing**—Students represent an event or period through illustration, including cartoons.
- **Posters and Murals**—Posters and murals may include maps, time lines, diagrams, illustrations, photographs, and written explanations that reflect students' understanding of the information.
- **Videotapes**—Students film a video to show a simulation of an event.
- **Multimedia Presentation**—Students create a computer-generated presentation or slide show containing information and analysis.

How Are Performance Assessments Scored?

There are a variety of means used to evaluate performance tasks. Some or all of the following methods may be used:

- **Scoring Rubrics**—A scoring rubric is a set of guidelines for assessing the quality of a process and/or product. It sets out criteria used to distinguish acceptable responses from unacceptable ones, generally on a scale from excellent to poor. Rubrics may be used as guidelines as the students prepare their products. They are also commonly used for peer-to-peer assessment and self-assessment.
- **Models of Excellent Work**—Teacher-selected models of excellent work concretely illustrate expectations and help students set goals for their own projects.

- **Student Self-Assessment**—Common methods of self-assessment include ranking work in relation to the model, using a scoring rubric, and writing goals and then evaluating how well the goals have been met. Regardless of which method or methods students use, they should be encouraged to evaluate their behaviors and processes, as well as the finished product.
- **Peer or Audience Assessment**—Many of the performance tasks target an audience other than the classroom teacher. If possible, the audience of peers should give feedback. Have the class create rubrics for specific projects together.
- **Observation**—As students carry out their performance tasks, you may want to formally observe them at work. Start by developing a checklist, identifying all the specific behaviors and understandings you expect students to demonstrate. Then, observe students as they carry out performance tasks and check off behaviors as you observe them.
- **Interviews**—As a form of ongoing assessment, you may want to conduct interviews with students, asking them to analyze, explain, and assess their participation in performance tasks. When projects take place over an extended period of time, you can hold periodic interviews as well as exit interviews. In this way, the interview process allows you to gauge the status of the project and to guide the students' efforts along the way.

Prepare **Your Students** to **Improve** Their *Performance*

Test-Prep Strategies

Students can follow the steps below to prepare for the standardized assessments they are required to take.

- **Read About the Test**—Students can familiarize themselves with the format, the types of questions, and the amount of time they will have to complete the test. Emphasize that it is very important for students to budget their time during test-taking.

- **Review the Content**—Consistent study will help students build knowledge and understanding. If there are specific objectives or standards that are tested on the exam, help students review facts or skills.

- **Practice**—Provide practice, ideally with real tests, to build students' familiarity with the content, format, and timing of the real exam. Students should practice all the types of questions they will encounter on the test.

- **Pace**—Students should pace themselves differently depending on how the test is administered. As students practice, they should try to increase the number of questions they can answer correctly. If students have trouble with an item, they should mark it and come back to it later.

- **Analyze Practice Results**—Help students improve test-taking performance by analyzing their test-taking strengths and weaknesses. Help students identify what kinds of questions they found most difficult. Look for patterns in errors and tailor instruction to review the appropriate test-taking skills or content.

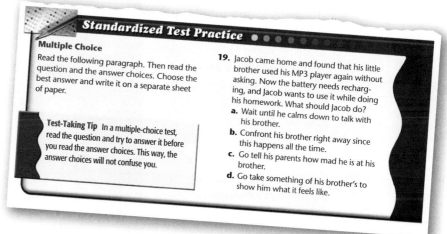

Standardized Test Practice

Multiple Choice

Read the following paragraph. Then read the question and the answer choices. Choose the best answer and write it on a separate sheet of paper.

Test-Taking Tip In a multiple-choice test, read the question and try to answer it before you read the answer choices. This way, the answer choices will not confuse you.

19. Jacob came home and found that his little brother used his MP3 player again without asking. Now the battery needs recharging, and Jacob wants to use it while doing his homework. What should Jacob do?
   a. Wait until he calms down to talk with his brother.
   b. Confront his brother right away since this happens all the time.
   c. Go tell his parents how mad he is at his brother.
   d. Go take something of his brother's to show him what it feels like.

Test-Taking Strategies

It's not enough for students to learn facts and concepts. They must be able to show what they know in a variety of test-taking situations.

Objective Tests

Apply the following strategies to help students do their best on objective tests.

Multiple-Choice Questions

- Students should read the directions carefully to learn what answer the test requires—the best answer or the right answer. This is especially important when answer choices include "all of the above" or "none of the above."
- Advise students to watch for negative words in the questions, such as not, except, unless, and never.
- Students should try to mentally answer the question before reading the answer choices.
- Students should read all the answer choices and eliminate those that are obviously wrong.

True/False Questions

- It is important that students read the entire question before answering. For an answer to be true, the entire statement must be true. If one part of a statement is false, the answer should be marked false.
- Remind students to watch for words such as all, never, every, and always. Statements containing these words are often false.

Matching Questions

- Students should read through both lists before they mark any answers.
- Unless an answer can be used more than once, students should cross out each choice as they use it.
- Using what they know about grammar can help students find the right answer. For instance, when matching a word with its definition, the definition is often the same part of speech (noun, verb, adjective, or adverb) as the word.

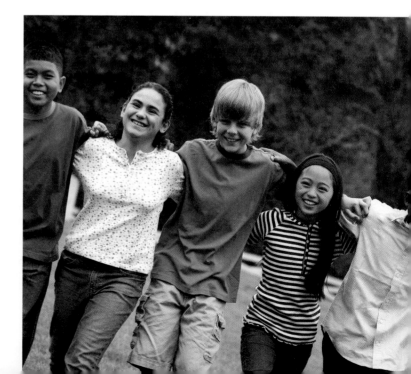

Essay Tests

Essay tests require students to provide thorough and well-organized written responses, in addition to telling what they know. Help students use these strategies on essay tests.

Read the Question

The key to writing successful essay responses lies in reading and interpreting questions correctly. Teach students to identify and underline key words to guide them in understanding what the question asks.

Plan and Write the Essay

Students should follow the writing process to develop their answer. Encourage students to follow these steps to plan and write their essays.

1. Map out an answer. Make lists, webs, or an outline to plan the response.
2. Decide on an order in which to present the main points.
3. Write an opening statement that directly responds to the essay question.
4. Write the essay. Expand on the opening statement. Support key points with specific facts, details, and reasons.
5. Write a closing statement that brings the main points together.
6. Proofread to check for spelling, grammar, and punctuation.

The table below defines purposes for different writing strategies.

Writing Strategies	
Analyze	To analyze means to systematically and critically examine all parts of an issue or event.
Classify or Categorize	To classify or categorize means to put people, things, or ideas into groups, based on a common set of characteristics.
Compare and Contrast	To compare is to show how things are similar, or alike. To contrast is to show how things are different.
Describe	To describe means to present a sketch or impression. Rich details, especially details that appeal to the senses, flesh out a description.
Discuss	To discuss means to systematically write about all sides of an issue or event.
Evaluate	To evaluate means to make a judgment and support it with evidence.
Explain	To explain means to clarify or make plain.
Illustrate	To illustrate means to provide examples or to show with a picture or other graphic.
Infer	To infer means to read between the lines or to use knowledge and experience to draw conclusions, make a generalization, or form a prediction.
Justify	To justify means to prove or to support a position with specific facts and reasons.
Predict	To predict means to tell what will happen in the future, based on an understanding of prior events and behaviors.
State	To state means to briefly and concisely present information.
Summarize	To summarize means to give a brief overview of the main points of an issue or event.
Trace	To trace means to present the steps or stages in a process or event in sequential or chronological order.

Base Your Teaching on Best Practices

Critical Thinking

One of the factors that determines students' success is a their ability to deal with the varied demands of day-to-day life. This requires insightful decision making, creative problem solving, and interactions with diverse groups. Thus, teaching critical thinking equips your students with the skills necessary to achieve success.

Cognitive Development

All learning requires thinking. Benjamin Bloom's Taxonomy of the Cognitive Domain is probably the most widely recognized schema of levels of thinking.

Each of Bloom's six cognitive categories lists various thinking skills and indicates the types of behavior students are expected to perform to fulfill specific learning goals. See the chart below.

The Value of Critical Thinking

Critical thinking is the process of reasonably or logically deciding what to do or believe. It involves the ability to:

- Compare and contrast
- Solve problems
- Make decisions
- Analyze and evaluate
- Synthesize and transfer knowledge
- Engage in metacognition

CATEGORY	GOAL	EXPECTED STUDENT RESPONSE	APPROPRIATE QUESTIONS/PROMPTS
Knowledge	Identify and recall information	Define, recognize, recall, identify, label, show, collect, understand, examine	Who…? What…? When…? Where…? How…? Describe….
Comprehension	Organize and select facts and ideas	Translate, interpret, explain, describe, summarize, extrapolate	Retell in your own words…. What is the main idea of…?
Application	Use facts, rules, and principles	Apply, solve, show, experiment, predict	How is…an example of…? How is…related to…?
Analysis	Separate a whole into component parts	Connect, relate, differentiate, classify, arrange, check, group, distinguish, organize, categorize, detect, compare, infer	Classify…according to…. How does… compare/contrast with…?
Synthesis	Combine ideas to form a new whole	Produce, propose, design, construct, combine, formulate, compose, plan, hypothesize	What would you predict/infer from…? What might happen if you combined…with…?
Evaluation	Develop opinions, judgments, or decisions	Appraise, judge, criticize, decide	What do you think about…? Prioritize….

and Your Students Will Benefit

Critical thinking skills are important for these reasons:

- They help students investigate their own problem-solving mechanisms.
- They help students find creative resolutions.
- They lead students to compare and contrast what they know with unknowns.
- They allow students to make decisions about their own learning while making them aware of their learning processes.

Cooperative Learning

Studies show that students learn faster and retain more information when they are actively involved in the learning process. Cooperative learning is one method that gets students actively involved in learning and at the same time allows for peer teaching.

Using Cooperative Learning

Your family and consumer sciences course provides many opportunities for students to learn and apply the skills necessary for positive interpersonal relationships. Through the use of cooperative learning, you can offer a structured method of teaching team-building, collaborative social skills, and team decision making while teaching basic concepts—essential skills for making nutrition and wellness choices.

Cooperative Learning in This Text

In *Discovering Life Skills*, students and teachers have a variety of materials to assist with cooperative learning activities.

The Benefits of Cooperative Learning

- Cooperative learning emphasizes working toward group goals rather than the traditional emphasis on individual competition and achievement.
- Students discover that not only must they learn the material themselves, but they are also responsible for helping everyone in the group learn.
- Cooperative learning increases academic achievement and develops essential social skills.
- Students learn valuable problem-solving, team-building, and creativity skills that transfer to real-world environments and situations.
- People who help each other and work together toward a common goal generally begin to feel more positive about themselves and each other.
- Students have the opportunity to perceive other students as colleagues rather than competitors. They recognize the value of helping others.

Research-Based Classroom Solutions

Technology

Technology affects how all people work, interact, and live. Technology will affect your students in the real world. For example, they may keep records using a computer or apply for a job over the Internet. It will also affect your students as consumers. An increasing number of people market, buy, and sell products on the Web. It is critical that your students become familiar and comfortable with technology now in order to prepare for success in life.

Activities

Discovering Life Skills helps you integrate technology into your teaching with technology-based activities:

- Features and assessments provide a link to the *Discovering Life Skills* Online Learning Center (OLC) at **glencoe.com** to assist students in finding answers and to further research the topic or find a project.

- The chapter-opening **Reading Guide** provides a link to the OLC for students to download the printable graphic organizer.
- The in-chapter features **Hands-On Lab** and **Discovering Careers** send students to the OLC for helpful links or an extension activity.
- The **Real-World Skills and Applications** section in the Chapter Review and Applications assessment contains a Technology Application in alternating chapters.
- Students can use assessment rubrics on the OLC to self-evaluate their **Unit Life Skills Projects**.

Using the Internet Effectively

Give these tips to your students to help them use the Internet effectively in the classroom:

- Look for sites that are created by the government or universities (their URLs typically end in .gov or .edu). These are reliable sites with factual integrity and stability.
- Find out who created the site. If the purpose and creator of the Web site are unclear, its content may be unreliable.
- Use multiple search engines when looking for information on a topic. This will call up as many of the pertinent sites as possible.
- Combine Internet research with traditional research methods. Have students ask librarians and experts for information and sources. Use books and magazines.

Diversity

Discovering Life Skills is designed to help students recognize and discuss issues of cultural diversity. During class activities, you may also find it appropriate to integrate questions related to cultural diversity. For example, you might expand a class discussion by asking:

- Would your response change if a classmate did not speak the same native language as you speak? If so, how?
- Would you speak to your classmate differently if his or her ethnic background were different from yours?
- Would your decision change if your classmate were a male or female? From your own ethnic background? From a different background? Why?

Integrating Cultural Diversity

Your students will be faced with a diverse world, meeting people of many different cultures. Cultural knowledge may be the difference between success and failure in our global economy. For students to become productive and responsible citizens, they must be open to cultural differences.

As students learn about skills needed to be successful, they should keep in mind the wide diversity of the people they are likely to encounter in every aspect of their working and personal lives. In the classroom and in one-on-one conferences, you can help your students consider the diversity of the U.S. population, not only in terms of ethnicity, but also in terms of customs, attitudes, religious beliefs, language backgrounds, and physical capabilities. High school students need to understand that ability and success are not related to skin color or gender.

Multicultural Education

Multicultural education incorporates the idea that all students—regardless of their gender and social class, and their ethnic, racial, or cultural characteristics—should have an equal opportunity to learn in school. Learning about other cultures concurrently with their own culture helps students recognize similarities and appreciate differences, without perceiving inferiority or superiority of one or the other. To foster cultural awareness:

- Recognize that all students are unique, having special talents and abilities.
- Promote uniqueness and diversity as positive traits.
- Know, appreciate, and respect the cultural backgrounds of your students.
- Use authentic situations to provide cultural learning and understanding.
- Make sure people of all cultures are represented fairly and accurately.
- Make sure that historical information is accurate and nondiscriminatory.
- Make sure that materials do not include stereotypical roles.
- Make sure there is gender equity.
- Welcome family and community involvement.
- Use current news stories, advertisements, or other forms of media to call students' attention to cultural differences that influence businesses, communities, and families.

Ethics

Helping students learn about ethical behavior and how to consider the effects of a decision before it is made are important life skills for your students preparing for the real world.

The Benefits of Integrating Ethics

The goal of teaching ethical decision-making skills is not to teach values. It is to help students clarify their ethical beliefs and learn how to evaluate ethical situations. Make your classroom a risk-free environment in which students can discuss issues and make ethical decisions. Students need to learn how to evaluate their actions and to ask questions such as, "Will I be proud of myself if I take this action?" and "Would I want others to know about my actions?"

The Ethical Decision Model

Your students will learn to analyze ethical situations better if they have a model to use in deliberating the issues that helps them to understand how a decision can affect others. Several decision models exist, but the basic steps for an ethical decision model are as follows:

1. Determine the ethical issue.
2. Identify the actions for handling the situation.
3. Identify the people affected by the situation.
4. Analyze how the situation affects the people involved.
5. Decide which of the actions to take.

Classroom Strategies

Discovering Life Skills provides real-world situations that sometimes pose ethical conundrums. These can be catalysts for lively classroom discussion. In addition, you might lead discussion about topical ethics issues or have students bring in newspaper or magazine articles that suggest ethical dilemmas. Have students analyze the situations in class and, perhaps, write short reports on their analyses and conclusions. Some formats, such as learning groups, role plays, and debates, are particularly well suited to teaching students about ethics.

Cooperative Learning Groups

Small groups of students are especially well suited to discuss cases and share their ideas about ethical issues. Divide students into groups of four or five. Observe groups and encourage all students to participate. Allow each group to reach its own conclusions, and then ask a member of each group to share the group's ideas with the class.

Role Plays and Debates

Have your students role play ethical situations, using their own ideas about how to respond to a given situation. Discuss class responses to the role play, guiding students in using the ethical decision model. Set up debate teams to present different sides of an ethical issue.

Focus on You

Unit Overview

This unit introduces students to the factors that make them who they are. Students will learn about personal care, family structure and support, the importance of friendship, and how to identify and respond to both positive and negative peer pressure.

Chapter 1 *Discover Yourself* In this chapter, students will learn that many parts of their lives come together to make them unique and individual people. They will also learn about the importance of grooming and personal care.

Chapter 2 *Your Family* In this chapter, students become familiar with how families can provide structure and support in their lives. They will be introduced to the different types of changes their families might face and how they can adjust to these changes positively.

Chapter 3 *Your Friendships* In this chapter, students will learn why friendship is important and how to be a good friend. They will also learn how to identify and handle peer pressure and avoid high-risk behaviors.

Life Skills Project Preview

Your Role Models

Tell students that as part of this unit, they will learn that behaving like people they respect can help them grow into better people. They will learn how to identify traits that they admire. They will learn how to photograph and interview someone they admire and present a collage to the class to share what they have learned.

FCCLA provides programs to guide students through projects, enhance their personal growth, and build leadership skills that can make a difference in their lives, their families, and their communities.

Families First is a program through which young people gain a better understanding of how families work and learn skills to become strong family members. Families First focuses on understanding families, strengthening relationships, overcoming obstacles, managing responsibilities, and nurturing children.

Manage Tasks Form students into groups. Tell groups that they own a day care center together. Ask them to decide who will handle the different tasks of the day care: management, cleanliness, food preparation, and safety. Ask them to explain how they decided on their responsibilities and what skills they will need. Students may make their decisions based on individual preferences or specialized skills. Skills may include organization, leadership, customer service, writing or math skills, and knowledge of safety issues.

Professional Development

MINI CLIP VIDEO LIBRARY

Targeted professional development is correlated throughout *Discovering Life Skills*. **The McGraw-Hill Professional Development Mini Clip Video Library** provides teaching strategies to strengthen academic and learning skills. Log on to **glencoe.com**.

In this Unit, you will find these Mini Clips.

CHAPTER 1 Discover Yourself

READING
- **Building Vocabulary** A teacher plays vocabulary games with students. **(p. TM66)**
- **During and After Reading** A teacher models for her students and then has them practice what a good reader "thinks about." **(p. TM68)**

ENGLISH LANGUAGE LEARNERS
- **Language Practice** Students who have varying language proficiencies work together to review the content they have just read. **(p. TM67)**

MATH
- **Problem Solving—Order of Operations** A teacher uses real-life contexts to introduce order of operations. **(p. TM67)**
- **Probability and Fairness** A teacher introduces a probability activity, asking students to determine the fairness of a game by finding the probabilities of the various outcomes. **(p. TM69)**

CHAPTER 2 Your Family

READING
- **Fluency Development** A teacher uses three different instructional strategies to help develop her students reading fluency. **(p. TM73)**

ENGLISH LANGUAGE LEARNERS
- **Content Vocabulary** A teacher provides students with opportunities to practice academic vocabulary and develop concepts. **(p. TM71)**

- **Group Discussions** Students discuss academic content they have just read. **(p. TM71)**

MATH
- **Communications in Mathematics** Bea Moore-Harris explains the importance of student communication in the mathematics classroom. **(p. TM72)**

CHAPTER 3 Your Friendships

READING
- **Planning and Classroom Management** Nancy Frey, Ph.D., teacher, educator, and author, discusses instructional strategies that support a differentiated classroom. **(p. TM77)**
- **Lesson Reflections** A narrator discusses various instructional strategies suitable for use with English learners. **(p. TM77)**
- **Flexible Groupings** Teachers use the strategies of flexible groupings and partner sharing to encourage student discussions. **(p. TM78)**

ENGLISH LANGUAGE LEARNERS
- **Collaborative Work** Students work in groups to complete a science lab, requiring them to use academic vocabulary. **(p. TM76)**
- **Another Point of View** Emily M. Schell, Ed.D., educator, and author, discusses teacher collaboration as it applies to standards-based instruction. **(p. TM78)**
- **Language Practice** Students of varying language proficiencies work together to review the content they have just read. **(p. TM78)**

Discover Yourself

Section 1.1 *You Are Unique*

In this section, students will learn about factors that contribute to individual identity, qualities that make them unique, and emotional and physical changes that happen during adolescence.

Section 1.2 *Grooming and Personal Care*

In this section, students will learn how to groom their skin, hair, teeth, and clothing and how to make a positive first impression with their appearance and behavior.

Classroom Solutions

Print Resources

 Student Edition
 Teacher Annotated Edition
Student Activity Workbook
Student Activity Workbook
Teacher Annotated Edition

Technology Resources

ExamView *ExamView Assessment Suite CD* allows you to create and print out customized tests or ready-made unit and chapter tests, complete with answer keys.

Lesson Planner *Plus Lesson Planner Plus! CD** is and electronic lesson planner that provides instant access to teacher resources in one convenient package.

- Projects and Activities*
- Food Labs*
- Sewing Labs*
- Career Investigations*
- Reteaching Activities*
- Enrichment Activities*

Presentation Plus! PowerPoint™ Presentations can be edited and customized to meet the needs of students.

Online Learning Center includes resources and activities for students and teachers. Also includes Online Student Edition.

Interactive Student Edition

*ELECTRONIC RESOURCES ARE AVAILABLE ON LESSON PLANNER PLUS AND THE ONLINE LEARNING CENTER.

Writing Activity Answer

Freewriting Freewrites should include details that are personally relevant to the student, be written without stopping, and show that the student understands the concept of dependability.

Discovering Careers Answers ▼

1. Answers will vary. Students should write a summary of the education, training, and experience needed for the selected careers.
2. Pamphlets should include: use a soft-bristled brush, use fluoride toothpaste, use up-and-down strokes to clean between teeth, floss daily, eat nutritious food, and get regular dental checkups.
3. Answers will vary. Sample answers: honesty shows that you are sincere and trustworthy; thoughtfulness means you think about how your actions affect coworkers and customers; cheerfulness makes customers feel welcome; responsibility means you do the work you are assigned and you are on time.
4. Answers will vary. Students should present a summary of what they learned about the person's typical work day.

Section **1.1** Lesson Plan

You Are Unique

FOCUS

Discussion Starter

Ask students to name a quality that makes them unique. Explain that in this lesson they will learn more about what makes people unique. Answers will vary, but should be a quality of the answerer, not someone related to them. For example, "My mom works at the zoo" does not make the student unique, but "I help my mom with her work at the zoo" does.

Bell Ringer Activity

Your Unique Qualities Have students list the factors that influence who a person is. Then, next to each factor, have students list one way in which that factor influences who they are. Discuss as a class and have students compare answers to see how different factors combine in different ways to make each person an individual.

TEACH

S Skill Practice

Independent Practice

L1 List Have students list five of the qualities that can help build a positive self-concept. Students may list any qualities that help build positive self-concept, including: honesty, thoughtfulness, cheerfulness, responsibility, self-control, adaptability, compassion, cooperation, courtesy, dependability, enthusiasm, friendliness, generosity, and sincerity.

L2 Explain Have students write a paragraph that explains how heredity contributes to each individual's identity. Heredity is the passing on of traits from parents to children and determines which physical characteristics you inherit from your parents, such as eye, hair and skin color and body size. It also can play a part in determining your intelligence.

L3 Apply Tell students to keep a journal. Have them write down their feelings and brainstorm appropriate ways to deal with them. After a week, ask students to assess if the journal has made a difference in how they dealt with emotions. Students should write in their journals at least once a day about at least one emotional experience.

Professional Development — McGraw Hill — Mini Clip
Reading Building Vocabulary

U Universal Access

Students with Visual Impairments Students with visual impairments are constantly challenged because a large part of tradition learning is visual. Plan for these challenges by giving detailed verbal descriptions of concepts in the text, or have students take turns reading portions of the text aloud.

ASSESS

Quiz

Ask students to answer the following questions:

1. What are role models, and what type of people are role models? Role models are people who help you see what is expected of you, and can be anyone who is mature or experienced.

2. What are the ways you show your personality to others? Your personality shows in the way you look, communicate, and act.

3. What is a healthy way to deal with anger? If you are angry with another person, wait until you have cooled off before talking to them. Tell the person how you feel and what you need or want.

RETEACH

R Reading Strategy

Create a List Ask students to create a list of emotions and categorize them as "good" and "bad." Have them describe some causes of those emotions, as well as a healthy way to respond to each. Students should list at least five emotions and deem them positive or negative. An example might be nervousness, caused by a test or a sporting event, and one way to respond might be to do something relaxing, like take a bath or a walk.

C Critical Thinking

Draw Conclusions Self-esteem is not just a matter of talking or acting a certain way. It is important to distinguish between genuine self-esteem and a false sense of self-worth. Ask students to share thoughts on what might indicate a false sense of self-worth. Answers should indicate a person who truly feels comfortable with who they are as opposed to someone who is covering up insecurity by bragging or comparing others unfavorably to themselves.

ASSESS

Section 1.1 Review Assign the Section 1.1 After You Read activities.

 Student Activity Workbook Assign the Section 1.1 Activities.

Online Study Tools Have students go to the Online Learning Center at glencoe.com to:

■ Take the Section 1.1 **Practice Test**.

■ Download **Study-to-Go** content. 📕

Section 1.1 After You Read

Answer Key

1. Answers may include eye color, facial features, body build, or intelligence.

2. Answers may include the way you dress, communicate, and behave.

3. Answers will vary but may include becoming easily irritated, hurt, or embarrassed, and experiencing sudden mood swings.

4. Answers may include changes to height, weight, or body shape.

5. Lists may include inherited traits such as eye color, hair color, skin color, and body type; cultural traits may include holiday celebrations, language, and food preferences.

6. Paragraphs may include: attend religious services, be a good role model, participate in cultural events, take pride in your family and heritage, and offer to help with chores and homework.

CLOSE

Culminating Activity

What Makes Us Unique Now that they have learned qualities that make a person unique, have students discuss qualities that make them unique. Have each student pick one other student and describe something that they like about that person that makes them unique. Each student should think of at least one positive quality about another student. This exercise should help build self-confidence as students see their unique qualities described in a positive light.

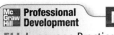

McGraw Hill **Professional Development** **Mini Clip**
ELL Language Practice

Grooming and Personal Care

FOCUS

Discussion Starter

Discuss with the class their morning routine. How long does it take them to get ready? What is their morning routine? Discuss why some people take longer than others to groom themselves. Students' routines will vary. Some might have a longer routine because they have more hair, or because they have a special skin care regimen or many other reasons.

Bell Ringer Activity

Grooming Demonstration Have volunteers pantomime how they perform the following activities: washing and caring for their face, washing and grooming their hair, and cleaning their teeth and gums. After, discuss what the students did alike and what they did differently.

TEACH

S Skill Practice

Independent Practice

L1 **List** Have students list five actions that can be taken to create a positive attitude. Possible actions can include: take positive action; talk positively and learn from mistakes; accept yourself; stay open to learning; reach out to others; assert yourself, but do not be offensive or hurtful; and accept and respect others as they are.

L2 **Explain** Ask students to explain how to care for clothing. Clean clothes after wearing them, and change clothes daily. If you get a stain, treat it as soon as possible. If clothing rips, fix it before it gets worse. Choose appropriate clothing for the occasion. Mix and match pieces for a new combination.

L3 **Apply** Have students choose one area of grooming or personal hygiene and locate tips for improving the techniques they use. Tell students to practice using the tips and note how it improves their routines. Students should use the tips to improve their grooming practices and recognize how they have improved.

McGraw Hill **Professional Development** **Mini Clip**
Math Problem Solving—Order of Operations

U Universal Access

English Language Learners Locate pictures of grooming supplies and have English language learners identify the names for the objects both in their native language and in English. If they cannot think of the name in English, have a student volunteer teach it to them. **ELL**

ASSESS

Quiz

Ask students the following questions:

1. **What should you do if you have severe acne?** Follow the tips for caring for their skin and consult a dermatologist.

2. **What are first impressions and why are they important?** First impressions are instant opinions formed about a person based on look, dress, speech, and behavior. They are important because they help people decide whether they want to know you better.

3. **How can attitude affect your appearance?** Positive facial expressions can make you more attractive to people who will feel positive in your presence, while negative facial expressions can affect your appearance negatively.

RETEACH

R Reading Strategy

Use Reference Materials Choose one type of grooming and use reference materials such as books or magazines that contain personal hygiene and grooming advice. Put together a hygiene routine based on what you learned. Students should use the reference materials to expand on the information learned from the lesson. They should put together a regimen for one type of grooming and evaluate what they learned from the reference materials.

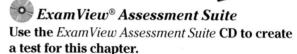

C Critical Thinking

Evaluate Information Present students with two photographs, one showing a person with a neat and clean appearance and the other showing a person who looks sloppy or dirty. Have them evaluate the first impressions they get from the two pictures and describe the kind of person they think each is. Put-

ting the two pictures together should help students understand the power of first impressions. The students should have two very different impressions of the two people in the photographs.

ASSESS

Section 1.2 Review Assign the Section 1.2 After You Read activities.

Student Activity Workbook Assign the Section 1.2 Activities.

 Online Study Tools Have students go to the Online Learning Center at **glencoe.com** to:

■ Take the Section 1.2 **Practice Test**.

■ Download **Study-to-Go** content.

ExamView® Assessment Suite
Use the *ExamView Assessment Suite* **CD to create a test for this chapter.**

Chapter Review Have students complete the Chapter 1 Review and Applications.

Section 1.2 After You Read

Answer Key

1. Skin, hair, hands, feet, nails, teeth, clothing.

2. Answers may include the way the person speaks, behaves, dresses, and cares for his or her overall appearance.

3. Posters will vary depending on which option is selected, but should include images of skin, hair, hands and feet, or teeth, and descriptions of how to care for the chosen option.

4. Paragraphs will vary. Look for specific details about the first impression, such as friendliness, confidence, attitude, and grooming. Students may also notice cultural aspects, such as manner of speech or way of dressing.

CLOSE

Culminating Activity

Grooming Routine Now that students have learned more about grooming and personal hygiene, have them discuss ways in which they have changed their grooming regimen. Students may have made permanent changes, such as beginning to floss every day instead of just brushing, or one-time changes, such as going through their closets and getting rid of clothes that are old, damaged, or no longer fit.

Words You Learned

1. Students should use each of the content vocabulary words and academic vocabulary words in a sentence.

Review Key Concepts

2. Heredity, family, environment, experiences, roles, culture.

3. Self-concept, self-esteem, responsibility, values.

4. By understanding your emotions and why they change, you will better understand yourself.

5. Answers should describe changes in height, weight, and body shape.

6. Personal grooming is important to your health and positive self-concept.

7. People form an opinion about you the first time they meet you, based on the way you look, dress, talk, and behave. First impressions are important because they help people decide whether they want to know you better.

Critical Thinking

8. Answers will vary. Sample answer: Finishing your homework even though you want to watch television shows that you value good grades.

9. Physical and emotional needs, such as food, shelter, and affection, are basic to all people and required for survival. Wants are things that you would like to have but do not need for survival.

Real-World Skills and Applications

10. Answers may include that Sarah should read the ingredients, compare brands and prices, and make sure the product is appropriate for her hair type before she buys anything. Since her hair may be damaged from using a straightener, she should look for products for damaged hair. A product that works for her friend may not work for her.

11. Answers should include information about physical changes such as growth spurts, hormonal changes, vocal changes, and acne. These changes can make teens feel awkward. It helps to remember that teens experience changes at different rates and times. Students may also mention that it helps to talk to friends and family.

Financial Literacy

12. Answers will vary, but students should explain that the price per ounce determines the best buy.

Active Learning

13. Collages will vary but may include images of families, sports, pets, hobbies, advertisements, and cultural events or imagery.

14. Guides will vary but may include stains such as grass, blood, ink, mustard, ketchup, oil, and makeup. Students should provide information on how to remove stains, such as pre-treating, soaking, or using vinegar. Encourage students to use illustrations.

Net Connection

15. Answers will vary, but should describe another culture's traditions, foods, and beliefs.

Academic Skills

16. Call on each group to act out their situation. Effective constructive criticism helps people grow and improve themselves. Have the rest of the class evaluate if the criticism is constructive.

17. Charts may include plaque build up, tooth decay, bad breath, and gum disease (gingivitis). Tips may include: use a soft-bristled brush to brush regularly, use toothpaste with fluoride, floss daily, eat a balanced diet, get regular check-ups.

18. $300.00 is spent on wants. Students should multiply $2,000 \times 15\% = \$2,000 \times .15 = \$300.00$.

Standardized Test Practice

19. Answers will vary depending on the quality chosen. Sample answer: Responsibility is important because it shows trust, reliability, and accountability. Honoring commitments, doing assignments on time, and accepting the consequences of actions shows responsibility.

Mc Graw Hill Professional Development **Mini Clip**
Math Probability and Fairness

Your Family

Section 2.1 Family Characteristics

In this section students will learn about the different types of families. They will also learn skills to get along with others in a family and how to take responsibility as part of a family.

Section 2.2 Changes in the Family

In this section, students will learn about some of the changes that can take place in a family. They will also learn how to adjust to the changes that can take place within a family.

Classroom Solutions

Print Resources

 Student Edition
 Teacher Annotated Edition
 Student Activity Workbook
Student Activity Workbook Teacher Annotated Edition

- Projects and Activities*
- Food Labs*
- Sewing Labs*
- Career Investigations*
- Reteaching Activities*
- Enrichment Activities*

Technology Resources

ExamView **ExamView Assessment Suite CD** allows you to create and print out customized tests or ready-made unit and chapter tests, complete with answer keys.

Lesson Planner Plus **Lesson Planner Plus! CD*** is and electronic lesson planner that provides instant access to teacher resources in one convenient package.

Presentation Plus! PowerPoint™ Presentations can be edited and customized to meet the needs of students.

Online Learning Center includes resources and activities for students and teachers. Also includes Online Student Edition.

Interactive Student Edition

*ELECTRONIC RESOURCES ARE AVAILABLE ON LESSON PLANNER PLUS AND THE ONLINE LEARNING CENTER.

 Writing Activity Answer

Prewriting Lists may include: help siblings with homework, help with the care of younger siblings or elderly relatives, take turns fixing dinner, offer to help without being asked, and listen when other family members talk

Discovering Careers Answers ▼

1. Answers will vary. Students should write a summary of the education, training, and experience needed for the selected careers.
2. Answers may include kind, patient, supportive, sense of humor, enthusiastic, understanding.
3. Paragraphs will vary but should express that clients, patients, children, and families need to feel secure in order to freely share their thoughts.
4. Answers will vary. Students should present a summary of what they learned about the person's typical work day.

Family Characteristics

FOCUS

Discussion Starter

Discuss with students the structure of their families. Who do they live with? Do they alternate between homes? Who is part of their family? Family structures may be very different or mostly alike. Discuss the similarities and differences and what causes them. Explain that in this lesson they will learn about characteristics of different families.

Bell Ringer Activity

Class Demographics Have the class look at Figure 2.1 and decide which types of families apply to them. Take a tally of the class to see where the majority of the students fall and whether any categories have no students. Determine the classroom family demographic from the results and discuss. What does this tell them about families today?

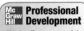
McGraw Hill Professional Development | **Mini Clip**
ELL Content Vocabulary

TEACH

S Skill Practice

Independent Practice

L1 List Have students list three characteristics of a positive family relationship and three ways to enrich family life. Characteristics of a postive family relationship: support one another; laugh and play together; share responsibilities; respect one another. Ways to enrich family life: share games and hobbies, attend religious services; create traditions; plan celebrations.

L2 Explain Ask students to explain how a person can show that he or she is reliable and explain the benefits of being reliable. You can show that you are reliable by doing what you say you will do and by keeping your word. If you are reliable, people will know they can depend on you.

L3 Apply Each day for a week, have students schedule time to talk their parents or guardians about their lives. Have them observe the effect of this on their relationships. After the week, discuss students' observations about how setting aside time to talk each day affected their relationship with their parents or guardians.

McGraw Hill Professional Development | **Mini Clip**
ELL Group Discussions

U Universal Access

Students with Physical Impairments Students with physical impairments may have uncontrollable body movements, the loss of use of one or more limbs, or other symptoms. Have these students prepare assignments electronically, if possible. If computers are available, have students use software and other assistive technology to take notes.

ASSESS

Quiz

Ask students to answer the following questions:

1. **What is a blended family?** A blended family is when two people marry and at least one has a child or children from a previous marriage.

2. **What are the guidelines for successfully sharing space with others?** Be considerate, be reliable, and respect the privacy of others.

3. **Why is communication with parents important during the teen years?** It helps parents be supportive of teens and helps teens and parents understand each other's feelings.

RETEACH

R Reading Strategy

Understand Words in Context Have students find an article about a unique family. Encourage students to look up the meaning of words that are unfamiliar to them. Have students share what they learned in a five-minute oral presentation. Students might locate articles about foster families, adoptive parents, large families, same-sex parents, or other unique family situations. Discuss the different family types.

C Critical Thinking

Make Connections Ask students what behaviors they can practice at school that could also be used at home. Ask students to list these behaviors and share them. Students should think of behaviors that would help them get along with others, such as sharing what they have with those who have less, helping people in need, and keeping classrooms neat.

ASSESS

Section 2.1 Review Assign the Section 2.1 After You Read activities.

 Student Activity Workbook Assign the Section 2.1 Activities.

 Online Study Tools Have students go to the Online Learning Center at glencoe.com to:

- Take the Section 2.1 **Practice Test**.
- Download **Study-to-Go** content. *STUDY TO GO*

Section 2.1 After You Read

Answer Key

1. Answers may include holiday celebrations, religious events, yearly activities.
2. Answers will vary but may include: play games, watch movies, prepare a meal together, attend religious services, plan a celebration.
3. Respect, consideration, cooperation, and reliability are learned from family. These qualities are necessary for life away from home.
4. Answers will vary. Paragraphs should include details about who was interviewed, how the tradition began, and should describe how their family continues the tradition today.
5. Answers will vary. Learning about other cultures can help you see that people around the world may do some things differently, but that does not mean they are wrong.

CLOSE

Culminating Activity

Improving Relationships Now that students have learned about getting along with others and taking responsibility, have a class discussion. Ask volunteers to talk about one thing that they will do to improve their relationship with a family member. Students should choose actions such as playing more with a younger sibling, helping out with an extra chore, or visiting a grandparent.

Section **2.2** Lesson Plan

Changes in the Family

FOCUS

Discussion Starter

Ask students to think about the changes that have taken place in their family since they were born.

Discuss these changes. What changes do they think might take place in the next few years? Answers will vary. Students may have experienced any of the common changes, such as divorce, remarriage, a move, or new siblings.

Bell Ringer Activity

Family Timeline Have students create a timeline, starting with the year their parents married. Mark the years that the family entered each stage of the family life cycle. Have them predict years for stages that may not have happened yet, such as the launching stage.

> **McGraw Hill Professional Development** **Mini Clip**
> **Math** Communications in Mathematics

TEACH

S Skill Practice

Guided Practice

L1 List Divide students into small groups, and have them list and describe positive ways to accept changes in their lives. Plan ahead for changes that you know are coming; discuss your feelings; look for the positive aspects of the change; and be supportive of other family members.

L2 Explain Have students form small groups. Tell the groups to imagine they are siblings, and that their mother has just lost her job. Ask them to write a paragraph that explains how they could help their mother and the rest of the family deal positively with this change. Students could discuss their feelings with their parents and offer support; cut back on what they spend; and possibly get a part-time job or do odd jobs to make extra money.

L3 Apply Remind students that it is not possible to control many of the changes that affect their lives, but it is possible to control how they react. Divide students into groups. Ask the groups to discuss positive and negative changes that affect families, such as moving, divorce, death, or the addition of new family members. Have each group present a skit to show constructive ways to react to these situations. Skits should demonstrate that family members need to talk to each other about their feelings and acknowledge that by working together and supporting each other, they can get through the difficult times.

U Universal Access

Students with Learning Disabilities Students with learning disabilities may require additional guidelines or study aids to get the most out of text material. You may wish to read aloud for students who find written text difficult to use. Elicit the help of classmates who have clear voices.

ASSESS

Quiz

Ask students to answer the following questions:

1. What is the first stage in the family life cycle? The first stage in the family life cycle is the Beginning Stage, where newlyweds get to know each other before children are born.

2. What are some positive ways to deal with a relative with a disability? Be understanding, supportive, and loving towards them. Look for ways to be helpful. Encourage independence if it is appropriate.

3. What types of people might you talk to when trying to deal positively with changes in your life? Teachers, counselors, coaches, religious leaders, and family service workers.

RETEACH

W Writing Strategy

More Changes Ask students to create a list of changes that might occur in a family other than those listed in the lesson. Have them brainstorm positive ways to deal with these new changes. Other changes that could occur in a family include: an unexpected job change, bankruptcy, relocation, new friends and neighbors, natural disasters, military deployment, losing a pet or getting a new pet, receiving a large inheritance. For each item on the list, students should provide a positive way to handle the change.

C Critical Thinking

Make Inferences The text tells you that you will have to adjust to both positive changes and negative changes. Ask students what they can infer about the effect of positive changes on a person. If positive changes as well as negative changes require an adjustment period, then the inference is that although a positive can make you happy, it is still a change and will require some getting used to.

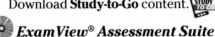

Professional Development | **Mini Clip**
Reading Fluency Development

ASSESS

Section 2.2 Review Assign the Section 2.2 After You Read activities.

Student Activity Workbook Assign the Section 2.2 Activities.

Online Study Tools Have students go to the Online Learning Center at glencoe.com to:

- Take the Section 2.2 **Practice Test**.
- Download **Study-to-Go** content.

 ExamView® Assessment Suite
Use the *ExamView Assessment Suite* **CD to create a test for this chapter.**

Chapter Review Have students complete the Chapter 2 Review and Applications.

Section 2.2 After You Read

Answer Key

1. Beginning stage, parenting stage, launching stage, and senior stage.

2. Changes and how you deal with them can help you grow. You learn from experience. Every change brings a new experience that can help you prepare for future changes.

3. Answers will vary. Students should describe what event caused the change, and should include details about how it affected them and their families.

4. Answers will vary. Students should write details about the person's life experiences and how their own lives have been affected.

CLOSE

Culminating Activity

Role Play Have students divide into groups and roleplay a family dealing with some of the different changes they have learned about in the section. There should be at least a parent and a child role in each group, with other roles added as appropriate. They should roleplay the announcement of the change and how each family member deals with it. Roleplays should provide positive examples of ways to deal with the changes.

Words You Learned

1. Students should write the vocabulary words and definitions on index cards, and work in pairs to match words and definitions.

Review Key Concepts

2. Nuclear, single-parent, blended, adoptive, foster, extended, legal guardian.

3. Consideration, cooperation, reliability, respect.

4. Be dependable, make wise choices, do chores, follow rules, show respect.

5. Divorce: legal end to a marriage; Remarriage: a divorced parent marries again and may bring new children into the family; Disability: emotional, mental, or physical impairment; Job Loss: parent loses a job and income; Serious Illness: a family member becomes ill and may need long-term care; Death: a family must cope with the loss of a loved one.

6. Plan ahead when a change is expected. Talk about your feelings. Look for the positive. Be supportive of your family members.

Critical Thinking

7. All people need to be encouraged, supported, valued, guided, and loved to be responsible members of society.

8. By sharing ideas with a variety of people, you can learn more about them and they can learn about you.

9. Answers will vary. Sample answers: The senior stage is the most difficult because parents have to say goodbye to their children. The beginning stage is the easiest because you do not yet have the responsibility of raising children.

Real-World Skills and Applications

10. List may include the school's Web site, the town's Chamber of Commerce, and calling the school to request newsletters or pamphlets.

11. Web pages should include tips such as being considerate, reliable, cooperative, and respectful. Encourage students to be creative and add drawings, cartoons, and attention-grabbing language.

Financial Literacy

12. The museum is cheaper. The two parents and the 14-year-old will have to pay full price ($6) at the cultural festival, while the remaining 3 kids will get in at the discounted price ($3). The total cost of the festival is ($6 × 3) + ($3 × 3) = $18 + $9 = $27. The museum costs $7 for every 2 people, or $7/2 = $3.50 for every 1 person. The entire family can get into the museum for $3.50 × 6 = $21.00.

Active Learning

13. Presentations will vary. Students should describe the tradition, its importance and meaning, when and how they will incorporate the tradition, and how it shows their unique family identity. Sample answer: Light a candle on the anniversary of an adopted child's homecoming to honor the child's birth family

14. Family trees will vary, but should include as much detail as possible, such as dates, marriages, and births, and interesting anecdotes. If there are adopted or foster students in your class who may not have this information available, modify the activity to include them. For example, instead of a tree with branches, have students draw a row of bushes to represent their adoptive or foster family, and roots to represent their biological family.

Net Connection

15. Information gathered will vary. Include all family types in this activity and modify as needed.

Academic Skills

16. Letters will vary, but students should clearly state their position and then support it with details about what families provide for children, such as love, comfort, food, shelter, guidance, security, and support.

17. Answers will vary. Students should map a logical travel plan and correctly estimate mileage. Students might use an online map Web site to confirm their answers.

18. Answers will vary for each student, but each student should list the ages of his fellow students' siblings along the horizontal axis, while the vertical axis should reflect the quantity that fall into each age. For example, if three students reported having 9-year-old siblings, then the bar above the age 9 should extend 3 units high.

Standardized Test Practice

19. F
20. T
21. F

Your Friendships

Section 3.1 Friends

In this section, students will learn how to make new friends. They will also learn how to be a good friend to the friends they already have, and how to deal with changes in a friendship.

Section 3.2 Peer Pressure

In this section students will learn how peer pressure can affect their decision-making process. They will learn how to stay safe by saying no to high-risk behavior. Finally, they will learn how to be assertive.

Classroom Solutions

Print Resources

- Student Edition
- Teacher Annotated Edition
- Student Activity Workbook
- Student Activity Workbook Teacher Annotated Edition

- Projects and Activities*
- Food Labs*
- Sewing Labs*
- Career Investigations*
- Reteaching Activities*
- Enrichment Activities*

Technology Resources

ExamView Assessment Suite **ExamView Assessment Suite CD** allows you to create and print out customized tests or ready-made unit and chapter tests, complete with answer keys.

Lesson Planner *Plus* **Lesson Planner Plus! CD*** is and electronic lesson planner that provides instant access to teacher resources in one convenient package.

PRESENTATION **Plus! Presentation Plus!** PowerPoint™ Presentations can be edited and customized to meet the needs of students.

Online Learning Center includes resources and activities for students and teachers. Also includes Online Student Edition.

Interactive Student Edition

*ELECTRONIC RESOURCES ARE AVAILABLE ON LESSON PLANNER PLUS AND THE ONLINE LEARNING CENTER.

Writing Activity Answer

Journal Entry Answers will vary. Students should include details about their best friend's qualities and what activities they enjoy together.

Discovering Careers Answers ▼

1. Answers will vary. Students should write a summary of the education, training, and experience needed for the selected careers.
2. Students should have a map of their home that shows how all family members should exit.
3. Answers may include: keep walkways free of clutter; do not let papers pile up; make sure electrical cords (such as on computers) are in good repair; turn off equipment at the end of the day; wear appropriate protective gear; set out caution signs when mopping;
4. Answers will vary. Students should present a summary of what they learned about the person's typical work day.

Section **3.1** **Lesson Plan**

Friends

FOCUS

Discussion Starter

Ask for volunteers to talk about a good friend or group of friends and describe the relationship, what makes them best friends, and how they became friends. Students will have different stories that illustrate what makes a friendship strong and how people become friends. Hearing these stories might help students who have a harder time making friends by showing them how people meet and make friends.

 Bell Ringer Activity

The Friend Wish List Have students divide a piece of paper into two columns. In one column, have them list the qualities that they want in a friend. In the other, have them list the qualities that they like to bring to a friendship. Ask them to compare and see how well the two columns match. Discuss the lists.

TEACH

S Skill Practice

Independent Practice

L1 List Have students list things that friends do for each other. Friends share good times, help each other during bad times, accept each other as they are, listen, and depend on each other.

L2 Explain Tell students to write a paragraph that explains what makes a good friend, and how to be a good friend. A good friend is supportive, caring, trustworthy, and dependable. Good friends accept each other for who they are and keep each other's secrets. To be a good friend, you must have these qualities, and you should praise friends when they do well, and encourage them when they do not.

L3 Apply Ask students to make an effort in the next week to introduce themselves to someone at school that they do not know. Have them evaluate the experience and share their insights. Students should practice getting comfortable with meeting and speaking to new people, which is the first step in making new friends.

U Universal Access

Students with Behavior Disorders Students who have attention difficulties may find it easier to stay on target if they are actively involved in learning. Have students select one section of this chapter to teach to another student. Afterward, discuss with the students whether they learn better when they are the teacher or the student.

ASSESS

Quiz

Ask students to answer the following questions:

1. **What is a friend?** A friend is someone you like and who likes you. It is someone you can talk to who shares similar interests and goals.

2. **What are the benefits of being part of a peer group?** A peer group provides companionship and support and opportunities to practice social skills, such as communication, conflict resolution, and compromise.

3. **What should you do if you feel jealous of a friend's achievements?** You should do something that makes you feel good about yourself.

RETEACH

R Reading Strategy

Expand the Concept Ask the class to review the section on making new friends. Discuss situations where it might be possible to make a new friend and list these on the board. Ask the class to brainstorm ways to make an acquaintance in each situation. Possible answers might include a new class at school, a party, or a vacation. They should list ways to meet a new person for each situation.

McGraw Hill Professional Development **Mini Clip**
ELL Collaborative Work

C Critical Thinking

Being a Friend You may make a friend who has a disability. Brainstorm ways to be a good friend to someone with a disability. Students should understand that a friend with a disability is the same as any other friend, but may have extra challenges. They should treat such a friend as they would anyone else. If they think their friend needs help, they should offer, but not without asking first. They should be there if their friend needs to talk about anything.

ASSESS

Section 3.1 Review Assign the Section 3.1 After You Read activities.

📁 **Student Activity Workbook** Assign the Section 3.1 Activities.

🧭 **Online Study Tools** Have students go to the Online Learning Center at glencoe.com to:

- ■ Take the Section 3.1 **Practice Test**.
- ■ Download **Study-to-Go** content.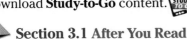

📖 **Section 3.1 After You Read**

Answer Key

1. An acquaintance is a person you greet or meet fairly often but do not have a close relationship with. A friend is someone you have a close relationship with.

2. Peers provide a sense of belonging and can increase self-esteem.

3. Someone to confide in, trust, and share common interests with.

4. Students should use information from the text and personal experience to determine the qualities of a good friend. Sample interview questions: What do you like most about your best friend? What qualities in your friendship keep you together? How do you resolve disputes?

5. Lists may include: research the new student's culture; talk about cultural differences as well as what you have in common; remember that different does not mean better or worse or wrong.

CLOSE

Culminating Activity

Role-play Divide students into pairs. Ask them to imagine that they are two people meeting for the first time. They should determine the occasion where they are meeting and role-play the meeting and how they would interact. Role-playing interactions should show the students being friendly, asking questions, and giving responses designed to get to know a new person.

Mc Graw Hill Professional Development **Mini Clip**
Reading Planning and Classroom Management

Peer Pressure

FOCUS

Discussion Starter

Ask the class whether any of them have ever felt pressured to do something or to not do something by others. What happened, and how did they respond. Many students may not feel comfortable talking about this so make sure that confidentiality is stressed before the exercise begins. You may want to start with a story of your own.

🔔 **Bell Ringer Activity**

What To Watch For As a class, brainstorm situations where peer pressure might arise. Come up with ways to prepare for each. Situations might include breaks at school, parties, sporting events, or other social situations where teens might be unsupervised. Students should come up with comebacks to situations that will help them decline gracefully but forcefully.

TEACH

S Skill Practice

Independent Practice

L1 List Have students list ways that they can positively handle negative peer pressure. Planning ahead for certain situations, suggesting safe and healthy alternate activities, choosing friends that share your values and interests, and talking to parents and counselors if you have problems.

L2 Explain Ask students to write a paragraph explaining how alcohol and drugs can negatively affect your life. These substances can cause you to become addicted, and addiction can lead to violence, crime, job loss, and even death. Students may also think of other negative outcomes, such as the loss of relationships and financial loss.

L3 Apply Have students create a list of what they will say to resist peer pressure in common situations. Have them choose one situation and write a dialogue. Scripts should demonstrate ways to positively resist peer pressure without giving in or turning it into a hostile situation.

Mc Graw Hill Professional Development **Mini Clip**
Reading Lesson Reflections

Universal Access

Interpersonal and Intrapersonal Learners Divide students into groups and ask each group to practice techniques for being assertive. They can discuss the techniques or role-play. Ensure that groups are balanced, containing both outgoing, interpersonal learners as well as reflective, intrapersonal learners.

ELL Another Point of View

ASSESS

Section 3.2 Review Assign the Section 3.2 After You Read activities.

Student Activity Workbook Assign the Section 3.2 Activities.

Online Study Tools Have students go to the Online Learning Center at glencoe.com to:

- Take the Section 3.2 **Practice Test**.
- Download **Study-to-Go** content.

ExamView® **Assessment Suite**
Use the *ExamView Assessment Suite* **CD to create a test for this chapter.**

Chapter Review Have students complete the Chapter 3 Review and Applications.

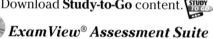
Reading Flexible Groupings

ASSESS

Quiz

Ask students to answer the following questions:

1. **How can peer pressure influence you positively?** It can make you feel better about yourself, make you feel like you belong, and encourage you to do positive things.

2. **What are some examples of high risk behaviors?** Drunk driving, sexual activity, and substance abuse.

3. **What is the "fight or flight" response?** This is your body's physical and mental response to a threat, resulting from an adrenaline release.

RETEACH

R Reading Strategy

Research Consequences Have students choose one type of high-risk behavior and research the potential consequences. Students should write a short report, citing sources. Students should locate reliable sources. Their report should be clear and concise and accurately explain the potential consequences of engaging in the type of behavior they have chosen.

C Critical Thinking

Connect to Community Have students set up peer counseling groups to help fellow students deal with peer pressure. They will act as group leaders and apply the lessons they have learned from the section to the particular problems of their peers. Emphasize the importance of confidentiality when acting as a counselor to peers. Remind them that they can encourage students to talk to an adult if the situation is over their head.

 Section 3.2 After You Read

Answer Key

1. Friends who cheer for you when you are on a team are showing positive peer pressure.
2. Say no and walk away.
3. A bully is a person who physically or verbally abuses someone and intends to cause injury.
4. Students can use costumes, music, or graphics to capture the attention of children.
5. Students should include details about the situation, how they reacted, how the other group or individual reacted, and how they would handle a similar situation.

CLOSE

Culminating Activity

Role-play Divide students into pairs or small groups. Ask them to imagine that one or more of them is peer pressuring the others. They should determine the location and what the peer pressure is regarding. Then they should role-play the situation and how they would respond. Role-playing interactions should show the students being assertive and resisting the peer pressure without becoming aggressive.

ELL Language Practice

Words You Learned

1. Students should use each of the content vocabulary words and academic vocabulary words in a sentence.

Review Key Concepts

2. Spend time sharing common interests to get to know each other better.

3. Good friends are supportive, caring, trustworthy, dependable, and reliable. They do not ask you to participate in harmful activities, and they accept you as you are.

4. Change can help you grow, learn, and understand more about yourself and others. It can also cause friends to drift apart as they develop new interests and make new friends.

5. Teens want to be accepted by peers. They may use acceptance as a basis for making decisions.

6. By saying no to cigarettes, alcohol, other drugs, and sexual behavior, teens can prevent injury or death.

7. Assertive teens are confident, do not give in to others, and stand up for what they believe.

Critical Thinking

8. Both involve the influence of friends. Positive peer pressure encourages teens to choose safe and healthful activities. Negative peer pressure encourages teens to participate in unsafe, illegal, or unhealthful activities.

9. Addicts can be abusive to themselves and their families. They may steal to pay for their habits, commit other crimes and end up in prison, lose their jobs and depend on others to pay their bills, or end up homeless.

Real-World Skills and Applications

10. Students may suggest that Lucas decide ahead of time what to do, such as suggest other activities and practice refusal skills. Some students may suggest that Lucas simply not go to the party.

11. Students may choose situations such as drinking alcohol, cheating on a test, or getting into a car with someone who does not have a license. Students should then role-play one of the situations using refusal skills and planning strategies. After, encourage a discussion about what worked and what could be improved.

Financial Literacy

12. Cole's budget allows him to spend 100% −

50% − 30% = 20% of his monthly income on entertainment, or 0.20 × $150 = $30. He can see $30 ÷ $10/movie = 3 movies in a month, or bowl $30 ÷ $3/game = 10 games in a month. If he bowls three games, he will spend 3 × $3 = $9, leaving $30 − $9 = $21 to spend on movies. $21 will buy 2 movie tickets (with $1 left over).

Active Learning

13. Students should present a T-shirt decorated with drawings and words to describe their friend.

14. Students should present a poem or other writing from a historical period, describing how friendship was symbolized and including words to illustrate friendship. They should discuss whether they would use similar terms to describe their own friendships

Net Connection

15. Essays should include a synopsis of the story and a discussion about the pressures teens faced then compared to those they face today.

Academic Skills

16. Letters will vary but may include how the friend can use refusal skills, and tips such as thinking ahead, suggesting other activities, and choosing friends carefully.

17. Answers will vary. Sample answer:

Negative Consequences of Alcohol	Ways to Say No
Drunk driving accident	I value my life too much to get into the car with someone who has been drinking.
Might become addicted	I don't want to get hooked on alcohol or drugs.
Loss of inhibitions	I don't want to do something I will regret later.

18. 100 × .08 = $8.00; $8.00 + $100.00 = $108.00. Gary will owe you $108.00.

Standardized Test Practice

19. Answers may include sentences about loyalty, compassion, empathy, and understanding.

20. Friends meet others and make new friends; develop different interests; move away or attend a different school; devote more time to romantic relationships

21. When you avoid high-risk behaviors and activities, you are not exposed to dangerous diseases and harmful chemicals.

FOCUS

Introduce the Project

In this project, students will identify their role models. Ask students how their role models reflect their personalities. Answers will vary, but may refer to admirable traits their role models possess such as: honesty, respect, fairness, fame, success in business, or success in raising a family.

Build Background

Heroes Ask students to list traits that someone must possess to be considered a hero. Then ask students to list some of their heroes. Write names next to corresponding traits. Discuss how heroes inspire us to become better people. Traits will vary, but may include honesty, courage, altruism, thinking out of the box, or standing up for what is right.

TEACH

S Skill Practice

Guided Practice

L1 **List** Ask students to list the positive qualities of others in the class who are role models. Have volunteers share their lists, and let other class members guess what person they are describing based on the qualities and traits described. Lists will vary but students may refer to a class member as loyal, friendly, a good listener, a great athlete, or a smart student.

L2 **Identify** Have students identify qualities they have been inspired to achieve from studying their role models. Students should then write a suggestion as to how to attain these traits. Traits may vary such as honesty, caring, good business sense, athleticism. Suggestions may be practical, such as getting proper education, giving to charity, working out, or being a better listener.

L3 **Imagine** Ask students to imagine themselves many years in the future as role models. Each student should draw the picture they imagine. Underneath the picture, ask them to write a paragraph explaining how they developed the traits that make them role models. Scenarios will vary but answers should show that students considered personal values, family values, and success.

C Critical Thinking

Who Are Your Heroes? Have students take a survey of friends, classmates, and relatives, asking who their heroes are and why. Ask students to consider age and gender, to predict the results. Answers will vary depending on survey results. For example, students may predict that many of their peers will choose celebrity role models based on their fame and fortune and that older people may choose notable historical figures or world leaders.

ASSESS

Quiz

Ask students to answer the following questions:

1. What kind of traits might a role model have that may not be possible for you to achieve? Physical traits like height, eye color, or certain body type and talent for things like music and art.

2. What are qualities of someone who is a bad role model? Lying, cheating, unreliability, poor hygiene, inability to control anger, or giving into peer pressure.

3. Are your best role models your age or older than you? Why? Our best role models are usually older, because they have more experience, and can offer the wisdom of their past success and failure.

CLOSE

Culminating Activity

Project Assessment In this activity, students identified people they consider role models. Have students write a paragraph about the difference between envy and admiration. Ask them to include an example of a person they envy and a person they admire. Choice of examples may vary, but should reflect the notion that envy is when you want something that someone else has. Admiration is when you wish to achieve the thing that another has achieved. Activity should suggest avoiding envy, and embracing admiration.

Take Charge of Your Life

Unit Overview

This unit introduces students to ways in which they can control their lives through efficient communication, conflict resolution, being responsible citizens, strong leadership skills, and learning how to set goals and make smart decisions.

Chapter 4 *Communicate with Others* In this chapter, students will learn how to communicate more effectively by improving their verbal and nonverbal communication skills. They will also learn about the causes of conflicts and how to prevent and resolve them.

Chapter 5 *Citizenship and Leadership* In this chapter, students are taught about their rights and responsibilities as citizens and how these build strong communities. They will also develop their leadership skills and learn how those skills help leaders guide groups.

Chapter 6 *Goals and Decision Making* In this chapter, students learn how to set both short- and long-term goals and why goal setting is an important aspect to achieving success. They will also work on their decision-making skills.

Life Skills Project Preview

Your Point of View

Tell students that as part of this unit, they will learn that forming their own points of view lets people know they are thoughtful and responsible citizens. They will learn how to consider all sides of an issue, interview a community leader, and present a campaign poster and speech about their issue as if they were running for elected office.

FCCLA provides programs to guide students through projects, enhance their personal growth, and build leadership skills that can make a difference in their lives, their families, and their communities.

Dynamic Leadership provides information, activities, and project ideas to help young people build, practice, and recognize the lifelong benefits of leadership skills. Dynamic Leadership helps young people master the six essentials of leadership: modeling good character, solving problems, fostering positive relationships, managing conflict, building teams, and educating peers.

Encourage Self-Esteem Have students form groups and come up with ideas for presentations to give to their peers that encourage positive attitude, self-esteem, personal growth, and development. Ideas might include puppet shows, music, poetry, skits, or speeches. Groups should perform in front of the class. Presentations should demonstrate and emphasize positive attitude, self-esteem, personal growth, and development in their peer group. They should be presented in a way that engages other teens.

McGraw Hill Professional Development

MINI CLIP VIDEO LIBRARY

Targeted professional development is correlated throughout *Discovering Life Skills*. **The McGraw-Hill Professional Development Mini Clip Video Library** provides teaching strategies to strengthen academic and learning skills. Log on to **glencoe.com**.

In this Unit, you will find these Mini Clips.

CHAPTER 4 Communicate with Others

READING

- **Vocabulary** Author Josefina Tinajero describes the critical importance of academic language. (p. TM84)
- **On Workshops** Doug Fisher, Ph.D., author and teacher educator, discusses the Workshop Approach to teaching. (p. TM85)
- **Bridging Cultural Gaps** A teacher models the use of context clues to determine the meaning of an unknown word. (p. TM86)

ENGLISH LANGUAGE LEARNERS

- **Low Risk Environment** Author Josefina Tinajero discusses the importance of creating a low-risk environment for English language learners. (p. TM84)

CHAPTER 5 Citizenship and Leadership

ENGLISH LANGUAGE LEARNERS

- **Words in Action** Students act out or mime the words they are trying to learn. (p. TM89)
- **Providing Clear Directions** A teacher provides clear written and oral directions for a classroom assignment and checks for student understanding. (p. TM89)
- **Group Discussions** Students discuss academic content they have just read. (p. TM91)

MATH

- **Communications in Mathematics** Bea Moore-Harris explains the importance of student communication in the mathematics classroom. (p. TM90)

CHAPTER 6 Goals and Decision Making

READING

- **Obstacles to Achievement** Teachers work together to determine why their students are struggling with mastery of a particular standard. (p. TM95)
- **Flexible Groupings** Teachers use the strategies of flexible groupings and partner sharing to encourage and promote student discussions. (p. TM95)

ENGLISH LANGUAGE LEARNERS

- **Academic Language** Authors Jana Echevarria and Josefina Tinajero discuss the importance of addressing academic language when teaching English language learners. (p. TM94)
- **Scaffolding Questions** A teacher uses a series of questions to lead a student to an appropriate verbal response. (p. TM95)

MATH

- **Guiding Questions** A teacher uses guiding questions to help students review vocabulary necessary for the lesson she will teach on polynomials. (p. TM96)

Communicate With Others

Section 4.1 *Listening and Speaking Skills*

In this section students will learn the basics of verbal and non-verbal communication. They will learn to be active listeners. They will also learn how to conduct a conversation by asking questions and avoiding gossip.

Section 4.2 *Handle Conflict*

In this section, students will explore the causes of conflict. They will learn to prevent and avoid conflict. They will also learn to resolve conflict through compromise and negotiation, or to walk away if necessary.

Classroom Solutions

Print Resources

 Student Edition
Teacher Annotated Edition
Student Activity Workbook
Student Activity Workbook Teacher Annotated Edition

Technology Resources

ExamView Assessment Suite **ExamView Assessment Suite CD** allows you to create and print out customized tests or ready-made unit and chapter tests, complete with answer keys.

Lesson Planner *Plus* **Lesson Planner Plus! CD*** is and electronic lesson planner that provides instant access to teacher resources in one convenient package.

- Projects and Activities*
- Food Labs*
- Sewing Labs*
- Career Investigations*
- Reteaching Activities*
- Enrichment Activities*

PRESENTATION *Plus!* **Presentation Plus!** PowerPoint™ Presentations can be edited and customized to meet the needs of students.

Online Learning Center includes resources and activities for students and teachers. Also includes Online Student Edition.

Interactive Student Edition

*Electronic Resources are available on Lesson Planner Plus and the Online Learning Center.

 Writing Activity Answer

A Good Way to Communicate Answers will vary. Sample answer: The best way to communicate is face to face. People who talk face to face can see each other's facial expressions. They can hear the other person's tone of voice. It is the most personal way to have a conversation.

 Discovering Careers Answers ▼

1. Answers will vary. Students should write a summary of the education, training, and experience needed for the selected careers.
2. Newscasts will vary but should include events or activities going on in their families. Ask volunteers to read their newscasts in class.
3. Lists will vary but may include: integrity, fairness, ethics, writing skills, reporting skills, ability to use good judgment, ability to keep his or her personal opinions from influencing the story, good spelling and grammar.
4. Answers will vary. Students should present a summary of what they learned about the person's typical work day.

Listening and Speaking Skills

FOCUS

Discussion Starter

Ask students to discuss various ways they communicate with others, and list them on the board. Modes of communication might include talking in person or on the phone, writing letters, e-mail, text messaging, Internet chat, sign language, eye contact, touch, and body language.

 Bell Ringer Activity

Charades Have students write down words on pieces of paper and put them in a container. Have volunteers draw one and try to get the class to guess their word. They can use body language and facial expressions, but no sounds or talking. Discuss how gestures and expressions can be communicative, but how it is difficult to communicate without words.

Professional Development
Reading Vocabulary

TEACH

S Skill Practice

Guided Practice

L1 List Divide students into small groups. Have each group list as many ways as they can to communicate without words. Lists should contain not only body language, posture, and personal space, but also other methods such as eye contact, facial expressions, and physical appearance (style of clothing, hair, and makeup).

L2 Discuss Have students work in groups. Instruct them to discuss what it means to be an active listener. Making an effort to understand what is being said, responding to the speaker to show understanding, and restating to make sure they understand. An active listener does not interrupt.

L3 Apply Divide students into pairs to practice asking questions during a conversation. Students should take turns choosing a topic and discussing it while the other asks questions. Students should ask questions that show they are actively listening and participating in the conversation, but should not interrupt.

U Universal Access

Interpersonal and Intrapersonal Learners Divide students into groups and have them review the information on how to be a good communicator and listener. Have them practice conversational skills. Ensure that groups are balanced, containing both outgoing, interpersonal learners as well as reflective, intrapersonal learners.

Professional Development Mini Clip
ELL Low Risk Environment

ASSESS

Quiz

Ask students to answer the following questions:

1. How does personal space serve as a nonverbal communication? The more distant you keep yourself from people, the less interested you appear.

2. What are the characteristics of an assertive communicator? An assertive communicator gets his or her point across without dominating the conversation and generally speaks and listens in equal amounts.

3. What is an open-ended question? A question that requires more than a yes or no answer, usually an explanatory answer.

RETEACH

W Writing Strategy

Prepare for a Meeting Ask students to prepare a list of questions they would ask if they were meeting a potential employer, a friend of a friend, a relative's fiancé, or a simply a person they have never met before. Students should come up with questions that are appropriate to each situation and designed to start a conversation and keep it going.

C Critical Thinking

Values and Interests Discuss with the class how to have a successful conversation even if the other person has different values and interests than you. People with different values and interests will be less likely to agree. This can lead to arguments, or to an imbalance of interest in the conversation topic. The speakers should not take each other's reactions personally.

ASSESS

Section 4.1 Review Assign the Section 4.1 After You Read activities.

 Student Activity Workbook Assign the Section 4.1 Activities.

Online Study Tools Have students go to the Online Learning Center at glencoe.com to:

- Take the Section 4.1 **Practice Test**.
- Download **Study-to-Go** content.

Section 4.1 After You Read

Answer Key

1. Speak for yourself; be clear and direct; be aware of your listener; ask questions.

2. Give full attention to the speaker; concentrate on what the speaker is saying; listen for overall meaning; remember to notice nonverbal cues; avoid making quick judgments; resist distractions; give feedback to indicate understanding.

3. Talking about people and their personal lives can destroy friendships and ruin reputations.

4. Paragraphs will vary. Students should describe a conversation they observed, with details about who said what to whom. They should include a description of how things were said, such as whether or not body language was used, what perceptions may have existed, or if tone of voice was a factor. They should conclude with an evaluation.

5. Answers may include that cell phones, email, text messages, and instant messages have replaced landline telephones, letters, and greeting cards. Some students may say the changes are positive because communication is easier and faster; others may say the changes are negative because communication is less personal.

CLOSE

Culminating Activity

Practice Makes Perfect The best way to become a good conversationalist is to practice. Have half of the students sit at their desks, while the other half rotates between desks at your direction every five minutes. Have students practice having short conversations with each other. By having many short conversations, students will learn how to think quickly to start a conversations and how to see what was successful and what was not.

Handle Conflict

FOCUS

Discussion Starter

Ask volunteers to discuss conflicts they have been in recently. Ask them to identify the cause, the arguments and the resolution/outcome. Looking back, do they think they could have done something differently to get a better outcome? Students should think critically about their behavior in order to identify possibilities for a better resolution to conflict. Perhaps they could have kept their voice down or listened more.

 Bell Ringer Activity

Causes of Conflict As a class, brainstorm possible causes of conflict. List as many situations as students can think of on the board. Discuss ways to prepare for the situations listed.

TEACH

S **Skill Practice**

Independent Practice

L1 **List** Have students list ways that anger can be controlled to avoid a conflict. Writing in a journal, listening to or playing music, making something creative, exercising, taking a nap, or talking about it. Students may also come up with other constructive solutions.

L2 **Explain** Ask students to write a paragraph that explains how compromise can help resolve conflicts. Compromise is an agreement in which each person gives up something in order to reach a solution that satisfies everyone. If two conflicting parties can come to a compromise, then the conflict can end without hard feelings.

L3 **Apply** Choose a topic for students to debate. Set up two teams. Give them a specific time in which to present their arguments. Evaluate how well they were able to keep the debate under control. Debating can help students understand how to argue without getting heated. By following rules and separating logic from emotion, one can learn how to argue without causing genuine conflict.

U Universal Access

Students with Hearing Impairments Arrange for a reliable classmate to take notes for a student with hearing impairments, so that he or she can concentrate on lip reading or following an interpreter.

ASSESS

Quiz

Ask students to answer the following questions:

1. **How can gossip cause conflict?** The person gossiped about may feel hurt and angry if they find out, and the gossip may not be true.

2. **What is the best way to prevent conflict?** Pay attention to your own behavior and try to see it from other people's points of view.

3. **What is the last resort if you are faced with a conflict you cannot resolve?** The last resort is to simply walk away and then to talk to an adult at school or home about the problem.

RETEACH

R Reading Strategy

Model Have students review the information on peer mediation. Ask three volunteers to model the process. Have two students play the part of the people in conflict and one student play the part of the peer mediator. Have the mediator work to resolve the conflict. All of the students modeling the peer mediation process should demonstrate an understanding of the process through their behavior during the exercise.

C Critical Thinking

Conflict Online There are often conflicts when people communicate online. Ask students: What are the characteristics of online communication that can lead to conflict. How can you try to avoid that conflict? You cannot see a person's facial expressions or hear their tone, so misunderstandings are more frequent. Anonymity can cause some people to be more confrontational. To avoid this, be clear about your tone, and ignore people who are being confrontational.

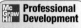
Professional Development **Mini Clip**
Reading Bridging Cultural Gaps

ASSESS

Section 4.2 Review Assign the Section 4.2 After You Read activities.

 Student Activity Workbook Assign the Section 4.2 Activities.

Online Study Tools Have students go to the Online Learning Center at glencoe.com to:

- Take the Section 4.2 **Practice Test**.
- Download **Study-to-Go** content.

ExamView® Assessment Suite
Use the *ExamView Assessment Suite* **CD to create a test for this chapter.**

Chapter Review Have students complete the Chapter 4 Review and Applications.

Section 4.2 After You Read
Answer Key

1. Gossip is unkind and can lead to rumors, damage friendships, and ruin reputations.

2. Write in a journal, listen to or play music, exercise, get some rest, or talk to someone.

3. Negotiation is when people discuss the conflict for the purpose of resolving it. Sometimes they use a mediator. Together, they can compromise and come to an agreement.

4. Emails should include details about the disagreement and how it began. Students could suggest a place and time to meet their friend to talk about possible compromises.

5. You would probably feel hurt, angry, and disappointed. The person could miss out on a friendship because he or she allowed stereotypes to interfere with accepting you for who you are.

CLOSE

Culminating Activity

Conflict Role Play Divide students into pairs or small groups. Give each group a cause of conflict and have them role-play the conflict and how they would resolve it. Students should practice the techniques for resolving conflict that they learned from the text. Each group should come to a satisfactory resolution. If they do not, discuss what could have been done differently.

Words You Learned

1. Students should write their own definition for each of the content and academic vocabulary words.

Review Key Concepts

2. You can speak and write to express yourself. You can also express yourself through body language and facial expressions. Both can show others how you feel.

3. Listening is not the same as hearing. When you hear, you are aware of the words being said. When you listen, you make an effort to understand the message.

4. Ask open-ended questions to keep a conversation moving.

5. Misunderstandings, differing opinions, gossip, jealousy, prejudice.

6. Try to head off problems before they start. Examine your own behavior. Look at situations from the other person's point of view.

7. Open communication lines, use "I" statements, listen carefully, pay attention to your body language, control your anger, negotiate a solution, compromise to reach an agreement.

Critical Thinking

8. Answers will vary but should show that students understand how the skill they chose will be useful and necessary when attempting to communicate effectively with the family member.

9. Answers will vary but may include lack of understanding, jumping to conclusions, making incorrect assumptions, not listening or showing respect.

Real-World Skills and Applications

10. Answers will vary. Paul could start by telling his parents that he wants to have better control of his temper, and he could ask for their help. He can work on heading off conflicts before they start or get worse. For example, he can write in a journal, listen to or play music, find a creative outlet, exercise, get some rest, or talk to someone.

11. Answers will vary. Students' comparisons should include details about the conversation and the letter, and which communication method they prefer and why. For example, they may say the conversation works better because you can hear tone of voice and see facial expressions and body language.

Financial Literacy

12. Answers will vary depending on store visited. Lists may include sale items, promotions, salespeople, displays, and specials. Without these forms of communication, shoppers would not know about sales or special offers. If shoppers buy something they were not planning to buy, students will conclude that the methods are effective, but that it may cause shoppers to spend more rather than save.

Active Learning

13. Handbooks will vary but should include information from the text and other sources about facing, preventing, avoiding, and resolving conflict.

14. Answers will vary depending on conflict chosen. Students should list the circumstances that caused the conflict, the participants, the issues in question, and how the conflict was resolved.

Net Connection

15. Answers will vary, but may include tips such as: give feedback in a timely fashion; praise someone's accomplishments in front of others; give negative feedback in private; be specific; consider the other person's feelings before speaking; be sincere.

Academic Skills

16. Presentations will vary. Students may choose to do a role-play demonstration of emotions, such as showing happiness with a big smile or frustration with an angry expression. They can use exaggerated posture and gestures, such as hands on hips for impatience, or folded arms and stomping for anger, and ask the 4th graders to guess the meaning.

17. Answers will vary, but may include a religious or local community organization. Paragraphs should include specific conflict resolution strategies that the organization or group uses.

18. The equation $x + 2x + 4x = \$168.21$ can be simplified to $7x = \$168.21$, or $x = \$24.03$. Thus, Dale's share ($x$) is \$24.03. Harry's share ($2x$) is $2 \times \$24.03 = \$48.06$. Benjamin's share ($4x$) is $4 \times \$24.03 = \$96.12$.

Standardized Test Practice

19. a

Citizenship and Leadership

Section 5.1 Good Citizenship

In this section, students will learn about the concept of citizenship. They will learn how to take responsibility in their community. They will also learn how to show respect for others.

Section 5.2 Leadership Skills

In this section, students will learn how to be a leader by motivating others, sharing responsibility, having a positive attitude and making good decisions. They will also learn about different leadership styles and teamwork.

Classroom Solutions

Print Resources

 Student Edition
 Teacher Annotated Edition
Student Activity Workbook
 Student Activity Workbook
Teacher Annotated Edition

Technology Resources

ExamView Assessment Suite **ExamView Assessment Suite CD** allows you to create and print out customized tests or ready-made unit and chapter tests, complete with answer keys.

Lesson Planner *Plus* **Lesson Planner Plus! CD*** is and electronic lesson planner that provides instant access to teacher resources in one convenient package.

- Projects and Activities*
- Food Labs*
- Sewing Labs*
- Career Investigations*
- Reteaching Activities*
- Enrichment Activities*

 Presentation Plus! PowerPoint™ Presentations can be edited and customized to meet the needs of students.

Online Learning Center includes resources and activities for students and teachers. Also includes Online Student Edition.

Interactive Student Edition

*Electronic Resources are available on Lesson Planner Plus and the Online Learning Center.

Writing Activity Answer

Leadership Qualities Answers will vary. To evaluate paragraphs, use the following criteria: Does the paragraph include a strong sentence? Does it convey a mood that is supported by its details? Does it present details in a logical order? Does it include precise transition words?

Discovering Careers Answers ▼

1. Answers will vary. Students should write a summary of the education, training, and experience needed for the selected careers.
2. Outlines may include details about their family's genealogy, places where they have lived, and family stories.
3. Lists may include traffic, crime, environment, education, taxes, and waste management.
4. Answers will vary. Students should present a summary of what they learned about the person's typical work day.

Section 5.1 Lesson Plan

Good Citizenship

FOCUS

Discussion Starter

Being a good citizen means participating in your community and contributing to your country's well-being. Ask volunteers to discuss ways in which they have been a good citizen. Some may volunteer and others may be old enough to vote. Obeying laws is another way to be a good citizen.

Bell Ringer Activity

Locate Opportunities Have each student use the local newspaper or the Internet to locate opportunities to volunteer in their community. Ask them to provide the name and contact information of the organization, its purpose, and available volunteer opportunities. Compile the information and encourage the students to contact one of the organizations and volunteer.

TEACH

S Skill Practice

Independent Practice

L1 **List** Have students list ways to volunteer in the community. The book gives examples of ways to volunteer on page 98. In addition, students may come up with other ideas of their own.

L2 **Demonstrate** Have students write a dialogue between two fictional people that demonstrates how to show respect for others. You show respect for others by treating them as you would like to be treated. Speak politely to people, and think of their desires as well as your own.

L3 **Apply** Have students select one day this week to pay special attention to their role as a citizen of this community. Tell students to look for opportunities to practice the suggestions given in the chapter and to be aware of treating people with respect. Have them prepare a brief presentation. Presentations should reflect acts of kindness and respect throughout the day, as well as sensitivity to how these actions were received.

Professional Development — Mini Clip
ELL Words in Action

U Universal Access

Students with Orthopedic or Visual Impairments Students with orthopedic or visual impairments may be limited in their use of body language, such as eye contact or hand gestures. Such students may have a difficult time communicating with new people. Encourage them to volunteer with a friend to meet new people.

ASSESS

Quiz

Ask students to answer the following questions:

1. What must you do in return for the rights that this country allows you to enjoy? Citizens have responsibilities that include obeying laws and rules.

2. Why is taking care of shared property part of being a good citizen? It ensures that everyone has a chance to use and enjoy that property.

3. What are the rewards of citizenship? It can make you feel proud, satisfied, and good about yourself.

Professional Development — Mini Clip
ELL Providing Clear Directions

RETEACH

R Reading Strategy

Identify Ask students to list their favorite hobbies. Have them research opportunities that would allow them to contribute to the community while enjoying their hobbies. Have students present their findings. There are many ways to contribute to community while doing something you enjoy. For example, someone who enjoys reading might volunteer at the library, and someone who enjoys sports might volunteer to coach children.

C Critical Thinking

Synthesize Have students survey their friends and relatives, asking what improvements they would like to see around the community. Tally them to see what kind of responses come up more often. Create an action plan for how your class could help improve the community. Students should try to survey a variety of people, not just their friends. As a class, students should pick a popular answer that is something they can conceivably contribute to.

ASSESS

Section 5.1 Review Assign the Section 5.1 After You Read activities.

 Student Activity Workbook Assign the Section 5.1 Activities.

 Online Study Tools Have students go to the Online Learning Center at glencoe.com to:

- Take the Section 5.1 **Practice Test**.
- Download **Study-to-Go** content.

Section 5.1 After You Read
Answer Key

1. Any three: vote, express opinions freely and publicly, receive an education, travel freely within the country, receive a fair and speedy trial, enjoy equal protection under the law.

2. Read to people in a hospital or nursing home; record reading for people with visual impairments; clean parks; care for pets of out-of-town neighbors; return lost items.

3. PSAs will vary but may include volunteer opportunities in animal shelters, hospitals, libraries, senior citizen centers, disaster relief centers, food banks, and fundraisers.

4. Paragraphs will vary. Students should choose an amendment, interpret it, and describe how it is important to them. Sample answer: The First Amendment includes freedom of speech. This means citizens are free to communicate an idea or opinion without fear of punishment. This is important because it means people can share ideas and learn about other viewpoints.

CLOSE

Culminating Activity

Be Active As a class, do something positive to improve the school. Choose something that everyone can participate in and that will make the school a better place. Get the permission you need from the principal, and invite other people if you like. Students might plan a day to pick up trash or make more permanent improvements, such as repainting or planting trees.

Section 5.2 Lesson Plan

Leadership Skills

FOCUS

Discussion Starter

Ask student volunteers to discuss situations where they have had to work as a team. Ask them to describe the situation, why it was necessary to work in a team, and how they worked together to accomplish their goal. Students may describe any situation in which they had to work as part of a group to accomplish a goal and should explain why it could not be done alone.

Bell Ringer Activity

A Good Leader Ask the class to imagine they must elect a leader of the class. The leader will be their representative and the person who communicates the feelings of the class to the teacher and the administration. Ask the class to list qualities that they would want this leader to have. Write the list on the board for the class.

TEACH

S Skill Practice

Independent Practice

L1 List List the things a good leader will do in order to accomplish goals. Motivate the members of his or her group, share responsibilities and rewards, have a positive attitude, and make sound decisions.

L2 Explain Write a paragraph explaining how a democratic leader works. A democratic leader does not make decisions on his or her own, seeks input from the group, and will usually go with what the majority of the group wants, rather than with their own personal wishes.

L3 Apply Bring a set of Legos, blocks, or some other building material to class. Divide the students into teams and have them work together to construct something out of the toys. Have them elect a leader to direct the construction. Students should elect a leader and then work together under their leader to build a creative structure.

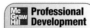
Professional Development **Mini Clip**
Math Communications in Mathematics

U Universal Access

Visual Learning With the students, compile a list of traits of a successful team on the board. Categorize them under leadership qualities and cooperative qualities. As a class, discuss the value of each and how the two types of qualities combine to form a successful team.

ASSESS

Quiz

Ask students to answer the following questions:

1. How can a leader motivate his or her group? Be upbeat about the task, and set an example by being the first person to jump in and work on the project.

2. How does an autocratic leader lead a group? An autocratic leader makes every decision themselves. The group has no input; they are just given orders to carry out.

3. Why is being a strong team member just as important as being a good leader? A group cannot succeed unless the team members are strong. If everyone is trying to be a leader, nothing will get done.

RETEACH

R Reading Strategy

Assess Priorities Ask: Which of the characteristics of a good leader are most and least important when working as a member of a team? List the characteristics given in the text in order of importance, from most to least important. Students should review the characteristics of a good leader in the lesson and decide which would help them most as a member of a team. They should arrange the characteristics from most to least important. Compare lists.

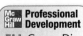
Professional Development **Mini Clip**
ELL Group Discussions

C Critical Thinking

Conduct Research Have students choose a career that requires leadership skills and research that career online or at the library. Have them write a short essay explaining what skills the career requires and why it is important to be a good leader when employed in that career. Students should take the leadership skills they learned about in this lesson and connect them to job duties and required skills for certain careers. Professions might include teachers, business executives, or politicians.

ASSESS

Section 5.2 Review Assign the Section 5.2 After You Read activities.

Student Activity Workbook Assign the Section 5.2 Activities.

 Online Study Tools Have students go to the Online Learning Center at glencoe.com to:

- Take the Section 5.2 **Practice Test**.
- Download **Study-to-Go** content.

 ExamView® Assessment Suite
Use the *ExamView Assessment Suite* **CD to create a test for this chapter.**

Chapter Review Have students complete the Chapter 5 Review and Applications.

Section 5.2 After You Read
Answer Key

1. A leader needs to motivate his or her team to keep them interested, enthusiastic, and committed

2. Technical skills, people skills, thinking skills

3. Without the cooperation and support of all members, a team cannot operate effectively.

4. Answers may include: What leadership roles have you held in other groups? What do want to accomplish as president? What do you do if someone criticizes you? How will you work to involve all students in school activities?

5. Answers will vary. Lists should be comprehensive, and actions should reduce waste.

CLOSE

Culminating Activity

Work as a Team Have the class plan an event, such as a bake sale. Have them elect a leader who assigns tasks. They should work together to successfully put on their event. Students should use the information they learned in this lesson to help them elect a leader and work together to follow their leader and plan and implement an event.

Words You Learned

1. Students should use each of the content and academic vocabulary words to create a cross-word puzzle.

Review Key Concepts

2. Obey the laws.

3. The sense of pride you can feel when you help and support others in your community can give you a strong connection to your community.

4. A good leader can guide by motivating others, encouraging others, sharing responsibilities and rewards, having a positive attitude, and making sound decisions.

5. Autocratic leadership is when the leader makes all the decisions. Democratic leadership is when the group works together to make decisions.

6. Participate in a school fundraiser, play on a sports team, join the student council, pitch in to help your family with yard work, take part in a walk-a-thon.

Critical Thinking

7. Answers will vary but may include: popularity can motivate followers. A popular person may be more likely to get a position of authority. Popularity may also be a replacement for skills and ideas. Being popular does not mean a person has good leadership skills.

8. All citizens. They pay through the lost use of the property, in taxes, in higher insurance rates, and through the costs involved in finding and prosecuting vandals.

9. Answers will vary, but may include: they think their efforts will not make a difference; they have too many other obligations and do not have time to volunteer; they do not want the responsibility.

Real-World Skills and Applications

10. Answers will vary but should include pros and cons for each kind of leadership style they observed in two different teams. They should explain why one style of leadership is better than the other. Some students may say that both styles are effective or ineffective for different reasons.

11. Answers will vary based on what is offered in your community, but may include animal shelters, soup kitchens, food banks, libraries, walks or runs for charity.

Financial Literacy

12. Answers will vary based on the organizations selected. Students should be able use the Internet or other sources to obtain annual reports for the two charities, which should allow them to find the percentages that each charity allocates for administrative expenses, fundraising expenses, and for the cause itself.

Active Learning

13. Reports will vary but should include details about the reactions students received and explanations about why the task was easy or difficult.

14. Answers will vary depending on leader chosen. Presentations should include details about the leader's style and include two examples of how the leader worked with other countries. Students should explain how they decided if the leadership style is effective or not.

15. Answers will vary. Students should create a list of three quotations about leadership that apply to concepts discussed in the chapter or in class.

Academic Skills

16. Paragraphs will vary. Students may say that they felt satisfied knowing that they made a child happy by spending time with him or her and by giving the book as a gift.

17. Answers will vary depending on the location. The percentage is apt to be low unless the last election was for President. Students should logically defend their answer about whether or not the voting percentage is acceptable.

18. The amount of Claire's tip was $110 − $92.50 = $17.50. Calculate the percentage by dividing $17.50 by $92.50, which results in 0.189189, or approximately 18.9%.

Standardized Test Practice

19. Students should have a clear thesis statement that defines the ideal leader to them. The essay should include examples of the kind of leadership they would look for to vote for a presidential candidate. The essay should conclude with a strong closing statement.

Goals and Decision Making

Section 6.1 Goals

In this section, students will learn how to set and achieve goals. They will learn about long-term and short-term goals and how to set realistic goals. They will also learn how to deal with both success and disappointment.

Section 6.2 Decisions

In this section, students will learn about the different types of decisions they may have to make. Then they will learn practical advice to help them learn to make good decisions.

Classroom Solutions

Print Resources

- Student Edition
- Teacher Annotated Edition
- Student Activity Workbook
- Student Activity Workbook Teacher Annotated Edition

Technology Resources

ExamView **ExamView Assessment Suite CD** allows you to create and print out customized tests or ready-made unit and chapter tests, complete with answer keys.

Lesson Planner Plus Lesson Planner Plus! CD* is and electronic lesson planner that provides instant access to teacher resources in one convenient package.

- Projects and Activities*
- Food Labs*
- Sewing Labs*
- Career Investigations*
- Reteaching Activities*
- Enrichment Activities*

 Presentation Plus! PowerPoint™ Presentations can be edited and customized to meet the needs of students.

Online Learning Center includes resources and activities for students and teachers. Also includes Online Student Edition.

Interactive Student Edition

*Electronic Resources are available on Lesson Planner Plus and the Online Learning Center.

Writing Activity Answer

Autobiography Answers will vary. Students should have an introduction, three paragraphs with details that support the introduction, and a conclusion.

Discovering Careers Answers ▼

1. Answers will vary. Students should write a summary of the education, training, and experience needed for the selected careers.
2. Students should draw a map of their home marked with an escape route and a meeting location.
3. Lists will vary. Sample answers: an airline pilot needs to decide whether or not to fly in bad weather; a store manager needs to decide how much product to order; a doctor needs to decide what kind of treatment to give a patient.
4. Answers will vary. Students should present a summary of what they learned about the person's typical work day.

Section **6.1** Lesson Plan

Goals and Decision Making

FOCUS

Discussion Starter

Discuss goals with the class. Ask volunteers to describe a goal that they have. It can be either a long-term or a short-term goal. How do they plan to achieve their goal? Goals could be anything from getting a good grade on test to fulfilling the requirements for the career of their choice. They should have some idea of how they can achieve their goal.

Bell Ringer Activity

Long- and Short-Term Goals Have students make two columns on a piece of paper, "Short-Term Goals" and "Long-Term Goals." Have them list examples of each in the appropriate column. The long-term goals should take months or years to reach, while the short-term goals should take only days or weeks. Students should come up with examples other than those given by the text.

> **Mc Graw Hill Professional Development** **Mini Clip**
> **ELL** Academic Language

TEACH

S Skill Practice

Independent Practice

L1 List Have students list the characteristics of a realistic goal. A realistic goal is: specific and clear; challenging, but at the same time, achievable; active; thought-out, so you are prepared to deal with problems that arise; and flexible.

L2 Explain Ask students to write a paragraph that explains how attitude can contribute to success in meeting goals. A positive attitude can get you through the rough portions of working toward your goal; help you do your best, even when you do not enjoy the task, and keep you going after setbacks.

L3 Apply Have students choose a goal they are working toward and create an action plan for meeting their goal. Have them write down the goal, and the steps required to reach it, and a timeline for completing each task. The action plans should be well thought-out, realistic, and useful.

U Universal Access

Verbal Learning Have students choose one portion of the lesson and create a short, motivational speech on that topic. Then have students give their speeches in front of the class. Afterwards, discuss what was learned from the speeches.

ASSESS

Quiz

Ask students to answer the following questions:

1. Why must a realistic goal be flexible? You cannot plan for everything. If your goal is not flexible, you may have difficulty achieving it if something you did not plan for occurs.

2. What are the personal benefits gained from achieving a goal? Achieving a goal helps you feel good about yourself and inspires you to set new goals and try new things.

3. Why do you sometimes have to prioritize in order to achieve a goal? If you have more than one goal, you will have to decide which is more important, so you can organize your time.

RETEACH

W Writing Strategy

Evaluate Why do we set goals? Why not just wait and see what happens? Explain why one would want to set goals and work toward achieving them. Having goals is necessary for success in life. Goals are things that you want, so if you do not set goals, you are less likely to get the things you want. Having goals will give you something to focus on and will boost your self-confidence.

C Critical Thinking

Deal with Setbacks Suppose your goal is to get into the local college. While applying, you discover that your grades are not high enough for the requirements. What could you have done differently to avoid this setback? What can you do now? The admission requirements should have been checked when the goal was first set and the student should have gotten tutoring or prioritized studies in order to get better grades. Now they must either find another school or speak to the admissions office to see what they can do.

ASSESS

Section 6.1 Review Assign the Section 6.1 After You Read activities.

 Student Activity Workbook Assign the Section 6.1 Activities.

Online Study Tools Have students go to the Online Learning Center at glencoe.com to:

- Take the Section 6.1 **Practice Test**.
- Download **Study-to-Go** content.

Section 6.1 After You Read

Answer Key

1. Setting a realistic goal can help prevent you from getting discouraged or giving up.

2. A positive attitude can help you tackle a difficult job rather than put it off, and it can help you be flexible.

3. Answers will vary, but students should write about a short-term goal and the resources they would use to meet the goal. Their answers may include any of the resources listed in the text: time, money, energy, knowledge, skills, family, friends.

4. Answers will vary depending on invention or event researched. Students should list key individuals involved in the accomplishments and what goals were likely set and reached along the way.

CLOSE

Culminating Activity

Revisit Goals Ask the class to think back to the goals they discussed in the discussion starter. Have any of them reached their goals? Have any of them changed the way they are pursuing their goal? Hearing from students who have been successful will encourage the other students. Discussing ways that students have changed the pursuit of their goals might encourage other students to follow the advice from the lesson.

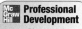 **Professional Development** **Mini Clip**
Reading Obstacles to Achievement

Decisions

FOCUS

Discussion Starter

Ask the class to think about the decisions they make every day. Some decisions are very hard while some are so routine they may not notice them. Ask volunteers to discuss those decisions and how they made their choice. Students can talk about any type of decision, whether it is large, like where to go to college, or small, like what to have for lunch.

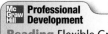 **Professional Development** **Mini Clip**
Reading Flexible Groupings

 Bell Ringer Activity

Decision Types Ask students to imagine that they are choosing a restaurant to take a friend from out of town to. Write down the different ways of making decisions and give an example of each as it applies to this decision. Students should think of one example for each. For example, an emotional decision might mean choosing your favorite restaurant without considering whether your friend would like it.

 Professional Development **Mini Clip**
ELL Scaffolding Questions

S **Skill Practice**

Independent Practice

L1 **List** Have students list the steps to follow in order to make a good decision. Use good timing; do not make decisions too quickly; consider all consequences; be willing to make mistakes; seek advice; accept responsibility.

L2 **Describe** Ask students to write a paragraph that describes how to make proactive decisions. Think ahead and take action right away to prevent problems instead of letting them happen and dealing with the aftermath. Proactive people do not hesitate for fear of making the wrong decision.

L3 **Apply** Have students choose one decision they are currently making or think they will have to make in the future and create a list of pros and cons. Pro/con lists are useful decision-making tools. They allow you to organize your thoughts and make a visual representation of the consequences of each decision.

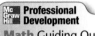 **Universal Access**

Logical/Mathematical Learners Have students create a chart or spreadsheet to organize their decision-making process. The chart should list each step of the process that works for them.

ASSESS

Quiz

Ask students to answer the following questions:

1. **What kind of decisions become habits?** Simple decisions that you make every day, and which do not require much thought become habits. These include things like brushing your teeth or doing homework.

2. **Why is evaluating the decision a part of the decision-making process?** Because you may have to make similar decisions in the future, and evaluation can help you be prepared.

3. **What are the consequences of making a decision too quickly?** You may not have time to consider all consequences, and your decision may have an unexpected result.

RETEACH

R Reading Strategy

Make A List Review the feature on page 125. For each step, list items that can help you make the decisions, such as graphic organizers, checklists, or questions to ask yourself. For each step, students should come up with at least one tool. For example, for step one, they might use a mind map to divide a big decision into parts, or a step-by-step checklist.

C Critical Thinking

Stay Organized It is important to be organized when you have an important decision to make. Brainstorm methods of maintaining efficient organization. Some methods of maintaining organization are to keep a notebook, computer file, or a personal organizer where you enter important dates, tasks to complete, notes, and lists.

ASSESS

Section 6.2 Review Assign the Section 6.2 After You Read activities.

Student Activity Workbook Assign the Section 6.2 Activities.

 Online Study Tools Have students go to the Online Learning Center at glencoe.com to:

■ Take the Section 6.2 **Practice Test**.

■ Download **Study-to-Go** content.

ExamView® *Assessment Suite*
Use the *ExamView Assessment Suite* **CD to create a test for this chapter.**

Chapter Review Have students complete the Chapter 6 Review and Applications.

Section 6.2 After You Read
Answer Key

1. You leave the outcome to chance.

2. Use good timing; consider the consequences; be willing to make mistakes and learn from them; seek advice when you need it; accept responsibility for your decisions.

3. Answers will vary depending on the character and the decision. Students can refer to the feature on page 125. Paragraphs should include details about the steps taken by the character to solve his or her problem. Students should discuss the outcome and evaluate the decision to determine what, if anything, they would do differently if they were faced with the same decision.

4. Answers will vary depending on the leader selected. Presentation should include specifics about the leader chosen, the factors that lead to the decision, and the outcome of the decision.

CLOSE

Culminating Activity

Make a Plan Ask students to choose a decision they are currently making or expect to have to make in the future. Have them create an action plan for making their decision. Students should use the advice that they learned from this lesson to create an action plan that will prepare them to make a decision. Their plan should take them through the steps of making a decision.

Words You Learned

1. Students should use each of the content vocabulary words and academic vocabulary words in a sentence.

Review Key Concepts

2. A long-term goal can take months or years to reach; a short-term goal can be reached in days or weeks.

3. A positive attitude can help you do your best, even if the task is something you do not enjoy. It can inspire you to keep working toward your goal, even if you hit snags along the way.

4. Planned, default, impulse, emotional, and resistance.

5. The outcome from decisions you make now can affect your future choices in positive and negative ways.

Critical Thinking

6. Answers will vary but may include: waiting longer could give you more time to think about your choices; more information may become available; some problems may work themselves out naturally.

7. Answers will vary but may include: the person had good self-esteem, positive role models, good decision-making skills, and the ability to set and achieve goals.

8. Students should list the steps (identify decision or problem; consider the alternatives; choose the best alternative; act on the decision; evaluate the decision) and a tip for each. Tips will vary depending on decision to be made, but should relate to the step it is associated with.

9. Answers will vary but may include: changes in the job market; your family and personal needs may change; you might develop new interests and skills.

Real-World Skills and Applications

10. Jacob could list the pros and cons of each activity. He should ask himself if either activity contributes to his long-term goals and should consider other alternatives, such as playing football this year and joining the band next year.

11. Templates should be based on the information in Figure 6.1 on page 118. Students should include tips related to the steps.

Financial Literacy

12. Answers will vary depending on the jobs selected by each student. The salaries found by students will also have varying effects on their long-term goals. For example, salary levels could impact the type of home they want to live in, the number of children they wish to have, or the location where they want to live.

Active Learning

13. Answers will vary. Students should notice a pattern and decide if they need to make a change in the way they approach decision making.

14. Students may identify the Internet, television and radio ads, videos, libraries, job fairs, recruitment offices, telephone directories, teachers, parents, other relatives, experienced adults, and teachers as resources. They should rank the information sources and give logical explanations for their rankings.

Net Connection

15. Answers will vary, but students will find a wide variety of Web sites devoted to goals and goal setting. Some Web sites are general, while others may offer advice geared toward specific goals. Students should explain which Web sites are the most useful and why.

Academic Skills

16. Pamphlets will vary. Students should use information from the text to create an appealing pamphlet that encourages and teaches responsible decision making for teens.

17. Students should create a chart that records body language (for example, wrinkling the brow, putting a finger up on the chin, or folding arms) that people display when making a decision.

18. Elena should spend no more than 36 seconds per slide. (15 x 60 = 900 seconds; 900 ÷ 25 = 36 seconds)

Standardized Test Practice

19. English and German are in the same language family.

FOCUS

Introduce the Project

In this project, students will formulate their points of view on a specific issue. Ask students about local issues they care about and why. Answers will vary, but may include pollution in their neighborhoods, homelessness on their city streets, poverty and hunger of less fortunate citizens, or crime rates in their community.

Build Background

Politics Ask students to name politicians they have seen in newspapers and on television. Explain that politicians are experts at stating their opinions. Then ask what methods politicians use to convince people of their points of view. Write the politicians' names and methods. Discuss which methods are most effective and why. Methods may include speeches, campaign commercials, posters, and debating other candidates.

TEACH

S Skill Practice

Guided Practice

L1 Identify Have students identify five issues most important to their age group. Identify which issue came up the most. Discuss why this issue is important today and why it may not have been in the past or may not be in the future. Lists may include global warming, crime, or overbearing parents. Discussion may reveal that communities constantly change and solving one problem sometimes creates new ones.

L2 Apply Suggest an opinion with which students most likely do not agree: "Soda should be illegal." Ask students to write supporting arguments for that opinion. Arguments may include facts about diseases associated with sugar or caffeine or that soda often replaces healthy foods.

L3 Imagine Ask students to imagine they are the Mayor of their city or town. A construction company wants permission to build a shopping mall on the site of a playground. The mall will bring needed jobs to the community but take away a place for kids to play. Have them write a paragraph about whether or not they would issue a permit to the company. Decisions will vary but answers should show that students considered the value of jobs for the community versus the need for the community's children to have a safe place to play.

C Critical Thinking

Compromise Explain that sometimes opinions clash. Ask two students to role-play a situation in which both want to sit in a certain chair. One wants it to see the board better, but the other wants it to sit next to a friend. Ask the class to suggest ways to compromise. Compromise suggestions may include taking turns daily, agreeing that neither of them should sit in chair, or asking the friend to move to a different part of the classroom.

ASSESS

Quiz

Ask students to answer the following questions:

1. What are nonverbal ways to communicate while you deliver a speech? Smiling, frowning, appropriate gestures, and relaxed posture.

2. What skills would a good leader use to convince people of his opinion? Listen to other opinions, be diplomatic, be positive, and allow others to make some decisions.

3. What are some ways to resolve conflict when points of view differ? Control anger, open lines of communication, encourage compromise, negotiation, and peer mediation.

CLOSE

Culminating Activity

Get Perspective In this activity, students developed a point of view about an issue. When you defend your opinion, you want people to believe you are right. However there is a difference between winning an argument and being right. Often it is hard to admit you are wrong. Ask students to write a paragraph about a time they were wrong and what they learned from that experience. Answers will vary, but may include the ability to see an issue from another perspective, understanding their limitations, and doing more research before forming an opinion.

Make Your Career Plan

Unit Overview

This unit introduces students to career planning and focuses on how students can start preparing for their careers now and develop the necessary skills to be responsible workers.

Chapter 7 *Explore Careers* In this chapter, students learn that it is never too soon to start thinking about the careers they might want to have one day. They are also taught how to best plan and prepare for the world of work.

Chapter 8 *Enter the Workplace* In this chapter, students will learn how to interview successfully and be responsible and flexible workers. They will also learn how reading, writing, math, science, speaking, listening, and technology skills contribute to success in the workplace.

Life Skills Project Preview

You in Ten Years

Tell students that as part of this unit, they will learn how to choose a job or career. They will learn how to explore their own skills and talents, interview someone who has a job that interests them, and present a project to the class to share what they have learned.

FCCLA provides programs to guide students through projects, enhance their personal growth, and build leadership skills that can make a difference in their lives, their families, and their communities.

Career Connection helps students discover their strengths, target career goals, and initiate a plan for achieving the lifestyles they desire. It focuses on career development aspects such as linking personal interests, skills, and goals to careers; preparing with education, leadership, and experience; learning to find a job; practicing productivity on the job; and managing roles in families, careers, and communities.

Skills Questionnaires Have students create questionnaries which uncover skills and personality traits. Each should have at least ten questions, and answers should enable students to make career suggestions. Divide students into pairs, and have them give each other their questionnaires. Then, have students make career suggestions, based on their responses. Questionnaires will vary, but questions should uncover skills and traits. For example, "Do you like being inside, working on a computer, or are you only happy outside, being active?" Based on answers, students should be able to make career suggestions. For example, if the student does not like being inside or inactive, suggested jobs could be a forest ranger or personal trainer.

Professional Development

MINI CLIP VIDEO LIBRARY

Targeted professional development is correlated throughout *Discovering Life Skills*. **The McGraw-Hill Professional Development Mini Clip Video Library** provides teaching strategies to strengthen academic and learning skills. Log on to **glencoe.com**.

In this Unit, you will find these Mini Clips:

CHAPTER 7 Explore Careers

READING
- **Flexible Groupings** Teachers use the strategies of flexible groupings and partner sharing to encourage and promote student discussions. (p. TM102)

ENGLISH LANGUAGE LEARNERS
- **Previewing a Text** A teacher previews a text with students, pointing out features and strategies that will promote student comprehension. (p. TM102)
- **Group Discussions** Students discuss academic content they have just read. (p. TM103)
- **Words in Action** Students act out or mime the words they are trying to learn. (p. TM104)

CHAPTER 8 Enter the Workplace

READING
- **Prereading Strategies** A teacher assesses her students prior knowledge about a text selection they are about to read. (p. TM107)
- **During and After Reading** A teacher models for her students and then has them practice what a good reader "thinks about" as they read. (p. TM108)
- **Exploring the Big Idea** Students share, in the format of their choice, their answer to a lesson's "Big Question." (p. TM109)

ENGLISH LANGUAGE LEARNERS
- **Comprehension and English Learners** Author Josefina Tinajero discusses comprehension strategies that are appropriate for English learners. (p. TM108)
- **Vocabulary Activities** Students practice vocabulary using synonyms, antonyms, defintions, and words in context. (p. TM109)

MATH
- **Problem Solving—Order of Operations** A teacher uses real-life contexts to introduce the order of operations concept. (p. TM110)

Explore Careers

Section 7.1 Plan Your Career

In this section, students will learn how to explore their options and research potential careers. They will learn how to use networking, professional organizations, and the Internet to search for jobs.

Section 7.2 Prepare For Work

In this section, students will learn about the working world and how to prepare for their future careers. They will learn why people work and how to find a job that they will enjoy.

Classroom Solutions

Print Resources

 Student Edition
 Teacher Annotated Edition
 Student Activity Workbook
Student Activity Workbook
Teacher Annotated Edition

Technology Resources

ExamView *ExamView Assessment Suite CD* allows you to create and print out customized tests or ready-made unit and chapter tests, complete with answer keys.

Lesson Planner Plus *Lesson Planner Plus! CD** is and electronic lesson planner that provides instant access to teacher resources in one convenient package.

- Projects and Activities*
- Food Labs*
- Sewing Labs*
- Career Investigations*
- Reteaching Activities*
- Enrichment Activities*

Presentation Plus! PowerPoint™ Presentations can be edited and customized to meet the needs of students.

Online Learning Center includes resources and activities for students and teachers. Also includes Online Student Edition.

Interactive Student Edition

*Electronic Resources are available on Lesson Planner Plus and the Online Learning Center.

Writing Activity Answer

Work in the News Summaries will vary depending on the article chosen. Paragraphs should include the main points and most important supporting details.

Discovering Careers Answers ▼

1. Answers will vary. Students should write a summary of the education, training, and experience needed for the selected careers.
2. Answers will vary. Sample answer: older brother's job at home includes washing the car, mowing the lawn, taking care of the dog, washing dishes, and cleaning the garage.
3. Answers will vary. Students should present a list of jobs that meet their career interests.
4. Answers will vary. Students should present a summary of what they learned about the person's typical work day.

Chapter 7 Lesson Plan

Section 7.1 Lesson Plan

Plan Your Career

FOCUS

Discussion Starter

Ask students to discuss their career plans. How many of them have career goals? What are they doing to prepare themselves? For the students that have a career goal, encourage them to find out the requirements for that career path now so that they can prepare themselves.

Bell Ringer Activity

Help Wanted As a class, look at employment ads in the newspaper or on the Internet. Pick out the job requirements for each job. Some requirements may be stated explicitly, while some may have to be inferred. For example, some will state the education level required, while some will not.

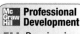
Mc Graw Hill Professional Development **Mini Clip**
ELL Previewing a Text

TEACH

S Skill Practice

Guided Practice

L1 List Divide students into small groups to list things to look for when researching employment opportunities. Lists may include: educational requirements, job responsibilities, starting salary, promotion opportunities, working conditions, and the future of the field.

L2 Discuss Have students work in groups to discuss how networking can help people find jobs and the benefits for the job seeker and contact. Let contacts know that you are looking for a job, the type of job, and your qualifications. They may recommend you for jobs at their company or with friends. Job seekers benefit by increasing opportunities, and contacts benefit by helping their employers.

L3 Apply Have students select a job that they would like to have and locate job listings so they can see the skills and educational requirements for the job. Which skills would they need to learn? Divide the class into groups and have the groups offer suggestions about how they can acquire the necessary skills. Students should determine what

they need to learn and discuss with their groups how they can acquire these skills. Suggestions may include: finish high school, enroll in college or a trade school, get a part-time job, join the military, volunteer in the field.

Mc Graw Hill Professional Development **Mini Clip**
Reading Flexible Groupings

U Universal Access

Gifted Learners Have students visit and assess the school's career center. Have gifted students work in groups to create a proposal to improve the career counseling services. What improvements would they suggest? What budget and resources are necessary to implement those changes?

ASSESS

Quiz

Ask students to answer the following questions:

1. What factors should you consider to help you find work that you enjoy? Consider your interests, abilities, values, and goals.

2. How does apprenticeship lead to a career? An apprentice serves as an assistant to a professional while learning the trade.

3. What kinds of people are good networking resources? Family, friends, classmates, teachers, coworkers, or anyone who can recommend you.

RETEACH

R Reading Strategy

Assess an Employer Have students select and gather information on their dream job from online or print resources. What kind of information would they want to have before going to an interview? Information could come from the company's Web site, the news, or people that work for the employer. They might look for information on salary, required skills, promotion opportunities, job responsibilities, and work culture.

C Critical Thinking

Stay Organized An employee who is organized will be more efficient. Brainstorm methods of maintaining efficient organization. Methods might include keeping a calendar, keeping a to-do list, having a neat filing system, and setting aside time each day to clean your workspace.

ASSESS

Section 7.1 Review Assign the Section 7.1 After You Read activities.

 Student Activity Workbook Assign the Section 7.1 Activities.

 Online Study Tools Have students go to the Online Learning Center at glencoe.com to:

■ Take the Section 7.1 **Practice Test**.

■ Download **Study-to-Go** content.

Section 7.1 After You Read

Answer Key

1. Strengths, interests, abilities, values, and goals.

2. It is one of the most direct ways to find a job. When you seek job information from people you know, you have a good chance of going into the job application process informed and confident.

3. Answer will vary, but should be supported logically. People tend to be happier when they do work they enjoy. On the other hand, they may not make enough money or be able to find work they enjoy. These circumstances could lead a person to choose a career that does not match their interests.

4. Students should choose a professional organization that fits their career aspirations. Summaries should include their research findings about the benefits the organization offers for career planning.

CLOSE

Culminating Activity

Networking Roleplay Assign half of the students to be jobseekers and the other half to be employers in an industry they choose. Have them roleplay a networking event and practice their networking skills. Students playing employers should ask questions designed to learn the skills and potential of the employees, while the employees should try to show themselves in their best light and learn about the employers to see if they are a good match.

Section **7.2** **Lesson Plan**

Prepare for Work

FOCUS

Discussion Starter

Discuss with the class why it is important to prepare for the working world now, while they are still in school. What are some problems that could arise if they do not start early? Some jobs require a certain type of education and experience. Knowing what is required to get the desired job will help students determine their present education and activities.

Professional Development
ELL Group Discussions

Bell Ringer Activity

Career Poll Poll the class to find out how many of them have an idea of what kind of career they want. Tally the numbers. Then poll those students on what careers they are interested in. Make a note of what students are interested in so that you incorporate those interests into the lesson. Encourage the students who are undecided to think about it as they go through the lesson.

TEACH

S Skill Practice

Independent Practice

L1 List Have students list ways to prepare for the world of work. Attend college, enroll at a career or technical center, get on-the-job training, join a branch of the military, or volunteer.

L2 Explain Write a paragraph that explains how technology can help you in your work. Technology often makes a job faster and less strenuous. It can save time by eliminating tasks that would be done manually, and it allows you to do more at once.

L3 Apply Have students create a simple business plan for a business they would like to create. Have them draw a mock-up of a business card or flyer to accompany their plan. Business plans should state the type of business, location, employees, and the product. Business cards or fliers should include contact information, description of services offered, and prices if applicable.

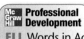 **Universal Access**

Kinesthetic Learners Have students work in groups to create and present skits dealing with the contrast between working at a job where you enjoy the work vs. working at a job where you do not.

Mc Graw Hill **Professional Development** **Mini Clip**
ELL Words in Action

ASSESS

Quiz

Ask students to answer the following questions:

1. **Why do people work?** To earn a living, for a sense of accomplishment, to feel good about what they do for others, and to meet people and make friends.

2. **How can joining the military prepare you for a career?** In the military, you can get training in specified fields and save money for college. The military also can provide a lifelong career.

3. **What does an entrepreneur do?** Instead of working for someone else, an entrepreneur starts and runs his or her own business. They create and plan the business and then operate it.

RETEACH

W Writing Strategy

Make a List According to some surveys, about half of the new businesses started each year will fail in their first five years. Ask students to brainstorm possible causes for this and present ideas to improve the chances of success when starting a new business. Have them summarize the information in one or more paragraphs. Some causes of failure could be underestimating the cost of your business, trying to grow too quickly, or failing to market well enough. Student ideas might suggest keeping the business small, building up savings, keeping costs at a minimum, and doing market research.

C Critical Thinking

Identify Your students may be participating in activities that are not directly career-related, but are training them in valuable skills for a future career. Ask them to think about the activities they participate in and what aspects of that activity might be useful to prepare them for a career. Many activities are useful in practicing job skills. Playing team sports teaches you discipline and teamwork. Babysitting teaches you how to supervise others. Being on student government teaches you to work with your peers and leadership skills.

ASSESS

Section 7.2 Review Assign the Section 7.2 After You Read activities.

Student Activity Workbook Assign the Section 7.2 Activities.

 Online Study Tools Have students go to the Online Learning Center at glencoe.com to:

- Take the Section 7.2 **Practice Test**.
- Download **Study-to-Go** content. STUDY TO GO

 ExamView® Assessment Suite

Use the *ExamView Assessment Suite* **CD to create a test for this chapter.**

Chapter Review Have students complete the Chapter 7 Review and Applications.

Section 7.2 After You Read

Answer Key

1. Learn to get along with others; find out how you like a certain type of work; gain work experience that will be helpful when you apply for a full-time job.

2. You are your own boss. You get credit for your successes. You are responsible for every part of your business.

3. Answers will vary. Summaries should be a comprehensive list of local opportunities.

4. Students should research an entrepreneur who went against the norm, such as Frank Lloyd Wright or Ben Franklin. The presentation should include details about their successes and their impact on society.

CLOSE

Culminating Activity

Job Searching Have students look through local employment listings and pick out five jobs that they think they would be qualified for. Have them explain why they would be suited for each job. Most jobs will probably be entry level or part-time jobs. Students should understand the qualifications and be able to articulate the skills and qualities that make them suitable for the job.

Words You Learned

1. Students should use each of the content vocabulary words and academic vocabulary words in a sentence.

Review Key Concepts

2. Identify the careers that interest you; learn about the kind of education and training you will need; collect occupational and labor market information about each career; consider your values and goals.

3. Most people spend about 40 years working. It is important to research as much as possible to pick the career that is best for you.

4. People work to earn a living, for job satisfaction, and to meet people and make friends.

5. Attend college, enroll at a career or technical center, get on-the-job training, join a branch of the military, and volunteer.

Critical Thinking

6. Both careers and jobs pay wages or salaries. Both can be based on personal interests, but generally, a job is something you do to learn a skill and pay the bills. A career is usually the result of several jobs and your long-term work goals. Examples may include: a job as a sales clerk could lead to a retail management career; someone may work at several jobs related to books and find a career in publishing.

7. Answers will vary, but should be explained. Job satisfaction may not seem so important when you are struggling financially. On the other hand, doing something you love can be more satisfying than having a lot of money from a job you do not like.

8. Answers will vary, but may include: to research jobs that suit your personality; to find out what jobs are available; to learn about the job outlook for a particular field; to submit résumés; to network with others in the field.

9. Lists will vary, but may include an interest in fostering the growth of young people and a desire to help students make the best of themselves. Counselors should be patient, understanding, caring, and have strong communication skills.

Real-World Skills and Applications

10. Students should present the results of their aptitude test, plus an evaluation of how the information will help them plan their career path, such as what classes to take, what kind of special training might be required, and part-time jobs that could help them learn nessary skills.

11. Groups should present two checklists that illustrate the steps needed to prepare for two particular careers. For example, if a group chooses physician, they should include such steps as: finish high school, work part-time or volunteer in the medical field, complete a 4-year degree, attend medical school, get an internship, and become a resident. They should choose which of their career choices would be the most challenging and explain why. Discuss results as a class.

Financial Literacy

12. At $26,000 a year, Gustavo would make $26,000 ÷ 52 = $500 a week. Vacation and sick time should be valued at the same rate, so 2 weeks of vacation = 2 + $500 = $1,000. One week of personal time is $500, and one week of sick time is $500. His total compensation would be $26,000 + $5,000 + $1,000 + $500 + $500 = $33,000 per year.

Active Learning

13. Students should fill out job applications. Help them fill in any blanks, correct spelling or grammar, and explain anything they do not understand.

14. Lists will vary, but may include computers and technology, construction and engineering, legal and law enforcement, mechanics, medical and emergency services, transportation and aviation. Skills learned in these jobs can be applied to non-military careers, such as working at a law firm, hospital, auto repair shop, or for commercial airlines.

Net Connection

15. Students should have an overview of a career that interests them, including education, responsibilities, working conditions, and employment outlook.

Academic Skills

16. Paragraphs will vary, but should include details about the other person's aptitudes, abilities, interests, and values.

17. Students should have a one-page report that compares a desert biome with where they live now. They should explain where they would prefer to live and work, and why.

18. The ratio of volunteer work to paid work is 1/5 (400/2,000). The ratio of volunteer work to total work is 1/6 (400/2,400).

Standardized Test Practice

19. b

Enter the Workplace

Section 8.1 Your Job Search

In this section, students will learn to develop the skills that are necessary for getting a job. They will learn how to prepare for their job search and how to apply for jobs.

Section 8.2 On the Job

In this section, students will learn how to be responsible employees. They will learn how to leave a job gracefully by giving either notice or a letter of resignation.

Classroom Solutions

Print Resources

 Student Edition
 Teacher Annotated Edition
Student Activity Workbook
Student Activity Workbook
Teacher Annotated Edition

- Projects and Activities*
- Food Labs*
- Sewing Labs*
- Career Investigations*
- Reteaching Activities*
- Enrichment Activities*

Technology Resources

ExamView Assessment Suite *ExamView Assessment Suite CD* allows you to create and print out customized tests or ready-made unit and chapter tests, complete with answer keys.

Presentation Plus! PowerPoint™ Presentations can be edited and customized to meet the needs of students.

Lesson Planner *Plus Lesson Planner Plus! CD** is and electronic lesson planner that provides instant access to teacher resources in one convenient package.

Online Learning Center includes resources and activities for students and teachers. Also includes Online Student Edition.

Interactive Student Edition

*ELECTRONIC RESOURCES ARE AVAILABLE ON LESSON PLANNER PLUS AND THE ONLINE LEARNING CENTER.

Writing Activity Answer

Cover Letter Answers will vary, but should follow a similar format. Students should include an introduction that states how they found out about the position, a body which includes their specific qualities, skills, and experiences, and a closing paragraph with a thank-you and how they will follow up.

Discovering Careers Answers ▼

1. Answers will vary. Students should write a summary of the education, training, and experience needed for the selected careers.

2. Answers will vary depending on the product selected. Students should provide details about the product's research, such as collecting surveys, analyzing competitor's products, improving current products, and keeping up with trends and technology.

3. Answers will vary. Skills should fit logically under each of the seven headings.

4. Answers will vary. Students should present a summary of what they learned about the person's typical work day.

Your Job Search

FOCUS

Discussion Starter

Ask if any students have a job or have had a job before. Ask for volunteers who have jobs or have had them in the past to discuss how they got their jobs. Write the different ways on the board. Based on the responses you get, either discuss the variety of ways that people get jobs, or note whether one method seems to be more common in the class.

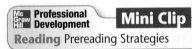

McGraw Hill **Professional Development** **Mini Clip**
Reading Prereading Strategies

Bell Ringer Activity

What Is Your Skill Level? Have students write each of the skills discussed in a lesson on a piece of paper: reading, writing, math, science, speaking, listening, and technology. Have the students rate themselves in each skill. Explain that their skill level in each area will help determine which jobs they are better suited for. They may have to improve some skills to get a job they want.

TEACH

S Skill Practice

Guided Practice

L1 List Divide students into small groups. Have groups list the types of legal documents required in order to be employed in the United States of America. Lists should include a social security card, a birth certificate, proof of citizenship, and a work permit if you are under a certain age.

L2 Discuss Have students work in groups. Ask groups to come up with at least five skills that are necessary in order to qualify for most jobs. Tell them to discuss why each skill is essential. Students may list any five of the following skills: reading, writing, math, science, speaking, listening, and technological. Groups should come up with at least one application for each skill, such as using reading and writing to fill out an application, math for making change, or technological skills for using computers.

L3 Apply Divide students into pairs and have them practice conducting job interviews. Bring a list of typical questions that the interviewer can use. After one partner interviews, have them switch places. This exercise should help students get comfortable with the interview and some of the common questions.

U Universal Access

Visual/Spatial Learners Have visual learners prepare a bulletin board display illustrating the common questions asked in interviews by potential employers and suggested questions for potential employees to ask. Hang the posters to remind students of the questions they should expect when they interview for a job.

ASSESS

Quiz

Ask students to answer the following questions:

1. What type of science skills are necessary for basic employability? Knowing how chemical and physical reactions occur, about your physical environment, and how weather occurs.

2. What are the labor laws regarding minors? 14- and 15-year-olds can be employed for 3 hours/day and 18 hours/week during the school year, and 8 hours/day and 40 hours/week during breaks.

3. What are the appropriate responses to a job offer? Accept the offer, ask for time to consider, or thank the employer but turn down the job.

RETEACH

R Reading Strategy

Make Connections Ask students to pick five jobs. For each, have them list the basic skills in order of importance. Ask: Do you think there is a connection between the skills and the amount of money that the job pays? Lists will vary, but students should come to the conclusion that jobs requiring more skills will likely pay more money.

C Critical Thinking

Analyze Ask: Why might it be a good idea to re-examine your career goals every so often? How often should you re-examine your goals and the job market to see if you still want to continue to pursue the same goals? The job market is ever changing, and it is a good idea to re-examine every so often because you might find new jobs or you might discover that a certain job is saturated.

ASSESS

Section 8.1 Review Assign the Section 8.1 After You Read activities.

 Student Activity Workbook Assign the Section 8.1 Activities.

 Online Study Tools Have students go to the Online Learning Center at glencoe.com to:

- Take the Section 8.1 **Practice Test**.
- Download **Study-to-Go** content.

Section 8.1 After You Read
Answer Key

1. Survey, question, read, recite, and review.
2. To compare prices, prepare a meal, or remove stains from clothes.
3. Concentrate on what the other person is saying; let the other person know you are listening; allow the other person to finish without interrupting; listen even if you do not agree.
4. Answers will vary, but may include questions such as: What are your career goals? Why are you the best person for the job? Why did you apply here? Do you enjoy working with people? Students should answer in a way that convinces the employer to hire them.
5. Answers will vary. Students should explain how the family member's attitude toward work might play a part in the students' career choices. For example, a mother who enjoys her job as a reporter might inspire the student to work in journalism.

CLOSE

Culminating Activity

Develop Skills Discuss basic employability skills with the class Ask them which skills they want to improve after reading the lesson. How do to improve those skills? Come up with a plan with students to improve at least one of their basic employability skills, such as reading the newspaper every day to improve reading skills, or taking a writing class to improve writing skills

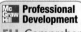 **Professional Development Mini Clip** **ELL** Comprehension and English Learners

---

Section 8.2 Lesson Plan

On the Job

FOCUS

Discussion Starter

Discuss the characteristics of a good employee. Have students volunteer qualities and explain why those qualities make a person a good employee. List the characteristics on the board. Students may list qualities such as responsible, organized, punctual, dedicated, intelligent, creative, or loyal. They should explain why those are good qualities of an employee.

 Bell Ringer Activity

Leaving a Job Ask the class to imagine that they have a job they like, but have been offered another job with more responsibility and higher pay. However, they want to be able to come back to the company where they work. How would they handle leaving their present job? Students should think of tactful ways to leave their job so that they may be welcome back in the future.

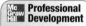 **Professional Development Mini Clip** **Reading** During and After Reading

TEACH

S **Skill Practice**
Independent Practice

L1 **List** Have students list the characteristics of a responsible employee. Carries out job duties, accepts diversity, does not discriminate against anyone, does not harass co-workers, and constantly evaluates his or her own performance.

L2 **Define** Ask students to write a paragraph that defines work ethic and explains how an employee can develop a positive work ethic. Work ethic is a personal commitment to doing one's very best. An employee can develop a positive work ethic by being responsible, flexible, and a team player.

L3 **Apply** Have students write a practice resignation letter to an employer. You may supply the details or have students choose them. The letter should state the last day of employment, thank the employer, and contain a brief explanation for leaving.

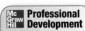 Universal Access

Verbal/Linguistic Learning Ask students to find the origin of the word *harass* and relate the original meaning to the concept of *harassment* at work. *Harass* comes from the French word *harer,* which means to *set a dog on.* It refers to hunting dogs chasing a rabbit.

Mc Graw Hill Professional Development **Mini Clip**
ELL Vocabulary Activities

ASSESS

Quiz

Ask students to answer the following questions:

1. **What is sexual harassment?** Unwelcome behavior of a sexual nature, whether physical or verbal, including any sort of teasing, intimidation, or threats.

2. **What role does teamwork play in being a responsible employee?** When coworkers cooperate and work well as a team, they can reach their goals more effectively.

3. **What is the proper way to give notice when leaving a job?** You should give notice soon enough for the employer to find a replacement, usually two weeks or more.

RETEACH

W Writing Strategy

Identify Personal Data Ask students to list five of their traits. Have them describe how each trait would make them a more or a less responsible employee. Ask: For the qualities that might make you less responsible, what could you do to improve? Students should be honest when listing their traits. If the trait would hurt, they should come up with solutions. For example, if they are often late, they should set an alarm.

C Critical Thinking

Set Personal Goals Emphasize the need to set personal goals as well as career goals. Some students may need to improve communication skills or their attitudes. Why is it important to have personal goals? Having personal goals will not only help you advance in the workforce, but also keep you well-rounded. Personal goals can also help if you decide to make a career change.

ASSESS

Section 8.2 Review Assign the Section 8.2 After You Read activities.

Student Activity Workbook Assign the Section 8.2 Activities.

 Online Study Tools Have students go to the Online Learning Center at **glencoe.com** to:

■ Take the Section 8.2 **Practice Test**.
■ Download **Study-to-Go** content. STUDY TO GO

ExamView® **Assessment Suite**
Use the *ExamView Assessment Suite* **CD to create a test for this chapter.**

Chapter Review Have students complete the Chapter 8 Review and Applications.

Section 8.2 After You Read
Answer Key

1. Tell the harasser to stop, and report the situation to your supervisor.

2. The exact date of your last day of employment, a thank-you to the employer for his or her help during your time with the company, and a brief explanation of why you are leaving.

3. Letters should be addressed to supervisors and include the last date of employment, a thank-you, and an explanation of why you are leaving.

4. Answers may vary depending on regulations in the area. Sample answers: Former employers are only allowed to confirm dates that the employee worked and his or her salary. Work records can be viewed only by the employee, human resources, and the employee's supervisors.

CLOSE

Culminating Activity

What Would a Responsible Employee Do? Ask for volunteers to provide common problems that occur at work, such as an angry customer. Ask the class to describe how a responsible employee would handle each situation. Students should provide thoughtful answers. For example, if there is an angry customer, a responsible employee might remain polite, listen, and put the customer in touch with the manager.

Mc Graw Hill Professional Development **Mini Clip**
Reading Exploring the Big Idea

Words You Learned

1. Students should write their own definitions for each of the content and academic vocabulary words.

Review Key Concepts

2. Basic reading, writing, math, science, speaking, listening, and technology skills help you function in life and at work.

3. A social security card and a copy of your birth certificate or other proof that you are a United States citizen; a work permit or employment certificate if you are under the age of 16 or 18.

4. Fill out a job application, submit a résumé and cover letter, compile references.

5. Arrive on time, follow rules, and do your work.

6. It is important to show courtesy, respect, and appreciation to your employer to give them enough notice so they can find a replacement. Write a formal letter of resignation and thank your supervisor.

Critical Thinking

7. Answers will vary, but may include: you will be easy to work with; your supervisors will notice that you are serious about your work; coworkers will respect you; others will be able to rely on you; you may be considered for a promotion.

8. The interviewer spent time reviewing your application and talking to you; it is polite, courteous, and professional to thank him or her for time and consideration; you may change your mind and want to reapply in the future.

9. Answers will vary, but may include: present an attitude of confidence, not arrogance; be honest; explain what you can do in a matter-of-fact way; use concrete examples of your success, such as how your strong writing skills helped you write a training manual for new employees.

Real-World Skills and Applications

10. Résumés will vary but should follow the résumé format on page 165.

11. Student teams should present a prioritized list of positions available for teen employment in their area.

Financial Literacy

12. Casey will earn $242.25. He worked one hour $(9-8=1)$ of overtime on Monday, two hours $(10-8=2)$ of overtime on Wednesday, and no overtime on Friday, for a total of 3 overtime hours. He also worked 8 hours of regular time each of the three days, for a total of $8 \times 3 = 24$ regular hours. For the regular hours, he earned $24 \times \$8.50 = \$204$. His overtime pay rate is $1.5 \times \$8.50 = \$12.75$ per hour, meaning that he earned $3 \times \$12.75 = \$38.25$ for his overtime hours. His total pay for the week was $\$204 + \$38.25 = \$242.25$.

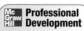

Professional Development **Mini Clip**
Math Problem Solving—Order of Operations

Active Learning

13. Posters will vary, but may include such tips as: listen to other people's ideas; discuss ideas with the team; ask questions; talk about goals; treat others with respect; help and support one another; encourage all members to participate.

14. Answers will vary. Students should discuss a relatively new job or field that did not exist twenty or thirty years ago, such as videogame designers or laser eye surgeon. They should include information about the job or field, its requirements, and what led to the development of the job or field.

Net Connection

15. Students should create a spreadsheet that lists three jobs they are interested in with categories for information about the company, the qualifications, salaries, benefits, job requirements, and their own preparation for the position.

Academic Skills

16. Students should present a one-minute speech on why they think employability skills are important. The focus should be more on presentation rather than content. Help students feel comfortable and at ease in front of the class.

17. Letters will vary. Students may suggest that the owner invest in ramps and remodel part of the bathroom to accommodate people with disabilities. They may also suggest that the manager visit the ADA Web site for information.

18. If she selects the first type of paper, Tanya can make $\$6.00 \div \$0.05/\text{copy} = 120$ copies. If she selects the second paper, she can make $\$6.00 \div \$0.06/\text{copy} = 100$ copies

Standardized Test Practice

19. c

FOCUS

Introduce the Project

In this project, students will explore what they may do for a living. Ask students what subjects they should consider when thinking about their future job. Answers will vary, but may include salary, hours of work, years of education needed, their own talents, free time, or whether job is fun.

Build Background

Parents' Jobs Ask students to volunteer to explain what their parents or guardians do for a living. Write down the job titles, and then ask what skills make them good at their job. Discuss why they chose those positions and how they are suitable to their personalities. Job titles and skills will vary. Example job titles: singer, doctor, or custodian. Example skills: organized, creative, good at science, curious, or caring.

TEACH

S Skill Practice

Guided Practice

L1 Identify Ask students to identify qualities that would make an employer want to hire them. Write the qualities, and discuss why each one is valuable. Lists will vary, but may include responsible, organized, creative, on-time, friendly, and experienced.

L2 Imagine Tell students to write three interview questions that an employer may ask when interviewing them. Have students pair up and take turns interviewing each other. Encourage them to greet with a firm handshake and make eye contact. Discuss the results afterwards for feedback. Questions may vary, but may include: Why do you want to work here? Where did you train for this job? What makes you the best candidate? What are your strengths and weaknesses? Can you tell me about a time that you demonstrated leadership skills?

L3 Apply Explain that after an interview, it is important to follow up with an employer. Have students write a practice follow-up letter to a prospective employer, thanking them for an interview. Letters should be formatted properly in business style, asking for feedback about the interview and thanking the employer for their consideration.

C Critical Thinking

Odd Jobs Ask students to search on the Internet and make a list of at least three unusual jobs that they have never heard of before. Write down some of the jobs, and discuss what makes them unusual. Brainstorm the unusual qualifications one might need to be qualified for each job. Answers will vary, but may include furniture tester, fortune cookie writer, rodeo clown, chimney sweeper, and alligator wrangler. Sample unique qualification: a rodeo clown would need to be daring.

ASSESS

Quiz

Ask students to answer the following questions:

1. **What are some of the basic employability skills?** Reading, writing, math, science, speaking, listening, and technology.

2. **Who are people you can network with to help find a job?** Friends and classmates, teachers and mentors, employers and coworkers, school organizations, community organizations, and recruiters at job fairs.

3. **What is an entrepreneur, and what is an advantage to being one?** An entrepreneur is a person who runs his or her own business. One advantage is you get to be your own boss.

CLOSE

Culminating Activity

Twenty Years and Beyond In this activity, students imagined themselves in a job they were interested ten years from now. Now ask students to write a paragraph about their lives twenty years in the future. Answers will vary, but students should consider promotions they could get, a career change, how having a spouse and family might affect their work, and when they might expect to retire.

Children and Parenting

Unit Overview

This unit introduces students to the basics of child care and the challenges of parenthood. Students will become familiar with the different stages of childhood and how to keep children safe.

Chapter 9 *Caring for Children* In this chapter, students will learn the skills necessary to be a successful parent and what to expect from children in the different stages of childhood: infants, toddlers, and pre-schoolers.

Chapter 10 *Child Care Basics* In this chapter, students will learn how to keep children safe, specifically focusing on childproofing, accident prevention, and first aid. They will also learn the skills necessary to becoming a successful babysitter and the benefits of babysitting.

Life Skills Project Preview

Your Relationship with Children

Tell students that as part of this unit, they will study how children learn by playing with toys appropriate to their age. They will learn how to design a toy for children, interview someone who takes care of children, and present a toy or game design of their own to the class.

FCCLA provides programs to guide students through projects, enhance their personal growth, and build leadership skills that can make a difference in their lives, their families, and their communities.

STOP the Violence empowers youth with attitudes, skills, and resources to recognize, report, and reduce youth violence. Students learn to reach their peers with violence prevention education; recognize warning signs of potential youth violence; encourage young people to report troubling behavior; and collaborate with school and community resources to address youth violence.

Violence Awareness Ask students to research an aspect of youth violence in their communities. Working in groups, have students create presentations that relate to that aspect and which provide information, increase awareness, and educate on ways to prevent or decrease this type of violence. Presentations should be preformed in front of the class, allowing time for discussion and feedback. Presentations should be about an aspect of youth violence (such as bullying, gangs, or child abuse) and relay information to the audience which will increase awareness and provide ways to prevent the violence (such as, counseling, youth groups, after-school activities, or community resources). Students should perform their presentations and have class discussions about them.

UNIT 4 Planning Guide

Professional Development

MINI CLIP VIDEO LIBRARY

Targeted professional development is correlated throughout *Discovering Life Skills*. **The McGraw-Hill Professional Development Mini Clip Video Library** provides teaching strategies to strengthen academic and learning skills. Log on to **glencoe.com**.

In this Unit, you will find these Mini Clips.

CHAPTER 9 Caring for Children

READING
- **Another Point of View** Emily M. Schell, Ed.D., educator and author, discusses teacher collaboration as it applies to standards-based instruction. **(p. TM115)**
- **Fluency Development** A teacher uses three different instructional strategies to help develop her students reading fluency. **(p. TM117)**
- **Assessment in Standards-Based Instruction** Lois Moseley, author and educator, discusses the role of assessment in standards-based instruction. **(p. TM117)**

ENGLISH LANGUAGE LEARNERS
- **Understanding Proficiency** Author Jana Echevarria discusses the meaning of proficiency and describes the various levels of proficiency that can be applied to English learners. **(p. TM115)**
- **Words and Pictures** A teacher uses words and media examples to help her students learn new vocabulary. **(p. TM116)**

CHAPTER 10 Child Care Basics

READING
- **Extending the Big Idea** A teacher assigns group collaborations and consensus-building activities to promote student discussions about a reading selection. **(p. TM121)**

ENGLISH LANGUAGE LEARNERS
- **Providing Clear Directions** A teacher provides clear written and oral directions for a classroom assignment and checks for student understanding. **(p. TM120)**
- **Graphic Organizers** Students use graphic organizers to distinguish between major and minor details in a reading selection. **(p. TM122)**

MATH
- **Real-Life Ratios** A teacher discusses a real-life application of ratios. **(p. TM123)**

Caring for Children

Section 9.1 Responsible Parenting

In this section students will learn what is involved with being a parent. They will learn about children's needs and how to meet them. They will also learn about child abuse and neglect.

Section 9.2 Child Development

In this section, students will learn about the developmental stages of children and about children with special needs. They will also learn how children learn and how to teach children through play.

Classroom Solutions

Print Resources

- Student Edition
- Teacher Annotated Edition
- Student Activity Workbook
- Student Activity Workbook Teacher Annotated Edition

Technology Resources

ExamView **ExamView Assessment Suite CD** allows you to create and print out customized tests or ready-made unit and chapter tests, complete with answer keys.

Lesson Planner *Plus* **Lesson Planner Plus! CD*** is and electronic lesson planner that provides instant access to teacher resources in one convenient package.

- Projects and Activities*
- Food Labs*
- Sewing Labs*
- Career Investigations*
- Reteaching Activities*
- Enrichment Activities*

 Presentation Plus! PowerPoint™ Presentations can be edited and customized to meet the needs of students.

 Online Learning Center includes resources and activities for students and teachers. Also includes Online Student Edition.

Interactive Student Edition

*ELECTRONIC RESOURCES ARE AVAILABLE ON LESSON PLANNER PLUS AND THE ONLINE LEARNING CENTER.

Writing Activity Answer

Unified Paragraph Answers will vary. Students should write a topic sentence about parental quality, followed by supporting examples and details that connect the examples to the topic sentence.

Discovering Careers Answers ▼

1. Answers will vary. Students should write a summary of the education, training, and experience needed for the selected careers.
2. Lists will vary, but should include a variety of toys used at each stage.
3. Answers may include psychology, science, sociology, child development, nutrition, and human behavior.
4. Answers will vary. Students should present a summary of what they learned about the person's typical work day.

Section 9.1 Lesson Plan

Responsible Parenting

FOCUS

Discussion Starter

Ask the class to discuss the ways in which their parents fulfill their parental responsibilities. What qualities do the students hope to bring to their own parenting in the future? Students should discuss the ways their parents meet their needs, communicate with them, encourage independence, and provide guidance.

 Bell Ringer Activity

Parent Visit Invite a mother and her infant to class, and have the class observe her as she interacts with her child. Have her talk to the class about parenting and answer questions. This should give students an idea of what a parent's day is like and the responsibility involved.

TEACH

S Skill Practice

Independent Practice

L1 List Have students list causes of abuse and neglect. Angry outbursts; expectations that are too high; inability to cope with personal problems; substance abuse; abuse in the abuser's past.

L2 Express Have students write a paragraph expressing how parents can encourage independence in their children. Parents can encourage their children to be independent by making it possible for them to do tasks by themselves, giving them the tools to accomplish tasks without help, allowing children to make mistakes, and permitting them to make decisions.

L3 Apply Encourage students to spend time with a young child they know and practice interacting with them in ways that meet their needs. Spending time with a young child under supervision will help students become comfortable interacting with children and learn how to meet their emotional, physical, and intellectual needs.

U Universal Access

English Language Learners English language learners may need more help understanding the concepts of physical, emotional, and intellectual needs. Explain these concepts in simple terms, such as the needs of the body, the need for love and attention, and the needs of the brain.

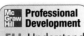
McGraw Hill **Professional Development** **Mini Clip**
ELL Understanding Proficiency

ASSESS

Quiz

Ask students to answer the following questions:

1. What is the most important thing to communicate to children to meet their emotional needs? Children need to feel loved. Hold, touch, and talk to them to communicates love.

2. What are two ways to positively communicate with children? Speak to children using positive statements rather than negative ones, and praise them instead of pointing out flaws.

3. What should you do if you suspect that a child is being abused or neglected? Tell a trusted adult, make an anonymous report to a child protective services agency, or call 9-1-1 if there is immediate danger.

RETEACH

R Reading Strategy

Draw Conclusions After reviewing the section on encouraging independence, ask students why encouraging independence is an important part of child development. It is necessary for children to develop the ability to face life on their own. Allowing children to attempt tasks and activities on their own and make their own decisions will give them confidence and a sense of self-worth.

C Critical Thinking

Draw Conclusions The text notes that parenting is a full-time job. How do you think being a parent would conflict with being a student? Being a parent requires that you be on call 24 hours a day. This means you might have to miss class for an emergency. You would have to give up most of your free time, social life, and extra-curricular activities to take care of a child.

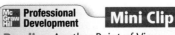
McGraw Hill **Professional Development** **Mini Clip**
Reading Another Point of View

ASSESS

Section 9.1 Review Assign the Section 9.1 After You Read activities.

 Student Activity Workbook Assign the Section 9.1 Activities.

Online Study Tools Have students go to the Online Learning Center at glencoe.com to:

- Take the Section 9.1 **Practice Test**.
- Download **Study-to-Go** content.

Section 9.1 After You Read

Answer Key

1. Children need to know what to expect. If you are not consistent, children will not take you seriously.

2. Emotional outbursts of anger and frustration; unrealistic expectations of children; inability to cope with personal problems; substance abuse; the abuser may have been abused as a child; financial or emotional stress.

3. Flyers will vary, but should address physical, intellectual, and emotional needs. For children's physical needs, they need healthful food, appropriate clothing, rest and sleep, and a safe environment. For their intellectual needs, provide interesting environments, read books out loud to them, and help them play with toys. For their emotional needs, children need to be held, cuddled, and comforted.

4. Presentations will vary. Some of the long-term effects may include depression, anxiety, insomnia, the possibility of becoming an abuser, inability to form close relationships, lack of trust, and an increased chance of abusing alcohol and other drugs.

CLOSE

Culminating Activity

Preventing Abuse There are many organizations that are set up to help prevent child abuse. As a class, locate information about any such organizations in your area, and encourage students to volunteer their time with these organizations. Some organizations need volunteers to play and spend time with children who have been abused or simply to help out with their activities or office work. Through volunteering, students can learn more about child abuse and how to prevent it.

Section 9.2 Lesson Plan

Child Development

FOCUS

Discussion Starter

Ask students to recall their first memory of learning. What did they learn and how did they learn it? Memories could be learning how to read in school, learning how to tie shoes at home, or learning from experience, such as getting burned and learning to avoid hot things.

Bell Ringer Activity

Stages of Development Draw or find pictures of infants, toddlers, and pre-schoolers. Attach them to a poster and have students write the characteristics of each stage of development on the poster. Explain that they will learn more about these stages during the lesson. Answers will vary, but may include: Infants laugh; roll over; put objects in mouth; and crawl. Toddlers walk; feed selves with spoon; climb stairs; and begins toilet learning. Pre-schoolers dress selves; recognize colors; brush teeth; and speak in sentences.

McGraw Hill **Professional Development** **Mini Clip**
ELL Words and Pictures

TEACH

S Skill Practice

Guided Practice

L1 **List** Have students work in groups to list milestones for a toddler. Walk, learn the meaning of "No," follow simple instructions, feed self with spoon, identify pictures, climb stairs, undress self, play beside others, put words into sentences, and begin toilet training.

L2 **Discuss** Divide students into groups to discuss how having special needs affects a child's development. They may be slower to develop in one area or have an impairment. As they develop, they need to be encouraged to be independent to develop a positive self-concept.

L3 **Apply** Arrange with a local preschool teacher for students to visit the class and practice teaching preschoolers through play. Students should play with the preschoolers cooperatively, helping them learn through creative play.

U Universal Access

Students with Visual Impairments For students with visual impairments, consider pairing them with another student who is patient and understands the material. Have the partner describe the visual elements of the chapter, such as the figures, and review any parts they had trouble with.

ASSESS

Quiz

Ask students to answer the following questions:

1. **How often do infants eat and sleep?** A newborn baby eats every few hours and sleeps 16 to 20 hours each day.

2. **What is most important for children with special needs as they develop?** That they learn how to develop their abilities and enjoy life.

3. **What kinds of toys are best for toddlers?** They need toys for both active and quiet play that help them develop socially and physically and use their imagination.

RETEACH

R Reading Strategy

Conduct Research Have students conduct research on interaction with children by reading parenting magazines and locating articles about communicating with children. Have them choose some articles and compare that information with what they learned in the lesson. Articles can be on any subject as long as they deal with communicating with children. They should compare the information with that in the book.

McGraw Hill **Professional Development** **Mini Clip**
Reading Fluency Development

C Critical Thinking

Evaluate Information Some companies claim to make infants smarter if you let them watch a certain video. Research these products and compare them to interaction and play. Which do you think is better? Answers will vary. Some studies will indicate that these types of videos will increase language skills in infants. However, these types of videos cannot replace face-to-face interaction; they can only supplement it, and they may not be more effective than quality face-to-face interaction.

ASSESS

Section 9.2 Review Assign the Section 9.2 After You Read activities.

📁 **Student Activity Workbook** Assign the Section 9.2 Activities.

�ⁿ **Online Study Tools** Have students go to the Online Learning Center at **glencoe.com** to:

■ Take the Section 9.2 **Practice Test**.

■ Download **Study-to-Go** content.

💿 *ExamView®* **Assessment Suite**
Use the *ExamView Assessment Suite* **CD to create a test for this chapter.**

McGraw Hill **Professional Development** **Mini Clip**
Reading Assessment in Standards-Based Instruction

📖 **Chapter Review** Have students complete the Chapter 9 Review and Applications.

📖 Section 9.2 After You Read

Answer Key

1. Every child is unique and grows at his or her own rate, even in the same family.

2. By exploring their environment; using their senses; playing with toys; practicing and repeating tasks; and observing others.

3. Students should present an illustrated "How To" guide about what kind of toys and activities are appropriate for an infant.

4. Physiological: children need food, clothing, and shelter. Safety: children need to be protected. Social: children need to feel loved. Esteem: children who are loved and praised for their accomplishments will feel good about themselves. Actualization: a person whose needs were met in childhood will have a better chance of reaching full potential.

CLOSE

Culminating Activity

Create Activities Ask students to come up with an appropriate activity they might do with a child. Have the students share their activities, and encourage them to try the activities with relatives or children of friends. Students should come with activities that are age-appropriate for each stage of development and stimulate communication and learning between the older person and the child.

Words You Learned

1. Students should use each of the content vocabulary words and academic vocabulary words in a sentence.

Review Key Concepts

2. Parenting lasts well beyond a child's eighteenth birthday. Parents need to care for their children's emotional, physical, social, and intellectual needs until they are grown. Then parents need to be there for support, advice, and friendship.

3. Possible causes: emotional outbursts, anger, frustration, temper loss, unreasonable expectations, substance abuse, adults were abused as children. Prevention: leave children alone only with reliable, responsible people; take parenting courses; join parent support groups; call a child protective service agency for help.

4. Infant: birth to one year; toddler: one to three years; preschooler: three to five years.

5. Children at every stage of development can benefit from playing with parents, caregivers, siblings, and other children. Playtime helps children develop motor skills as well as their emotional, social, and intellectual skills

Critical Thinking

6. Parents should teach children to treat others as they would like to be treated. Children should be taught that it is good to feel proud and confident as long as it is not at the expense of others. Parents are responsible for setting examples that teach children to care about other people.

7. The food provides nourishment for physical growth; conversation promotes intellectual growth; good manners at the table help social growth; positive interactions encourage emotional growth.

8. Children may fail to obey and respect parents, lose respect for rules and laws in general, and come to believe that parents do not care enough to offer discipline and guidance

9. Independent play is playing alone and showing little interest in interacting with other children. Cooperative play is playing together with one or two other children and sharing toys. Both are necessary for developing independence and teamwork.

Real-World Skills and Applications

10. Answers will vary, but may include: negotiate to create rules; discuss the need to work together for consistency; see a counselor to help them with parenting skills.

11. Scenes will vary, but students should demonstrate positive interaction through kind words, questions that indicate an interest in the children, and modeling good manners and social behavior

Financial Literacy

12. Answers will vary depending on the schools selected. The current cost of the average four-year private university is about $22,000, so the cost in 18 years will be $22,000 \times 3.40 = \$74,800$, or close to $300,000 for all four years. The current cost of a four-year public school is around $5,500, so in 18 years the annual cost would be $5,500 \times 3.40 = \$18,700$, or about $75,000 for all four years. The current cost of the average two-year school is $2,000. In 18 years, that cost will be $2,000 \times 3.4 = \$6,800$ per year, or near $14,000 for both years.

Active Learning

13. Students should present musical shakers appropriate to share with children. If possible, provide the opportunity to make the shakers with younger elementary or preschool children.

14. Answers will vary. Students should identify what is taught and how it is taught. They should determine whether they would want their child to watch the programs and explain why or why not.

Net Connection

15. Lists will vary, but should include ten educational toys or games with reasonable descriptions of the educational value of each toy or game.

Academic Skills

16. Answers will vary. Students should write an accurate summary of the article and describe what the article advises readers to do. Students should logically explain whether or not they think the advice is realistic.

17. Paragraphs will vary, but most students will probably discover that excessive videogame playing can lead to inactivity and an increased chance of weight gain. Students should recognize that active play is a healthier alternative.

18. Peter's weight at 5 months is $7 \times 2 = 14$ pounds. His weight at 12 months is $7 \times 3 = 21$ pounds. His weight at 2 years is $7 \times 4 = 28$ pounds.

Standardized Test Practice

19. False
20. False
21. True

Child Care Basics

Section 10.1 Child Safety

In this chapter, students will learn how to keep children safe and how to prevent accidents. They will learn what to do in case of intruders, falls and injuries, fires, and poisoning.

Section 10.2 Babysitting

In this chapter, students will learn about the responsibilities a babysitter has for children at different stages of development. In particular they will learn how to hold, change, feed, and watch an infant.

Classroom Solutions

Print Resources

 Student Edition
Teacher Annotated Edition
Student Activity Workbook
Student Activity Workbook
Teacher Annotated Edition

Technology Resources

ExamView *ExamView Assessment Suite CD* allows you to create and print out customized tests or ready-made unit and chapter tests, complete with answer keys.

Lesson Planner Plus *Lesson Planner Plus! CD** is and electronic lesson planner that provides instant access to teacher resources in one convenient package.

- Projects and Activities*
- Food Labs*
- Sewing Labs*
- Career Investigations*
- Reteaching Activities*
- Enrichment Activities*

Presentation Plus! PowerPoint™ Presentations can be edited and customized to meet the needs of students.

Online Learning Center includes resources and activities for students and teachers. Also includes Online Student Edition.

Interactive Student Edition

*Electronic Resources are available on Lesson Planner Plus and the Online Learning Center.

Writing Activity Answer

Coherent Paragraph Paragraphs will vary. The topic sentence should state the task, and the paragraph should follow a logical order. Look for transitions, parallel structure, and repeated key words.

Discovering Careers Answers ▼

1. Answers will vary. Students should write a summary of the education, training, and experience needed for the selected careers.

2. Job descriptions will vary, but may include: change diapers; feed and clothe; play games; teach skills; participate in activities; and provide love, affection, and security.

3. Answers may include preschool teacher, in-home daycare provider, nanny, pediatric dentist, playground director, dance instructor, tutor, and social worker.

4. Answers will vary. Students should present a summary of what they learned about the person's typical work day.

Child Safety

FOCUS

Discussion Starter

Ask the class to discuss common dangers for children in a household. For each danger, ask for ideas on how to prevent the child from getting hurt. Explain that in this lesson, students will learn more about keeping a child safe. Answers will vary, but should consist of common household dangers, such as poisons, and logical means of avoiding those dangers, such as keeping poisons out of reach.

Bell Ringer Activity

Childproof Your House Ask students to envision their house and the potential dangers in their homes and come up with a list of five ways they could childproof the house. Lists will vary according to each child's home, but they should be able to identify five areas of their home that could be made safer, and ways to make that area safer. These could include safety latches on cabinet doors and drawers, safety gates at the top and bottom of stairs, safety covers on electrical outlets.

TEACH

S Skill Practice

Independent Practice

L1 List Ask students to list the basic things to do when childproofing a home Put safety latches on cabinets and drawers, put safety gates at the bottom and top of stairs, put safety covers on electrical outlets, move dangerous items out of reach, and remove poisonous plants.

L2 Describe Have students write a paragraph describing why it is important to monitor small children at all times. Toddlers are adventurous and do not know yet what it means to be careful. Preschoolers are starting to learn what it means to be careful, but still need constant reminders.

L3 Apply Ask students to imagine that a friend is bringing a child over to their house. Have them a plan for how to ensure the child's safety. Plans should include measures for making the house safer before the child comes over as well as procedures for safety while the child is in the house.

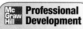

Professional Development **Mini Clip**
ELL Providing Clear Directions

U Universal Access

Students with Physical Impairments Students with physical impairments may have greater insight into the types of safety precautions that are especially important or any extra safety precautions needed for children who are disabled. Have them share their knowledge with the class.

ASSESS

Quiz

Ask students to answer the following questions:

1. What is the leading cause of accidental deaths in the home in the United States? Falls are the leading cause.

2. What should you do if you smell smoke or see a fire while you are caring for children? Get the children out safely. Then call the fire department (9-1-1).

3. What should you do with poisonous items in the house? Keep them in locked cabinets or on a high shelf, out of the reach of children.

RETEACH

W Writing Strategy

Activate Prior Knowledge Ask students what they were taught about being safe when they were children? Have them write a paragraph discussing how what they learned as children relates to what is being taught in this lesson? Students may discuss safety lessons such as not talking to strangers or keeping away from stoves and dangerous appliances. These lessons relate to this lesson, because the caregiver and the child need to work together to keep a child safe.

C Critical Thinking

Assess a Situation Explain to students that while a parent can childproof the home, they cannot guarantee that other places are safe for children. Ask students to describe what they would do when taking their child to someone else's home. Walk through the house and look for potential hazards so you have an idea of what areas you want to keep the child away from and where they will need to be watched more carefully.

ASSESS

Section 10.1 Review Assign the Section 10.1 After You Read activities.

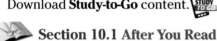 **Student Activity Workbook** Assign the Section 10.1 Activities.

Online Study Tools Have students go to the Online Learning Center at glencoe.com to:

- Take the Section 10.1 **Practice Test**.
- Download **Study-to-Go** content.

Section 10.1 After You Read

Answer Key

1. Check that all doors and windows are locked. Do not open the door for strangers. Do not tell callers that you are alone with the children. Call a neighbor, another trusted adult, or dial 9-1-1 if a stranger does not go away.

2. Falls and fire.

3. Guide should include tips from the book, as well as ideas from other sources. Encourage students to illustrate their guides.

4. Research will vary depending on the person's culture and the values named. Reports should list three values, such as religion, close family ties, or education. Students should explain how each value affects childcare.

CLOSE

Culminating Activity

Childproofing Ask students to imagine that a group of children are coming in to visit the class. Ask them to describe how they would child-proof the room to make it safer for the children. Answers will vary depending on the character-istics of the room. Answers should reflect basic safety advice, such as locking up cabinets, putting dangerous items out of reach, removing any poisonous plants, covering electric outlets, and other basic safety precautions.

Mc Graw Hill Professional Development **Mini Clip**
Reading Extending the Big Idea

Babysitting

FOCUS

Discussion Starter

Ask the class who has babysat before. For those who have, ask them what age level they babysat and what were their favorite and least favorite parts. Have babysitters discuss their experiences so that students without babysitting experience can understand what it is like.

Bell Ringer Activity

Change a Diaper Bring in diapers and a model baby or doll, and have students practice changing an infant's diaper. Have them gather everything they will need before beginning. Remind them to treat the doll like a real infant and handle it care-fully. They should practice cleaning the infant as well as changing the diaper.

TEACH

S Skill Practice

Guided Practice

L1 **List** Divide students into small groups to list the rules they should go over with parents in front of the child they are babysitting before the parents leave the house. Ask the parents to go over the rules about television viewing, doing homework, telephone use, visits from friends, having snacks, and when to go to bed.

L2 **Explain** Have students work in groups to explain how to show parents that they are reliable babysitters. Keep a careful eye on the children; ask questions to show you are serious; leave the home as you found it; do not allow friends to visit; do not open the door for strangers.

L3 **Apply** Ask students to imagine that a fam-ily friend has asked them to babysit her toddler. Instruct them to write a plan for the evening, beginning with arriving at the house and ending with the child's bedtime. Divide the class into groups to share their plans. Plans will vary, but should include what they will ask the parent, what types of activities they will do, and how they will put the child to bed.

Universal Access

Students with Learning Disabilities Students with learning disabilities may require additional guidelines or study aids to get the most out of text material. You may wish to make charts and/or conduct demonstrations with an infant doll in order to reinforce the information given in this lesson about caring for an infant.

Professional Development **Mini Clip**
ELL Graphic Organizers

ASSESS

Quiz

Ask students to answer the following questions:

1. **How should you support an infant's head when holding it?** Place one hand under its head and the other hand and arm under the lower part of its back.

2. **How should you feed a toddler?** Feed a toddler soft food, cut into small pieces, to avoid choking. Monitor the toddler's eating.

3. **What can you do to make a preschooler more willing to sleep when it is bedtime?** Keep the preschooler active throughout the day so they are more willing to go to sleep at bedtime.

RETEACH

W **Writing Strategy**

Compare and Contrast Ask students to compare and contrast the type of care a toddler needs with the type a preschooler needs. Toddlers need a lot of attention, but have short attention spans. They can eat food that adults eat, as long as it is soft and cut into small pieces. Toddlers may need help using the toilet. Preschoolers are curious and like to spend time with others. They may be picky eaters.

C **Critical Thinking**

Make Inferences The text tells you that you should ask the parents to go over household rules with you in front of the children. Ask students why they think this is important. If parents do not review the rules in front of the children, the child might be more inclined to argue about the rules. Discussing them in front of the child establishes that everyone knows the same rules.

ASSESS

Section 10.2 Review Assign the Section 10.2 After You Read activities.

Student Activity Workbook Assign the Section 10.2 Activities.

Online Study Tools Have students go to the Online Learning Center at glencoe.com to:

■ Take the Section 10.2 **Practice Test**.
■ Download **Study-to-Go** content.

ExamView® Assessment Suite
Use the *ExamView Assessment Suite* CD to create a test for this chapter.

Chapter Review Have students complete the Chapter 10 Review and Applications.

 Section 10.2 After You Read
Answer Key

1. Television viewing, homework, phone use, visits from friends, snacks, and bedtime
2. Place one hand under its head and the other hand and arm under the lower part of the back.
3. Toddlers are still learning the proper ways to eat, chew, and swallow.
4. Keep him or her busy with fun activities.
5. Flyers will vary, but should include specific information about experience, such as number of years, how many families, and ages of children. Special skills might include first-aid. Fees will vary by location.
6. Daycare is for children whose parents work outside the home. It is provided in private homes, school-like facilities, or by nannies. This topic can be controversial, so students might find positive and negative effects. Possible answers: children are better prepared for school; socialization skills start early; children get sick more; daycare causes behavioral problems.

CLOSE

Culminating Activity

Caring for an Infant Choose an object to represent an infant, like a doll or an egg. Distribute one to each student, and have them care for the object as if it were an infant. Students should practice caring for their object, including holding, changing, feeding, and putting it to sleep. Using a fragile object can help remind them to be careful.

Words You Learned

1. Students should use each of the content vocabulary words and academic vocabulary words in a sentence.

Review Key Concepts

2. Put safety latches on cabinets and drawers; use safety gates; cover outlets; move dangerous household products out of the reach of children; remove poisonous plants; use age-appropriate toys; keep electrical cords out of reach.

3. Knowing first aid can help you take care of minor injuries that do not require emergency care.

4. Number and ages of children; the time you should arrive; how long the parents plan to be gone; the rate of pay you will receive.

5. Holding, changing, feeding, and sleeping.

6. Redirect his or her attention with a favorite toy, game, or puzzle.

7. Have a list of back-up activities for preschoolers to keep them entertained.

Critical Thinking

8. It is important to make sure that toys are age-appropriate. A toy for a 3-year-old may contain small parts or parts that could pinch. Even a well-coordinated 18-month-old still puts things in his or her mouth and does not yet know what could be dangerous.

9. Use your first-aid knowledge to immediately wash the affected skin, apply wet compresses or soak in cool water, and treat with calamine lotion. Call the child's parent or doctor if the rash worsens.

Real-World Skills and Applications

10. Questions will vary but may include: How many children do you have? How old are the children? How much will I be paid? How long will you be out? Will you pick me up and take me home? Will I need to prepare dinner? What kind of personalities do your children have? What kinds of activities do they enjoy?

11. Answers will vary, but may include questions about: responsibility, promptness, reliability, attitude, creativity, ability to follow directions and rules, and interaction with children. Format should be user-friendly for the person who fills out the evaluation.

Financial Literacy

12. The total expenses are $350 + $89 + $65 = $504, so your ½ share amounts to $252. There are $3 \times 4 = 12$ weeks until the dance, so you will need to make $252 \div 12 = $21 per week. You will need to baby sit $21 \div $7/hour = 3 hours per week.

Active Learning

13. Puppets will vary, but should be creative and fun for children.

14. Presentations will vary, but should include research on the history of childcare. Students should explain who cared for children during their chosen time period, including any details they found.

Net Connection

15. Answers will vary depending on what is available in your area. Students will probably find CPR and first-aid classes offered in hospitals or community centers. Community colleges may offer classes in childcare and child development.

Academic Skills

16. Ads will vary, but should include the qualities of a good babysitter, such as reliable, responsible, trustworthy, caring, prompt, experienced, and familiar with first aid.

17. Reports should show that the student located information about the development and evolution of car seats, what the current standards are (such as a 5-point harness), how they should be installed (some communities offer free installation through fire departments), and how they work to keep children safe. Student should also include information about legal requirements. For example, newborns are not allowed to leave the hospital without having safe transportation.

18. The ratio of Aquino to Brooks nights was 2/4, which reduces to ½. She worked a total of $2 + 4 = 6$ nights; therefore, there was just one night she did not work. Thus, the ratio of nights off to nights worked was 1/6.

McGraw Hill **Professional Development** **Mini Clip**
Math Real-Life Ratios

Standardized Test Practice

19. b

FOCUS

Introduce the Project

In this project, students will design a toy for an infant, toddler, or preschooler. Ask students what skills some toys and games helped them learn as they grew up. Skills learned will vary, but may include reading from books, art from crayons, and throwing, kicking, and running from balls.

Build Background

Toy Commercials Ask students to describe toy commercials they have seen, the name of the show they were watching, and what age group normally watches that show. Discuss why most toys are only appropriate for specific age groups. Examples of commercials will vary, but should indicate that advertisers target the age group that is the primary audience of the show. Discussion should focus on how children will outgrow toys as they reach developmental milestones.

TEACH

S Skill Practice

Guided Practice

L1 List Inform students that toy store Web sites are often organized so shoppers can select toys by age group. Ask students to visit a site and search for toys in three separate age groups. Have them record the age groups they searched and list three toys found in each group. Discuss why toys are targeted for that particular age. Search results may vary, but discussion may take into account brightness of colors, abilities of child age, and size of toy parts for safety.

L2 Demonstrate Have students write a paragraph that demonstrates how developmental tasks of toddlers change as they grow into preschoolers. Sample answer may describe how toddlers go from playing alone, putting words into sentences, and following simple instructions to preschoolers who play interactively, talk more often, and play pretend games.

L3 Imagine Ask students to imagine they have been employed to babysit a toddler. To make a good impression, they should bring a toy that is age-appropriate. What should they consider when choosing a toy to bring? Write down toy ideas and discuss. Toys will vary, but should account for toddler specific age behavior, such as walking, following simple instructions, identifying pictures, and putting words into sentences.

C Critical Thinking

Playing With Younger Kids Tell students to describe a time they played with a younger child. Ask them to write a description of the experience and how it was different from hanging out with friends their own age. Experiences will vary, but may include talking about simpler subjects, using simpler vocabulary, the need to teach things, being bored, and being nervous.

ASSESS

Quiz

Ask students to answer the following questions:

1. What are the four types of children's needs? Four types of children's needs are physical needs, emotional need, social needs, and intellectual needs.

2. What is a developmental task? A developmental task is an achievement, such as walking or talking, which can be expected at specific ages and stages of growth.

3. What are some toys that are fun for most preschoolers? Some toys that are fun for most preschoolers are clay dough, puzzles, dolls, construction sets, crayons, and paints.

CLOSE

Culminating Activity

Fun and Learning In this activity, students designed a toy for a specific age group which helps those children learn through play. Have students write a paragraph that explains why teaching with a toy may be more effective than simply showing or talking about a subject. Sample answer may cite how it is always easier to learn when one is interested in the subject. Since kids are generally interested in having fun, teaching with toys is a great way to keep them involved.

Management Skills

Unit Overview

This unit introduces students to the skills they will need to manage their money, their time, and their personal, community, and material resources. They will also become familiar with different methods of dealing with stress.

Chapter 11 *Manage Your Money* In this chapter, students will learn how to evaluate advertisements and carefully consider what they want and need from the products they purchase. They will also become familiar with their rights and responsibilities as consumers.

Chapter 12 *Manage Resources, Time, and Stress* In this chapter, students will learn that being organized and planning ahead can help them manage their resources. They will also learn how to manage their time, balance their lives, and avoid stress.

Life Skills Project Preview

Your Shopping Skills

Tell students that as part of this unit, they will learn shopping is a skill that uses math, research, and common sense. They will learn how to analyze their grocery needs and shop for the family groceries, interview someone who is an experienced shopper, and present a project to the class to share what they have learned.

FCCLA Family, Career and Community Leaders of America

FINANCIAL FITNESS

FCCLA provides programs to guide students through projects, enhance their personal growth, and build leadership skills that can make a difference in their lives, their families, and their communities.

Financial Fitness involves young people teaching one another how to make, save, and spend money wisely. Students plan and carry out projects that help them and their peers learn to become wise financial managers and smart consumers. Financial Fitness focuses on learning banking basics, tracking and planning personal spending, making money, becoming a savvy spender, and financing the future.

Take Action Tell students to imagine they have $100. Have them choose a local bank, find out the interest rate for a savings account, and calculate the interest that would be earned on $100 in ten years. Then have students use a newspaper or the Internet to choose a stock and find out that stock's interest rate. Assuming the interest rate does not change, have them calculate the profits for the $100 invested in that stock over 10 years. Have a class discussion about which scenario will result in more money. What else should be taken into consideration besides money earned? Be prepared with suggestions of local financial institutions and investment opportunities. Students should be able to calculate which scenario will result in more interest earned. Discuss the advantages and disadvantages of investing money versus opening a savings account. Students should be able identify whether they are risk inclined or risk averse.

Professional Development

MINI CLIP VIDEO LIBRARY

Targeted professional development is correlated throughout *Discovering Life Skills*. **The McGraw-Hill Professional Development Mini Clip Video Library** provides teaching strategies to strengthen academic and learning skills. Log on to **glencoe.com**.

In this Unit, you will find these Mini Clips.

CHAPTER 11 Manage Your Money

READING
- **Planning and Classroom Management** Nancy Frey, Ph.D., teacher, educator, and author, discusses the instructional strategies that support a differentiated classroom. **(p. TM130)**

ENGLISH LANGUAGE LEARNERS
- **Using Manipulatives** A teacher uses concrete objects to illustrate lesson concepts. **(p. TM129)**
- **Collaborative Work** Students work in groups to complete a science lab. This requires them to discuss and record their findings using academic vocabulary. **(p. TM129)**

MATH
- **Problem Solving with Algebra and Measurement** Curriculum supervisor Mary Esther Reynosa suggests various ways to build students problem-solving abilities. **(p. TM128)**
- **Communication in Mathematics** Bea Moore-Harris explains the importance of student communication in the mathematics classroom. **(p. TM128)**

CHAPTER 12 Manage Resources, Time, and Stress

READING
- **Standards-Based Instruction** Emily M. Schell, Ed.D., educator and author, discusses standards-based instruction. **(p. TM133)**
- **Obstacles to Achievement** Teachers work together to determine why their students are struggling with mastery of a particular standard. **(p. TM134)**
- **Strategic Readers** Author Scott Paris discusses the characteristics of strategic readers. **(p. TM134)**

ENGLISH LANGUAGE LEARNERS
- **Elaborating on Student Responses** A teacher elaborates on a student response using explanatory language. **(p. TM135)**

Manage Your Money

Section 11.1 *Be a Smart Consumer*

In this section, teens will learn how to be wise consumers. They will learn how to make smart buying decisions and how to evaluate the claims of advertisers.

Section 11.2 *Spending and Saving Basics*

In this section, students will learn good shopping skills. They will learn about their rights and responsibilities as consumers. They will also learn how to manage their money.

Classroom Solutions

Print Resources

- Student Edition
- Teacher Annotated Edition
- Student Activity Workbook
- Student Activity Workbook
  Teacher Annotated Edition

Technology Resources

ExamView *ExamView Assessment Suite CD* allows you to create and print out customized tests or ready-made unit and chapter tests, complete with answer keys.

Lesson Planner *Plus* *Lesson Planner Plus! CD* is and electronic lesson planner that provides instant access to teacher resources in one convenient package.

- Projects and Activities*
- Food Labs*
- Sewing Labs*
- Career Investigations*
- Reteaching Activities*
- Enrichment Activities*

Presentation Plus! PowerPoint™ Presentations can be edited and customized to meet the needs of students.

Online Learning Center includes resources and activities for students and teachers. Also includes Online Student Edition.

Interactive Student Edition

*Electronic Resources are available on Lesson Planner Plus and the Online Learning Center.

Writing Activity Answer

Essay Answers will vary. Essays should have a clear introduction, a body that supports the introduction with details and examples, and a conclusion that restates the introduction. Essays should show an understanding of resourcefulness.

Discovering Careers Answers ▼

1. Answers will vary. Students should write a summary of the education, training, and experience needed for the selected careers.
2. Answers may include groceries, utilities, entertainment, and car payments.
3. Answers may include office supplies, equipment, computers, telephone and Internet service, mail and package delivery services, break room supplies, and cleaning supplies.
4. Answers will vary. Students should present a summary of what they learned about the person's typical work day.

Be a Smart Consumer

FOCUS

Discussion Starter

Ask the class to discuss the things they purchase for themselves, as opposed to the things their parents purchase it for them. How do they decide what to purchase? Explain that they will learn more about purchasing decisions in this lesson. Students should be able to think of items they purchase for themselves and describe the process by which they decide what to purchase.

Bell Ringer Activity

Targeted Marketing Find one example each of products that are marketed to teens or adults. You might choose clothing, beauty products, school/office supplies, or any other product where there is a clear difference between an item aimed at teenagers and an item aimed at adults. Ask the students to explain what features of the product appeal to its target market.

 Professional Development Mini Clip
Math Problem Solving with Algebra and Measurement

TEACH

S Skill Practice

Independent Practice

L1 List Ask students to list the techniques that advertisers use to sell products or services. Slogans, jingles, and catchy songs; endorsements by famous people; cartoon characters and cute mascots; and appeals to emotion.

L2 Demonstrate Ask students to write a paragraph demonstrating how trends can affect people's buying decisions. When a trend is started, many people will want to buy that product because they feel it will make them more popular or identify them with a particular style or person they admire.

L3 Apply Find examples of different brands of certain products, such as shoes, jeans, backpacks, or makeup. Ask students to look at each brand and available product information and explain which they would purchase and why. Students

should provide reasoning for their decision, such as a reasonable price, durability, or good value.

U Universal Access

Students with Behavior Disorders Students who have attention difficulties may find it easier to stay on target if they are actively involved in learning. When discussing advertisements, ask students to bring in an advertisement that appeals to them, present it to the class, and discuss why it is appealing.

ASSESS

Quiz

Ask students to answer the following questions:

1. **What are goods and services?** A good is an object that you purchase, while a service is an action that someone performs.

2. **Name three things that can influence buying decisions.** Advertising, celebrity endorsements, the latest trends, and what your friends buy.

3. **What are the advantages and disadvantages of advertising?** Advantages: introduce you to new products or deliver a public service announcement. Disadvantages: mislead or persuade you to buy things you do not need.

RETEACH

W Writing Strategy

Make a List Ask students to create a list of questions to ask when evaluating an advertisement that they can fill out when looking at an advertisement. Students should come up with questions to help them evaluate an advertisement. Example questions: What are the claims being made? What are the qualifications of the endorser? Are there emotional appeals? What further information do I need?

C Critical Thinking

Get Financial Help Ask students to imagine that they are having trouble saving money. What can they do to manage their spending? Who can they ask for help? Students might implement a weekly allowance for themselves, ask their parents to help them by taking charge of their funds, or see if their bank offers financial counseling

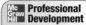 **Professional Development Mini Clip**
Math Communication in Mathematics

ASSESS

Section 11.1 Review Assign the Section 11.1 After You Read activities.

 Student Activity Workbook Assign the Section 11.1 Activities.

Online Study Tools Have students go to the Online Learning Center at glencoe.com to:

- Take the Section 11.1 **Practice Test**.
- Download **Study-to-Go** content.

 Section 11.1 After You Read

Answer Key

1. What to buy, where to buy, and when to buy.
2. Advertising, friends, trends, and habits.
3. Information ads and image ads.
4. Answers will vary depending on product or service selected. Reports should include product descriptions, how they are advertised in the two media chosen, and what the similarities and differences are in the advertising method.
5. Online advertising reaches consumers in the form of banners, pop-up ads, and spam. Consumers can make instant purchases from Web sites created by established brick-and-mortar companies, or they can buy from companies that exist only online. Unlike traditional advertising, the consumer is usually in control of the ads he or she wants to view.

CLOSE

Culminating Activity

Evaluate Advertising Bring in examples of ads that appear in different magazines geared towards teenagers. Choose some examples from magazines for teenage girls and some from magazines for boys, such as sports or video game magazines. Have the students analyze the ads. Students should identify the different techniques being used in the ads to sell the products and evaluate the claims being made, such as benefits the product is said to give or celebrities endorsing the product.

Section 11.2 Lesson Plan

Spending and Saving Basics

FOCUS

Discussion Starter

Discuss with the class the types of stores they like to shop in. Why do they like these stores? Students should be able to articulate their reasons for choosing their favorite stores. Perhaps they carry brands that they like or have a fun atmosphere

Bell Ringer Activity

Read Labels Bring in food and clothing labels for students to review. Look for ingredients or materials that the class does not understand and research them. Look for information that could affect a customer's decision, such as special laundering instructions. Encourage students to read labels before purchasing any food or clothing item.

Professional Development | **Mini Clip**
ELL Using Manipulatives

TEACH

S Skill Practice

Guided Practice

L1 **List** Divide students into groups to list their responsibilities as consumers. Be courteous to the staff, behave responsibly when handling and using merchandise, and be honest.

L2 **Discuss** Have students work in groups to discuss how to properly obtain a refund or exchange. Read the store's policy before you purchase the item. Keep your proof of purchase. Determine whether you are entitled to a refund. Bring the item to the store to process your claim.

L3 **Apply** Ask students to choose an item they will purchase in the near future and practice comparison shopping for it. Divide the class into groups to work together to share ideas on how to comparison shop for their items. Students should go through the process of comparison shopping as if they were really purchasing the item, explaining the factors they considered.

Professional Development | **Mini Clip**
ELL Collaborative Work

U Universal Access

Interpersonal and Intrapersonal Learners Divide students into groups and ask each group to design a brochure for consumers about their rights and responsibilities. Try to see that the groups are balanced, containing both outgoing, interpersonal learners as well as reflective, intrapersonal learners.

Professional Development **Mini Clip**

Reading Planning and Classroom Management

ASSESS

Quiz

Ask students to answer the following questions:

1. How can you be an informed shopper? Read labels, compare prices between stores and brands, check for warranties, and research product information.

2. What are your rights as a consumer? The right to safety, to be informed, to choose, to be heard, to redress, and to consumer education.

3. What is a savings plan? The part of the budget that helps you put money aside for emergency needs and future use.

RETEACH

R Reading Strategy

Find Details Ask students to look at financial magazines or the finance section of the newspaper to find articles about using credit cards responsibly. Ask them to read the articles and find details about credit card use. Students might locate information about how to deal with debt or how to spend wisely. They should locate specific details that give them useful information.

C Critical Thinking

Connect to Community Have students evaluate local merchants. Have them decide on categories of businesses that teenagers frequent. Then have them survey their fellow students on their experiences with businesses in those categories. Discuss as a class how the results of their survey have affected their opinions of local merchants. Students should gather positive and negative comments about local merchants and evaluate the collective comments of their peers to see how their opinions change.

ASSESS

Section 11.2 Review Assign the Section 11.2 After You Read activities.

Student Activity Workbook Assign the Section 11.2 Activities.

 Online Study Tools Have students go to the Online Learning Center at glencoe.com to:

■ Take the Section 11.2 **Practice Test**.

■ Download **Study-to-Go** content.

ExamView® Assessment Suite
Use the *ExamView Assessment Suite* **CD to create a test for this chapter.**

Chapter Review Have students complete the Chapter 11 Review and Applications.

Section 11.2 After You Read
Answer Key

1. Read labels. Compare prices and brands. Inspect merchandise. Find out if the manufacturer will replace or repair the item.

2. Responsible consumers are polite. If there is a problem, calmly explain the problem and how you would like to resolve it.

3. A savings plan helps you put money aside for unexpected needs and future use. Plan ahead and save regularly to achieve your financial goals.

4. Pamphlet designs will vary, but should include information from the chapter about savings, written in a way that teens will understand.

5. Answers will vary by state. Sample answer: The "Lemon Law" varies from state to state, but in general it refers to laws protecting consumers against the purchase of vehicles found to be persistently defective.

CLOSE

Culminating Activity

Create a Budget Have students create a budget for the next month. Have them determine the amount of money they will receive from allowance or a job and create a spending budget that fits within that amount. Students should include all of the things that they typically spend money on in a month. They should make sure that they are not spending more than they are getting, and should try to have some money left over.

Words You Learned

1. Students should write their own definition for each content and academic vocabulary term.

Review Key Concepts

2. Decide what to buy, where to buy, when to buy, and how to get the best value for your money.

3. If you always shop at the same store, you may be passing up good prices offered at another store. If you always buy the same brand, you may be missing out on other good products and good deals.

4. Advertising is designed to catch the attention of consumers and convince them to buy a product or service.

5. Discount stores, factory outlets, chain stores, specialty stores, department stores, catalogs, and the Internet.

6. Consumer rights protect consumers from false advertising and unsafe products. Consumer responsibilities: be courteous, behave responsibly, be honest, and understand refund and exchange policies before buying.

7. Know the source of your income; determine how much money you will have; look at how much money you are spending; evaluate what you are buying.

Critical Thinking

8. Finance charges will add up on the unpaid balance; your credit can be damaged; you may not be able to get a loan for a car or a home, and if you do get a loan, your interest rates will be higher; renting an apartment may be difficult.

9. Advertisements aimed at teens and pre-teens often use popular music, teen role models from the media, teens that look and act like real teens, or scenarios that teens can relate to. Media may include television, teen-themed magazines, radio, and the Internet.

Real-World Skills and Applications

10. Consider the brands, but do not base your decision on brand alone. Ask a salesperson for a recommendation based on your needs. Read the information card attached to the shelves or on the product boxes to compare prices and features. Ask about the return policy.

11. Answers will vary, but students should determine the dominant influence and explain why this is the case. For example, if friends are the biggest influence, students may say that it is because teens often feel the need to fit in with their peers.

Financial Literacy

12. At 4%, Shannon's money will double in about $72 \div 4 = 18$ years. The formula can be used in reverse for the second problem, which states that $72 \div x = 2$ years, with x standing for the interest rate percentage. Multiply both sides by x to get $72 = 2x$, and divide both sides by 2 to get $x = 36$. It will take an interest rate of 36% to double her money in two years.

Active Learning

13. Cards will vary depending on the banks chosen. Students should include details about the accounts offered. Students will probably come across unfamiliar terms such as high yield, eligible, IRA, and APR. Compile a list of these terms, and define them as a class.

14. Answers will vary, but students should identify advertising techniques and determine the effectiveness of each. They should logically discuss how, if at all, their new knowledge about advertising affects the way they react to ads and why.

Net Connection

15. Lists will vary, but should include sensible tips for someone with a small or limited income to save money.

Academic Skills

16. Brochures will vary, but should include accurate information that would be useful for young adults starting out on their own. Encourage students to create an interesting design and layout.

17. Information in charts will vary depending on condiments chosen. Students should include ingredient lists for both brand-name and generic products and determine how the items compare.

18. John will pay $441 each year. When he turns 21, he will pay $90\% \times \$500 = \$450$ per year for his insurance. If he also takes the safe driving course, his insurance premium will drop to $98\% \times \$450 = \$441$ per year.

Standardized Test Practice

19. Essays will vary. Students should explain how they make a major purchasing decision, and should include specific details and examples to support the explanation.

Manage Resources, Time, and Stress

Section 12.1 *Manage Resources*

In this lesson, students will learn what the management process is. They will also learn how to manage personal resources, material resources, and community resources.

Section 12.2 *Manage Time and Handle Stress*

In this lesson, students will learn time management skills and how to handle stress. They will learn how to make their time count and will also learn good study skills.

Classroom Solutions

Print Resources

 Student Edition
Teacher Annotated Edition
 Student Activity Workbook
 Student Activity Workbook
Teacher Annotated Edition

- Projects and Activities*
- Food Labs*
- Sewing Labs*
- Career Investigations*
- Reteaching Activities*
- Enrichment Activities*

Technology Resources

 ExamView Assessment Suite CD allows you to create and print out customized tests or ready-made unit and chapter tests, complete with answer keys.

Lesson Planner *Plus* Lesson Planner Plus! CD* is and electronic lesson planner that provides instant access to teacher resources in one convenient package.

 Presentation Plus! PowerPoint™ Presentations can be edited and customized to meet the needs of students.

Online Learning Center includes resources and activities for students and teachers. Also includes Online Student Edition.

Interactive Student Edition

*ELECTRONIC RESOURCES ARE AVAILABLE ON LESSON PLANNER PLUS AND THE ONLINE LEARNING CENTER.

Writing Activity Answer

Dialogue Answers will vary. Dialogues should sound sincere, use realistic language, and include a logical discussion about time use and studying.

Discovering Careers Answers ▼

1. Answers will vary. Students should write a summary of the education, training, and experience needed for the selected careers.
2. Schedules should demonstrate an understanding of arranging activities within a specified time period.
3. Lists will vary. Sample answers: spreadsheet and word-processing applications can help with managing tasks; graphics applications can help develop creative flyers and newsletters; e-mail skills can help with communication on the job.
4. Answers will vary. Students should present a summary of what they learned about the person's typical work day.

Section **12.1** Lesson Plan

Manage Resources

FOCUS

Discussion Starter

Ask students if they ever feel like there is not enough time in the day, they do not get enough sleep, or they have difficulty making time for all of their friends and family. Explain that this chapter will help them learn how to manage these resources. Have students describe which aspect of their life they feel they have difficulty managing and why.

Bell Ringer Activity

Identify Resources Have students skim the information on resources and list five examples of their personal resources and five of their material resources. Have them also list five examples of community resources. Students should list examples of their personal and material resources, such as their parents or a bicycle. They should also come up with community resources, such as the local police.

TEACH

S Skill Practice

Guided Practice

L1 **List** Have the students work in groups to list the steps in creating a management plan. 1. Decide on the goal and write it down; 2. Make a plan to achieve the goal. Divide the goal into smaller goals, if necessary; 3. Put the plan into action; 4. Evaluate the results of your plan.

L2 **Describe** Divide the students into small groups to describe why it is useful to write out a management plan. Having a written list gives you a visual reminder of what you need to do and helps you organize your ideas. Writing something down can help you remember it better.

L3 **Apply** As a class, come up with a goal. It might be academic, such as having everyone score high on the next test, or social, such as going on a field trip. Instruct the students to follow the management process to come up with a plan. Students should create a realistic plan for meeting the goal they choose.

U Universal Access

Students with Hearing Impairments Have a reliable classmate make an outline of the management process for a student with hearing impairments that he or she can follow while the class learns about the process. Making the outline can also serve as reinforcement for the student making it.

ASSESS

Quiz

Ask students to answer the following questions:

1. **What are your personal resources?** Available time, energy level, knowledge and education, learned skills and natural talents, and relationships with friends, family, and others.

2. **How can personal possessions make life easier?** They can provide satisfaction and enjoyment, which can reduce stress and save time by making tasks easier.

3. **What are community resources?** Services that the local community provides to enrich the lives of its citizens, such as education or entertainment, or to help and support those with special problems.

RETEACH

W Writing Strategy

Evaluate Have students choose a small goal and apply the management process. For the final step, ask them to write down their evaluation in the form of a short essay and turn it in. Students should choose an easily-accomplished goal, such as getting a good grade. The evaluation should focus on what students were satisfied with and what they would do differently.

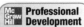

McGraw Hill **Professional Development** **Mini Clip**
Reading Standards-Based Instruction

C Critical Thinking

Assess Personal Resources Have students evaluate their management of time, energy, knowledge, skills, and people. For each, have them list the ways in which they are successful and the ways in which they need improvement. Students should be able to figure out strong and weak areas when it comes to managing their resources. For example, they might realize they sometimes take too long a break when they come home from school before studying.

ASSESS

Section 12.1 Review Assign the Section 12.1 After You Read activities.

 Student Activity Workbook Assign the Section 12.1 Activities.

 Online Study Tools Have students go to the Online Learning Center at glencoe.com to:

■ Take the Section 12.1 **Practice Test**.

■ Download **Study-to-Go** content.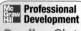

Section 12.1 After You Read

Answer Key

1. Management is the skillful use of resources to accomplish a task

2. Enjoyment and satisfaction, and they can make your life easier.

3. Answers will vary based on the student's goal. Students should have a detailed outline of their goal that includes all four steps listed in the How To Make a Management Plan feature on page 260.

4. Answers will vary. Students should include details that demonstrate how meeting someone from another culture can offer an exchange of thoughts, ideas, or knowledge. Benefits for both teens may include new knowledge, inspiration to try new things, exposure to a different culture, and elimination of stereotypes.

CLOSE

Culminating Activity

Manage a Resource Have students choose one personal resource (time, skills, energy, knowledge, or people) and use the first two steps of the management process to create a plan for managing that resource. Students should choose one personal resource, decide what their goal is, and create a plan to reach that goal. For example, if students want to manage time better, they might decide their goal is to make a schedule and keep to it.

Mc Graw Hill Professional Development **Mini Clip**
Reading Obstacles to Achievement

Section 12.2 Lesson Plan

Manage Time and Handle Stress

FOCUS

Discussion Skills

Ask students to discuss the things that make them feel stressed. List the stressors on the board. Discuss the ones that come up more often, which are likely to be common sources of stress for teenagers. Encourage the students to work together to develop coping skills. Student answers will vary, but may include common stressors like schoolwork, athletic teams, and social pressures.

 Bell Ringer Activity

Create a Schedule Ask students to think about what they did yesterday and recreate their schedule from memory. How did they use their time? Can they think of a more efficient way they could have organized their time? How would they revise their schedule? Ask them to create a schedule for the next day that they think will be more efficient.

TEACH

S Skill Practice

Independent Practice

L1 **List** Have students list the things a person with effective study skills does to make the most of their studying time. Practices reading, note-taking, test-taking, listening, and computer skills; organizes and prioritizes homework, projects, and test preparation time; keeps track of where they need improvement; and asks for help if they need it.

L2 **Explain** Have students write a paragraph explaining how getting organized can help save time. You will already have everything you need and will not have to interrupt to go get items. Organizing again at the end will save even more time next time you do the task.

L3 **Apply** Have students keep a stress journal for one week. Whenever they feel stressed, they should write down the cause, how they tried to relieve the stress, and the result. Students should have at least one entry per day that describes the cause of stress and their coping mechanisms.

Mc Graw Hill Professional Development **Mini Clip**
Reading Strategic Readers

U Universal Access

Students with Orthopedic or Visual Impairments
Students with orthopedic or visual impairments may have sources of stress that are different from other students. Encourage such students to talk about sources of stress that may not be apparent to a sighted person.

ASSESS

Quiz

Ask students to answer the following questions:

1. Can you make more time by sleeping less? No, you cannot, because if you sleep less, you will be tired and unfocused so you will be less productive.

2. How can you improve your study skills? Prioritize your time, make a to-do list, remove distractions, and gather supplies in advance.

3. What causes stress? Stress is a natural reaction to the changes in your life or to pleasant or unpleasant events.

RETEACH

W Writing Strategy

Anticipate Study Schedule Ask students to think ahead to their final exams or midterms. Have them review the advice on studying and prepare a study schedule including what will be studied, what will be done to prepare, and what materials will be needed. Student study plans should reflect the advice given in the book, as well as recognition of how much time they will need to study and what materials are needed.

McGraw Hill **Professional Development** **Mini Clip**
ELL Elaborating on Student Responses

C Critical Thinking

Connect to Technology Ask students how they can use technology to help manage their time more effectively. Computer software can save you time in your work and also help you create schedules and to-do lists. There are technology products such as personal digital assistants that keep all of your data in a portable form and allow you to take information from your computer with you.

ASSESS

Section 12.2 Review Assign the Section 12.2 After You Read activities.

Student Activity Workbook Assign the Section 12.2 Activities.

Online Study Tools Have students go to the Online Learning Center at glencoe.com to:

- Take the Section 12.2 **Practice Test**.
- Download **Study-to-Go** content.

ExamView® Assessment Suite
Use the *ExamView Assessment Suite* **CD to create a test for this chapter.**

Chapter Review Have students complete the Chapter 12 Review and Applications.

Section 12.2 After You Read
Answer Key

1. Rank tasks by importance. As you complete each task, cross it off. It can motivate you to see what you have accomplished.

2. Any five of the following: talk to someone you trust; spend time on a hobby; exercise; participate in a sport; spend time with a pet; eat nutritious food; get plenty of rest; take quick breaks; take deep breaths; plan ahead for events; think positive.

3. E-mails may include such tips as make to-do lists, prioritize tasks, make a list of pros and cons when she has too many choices, ask parents for help, take a few minutes to relax, reevaluate her schedule, or postpone an activity until she has more time.

4. Paragraphs should communicate how family members manage time, how students are influenced by the management styles within their families, and the similarities and differences in time-management skills between themselves and family members.

CLOSE

Culminating Activity

Practice Study Skills Ask students to follow the study skills advice provided by the lesson. Discuss how the process differed from their normal study routine and how it affected their performance. Students might find that small changes make a big difference in their efficiency.

Words You Learned

1. Students should create a fill-in-the-blank sentence for each of the vocabulary words. The sentence should contain enough information to help determine the missing word.

Review Key Concepts

2. Step 1—Decide on your goal: write it down to help you commit to it. Step 2—Make a plan: decide how you want to achieve the goal, and break it down into short-term goals that are easier to reach. Step 3—Put the plan into action: start working on it now. Step 4—Evaluate the results: decide what you would do differently next time.

3. Personal resources: time, energy, knowledge and education, skills and talents, people; Material resources: possessions, objects, money; Community resources: parks, libraries, recreation facilities, shelters, youth programs, hospitals.

4. Good time-management skills can help you meet deadlines and stay on schedule, and they can help you deal with problems that may arise.

5. Get away from the routine; set priorities; seek out your support system; take care of yourself; participate in a physical activity; adjust your attitude.

Critical Thinking

6. Answers may include: divide and alternate chores, keep daily planners or schedules, stay in touch throughout the day.

7. Material resources are objects, possessions, and money. They are not essential for survival like food, water, and shelter are. Personal resources are unique to you, such as your time, energy, knowledge, skills, and the people in your life. Both can help you manage your life.

8. The stress can build up and lead to moodiness, arguments, physical problems such as headaches and sleeplessness, and inability to focus.

9. Stress can make you feel challenged and motivated, giving you an extra push to achieve goals.

Real-World Skills and Applications

10. Answers may include: eliminate an activity until next year; keep a daily planner and make to-do lists; offer to trade chores when he has to study; make sure his study area is organized and neat; suggest that he negotiate with your parents about his work load at home.

11. Planners will vary, but students should recognize where they need to improve their management skills.

Financial Literacy

12. Andre would spend $20 \times 12 = 240$ minutes a year organizing his financial paperwork. But he would no longer waste $15 \times 52 = 780$ minutes a year looking for things, so his net time savings would be $780 - 240 = 540$ minutes (or $540 \div 60 = 9$ hours).

Active Learning

13. Encourage students to be creative and to have fun as they create ways to help them organize their study supplies at home.

14. Tips will vary, but students should present a list of stress-handling tips based on their interviews with a working person.

Net Connection

15. Lists may include: learn general concepts first, then learn the details; take notes and summarize important ideas as you read; review the material right after class while it is fresh; read for comprehension, not just to hurry to the end; study when you are most alert; avoid studying at bed time; and only study with others who are serious about studying.

Academic Skills

16. Students should present workspace designs suited to their personal study needs. Lists should include useful study tools and resources such as: a planner or calendar; file organizer; places for pens and other small items; notebooks; and folders. They should explain how their designs will help with time and stress management.

17. Physical problems caused by stress may include: headaches, backaches, muscle tension, nausea, dizziness, insomnia, chest pain, rapid heartbeat, weight gain or loss, skin breakouts, and frequent colds. Stress management tips may include: learn how to say no; limit contact with people who cause stress; take control of your environment; reevaluate your schedule, responsibilities, and daily tasks; express feelings instead of bottling them up; be willing to compromise.

18. Chiyoko spends $3 \div 24 = 0.125 = 12.5\%$ of his day watching television. He spends $45 \div (24 \times 60) = 45 \div 1,440 = 0.03125 = 3.125\%$ of his day playing videogames.

Standardized Test Practice

19. c. sleep:alertness. (The relationship is cause and effect.)

FOCUS

Introduce the Project

In this project, students will learn shopping skills. Ask students what knowledge and skills they think they will need to make a list and shop for their family. Answers will vary, but may include math skills to compute prices and keep a budget, nutrition knowledge to compare health labels, and organization to keep lists and coupons.

Build Background

Brand Names Ask students to name brands of grocery items they are aware of. Then ask what qualities the brand claims makes them better than other brands. Write the brand names and the qualities. Discuss whether brand claims can be verified and whether they should influence students' shopping choices. Brands will vary, but claims may be lite, new, diet, more absorbent, bigger, fresh, or quick-cooking.

TEACH

S Skill Practice

Guided Practice

L1 Identify Ask students to identify five items their family regularly buys at the market that they do not really need. Have volunteers share their items and pick two that they could most easily live without. If possible, determine how much money this would save their family or if there is a health benefit to gain. Lists will vary, but may include candy and sweets, soda, prepared snacks, ready-to-eat meals, magazines, books, or CDs.

L2 Compare Show students two cartons of orange juice. One is larger in volume and costs more. The other costs less, but has less volume. Compare them. What factors would determine the better value? Answers include price per liter, if family drinks enough to buy larger container, if any will go to waste, and room in the refrigerator.

L3 Apply Challenge students to pair up and use the Internet to find the lowest prices of the same quantity of bread, milk, butter, and eggs. See who can find the market with the lowest prices on all four items. Challenge another group to compare labels and choose the healthiest items. Prices will vary, but students should take into account container sizes, weight, and volumes before determining best value.

C Critical Thinking

Price vs. Value Ask students to compare similar items with different prices. Although one is less expensive, it may not be a better value. For example, one roll of paper towels may cost less, but another may be more absorbent. What other qualities besides price determine a product's value? Answers will vary, but may include freshness, better taste, better for health, lasts longer, more effective at its purpose.

ASSESS

Quiz

Ask students to answer the following questions:

1. What does "impulse buying" mean, and what are its risks? Buying something you did not plan to purchase. You risk wasting your money and not following your budget.

2. What are alternative ways to shop, besides going to the market? Buying products from catalogs and electronic shopping on the Internet.

3. What are your responsibilities if you want to return or exchange something? Know the store's policy, keep proof of your purchase, determine whether you are entitled to a refund, and be ready to process your claim.

CLOSE

Culminating Activity

Letter of Commendation In this activity, students shopped for their family, looking for bargains and better values. Ask students to choose the product they bought that is the best value and write a letter to the company that makes it, explaining what makes their product such a good buy. Students should use proper letter format and consider price, nutritional benefits, time-saving merits, and comparison to other brands.

Your World

Unit Overview

This unit introduces students to their living spaces and the environment and provides them with tips on how to make their homes safe, comfortable, and unique. It also gives information on how to conserve natural resources and protect the environment.

Chapter 13 *Your Living Space* In this chapter, students will learn not only how to make their homes functional, safe, and organized, but also how to use design elements to make their living spaces reflect their personal, unique styles.

Chapter 14 *Your Environment* In this chapter, students will be introduced to the different types of natural resources. They will be taught how to conserve these resources and how to limit waste, and use air, water, land, and energy wisely.

Life Skills Project Preview

Improve Your Home

Tell students that as part of this unit, they will learn about the importance of having a functional, safe, and appealing living space. They will learn how to identify problems in a home, suggest solutions, interview someone who builds or designs homes, and present a project to the class to share what they have learned.

FCCLA provides programs to guide students through projects, enhance their personal growth, and build leadership skills that can make a difference in their lives, their families, and their communities.

Community Service guides students to develop, plan, carry out, and evaluate projects that improve the quality of life in their communities. This program helps young people build skills for family, career, and community roles and encourages young people to develop the positive character traits of trustworthiness, respect, responsibility, fairness, caring, and citizenship.

Help Others Most communities have nonprofit organizations with volunteer opportunities, and many will even have positions specifically geared toward teens. Have students research volunteer opportunities in the community, and choose one that they would like to volunteer for. Possibilities may include tutoring, working in a hospital, delivering meals, or making audio recordings of books for people with visual impairments. Students should volunteer at one of these places, and write a short description of their experiences. Did they enjoy it? Why or why not? Did they feel they made a difference? What did they learn? Students should pick a volunteer opportunity suited to their interests and personalities (for example, if the student loves animals, he or she could volunteer at a local animal shelter). Students should then write about their experience, describing it and explaining whether or not they enjoyed it and what they learned.

Professional Development

MINI CLIP VIDEO LIBRARY

Targeted professional development is correlated throughout *Discovering Life Skills*. **The McGraw-Hill Professional Development Mini Clip Video Library** provides teaching strategies to strengthen academic and learning skills. Log on to **glencoe.com**.

In this Unit, you will find these Mini Clips.

CHAPTER 13 Your Living Space

READING
- **Extending the Big Idea** A teacher assigns group collaborations and consensus building activities to promote student discussions about a reading selection. (p. TM142)
- **On Workshops** Doug Fisher, Ph.D., author and teacher educator, discusses the Workshop Approach to teaching. (p. TM142)

ENGLISH LANGUAGE LEARNERS
- **Using Manipulatives** A teacher uses concrete objects to illustrate lesson concepts. (p. TM141)

MATH
- **Small Group Work** Students work in cooperative groups to graph an equation. (p. TM143)

CHAPTER 14 Your Environment

READING
- **Bridging Cultural Gaps** A teacher models the use of context clues to determine the meaning of an unknown word. (p. TM148)

ENGLISH LANGUAGE LEARNERS
- **Using Realia** A teacher uses realia to make lesson concepts more real to students. (p. TM146)
- **Elaborating on Student Responses** A teacher elaborates on a student response using explanatory language. (p. TM147)

MATH
- **Unknowns in Equations** A Grade 6 teacher uses a warm up activity to check her student's knowledge of equations. (p. TM146)

Your Living Space

Section 13.1 Home Organization and Safety

In this lesson, students will learn how to organize their living space and how to keep a neat and clean environment at home. They will also learn about safety in the home and community.

Section 13.2 Home Design

In this lesson, students will learn about the elements and principles of interior design. They will also learn how to accessorize and decorate to create a look that suits their style.

Classroom Solutions

Print Resources

- Student Edition
- Teacher Annotated Edition
- Student Activity Workbook
- Student Activity Workbook Teacher Annotated Edition

Technology Resources

 ExamView Assessment Suite CD allows you to create and print out customized tests or ready-made unit and chapter tests, complete with answer keys.

 Lesson Planner Plus! CD* is and electronic lesson planner that provides instant access to teacher resources in one convenient package.

- Projects and Activities*
- Food Labs*
- Sewing Labs*
- Career Investigations*
- Reteaching Activities*
- Enrichment Activities*

Presentation Plus! PowerPoint™ Presentations can be edited and customized to meet the needs of students.

Online Learning Center includes resources and activities for students and teachers. Also includes Online Student Edition.

Interactive Student Edition

*ELECTRONIC RESOURCES ARE AVAILABLE ON LESSON PLANNER PLUS AND THE ONLINE LEARNING CENTER.

 Writing Activity Answer

Descriptive Paragraph Answers will vary. A sample answer might include: A room with the feeling of a log cabin might have large wooden furniture, a fireplace, warm colors, lanterns, and accessories inspired by nature.

 Discovering Careers Answers ▼

1. Answers will vary. Students should write a summary of the education, training, and experience needed for the selected careers.

2. Lists may include: painting, landscaping, electrical repair, home improvement, tile installation, carpet cleaning, and carpet or other flooring installation.

3. Answers may include: color selection for walls and carpet to create a mood; use of accessories such as wall hangings, plants, and lighting; functional arrangement and style of office furniture and workspaces; or decorative items in a reception area or lobby. Workers might decorate their workspaces with personal items.

4. Answers will vary. Students should present a summary of what they learned about the person's typical work day.

Section **13.1** Lesson Plan

Home Organization and Safety

FOCUS

Discussion Starter

Discuss home safety with the class. How safe do the students think their homes are? Ask them to visualize their home and describe areas that are set up for safety and/or areas that could be made safer. Students might point out ways in which their homes are made safe, such as having emergency supplies or a fire escape, and areas where it could be improved, such as eliminating slip-and-fall hazards.

Bell Ringer Activity

Create a Cleaning Schedule Ask students to think of the tasks they have to do in order to keep their personal space clean at home. Ask them to create a schedule with each of the chores and the time that the student performs that chore. Ask them to think about the best time for each. Some might be better to do at night and some in the morning.

TEACH

S Skill Practice

Independent Practice

L1 List Ask students to list the benefits of keeping a neat and safe home. Save time and energy; make your clothes and other possessions last longer; help family members stay healthier; help prevent accidents; and help keep a home safe from intruders.

L2 Express Have students write a paragraph expressing what to do in the bathroom to keep the shared space neat and tidy. Each person who uses the bathroom should: rinse the bathtub and sink after each use; hang towels after each use; wipe up spills and water; and return personal grooming items to their proper place.

L3 Apply Ask students to make their homes more "fall-proof." Have them list the things they did and report to the class. Students should follow the advice given in the lesson about preventing falls. If they did not make any changes, they should report on what they found satisfactory.

U Universal Access

Visual Learning Have visual learners create floor plans or models of rooms to demonstrate organization. You can also reinforce lessons about safety and cleaning by using visual aids such as posters, videos, and images to demonstrate cleaning techniques and safety procedures.

McGraw Hill **Professional Development** | **Mini Clip**
ELL Using Manipulatives

ASSESS

Quiz

Ask students to answer the following questions:

1. **What concepts should you consider when arranging your space?** Think about the traffic pattern in the room, necessary space around furniture, making functional arrangements, and grouping related items together.

2. **What can you do when you run out of room in your storage space?** For usable items, give away items to family members; have a yard sale; or donate to charity. Recycle or throw away things that are broken or unusable.

3. **What is a cleaning plan?** A list of daily, weekly, and occasional household jobs, and a list of the family member responsible for each job.

RETEACH

W Writing Strategy

Make a List Based on the information in the lesson, ask students to think about their homes and make a list of cleaning tasks that need to be performed in both their own space and the shared spaces. Have the students rate the items on a scale of 1 to 10 with 1 being the most important. Students should provide a thorough list of the cleaning tasks and number these tasks in order of importance.

C Critical Thinking

Synthesize Ask students to have a family meeting regarding chores. Ask them to poll their family members on which chores they enjoy doing and which they do not. Then have them try to come up with a chore schedule to divide chores fairly, with people voluntarily doing chores they like better, and taking turns doing chores nobody likes. Students should analyze the data they gather and use their diplomacy skills to try to come up with a chore schedule that everyone agrees to.

ASSESS

Section 13.1 Review Assign the Section 13.1 After You Read activities.

 Student Activity Workbook Assign the Section 13.1 Activities.

Online Study Tools Have students go to the Online Learning Center at glencoe.com to:

- Take the Section 13.1 **Practice Test**.
- Download **Study-to-Go** content.

Section 13.1 After You Read
Answer Key

1. Organize rooms for more than one function to make the best use of space, equipment, and furniture.
2. A floor plan is a drawing of a room and its furniture arrangement. It allows you to see how furniture fits together without moving it.
3. Wash dishes, make beds, keep rooms picked up, and hang up clothes.
4. It will be easier to spot suspicious activity by strangers. If there is an emergency, you will know which neighbors you can call for help.
5. Posters should be illustrated and have accurate information written in a way that is easy to read and understand. If possible, display the posters in your classroom.
6. Answers will vary. Students should make sensible predictions about what a home of the future may include, such as advances in security, entertainment, communication, and convenience.

CLOSE

Culminating Activity

Safety in the Class As a class, discuss the safety procedures for your classroom for various emergencies. Make sure everyone understands the procedures and create posters to illustrate the procedures. By the end of the discussion, students should be familiar with the classroom safety procedures and also have made posters so that if an emergency happens, they will be prepared and less likely to panic.

Professional Development Mini Clip
Reading Extending the Big Idea

Section 13.2 Lesson Plan

Home Design

FOCUS

Discussion Starter

Ask students to think about which aspects of their bedroom's decoration were contributed by themselves and which by others. How would they change their rooms? What do they like best about their rooms? Students should discuss which parts of their rooms are part of their personal style and which are due to their parents' or others' influence.

Professional Development Mini Clip
Reading On Workshops

Bell Ringer Activity

Design Elements Have students look at the classroom and identify spaces, shapes, lines, textures, and colors. Ask the students to describe what they like or do not like about the elements, and what they would prefer. For example, students may point out the color of the walls and either describe why they like it or suggest a color that is more fun.

TEACH

S Skill Practice
Guided Practice

L1 List Divide students into groups of two and ask them to list five different accessories that can be used to personalize a room. Curtains, handmade items, quilts, pillows, posters and pictures, collections and mementos, trophies and awards, baskets, and rugs.

L2 Discuss Have students work in groups to discuss the effect of different lines in a design. Straight lines make objects seem strong and dignified. Curved lines are softer and more graceful. Vertical lines give the appearance of height. Horizontal lines make objects appear wider. Lines that are set at a diagonal suggest movement.

L3 Apply Ask students to imagine that they are allowed to redecorate the classroom. Divide the class into groups to share ideas and work together to explain the changes they would make. Students should be creative and consider their personal style, but should not forget to consider the room's function as a classroom.

U Universal Access

Verbal Learning Have students watch television shows or recordings on interior design. Ask them to relate the shows to the information about elements and principles of design in the text.

ASSESS

Quiz

Ask students to answer the following questions:

1. How can texture affect the design of a room? Texture provides visual variations, adds more interest, and affects the mood.

2. How do you add rhythm to a room design? Create a visual path through a room by placing elements carefully. Place elements so that the eye is drawn from one to the other.

3. What factors should you consider when planning a room design? You should consider the mood you want to create, your interests, and what you want to accomplish with the design.

RETEACH

W Writing Strategy

Create a List Have students make a list of characteristics of their personal style and give an example for each of how they could show that characteristic in their room decor. Student lists should contain the style characteristic and an example of how it could be shown through decoration. For example, if they have a favorite color, they might paint the wall with it.

C Critical Thinking

Conduct Research Have students choose one design principle and research it to expand on the information in the lesson. Then ask them to explain how they would apply that principle to improve the classroom. Students should gather information from design magazines and Web sites on how to apply the principle they have chosen. Then they should apply that principle to the classroom to come up with creative decorating ideas.

ASSESS

Section 13.2 Review Assign the Section 13.2 After You Read activities.

📁 **Student Activity Workbook** Assign the Section 13.2 Activities.

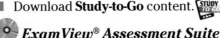 **Online Study Tools** Have students go to the Online Learning Center at glencoe.com to:

- Take the Section 13.2 **Practice Test**.
- Download **Study-to-Go** content.

💿 ***ExamView® Assessment Suite***
Use the *ExamView Assessment Suite* **CD to create a test for this chapter.**

📝 **Chapter Review** Have students complete the Chapter 13 Review and Applications.

📖 **Section 13.2 After You Read**
Answer Key

1. Light colors make a room look larger. Darker colors make a room seem smaller. Red, yellow, and orange are warm, comfortable colors. Blue, green, and violet are cool, restful colors.

2. Think about the look you want; if you share your space, consider the other person; consider your interests, hobbies, and whether you want a warm or cool environment. Planning is important as you will probably have to live with your choices for a long time.

3. Students should present a collage that represents their ideal living space. Floor plans should show furniture arrangement. Action plans may include: check with parents, cost consideration, and use of creativity.

4. Answers may include: budget, safety, geography, climate, amount of land, purpose of the buildings (administrative, classroom, library, restroom), playground areas, number of students and staff. Students should include specific design elements noticeable in your school.

CLOSE

Culminating Activity

Decorating Plan Ask students to imagine they have $1,000 to redo their bedroom. Since they will provide the labor, only the materials will cost money. Have them come up with a plan and budget for redecorating their room. Students should be creative but practical when redecorating their rooms. They should stick to the budget, providing a list of materials and their costs.

Words You Learned

1. Students should create a fill-in-the-blank sentence for each of the vocabulary terms. The sentence should contain enough information to help determine the missing word.

Review Key Concepts

2. Homes also provide comfort, security, and a place for entertainment and self-expression.

3. Furniture is used for comfort and convenience and can also be decorative. Storage space is for holding and organizing everything from paperclips to linens to tools to cleaning supplies.

4. It saves time and energy. Clothes and other possessions last longer. Family members stay healthier. You can help prevent home accidents.

5. Fire: escape route, extinguisher, smoke alarm, kitchen and fireplace safety. Falls: wipe up spills, use nonskid pads, keep stairs and walkways free of clutter, secure windows. Online: never reveal personal information, tell an adult if you feel threatened. Be careful around poisonous substances, tools, electrical appliances.

6. Elements: space, shape, line, texture, color. Principles: balance, emphasis, proportion, rhythm, unity.

7. Accessories such as pillows, posters, pictures, baskets, and trophies personalize a room. Decorating can show off your style and creativity.

Critical Thinking

8. Answers may include: you risk ending up with a lack of balance or proportion; your color choices may not work together; the room may seem too cramped or too bare.

9. Answers will vary depending on your region. Students should have appropriate emergency plans for the conditions in your region.

Real-World Skills and Applications

10. Some students may prefer buying inexpensive new furniture. Other students may prefer used but better-quality items.

11. Lists will vary. Students should present 5 realistic problems, and work together to come up with reasonable solutions. Sample: for kitchen cleaning, roommates might alternate tasks.

Financial Literacy

12. Students should present a summary of prices and locations for their items. They should determine how to get the best bargain and indicate whether the least expensive option is actually their best option.

Active Learning

13. Herb gardens are decorative because the plants are attractive, and the pots can complement your home design. The garden is functional because the herbs can be used for cooking.

14. Lists will vary, but may include: victim assistance services, park patrol, security guard services, crime tip rewards, regular neighborhood meetings with law enforcement representatives, disaster preparation information, graffiti clean up.

Net Connection

15. Answers will vary depending on style chosen. Styles could include traditional, eclectic, modern, contemporary, country, romantic, retro, or cottage. Students should describe how the style would affect the look and feel of the room, how their current accessories would mix with the style, and how visitors would respond.

Academic Skills

16. Promises may include: I will talk with my parents about rules for going online; I will keep my identity and location private; I will never respond to anyone who makes me feel uncomfortable; I will never agree to a face-to-face meeting with someone I do not know; I will behave appropriately while online.

17. Mold can cause allergic reactions such as nasal stuffiness, throat irritation, coughing and eye and skin irritation. People with asthma or immune deficiencies may get serious infections in their lungs when exposed to mold. Mold can only grow when moisture is present, so indoor mold growth can be prevented by controlling moisture. Make sure pipes and faucets are working, allow wet materials to dry before they are put away, and check for leaks.

18. One gallon is not enough to cover the four walls. The perimeter of Amanda's room is $(2 \times 12$ ft.$) + (2 \times 9$ ft.$) = 24 + 18 = 42$ ft, so the area of all four walls equals 42 ft. $\times$ 10 ft. = 420 sq. ft., which is more than 350 sq. ft. She will actually need $420 \div 350 = 1.2$ gallons of paint.

Standardized Test Practice

19. b

Your Environment

Section 14.1 *Resources and Conservation*

In this lesson, students will learn about the natural resources of air, water, soil, and energy. They will also learn how to conserve these resources, particularly water and energy.

Section 14.2 *Protect the Environment*

In this lesson, students will learn how to do their part to protect the environment. They will learn about the process of waste removal and how to limit waste by reducing, reusing, and recycling.

Classroom Solutions

Print Resources

- Student Edition
- Teacher Annotated Edition
- Student Activity Workbook
- Student Activity Workbook Teacher Annotated Edition

Technology Resources

ExamView Assessment Suite **ExamView Assessment Suite CD** allows you to create and print out customized tests or ready-made unit and chapter tests, complete with answer keys.

Lesson Planner *Plus* **Lesson Planner Plus! CD*** is and electronic lesson planner that provides instant access to teacher resources in one convenient package.

- Projects and Activities*
- Food Labs*
- Sewing Labs*
- Career Investigations*
- Reteaching Activities*
- Enrichment Activities*

Presentation *Plus!* **Presentation Plus!** PowerPoint™ Presentations can be edited and customized to meet the needs of students.

Online Learning Center includes resources and activities for students and teachers. Also includes Online Student Edition.

Interactive Student Edition

*ELECTRONIC RESOURCES ARE AVAILABLE ON LESSON PLANNER PLUS AND THE ONLINE LEARNING CENTER.

Writing Activity Answer

Explanation Answers will vary depending on the area chosen. Paragraphs may begin with a statement like, "The pollution on the beach in my town is caused by people and businesses that litter and dump into the water." The statement should be followed by supporting details.

Discovering Careers Answers ▼

1. Answers will vary. Students should write a summary of the education, training, and experience needed for the selected careers.
2. Lists will vary, but should include items that can be reused or recycled.
3. Lists may include veterinarian, zookeeper, aquarium designer, animal welfare advocate, farm inspector, kennel manager, and wildlife rescue educator.
4. Answers will vary. Students should present a summary of what they learned about the person's typical work day.

Section 14.1 Lesson Plan

Resources and Conservation

FOCUS

Discussion Starter

Ask students to discuss the ways their families try to conserve at home. Have volunteers talk about ways they save water and energy. Students should give examples of things they do at home to conserve, such as turning off lights, using blankets instead of heat, limiting shower time, or recycling.

Bell Ringer Activity

How To Conserve More Ask students to evaluate their family's activities and locate areas where their families waste energy or water. Then have students come up with ideas for how they can correct the waste. Students should come up with thoughtful ways to either correct or offset their wasteful behavior. For example, opening windows instead of running the air conditioner.

 Professional Development **Mini Clip**
ELL Using Realia

TEACH

S Skill Practice

Independent Practice

L1 List Ask students to list three ways to conserve water. Turn off water when brushing teeth; take showers instead of baths; install water-saving showerheads and toilets; repair leaky faucets; run washing machine only with a full load; change level of water in the washing machine according to the amount being washed.

L2 Explain Instruct students to write a paragraph explaining how to conserve energy. Purchase appliances that use less energy and look for ways to use less energy with the appliances that you already have, such as using less hot water or altering your house to conserve heat.

L3 Apply Ask students to create a plan to conserve water and energy in the classroom. Write the plan on a posterboard and follow the plan. Students should first assess the appliances and water used in the classroom, and then come up with a plan to use less energy.

U Universal Access

Logical/Mathematical Learners Have logical/mathematical learners estimate how much energy is used in their home by looking at the energy usage of their appliances and how often they are used. Then have them create a chart detailing the energy use and determine the appliances that use the most energy.

 Professional Development **Mini Clip**
Math Unknowns in Equations

ASSESS

Quiz

Ask students to answer the following questions:

1. Which natural resources do we depend on for day-to-day living? Air, water, soil, and energy derived from coal, oil, and gas.

2. What are the three main causes of air pollution? Poisonous gases, such as car exhaust fumes; smoke from fireplaces, fires, barbecues, or burning leaves; and gardening and household or industrial chemicals.

3. Why is soil an important resource for humans? Plants get the nutrients they need from the soil, and people need the nutrients that plants provide in order to live.

RETEACH

R Reading Strategy

Understand Words in Context Have students look up the word *resource* in the dictionary and discuss its definitions. Discuss the ways that *natural resource* does and does not fit into each definition. Go through each definition and discuss how natural resources match or do not match. Have students give details about what characteristics make natural resources fit or not.

C Critical Thinking

Overcome Setbacks Ask students to imagine that their electric bill is very high. However, they do not have enough money to replace their appliances with more efficient ones. What can they do to save electricity and lower the bills? Answers might include going to sleep and waking up earlier to use natural light and doing activities that do not require electricity such as playing cards.

ASSESS

Section 14.1 Review Assign the Section 14.1 After You Read activities.

 Student Activity Workbook Assign the Section 14.1 Activities.

 Online Study Tools Have students go to the Online Learning Center at glencoe.com to:

- Take the Section 14.1 **Practice Test**.
- Download **Study-to-Go** content.

Section 14.1 After You Read

Answer Key

1. Human wastes, detergents, and chemicals.

2. Energy-efficient appliances offer guides that consumers can use to compare energy costs and savings per year.

3. Students should list how their family uses water, such as for drinking, bathing, cooking, garden care, and toilet flushing, and how they use energy, such as for gasoline, electricity, heating, and cooling. Students' plans will vary, but should include tips that would help their families conserve energy and water.

4. Lists will vary but may include such issues as rainforest destruction, endangered animals, global warming, recycling, hazardous wastes, and the use of oil and gas. Students' suggestions will vary. Sample answers: volunteer at a zoo or wildlife preserve to educate people about animals, recycle at home and school, or put litter where it belongs.

CLOSE

Culminating Activity

Become Energy Efficiency Ambassadors Have students research simple ways to save energy and come up with short demonstrations; then arrange to visit a local elementary school and promote energy efficiency to the elementary students. Students should come up with demonstrations that illustrate easy ways for younger children to save energy, such as turning off lights. The lesson should be written and presented in a manner that is appropriate for the age group.

Section 14.2 Lesson Plan

Protect the Environment

FOCUS

Discussion Starter

Discuss with students the things they do at home with their family to help protect the environment. Ask them to describe these measures. Students should describe anything their families do that is healthy for the environment and explain why the action helps, such as biking instead of driving.

Bell Ringer Activity

Environmental 20 Questions Have students choose one topic that involves environmental issues, such as pollution, global warming, or endangered species. Have them play twenty questions to see if they can guess their topic. At the end of each round, have students say what they know about the topic they chose to the class. You may wish to bring in small prizes.

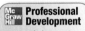

Mc Graw Hill **Professional Development** **Mini Clip**
ELL Elaborating on Student Responses

TEACH

S Skill Practice

Guided Practice

L1 **List** Divide students into groups to list three ways to reduce the amount of waste they create. Use both sides of paper; do not uses paper plates, avoid disposable products; or use cloth grocery bags.

L2 **Consult** Have students work in groups to consult about how recycling can reduce waste. Reuse materials for new purposes or give them away to someone else. These actions help keep the items out of landfills.

L3 **Apply** Encourage the class to choose a behavior change that is good for the environment and implement it. Have them discuss why they chose that change and how it helps the environment. Students should choose small changes they can easily implement, such as bringing lunch in reusable containers.

U Universal Access

Gifted Learners Have gifted students work together to create a proposal to make their school more environmentally-friendly. Ask them to consider building materials, waste, energy and water use, landscaping, and to include cost estimates.

ASSESS

Quiz

Ask students to answer the following questions:

1. List four natural resources. Air, water, soil, and the energy derived from coal, oil, and gas.

2. Name some ways that you can conserve water. Turn off the water when brushing teeth; take showers instead of baths; repair leaky faucets; run the washing machine only with a full load; change the level of water in the washing machine according to the load.

3. What is the definition of "pollution"? The changing of air, water, and land from clean and safe to dirty and unsafe.

RETEACH

W Writing Strategy

Recognize Environmental Impact Ask students to observe actions and situations at school that they think impact the environment, positively or negatively. Have them list the actions and situations and explain the environmental impact. Students should take note of things around the school that impact the environment, such as recycling, use of water, any sources of pollution, or the amount of greenery.

McGraw Hill **Professional Development** **Mini Clip**
Reading Bridging Cultural Gaps

C Critical Thinking

Make Smart Choices Students can make smart choices for the environment when choosing school supplies. Ask students to look at different school supplies and determine which items are more and less environmentally-friendly. Students should accurately assess the relative environmental impact of school supplies. For example, recycled paper is more environmentally-friendly than non-recycled paper. PVC and vinyl backpacks are less environmentally-friendly than bags made of natural fibers.

ASSESS

Section 14.2 Review Assign the Section 14.2 After You Read activities.

Student Activity Workbook Assign the Section 14.2 Activities.

Online Study Tools Have students go to the Online Learning Center at glencoe.com to:

- Take the Section 14.2 **Practice Test**.
- Download **Study-to-Go** content.

ExamView® Assessment Suite
Use the *ExamView Assessment Suite* **CD to create a test for this chapter.**

Chapter Review Have students complete the Chapter 14 Review and Applications.

Section 14.2 After You Read
Answer Key

1. Use air, water, land, and energy wisely; be energy-efficient at home; work with others to keep the environment clean.

2. When waste is burned, it can release poisonous smoke and contribute to air pollution

3. Throw away less paper; buy reusable products; pre-cycle; use cloth grocery bags; buy biodegradable products.

4. Letters will vary, but may include suggestions such as shop at thrift shops; reuse household items; and encourage family members to recycle. The efforts of all individuals, no matter how small, combine to make a big difference.

5. Answers will vary depending on the level of your school's involvement in a recycling program. Students should include their recommendations for improvement.

CLOSE

Culminating Activity

Environmental Awareness Day Have the students in the class put together an environmental awareness day, in which they will participate in activities designed to promote awareness to their fellow students. Make sure students get the appropriate permission from the school. Encourage them to be creative and entertaining in the activities they choose to make other members of the school more aware of environmental issues.

Words You Learned

1. Students should write a sentence using two or more of the vocabulary words. The sentence should show how the words are related.

Review Key Concepts

2. Air, water, soil, and energy must be protected for our health and our survival.

3. To save water: turn off water when brushing teeth; take showers instead of baths; run the washing machine and dishwasher only with a full load. To save energy: do not leave refrigerator door open; seal cracks around doors and windows; turn off lights.

4. Items are used only once, then thrown away.

5. Landfills take up huge amounts of space, and no one wants to live near one. When poisonous waste is incinerated, its smoke is dangerous.

6. Reduce, reuse, recycle.

Critical Thinking

7. Answers may include: save money; personal satisfaction knowing that you are doing your part; enjoyment of a clean and safe environment.

8. Paper products can be reduced; glass jars can be reused; cans, glass bottles, and plastic containers can be recycled. Kitchen scraps from food waste can be composted.

9. Washing a ceramic cup keeps non-biodegradable foam out of landfills, but it uses extra water. Foam cups add to landfills and do not break down, but using them can conserve water. Students' opinions on which is better will vary.

Real-World Skills and Applications

10. Remove litter; plant trees or wildflowers; remove graffiti; trim and maintain plants.

11. Deforestation is the removal of trees from an area of land. It occurs through fire, logging, cattle grazing, and when land is cleared for agriculture. Effects: animals and plants die because their homes are destroyed; rainfall that comes from rainforests is lessened which leads to drought; trees are no longer around to remove carbon dioxide from the air. Many experts believe that deforestation is a major contributor to global warming.

Financial Literacy

12. Answers will vary based on the students' consumption of drinks. Once they figure out the average for a week by multiplying the number of containers they consume by the appropriate state recycling rate, students should multiply that figure by 4 and 52 for the monthly and yearly totals.

Active Learning

13. Pressed flowers can be used for scrapbook decoration, greeting cards, wall hangings, gift bags, candle making, picture frames, lamp shades.

14. Nuclear fusion: energy is released when atoms are combined to form a larger atom. Nuclear fission: energy is released when atoms are split apart to form smaller atoms. Nuclear energy is cleaner because it does not produce air pollution or carbon dioxide.

Net Connection

15. Lists may include: paint, motor oil, turpentine, bleach, batteries, cleaning products. Tips may include: Do not store hazardous products in food containers; keep them in original containers and never remove labels; never mix leftover hazardous products together; follow product labels for use and disposal; learn about local drop-off programs.

Academic Skills

16. Articles should provide details about any relevant topic the student chooses. They should be written in a format that resembles a newspaper article, and should be well-organized and clearly-written.

17. Summaries will vary depending on interview results. Students should include details about how their family members viewed environmental concerns when they were younger, and how and why their attitudes have changed since then.

18. Vanessa could fill 16.2 two-liter soda bottles with the water that dripped. There are $3 \times 24 \times 60 = 4,320$ minutes in three days. There were 4,320 min. $\times$ 30 drips/min. = 129,600 drips during that period. Those drips could fill $129,600 \div 8,000 = 16.2$ soda bottles.

Standardized Test Practice

19. It can help you feel like you are making a difference, is good for the environment, and can help you save resources and money.

20. Products that can be broken down and absorbed by the environment.

21. They save costs and energy.

FOCUS

Introduce the Project

In this project, students will improve a room. Ask students how the space they live in affects them on a daily basis. Answers will vary, but may include how design, color and cleanliness affect their mood, how they use or waste energy, how they need more privacy, or how furniture layout prohibits easy movement.

Build Background

Dream Homes Ask students to imagine their dream home. What rooms would it have? Where would it be located? What features would they put in it? Write down ideas. Then discuss the impact students' imagined homes may have on their lives and on the world. Impact on life may be: expensive to buy or maintain, difficult to clean, too remote. Impact on world may be: uses a tremendous amount of electricity, water, gas, creates unnecessary waste.

TEACH

S Skill Practice

Guided Practice

L1 List Ask students to list three ways their home creates pollution or wastes natural resources. Have volunteers offer possible solutions. Lists will vary, but may include trash from food packaging, water use in home and garden, gas and oil burning for heat and cooking. Solutions may be to recycle, conserve water, and lowering thermostat.

L2 Describe Have students research and write a step-by-step instruction booklet about how to clean a bathroom. Instructions should be clear, concise, and easy-to-follow, and may include details about toilets, showers, floors, and mirrors. They should mention what types of cleaners and tools might be necessary.

L3 Apply Have students redesign the floor plan of the classroom. Ask them to take into consideration the way students interact with one another, the necessity of being able to see the teacher, and the classroom's traffic pattern. Rearrange the furniture, and critique the new layout. Redesign will vary, but may include creating staggered rows,

grouping chairs together for easier teamwork, or placing the teacher's desk in the center of the classroom.

C Critical Thinking

Kitchen Conservation Have students analyze the environmental impact of their kitchen. Ask them to record how much trash is created daily and list appliances that use water, gas, and electricity. What are three methods to conserve and reduce trash? Amount of trash created will vary, but appliances that use resources are sink, dishwasher, electric or gas stove or oven, light fixtures, trash compactor, and food processor. Methods to conserve include recycling, turning off lights, and turn water off between rinsing dishes.

ASSESS

Quiz

Ask students to answer the following questions:

1. What are some ways to organize space in your closet? Double up hanging space, add shelves, use floor space, hang hooks, use door to hang shoes, and store items in boxes or baskets.

2. What are the five elements of design you can use to create a desired look in a room? Space, shape, line, texture, and color.

3. What are some natural resources you use in your home, and why should we conserve them? Water, air, oil and gas. We should conserve them because they can be used up and no longer be available.

CLOSE

Culminating Activity

Take Two In this activity, students redesigned a room. Ask students to use the knowledge they have learned in this unit, and imagine they could start over and build the room from scratch with unlimited resources. Have them write a paragraph describing the features the new room would have. Answers will vary, but in addition to reorganization, students may now consider new elements such as amount of windows, doors, skylights, new furniture, carpeting, and appliances.

Clothing Choices

Unit Overview

This unit introduces students to clothing, focusing on students' personal styles, how they can better express themselves through their clothing choices, and how to select and care for high-quality clothing.

Chapter 15 *Your Fashion Statement* In this chapter, students will learn how to expand their wardrobes through accessorizing and evaluating what they already own. They will also be taught how color, line, and texture can make their wardrobe more flattering and flexible.

Chapter 16 *Clothing Basics* In this chapter, students will learn about making smart clothing choices when they shop, and they will also be introduced to the basics of clothing care which will help make their clothes last longer.

Life Skills Project Preview

Your Personal Style

Tell students that as part of this unit, they will discover how developing their own style is important for self-expression and confidence. They will learn how to explore and create their personal style, interview someone whose style they admire, and present a project to the class to share what they learned.

FCCLA provides programs to guide students through projects, enhance their personal growth, and build leadership skills that can make a difference in their lives, their families, and their communities.

Power of One helps students find and use their personal power. Members set their own goals, work to achieve them, and enjoy the results. The skills students learn help them now and in the future in school, with friends and family, at college, and on the job. Power of One focuses on improving personal traits, getting along better with family members, exploring work options, and developing leadership qualities.

A Family Festival Have students work together to plan a family festival for the community. For example, a spring carnival theme may have balloons, flowers, and bright colors. Students should develop ideas for activities, asking family members and other school groups to participate. Food classes may handle food booths. Members in child development classes could set up storytelling, face-painting, and other activities for young children. Students should work together to plan a family festival of some sort. They should focus on organizing the festival, being sure to include activities which will be enjoyable for the entire family and different age groups. This activity should help students develop their leadership and organizational skills, and it should also promote family bonding. Additionally, it should allow students to work on their teambuilding skills.

Professional Development

MINI CLIP VIDEO LIBRARY

Targeted professional development is correlated throughout *Discovering Life Skills*. **The McGraw-Hill Professional Development Mini Clip Video Library** provides teaching strategies to strengthen academic and learning skills. Log on to **glencoe.com**.

In this Unit, you will find these Mini Clips.

CHAPTER 15 Your Fashion Statement

READING
- **Focus Lesson** A teacher models how to find the main idea or theme of a selection by identifying the major and minor details. (p. TM154)
- **Flexible Groupings** Teachers use the strategies of flexible groupings and partner sharing to encourage and promote student discussions. (p. TM155)

ENGLISH LANGUAGE LEARNERS
- **Words in Action** Students act out or mime the words they are trying to learn. (p. TM154)
- **Using Manipulatives** A teacher uses concrete objects to illustrate lesson concepts. (p. TM156)

CHAPTER 16 Clothing Care Basics

READING
- **Obstacles to Achievement** Teachers work together to determine why their students are struggling with mastery of a particular standard. (p. TM160)
- **Building Vocabulary** A teacher introduces and plays two vocabulary building games with her students. (p. TM160)
- **Connecting the Pieces** A teacher helps students develop predictions and inferences about characters in a story. (p. TM161)

ENGLISH LANGUAGE LEARNERS
- **Graphic Organizers** Students use graphic organizers to distinguish between major and minor details in a reading selection. (p. TM159)
- **Strategies for English Learners** Author Jana Echevarria discusses strategies for teaching English learners. (p. TM161)

Your Fashion Statement

Section 15.1 Selecting Your Clothes

In this section, students will learn what to consider when making clothing choices. They will also learn how to assess their clothing needs. Finally, they will learn how to add accessories to their outfits.

Section 15.2 Color, Lines, and Texture

In this section, students will learn how to create a color scheme with their clothing. They will also learn how to take into account lines and appearance, as well as clothing texture when choosing clothing.

Classroom Solutions

Print Resources

 Student Edition
 Teacher Annotated Edition
Student Activity Workbook
 Student Activity Workbook
Teacher Annotated Edition

- Projects and Activities*
- Food Labs*
- Sewing Labs*
- Career Investigations*
- Reteaching Activities*
- Enrichment Activities*

Technology Resources

ExamView Assessment Suite *ExamView Assessment Suite CD* allows you to create and print out customized tests or ready-made unit and chapter tests, complete with answer keys.

Lesson Planner *Plus* *Lesson Planner Plus! CD** is and electronic lesson planner that provides instant access to teacher resources in one convenient package.

PRESENTATION *Plus!* *Presentation Plus!* PowerPoint™ Presentations can be edited and customized to meet the needs of students.

 Online Learning Center includes resources and activities for students and teachers. Also includes Online Student Edition.

○ Interactive Student Edition

*ELECTRONIC RESOURCES ARE AVAILABLE ON LESSON PLANNER PLUS AND THE ONLINE LEARNING CENTER.

Writing Activity Answer

Step-by-Step Guide Steps may begin with outfit selection, followed by personal grooming steps, shoe and accessory selection, and transportation arrangement. Steps should be easy-to-follow and ordered logically.

Discovering Careers Answers ▼

1. Answers will vary. Students should write a summary of the education, training, and experience needed for the selected careers.

2. Lists may include: old, comfortable clothes for doing housework; coveralls for working in the garage; rubber gloves for doing dishes; and a sun hat or visor for gardening.

3. Answers will vary. Sample answers: uniforms and workout wear for a professional ballplayer; suits or business casual for a corporate career; swimsuit for a lifeguard; lab coat for scientists; scrubs for nurses and doctors; and uniforms for firefighters and police officers.

4. Answers will vary. Students should present a summary of what they learned about the person's typical work day.

Chapter 15 Lesson Plan

Section 15.1 Lesson Plan

Selecting Your Clothes

FOCUS

Discussion Starter

Ask students to discuss how they choose what to wear each day. Do they have a certain process or do they choose at random? What types of factors do they consider? Students should detail their process for choosing clothing. If they have no process for choosing clothing, explain that this lesson will give them some guidance by offering them things to think about when selecting an outfit.

Bell Ringer Activity

What to Wear? Bring in pictures of clothing items for male and female teenagers. Propose scenarios, such as an interview, school, dinner party, or day at the beach. Ask students to choose clothing to make an outfit appropriate to the occasion. Students should choose outfits that are appropriate and explain why.

TEACH

S Skill Practice

Guided Practice

L1 List Divide students into small groups to list the reasons that people wear clothing. To protect themselves from the weather or from occupational hazards, to adorn themselves and express their creativity, to identify themselves as part of a group, to suggest modesty, or to show a person's status.

L2 Define Have students work in groups to define a fad and discuss how to handle fads when buying clothing. A fad is a fashion that is very popular for a short time. They are fun, but go out of style quickly. You should purchase fad items sparingly and spend more on classic items.

L3 Apply In pairs, have students describe three different events they will attend this week, choose an outfit for each, describe the outfit, and explain why they chose that outfit. Students should use their actual wardrobes to choose their outfits. The events can be ordinary, such as going shopping with friends, or special, such as a party.

U Universal Access

Kinesthetic Learners Have students work in groups to create and present skits on choosing clothes to buy in a store. Have some students play the salespeople and give advice, while the others play the customers and ask questions.

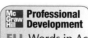
Professional Development **Mini Clip**
ELL Words in Action

ASSESS

Quiz

Ask students to answer the following questions:

1. How can you keep up with fashions without spending too much money? Alter clothes to change their style and get a fresh, new look.

2. What can you do with clothes that no longer fit so that they do not have to be thrown away? Alter the items so they fit or give them away to someone who will wear them.

3. What is the purpose of accessories? Accessories can give a well-worn outfit a new look, or draw attention to your best features or away from features you do not want to emphasize

RETEACH

R Reading Strategy

Make a List Have students make a list of people wearing clothing for protection, adornment, identification, modesty, and status. Ask students to explain why each is important. Students should list specific examples, such as an exterminator wearing a special suit for protection from chemicals, an actress wearing jewelry to complement a dress at an awards show, or someone in the military wearing insignia to show status.

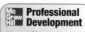
Professional Development **Mini Clip**
Reading Focus Lesson

C Critical Thinking

Categorize Clothing Ask students to inventory their closets and categorize their clothes into: wear often, never wear, do not fit, and need repair. Then have them make a plan for cleaning out their closets. Students should come up with a plan for the clothes they no longer wear or that do not fit them so that the clothes do not go to waste.

ASSESS

Section 15.1 Review Assign the Section 15.1 After You Read activities.

📁 **Student Activity Workbook** Assign the Section 15.1 Activities.

🔲 **Online Study Tools** Have students go to the Online Learning Center at glencoe.com to:

■ Take the Section 15.1 **Practice Test**.

■ Download **Study-to-Go** content. 📱

📖 **Section 15.1 After You Read**

Answer Key

1. Style is the design of a garment. Fashion is a style of clothing that is popular at a particular time.

2. Clothes that you wear often; clothes that do not fit; clothes that you never wear; clothes in need of repair.

3. Presentations will vary. Students should state their opinion and support it with logical details.

4. Posters will vary depending on the fad selected. Students should present one or more images of the fashion and include details about how it started, how people learned about it, and who was most influenced by it.

CLOSE

Culminating Activity

Express Yourself Bring in pictures of several different people wearing various types of outfits. Ask the students to discuss the personality traits that they believe each person has based on the outfits they are wearing. Students should come to realize through this exercise how much their clothing choices can project about them to the outside world. Encourage them to make wise clothing choices so that they present the image that they would like to.

 Section 15.2 Lesson Plan

Color, Lines, and Texture

FOCUS

Discussion Starter

Bring in pictures of styles from different decades. Ask students to identify the differences in the colors, texture, and lines and discuss how these contribute to the overall look. Students should notice changes in these aspects of fashion over the decades. For example, in the 1960s, A-lines were in fashion, while in the 1970s, peasant skirts were.

🔔 **Bell Ringer Activity**

Design an Outfit Bring in various papers and cloth trimmings of different textures. Ask students to design a simple outfit using the materials. Ask them to think about the shape of the clothing as well as the texture and color. Have each student show and describe his or her design to the class, and then display the designs.

Professional Development **Mini Clip**
Reading Flexible Groupings

TEACH

S **Skill Practice**

Independent Practice

L1 **List** Ask students to list and describe the different color schemes. Monochromatic: an outfit made of one hue; complementary: combines colors that are opposite each other on the color wheel; analogous: the colors have a common hue; and accented neutral: neutral colors with one other color as an accent.

L2 **Explain** Ask students to write a paragraph explaining how the lines of clothing can change the way you look. Vertical lines can make you look taller and thinner. Horizontal lines can make you look shorter and wider. Diagonal lines can do either, depending on the length and angle of the lines.

L3 **Apply** Ask students to visualize their favorite outfit and describe the colors, lines, and textures. Ask them to describe how they feel when wearing the outfit and why it is their favorite. Students should deconstruct their favorite outfit to figure out why it makes them feel comfortable or attractive.

U Universal Access

Musical Learners Play songs from a variety of musical styles, and ask students to describe what the person who performs that type of music wears. Have students write down their visions of the colors, textures, and lines of the clothing. Then ask them what made them choose the clothing they described.

ASSESS

Quiz

Ask students to answer the following questions:

1. What are the three basic hues and what are they called? Red, yellow, and blue. These are called primary colors because all other colors can be made from them.

2. How can colors affect your appearance? Light, warm, and bright colors can make you look larger. Dark, cool, and dull colors can make you look smaller.

3. How is texture created? Texture can be made heavy or light, rough or smooth, by choosing different yarns and weaves in making fabric.

RETEACH

W Writing Strategy

Conduct Research Ask students to choose one type of yarn and research it. In particular, ask them to describe the texture that can be created with that yarn. Some suggestions include boucle, loop yarn, or chenille. Students should write the results of their research. Students should describe the yarn and the texture it creates. For example, if they chose boucle, they might say that boucle is a yarn of three plies with one loose thread that gives it a rough feeling and bulky look.

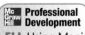
Mc Graw Hill **Professional Development** **Mini Clip**
ELL Using Manipulatives

C Critical Thinking

Analyze Ask students why it is important to consider lines, texture, and color when choosing clothing. What might be the result if they fail to consider these qualities before purchasing clothing? Failing to consider any of these qualities could result in a purchase that is unflattering. If you fail to consider texture, you might choose a texture that makes you look bulky or does not suit your climate, for example.

ASSESS

Section 15.2 Review Assign the Section 15.2 After You Read activities.

📁 **Student Activity Workbook** Assign the Section 15.2 Activities.

 Online Study Tools Have students go to the Online Learning Center at glencoe.com to:

■ Take the Section 15.2 **Practice Test**.
■ Download **Study-to-Go** content.

💿 *ExamView® Assessment Suite*
Use the *ExamView Assessment Suite* **CD to create a test for this chapter.**

📝 **Chapter Review** Have students complete the Chapter 15 Review and Applications.

📖 **Section 15.2 After You Read**
Answer Key

1. Primary: red, blue, and yellow. Secondary: violet, green, and orange.

2. Lines can be formed by the seams and waistlines of a garment, or they can be part of the fabric's design, such as stripes or plaids.

3. Texture is created by using different yarns and weaves in making fabric.

4. Answers will vary, but should include details about appropriate colors, flattering lines, and the use of texture to create a professional-looking outfit.

5. Answers will vary depending on culture chosen. Sample answer: in parts of Northern China, red is the color for the woman's wedding dress. Red is considered a powerful color that can keep away evil spirits and bring good luck.

CLOSE

Culminating Activity

Design with Texture Bring fabric swatches of different textures to class. Have the students look at and feel each and create ideas for an item of clothing made with that fabric. Have the class compare ideas. Students should be able to explain the reason behind their clothing ideas. This exercise should show the variety of clothing items that can be created with a fabric.

Chapter 15 Answer Key

Words You Learned

1. Students should create a true-false quiz based on the content and academic vocabulary words. Have them exchange quizzes with a classmate and complete.

Review Key Concepts

2. Protection, adornment, identification, modesty, status, family, friends, media, personal preferences.

3. Take a clothing inventory; add accessories; experiment with mixing and matching.

4. Colors can affect your mood, energy level, and appetite. Colors can be bright and cheerful, or quiet and peaceful.

5. Vertical lines can make you look taller and thinner; horizontal lines can make you look shorter and wider; diagonal lines can make you look taller and thinner or shorter and wider, depending on the length and angle of the lines.

6. Texture is the feel and appearance of the fabric's surface. Examples: wool, flannel, silk, satin, corduroy, denim, and tweed.

Critical Thinking

7. Answers will vary. Budget and values should be considered when making such a decision. Students should support their opinion with logical statements.

8. The appearance of others can affect the dining atmosphere. Nicely-dressed people may be annoyed that they took the time to dress up and others did not. However, people are allowed to wear any clothes that are acceptable to the restaurant.

9. People get tired of seeing the same color; celebrities, movies, or televisions shows may popularize a certain color; designers may promote "new" colors.

Real-World Skills and Applications

10. Try to find humor in the situation. Perhaps you can make a joke about missing the "rules." Next time, ask the host or other guests what they plan to wear. If you cannot find out ahead of time, choose an outfit somewhere in between dressy and casual.

11. Posters will vary. Celebrities and athletes wear inspirational clothing, but in some cases they promote certain designers, or even design clothing themselves. Many people like to be associated with celebrities, so they follow what celebrities wear. Movies and television shows can influence fashion trends because they reach a large audience.

Financial Literacy

12. Answers will vary based on the three companies selected. Students should understand that not every clothing company will have a publicly-traded stock available, but should pick three companies that do. They should use the Internet or a newspaper to determine a current share price for each company, and, if possible, make the comparison to the price one year ago.

Active Learning

13. Designs will vary. Students should present a design that represents their ideas about America.

14. Answers will vary. Students should determine the room's color scheme and offer ideas to adapt the existing colors to another scheme. For example, a room with an accented neutral scheme could become complementary by adding a color opposite the accent color.

Net Connection

15. Answers will vary depending on designer chosen. Students should summarize the designer's beginnings, inspirations, clothing creations, and the people who wear the clothes (for example, teens, celebrities, men, women, children).

Academic Skills

16. Lists of items will vary. Students may include influences such as friends, family, media, advertising, fashion trends, personal preferences, climate, a special occasion. Students may regret buying certain items because they are no longer in fashion, they did not fit properly, or the color did not look good on them.

17. Answers will vary depending on clothing and cultures selected. Answers should reflect an understanding of how cultural values can determine the style and function of clothing.

18. It would take Andrea a little less than $4\frac{1}{2}$ months to pay off her credit card ($250 − $35 = $215; $215 ÷ $25 = 8.6 payments. 8.6 ÷ 2 = 4.3 months.)

Standardized Test Practice

19. a

Chapter 15   Answer Key   **TM157**

Clothing Basics

Section 16.1 *Quality Clothing*

In this lesson, students will learn how to recognize quality fabrics. They will learn how to select the appropriate size. They will also learn how to prepare for clothes shopping.

Section 16.2 *Clothing Care Basics*

In this lesson, students will learn how to read care labels on clothing. They will also learn how to make the most of their clothing budget and how to properly clean clothes.

Classroom Solutions

Print Resources

 Student Edition
Teacher Annotated Edition
Student Activity Workbook
Student Activity Workbook
Teacher Annotated Edition

- Projects and Activities*
- Food Labs*
- Sewing Labs*
- Career Investigations*
- Reteaching Activities*
- Enrichment Activities*

Technology Resources

ExamView *ExamView Assessment Suite CD* allows you to create and print out customized tests or ready-made unit and chapter tests, complete with answer keys.

Lesson Planner *Plus* *Lesson Planner Plus! CD** is and electronic lesson planner that provides instant access to teacher resources in one convenient package.

Presentation Plus! PowerPoint™ Presentations can be edited and customized to meet the needs of students.

 Online Learning Center includes resources and activities for students and teachers. Also includes Online Student Edition.

Interactive Student Edition

*ELECTRONIC RESOURCES ARE AVAILABLE ON LESSON PLANNER PLUS AND THE ONLINE LEARNING CENTER.

Writing Activity Answer

Character Analysis Character analyses should describe his or her words and actions and the reactions of others. Supporting details should show an understanding of the concept of diligence. Sample answer: "My sister talks about getting value for her money. She shops for clothes at thrift stores and hunts for bargains. People think she is smart for shopping wisely."

Discovering Careers Answers ▼

1. Answers will vary. Students should write a summary of the education, training, and experience needed for the selected careers.

2. Dry clean, hand-wash, machine wash, no bleach, delicate cycle, dry flat, cool iron, drip dry.

3. Likely stains: fruit juice, perspiration. Stain removal: check the uniform label for any specific instructions. Fruit juice: soak in cold water, pre-treat remaining stain, wash; perspiration: use a pre-wash stain remover, sponge ammonia, or white vinegar, then rub detergent into stain and wash with the hottest water safe for fabric.

4. Answers will vary. Students should present a summary of what they learned about the person's typical work day.

Section **16.1** Lesson Plan

Quality Clothing

FOCUS

Discussion Starter

Ask students to name and describe the fabrics they know and describe the relative quality of each fabric. Explain that in this chapter, they will learn more about fabrics to help them choose clothes of high quality. Students should list fabrics they are familiar with, such as denim, corduroy, flannel, silk, and satin. They should have an idea of the relative quality of the fabrics based on which fabrics they are.

 Bell Ringer Activity

Experience Fabrics Bring in swatches or clothing items made of several different fabrics of different qualities. Have students look at and feel each fabric. Discuss the differences in looks and texture of each and what causes those differences. Give students the relative price of each fabric or items made with each fabric. Have students discuss their ideas about what characteristics are indicators of higher and lower quality fabrics.

McGraw Hill **Professional Development** **Mini Clip**
ELL Graphic Organizers

TEACH

S **Skill Practice**

Independent Practice

L1 **List** Ask students to list the features they would check to make sure that clothing fits comfortably. Whether sleeves are the right length and not too tight, if the neck opening is the right size, shoulder seams, fasteners that lie smoothly, waistband and hips are comfortable, and hemline is the right length.

L2 **Describe** Ask students to write a paragraph describing how to choose clothing that is the correct size for them. Try on various sizes until you find one that feels comfortable. Look in a full-length mirror from the front and back. Sit, bend, walk, and reach while wearing the garment to make sure it feels comfortable as you move around.

L3 **Apply** Have students imagine that they are about to shop for the new school year. Have them create a shopping plan. Students should create a plan that includes a reasonable clothing budget, a purchase plan that fits the budget, and a list of stores and items to look for.

U **Universal Access**

Visual/Spatial Learners Have visual learners prepare a poster illustrating quality fabrics, the proper fit for clothes, or an example shopping plan. Place the displays on the wall, and ask students to explain theirs to the class.

ASSESS

Quiz

Ask students to answer the following questions:

1. What are the two types of fibers that clothing is made from? Natural fibers, made from plant and animal products, and synthetic fibers, manufactured from substances such as wood pulp and petroleum.

2. What are the different types of sizes for girls' and women's clothing? Female clothing is sold in girls', juniors', misses', women's, and plus sizes. Each size level is increasingly larger.

3. What is a shopping plan? A strategy, or way to prepare, for spending the money you have to buy the clothing you need or want.

RETEACH

R **Reading Strategy**

Conduct Research Have students choose a type of fabric and research information on that fabric, such as how it is made, whether it is natural or synthetic, and the relative cost and quality. Ask students to share their findings. Students should choose a type of fabric and read about that fabric. They should present the information they learned clearly and with a logical organization.

C **Critical Thinking**

Quality vs. Quantity Explain to students that quality clothing is generally more expensive than clothing of lesser quality. Ask them to discuss the pros and cons of purchasing fewer items of higher quality or more items of lesser quality. Quality clothing is more durable, and will keep its looks longer. Lesser quality clothing will not be wearable for as long. In the long run, spending more on a few quality items may save you money since you will not have to keep replacing clothes.

ASSESS

Section 16.1 Review Assign the Section 16.1 After You Read activities.

 Student Activity Workbook Assign the Section 16.1 Activities.

Online Study Tools Have students go to the Online Learning Center at glencoe.com to:

- Take the Section 16.1 **Practice Test**.
- Download **Study-to-Go** content.

Section 16.1 After You Read

Answer Key

1. Plain, twill, and satin.

2. Look in a full-length mirror from the front and back. Sit, bend, walk, and reach while wearing the garment to make sure it feels comfortable as you move around.

3. Parents can help you determine how much money should be used to buy the clothes you need, as well as how much money you can spend for items you want.

4. Illustrations should include information about how to check for comfort and fit at the neck, wrists, shoulders, hips, and waist. Students should include how fasteners work and how to check for the comfort and fit of shoes

5. Answers may include: antibacterial or antiseptic finishes to reduce or prevent germ growth; antistatic finishes to reduce static electricity; water- and stain-repellant finishes to keep clothes drier and cleaner; waterproof finishes; wrinkle-resistant finishes to reduce or eliminate the need for ironing.

CLOSE

Culminating Activity

Plan a Basic Wardrobe Ask students to imagine they must build a wardrobe for themselves of only ten items. Have them look on the Internet or in catalogs and choose the ten items that would make up their wardrobe. Students should choose items of good quality, that they can mix and match and make multiple uses of, since they will have a limited wardrobe. Each item of clothing should go with several of the others.

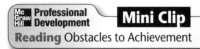

McGraw Hill **Professional Development** **Mini Clip**
Reading Obstacles to Achievement

Section 16.2 Lesson Plan

Clothing Care Basics

FOCUS

Discussion Starter

Ask students if they are responsible for caring for their own clothes or if someone else does it for them. Encourage them to take a more active role in caring for their clothes. Some students will care for their own clothes, while some will not. Encourage the students who care for their own clothes to discuss what they do to care for their clothes.

McGraw Hill **Professional Development** **Mini Clip**
Reading Building Vocabulary

Bell Ringer Activity

Sort the Laundry Bring in examples of different clothing labels, both more-detailed and less-detailed. Go over them with the students, and as a class, decipher each one to determine the laundry regimen. Ask students to imagine that these items are their laundry for the week. How would they sort and handle all of the clothes? Students should correctly sort the clothes according to their labels.

TEACH

S Skill Practice

Independent Practice

L1 List Ask students to make a list of the information to look for on a garment label. The fiber content, the correct way to clean the garment, a no bleach warning, a no ironing label, and whether the garment is colorfast.

L2 Suggest Ask students to write a paragraph suggesting how someone can save money by caring for his or her clothes. Wear clothing that is suitable for the activity, dress and undress carefully, inspect clothes carefully after wearing, make repairs, and treat any stains as necessary.

L3 Apply Have students revisit the shopping plan they created in the previous lesson. Ask them to review the budget section in light of the new information they learned in this section and revise their plan accordingly. Students should revise the plan to include things like sales or accessories to help them make the most of their wardrobe budget.

U Universal Access

Bodily/Kinesthetic Learners Have students demonstrate the process of sorting, washing, drying, and folding laundry. Set up two desks, and label them as washer and dryer. Have objects represent detergent, bleach, fabric softener, and stain remover.

ASSESS

Quiz

Ask students to answer the following questions:

1. Why should you check clothing care labels before you buy an item of clothing? It helps you determine the quality, durability, and care of garments, which saves time and money.

2. How can learning how to sew help you with your clothing budget? Making simple clothing items can save money. If you know how to make simple repairs, your clothes last longer.

3. What is the first step in doing the laundry? Pre-treat stains, sleeve cuffs, and the fold line on collars.

RETEACH

W Writing Strategy

Conduct Research Have the students research clothing construction to determine what to look for. Ask them to write a one-page report on good clothing construction and what they would look for when choosing well-constructed clothes. In general, clothes should retain functionality, be durable, and construction details should be inconspicuous. Students might also find information on buttons, collars, darts, gathers, hems, lining, and pockets.

C Critical Thinking

Draw Conclusions Discuss with the class what might happen if each step of the laundering procedure is not followed. If stains are not pre-treated, they could become permanent. If clothes are not sorted, they could get discolored. If the wrong temperature is used, clothes could shrink. If you do not use the correct load size, you might overload. If you use an incorrect amount of detergent, clothes may not get clean. If you do not use fabric softener, you will get static cling.

Professional Development Mini Clip
Reading Connecting the Pieces

ASSESS

Section 16.2 Review Assign the Section 16.2 After You Read activities.

 Student Activity Workbook Assign the Section 16.2 Activities.

Online Study Tools Have students go to the Online Learning Center at glencoe.com to:

- Take the Section 16.2 **Practice Test**.
- Download **Study-to-Go** content.

ExamView® Assessment Suite
Use the *ExamView Assessment Suite* CD to create a test for this chapter.

Chapter Review Have students complete the Chapter 16 Review and Applications.

Section 16.2 After You Read

Answer Key

1. To help you determine the quality, durability, and care of garments.

2. Wear appropriate clothing for the activity; dress and undress carefully; inspect your clothes for rips or stains after each wearing.

3. Line-drying saves energy and money but takes longer. Machine-drying is quick and convenient, but it uses energy and therefore costs more.

4. Answers will vary depending on clothing selected. Students should include how they would sort, clean, dry, press, and store each item according to the instructions.

5. Wearing used clothing has become more acceptable and even fashionable when it is labeled "vintage clothing." The rising interest in used clothing may also be due to awareness of environmental issues and the need to save money.

CLOSE

Culminating Activity

Laundry Game Bring in several clothing items or photocopied labels, and set up baskets labeled: Whites, Brights, Lights, Darks, Handwash, and Dry Clean. Have the students work in teams to sort the laundry items, and see who can correctly sort their items the fastest.

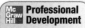
Professional Development Mini Clip
ELL Strategies for English Learners

Words You Learned

1. Students should arrange the vocabulary words into groups of related words and explain why they grouped the words together.

Review Key Concepts

2. Fiber type, grain, and finish.

3. Fit, fabric, and style.

4. Check your budget, make a purchase plan, and evaluate your shopping options.

5. Labels provide information about the clothing quality, durability, fiber content, where it was made, and how to care for it.

6. Start with two or three classic styles and colors; make the best use of what you have; take good care of your clothes; compare cost and quality; take advantage of sales; learn to sew

7. Pre-treat stains; sort clothes before washing; use the correct water temperature; choose the correct load size; use the correct amount of detergent; use a fabric softener.

Critical Thinking

8. Compare the fabric to a similar item that has care instructions; hand-wash to be safe; ask a dry cleaner for advice.

9. Consumers might think designer clothes are better because of the high price, but this may not be true. Other shoppers might believe they are the same quality but cost more simply because of the designer name.

Real-World Skills and Applications

10. Ask her: What is your budget? Does the outfit cost the entire amount? How do you plan to pay for the outfit? What do you have at home that you could use? Are there less expensive places to shop?

11. Presentations will vary, but students should include details about checking for quality fabric and construction, choosing the right size, checking for comfort and flattering style, making a shopping plan, stretching their budget, and properly caring for clothes.

Financial Literacy

12. Answers will vary depending on the options selected, which can include outlet stores, discount stores, warehouse (club) stores, Internet sites, thrift stores, and garage sales. The pros for each one should include lower prices, while cons might include limited selection, outdated styles, poor clothing condition, or, in the case of the Internet, potential fraud.

Active Learning

13. Collages will vary. Students should choose items that coordinate with what they already have.

14. Charts may include: Rayon—absorbent, soft, comfortable, drapes easily, wrinkles and shrinks easily, may require dry cleaning; suitable for dresses, skirts, shirts. Polyester—resists wrinkles and shrinking but not absorbent, washable and fast-drying but attracts oily stains; suitable for pants and suits. Nylon—strong, lightweight, holds shape, washable and fast-drying but sensitive to heat; suitable for hosiery. Acrylic—soft, warm, resists wrinkling; suitable for most types of casual clothing. Acetate—looks like silk, may wrinkle and fade, may require dry cleaning; suitable for scarves. Spandex—elastic, stretchy fiber usually combined with other fibers; suitable for bathing suits and exercise wear.

Net Connection

15. Lists may include fabrics that are waterproof, insect resistant, mold and mildew resistant, extra thin but strong for swimmers and runners, soil and stain resistant. Students may also find information about fabrics used to make protective gear for medical professionals and for people who work in hazardous conditions.

Academic Skills

16. Descriptions will vary, but students should submit a description that follows the general format of a catalog entry.

17. Students should present a list of ingredients and label descriptions from an environmentally-friendly brand of laundry detergent. Product may claim to use only natural ingredients, work in cold water, and be gentle on fabrics. Summaries will vary depending on the results of the experiment.

18. Rewriting 25% as a fraction results in 25/100, or ¼. ¼ × $320 = $320/4, or $80. The original deposit will be $80, and all subsequent payments (including the service charge) will be $85.

Standardized Test Practice

19. T
20. F
21. T

FOCUS

Introduce the Project

In this project, students will explore their personal style. Ask students how their clothing choices reflect their personalities. Answers will vary, but may include their desire to express individuality, the need to fit in, or their desire to make a personal statement about what they enjoy, such as sports, music, or other activities.

Build Background

Celebrity Style Ask students to name celebrities whose fashion style makes a strong statement. Then ask what the clothing and grooming choices made by these celebrities suggest about their personalities. Write the personality traits next to the name. Discuss what conclusions might be drawn about personality based on how one dresses. Traits may be positive or negative, and may include confident, proud, elegant, modest, laid-back, sporty, arrogant, or vain.

TEACH

S Skill Practice

Guided Practice

L1 List Ask students to make a list of their five favorite clothing items or accessories. Have volunteers tell the class why the items are their favorites. Lists will vary, but may say that the clothes are stylish, make them feel confident, are comfortable, go with other items in their closets, or hold up to wear and tear.

L2 Explain Have students write a two-paragraph article for the school newspaper about making sensible clothing decisions. Articles should include a lead that summarizes the main idea, supporting details, and helpful tips for making wise clothing choices.

L3 Imagine Tell students to imagine they work in a department store as a Personal Shopper. A client is starting a job as a legal assistant. He wants to make a good impression and appear professional, but he also wants to express his personality. Have students write a scenario in which they make suggestions to the client for his new wardrobe. Scenarios will vary, but answers should show that students considered the client's age, interests, goals, and personal style.

C Critical Thinking

Where Do You Shop? Have students take a survey of friends, classmates, and relatives, asking where they shop for clothes and why. Ask students to consider age, gender, and income to predict results. Analyses will vary depending on survey results. For example, students may find that many of their peers shop at trendy stores because they want to fit in or that their parents shop at discount stores because they want to save money.

ASSESS

Quiz

Ask students to answer the following questions:

1. What can you wear other than clothing to express your style? Shoes, jewelry, cosmetics, hats, eyeglasses, hair accessories, and scarves.

2. Why is it important to develop your own style? Creating your own look helps you express yourself and look your best. Looking your best helps you feel confident.

3. Is it better to spend more of your clothing budget on classic styles or fads? Fads can be fun, but it is better to invest more of your clothing money in classic styles because they will last longer and are more versatile.

CLOSE

Culminating Activity

Project Assessment In this activity, students identified and interviewed someone whose style they admire. Have students write a paragraph comparing and contrasting the person they interviewed with someone whose style is completely different. Answers will vary, but students should consider clothing styles, accessory choices, colors, and the personal traits reflected by the differing styles.

Prepare to Sew
Unit Overview

This unit introduces students to the basics of starting a sewing project. Students will learn how to choose and plan a sewing project, prepare materials, and use equipment to complete a sewing project.

Chapter 17 *Plan Sewing Projects* In this chapter, students will learn how to operate a sewing machine and what to look for when choosing a sewing project. They will also learn how to select appropriate patterns, notions, and fabrics.

Chapter 18 *Learn How to Sew* In this chapter, students prepare fabric and patterns and start sewing. They will learn about hand-sewing techniques, basic machine sewing, and how to make basic repairs and alternations

---

Life Skills Project Preview

Design Your Own Clothing

Tell students that as part of this unit, they will learn that sewing is a life skill that they can use to be creative. They will learn how to design something to wear, interview someone who sews as part of his or her job, and present their clothing design pattern to the class to share what they have learned.

FCCLA provides programs to guide students through projects, enhance their personal growth, and build leadership skills that can make a difference in their lives, their families, and their communities.

STAR Events (Students Taking Action with Recognition) are competitive events in which members are recognized for proficiency and achievement in chapter and individual projects, leadership skills, and career preparation. STAR Events offer individual skill development and application of learning through cooperative work, individualized work, and competition.

Fresh Fashion Divide students into small groups and have them think about current fashion trends for their age group. Working together, have them design a new fashion item, either a piece of clothing or an accessory. They should provide a detailed sketch, a list of materials required, and a description of how the item would be created. They should also be very clear about why this new item would appeal to teens and how it fits in or moves beyond current fashion trends. Teams should prepare a presentation to do in front of the rest of class. Students should think carefully about current fashion trends, and, working together, come up with a new fashion item, along with a sketch of the item, a list of materials, a description of how the item will be put together, and why the item will appeal to teens. Students should present their idea to the rest of the class. You may want to judge or have the students judge and pick a winner and a runner-up.

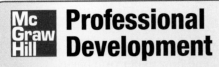

Professional Development

MINI CLIP VIDEO LIBRARY

Targeted professional development is correlated throughout *Discovering Life Skills.* **The McGraw-Hill Professional Development Mini Clip Video Library** provides teaching strategies to strengthen academic and learning skills. Log on to **glencoe.com**.

In this Unit, you will find these Mini Clips.

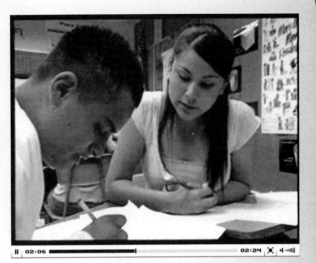

CHAPTER 17 Plan Sewing Projects

READING
- **Lesson Reflections** A narrator discusses various instructional strategies suitable for use with English learners. (p. TM167)
- **Building Vocabulary** A teacher introduces and plays two vocabulary building games with her students. (p. TM168)

ENGLISH LANGUAGE LEARNERS
- **Reading Aloud** A teacher reads aloud, modeling fluency, pronunciation, expression, and comprehension strategies. (p. TM167)
- **Previewing a Text** A teacher previews a text with students, pointing out features and strategies that will promote student comprehension. (p. TM169)

CHAPTER 18 Learn How to Sew

READING
- **Strategic Readers** Author Scott Paris discusses the characteristics of strategic readers. (p. TM173)

ENGLISH LANGUAGE LEARNERS
- **Content Vocabulary** A teacher provides students with opportunities to practice their academic vocabulary. (p. TM172)
- **Providing Clear Directions** A teacher provides clear written and oral directions for a classroom assignment and checks for student understanding. (p. TM174)

MATH
- **Real-Life Connection—Proportion** A teacher introduces and models scale factors and similar figures using real-life examples. (p. TM172)

Plan Sewing Projects

Section 17.1 *Sewing Machine Basics*

In this section, students will learn how to operate a sewing machine. They will learn about the machine's basic functions by looking at the operating manual and how to perform basic stitches.

Section 17.2 *Patterns, Fabrics, and Notions*

In this section, students will learn how to select a pattern for a sewing project. They will also learn how to select an appropriate fabric, as well as how to select appropriate notions.

Classroom Solutions

Print Resources

 Student Edition
 Teacher Annotated Edition
 Student Activity Workbook
 Student Activity Workbook
Teacher Annotated Edition

Technology Resources

ExamView *Assessment Suite* **ExamView Assessment Suite CD** allows you to create and print out customized tests or ready-made unit and chapter tests, complete with answer keys.

Lesson Planner *Plus* **Lesson Planner Plus! CD*** is and electronic lesson planner that provides instant access to teacher resources in one convenient package.

- Projects and Activities*
- Food Labs*
- Sewing Labs*
- Career Investigations*
- Reteaching Activities*
- Enrichment Activities*

PRESENTATION *Plus!* **Presentation Plus!** PowerPoint™ Presentations can be edited and customized to meet the needs of students.

Online Learning Center includes resources and activities for students and teachers. Also includes Online Student Edition.

Interactive Student Edition

*ELECTRONIC RESOURCES ARE AVAILABLE ON LESSON PLANNER PLUS AND THE ONLINE LEARNING CENTER.

Writing Activity Answer

"How To" Paper Papers should include an introduction; a list of materials such as thread, needle, scissors, button, sewing machine, pins; a list of detailed steps in the correct order; transition words that guide the reader from step to step; and a conclusion.

Discovering Careers Answers ▼

1. Answers will vary. Students should write a summary of the education, training, and experience needed for the selected careers.
2. Answers may include missing or loose buttons, torn hems, broken zippers, or rips and tears. Students should suggest hand-stitching or machine sewing techniques to fix the repairs on their lists.
3. Lists may include office furniture upholstery, curtains, work uniforms and aprons, and cleaning towels.
4. Answers will vary. Students should present a summary of what they learned about the person's typical work day.

Plan Sewing Projects

FOCUS

Discussion Starter

Ask students if any of them have ever sewn before. If any of them have, ask them to describe the project and how they made it. If they have not, discuss what they would like to make if they could sew something for themselves. Discussing former projects can help students new to sewing become more familiar with it, while discussing imagined projects can help get them enthusiastic.

Bell Ringer Activity

Demonstrate Stitches Demonstrate the use of a sewing machine by making basic stitches on a piece of fabric. Have the students watch as you make the stitches and explain how you prepared and operated the sewing machine. Then have volunteers practice making stitches as you guide them.

TEACH

S Skill Practice

Independent Practice

L1 List Ask students to list the safety rules for using supplies and equipment in the sewing lab. Keep fingers away from the path of the needle; do not use the machine if it is jammed or making an unusual noise; do not hold pins or needles in your mouth; and keep scissors closed when not in use.

L2 Explain Ask students to write a paragraph explaining how to make a hem. Turn the raw edge of fabric to the inside of the garment and stitch it in place. Students should summarize the instructions on page 376.

L3 Apply Have students practice making hems by following the instructions given in the section. Evaluate their work. Students should each make at least one practice hem. Evaluate the hems and point out what they did well and what still needs improvement. Encourage them to practice once more if there is time, incorporating the advice from the evaluation.

U Universal Access

Verbal/Linguistic Learning Have verbal learners look at the operating manual for the sewing machines available to the class and see if they can figure out how to use the machine from reading the instructions. Answer any questions, and then have them practice with the machine.

ASSESS

Quiz

Ask students to answer the following questions:

1. How does a sewing machine operate? A needle moves up and down through the fabric, and two sets of threads interlock to form closely fitted stitches.

2. What is the most common way to make a hem? Turn the raw, or unfinished, edge of fabric to the inside of the garment and stitch it in place.

3. What are the different ways that you can finish the raw edge of a hem? The raw edge can be pinked, zigzag stitched, edgestitched, or overlapped with hem tape.

RETEACH

R Reading Strategy

Types of Stitches Have students look up different types of stitches and choose one type to read about. Then ask them to describe the stitch, what it is used for, what it looks like, and any history attached to it. Have them write short descriptions and share them with the class. There are several different stitches to choose from, including basting stitch, blanket stitch, zig-zag stitch, buttonhole stitch, embroidery stitch, or running stitch.

C Critical Thinking

Evaluate Information Bring in operating manuals for sewing machines and have students review the safety warnings and precautions. Discuss why these warnings are there, and ask about what kind of things could happen if the warnings are not followed. Common safety warnings include keeping your hand away from the needle, keeping safety guards on, always turning off and unplugging the machine when not in use. Various injuries could occur if these safety precautions are not observed.

ASSESS

Section 17.1 Review Assign the Section 17.1 After You Read activities.

 Student Activity Workbook Assign the Section 17.1 Activities.

Online Study Tools Have students go to the Online Learning Center at glencoe.com to:

- Take the Section 17.1 **Practice Test**.
- Download **Study-to-Go** content.

Section 17.1 After You Read

Answer Key

1. Organization, preparation, and consideration.

2. Keep the stitches loose so that the hemline does not pucker.

3. Answers will vary depending on projects selected. Students should recognize that the advanced project requires skill, experience, and knowledge of sewing terms that a beginner would not yet know.

4. Summaries will vary depending on time period selected. Answers should include details about the materials and techniques used for making or obtaining clothing. Students may wish to focus on a certain group of people.

CLOSE

Culminating Activity

Choose an Activity Have students research a simple sewing project, such as a pillowcase, curtain, or bag. Have them obtain the instructions and attempt to make the item they have chosen using a sewing machine. If students are less experienced with a sewing machine, you may want to have them work in small groups. Students should put what they learned in the chapter to practice by using the sewing machine to create a simple item.

Section 17.2 Lesson Plan

Patterns, Fabrics, and Notions

FOCUS

Discussion Starter

Have students look over the chapter headings and discuss what they know about each. Have students that know something about a topic discuss what they know. Have the other students write down questions. If all students are unfamiliar with a certain topic, ask them to write down what they would like to learn.

Reading Building Vocabulary

 Bell Ringer Activity

Choose a Pattern Bring in different patterns for the class to look at. Ask them to imagine that they are choosing a sewing project. Which pattern would they choose? Have students explain why they made the choice they did. Explain that in this lesson, they will learn about choosing patterns.

TEACH

S Skill Practice

Independent Practice

L1 List Ask students to list the things you should consider when choosing a pattern. The purpose of the project, your sewing skills and experience, whether you have enough time, and how much money you have to spend.

L2 Descibe Ask students to write a paragraph describing what information they can find on the pattern envelope. A drawing of the pattern pieces and construction features, a chart of how much fabric to buy, recommendations for fabric type, additional materials needed, and a picture of the completed project.

L3 Apply Ask students to imagine they are choosing a pattern for their first sewing project. What should they consider while choosing? Students should look for patterns with fewer pieces, fewer seams, looser fits, and elastic waists.

U Universal Access

Students with Visual Impairments Discuss challenges faced by people with visual impairments doing a sewing project. Brainstorm possible solutions. For example, they may need a friend to read pattern envelopes to them.

ASSESS

Quiz

Ask students to answer the following questions:

1. **What items does a pattern contain?** A pattern contains paper shapes of the various pieces and instructions for sewing.

2. **What should you evaluate when choosing a quality fabric?** The fiber content, how the fabric is made, any finishes that have been added, and the quality of the fabric grain.

3. **What are notions?** The small items that become a permanent part of the finished product, such as thread, fasteners, elastic, decorative trim, and interfacing.

RETEACH

R Reading Strategy

Provide Examples Bring out your sample pattern envelopes and ask students to look at five of them and then list examples of fabrics that could be used to create each project. Ask them to list the fabric type and the reason it is appropriate with that pattern. Students should list appropriate fabrics and explain how they fit with their experience, the intended use of the item, and what type of care is needed for the fabric.

Mc Graw Hill **Professional Development** **Mini Clip**
ELL Previewing a Text

C Critical Thinking

Make Connections Ask students to discuss how details like the notions can change the overall look and construction of a garment. Ask them how notions affect the final outcome of a project and why choosing notions is an important part of planning a project. Notions can cause an otherwise well-crafted product to appear sloppy or poorly-constructed, if they are not chosen with care. For example, the wrong color thread will stand out and clash with the fabric.

ASSESS

Section 17.2 Review Assign the Section 17.2 After You Read activities.

 Student Activity Workbook Assign the Section 17.2 Activities.

Online Study Tools Have students go to the Online Learning Center at glencoe.com to:

- Take the Section 17.2 **Practice Test**.
- Download **Study-to-Go** content.

ExamView® Assessment Suite
Use the *ExamView Assessment Suite* **CD to create a test for this chapter.**

Chapter Review Have students complete the Chapter 17 Review and Applications.

Section 17.2 After You Read

Answer Key

1. Number of pattern pieces, number of seams, garment fit, and closures.

2. Crosswise threads, pattern, weave, color, finish, and label.

3. It is strong and smooth, has even thickness, and resists tangling.

4. Answers will vary depending on the outfit selected. Students should have an accurate list of fabric, equipment, tools, and notions needed for their particular project. They should present the information as a "How To" report with detailed and logical steps.

5. Samples may include any fabric that is unique to or typical of certain cultures, such as Guatemalan weavings used for blankets, Chinese or Indian silk used for clothing or home furnishings, or Indonesian batiks used for quilting.

CLOSE

Culminating Activity

Plan a Project. Have students imagine that they are going to create a sewing project. Have them choose a pattern, fabrics, and notions. Then have them write down their plan and explain the reasons behind their choices. Students should choose a pattern and all of the fabrics and notions necessary to complete the design. They should give logical reasons for their choices, using the factors given in the section.

Words You Learned

1. Students should create multiple-choice test questions using each of the content vocabulary words and academic vocabulary words.

Review Key Concepts

2. A needle moves up and down through the fabric, and two sets of threads interlock to form closely fitted stitches.

3. A hem is an edge made by folding fabric over and stitching it down.

4. Purpose, sewing skills and experience, time, and cost.

5. Evaluate your sewing experience, who will use the item, when the item will be used, how the item will be used, and the type of care needed.

6. Thread, fasteners (snaps, zippers, buttons, buckles, and hook-and-eye closures), tapes and trims, elastic, linings, and interfacings.

Critical Thinking

7. Christa might be assuming that her clothes will never need to be repaired or that she will never want to make her own clothes. She may assume someone else will do it for her. Students may tell Christa about the value of knowing how to sew, hem, and make repairs.

8. Consequences may include: a garment that does not fit well, has puckered seams, does not hang correctly, or shrinks when washed; wasted time and money; lost interest in sewing because of poor results.

9. Shorten the length of sleeves, pants legs, or skirt; change the buttons; add decorative trims.

Real-World Skills and Applications

10. Answers will vary depending in patterns selected, but may include step-by-step directions, illustrations, a basic style, and limited notions.

11. Information should include a description of the project, when it will be worked on, who will be assigned to each task, how long the tasks are expected to take, a back-up plan for absent students, and a list of supplies and resources.

Financial Literacy

12. Students should present their information in a spreadsheet or worksheet that shows the categories and prices gathered from their research. Summaries should include an explanation of which is the better value. Answers regarding the value may vary depending on students' opinions and research, but they should be able to present logical reasoning.

Active Learning

13. Students should create an attractive arrangement of fabric samples with brief descriptions.

14. Presentations should include details about the types of fabric commonly used for curtains, upholstery, pillows, tapestries, and other home decorating projects. Students will probably notice that these fabrics are stronger, thicker, and more textured than the fabrics used for clothing.

Net Connection

15. Students should find a project that they can learn to do in the future and list the supplies they would need to complete it. They should also list any skills they would need to learn.

Academic Skills

16. Journal entries will vary. Students should describe their personal style and goals they have for sewing projects that would reflect their style.

17. Answers will vary depending on the function selected. Sample answer: Adding embroidery is not necessary, but it enhances the look of the product. Computerized embroidery may eliminate the need for some creativity, but you can still choose what kind of design and colors you want. Computerized functions can give the appearance of higher quality by making the product more professional-looking.

18. The rounded dollar amounts are $7, $11, $3, $3, and $8, for a total of $32.

Standardized Test Practice

19. a

Learn How to Sew

Section 18.1 *Fabric and Pattern Preparation*

Sewing is a fun and practical activity that can help expand and preserve your wardrobe. This section emphasizes the importance of planning and preparation to avoid mistakes during a sewing project. Students will learn how to preparing fabric and how to use a pattern.

Section 18.2 *Sewing and Serging Basics*

This section introduces students to ten basic sewing techniques and provides an overview of serger and sewing machine functions. Students will learn techniques to help them add a professional look to their sewing projects.

Classroom Solutions

Print Resources

- Student Edition
- Teacher Annotated Edition
- Student Activity Workbook
- Student Activity Workbook Teacher Annotated Edition

- Projects and Activities*
- Food Labs*
- Sewing Labs*
- Career Investigations*
- Reteaching Activities*
- Enrichment Activities*

Technology Resources

ExamView Assessment Suite *ExamView Assessment Suite CD* allows you to create and print out customized tests or ready-made unit and chapter tests, complete with answer keys.

Lesson Planner *Plus* *Lesson Planner Plus! CD** is and electronic lesson planner that provides instant access to teacher resources in one convenient package.

PRESENTATION *Plus!* *Presentation Plus!* PowerPoint™ Presentations can be edited and customized to meet the needs of students.

Online Learning Center includes resources and activities for students and teachers. Also includes Online Student Edition.

Interactive Student Edition

*ELECTRONIC RESOURCES ARE AVAILABLE ON LESSON PLANNER PLUS AND THE ONLINE LEARNING CENTER.

Writing Activity Answer

Cause and Effect Paragraphs should include a thesis statement, an introduction, and a conclusion; use transitions; and state a relationship between the two items. Paragraphs should identify the reasons for being prepared and the effects of planning and preparation.

Discovering Careers Answers ▼

1. Answers will vary. Students should write a summary of the education, training, and experience needed for the selected careers.
2. Students should present a selection of images from magazines to show to the family member who is playing the role of client.
3. Lists may include chef, medical professional, mail carrier, police officer, firefighter, military personnel, or airline staff.
4. Answers will vary. Students should present a summary of what they learned about the person's typical work day.

Section **18.1** Lesson Plan

Fabric and Pattern Preparation

FOCUS

Discussion Starter

Preparation is Key Ask students to discuss sewing projects they would like to try. List their ideas on the board, and discuss what kinds of planning and preparation they would need before sewing begins. Project ideas may include clothing items, accessories, and home fashions. Planning and preparation might include choosing the right fabric and notions, reading the pattern, and taking measurements.

 Bell Ringer Activity

Select a Pattern Distribute a variety of patterns to small groups and tell students to ask themselves: What is my experience level? How much time do I have to spend on this project? Where will I sew? What would I have to do to prepare?

Mc Graw Hill Professional Development **Mini Clip**
ELL Content Vocabulary

TEACH

S Skill Practice

Independent Practice

L1 List Ask students to create a list of the contents in a pattern envelope. Guide sheet, diagram of the pattern pieces, explanation of the pattern pieces, and layout.

L2 Explain Have students write a step-by-step guide explaining how to use a pattern guide sheet. (1) Study the diagram of the pattern pieces. (2) Circle the letters of the pieces needed for the item. (3) Circle the layout diagram that you will use for your size and style. (4) Read through all of the pattern directions before starting.

L3 Apply Have students practice measuring pattern pieces and comparing the measurements to their own body measurements. Tell them that very few people have measurements that match patterns exactly. Show students how to use the two parallel lines to lengthen or shorten and how to adjust the amount of ease in the pattern.

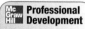
Mc Graw Hill Professional Development **Mini Clip**
Math Real-Life Connection—Proportion

U Universal Access

Gifted Students Tell students that sewing terms such as ease, facing, and bias have other meanings. Ask students to write a sewing-related sentence for each and a sentence using each with an alternate meaning. Sample answers: (1) The amount of *ease* in a pattern depends on how the garment will be worn. Gently *ease* the baby into her stroller. (2) Tailors use *facings* to finish the raw edges of a garment. Art students are painting a mural on the *facing* of the library wall. (3) You can straighten fabric by folding it on the *bias*. The results are inaccurate because of a gender *bias*.

ASSESS

Quiz

Ask students the following questions:

1. What can you use to check the grain? The selvages and the bias.

2. What is ease in a pattern? The amount of fullness added for movement and comfort.

3. What are the different marking methods used for different fabrics and types of marks? Tailor's chalk, tracing paper, air-soluble pens, and water-soluble pens.

RETEACH

R Reading Strategy

Explain Review the steps involved in preparing for a sewing project. Tell students, "I'm going to make a shirt. What should I do to get started?" Ask students to write the steps on the board. Prepare fabric, check grain, prepare pattern, read guide sheet, check measurements, and cut out pattern.

C Critical Thinking

Predict Emphasize the importance of positioning pattern pieces according to the grain line arrows as shown in Figures 18.1 and 18.2. Ask students to predict what might happen if a pattern piece is positioned across the grain. The fabric would probably stretch and hang unevenly. The product would not look professional, and you may need to redo it or start over.

ASSESS

Section 18.1 Review Assign the Section 18.1 After You Read activities.

 Student Activity Workbook Assign the Section 18.1 Activities.

Online Study Tools Have students go to the Online Learning Center at glencoe.com to:

- Take the Section 18.1 **Practice Test**.
- Download **Study-to-Go** content.

Section 18.1 After You Read

Answer Key

1. For proper fit, accurate measurements, appropriate fabric choice, and to determine if it matches your skill level.

2. Prepare fabric, prepare pattern, take measurements, cut pattern, and transfer markings.

3. Details should include laundering to preshrink fabric, pressing fabric, and checking the grain by matching the selvages and folding it on the bias.

4. Answers will vary. Samples: animal hides used for clothing and shelter by Native Americans; Kente cloth used in Africa to indicate status; ancient Egyptian clothing made from linen; and embroidered Chinese silk used for robes, theatrical costumes, purses, and shoes.

CLOSE

Culminating Activity

Putting Skills to Work Have students choose a sewing project that involves using a pattern. They can make a garment, accessory, or craft project for themselves, a friend, or family member. Tell them to take their project as far as cutting out and marking the fabric. They can work on finishing the project after completing Section 18.2.

Section 18.2 Lesson Plan

Sewing and Serging Basics

FOCUS

Discussion Starter

Ask students who have never used a sewing machine or serger to name a project that could benefit from the use of one of these machines. Students may name a variety of clothing items or accessories or they may name repairing damaged clothing.

Reading Strategic Readers

 Bell Ringer Activity

Now and Then Tell students to imagine that they are living 200 years ago, before the invention of the sewing machine. Discuss clothing that would have been difficult to make. Most contemporary clothing, especially clothing made with knits, silks, and sheers, would have been difficult to make.

TEACH

S **Skill Practice**

Guided Practice

L1 **List** Have students create a list of hand-stitching techniques and machine-stitching techniques. Hand-stitching: basting, slipstitch, hem, blanket, and backstitch. Machine stitching: straight seams, curved seams, turn corners, add seam finishes, darts, gather, ease, casings, facings, and buttons and snaps.

L2 **Explain** Have students explain why it is necessary to use hand-stitching techniques in some cases, even if a machine is available to use. Basting stitches are for temporarily holding pieces of fabric together; if you use a machine, the stitching would be difficult to remove. Slipstitching is used for nearly invisible finishes on pockets, linings, and trims. If the area to be slipstitched is small, it would be difficult on a machine.

L3 **Apply** Using the "How To Sew by Hand" feature on page 401, have students perform each stitch. Ask them to rank the stitching techniques from least to most difficult. Students' rankings will vary depending on experience.

Chapter 18 Lesson Plan

U Universal Access

Students with Physical Impairments Students with physical impairments may have a difficult time using sewing equipment. Work with students to think of activities that they can do, and go online to find examples of people with similar disabilities doing sewing activities.

ASSESS

Quiz

Ask students the following questions:

1. How can you prevent fabrics from raveling at the seam? Add a seam finish.

2. Describe the purpose of darts and where they would be used. Darts help shape fabric to the body, usually at the waistline, bustline, elbow, or back of the shoulder.

3. What are the three steps to sewing a shank button in place? (1) Sew five or six small stitches through the shank and into the fabric. (2) Fasten the thread securely. (3) Insert an eye fastener, and sew the eye in place.

RETEACH

R Writing Strategy

Compare Machines Have each student write three sentences describing a task done by a sewing machine, serger, or both. Have them exchange sentences and attempt to identify the machine that performs the tasks described. Sewing machines can sew a single line of locked stitches, insert zippers, and create darts, casings, gathers, and buttonholes. Sergers can sew, finish, and trim a seam in one step, and are useful for stretchy knits or silky fabrics. Both machines can sew conventional pant or skirt hems.

C Critical Thinking

Analyze Tell students they have a pair of pants that needs to be shortened. Instruct them find out what it would cost to have the alteration done by a professional tailor. Ask: When would be a good idea to pay for an alteration rather than do it yourself? Answers will vary, but may include: when you do not have the tools, equipment, or time to make the repair.

ASSESS

Section 18.2 Review Assign the Section 18.2 After You Read activities.

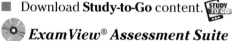 **Student Activity Workbook** Assign the Section 18.2 Activities.

Online Study Tools Have students go to the Online Learning Center at glencoe.com to:

- Take the Section 18.2 **Practice Test**.
- Download **Study-to-Go** content.

ExamView® Assessment Suite
Use the *ExamView Assessment Suite* CD to create a test for this chapter.

 Chapter Review Have students complete the Chapter 18 Review and Applications.

Section 18.2 After You Read
Answer Key

1. Fold-down casings are used for pull-on pants and skirts; applied casings are used at the waistline.

2. Sergers can save time and handle a variety of fabrics. They can also allow for movement in stretchy fabrics.

3. Paragraphs may include descriptions of the clothing and how students determined the type of seam.

4. Quilts can be a historical record because of the fabric used, such as feed and flour sacks during the Great Depression, to save money. Quilts can be made to honor individuals, such as a quilt made for a newborn baby, or to honor groups, such as soldiers.

CLOSE

Culminating Activity

Research Jobs Have students conduct research on three jobs in the clothing industry. Have them make a list of three skills a person would need to succeed in each of the jobs. Answers may include: ability to set up and operate sewing machines; know how to do fittings; knowledge of fashion trends; and know how to make alterations.

Words You Learned

1. Students should write complete sentences using each vocabulary term correctly.

Review Key Concepts

2. Fabric preparation helps you to avoid mistakes, saves time in the long run, and ensures that you have the right type of fabric for your project.

3. Fabric preparation includes laundering the fabric to preshrink it, pressing it to remove wrinkles, checking the grain matching selvages, and folding on the bias.

4. Stitch straight seams, stitch curved seams, turn corners, add seam finishes, make darts, gather fabric, ease fabric, make casings, make facings, and sew on buttons and snaps.

5. A serger is a machine that sews, trims, and finishes a seam in one step.

Critical Thinking

6. Some fabrics need to be preshrunk and pressed; others do not. Cleaning instructions vary and can be found on the bolt of the fabric. Different fabrics, such as knits, silks, and sheers, require different sewing techniques.

7. The garment may not fit properly, errors may be made in cutting or measuring, and materials may be wasted.

8. Sergers are high-speed machines that can save time and handle fabrics that are more difficult to work with, such as stretchy knits or slippery silks. Sergers keep edges from raveling on all fabrics. Unlike sergers, sewing machines can sew a single line of locked stiches. Sewing machines can create buttonholes, insert zippers, and some can do embroidery.

9. Answers will vary depending on students' experiences and opinions, but should demonstrate that the student understands both techniques and can clearly explain why one is more challenging than the other.

Real-World Skills and Applications

10. Evan should prepare his fabric and pattern. He should launder fabric according to instructions on the bolt, press if needed, and check the grain. He should read the pattern guides, measure and adjust the pattern as needed, and pin the pattern according to the layout. Then he can cut the pieces and begin sewing.

11. Answers will vary, but may include that the first practical sewing machine was patented in 1846 by Elias Howe in Massachusetts, based on designs by European inventors. Manufacturers used the first sewing machines. Students might mention that in 1851, Isaac Merritt Singer, a machinist from Boston, Massachusetts, introduced the first and most successful sewing machine created for home use.

Financial Literacy

12. Answers will vary depending on students' clothing selection and shopping choices.

Active Learning

13. Students should present a completed pillowcase.

14. Reports will vary, but should include details about historical clothing features, and who wore the clothing and why.

Net Connection

15. Examples will vary, but should include details about teen clothing styles from today, 10 years ago, and 100 years ago.

Academic Skills

16. Flyers will vary. Sample flyer: To encourage boys to join as well as girls, flyer advertises vests, cargo pants, backpacks, pajamas, shorts, carpentry aprons, and duffel bags. Date, time, location, and what to bring are included. Flyer is creative, relevant, and appealing to both genders. Advantages to joining are to meet people, learn more sewing techniques, share ideas, and have fun!

17. Answers will vary depending on students' opinions, but hypotheses should be stated clearly, and students should list facts that support the statement.

18. Each will spend an average of 240 minutes on the project.

Standardized Test Practice

19. c

FOCUS

Introduce the Project

In this project, students will design a sewing project for something they can wear. Ask students how possessing sewing skills may help them in their everyday life. Answers may include being able to repair tears, sewing a missing button, shortening pants, sewing their own clothing from fabric, or creating crafts.

Build Background

Famous Designer Clothes Ask students to name famous designers or popular labels. Then ask students to name qualities that make each designer easily recognizable. Write down names and qualities. Discuss the importance of both function and style to a successful clothing design. Names may vary. Qualities may include unique colors, interesting patterns, comfort, good for my body type, and easy to clean and care for.

TEACH

S Skill Practice

Guided Practice

L1 Compare Ask students to compare the merits and drawbacks of sewing clothing over purchasing it. Merits may be: less expensive, better choice of color, better choice of features, and ability to make perfect size. Drawbacks may be: takes a long time, difficult to make more complex designs, and not experienced enough.

L2 Apply Have students choose a partner, and take measurements for each other's clothing size. Males should measure for Neck, Chest, Arm, Waist, and Hips. Females should measure for Bust, Back Waist Length, Waist, and Hips. Measurements will vary, but students should record their findings and save them for use in their clothing design.

L3 Imagine Tell students to imagine they have been asked to design and sew a one-piece pajama for a newborn child. For safety, the clothing cannot have any buttons or snaps. How can they design the garment to have a snug fit? Answers will vary, but may include using stretchy material to avoid the need for fasteners, sewing loose elastic in the neckline, or creating a rear hatch opening so the top and bottom parts can be put on at the same time.

C Critical Thinking

How To Make Clothes Have students cut out an advertisement for clothing from a magazine and write an analysis of the methods, tools, and fabrics that would be needed to construct the garment. Ask students to use vocabulary they learned in the unit to help write their analysis. Analyses will vary, but vocabulary they may use could include bias, fabric grain, layout, guide sheet, pattern, hem, darts, ravel, hem, and notion.

ASSESS

Quiz

Ask students to answer the following questions:

1. What are the four basic stitches? Regular stitch, Basting stitch, Reinforcement stitch, and Zigzag stitch.
2. What factors should you consider before choosing a pattern for a sewing project? Purpose of project, your sewing skills and experience, whether you have enough time to finish, and how much the project will cost.
3. How can you identify "stitching lines" on a pattern, and what do you use them for? Stitching lines are broken or dotted lines that indicate where and in what direction to stitch fabric together.

CLOSE

Culminating Activity

Catalogue Description In this activity, students designed their own article of clothing. Ask students to imagine their finished clothing in a catalogue. Instruct them to write a description of the garment that would accompany a photograph, suggesting its appealing features and an appropriate price. Catalogue descriptions will vary, but may indicate purpose, size, colors, and account for age group of buyer. Price may account for cost of materials, hours of labor, and profit.

Nutrition and Your Health

Unit Overview

This unit introduces students to the Dietary Guidelines, MyPyramid, and the different food groups. It emphasizes the importance of eating healthful, balanced meals and the roles exercise and nutrition play in maintaining a healthy weight.

Chapter 19 *Nutrition and Wellness* In this chapter, students will learn the importance of eating healthful, balanced meals and about the different nutrients found in food. They will also learn how to use MyPyramid as a guide.

Chapter 20 *Health and Fitness* In this chapter, students will learn the importance of fitness to both their physical and mental well-beings. They will also be taught that a combination of a balanced meal plan and exercise regime will help them maintain a healthy weight.

Life Skills Project Preview

Play with Your Food!

Tell students that as part of this unit, they will learn that what they eat and how they exercise affect their health. They will learn how to write a play about a health topic that interests them, interview an expert on diet and fitness, and act out their play to share what they have learned.

FCCLA provides programs to guide students through projects, enhance their personal growth, and build leadership skills that can make a difference in their lives, their families, and their communities.

Student Body helps young people learn to eat right, be fit, and make healthy choices. Its goals are to help young people make informed and responsible decisions about their health. Student Body focuses on: exploring good nutrition, eating disorders, and healthy snacks; taking action related to lifelong exercise habits, obesity, and sports training; choosing a positive lifestyle by avoiding drugs, alcohol, and tobacco; and managing stress.

Stress Reduction Project Have students work together to plan a project that focuses on positive outlets for teen stress. Most communities have resources that can help establish stress-relief programs. Have students include some of the following in their project plan: exercise; improved nutrition; health/wellness; dramatic, musical, artistic, craft or other ideas for creative expression; peer support system; journal writing; and time management. Students should work together to come up with a project idea which will alleviate stress in teens. Ideas and projects should vary widely, but they should focus on some outlet for stress, be it physical, mental, or creative. For example, they could create a local sports team or a peer counseling group. Have students share their ideas with the other students, so everyone comes away with more possibilities for relieving stress.

Professional Development

MINI CLIP VIDEO LIBRARY

Targeted professional development is correlated throughout *Discovering Life Skills*. **The McGraw-Hill Professional Development Mini Clip Video Library** provides teaching strategies to strengthen academic and learning skills. Log on to **glencoe.com**.

In this Unit, you will find these Mini Clips.

CHAPTER 19 Nutrition and Wellness

READING

- **Guided Instruction** A teacher helps her students identify major and minor details from a selection she has read to them. (p. TM181)
- **Content Vocabulary** A teacher provides students with opportunities to practice their academic vocabulary. (p. TM181)

ENGLISH LANGUAGE LEARNERS

- **Vocabulary Activities** Students practice vocabulary using synonyms, antonyms, definitions, and words in context. (p. TM180)

MATH

- **Communication in Mathematics** Bea Moore-Harris explains the importance of student communication in the mathematics classroom. (p. TM182)

CHAPTER 20 Health and Fitness

READING

- **Flexible Groupings** Teachers use the strategies of flexible groupings and partner sharing to encourage and promote student discussions. (p. TM185)

ENGLISH LANGUAGE LEARNERS

- **Direct Vocabulary Instruction** A teacher has students create vocabulary cards to build a personal dictionary. (p. TM185)
- **Vocabulary Activities** Students practice vocabulary using synonyms, antonyms, definitions, and words in context. (p. TM186)
- **Words in Action** Students act out or mime the words they are trying to learn. (p. TM187)

Nutrition and Wellness

Section 19.1 Nutrients for Health

In this section, students will learn how to eat in order to look and feel good, while still satisfying their hunger. They will also learn about the functions of the various nutrients.

Section 19.2 Healthful Eating

In this section, students will learn about MyPyramid and the Dietary Guidelines. They will learn how to maintain a healthy weight. They will also learn how to maintain a healthy diet while eating out.

Classroom Solutions

Print Resources

- Student Edition
- Teacher Annotated Edition
- Student Activity Workbook
- Student Activity Workbook Teacher Annotated Edition

Technology Resources

ExamView **ExamView Assessment Suite CD** allows you to create and print out customized tests or ready-made unit and chapter tests, complete with answer keys.

Lesson Planner Plus **Lesson Planner Plus! CD*** is and electronic lesson planner that provides instant access to teacher resources in one convenient package.

- Projects and Activities*
- Food Labs*
- Sewing Labs*
- Career Investigations*
- Reteaching Activities*
- Enrichment Activities*

Presentation Plus! PowerPoint™ Presentations can be edited and customized to meet the needs of students.

Online Learning Center includes resources and activities for students and teachers. Also includes Online Student Edition.

Interactive Student Edition

*ELECTRONIC RESOURCES ARE AVAILABLE ON LESSON PLANNER PLUS AND THE ONLINE LEARNING CENTER.

Writing Activity Answer

Persuasive Paragraph Answers will vary, but should follow a similar format. The paragraph should be well-written and persuasive. It should clearly indicate the reasons eating a nutritious, balanced diet, even when extremely busy, is very important. It should be convincing and written so that it appeals to teenagers.

Discovering Careers Answers ▼

1. Answers will vary. Students should write a summary of the education, training, and experience needed for the selected careers.
2. Students should create a menu for a meal that they could prepare at home. It should follow the guidelines from MyPyramid.
3. Answers may include: bring their own lunch and snacks, avoid candy and soda vending machines, drink plenty of water, take frequent breaks, and take walks.
4. Answers will vary. Students should present a summary of what they learned about the person's typical work day.

Nutrients for Health

FOCUS

Discussion Starter

Give students a brief overview of what nutrients are, and ask them to name some nutrients. Write the named nutrients on the board, and have the students discuss what they know about each. Answers could include carbohydrates, fat, protein, water, and various vitamins. Students should know something about the nutrients. For example, carbohydrates and fats provide energy.

Bell Ringer Activity

Role of Nutrients Ask students what keeps a car running. Gasoline provides energy, and oil and other fluids keep it running smoothly and its parts in good repair. Nutrients play similar roles in the body. Some provide energy, and others keep everything working smoothly. They also help the body repair itself when necessary.

TEACH

S Skill Practice

Independent Practice

L1 List Ask students to list as many vitamins and minerals as they can and the food sources of each. Vitamin A, B-complex vitamins, vitamin C, vitamin D, and vitamin E. Minerals include calcium and iron. Examples of food sources are on pages 423-428.

L2 Contrast Ask students to write a paragraph contrasting hunger and appetite. Hunger is the physical need to eat. Appetite is the desire to eat. You can still have an appetite when your hunger has been satisfied. However, you should stop eating once your hunger has been satisfied.

L3 Apply Have students create a meal plan for one day that provides all of the nutrients listed in the section. Have the students list the nutrients that each food contributes. Meal plans should be balanced and contain each type of nutrient, but should not contain too much of any nutrient. Students should also be able to identify which nutrients come from which foods.

U Universal Access

English Language Learners Locate the names of the nutrients in all of the languages spoken by students in your class. Compare the names and discuss similarities and differences. For example, iron in Spanish is "hierro." The English comes from old English, while the Spanish comes from Latin.

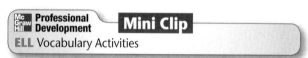

Professional Development **Mini Clip**
ELL Vocabulary Activities

ASSESS

Quiz

Ask students to answer the following questions:

1. **What are the functions of fat in the body?** Store energy; regulate body temperature; keep the skin smooth and the nervous system functioning; and carry vitamins.

2. **What is riboflavin?** A B-complex vitamin found in dairy foods, eggs, proteins, enriched breads and cereals. It helps keep eyes and skin healthy.

3. **Why is water an important nutrient?** It regulates body functions, carries nutrients to cells, aids in digestion, removes wastes, and helps control body temperature.

RETEACH

W Writing Strategy

Identify Nutrient Needs Ask students to write the types of foods they would eat more of if their doctor told them they were not getting enough: carbohydrates, fat, protein, vitamin B12, and calcium. Students should identify food sources for each. For example, food sources for calcium include milk, cheese, yogurt, green leafy vegetables, and fish with edible bones. Some food sources may provide more than one nutrient, like milk which provides calcium and fat.

C Critical Thinking

Evaluate Information The text gives food sources of vitamins and minerals. Some people take supplements to provide vitamins and minerals. Have students research the necessity of taking supplements and their effectiveness. The body does not absorb nutrients in supplements as readily as it does nutrients in food. Food is a better source of nutrients; however, supplements may be recommended for people with a particular deficiency.

Chapter 19 Lesson Plan

ASSESS

Section 19.1 Review Assign the Section 19.1 After You Read activities.

📁 **Student Activity Workbook** Assign the Section 19.1 Activities.

🖱 **Online Study Tools** Have students go to the Online Learning Center at glencoe.com to:

- Take the Section 19.1 **Practice Test**.
- Download **Study-to-Go** content.

 Section 19.1 After You Read

Answer Key

1. A balanced meal plan, physical activity, adequate rest, and personal hygiene.

2. Dark green, leafy vegetables, deep yellow vegetables, eggs, fruits, and dairy products.

3. Students should create a pamphlet that communicates the importance of minerals. They can mention any or all of the minerals discussed in the chapter, discuss how these minerals function in the body, and mention in which foods these minerals can be found. The pamphlet should incorporate graphics to make it more appealing.

4. Answers will vary, but should mention one or two traditions which incorporate food, such as cake on birthdays or ham or turkey at Thanksgiving. They could mention how food brings people together, both physically at the table, and as a shared experience.

CLOSE

Culminating Activity

Combine Nutrients in a Meal Ask students to bring in one recipe each, from a cookbook, magazine, newspaper, the Internet, or a family recipe. As a class, discuss the recipes and identify the nutrients in each. After learning about the different nutrients and their food sources, students should be able to identify some of the nutrients that would be provided by the various recipes they find. For example, any meat recipe would provide protein.

Mc Graw Hill **Professional Development** **Mini Clip**
Reading Guided Instruction

 Section 19.2 Lesson Plan

Healthful Eating

FOCUS

Discussion Starter

Ask students to discuss the ways they already follow nutrition guidelines, maintain a healthy weight, and eat right. Answers should include activities and food choices that promote healthful eating and maintain a healthy weight, such as paying attention to nutrition content, eating healthful snacks, or being physically active.

Mc Graw Hill **Professional Development** **Mini Clip**
Reading Content Vocabulary

🔔 **Bell Ringer Activity**

Know the Consequences Ask students to list the consequences of not eating healthfully. Explain that MyPyramid and the Dietary Guidelines can help them maintain healthy eating habits so they can avoid these consequences. Consequences: becoming overweight, heart disease, a weakened immune system, or physical weakness.

TEACH

S **Skill Practice**

Independent Practice

L1 **List** Ask students to list healthful whole-grain foods, vegetables, and fruits. Lists may include: brown rice and whole wheat bread for whole-grains; leafy greens, bell peppers, carrots, and zucchini for vegetables; and apples, oranges, bananas, and tomatoes for fruits.

L2 **Detail** Ask students to choose one of the Dietary Guidelines and write a paragraph detailing what changes they can make in their diets or lifestyles in order to follow that guideline. Students' answers will vary, but may include things like adding more healthful foods, adding physical activity to their schedule, or reducing sugar and fat.

L3 **Apply** Obtain nutrition information labels for various foods and have students evaluate the healthfulness of each. Ask them to arrange the labels from healthiest to least healthy and explain. Students should put items with more nutrient content and less calories, sugar, and fat at the top.

U Universal Access

Mathematical/Logical Learners Have students create a system for healthful eating; for example a series of charts detailing nutrient intake, physical activity, and/or nutrition information of foods eaten. Encourage them to use the system.

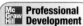

McGraw Hill Professional Development — Mini Clip
Math Communication in Mathematics

ASSESS

Quiz

Ask students to answer the following questions:

1. How can you know if your weight is healthy? Different people have different healthy weights, so you should consult with a doctor.

2. What are the effects of eating too much fat and cholesterol? It will increase your risk of heart disease and obesity.

3. What does sodium do, and why is it important not to eat too much of it? Sodium helps regulate the amount of fluid in the body, but too much can lead to high blood pressure.

RETEACH

W Writing Strategy

Conduct Research Part of the Dietary Guidelines involves handling foods safely. Have students choose a food such as chicken, eggs, or lettuce, and research food safety procedures. Have them write a paragraph about the proper procedures to use when handling that food. Students should demonstrate an understanding of the information they reviewed in the course of their research. The paragraph should include accurate information about safely handling and preparing meals with the ingredient chosen.

C Critical Thinking

Healthy Weight Ranges The text indicates that everyone's healthy weight is different. Have students look for different methods of evaluating whether one's weight is healthy and compare them. Do they have the same results? What conclusions can students draw? Students may find there are different opinions about healthy weight. Students should look at the source to evaluate credibility. The best way to determine healthy weight is to talk to a doctor.

ASSESS

Section 19.2 Review Assign the Section 19.2 After You Read activities.

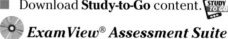

Student Activity Workbook Assign the Section 19.2 Activities.

Online Study Tools Have students go to the Online Learning Center at glencoe.com to:

- Take the Section 19.2 **Practice Test**.
- Download **Study-to-Go** content.

ExamView® Assessment Suite
Use the *ExamView Assessment Suite* CD to create a test for this chapter.

Chapter Review Have students complete the Chapter 19 Review and Applications.

 Section 19.2 After You Read
Answer Key

1. The person represents the physical fitness component of MyPyramid.

2. Consult your doctor.

3. High blood pressure.

4. Eat only until you feel satisfied. Remember most portions are larger than a serving. Select dishes low in fat, sugar, salt, and calories. Choose nutrient-dense dishes. Remember sauces add calories. Limit treats.

5. Students should prepare a presentation appropriate for elementary age children about using the MyPyramid. Coordinate with an elementary school to have your students share their presentations.

6. Answers may include droughts, flooding, very hot or very cold climates, bad soil quality, or fires. Students could mention storing extra food, irrigation, fertilizers, or providing relief to the affected area.

CLOSE

Culminating Activity

Physical Activity Discuss the physical activities that the students do. For students that do not do a lot of physical activity, ask them about their hobbies and have the class come up with physical activities that go along with their existing hobbies. Students who prefer sedentary hobbies such as reading or playing games, may have an interest in the activities they read about or see in their games, such as martial arts, horseback riding, or fencing.

Words You Learned

1. Students should use each of the content vocabulary words and academic vocabulary words in a sentence.

Review Key Concepts

2. Hunger is the physical need to eat. Appetite is the desire to eat.

3. Proteins are nutrients that are needed to build, repair, and maintain body cells and tissues. Carbohydrates are the starches and sugars that give the body most of its energy. Fats are an important source of energy.

4. MyPyramid reminds you how to make healthful food choices and increase physical activity.

5. High blood pressure, heart disease, stroke, diabetes, and cancer.

6. Whole grain breads, fruits, and vegetables.

7. Choose foods just as carefully when dining out as you do at home.

Critical Thinking

8. Answers may include: granola and low-fat yogurt, smoothies, milk, fruit, grilled chicken, and salads.

9. Answers should describe in what areas students are eating well and in what areas they could improve.

Real-World Skills and Applications

10. Answers will vary depending on the restaurants selected, but students should demonstrate an understanding of healthful meal planning while dining out.

11. Students should create a spreadsheet showing their intake of fruits and vegetables for a week.

Financial Literacy

12. Students will have two grocery lists: one with their families' usual items that may include processed and sugar-filled snacks and foods and another with healthful alternatives that follow MyPyramid and the Dietary Guidelines. They should make comparisons in price based on their shopping and be able to discuss which is more expensive and what changes they can make in their families' lifestyle.

Active Learning

13. Maps will vary depending on the region selected. Each state in the region should include an image of the food produced there.

14. Presentations may include any organization that supports the delivery of information or services related to nutrition and wellness.

Net Connection

15. Definitions of organic may vary depending on how it is defined in your region, but it generally refers to foods produced without the use of chemicals, fertilizer, and additives. Products in grocery stores may include fruits, vegetables, and grain products.

Academic Skills

16. Students should present a poster or advertisement for MyPyramid for their local newspaper. They should include colorful graphics, catchy phrases, and photos to communicate how to apply the guidelines for MyPyramid

17. Students should create an overview of the research they have done about food from a cultural background of their family. They should include the culture's diet and lifestyle, the results of this lifestyle on the culture, and the influence they see in their present family.

18. Jennifer consumed $9 \times 110 = 990$ calories of fat, which amounted to $990 \div 2{,}200 = 0.45 = 45\%$ of her total calories for the day. To limit her fat intake to 30%, no more than $0.3 \times 2{,}200 = 660$ calories can come from fat. Since there are 9 calories in every gram of fat, this amount translates to $660 \div 9 \approx 73$ grams of fat per day.

Standardized Test Practice

19. Answers will vary, but should give a description of the person's healthy lifestyle and bring this person to life.

Health and Fitness

Section 20.1 Physical Activity

In this section, students will learn how to stay healthy and fit by doing physical activity. They will learn about the benefits of fitness and what is necessary to reach and maintain a healthy weight.

Section 20.2 Body Weight and Health

In this section, students will learn about healthy weight and determining their healthy weight. They will learn about eating disorders, how to recognize them, and their consequences.

Classroom Solutions

Print Resources

 Student Edition
 Teacher Annotated Edition
 Student Activity Workbook
 Student Activity Workbook Teacher Annotated Edition

Technology Resources

ExamView **ExamView Assessment Suite CD** allows you to create and print out customized tests or ready-made unit and chapter tests, complete with answer keys.

Lesson Planner *Plus* **Lesson Planner Plus! CD*** is and electronic lesson planner that provides instant access to teacher resources in one convenient package.

- Projects and Activities*
- Food Labs*
- Sewing Labs*
- Career Investigations*
- Reteaching Activities*
- Enrichment Activities*

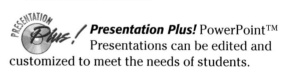 **Presentation Plus!** PowerPoint™ Presentations can be edited and customized to meet the needs of students.

Online Learning Center includes resources and activities for students and teachers. Also includes Online Student Edition.

Interactive Student Edition

*Electronic Resources are available on Lesson Planner Plus and the Online Learning Center.

Writing Activity Answer

Advertisement Students should create an advertisement for elementary-age children, which includes suggestions and explains the benefits of exercise. For example, a student could write about joining a community sports team, taking up horseback riding, or buying a bicycle. The students should emphasize that physical activity is important for a healthful lifestyle.

Discovering Careers Answers ▼

1. Answers will vary. Students should write a summary of the education, training, and experience needed for the selected careers.

2. Students should create a log of their family's physical activity for a week. If students find that their families should be getting more physical activity, they should come up with some suggestions (a family hike on the weekend or a family bike ride).

3. Students should list three ways healthy employees benefit the workplace (increased production, not missing work as often, more energy, and better ability concentrate).

4. Answers will vary. Students should present a summary of what they learned about the person's typical work day.

Section 20.1 Lesson Plan

Physical Activity

FOCUS

Discussion Starter

Ask students to discuss what they know about the benefits of physical fitness, the different physical activities they do, and why they choose to do that particular activity. Students should discuss physical benefits, such looking good and staying healthy, as well as other benefits, such as having fun and making friends. They should discuss their favorite activities and why they do them.

 Bell Ringer Activity

Find the Right Activity Ask students to describe a time they tried a physical activity for the first time. How did it feel on that first day? How do they feel about it now? Did they continue doing the activity? Explain that not all activities are for everyone. On the other hand, you may enjoy activities more as your skills improve.

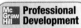
McGraw Hill **Professional Development** **Mini Clip**
ELL Direct Vocabulary Instruction

TEACH

S Skill Practice

Independent Practice

L1 List Ask students to list ways to engage in physical activity. Remind students to think about all types of physical activity, not just sports, but things like hiking, dancing, or yoga. Share the lists with the class to give students new ideas for activities they can try.

L2 Explain Ask students to write a paragraph explaining how exercise affects the body. Exercise builds muscle and burns fat. Exercising a specific part of your body will not burn fat and calories only from that part of the body, although it will build muscle in that area.

L3 Apply Ask students to use the advice in the "How To …" feature to create an exercise routine. Students should read about the different options and create an exercise routine that includes several sessions of one type of physical activity or different activities several times a week.

U Universal Access

Students with Physical Impairments Students with physical impairments may have extra challenges when it comes to physical activity. Discuss students' interests with them and assist them in locating ways to incorporate their interests into appropriate physical activity.

ASSESS

Quiz

Ask students to answer the following questions:

1. What are the benefits of physical activity? Burn calories, improve heart and lung function, tone muscles and skin, control appetite, and relieve tension and stress.

2. How can you burn fat from a specific body part? You cannot. Calories and fat are burned from your total body.

3. What are some types of indoor exercises you can do? Lift weights, work out on machines, dance, do yoga, or swim.

RETEACH

W Writing Strategy

Fitness Evaluation Have students pair up and act as fitness trainers for each other. First, they will interview each other about their fitness goals, their strengths and weaknesses, and their likes and dislikes. Then each will create a fitness plan for the other and write it down. Fitness plans should show that the partners listened to each other and incorporated knowledge from the chapter to create an appropriate plan.

McGraw Hill **Professional Development** **Mini Clip**
Reading Flexible Groupings

C Critical Thinking

Avoid Extremes Give students a description of four different people. One does no physical activity. The next does the minimum suggested level of activity. The third exercises for at least 60 minutes per day, 4-5 times a week. The last exercises for several hours every day. Have students evaluate how the lifestyles would affect health, relationships, and overall happiness. Students should recognize that the two extreme positions will have negative effects in each area, while the more moderate lifestyles will have positive effects.

ASSESS

Section 20.1 Review Assign the Section 20.1 After You Read activities.

 Student Activity Workbook Assign the Section 20.1 Activities.

Online Study Tools Have students go to the Online Learning Center at glencoe.com to:

- Take the Section 20.1 **Practice Test**.
- Download **Study-to-Go** content.

Section 20.1 After You Read

Answer Key

1. You have the energy to do your schoolwork and chores, with enough leftover to have fun too. You are confident about your abilities. You can keep your weight at the right level. You can deal with stress.

2. Burns calories; helps your heart and lungs work better; tones your muscles and skin; helps you control your appetite; relieves tension.

3. Essays should express that it is important for teens to be fit, follow with examples of the benefits of physical activity, and explain how fitness helps teens look and feel their best (tones muscles, manages weight, increases energy and the ability to concentrate, and improves self-esteem).

4. Research may show that a person needs both kinds of exercise. Organized exercise can be fun and motivating, but requires other participants, a place to meet, and sometimes special equipment. Participating in team sports may help people learn to communicate, work with others, and develop relationships, while individual exercise may help people develop self-confidence and build independence.

CLOSE

Culminating Activity

Keep A Good Attitude Ask students to come up with common excuses for not doing physical exercise. Write the excuses on the board, and brainstorm solutions. Common excuses might include things like, "I am too tired" or "I will make up for it tomorrow." Students should think up positive ways to counter those excuses.

Section **20.2** Lesson Plan

Body Weight and Health

FOCUS

Discussion Starter

Discuss with students why it is important to maintain a healthy weight. Ask them to name some of the dangers of being overweight and underweight. Being overweight creates a risk for health problems, including diabetes, high blood pressure, and stroke. It can also cause discomfort in breathing, walking, and sitting. Being underweight can also create health problems, such as bone loss and low blood pressure.

Mc Graw Hill Professional Development **Mini Clip**
ELL Vocabulary Activities

 Bell Ringer Activity

Teen Dieting What are the reasons for dieting? How many of the diets are for the purpose of losing weight versus gaining or maintaining weight? Why do the students think that so many people are dissatisfied with their weight? Are the diets healthful?

TEACH

S **Skill Practice**

Guided Practice

L1 **List** Work with the students to list and describe different types of eating disorders. Anorexia nervosa, when a person severely limits eating in order to lose weight; bulimia nervosa, when a person eats a large amount of food and then purges it; and binge eating, when a person eats a large quantity of food at one time.

L2 **Explain** Work as a class to explain some of the common causes of eating disorders. Low self-esteem, depression, troubled relationships, poor body image, and chemical imbalances in the brain.

L3 **Apply** Ask students to find information on three types of diets. Work as a class to list the different types of diets and evaluate each to determine how healthy it is and whether or not it is a fad diet. Students should use what they learned in the section to evaluate the diets they choose and determine whether they are fad diets.

U Universal Access

Students with Learning Disabilities Students with learning disabilities may require additional study aids to get the most out of the text. You may wish to supplement the book by giving yoga demonstrations or having guest speakers on eating disorders.

Mc Graw Hill **Professional Development** **Mini Clip**
ELL Words in Action

ASSESS

Quiz

Ask students to answer the following questions:

1. **What types of eating behavior do fad diets encourage?** Unhealthy ones like consuming only liquids, fasting, or using diet pills.

2. **What are the negative affects of bulimia nervosa?** Stained teeth, swollen cheeks, damage to the teeth, gums, and esophagus, kidney problems, heart failure, and death.

3. **What should you do if you think you or someone else has an eating disorder?** Talk to a parent, teacher, or counselor. It often takes medical, nutritional, and psychological counseling to defeat an eating disorder.

RETEACH

R Reading Strategy

Research Healthy Activities Gather local publications containing information about upcoming local events. Ask students to locate activities that promote health and fitness. Students should look for group activities or volunteer opportunities that are physically active or promote a healthy lifestyle, such as hiking groups, sports teams, volunteer cleanups, healthy cooking classes, or nutrition advocates.

C Critical Thinking

Evaluate Claims Ask students to find a description of a diet or other weight loss product. Have them determine what claims are made and how believable those claims are. Have them write a report evaluating the product. Students should learn to recognize that when a product makes extraordinary claims, it requires extraordinary evidence to be convincing. They should learn to look deeper into products that make such claims.

ASSESS

Section 20.2 Review Assign the Section 20.2 After You Read activities.

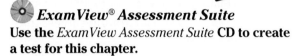 **Student Activity Workbook** Assign the Section 20.2 Activities.

Online Study Tools Have students go to the Online Learning Center at glencoe.com to:

- Take the Section 20.2 **Practice Test**.
- Download **Study-to-Go** content.

ExamView® Assessment Suite
Use the *ExamView Assessment Suite* **CD to create a test for this chapter.**

Chapter Review Have students complete the Chapter 20 Review and Applications.

Section 20.2 After You Read

Answer Key

1. A condition in which a person's weight is 20 percent or more above healthy weight.

2. You gain weight when you consume more calories than your body uses. You lose weight when your body uses more calories than you consume.

3. Anorexia nervosa, bulimia nervosa, and binge eating.

4. Talk to a parent, teacher, or counselor.

5. Students should identify which eating disorder they think the friend has, what signs or symptoms they see (for example, with anorexia nervosa, that the friend cuts food into small pieces, chews food for longer than is normal, or exercises too much), and what the long-term effects could be. The letter should encourage the friend to seek help.

6. Students should pick an eating disorder, examining how it develops, what contributes to its development, and how it is treated.

CLOSE

Culminating Activity

Peer Counseling Have some students imagine they are volunteers at an eating disorder hotline. Have other students "call in" with questions and ask the volunteer students to answer as best they can. Students should answer questions with information from the section. If there is a question they cannot answer, they should refer the caller to a real counselor or doctor.

Words You Learned

1. Students should create a fill-in-the-blank sentence for each of the vocabulary terms. The sentence should contain enough information to help determine the missing word.

Review Key Concepts

2. Fitness gives you energy to do your work and enjoy activities; helps you feel confident about your abilities; helps you make physical activity a part of every day; helps you maintain appropriate weight; and enables you to better handle stress.

3. Exercise regularly and incorporate fitness into your everyday lifestyle.

4. Obese people are at greater risk for such illnesses as diabetes and heart disease.

5. Take in fewer calories and exercise more.

6. Eating disorders can result in depression, anxiety, heart disease, stunted growth, brain damage, kidney problems, severe weight gain or loss, high blood pressure, diabetes, and even death.

7. Low self-esteem, depression, troubled relationships, poor body image, or chemical imbalances in the brain.

Critical Thinking

8. Being overweight can lead to heart disease and diabetes, while being underweight means you are not getting the nutrients your body needs.

9. Answers will vary, but students should have a plan that includes a target number of calories with a specific amount of exercise each day. Then they should come up with what they can eat within their range. To maintain a specific weight, the students' daily intake of calories should match how many they are burning through physical activity.

Real-World Skills and Applications

10. Answers will vary, but students will have a weekly schedule in which they have included exercise as a high priority. Perhaps they will fit exercising in early in the morning, during lunch, after school, or on the weekends.

11. Groups should create an advertisement for a fruit or vegetable that will convince people to buy (and eat) that fruit or vegetable. They can borrow ideas from the ads for junk food, but the students should be aware of the differences between selling junk food and selling healthful food.

Financial Literacy

12. Answers will vary. Students may elect to engage in cardiovascular exercises such as swimming at a public pool, jogging, or bicycling with equipment already on hand. Strength exercises can be done with cheaply-purchased weights, an exercise ball, household objects, or even without any outside objects (sit-ups and push-ups). Yoga and other activities can sometimes be viewed on television or can be offered at a local park for a small fee (or free).

Active Learning

13. Students should go to a park with friends where they will be involved with fitness activities. They should be able to report on the picnic and the benefits. They could mention how this activity compares to other, less beneficial activities (going to the movies and ordering a large popcorn or sitting on the couch and watching TV).

14. Students will make a brief presentation on a fruit or vegetable. They should present information, such as where and how it is grown and ways in which it can be prepared and served.

Net Connection

15. Students should provide information about a variety of activities and how many calories they expend during the activities.

Academic Skills

16. Students should write a short essay that expounds the benefits of physical activity for the mind. They should provide examples and details (for example, increases concentration, improves the ability to learn, helps people feel good about themselves, increases confidence, and provides an outlet for stress).

17. Students should create a physical fitness plan that incorporates cross training. It should incorporate both cardio activities and strength training activities, focus on creating variation, and avoid doing the same type of activity over and over.

18. Starting with $(80 + x) \div 5 = 20$, multiply both sides by 5 to get $80 + x = 100$. Subtract 80 from both sides to get $x = 20$ minutes.

Standardized Test Practice

19. a

FOCUS

Introduce the Project

In this project, students will write a play about nutrition and health. Ask students to identify habits they may have developed that are harmful. Answers will vary, but may include skipping breakfast, not getting enough exercise, eating too much junk food, not eating enough vegetables, and not getting enough sleep.

Build Background

Body Image The media often shows images of attractive people. Ask students to name famous people who they think have ideal bodies and explain why. Write names of celebrities and qualities that make them ideal. Remind students that very few people look like actors or models. Discuss what effects seeing perfect body types might have on your own body image. Names will vary; qualities may include thin body, muscular body, perfect skin complexion, or hourglass shape.

TEACH

S Skill Practice

Guided Practice

L1 List Remind students that exercise does not have to be boring and is easier to do if it is something they like doing. Ask students to list physical activities they enjoy. Lists will vary, but may include basketball, soccer, jogging, walking, swimming, rollerblading, skateboarding, or hiking.

L2 Think Have students think of favorite foods. Ask them to combine each favorite food with a food from a food group they are lacking to create an equally satisfying, but more balanced meal. Combination examples: peanut butter and celery, chocolate and strawberries, ice cream and wheat germ, or chocolate cake and milk.

L3 Imagine Tell students to imagine they have a friend who is overweight. They are concerned for his or her health, but are also worried that they may offend their friend if they bring up the issue. Ask students to write a letter to their friend to express their concern and suggest helpful and encouraging ways to manage the problem. Letters should be in proper format, and suggestions may include: eat less junk food, offer to exercise

together, bring lunch from home to control food choices, or eat only during regular meal times.

C Critical Thinking

Appetite vs. Hunger Remind students that hunger is the physical need to eat, and appetite is the desire. Have students list foods they want to eat, even when they are not hungry. Ask students to write a paragraph, suggesting ways to avoid eating junk food. Answers will vary, but may include swapping a healthier version for the less nutritious choice (veggie pizza instead of pepperoni), eating regularly, or saving a small portion of junk food as dessert after a healthy meal.

ASSESS

Quiz

Ask students to answer the following questions:

1. **What is the definition of obesity, and what are the risks?** Obesity is a condition in which a person's weight is 20 percent above healthy weight. Risks are illnesses, such as heart disease and diabetes.

2. **What are fad diets, and why are they often unhealthy?** Fad diets promise quick weight loss through unrealistic means and are not healthy because they are unbalanced and lack the nutrients you need.

3. **What is the role of minerals in a person's diet?** Minerals promote sturdy bones and teeth, maintain healthy blood, and encourage regular elimination of body wastes.

CLOSE

Culminating Activity

Looking Ahead In this activity, students identified health issues for their age group. Have students write a paragraph about ways their health needs will change as they become adolescents, young adults, middle adults, and older adults. Answers will vary, but each stage brings a new need. For example, adolescents need to increase calcium for bone growth. As age increases, health needs may be to exercise more, increase iron and calcium, maintain desirable weight, increase fiber intake, limit stress, and take essential vitamins.

Learn to Cook

Unit Overview

This unit introduces students to safe kitchen and food handling practices, accident prevention in the kitchen, meal preparation, food shopping, reading and following recipes, choosing ingredients, and cooking techniques.

Chapter 21 *Working in the Kitchen* In this chapter, students will learn how to handle food safely and keep the kitchen clean to help avoid food contamination. They will also be taught safe work habits to avoid common kitchen accidents.

Chapter 22 *Prepare to Cook* In this chapter, students will learn why it is important to plan meals ahead of time. They will also be introduced to the different recipe formats and the meanings of common recipe terms and abbreviations.

Chapter 23 *Cooking Basics* In this chapter, students learn how to add variety to dishes with herbs, spices, fruit, and vegetables. They are also introduced to a variety of cooking methods and will learn how to match cooking methods with appropriate foods.

Life Skills Project Preview

A Meal from Your Culture

Tell students that as part of this unit, they will discover how food can be an important part of their cultural identity. They will learn how to prepare a recipe that reflects their cultural background, interview someone who shares their heritage, and present a dish to the class.

FCCLA Family, Career and Community Leaders of America **DYNAMIC LEADERSHIP**

FCCLA provides programs to guide students through projects, enhance their personal growth, and build leadership skills that can make a difference in their lives, their families, and their communities.

Dynamic Leadership helps young people build leadership skills. It provides information, activities, and project ideas to help students learn about leadership; recognize the lifelong benefits of leadership skills; and become strong leaders for families, careers, and communities. Dynamic Leadership focuses on modeling good character, solving problems, fostering positive relationships, managing conflict, building teams, and educating peers.

Roll Out the Red Carpet In groups, have students come up with ideas for and organize a project to help freshman adjust to high school. Ideas could include: acting as tour guides at freshman orientation; creating a school Web site that gives information for adjusting to your school; or producing a brochure that describes activities and traditions of the student body. Students should come up with an idea for a project that will help welcome freshman into high school, providing them with information which will make their transitions smoother. This project should help both the freshman and the students organizing the event, as they will get to practice their leadership skills.

Professional Development

MINI CLIP VIDEO LIBRARY

Targeted professional development is correlated throughout *Discovering Life Skills*. **The McGraw-Hill Professional Development Mini Clip Video Library** provides teaching strategies to strengthen academic and learning skills. Log on to **glencoe.com**.

In this Unit, you will find these Mini Clips.

CHAPTER 21 Kitchen Safety

READING

- **Planning and Classroom Management** Nancy Frey, Ph.D., teacher, educator, and author, discusses the instructinal strategies that support a differentiated classroom. **(p. TM193)**
- **Differentiated Instruction** Nancy Frey, Ph.D., teacher, educator, and author, discusses the elements of a differentiated classroom. **(p. TM194)**

ENGLISH LANGUAGE LEARNERS

- **Group Discussions** Students discuss academic content they have just read. **(p. TM194)**
- **Words in Action** Students act out or mime the words they are trying to learn. **(p. TM195)**

CHAPTER 22 Prepare to Cook

READING

- **Guided Instruction** A teacher helps her students identify major and minor details from a selection she has read to them. **(p. TM198)**
- **Exploring the Big Idea** Students share, in the format of their choice, their answer to a lesson's "Big Question." **(p. TM199)**

ENGLISH LANGUAGE LEARNERS

- **Building the Context** A teacher models an activity that will provide students with background information they may need to understand the text they are about to read. **(p. TM198)**

- **Guided Instruction** A teacher helps her students identify major and minor details from a selection she has read to them. **(p. TM198)**
- **Low Risk Environment** Author Josefina Tinajero discusses the importance of creating a low-risk environment for English language learners. **(p. TM199)**

CHAPTER 23 Cooking Basics

READING

- **Lesson Reflections** A narrator discusses various instructional strategies suitable for use with English learners. **(p. TM205)**
- **Bridging Cultural Gaps** A teacher models the use of context clues to determine the meaning of an unknown word. **(p. TM203)**

ENGLISH LANGUAGE LEARNERS

- **Using Manipulatives** A teacher uses concrete objects to illustrate lesson concepts. **(p. TM203)**

MATH

- **Ways of Working—Solving Equations** A teacher uses partner work and whole group instruction to build students' understanding of the equation-solving process. **(p. TM203)**
- **Multiple Approaches to Problem Solving** A teacher and his students discuss various options for problem solving and then apply one of the options. **(p. TM204)**

Working in the Kitchen

Section 21.1 *Food Safety*

In this section, students learn about foodborne illnesses and their causes. They will also learn how to keep food safe by handling and storing it properly.

Section 21.2 *Kitchen Essentials*

In this section, students will learn about kitchen safety, including how to avoid falls, burns, fires, cuts, and electric shocks. They will also learn about the safe use of small and large equipment in the kitchen.

Classroom Solutions

Print Resources

 Student Edition
 Teacher Annotated Edition
 Student Activity Workbook
Student Activity Workbook
Teacher Annotated Edition

Technology Resources

ExamView *ExamView Assessment Suite CD* allows you to create and print out customized tests or ready-made unit and chapter tests, complete with answer keys.

Lesson Planner *Plus* *Lesson Planner Plus! CD** is and electronic lesson planner that provides instant access to teacher resources in one convenient package.

- Projects and Activities*
- Food Labs*
- Sewing Labs*
- Career Investigations*
- Reteaching Activities*
- Enrichment Activities*

 Presentation Plus! PowerPoint™ Presentations can be edited and customized to meet the needs of students.

Online Learning Center includes resources and activities for students and teachers. Also includes Online Student Edition.

Interactive Student Edition

*ELECTRONIC RESOURCES ARE AVAILABLE ON LESSON PLANNER PLUS AND THE ONLINE LEARNING CENTER.

Writing Activity Answer

Personal Narrative Students should write a narrative about an event or memory from childhood that took place in the kitchen. The thesis should state what the situation was and the point the student wants to make about the event. The student should explain why the event was so memorable. They should tell the story, using precise details about the event.

Discovering Careers Answers ▼

1. Answers will vary. Students should write a summary of the education, training, and experience needed for the selected careers.
2. Student answers should include a list of the safety procedures their family follows when cooking at home. They should conclude how safe their home kitchen is and if there are any improvements that can be made.
3. Answers will vary but may include a chef, server, bus boy, dishwasher, sous-chef, dessert chef, cook, manager, Maitre D', and valets.
4. Answers will vary. Students should present a summary of what they learned about the person's typical work day.

Section 21.1 Lesson Plan

Food Safety

FOCUS

Discussion Starter

Ask students to discuss what they know about food safety. Why is it important? When they prepare a meal, what do they do to make sure it is safe to eat? Food safety helps prevent foodborne illness. Answers should include basic safety procedures, such as washing hands with soap and water, washing produce, and making sure food has been properly stored.

Bell Ringer Activity

Take Precautions Ask volunteers to describe a time they made a mistake or had an accident. How could it have been prevented? What did they learn and how did it change their behavior? Explain that food safety rules have been developed in a similar way, by determining what behaviors lead to foodborne illness, and developing rules to avoid those behaviors.

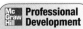
McGraw Hill Professional Development | **Mini Clip**
Reading Planning and Classroom Management

TEACH

S Skill Practice

Independent Practice

L1 List Ask students to make a list of food safety guidelines to be followed in their kitchen at home. Students should list common safety rules for keeping utensils, hands, and surfaces clean and avoiding contamination and cross-contamination. Ask students which rules they thought were most and least important.

L2 Detail Ask students to write a paragraph detailing how to store leftovers. Refrigerate or freeze leftovers promptly. Put leftovers in a tightly covered shallow container. Pack them in an airtight container, and label them with the name of the food and the date and freeze them.

L3 Apply Ask students to demonstrate kitchen safety by modeling how they would prepare before cooking, cook a meal, and store the leftovers. Students should demonstrate procedures that match the guidelines given in the chapter for preparing, handling, and storing food. Evaluate the student demonstrations.

U Universal Access

Kinesthetic Learners Choose a simple recipe and have students demonstrate how they would prepare that dish safely for the class, either using the actual ingredients, or pantomiming the steps of the preparation. Have them explain what they are doing and how it promotes food safety.

ASSESS

Quiz

Ask students to answer the following questions:

1. What are the symptoms of foodborne illness? The symptoms can feel like a mild flu and include diarrhea, nausea, stomach pain, headache, muscle pain, and fatigue.

2. What are perishable foods? Foods that are likely to spoil quickly, such as meat, poultry, fish, eggs, and dairy products.

3. How can you keep leftovers from spoiling? Refrigerate or freeze them promptly or immediately after the meal. Make sure they are tightly wrapped or in a sealed container.

RETEACH

W Writing Strategy

Self-Quiz Divide students into several small groups. Have each student develop and write down three questions about the material in this section, in either multiple choice, true/false, or short answer format. Have the groups answer each other's questions. The questions should be taken from this section, and the group should provide the correct answer to the question. You may want to do the quiz in the form of a contest.

C Critical Thinking

Outbreak Ask students to imagine that their family has had an outbreak of foodborne illness, and they are not yet sure of the source. Ask them to write up a procedure, including questions they would ask, things they would inspect, and recommendations they might make. Student procedures should reflect the common causes of foodborne illness. Questions should focus on what the family has eaten, and the report should include an inspection of the kitchen.

ASSESS

Section 21.1 Review Assign the Section 21.1 After You Read activities.

 Student Activity Workbook Assign the Section 21.1 Activities.

 Online Study Tools Have students go to the Online Learning Center at glencoe.com to:

- Take the Section 21.1 **Practice Test**.
- Download **Study-to-Go** content. STUDY TO GO

Section 21.1 After You Read
Answer Key

1. E. Coli can be found in contaminated water, raw or rare ground beef, and unpasteurized milk.

2. Freezer burn causes unappealing, dried-up white areas on food. To prevent it, keep foods airtight in freezer paper, heavy-duty foil, freezer-quality plastic bags, or plastic freezer containers.

3. Answers will vary, but students should mention some the safety techniques discussed in this chapter, including washing hands, keeping hair out of food, storing foods at proper temperatures and in proper containers, and cleaning up any spills immediately.

4. Students should present an overview of food safety regulations for community restaurants. They should discuss the guidelines, frequency of checks, and how the guidelines contribute to the public's safety (for example, restaurants are checked by an outside source to ensure that safe practices are used).

CLOSE

Culminating Activity

Apply Food Safety Find a simple recipe, and make a copy for each student. Have students determine where food safety guidelines would apply at each step of the recipe, and any special handling for the ingredients. Food safety guidelines might include: checking ingredients for proper storage and for spoilage, washing hands before and after touching food, washing produce thoroughly, following handling rules with meat, and cleaning surfaces and equipment.

Mc Graw Hill Professional Development **Mini Clip**
ELL Group Discussions

Section **21.2** **Lesson Plan**

Kitchen Essentials

FOCUS

Discussion Starter

Ask for volunteers to list accidents that occur in the kitchen. Discuss ways to prevent these accidents. Answers may include accidents such as burns and cuts, and ways to prevent these accidents, such as wearing oven mitts or handling and storing knives properly. Explain that students will learn more about preventing accidents in this section.

Bell Ringer Activity

Kitchen Rules Ask each student to create a list of rules to promote safety in their home kitchen. Ask volunteers to share their rules and explain why they are important. Compare lists. Working as a group, come up with a list of rules for safety in the classroom. Make a poster of the rules to hang on the wall.

Mc Graw Hill Professional Development **Mini Clip**
Reading Differentiated Instruction

TEACH

S Skill Practice
Independent Practice

L1 **List** Have students visualize their kitchens at home and list potentially dangerous objects or areas in their kitchens. Lists may include items such as knives, ovens/stoves, electrical appliances, cleaning supplies that contain hazardous substances, rugs, sharp corners, or other common kitchen hazards.

L2 **Explain** Ask students to explain what a convection oven is and how it works. A convection oven uses a high-speed fan to circulate hot air throughout the oven, evenly and continuously, which speeds up the cooking.

L3 **Apply** Divide students into groups and assign each group one type of kitchen accident. Using the section material, have the groups create a demonstration on how to prevent accidents of that type. Students should present accurate information about preventing falls, burns, fires, cuts, or electric shocks.

U Universal Access

Musical Learners Ask students to imagine that they are presenting a safety lesson to an elementary school class. Ask them to write a song to help the students remember kitchen safety tips. Have the students perform their songs for each other.

McGraw Hill **Professional Development** **Mini Clip**
ELL Words in Action

ASSESS

Quiz

Ask students to answer the following questions:

1. **What are the most common types of kitchen accidents?** Falls, burns, fires, cuts, and electric shocks.

2. **What happens if you put metal in a microwave oven?** Metal in a microwave creates sparks, which could result in a fire.

3. **What are some ways to prevent accidental knife cuts?** Cut food away from your body; wash knives separately; store knives in a knife holder; when cutting food, hold your hand so your fingertips are under your knuckles.

RETEACH

R Reading Strategy

Accident Prevention Have students review the information on common kitchen accidents. Go through the safety tips under each type of accident and have volunteers explain how each safety tip will prevent the accident that it refers to. Students should understand how the safety tips will help prevent the accident. For example, wearing potholders helps prevent burns by protecting your skin from hot surfaces.

C Critical Thinking

Self-Assessment Ask students to think about a task they perform often in the kitchen, whether it is making a simple meal, getting a snack, or washing dishes. Ask them to evaluate their behavior and write down ways in which they could perform their task more safely. Student assessments should show careful examination of their behavior and application of the chapter advice to improve it.

ASSESS

Section 21.2 Review Assign the Section 21.2 After You Read activities.

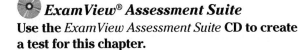 **Student Activity Workbook** Assign the Section 21.2 Activities.

Online Study Tools Have students go to the Online Learning Center at glencoe.com to:

- Take the Section 21.2 **Practice Test**.
- Download **Study-to-Go** content. STUDY TO GO

ExamView*® *Assessment Suite Use the *ExamView Assessment Suite* **CD to create a test for this chapter.**

Chapter Review Have students complete the Chapter 21 Review and Applications.

 Section 21.2 After You Read
Answer Key

1. Stand on a short stepladder or a sturdy step stool with a waist-high hand bar to get at high or hard-to-reach items. Turn pot and pan handles toward the center of the stove. Clean spills immediately. Keep cupboard doors and drawers closed when not in use.
2. Toasters, food processors, and blenders.
3. To learn how to use and care for appliances and to refer to later.
4. Students should create a poster focusing on how to avoid falls, burns, fires, cuts, or electric shocks. The poster should use graphics, photos, clip art and attention-grabbing copy.
5. Students should give a short presentation about a small kitchen appliance. Among the information they present should be who invented it, how it has developed (what the original version looked like and how it has changed over time), and how it is used.

CLOSE

Culminating Activity

Recipe Evaluation Locate a simple recipe and provide a copy to each of the students. Have them review the steps of the recipe and identify areas where accidents might occur and how could they prevent them. Common danger areas will be tasks that use knives (cuts) and tasks that involve the oven or stove (burns). Students should come up with safe ways to complete these dangerous steps.

Words You Learned

1. Students should use at least six of the content and academic vocabulary words in a short essay about food and kitchen safety.

Review Key Concepts

2. E. coli and salmonella.

3. Put leftovers in a tightly covered shallow container and refrigerate or freeze immediately.

4. Falls, burns, fires, cuts, and electric shocks.

5. They make food preparation much easier and often save us time and effort.

6. Refrigerators, dishwashers, stoves, convection ovens, and microwave ovens.

Critical Thinking

7. Answers may include: drink bottled water; cook meat, poultry, fish, and eggs fully; wash hands, knife, and cutting board when cutting meat, poultry, or fish; wipe up spills immediately; wash pots and pans in hot, soapy water; store perishable foods properly and immediately.

8. Students should evaluate how safe their kitchen at home is. If there are safety issues, they should suggest solutions. For example, perhaps there are dull knives in their kitchen that should be sharpened. If good safety precautions are followed in their kitchen at home, they should mention what those are.

9. Both cook food. A convection oven uses a high-speed fan to circulate hot air evenly and continuously, which speeds up cooking. Conventional ovens do not have a fan to circulate the heat, and so these tend to cook food slowly.

Real-World Skills and Applications

10. Treatment should mention cooling the burn by holding the burned area under cold water for at least five minutes to decrease the swelling. Additionally, the burn should be covered with a sterile gauze bandage, wrapped loosely. Neither ice nor butter should be applied, and formed blisters should not be broken.

11. Groups should create a brochure about kitchen safety. They should focus on one aspect of kitchen safety, such as how to avoid contamination or how to avoid accidents, such as burns, cuts or electric shocks.

Financial Literacy

12. The energy cost for Model A is $15 \times \$58 = \$870$, so the total lifetime cost is $\$870 + \$595 = \$1,465$. The energy cost for Model B is $15 \times \$35 = \$525$, so the total lifetime cost is $\$525 + \$715 = \$1,240$. Model B is less expensive.

Active Learning

13. Students should design a diagram/plan for their dream kitchen. They should include where appliances and utensils will be placed with regard to safety and convenience. They should think about the layout, where the cabinets and counters will be, where the sink and dishwasher will be, perhaps even where the refrigerator, toaster, and microwave will be. They should have reasons for why they designed their dream kitchen in the way they did.

14. Students should present information about either E. coli or salmonella. Their presentation should include causes, symptoms, and ways to prevent it. Students should provide detailed information in addition to what is in this chapter.

Net Connection

15. Students should provide a variety of table settings, including drawings of table settings organized by function.

Academic Skills

16. Students should create procedures for a safe dinner party. They should create a list with explanations written so that their classmates could follow the directions easily. Answers may include: fully cook meat; wash hands, cutting boards, and utensils with soap and hot water whenever you cut raw meat, fish, or poultry; clean as you cook; wipe spills immediately; handle perishable foods carefully; refrigerate leftovers immediately; and store leftovers in tightly covered shallow containers.

17. Students should create a short presentation about food safety during a historical period. They should provide examples of how safety was addressed, what procedures where followed, who did what, and the most prevalent risks.

18. $V = (3.14)(2 \text{ in.})(2 \text{ in.})(8 \text{ in.}) = 100.48$ cu. in. One container will not be enough to hold 115.5 cubic inches of soup.

Standardized Test Practice

19. a. $C = 5/9 \, (F\text{-}32)$

Prepare to Cook

Section 22.1 Meal Preparation

In this section, students will learn how to prepare before making a meal. They will learn how to plan the meal, shop for ingredients, and properly store ingredients.

Section 22.2 Recipe Basics

In this section, students will learn how to read and understand a recipe. They will also learn common abbreviations and mixing terms used in recipes and cooking.

Classroom Solutions

Print Resources

 Student Edition
Teacher Annotated Edition
Student Activity Workbook
Student Activity Workbook
Teacher Annotated Edition

Technology Resources

ExamView *ExamView Assessment Suite CD* allows you to create and print out customized tests or ready-made unit and chapter tests, complete with answer keys.

Lesson Planner *Lesson Planner Plus! CD** is and electronic lesson planner that provides instant access to teacher resources in one convenient package.

- Projects and Activities*
- Food Labs*
- Sewing Labs*
- Career Investigations*
- Reteaching Activities*
- Enrichment Activities*

Presentation Plus! PowerPoint™ Presentations can be edited and customized to meet the needs of students.

Online Learning Center includes resources and activities for students and teachers. Also includes Online Student Edition.

Interactive Student Edition

*ELECTRONIC RESOURCES ARE AVAILABLE ON LESSON PLANNER PLUS AND THE ONLINE LEARNING CENTER.

Writing Activity Answer

First Draft Students should write a first draft describing how to make one of their favorite recipes. The draft should mention the necessary ingredients and the steps to follow. It can be rough with spelling and punctuation errors that will be corrected in a later draft. Help the students critique their first draft by asking what they have left out and what they should delete.

Discovering Careers Answers ▼

1. Answers will vary. Students should write a summary of the education, training, and experience needed for the selected careers.
2. Student answers will vary based on the type of food they compare. Answers should include the order the ingredients are in, the amount of a particular ingredient, or actual different ingredients.
3. Student answers will vary, but may include cafeterias, vending machines, catering, fast-food, microwaves, toasters, and refrigerators.
4. Answers will vary. Students should present a summary of what they learned about the person's typical work day.

Section 22.1 Lesson Plan

Meal Preparation

FOCUS

Discussion Starter

Ask students to discuss how they plan their meals. Do they plan meals ahead, or do they make decisions at the last moment? Do they plan their own meals, or does someone else plan for them? Students should compare the types of meals they choose when making a split-second decision versus when their meal is planned and the meals they choose for themselves versus those chosen for them.

McGraw Hill Professional Development **Mini Clip**
Reading Guided Instruction

Bell Ringer Activity

Planning Procedures Ask students to brainstorm factors to consider when planning and shopping for a meal. Have students explain why each factor is important. Use the suggestions to create a procedure for planning a meal. List steps from start to finish, beginning with the idea for the meal and finishing with beginning preparation. Copy the list for each student.

TEACH

S Skill Practice

Guided Practice

L1 List Work as a class to list three foods from each food group. Students should list foods that fit into the meats and beans group, the grain group, the vegetable group, the fruit group, the milk group, and oils. For example for meat and beans, one could choose chicken or pinto beans.

L2 Brainstorm Work as a class to brainstorm ways to include variety in a meal. One way to add variety is to vary the way foods are prepared. Another way is to choose foods that provide different colors, sizes and shapes, textures, flavors, and temperatures. For example, adding different colored vegetables to a rice dish can add variety.

L3 Apply Work as a class to plan a dinner that is healthful, affordable, and fits into a schedule. Encourage students to attempt making the meal

you planned for their families. Students should gain experience in the process of meal planning, reading recipes, thinking about nutrition, and time management. Ask any students who actually prepare their meal to describe what happened.

U Universal Access

Verbal Learners Pair students and have one explain to the other how to incorporate special dietary needs into the meal planning process. Have the other explain how to read food labels.

ASSESS

Quiz

Ask students to answer the following questions:

1. **What types of foods are in the grain group, and how much of them should you eat each day?** Cereal, rice, pasta, breads, and grits; 6 ounces every day.

2. **What are generic brands?** Products with labels listing only the product name and nutritional information are generic brands. These often cost less than store and national brands.

3. **What can happen if you do not store food properly?** Heat, light, time, and moisture destroy nutrients. They can also affect flavor. Food can spoil, turn, or become stale.

RETEACH

W Writing Strategy

Assess Priorities Ask students to assess their priorities when it comes to shopping for food. What factors are most and least important to them? Ask them to write their answers. Students should prioritize the information they would look at when shopping. They should choose what is most and least important out of brand, nutritional content, and price, and explain their priorities.

C Critical Thinking

Make Inferences The text gives you some information about the difference between national brands, store brands, and generic brands. What can you infer about the relative quality of each of these brand types? Is one better than the others? Students should realize from the information given that while the price may differ, there is no indication of the relative quality of each.

McGraw Hill Professional Development **Mini Clip**
ELL Building the Context

ASSESS

Section 22.1 Review Assign the Section 22.1 After You Read activities.

 Student Activity Workbook Assign the Section 22.1 Activities.

Online Study Tools Have students go to the Online Learning Center at glencoe.com to:

- Take the Section 22.1 **Practice Test**.
- Download **Study-to-Go** content.

Section 22.1 After You Read

Answer Key

1. Vary the way foods are prepared or choose foods that provide different colors, sizes, shapes, textures, flavors, and temperatures.

2. Buy store or generic brands, compare brands, read labels and unit pricing information, use coupons, and check newspapers for sales.

3. Storing foods properly helps them keep their freshness and flavor.

4. Students should create a formal invitation to a dinner party. They should have a theme and include information so that their guests can arrive on time and dressed appropriately. They may also use graphics or clip art.

5. Students should pick a meal or food that they think is unique to their family and be able to explain the story/tradition behind it.

CLOSE

Culminating Activity

Working with Resources Divide students into five groups and assign each group a resource that they lack (skills, equipment, ingredients, money, or time). Have each group prepare a meal plan that accounts for the deficiency. Discuss their plans and how they address the deficiency. Plans should focus on making up for the lack of a resource by being simple to prepare, requiring little to no equipment or few ingredients, being low-cost, or being quick to prepare.

McGraw Hill **Professional Development** **Mini Clip**
Reading Exploring the Big Idea

Recipe Basics

FOCUS

Discussion Starter

Ask students how many of them have ever cooked a meal from a recipe. What was the most difficult thing they have prepared from a recipe? How did it turn out? How did they feel when it was served? Answers will vary depending on personal experiences. Students should discuss the meals or dishes they have prepared and what they did and did not do well. They should also discuss how it made them feel to prepare something difficult.

Bell Ringer Activity

Create a Basic Recipe Ask students to create a recipe for a simple dish, such as a sandwich or a salad. Have the students compare their recipes. How many different recipes did the students come up with? Did anyone create something similar? Compile the recipes into a book.

McGraw Hill **Professional Development** **Mini Clip**
ELL Low Risk Environment

TEACH

S Skill Practice

Independent Practice

L1 List Ask students to list five cooking terms and their definitions. Students should choose terms from Figure 22.4 on page 502, and provide a definition for each. For example, they might list baking, to cook in the oven without a cover.

L2 Explain Ask students to explain what the different recipe abbreviations stand for. Tsp. is teaspoon, Tbsp. is tablespoon, oz. is ounce, c. is cup, pt. is pint, qt. is quart, gal. is gallon, °F is degrees Fahrenheit, °C is degrees Celsius, mL is milliliter, L is liter, lb. is pound, and g. is gram.

L3 Apply Ask students to locate a recipe for soup and explain the abbreviations and terms in that recipe. Students should review the recipe and provide the full word for each abbreviation and give a definition for each cooking term. If any terms are unfamiliar to them, have them look them up.

U Universal Access

Students with Hearing Impairments Arrange for a reliable classmate to partner with a hearing impaired student. Have them compare their notes so that the hearing impaired student may fill in any information he or she may have missed.

ASSESS

Quiz

Ask students to answer the following questions:

1. **How does using a recipe make cooking easier?** Recipes provide ingredients, amounts of ingredients, and instructions that have been tested already, so using one will improve your chances of success when preparing a meal.

2. **Why is it important to know common cooking abbreviations?** Recipes use abbreviations to save space, and knowing them will prevent you from using the wrong amount of an ingredient.

3. **What does it mean to scald milk when cooking?** Heating milk until it steams and begins to bubble around the edge of the pan.

RETEACH

R Reading Strategy

Evaluate Have students review the guidelines for what they should look for in a recipe. Have them find three recipes and evaluate whether each meets those guidelines. Have them rate how easy each would be to follow. Students should go through each guideline and determine whether it matches the recipe they are evaluating. The more guidelines the recipe matches, the easier the recipe.

C Critical Thinking

Physical Impairments and Cooking Have students list the mechanical, technical, spatial, and motor skills they might need in order to cook in a home kitchen. Then ask them to brainstorm any aids or technology that could be used to assist a person with physical disabilities in the kitchen. Answers will vary, but answers might include specially designed kitchens or workspaces or special tools to help with reach.

ASSESS

Section 22.2 Review Assign the Section 22.2 After You Read activities.

Student Activity Workbook Assign the Section 22.2 Activities.

Online Study Tools Have students go to the Online Learning Center at glencoe.com to:

- Take the Section 22.2 **Practice Test**.
- Download **Study-to-Go** content.

ExamView® Assessment Suite

Use the *ExamView Assessment Suite* **CD to create a test for this chapter.**

Chapter Review Have students complete the Chapter 22 Review and Applications.

Section 22.2 After You Read

Answer Key

1. Knowing how to read and follow recipes.

2. Any five of: bake, boil, braise, broil, brown, chill, cook, cook by dry heat, cook by moist heat, deep-fat fry, fry, roast, sauté, scald, simmer, steam, stew, stir fry, and preheat.

3. Trim as little from fruits and vegetable as possible; keep food whole or in large pieces; cook food for right length of time; cook and serve food at the right temperature; and save cooking liquids to use in other foods.

4. Students should provide instructions, necessary ingredients and utensils, any preparation work, baking time, how many servings it makes, and why the recipe is special.

5. Students should bring in recipes from family members that were not written down before and share them with their classmates and family as part of their family history.

CLOSE

Culminating Activity

Abbreviations and Terms Have students choose one recipe from a cookbook or food magazine and identify the abbreviations and terms. Have them expand each abbreviation and define each term. Students should correctly identify each abbreviation and term and correctly expand the abbreviations and define the terms.

Words You Learned

1. Students should label each content and vocabulary term as a noun, verb, or adjective.

Review Key Concepts

1. Meats, beans, fish, and foods from the nuts group, grains group, vegetable group, fruit group, and milk and other calcium-rich group.

3. Name of food, manufacturer, nutritional content, serving size, calories, ingredients, weight, and trans fat amount.

4. Heat, light, time, and moisture.

5. You need to follow the steps so your dish will come out as expected, and you need to know what ingredients to use and how much of each.

6. Whip, blend, cream, stir, toss, combine, beat.

7. Suggestions may include: adding vegetables, adding calcium-rich foods, cutting back on fats, adding fiber, reducing added suger, and reducing sodium.

Critical Thinking

8. Answers will vary based on the recipe chosen. Students should point out if any information is missing (for example, if it does not list all the ingredients or utensils needed; if it does not list the amounts; if it does not indicate how many servings the recipe will yield). Students should also be able to assess what preparation needs to be done (for example, preheating the oven or greasing a pan).

9. Student answers will vary based on what they ate, but they should list everything they ate yesterday and from this list, draw a conclusion about whether their day contained enough variation and balance from all the food groups.

Real-World Skills and Applications

10. Students should provide label information from five foods they regularly eat. They should include serving size, nutritional content, calories, and ingredients. They should draw conclusions about whether these foods are healthful.

11. Students should have a meal together for which each person has prepared a dish. Allow time in class for eating and sharing the food and recipes. Students should share what the experience of preparing their dish was like.

Financial Literacy

12. Using the coupon to buy a 40-oz. jar is the cheapest option. If Michael uses the coupon with the 28-oz. jar, the cost per serving will be ($4.89 − $0.50) ÷ 28 ≈ $0.16. If he uses the coupon with the 40-oz. jar, the cost per serving will be ($5.99 − $0.50) ÷ 40 ≈ $0.14. If he uses the coupon with one 17-oz. jar, the cost per serving will be ($3.50 − $0.50) ÷ 7 ≈ $0.18, but if he buys two 17-oz. jars, the cost per serving will be $5.00 ÷ 34 ≈ $0.15.

Active Learning

13. Students will create a class cookbook by collecting contributions from classmates. Recipes should be in a standard format, with step-by-step instructions and correct abbreviations. Make copies of the cookbook for everyone. Students can share why they selected their particular recipe.

14. Students should present the history of a common food, sharing how the food has changed and how recipes with that food have evolved.

Net Connection

15. Students should create a list of healthy appetizers, such as raw vegetables and dip, pita bread and humus, fresh fruit, cheese, or nuts.

Academic Skills

16. Possible benefits are: families may be made stronger and more communicative since eating together allows them to share how their days went; eating in can save money, since the family is not eating at a restaurant; and eating in is usually a more nutritious option than eating out.

17. Students should be able to deduce that the necessary ingredients are flour, yeast, sugar, salt, and water. These ingredients work together to bond and make way for the rising of the bread.

18. The revised recipe should have $4 \times \frac{3}{4} = 3$ cups of rolled oats, $3/2 \times \frac{3}{4} = 9/8 = 1\ 1/8$ cups of wheat germ, $\frac{1}{2} \times \frac{3}{4} = 3/8$ cup of almonds, $3/8$ cup of coconut, $3/8$ cup of raisins, $1 \times \frac{3}{4} = \frac{3}{4}$ cup of honey, and $\frac{3}{4} \times \frac{1}{4} = 3/16$ cup of oil.

Standardized Test Practice

19. Sample answer: Being able to read a recipe will increase your success in the kitchen. You need to understand abbreviations and cooking and mixing terms. If you do not know what T. stands for, you may put too much or too little of a spice into a recipe.

20. Sample answer: When you plan your meals ahead of time, you can shop for the best prices and have the resources you need on hand. You can allot the right amount of time and money. It is hard when you start a meal and do not have an ingredient. It can change your meal entirely.

Chapter 23 Planning Guide

Cooking Basics

Section 23.1 Choose Your Ingredients

In this section, students will learn how to cook with basic ingredients. They will learn how to select quality fruits and vegetables. They will also learn how to use convenience foods.

Section 23.2 Cooking Techniques

In this section, students will learn basic cooking techniques for grains, fruits and vegetables, milk products, meat, poultry, fish, and other proteins, such as legumes and eggs.

Classroom Solutions

Print Resources

- Student Edition
- Teacher Annotated Edition
- Student Activity Workbook
- Student Activity Workbook Teacher Annotated Edition

Technology Resources

ExamView *ExamView Assessment Suite CD* allows you to create and print out customized tests or ready-made unit and chapter tests, complete with answer keys.

Lesson Planner *Plus Lesson Planner Plus! CD** is and electronic lesson planner that provides instant access to teacher resources in one convenient package.

- Projects and Activities*
- Food Labs*
- Sewing Labs*
- Career Investigations*
- Reteaching Activities*
- Enrichment Activities*

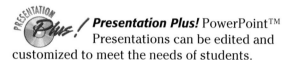

Presentation Plus! PowerPoint™ Presentations can be edited and customized to meet the needs of students.

Online Learning Center includes resources and activities for students and teachers. Also includes Online Student Edition.

Interactive Student Edition

*ELECTRONIC RESOURCES ARE AVAILABLE ON LESSON PLANNER PLUS AND THE ONLINE LEARNING CENTER.

Writing Activity Answer

Compare and Contrast Students should write an essay with a thesis/topic sentence that says one of the dishes is better than the other or identifies how they are different or similar. Students should provide specific details about each dish and use transitions when moving between descriptions of the two dishes.

Discovering Careers Answers ▼

1. Answers will vary. Students should write a summary of the education, training, and experience needed for the selected careers.

2. Students should prepare a meal with their family. Each person will have taken responsibility for a specific part of the meal. They should be able to discuss what technique they used and why they selected this technique for their section of the meal.

3. Students should provide three suggestions for healthy brown-bag lunches and compare them with other students.

4. Answers will vary. Students should present a summary of what they learned about the person's typical work day.

Section **23.1** Lesson Plan

Choose Your Ingredients

FOCUS

Discussion Starter

Ask students to think of the meals that they ate the day before. How many ingredients can they list from each? Have them say what the meal consisted of and list each ingredient. Students may find that although they know the main ingredients, they do not know all of the ingredients that combine to make up their meals.

Bell Ringer Activity

Name Ingredients Choose a common food, such as hamburger, taco, pizza, or salad and ask students to list the ingredients they would use if they were making the item. Note how each student's selections are similar and different. Students may choose different ingredients. For example, a vegetarian might use a vegetable patty. Some students may choose ground turkey instead of beef for health reasons.

Mc Graw Hill Professional Development **Mini Clip**
Reading Bridging Cultural Gaps

TEACH

S Skill Practice

Independent Practice

L1 List Ask students to list and describe five kinds of herbs and spices. Students should choose five herbs and/or spices from the list on page 54 and provide a description. For example, cinnamon comes from the bark of the laurel tree. Ground cinnamon is common in cakes, cookies, and specialty drinks.

L2 Describe Ask students to write a paragraph describing why it is better to purchase produce that is in-season. You get the best possible quality and save money. Produce that is available out-of-season is often more expensive. It may be less nutritious because it is artificially ripened or shipped a long distance.

L3 Apply Have students smell and taste various herbs and spices and come up with dishes that they would use them in. Students should imagine what dishes each herb or spice would enhance and explain why they chose as they did.

U Universal Access

Logical/Mathematical Learners Have students practice converting measurements from standard weights to metric weights. Explain that most recipes will be written using standard measurements, but European recipes may be written using metric. Encourage them to learn both systems.

Mc Graw Hill Professional Development **Mini Clip**
Math Ways of Working—Solving Equations

ASSESS

Quiz

Ask students to answer the following questions:

1. **What are the basic ingredients that are common to many recipes?** Some are flour, sugar, butter, milk, eggs, and spices.

2. **What are the benefits of eating fruits and vegetables?** They are full of essential nutrients, easy to include in meals, and high in fiber.

3. **What are the downsides of using convenience foods?** Convenience foods tend to cost more than fresh foods. Additionally, they may not taste as fresh, and often contain preservatives.

RETEACH

R Reading Strategy

Make a List Have students find ten recipes and note how many times each ingredient appears in the recipes. Then have the class group their results to see which ingredients appear in the most recipes overall, and make a list. Common ingredients will probably include things like flour, eggs, milk, sugar, and salt.

C Critical Thinking

Connect to Community See if you can find a farmer's market nearby that takes place on a weekday. Get the school's permission to take a field trip, and encourage students to talk to the vendors. Discuss shopping for produce in this way as opposed to at the grocery store. Many vendors in the farmer's market are knowledgeable about when produce is in season and what to look for regarding quality.

Mc Graw Hill Professional Development **Mini Clip**
ELL Using Manipulatives

ASSESS

Section 23.1 Review Assign the Section 23.1 After You Read activities.

 Student Activity Workbook Assign the Section 23.1 Activities.

 Online Study Tools Have students go to the Online Learning Center at glencoe.com to:

- Take the Section 23.1 **Practice Test**.
- Download **Study-to-Go** content. 📖

Section 23.1 After You Read

Answer Key

1. The basic ingredients are flour, sugar, shortening or butter, milk, eggs, and spices.

2. Serve them as main dishes, side dishes, snacks, salads, and garnishes.

3. They can be more expensive; they can taste less fresh; and they may contain preservatives.

4. Students should create a pamphlet attempting to sell spices. They should incorporate art of photos in order to grab people's attention. They should mention the benefits of spices such as that they add flavor, create variety, and can be healthful alternatives to salt, butter, and other less healthful flavor enhancers. They should mention specific spices and dishes in which these spices can be used.

5. Students should create a map of the U.S. that shows where fruits and vegetables are most commonly grown. They should use clip art, illustrations, or drawings to illustrate what fruits and vegetables are grown where.

CLOSE

Culminating Activity

Identify Herbs and Spices Copy recipes for the class that contain herbs and spices. Go through the ingredients and have students identify which are herbs and spices. Then have them describe each herb and spice. Students should be able to pick out the herbs and spices in an ingredient list and describe flavors and appearances. Write down the names of those they do not know so you can look them up at the end of the exercise.

Section 23.2 Lesson Plan

Cooking Techniques

FOCUS

Discussion Starter

Ask students to describe different cooking methods that they have used or that their families use. Have them describe the method and what type of food it is used for. Try to elicit a variety of cooking methods for all types of foods, such as baking, boiling, frying, or steaming, as well as the types of foods they use them on.

🔔 Bell Ringer Activity

Work with Ingredients Ask students to imagine that they have pasta, spinach, and chicken breast in their kitchen. How many ways can they think of to prepare those items? They may add other ingredients. See how many dishes the class can come up with. Students should come up with dishes, such as pasta with chicken and spinach, a casserole, or a salad.

> **McGraw Hill Professional Development** **Mini Clip**
> **Math** Multiple Approaches to Problem Solving

TEACH

S Skill Practice

Independent Practice

L1 **List** Ask students to list the components of a sandwich. A type of bread, such as sourdough, wheat or rye; a spread, such as mayonnaise; a filling; and ingredients that add extra flavor and texture, such as lettuce, spinach, avocado, relish, sprouts, tomatoes, peppers, and olives.

L2 **Explain** Have students write a paragraph explaining how to make pasta slippery and not sticky. Use a lot of water, heat to a boil before putting in pasta, stir, cook until tender but slightly firm, drain carefully, mix in any additional ingredients, and serve the pasta while it is still hot.

L3 **Apply** Ask students to imagine that they will make a soup. Have them describe what type of ingredients they would use and what they might have to do to prepare them. Students should choose vegetables and meats to go in their soups. They may need to pre-cook some ingredients.

U Universal Access

Students with Hearing Impairments Work with a student with a hearing impairment to make sure that they are not missing too much from the class lecture. You may want to include visual aids showing examples of the different types of food.

ASSESS

Quiz

Ask students to answer the following questions:

1. **What is the difference between a quick bread and a yeast bread?** In a quick bread, the leavening agent is baking powder or baking soda. In a yeast bread, the leavening agent is yeast.

2. **How can you prevent milk from curdling?** When milk curdles, it separates into particles. To avoid this, add ingredients very slowly and stir the milk constantly.

3. **What types of meat should be cooked using a moist heat method?** Chuck roast, corned beef, pork blade steak, pot roast, poultry, round steak, spareribs, and stew meat.

RETEACH

W Writing Strategy

Menu Analysis Provide students with menus from restaurants. Ask them to identify the main ingredient and the cooking method used. What kind of variety is on each menu? Students should identify the main ingredients and cooking method for each dish. For example, a hamburger has a main ingredient of ground beef and is grilled. Some restaurants may use mostly one cooking method, while others may use a variety.

C Critical Thinking

Predict Consequences Ask students to examine the following scenarios and predict consequences: (1) Jorge is baking a yeast bread. He only lets the dough rise once. (2) Jason is cooking a beef rib roast, and he stews it. (3) Ayesha is hard-boiling an egg. She takes it out of the water immediately after taking it off the burner. (1) The bread will be dense and hard; (2) The meat will be too tender and will fall apart during stewing; (3) The egg will not finish cooking and will be runny.

Professional Development **Mini Clip**
Reading Lesson Reflections

ASSESS

Section 23.2 Review Assign the Section 23.2 After You Read activities.

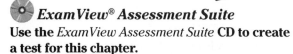 **Student Activity Workbook** Assign the Section 23.2 Activities.

Online Study Tools Have students go to the Online Learning Center at glencoe.com to:

- Take the Section 23.2 **Practice Test**.
- Download **Study-to-Go** content.

ExamView® Assessment Suite
Use the *ExamView Assessment Suite* **CD to create a test for this chapter.**

Chapter Review Have students complete the Chapter 23 Review and Applications.

Section 23.2 After You Read

Answer Key

1. Let it rise in a warm place outside the oven for an hour or more. Then punch it down, shape it, and let it rise in the pan before baking. Then let the dough warm to room temperature and rise until it is ready to be baked.

2. Simmering, steaming, baking, frying, stir-frying, and microwaving.

3. Use low to medium heat. Grate or shred hard cheeses before adding them to other ingredients. Add cheese at the end of the cooking time to avoid overcooking.

4. Beans and eggs.

5. The letter should provide specific information about fruit to support the stance. Ideas could include dried, cooked, or baked fruit.

6. Students should research a cooking technique covered in the section, and compare and contrast the technique with what we do now.

CLOSE

Culminating Activity

Practice Makes Perfect Divide students into groups, and have each group choose a simple recipe, prepare it, and serve it to the class. Students should put what they have learned into practice by preparing a recipe. If you do not have a classroom kitchen, you may try to plan a class potluck instead.

Words You Learned

1. Students should create a fill-in-the-blank sentence for each of the vocabulary terms. The sentence should contain enough information to help determine the missing word.

Review Key Concepts

2. Herbs and spices add taste, color, and aroma to foods.

3. Fruits that are frozen, canned, or dried are considered processed. Fruit juices are also processed.

4. They can save you time.

5. Quick breads and yeast breads.

6. They are valuable sources of carbohydrates, fiber, and many important vitamins and minerals.

7. To make soups, sauces, puddings, custards, cakes, pies, breads, and muffins.

8. Moist heat and dry heat.

Critical Thinking

9. You can prevent or minimize the loss of nutrients while cooking vegetables by: cooking until they are tender and crisp, not soft; using as little water as possible while cooking; using a lid to speed cooking time; avoiding overcooking; and making sure the color of the vegetable stays bright (for example, cooked green beans should be bright green, not olive green).

Real-World Skills and Applications

10. Broiling, pan-frying, and stir-frying are fast cooking methods. The chicken breasts could be cooked in all these ways. To increase the nutritional value of the meal, you could add vegetables as a side dish or to a stir-fry. Be careful not to overcook the vegetables which can result in the vegetables losing some of their nutrients.

11. Students should create a spreadsheet that lists spices and herbs for cooking, with suggestions for dishes and the best foods to use them with.

Financial Literacy

12. Answers will vary based on the recipes and products selected by students, although the finished cake will most likely be the most expensive item. Pros and cons should include the time required for each type of cake, the amount of control and customization over the appearance and ingredients of the cake, the nutritional value of the three different cakes, and the taste of the cakes.

Active Learning

13. Students should fill a basket with fruit and healthful snacks to give to a friend, teacher, or family member. The basket should also include a booklet of recipes for additional healthful snacks.

14. Answers will vary depending on spices chosen. Sample answer: Cinnamon originated in India and is made from the bark of the cinnamon tree. Original uses include drink flavoring, medicine, and as an embalming agent. Today it is used mainly in desserts, such as apple pies and cinnamon rolls, and in teas. It can also be used as a fragrance.

Net Connection

15. Lists may include: sweet potatoes, carrots, cantaloupe, squash, apricots, pumpkin, mangos, collard greens, broccoli, spinach, kale, tomatoes, soybean oil, watermelon, guava, papaya, apricots, pink grapefruit, liver, milk, egg yolks, mozzarella cheese, poultry, and fish.

Academic Skills

16. Students should create a poster of cooking techniques for vegetables. They should include graphics, photos, and instructions for each technique. Display the posters in your classroom. The six cooking methods mentioned in this chapter, which students will probably focus on, are simmering, steaming, baking, frying, stir-frying, and microwave cooking.

17. Students should write an overview of a family recipe, including its ingredients and origins. They should provide details to explain the importance of the recipe to their family's traditions and culture.

18. For the sourdough loaf, she will get $12 \div \frac{3}{4} = 12/1 \times 4/3 = 48/3 = 16$ slices. For the rye loaf, she will get $13\frac{1}{2} \div \frac{1}{2} = 27/2 \times 2/1 = 27$ slices.

Standardized Test Practice

19. b

FOCUS

Introduce the Project

In this project, students will cook a dish unique to their culture. Ask students what they consider to be their cultural identity. Answers will vary, but may include a nationality, ethnic group, religion, race, a combination of these, or that they simply follow unique family traditions.

Build Background

Favorite Restaurants Ask students to name their favorite restaurants. Restaurants usually categorize themselves according to culture or nationality. Ask them to describe their food and ambiance and to write their observations. Discuss what conclusions may be drawn about a culture from its style of food and ways of eating. Restaurants will vary, but may be Italian, Mexican, or Thai. Sample observations are that Italian food is served "family style" while Mexican food uses tortillas in many dishes.

TEACH

S Skill Practice

Guided Practice

L1 List Tell students to make a list of five foods that they used to dislike, but have now acquired a taste for. Choose students to read their lists and explain what changed their mind about the food. Discuss why tastes change as you get older. Lists will vary, but students may explain that they never tasted something or that pairing the food with something else gave it a different flavor.

L2 Identify Ask students to choose a holiday specific to their culture, religion, or nationality. Have students volunteer to explain the traditional foods that are eaten on that holiday. Holidays and meals may include turkey on Thanksgiving or candy on Halloween.

L3 Imagine Have students imagine they are giving a dinner party, but that some of the guests are vegans, which means the do not eat any meat or animal products (no eggs or dairy). Ask them to suggest a menu that includes an appetizer, a main course, and a dessert that all their guests can enjoy. Sample menu: green salad with oil and vinegar as an appetizer, black bean burritos as a main course, and fresh berrries as a dessert.

C Critical Thinking

Eating Ambiance Remind students that food stimulates two senses: smell and taste. What other senses may be critical to your eating experience? Ask students to compare and contrast the experience of eating in a noisy, crowded environment with eating in a spacious, quiet area. How important is the look, feel, and mood of the location in which they are eating? Answers will vary, but students may conclude that eating can be more satisfying when all of your senses are satisfied.

ASSESS

Quiz

Ask students to answer the following questions:

1. What are the six food groups you should include in your meals? Meats and Beans, Grains, Vegetables, Fruits, Milk, and Oils.

2. What do each of the following abbreviations stands for: Tbsp., pt., L, mL, lb.? Tablespoon, pint, liter, milliliter, and pound.

3. What is the difference between national brands, store brands, and generic brands? National brands cost most because of fancy packaging and advertising. Store brands are cheaper because their packaging is simpler. Generic brands are the least expensive because the label has only the name of the product and the nutritional information.

CLOSE

Culminating Activity

What is American Food? In this activity, students cooked a meal from their own culture. But we are all also part of the American culture. Have students write a paragraph suggesting what American food is and how it compares and contrasts with food from their other culture. Answers will vary, but may include pizza, hamburgers, apple pie, and ice cream. Comparisons may note that food is spicier in other cultures, or how many American dishes, like pizza, hot dogs, and hamburgers, are based on food from other cultures.

Discovering
LIFE SKILLS

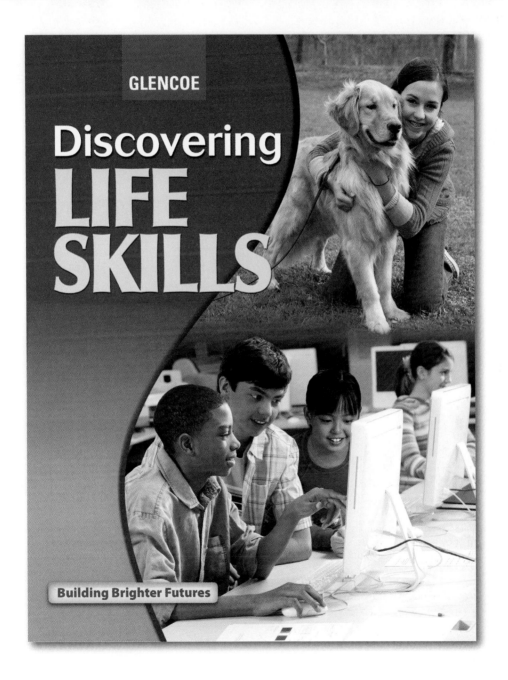

GLENCOE

Discovering
LIFE
SKILLS

Building Brighter Futures

Send all inquiries to:
Glencoe/McGraw-Hill
21600 Oxnard Street, Suite 500
Woodland Hills, CA 91367

ISBN: 978-0-07-888468-9   (Student Edition)
MHID: 0-07-888468-3   (Student Edition)
ISBN: 978-0-07-888469-6   (Teacher Annotated Edition)
MHID: 0-07-888469-1   (Teacher Annotated Edition)

1 2 3 4 5 6 7 8 9   079   11 10 09 08

Educational Reviewers

LeeLinda Baggett
Family and Consumer
 Sciences Teacher
Trickum Middle School
Lilburn, Georgia

Melinda Chambers
Family and Consumer
 Sciences Teacher
Romney Middle School
Romney, West Virginia

Tammy Clow-Kennedy
Family and Consumer
 Sciences Teacher
Hendrix Junior High School
Chandler, Arizona

Dawn Gary
Family and Consumer
 Sciences Teacher
Lafayette Parish
School Board
Lafayette, Louisiana

Janet Hartline
Family and Consumer
 Sciences Teacher
Fort Payne High School
Fort Payne, Alabama

Judy Henry
Family and Consumer
 Sciences Teacher
ROCORI Middle School
Cold Spring, Minnesota

Georgia Lash
Student Council Advisor
Family and Consumer
 Sciences Department
Hillcrest High School
Simpsonville, South Carolina

Angie Lustrick
Nutritionist–Personal
 Trainer
Angie's World
Riverside, California

Valerie Morgan
Family and Consumer
 Sciences Teacher
Water Valley High School
Water Valley, Mississippi

**Teddy Mwonyonyi-
Nantambi**
Family and Consumer
 Sciences Department
 Chair
Cleveland Municipal
School District
Cleveland, Ohio

Kimberly Myers
Family and Consumer
 Sciences Teacher
Aynor High School
Aynor, South Carolina

Bettie J. O'Shields
Family and Consumer
 Sciences Teacher
Durham Public Schools
Durham, North Carolina

Mary Lu Pennington
Family and Consumer
 Sciences Department
 Chair
Guion Creek Middle School
Indianapolis, Indiana

Jeanine M. Pope
Family and Consumer
 Sciences Teacher
Fort Morgan High School
Fort Morgan, Colorado

Marcia Jean Ritter
Family and Consumer
 Sciences Teacher, Retired
Pleasant Lea Middle School
Lee's Summit, Missouri

Patti Sanchez
Family and Consumer
 Sciences Teacher
Preston Junior High School
Fort Collins, Colorado

Jill Tolleson
Family and Consumer
 Sciences Teacher
Delight School System
Delight, Arkansas

Anne Weiss
Family and Consumer
 Sciences Teacher, Retired
Kimball Middle School
Elgin, Illinois

Technical Reviewers

Bill Dueease
Life Coach
Fort Myers, Florida

Vikki Jackson
Family and Consumer
 Sciences Teacher
Kathleen Middle School
Lakeland, Florida

Kathryn Oliver Russell
Family and Consumer
 Sciences Department
 Chair
Chickasha, Oklahoma

Scavenger Hunt

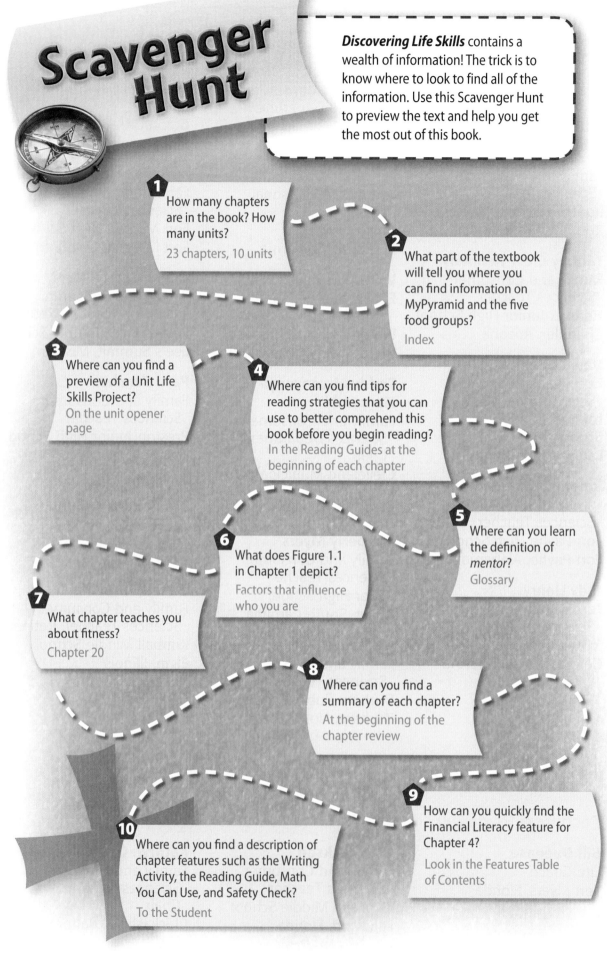

Discovering Life Skills contains a wealth of information! The trick is to know where to look to find all of the information. Use this Scavenger Hunt to preview the text and help you get the most out of this book.

1 How many chapters are in the book? How many units?
23 chapters, 10 units

2 What part of the textbook will tell you where you can find information on MyPyramid and the five food groups?
Index

3 Where can you find a preview of a Unit Life Skills Project?
On the unit opener page

4 Where can you find tips for reading strategies that you can use to better comprehend this book before you begin reading?
In the Reading Guides at the beginning of each chapter

5 Where can you learn the definition of *mentor*?
Glossary

6 What does Figure 1.1 in Chapter 1 depict?
Factors that influence who you are

7 What chapter teaches you about fitness?
Chapter 20

8 Where can you find a summary of each chapter?
At the beginning of the chapter review

9 How can you quickly find the Financial Literacy feature for Chapter 4?
Look in the Features Table of Contents

10 Where can you find a description of chapter features such as the Writing Activity, the Reading Guide, Math You Can Use, and Safety Check?
To the Student

Table of Contents

FOCUS ON **Reading Strategies**
Look for these reading
strategies in each chapter:

- Before You Read
- Graphic Organizer
- As You Read
- Reading Check
- After You Read

Table of Contents

Table of Contents

FOCUS ON **Academic Success**
To help you succeed in your classes and on tests, look for these academic skills:
- Reading Guides
- Writing Tips
- Math You Can Use
- Science You Can Use

Table of Contents

FOCUS ON

Project-Based Learning
Projects throughout the book can help you use your skills in real-life situations:

- Real-world scenarios
- Step-by-step instructions
- Independent and group activities

Table of Contents

Table of Contents

FOCUS ON **Assessment**
Look for review questions and activities to help you remember important topics:

- Reading Checks
- Section Reviews
- Chapter Reviews
- Life Skills Projects

Table of Contents

Features Table of Contents

Academic Skills for Life!

How much money can you save by recycling? How can you avoid the dangers of second-hand smoke? Do you know how to compare products to get the best value for your money? Use these academic features to succeed in school, on tests, and with life!

MATH YOU CAN USE

SCIENCE YOU CAN USE

Financial Literacy

Tips for Success Throughout Your School Years

Where can you go for extra help in a difficult subject? How can you organize your study space more effectively? What can you do to reduce your stress level? Look for the Succeed in School tips in every chapter to help you in every class you take.

SUCCEED IN SCHOOL!

What Do You Want to Do?

What career options are open to you? What do professionals in the Family and Consumer Sciences fields really do? Discover a world of possibilities!

Discovering Careers
Focus On Careers In...

Features Table of Contents

Life Skills for Every Day

Do you know what it is like to set up a business? How can you keep a young child entertained while you baby sit? What can you do to help the environment? How can safety practices help you in the kitchen or while you are online? These activities and ideas show you how to apply your new skills to everyday life.

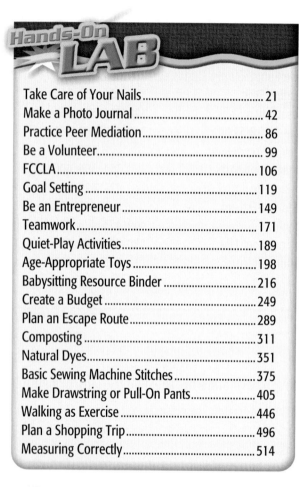

Hands-On LAB

Safety Check

How To...

Connect to Your Community – All Over the World!

Your world goes beyond your home and school. As you prepare to enter adulthood, you are learning that others can be affected by your actions. Community Connections gives you ideas for helping your community. Discover International shows how people all over the world are connected through common bonds.

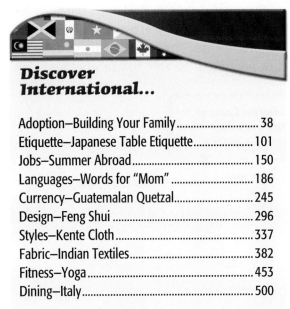

Discover International...

Take on New Responsibilities

What would you do if your coworker would rather chat on the phone than do his job? What if you and your sister could not agree on how to organize your shared bathroom? Use these features to develop your sense of responsibility for yourself and others.

Character Counts

To The Student

Begin the Unit | ## Discover the World of Life Skills

Successful readers first set a purpose for reading. *Discovering Life Skills* teaches skills you need to take care of yourself and to make plans for your future. Think about why you are reading this book. Consider how you might be able to use what you learn in your own life.

Read the Chapter Titles to find out what the topics will be.

Preview the Thematic Project at the end of the unit. A preview lets you know what is to come. Use the preview to think about how what you are learning applies to the project.

UNIT **2** Take Charge of Your Life

Chapter 4
Communicate With Others

Chapter 5
Citizenship and Leadership

Chapter 6
Goals and Decision Making

Unit Preview

This unit is about being in control of your own life. In this unit, you will learn about:

- Using verbal and nonverbal skills to communicate efficiently.
- Recognizing the causes of conflict.
- The duties of being a responsible citizen.
- The importance of leadership skills.
- Why setting goals is essential.
- Making smart decisions.

Explore the Photo
Achieving a goal can be a very fulfilling experience. *What are some of the things you should think about when setting goals?*

72 Unit 2 Take Charge of Your Life

Life Skills Project Preview

Your Point of View
When you are done studying this unit, you will complete a project in which you will:

✓ Discover an issue in your community that you care about.

✓ Interview someone who holds an elected office.

✓ Share your opinion on the issue with your class.

The prewriting activity below will help you get started.

My Journal

Prewriting Activity
Research Newspaper Stories

Find and read stories in your local newspaper about local issues that you care about. Cut out these stories for your journal, and write a summary of the article beside each one.

- What are the facts and issues discussed in each article?

- What are the different opinions about each issue? There are often two sides to an issue. If this is the case, summarize the opinion of each side.

73

Use the Photo to Predict what the unit will be about. Answer the question to help focus on unit topics.

Practice Your Writing in a personal journal. Your writing will help you prepare for the project at the end of the unit.

Close the Unit

What Did You Learn About Life Skills?

Every unit ends with a Life Skills Project that lets you explore an important issue from the unit. To complete each project, you will make decisions, do research, connect to your community, create a report, and present your project.

Read the Project Assignment and numbered steps. The assignment explains what you will need to do.

Follow the Project Checklist to make sure that you have done everything you need to complete your thematic project.

Evaluate Your Work A rubric is a scoring tool that lists the project criteria. You can find the Evaluation Rubric at the book's Online Learning Center at **glencoe.com**.

Apply Academic Skills that are behind the project.

To The Student

Begin the Chapter | What Is the Chapter All About?

Use the activities in the opener to help you connect what you already know to chapter topics. Think about the people, places, and events in your own life. Are there any similarities with those in your textbook?

Read the Main Ideas to preview the key ideas you will learn. Keep these in mind as you read the chapter.

Explore the Photo to jump-start your thinking about the chapter's main topics..

Chapter **6**

Goals and Decision Making

Section **6.1**

Goals
■ **Main Idea** You can accomplish your goals when you are focused and positive. Learn to set short-term and long-term goals to achieve success.

Section **6.2**

Decisions
■ **Main Idea** You make decisions every day. Decisions can be big or small. Making responsible decisions now can have a positive impact on your future.

Explore the Photo
Throughout your life, you will set goals and make decisions along the way. *What goals did you set for yourself this week?*

Writing Activity

Autobiography
Who Are You? An autobiography is a story about who you are. Writing about yourself may seem like an easy thing to do. However, it can be challenging to write about yourself because there is so much to tell. To write your autobiography, focus your ideas into three areas: your personality, your hobbies and activities, and your job goals.

Writing Tips To write a strong autobiography, follow these steps:
1. Write an introduction that states your name and what you will write about.
2. Write three short paragraphs with details about each of the three areas.
3. Write a conclusion that ties the paragraphs together.

115

114   Unit 2 · Take Charge of Your Life

Strengthen Your Writing Skills
Use the writing tips to continue to develop your writing.

Review the Chapter

Make Sure You Know and Understand the Concepts

Review what you learned in the chapter and see how this learning applies to your other subjects and other real-world situations.

Read the Chapter Summary to review the most important ideas that you should have learned in this chapter.

Review Vocabulary and Key Concepts to check your recall of important ideas.

Critical Thinking takes your knowledge of the chapter further. If you have difficulty answering these questions, go back and reread the related parts of the chapter.

Practice Academic Skills and connect what you learned to your knowledge of language arts, math, science, and social studies.

Apply Real-World Skills to situations that you might find in your day-to-day life.

Find More Activities Online at this book's Online Learning Center at **glencoe.com**.

Succeed on Tests with test-taking tips and practice questions.

Chapter 6 — Review and Activities

Chapter Summary

Section 6.1 Goals
A goal is something you want to achieve. When you set goals, you need to make sure that they are realistic. Goal setting requires planning and a positive attitude. Some goals will be more important to you than others. As you experience success in reaching your goals, you can feel good about yourself. If you do not achieve a goal, you can learn from the experience and improve your skills for the next goal.

Section 6.2 Decisions
Decision making is an important part of daily life. Sometimes you make decisions by responding to something that has happened. Other times you make decisions based on what you have already planned or considered. The decisions you make now can affect the choices you have in the future. Learning to make responsible decisions can give you a sense of control over your life.

Words You Learned
1. Use each of these content vocabulary words and academic vocabulary words in a sentence.

Content Vocabulary
- goal (p. 117)
- long-term goal (p. 117)
- short-term goal (p. 117)
- attitude (p. 120)
- priority (p. 120)
- trade-off (p. 120)
- decision (p. 123)
- alternative (p. 124)
- proactive (p. 124)
- consequence (p. 126)

Academic Vocabulary
- essential (p. 117)
- worth (p. 120)
- outcome (p. 124)
- integrity (p. 127)

Review Key Concepts
2. Differentiate between long-term and short-term goals.
3. Explain how attitude helps achieve goals.
4. Name the different ways that decisions are made.
5. Recognize how decisions you make now can affect your future.

Critical Thinking
6. Assess Is putting off making a decision always negative? When might it be better to put off making a decision?
7. Evaluate Why is it possible for someone who grew up with limited resources still be successful?
8. List Write a list of the steps in the decision-making process. N... write a tip that can help you make your next...
9. Predict Why should...

Chapter 6 — Review and Activities

Real-World Skills and Applications

Problem-Solving
10. Prioritize Jacob wants to play football and be in the band. During the fall, both activities hold their practices at the same time, so he has to choose one of the activities. How should he decide which activity to be involved in? What should Jacob consider as he prioritizes his activities?

Technology Applications
11. Design a Template A template is a model or an outline. Use word-processing or spreadsheet software to create a template people can use when they want to achieve a long-term goal. Refer to the steps in the decision-making process. Include helpful tips for each step ...ld take.

Financial Literacy
12. Set Career Goals You may already know what career you wish to have when you are finished with school. Even if you do, you may have the opportunity in the coming years to reconsider your decision. While money is not the only factor that should guide your career decisions, salaries do play a part in goal setting. Identify three jobs that you might like to have when you have completed your education. Conduct research to find out the typical starting salary for each of the three jobs you selected. How might those salaries affect other long-term goals that you may have? What trade-offs might you have to make?

13. The Impact of Your Choices Choose five decisions you have made in the last week. For each decision, make a list of all the people affected by your choice, including yourself. Put a plus sign next to each name if your choice had a positive effect on the person, or a minus sign if your choice had a negative effect. Rate yourself on how well you consider the consequences of your choices. Are you satisfied with the results?

14. Identify and Evaluate Resources Knowing how to gather information from various resources can help you make decisions and solve problems. Do you plan to attend college? Maybe you want to join a branch of the military, or perhaps you plan to enter the job market right away. List three things you want to do after high school. Then identify sources of information for each. Rank the information sources on your list from most useful to least useful and give reasons for your ranking.

15. Goal Setting Online With permission from your parents or teacher, go online to search for information about how to achieve goals. What advice can you find? Are there tips available online that apply to specific goals? Are there any Web sites about goal setting that you would recommend to a friend? If so, explain why you would recommend them. Write down useful goal-setting tips to share with your classmates and to include in your Life Skills Binder.

Academic Skills

English Language Arts
16. Advertise Your student council is launching a campaign to encourage students to make wise decisions by using the decision-making process. Create a pamphlet that that will teach your classmates how to use the decision-making process. What information should you include? What will the design be?

NCTE 8 Use information resources to gather information and create and communicate knowledge.

Science
17. Collect Data An important part of the scientific method is collecting data and studying it to see what it reveals about something. Collect your own data about what people do when they make decisions.
Procedure Choose a place, like a fast food restaurant or movie theater, to record the body language you observe while a person makes a decision.
Analysis Organize your findings in a chart. What conclusions can you draw?

NSES Content Standard A Develop abilities necessary to do scientific inquiry, understanding about scientific inquiry.

Mathematics
18. Calculate Elena is going to give a speech about setting goals at a luncheon for business executives. Her speech will be accompanied by a slide show. The presentation time limit is 15 minutes, and Elena figures she will use 25 slides. What is the average number of seconds she should spend on each slide without going over the time limit?

Math Concept Performing Calculations with Time When performing calculations with time, it is helpful to convert all numbers to the same units prior to calculating. Since a minute has 60 seconds, to convert minutes to seconds, multiply by 60. To convert seconds to minutes, divide by 60.
Starting Hint The average is the total time divided by the number of slides. Convert the number of minutes for the speech (15) to seconds by multiplying by 60. Divide the answer by the number of slides (25). Label your final answer with the correct unit of time.

NCTM Measurement Understand measurable attributes of objects and the units, systems, and processes of measurement.

Standardized Test Practice

Reading Comprehension Read the passage, then ans... the question that follows.

Test-Taking Tip Read the passage carefully, underlining key statements as you go. Answer the questions based only on what you just read in the passage, not based on your previous knowledge.

19. English has thousands of words borrowed from French. However, most of our basic English vocabulary is more similar to German. Compare English House and German Haus or English finger and German Finger. In fact, English is much more closely related to German than it is to French. English and German are both part of the Germanic language family.
According to this passage, why does English have many words that are similar to German?

To The Student

Begin the Section

Prepare with Reading Guides and Study Tools

Use the reading guide at the beginning of each section to preview what you will learn in the section. See if you can predict events or outcomes by using clues and information that you already know.

Take Notes and Study with graphic organizers. These help you find and identify relationships in the information you read.

Before You Read
Predict what the section will be about.

Check Vocabulary lists for words you do not know. You can look them up in the glossary before you read the section.

Look for Academic Standards throughout the text. You can apply what you learn to other subjects.

Section 7.1 Plan Your Career

Reading Guide

Before You Read

Check for Understanding If you have questions as you are reading, that means you are checking your understanding of the material. To get the most out of the text, try to answer those questions.

Read to Learn

Key Concepts
- ✓ **Describe** how to create a career plan.
- ✓ **Recognize** the importance of researching careers.

Main Idea
It is important to research and plan your career path.

Content Vocabulary
- ○ aptitude
- ○ portfolio
- ○ job shadowing
- ○ apprentice
- ○ networking
- ○ mentor

Academic Vocabulary
- ■ modify
- ■ reveal

Graphic Organizer
As you read, identify six factors to review when researching a career. Use a graphic organizer like the one shown to help you organize your information.

Job Research
1.
2.
3.
4.
5.
6.

Graphic Organizer Go to this book's Online Learning Center at glencoe.com to print this graphic organizer.

Academic Standards

English Language Arts
NCTE 5 Use different writing process elements to communicate effectively.

Science
NSES G Students should develop understanding of science as a human endeavor.

Social Studies
NCSS V G Individuals, Groups, and Instructions Analyze the extent to which groups and institutions meet individual needs and promote the common good in contemporary and historical settings.

NCTE *National Council of Teachers of English*
NCTM *National Council of Teachers of Mathematics*
NSES *National Science Education Standards*
NCSS *National Council for the Social Studies*

"**W**hat do you want to be when you grow up?" You have probably heard that question before. Have you really thought about your answer? Perhaps you are interested in becoming a gourmet chef or an astronaut. You have many choices. Whether you choose to be an attorney or a musician, it is not too soon to start thinking about the career you might want to have one day.

138   Unit 3   Make Your Career Plan

Review the Section

Check Your Comprehension with Self-Assessments

After you read, use the section closer to check your understanding. Make sure that you can answer the questions in your own words before moving on in the text.

The Internet

You can also learn about careers through the Internet. You can go online to get ideas, find out what jobs are available, and research specific job requirements. When you are ready, you can submit your résumé online. You will learn more about résumés in the next chapter.

Ask your parents, librarian, or teacher to help you:

- Search *The Occupational Outlook Handbook* or the *Dictionary of Occupational Titles.*
- Find job postings and job descriptions.
- Post a résumé.
- Locate professional organizations.
- Register with online employment agencies.

Find a Mentor Think about a person you admire and respect who has talents and skills you would like to learn. *How can a mentor help you with your career goals?*

Verify Your Understanding of key concepts in the section.

Practice Academic Skills with these cross-curricular activities.

Check Your Answers online at this book's Online Learning Center at **glencoe.com**.

Section 7.1 After You Read

Review What You Have Learned
1. **List** the factors you should consider when you think about career options.
2. **Explain** why it is important to network.

Practice Academic Skills

English Language Arts
3. Should a person ever choose a career that does not match his or her interests? Why or why not? Explain your answer in a short speech.

NCTE 5 Use different writing process elements to communicate effectively.

Social Studies
4. Locate professional organizations for a career that you are considering. What kinds of benefits do they offer for their members? Write a summary of how the organization could help you prepare for your career.

NCSS V G Analyze the extent to which groups and institutions meet individual needs and promote the common good in contemporary and historical settings.

Check Your Answers Check your answers at this book's Online Learning Center at

144   Unit 3   Make Your Career Plan

To The Student

As You Read | Use Reading Strategies and Visuals to Study Effectively

In addition to the reading guide at the beginning of each section, there are lots of reading strategies to help you comprehend the text.

Connect what you already know to the new ideas you learn as you read.

Keep a Vocabulary Journal Write down vocabulary words and then find definitions in the text and in the glossary at the back of the book.

Skim the Headings to help identify the main idea and supporting details.

Goal Setting

Goals are essential, or necessary, for success in life. A **goal** is something you want to achieve or accomplish. You will have many goals throughout your life. Some goals will be big, such as learn to fly a jet or get a college degree. Other goals will be smaller, such as pass tomorrow's math test or finish one more chapter in the book you are reading. Many other goals will fall somewhere in between. Personal goals can help you do your best and achieve the things you want and need.

As You Read

Connect What resources might you need to reach your goals?

Vocabulary You can find definitions in the glossary at the back of this book.

Long-Term and Short-Term Goals

You may not think often about setting goals, but it is something you do almost all the time. Some of your goals may take months or even years to reach. This kind of goal is called a **long-term goal**. Your long-term goals may include marriage, owning a car, going to college, or saving enough money to buy a new computer.

A **short-term goal** can be reached quickly, perhaps in a few days or weeks. Your short-term goals might include complete a science project, pass a math test, or make the cheerleading team.

Sometimes short-term goals can help you achieve a long-term goal. Set short-term goals, such as completing a CPR course, to prepare yourself for your long-term goal of becoming an emergency medical technician. What are your short-term goals? What are your long-term goals?

Set Realistic Goals

When you set goals, you need to make sure that they are realistic. If your goals are too hard to reach, you may become discouraged and give up. If they are too easy, you may lose interest in them. Realistic goals are both reachable and challenging. **Figure 6.1** on page 118 offers guidelines for setting realistic goals.

Personal Goals It can be very rewarding to reach a goal. *What do you think of first when you hear the word goal?*

Chapter 6 Goals and Decision Making **117**

Examine Visuals to reinforce content. Answer the questions so you can better discuss topics in the section.

The Management Process

People who manage well accomplish more with greater ease. They use their time and energy wisely. You may hear the word management and think of the workplace. However, you can apply management skills to all areas of your life. **Management** is the skillful use of resources to accomplish a task. Katie and Hassan are good managers. For example, Katie uses the time in her mom's car on the way to school to study. Hassan catches an early bus so he can get to school in time to spend 30 minutes in the computer lab.

You can be a good manager if you learn to follow the steps in the How To feature on page 260 . These steps work whether you are writing a report or organizing a fundraiser for the school band. Tasks, assignments, goals, and even unexpected events can be more manageable when you make a plan. Writing out your plan is useful for several reasons. Having a written list gives you a visual reminder of what you need to do. It helps you organize your ideas. The physical act of writing something down can help you remember it better than just thinking about it. What goals do you have for which the four-step management plan would be helpful?

As You Read

Connect Name a goal you achieved recently. What did you do to meet that goal?

Vocabulary You can find definitions in the glossary at the back of this book.

Reading Check **Explain** How can management skills help you get more accomplished?

Reading Checks let you pause to respond to what you have read.

Write It Down The key to management, whether in class, at home, or at work, is planning. *Why does writing down goals make planning easier?*

Chapter 12 Resources, Time, and Stress **259**

Study with Features

Skills You Can Really Use at School and in Life!

As you read, look for feature boxes throughout each chapter. These features build skills that relate to other academic subjects and prepare you for life on your own.

Make Math Simple You use math every day, even if it is just counting money to buy a drink at your campus store. See how to use starting hints break down math problems and solve them step by step.

MATH YOU CAN USE

+ − × ÷ ENTER

Calculate Measurement
You need to increase the waistline of your pattern by 4 inches. How much should you increase the measurement for each seam allowance?

Math Concept Multiply Fractions To multiply fractions, multiply the numerators and multiply the denominators. Mixed numbers must first be changed to improper fractions.

Starting Hint Rewrite the whole number representing the increase as a fraction. Then multiply that fraction by 1/a, with a representing the number of seam allowances. To increase a waistline by two inches, the formula would be 2/1 × 1/4 = 2/4. Then 2/4 would be reduced to = ½.

For more math help, go to the Math Appendix located at the back of this book.

NCTM Problem Solving Understand the meanings of operations and how they relate to one another.

Learn the Secrets of Science The secret is that it can be easy. You can use scientific principles and concepts in your everyday activities. Investigate and analyze the world around you with these basic skills.

SCIENCE YOU CAN USE

Research Advertisements
To complete a scientific investigation or experiment, you collect data. Scientists collect data as numbers and descriptions, and then organize that data in different ways. Use your science skills to research types of advertisements in magazines and newspapers.

Procedure Record the number of advertisements and what products or services are listed. Create a table like the one below to collect your data.

Type of Ad	Product	Service
Hairspray	X	
Yoga		X

Analysis Using the table, determine what types of products or services are most common. Do you notice any patterns in the data? What conclusions can you draw?

NSES Content Standard A Students should develop abilities necessary to do scientific inquiry, understandings and scientific inquiry.

Financial Literacy

Sewing Costs
Katie needs to buy materials for a sewing project, but she does not have a calculator. She has $25.00 to spend. Does she have enough money? Use rounding to determine the total cost of the following items.

Fabric .... $8.99   Thread 2.15
Pattern .... 6.50   Pins .... .99

Math Concept Cost Estimation To estimate the sum of a set of numbers, round the amounts to the same place-value position and add. When rounding, look at the first digit to the right of the decimal point. If the first digit to the right of the decimal point is 5 or greater, round up to the nearest dollar. If the digit is less than 5, round down.

Starting Hint: To round $8.99 to the nearest dollar, look at the number to the right of the decimal. Since 9 is more than 5, you would round $8.99 up to $9.00.

NCTM Number and Operation Compute fluently and make reasonable estimates.

For math help, go to the Math Appendix at the back of the book.

Your Money Matters! Learn the basics of personal finance to help make the most out of your money. Build a budget, compare costs, and find the best deals.

To The Student

Features (continued)

Put Your Skills to Work Hands-On Labs give you an opportunity to put your new skills to practical use. Some Labs can be done in class, while others can be completed in and around your home.

Step-by-Step Instructions Each Lab provides detailed steps to guide you through the activity.

How Did You Do? After you finish the lab, check your results to analyze your success and what you learned from the project.

Advice and Instructions Each unit includes a full-page *How To* feature to expand on the information in the unit.

Steps and Tips Learn a variety of useful skills, from changing a baby's diaper to choosing an exercise routine.

Hands-On LAB

Plan an Escape Route

In this activity you will plan an escape route for your family. In case of an emergency, it is important for your family to know what to do. Before you begin, read through the entire Hands-On Lab assignment. Write down any questions that you have about the assignment. Reread the text or ask your teacher for help if you need it.

Supplies
✓ Paper and pencil or pen

Develop Your Plan
- Sit down with all your family members.
- Make sure everyone in the family knows ways to get out of every room in your home.
- Teach younger children to crawl on their hands and knees and stay low under smoke.
- Teach younger children to shout their names out if they are trapped in a smoke-filled room.
- Plan your escape routes. Choose a place where everyone will meet outside in the event of a fire.
- Make sure everyone knows that they should never go back into the

- Assign an adult the responsibility for getting any pets out of the building.

Implement Your Plan
- Make a drawing of the layout of each floor of your home. Indicate where the windows and doors are. Mark the escape routes from each room.
- Hold a fire drill once a month.

Evaluate Your Results
How did your family react to creating the escape plan? After your family held a fire drill, did you find anything in the procedure that you wanted to change? If so, what? How will you change it? Write one or more paragraphs to explain your answer.

How To...

Make the Best of Your Interview

To be considered for a position, a potential employer will want to interview you. This is your opportunity to make the best impression possible and to convince the employer to hire you for the position.

Research the Employer Find out as much as you can about the employer. Ask people who work at the business why they like to work there. Check the company Web site for background information and details about the company. Know directions to the company ahead of time so you do not get lost, or make arrangements for transportation.

Make a Good Impression Choose appropriate clothing for the interview. Make sure it is clean and pressed. Keep jewelry to a minimum. Make sure you are clean, your hair is clean, your breath is fresh, and you have clean fingernails. If you do not appear professional, the employer will not take you seriously.

Prepare for the Interview Arrive at least 10 minutes early for the interview. Have some questions prepared to ask the interviewer about the job. For example, you may want to know what days and hours you would be expected to work, and what kind of training is offered. Bring your résumé and any other materials that were requested, such as your portfolio, or a list of references if you have not already provided them.

Be Professional During the Interview Turn off your cell phone or other electronic devices. Think before you answer each question. Smile, speak clearly, and be friendly and enthusiastic. Make eye contact. Practice good posture and good manners. Do not chew gum.

Follow Up after the Interview Send a thank-you letter after the interview. Tell the employer that you appreciate his or her consideration. Ask for feedback on how you did during the interview for future growth and development. If you decide that you do not want the job, it is still important to send a thank-you letter to thank the employer for his or her time.

166 Unit 3 Make Your Career Plan

Features (continued)

SUCCEED IN SCHOOL!

Note-Taking Skills

Main Points Your teacher will write the most important information, or the main points, on the board or on transparencies for the overhead projector. Include this information in your notebook, and then listen for the supporting details.

Tips for Success Each chapter includes tips for success in school. Use them in all of your classes, from today until you graduate!

SUCCEED IN SCHOOL!

Organization Skills

Arrange Your Papers Choose one place to put your papers for each subject. Create color-coded folders for each class. Arrange your papers in time order. Place your assignments that are due first on top.

Protect Yourself Safety is more than just first aid. There are steps you can take to stay safe online, in your food and sewing labs, and when you baby sit. Use these tips for safety at home, at school, and in your community.

Real-Life Scenarios Now that you are older and learning the importance of developing good character, you can solve problems in constructive ways. Read about common problems teens experience with friends and family, then recommend solutions.

Safety Check

Online Communication

Technology has changed the way we talk to our friends. It can be fast, easy, and fun to talk online through e-mail, instant messages, blogs, and social networking sites. However, it also can be dangerous. Even if you think your messages are private, it is still possible for others to access your information. Use these tips to stay safe online:

- Do not post your real name, phone number, home address, or school name.
- Do not open e-mail from a source you do not know.
- Only accept messages from people you know and trust.

Character Counts

Compromise

Yanett and Deenie are twins. Each sister has her own bedroom, and they share a bathroom. Both girls are neat and take care of their rooms, but they have different ideas about how to clean and organize the bathroom. Yanett thinks it is faster and easier to clean when the supplies are kept on the counter. If she does not see them, she forgets that she needs to clean. Deenie thinks it looks messy to have the supplies out in the open. To her, leaving supplies out is the same as not making a bed. Though Yanett and Deenie get along most of the time, the bathroom cleaning situation it bothering them, and it is bothering other members of the family who have to listen to them argue.

You Make the Call

Who is right? Who is wrong? Is there only one efficient way to clean a shared space? Write a paragraph explaining what Yanett and Deenie should do before their situation gets worse.

To The Student

Features (continued)

COMMUNITY CONNECTIONS

Donate Sometimes you have clothes that are clean and in good repair, but you simply do not wear them any longer. Donate these clothes to a thrift shop or a charitable organization to help families and individuals in need.

Get Involved Look for Community Connections throughout the book. These offer suggestions for how you and your family can contribute to your community.

COMMUNITY CONNECTIONS

Learn through Volunteering Volunteering in your community is a great way to introduce yourself to particular career field. Find opportunities to help others and explore your interests. For example, if you are interested in the health field, volunteer at a hospital. If you are interested in journalism, volunteer at a newspaper.

Common Bonds Discover something new about a particular culture or international experience in every unit. See what you have in common with people all over the world.

Discover International... Languages

Words for "Mom"

What do you call your mother? Is it Mom, mommy, or mama? People who study linguistics know that there are many names for "mother" around the world, and it is interesting to see how much the names are alike. For example, *ma* and *mama* are used in parts of the Middle East and Latin America. In much of North America, she is *mom* or *mommy*. In some parts of the United Kingdom, children call their mothers *mum* or *mummy*, and in other parts she is called *mam* or *mammy*. She may be called *maman* in France, or *maadar* in the Farsi-speaking world.

linguistics |liŋ-ˌgwis-tiks| the study of human language, including the nature, structure, and modification of language. Linguists study the words, the sounds, and the written representations of languages around the world.

NCTE 9 Develop an understanding of diversity in language use across cultures.

Features (continued)

Explore Careers in a wide variety of industries and fields. You can use the skills you develop in school to find career opportunities.

Discovering Careers

Focus on Careers in Emergency Response ▼

Do you work well under pressure? Are you able to make quick decisions? Do you want to help people in crisis? If you answered yes to any of those questions, you might want to consider a future in an emergency response career. The following chart explores several careers in the emergency response field.

Prepare for the World of Work It is not too early to start thinking about your career. These activities can help you learn about what kinds of jobs may be right for you.

Job Title	Job Description
Firefighter	Protect life and property from fires. Often the first emergency responders at traffic accidents. Firefighters are often required to treat injuries as well as fight fires.
Police Officer	Investigates complaints, maintains order, helps individuals, and identifies criminal offenders. Makes quick decisions in emergency situations.
Emergency Room Nurse	Cares for patients in various states of illness or injury. Helps decide which patients are in the most need of immediate care.
9-1-1 Operator	Answers calls from people in distress. Consults detailed manual to provide quick and often life-saving instructions to callers. Coordinates with fire, ambulance, and police services as needed.
Emergency Medical Technician (EMT)	Responds to emergency situations. Makes split-second decisions about patient care. Administers health care for accidents, injuries, and illness.

Career Activities ▼

At School

① Select three of the careers listed. Research the education, training, and work experience required for each career. Write a summary of your results.

At Home

② Create an emergency plan with your family in case of fire or other crisis. Make a map of your home with a planned escape route, and agree with you family on a specific place to meet.

At Work

③ Make a list of at least five jobs that require strong decision-making skills. Next to each job listed, write an example of a decision that might need to be made on the job.

In the Community

④ Contact and interview someone in your community who works in an emergency response career. Ask this person to describe what his or her typical work day is like. Share what you learned with your class.

Learn More Online 🅰 glencoe.com

Career Investigations Go to this book's Online Learning Center for activities and worksheets to help you explore careers.

128　Unit 2　Take Charge of Your Life

Check Out More Careers You can find more information about careers at this book's Online Learning Center at **glencoe.com**.

To The Student

Online Learning Center

Use the Internet to Extend Your Learning

Follow these steps to access the textbook resources at the *Discovering Life Skills* Online Learning Center.

Online Learning Center Icon Look for this icon throughout the text that directs you to the book's Online Learning Center for more activities and information.

Graphic Organizer Go to this book's Online Learning Center at glencoe.com to print out this graphic organizer.

Step 1
Go to glencoe.com.

Step 2
Select **your state** from the pull-down menu.

Step 3
Select **Student/Parent**.

Step 4
Select **Family and Consumer Sciences.**

Step 5
Click **ENTER.**

Step 6. Click **Discovering Life Skills.**

Step 7. Click **Student Center** to access student resources.

National Academic Standards

Prepare for Academic Success!

By improving your academic skills, you improve your ability to learn and achieve success now and in the future. It also improves your chances of landing a high-skill, high-wage job. The features and assessments in *Discovering Life Skills* provide many opportunities for you to strengthen your academic skills.

Academic Standards Look for this box throughout the text to know what academic skills you are learning.

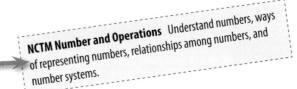

NCTM Number and Operations Understand numbers, ways of representing numbers, relationships among numbers, and number systems.

National English Language Arts Standards

To help incorporate literacy skills (reading, writing, listening, and speaking) into *Discovering Life Skills,* each section contains a listing of the language arts skills covered. These skills have been developed into standards by the *National Council of Teachers of English and International Reading Association.*

- Read texts to acquire new information.
- Read literature to build an understanding of the human experience.
- Apply strategies to interpret texts.
- Use written language to communicate effectively.
- Use different writing process elements to communicate effectively.
- Conduct research and gather, evaluate, and synthesize data to communicate discoveries.
- Use information resources to gather information and create and communicate knowledge.
- Develop an understanding of diversity in language use across cultures.
- Participate as members of literacy communities.
- Use language to accomplish individual purposes.

National Math Standards

You also have opportunities to practice math skills indicated by standards developed by the *National Council of Teachers of Mathematics**.

- Algebra
- Data Analysis and Probability
- Geometry
- Measurement
- Number and Operation
- Problem Solving

National Science Standards

The *National Science Education Standards* outline these science skills that you can practice in this text.

- Science as Inquiry
- Physical Science
- Life Science
- Earth and Space Science
- Science and Technology
- Science in Personal and Social Perspectives
- History and Nature of Science

National Social Studies Standards

The *National Council for the Social Studies* is another organization that provides standards to help guide your studies. Activities in this text relate to these standards.

- Culture
- Time, Continuity, and Change
- People, Places, and Environments
- Individual Development and Identity
- Individuals, Groups, and Institutions
- Power, Authority, and Governance
- Production, Distribution, and Consumption
- Science, Technology, and Society
- Global Connections
- Civic Ideals and Practices

*Standards are listed with permission of the National Council of Teachers of Mathematics (NCTM). NCTM does not endorse the content or validity of these alignments.

Reading Skills Handbook

► Reading: What's in It for You?

What role does reading play in your life? The possibilities are countless. Are you on a sports team? Perhaps you like to read about the latest news and statistics in your sports or find out about new training techniques. Are you looking for a part-time job? You might be looking for advice about résumé writing, interview techniques, or information about a company. Are you enrolled in an English class, an algebra class, or a business class? Then your assignments require a lot of reading.

> **Improving or Fine-Tuning Your Reading Skills Will:**
>
> ♦ Improve your grades.
> ♦ Allow you to read faster and more efficiently.
> ♦ Improve your study skills.
> ♦ Help you remember more information accurately.
> ♦ Improve your writing.

► The Reading Process

Good reading skills build on one another, overlap, and spiral around in much the same way that a winding staircase goes around and around while leading you to a higher place. This handbook is designed to help you find and use the tools you'll need **before, during,** and **after** reading.

> **Strategies You Can Use**
>
> ♦ Identify, understand, and learn new words.
> ♦ Understand why you read.
> ♦ Take a quick look at the whole text.
> ♦ Try to predict what you are about to read.
> ♦ Take breaks while you read and ask yourself questions about the text.
> ♦ Take notes.
> ♦ Keep thinking about what will come next.
> ♦ Summarize.

► Vocabulary Development

Word identification and vocabulary skills are the building blocks of the reading and the writing process. By learning to use a variety of strategies to build your word skills and vocabulary, you will become a stronger reader.

Use Context to Determine Meaning

The best way to expand and extend your vocabulary is to read widely, listen carefully, and participate in a rich variety of discussions. When reading on your own, though, you can often figure out the meanings of new words by looking at their **context,** the other words and sentences that surround them.

> **Look for clues like these:**
>
> ◆ A synonym or an explanation of the unknown word in the sentence:
>   *Elise's shop specialized in millinery, or hats for women.*
> ◆ A reference to what the word is or is not like:
>   *An archaeologist, like a historian, deals with the past.*
> ◆ A general topic associated with the word:
>   *The cooking teacher discussed the best way to braise meat.*
> ◆ A description or action associated with the word:
>   *He used the shovel to dig up the garden.*

Predict a Possible Meaning

Another way to determine the meaning of a word is to take the word apart. If you understand the meaning of the **base, or root,** part of a word, and also know the meanings of key syllables added either to the beginning or end of the base word, you can usually figure out what the word means.

Word Origins Since Latin, Greek, and Anglo-Saxon roots are the basis for much of our English vocabulary, having some background in languages can be a useful vocabulary tool. For example, *astronomy* comes from the Greek root *astro,* which means "relating to the stars." *Stellar* also has a meaning referring to stars, but its origin is Latin. Knowing root words in other languages can help you determine meanings, derivations, and spellings in English.

Prefixes and Suffixes A prefix is a word part that can be added to the beginning of a word. For example, the prefix *semi* means "half" or "partial," so *semicircle* means "half a circle." A suffix is a word part that can be added to the end of a word. Adding a suffix often changes a word from one part of speech to another.

Using Dictionaries A dictionary provides the meaning or meanings of a word. Look at the sample dictionary entry on the next page to see what other information it provides.

Thesauruses and Specialized Reference Books A thesaurus provides synonyms and often antonyms. It is a useful tool to expand your vocabulary. Remember to check the exact definition of the listed words in a dictionary before you use a thesaurus. Specialized dictionaries such as *Barron's Dictionary of Business Terms* or *Black's Law Dictionary* list terms and expressions that are not commonly included in a general dictionary. You can also use online dictionaries.

Glossaries Many textbooks and technical works contain condensed dictionaries that provide an alphabetical listing of words used in the text and their specific definitions.

Reading Skills Handbook

Dictionary Entry

Forms of the word

Part of speech

Numbered definitions

Example of use

Usage label

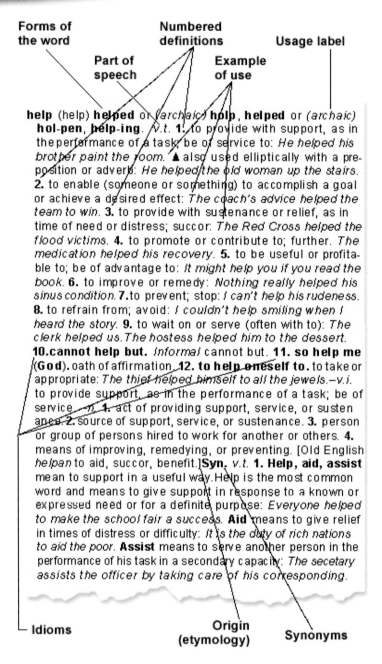

help (help) **helped** or *(archaic)* **holp**, **helped** or *(archaic)* **hol-pen**, **help-ing**. *v.t.* **1.** to provide with support, as in the performance of a task; be of service to: *He helped his brother paint the room.* ▲ also used elliptically with a preposition or adverb: *He helped the old woman up the stairs.* **2.** to enable (someone or something) to accomplish a goal or achieve a desired effect: *The coach's advice helped the team to win.* **3.** to provide with sustenance or relief, as in time of need or distress; succor: *The Red Cross helped the flood victims.* **4.** to promote or contribute to; further. *The medication helped his recovery.* **5.** to be useful or profitable to; be of advantage to: *It might help you if you read the book.* **6.** to improve or remedy: *Nothing really helped his sinus condition.* **7.** to prevent; stop: *I can't help his rudeness.* **8.** to refrain from; avoid: *I couldn't help smiling when I heard the story.* **9.** to wait on or serve (often with to): *The clerk helped us. The hostess helped him to the dessert.* **10. cannot help but.** *Informal* cannot but. **11. so help me (God).** oath of affirmation. **12. to help oneself to.** to take or appropriate: *The thief helped himself to all the jewels.* —*v.i.* to provide support, as in the performance of a task; be of service. —*n.* **1.** act of providing support, service, or sustenance. **2.** source of support, service, or sustenance. **3.** person or group of persons hired to work for another or others. **4.** means of improving, remedying, or preventing. [Old English *helpan* to aid, succor, benefit.] **Syn.** *v.t.* **1. Help, aid, assist** mean to support in a useful way. Help is the most common word and means to give support in response to a known or expressed need or for a definite purpose: *Everyone helped to make the school fair a success.* **Aid** means to give relief in times of distress or difficulty: *It is the duty of rich nations to aid the poor.* **Assist** means to serve another person in the performance of his task in a secondary capacity: *The secretary assists the officer by taking care of his corresponding.*

Idioms

Origin (etymology)

Synonyms

Recognize Word Meanings Across Subjects Have you learned a new word in one class and then noticed it in your reading for other subjects? The word might not mean exactly the same thing in each class, but you can use the meaning you already know to help you understand what it means in another subject area. For example:

Math Each digit represents a different place **value**.

Health Your **values** can guide you in making healthful decisions.

Economics The **value** of a product is measured in its cost.

▶ Understanding What You Read

Reading comprehension means understanding—deriving meaning from—what you have read. Using a variety of strategies can help you improve your comprehension and make reading more interesting and more fun.

Read for a Reason

To get the greatest benefit from your reading, **establish a purpose for reading.** In school, you have many reasons for reading, such as

- to learn and understand new information.
- to find specific information.
- to review before a test.
- to complete an assignment.
- to prepare (research) before you write.

As your reading skills improve, you will notice that you apply different strategies to fit the different purposes for reading. For example, if you are reading for entertainment, you might read quickly, but if you read to gather information or follow directions, you might read more slowly, take notes, construct a graphic organizer, or reread sections of text.

Draw on Personal Background

Drawing on personal background may also be called activating prior knowledge. Before you start reading a text, ask yourself questions like these:

- What have I heard or read about this topic?
- Do I have any personal experience relating to this topic?

Using a K-W-L Chart A K-W-L chart is a good device for organizing information you gather before, during, and after reading. In the first column, list what you already **know,** then list what you **want** to know in the middle column. Use the third column when you review and assess what you **learned.** You can also add more columns to record places where you found information and places where you can look for more information.

K (What I already know)	W (What I want to know)	L (What I have learned)

Adjust Your Reading Speed Your reading speed is a key factor in how well you understand what you are reading. You will need to adjust your speed depending on your reading purpose.

Scanning means running your eyes quickly over the material to look for words or phrases. Scan when you need a specific piece of information.

Skimming means reading a passage quickly to find its main idea or to get an overview. Skim a text when you preview to determine what the material is about.

Reading Skills Handbook

Reading for detail involves careful reading while paying attention to text structure and monitoring your understanding. Read for detail when you are learning concepts, following complicated directions, or preparing to analyze a text.

▶ Techniques to Understand and Remember What You Read

Preview

Before beginning a selection, it is helpful to **preview** what you are about to read.

> **Previewing Strategies**
> - Read the title, headings, and subheadings of the selection.
> - Look at the illustrations and notice how the text is organized.
> - Skim the selection: Take a glance at the whole thing.
> - Decide what the main idea might be.
> - Predict what a selection will be about.

Predict

Have you ever read a mystery, decided who committed the crime, and then changed your mind as more clues were revealed? You were adjusting your predictions. Did you smile when you found out you guessed the murderer? You were verifying your predictions.

As you read, take educated guesses about story events and outcomes; that is, **make predictions** before and during reading. This will help you focus your attention on the text and it will improve your understanding.

Determine the Main Idea

When you look for the **main idea**, you are looking for the most important statement in a text. Depending on what kind of text you are reading, the main idea can be located at the very beginning (news stories in newspaper or a magazine) or at the end (scientific research document). Ask yourself the following questions:

- What is each sentence about?
- Is there one sentence that is more important than all the others?
- What idea do details support or point out?

Taking Notes

Cornell Note-Taking System There are many methods for note taking. The **Cornell Note-Taking System** is a well-known method that can help you organize what you read. To the right is a note-taking activity based on the Cornell Note-Taking System.

Graphic Organizers Using a graphic organizer to retell content in a visual representation will help you remember and retain content. You might make a **chart** or **diagram,** organizing what you have read. Here are some examples of graphic organizers:

Venn diagrams When mapping out a compare-and-contrast text structure, you can use a Venn diagram. The outer portions of the circles will show how two characters, ideas, or items contrast, or are different, and the overlapping part will compare two things, or show how they are similar.

Flow charts To help you track the sequence of events, or cause and effect, use a flow chart. Arrange ideas or events in their logical, sequential order. Then, draw arrows between your ideas to indicate how one idea or event flows into another.

Cues	Note Taking

Summary

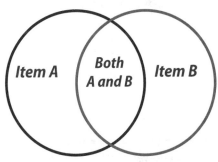

Item A | Both A and B | Item B

gather information → create outline → write essay

Visualize

Try to form a mental picture of scenes, characters, and events as you read. Use the details and descriptions the author gives you. If you can **visualize** what you read, it will be more interesting and you will remember it better.

Question

Ask yourself questions about the text while you read. Ask yourself about the importance of the sentences, how they relate to one another, if you understand what you just read, and what you think is going to come next.

Clarify

If you feel you do not understand meaning (through questioning), try these techniques:

> **What to Do When You Do Not Understand**
>
> ◆ Reread confusing parts of the text.
> ◆ Diagram (chart) relationships between chunks of text, ideas, and sentences.
> ◆ Look up unfamiliar words.
> ◆ Talk out the text to yourself.
> ◆ Read the passage once more.

Review

Take time to stop and review what you have read. Use your note-taking tools (graphic organizers or Cornell notes charts). Also, review and consider your K-W-L chart.

Monitor Your Comprehension

Continue to check your understanding by using the following two strategies:

Summarize Pause and tell yourself the main ideas of the text and the key supporting details. Try to answer the following questions: Who? What? When? Where? Why? How?

Paraphrase Pause, close the book, and try to retell what you have just read in your own words. It might help to pretend you are explaining the text to someone who has not read it and does not know the material.

▶ Understanding Text Structure

Good writers do not just put together sentences and paragraphs, they organize their writing with a specific purpose in mind. That organization is called text structure. When you understand and follow the structure of a text, it is easier to remember the information you are reading. There are many ways text may be structured. Watch for **signal words**. They will help you follow the text's organization (also, remember to use these techniques when you write).

Compare and Contrast

This structure shows similarities and differences between people, things, and ideas. This is often used to demonstrate that things that seem alike are really different, or vice versa.

Signal words: similarly, more, less, on the one hand / on the other hand, in contrast, but, however

Cause and Effect

Writers use the cause-and-effect structure to explore the reasons for something happening and to examine the results or consequences of events.

Signal words: so, because, as a result, therefore, for the following reasons

Problem and Solution

When they organize text around the question "how?" writers state a problem and suggest solutions.

Signal words: how, help, problem, obstruction, overcome, difficulty, need, attempt, have to, must

Sequence

Sequencing tells you in which order to consider thoughts or facts. Examples of sequencing are:

Chronological order refers to the order in which events take place.

Signal words: first, next, then, finally

Spatial order describes the organization of things in space (to describe a room, for example).

Signal words: above, below, behind, next to

Order of importance lists things or thoughts from the most important to the least important (or the other way around).

Signal words: principal, central, main, important, fundamental

▶ Reading for Meaning

It is important to think about what you are reading to get the most infor–mation out of a text, to understand the consequences of what the text says, to remember the content, and to form your own opinion about what the content means.

Interpret

Interpreting is asking yourself, "What is the writer really saying?" and then using what you already know to answer that question.

Infer

Writers do not always state exactly everything they want you to understand. By providing clues and details, they sometimes imply certain information. An **inference** involves using your reason and experience to develop the idea on your own, based on what an author implies or suggests. What is most important when drawing inferences is to be sure that you have accurately based your guesses on supporting details from the text. If you cannot point to a place in the selection to help back up your inference, you may need to rethink your guess.

Reading Skills Handbook

Draw Conclusions

A conclusion is a general statement you can make and explain with reasoning, or with supporting details from a text. If you read a story describing a sport where five players bounce a ball and throw it through a high hoop, you may conclude that the sport is basketball.

Analyze

To understand persuasive nonfiction (a text that discusses facts and opinions to arrive at a conclusion), you need to analyze statements and examples to see if they support the main idea. To understand an informational text (a text, such as a textbook, that gives you information, not opinions), you need to keep track of how the ideas are organized to find the main points.

Hint: Use your graphic organizers and notes charts.

Distinguish Facts from Opinions

This is one of the most important reading skills you can learn. A fact is a statement that can be proven. An opinion is what the writer believes. A writer may support opinions with facts, but an opinion cannot be proven. For example:

Fact: California produces fruit and other agricultural products.

Opinion: California produces the best fruit and other agricultural products.

Evaluate

Would you take seriously an article on nuclear fission if you knew it was written by a comedic actor? If you need to rely on accurate information, you need to find out who wrote what you are reading and why. Where did the writer get information? Is the information one-sided? Can you verify the information?

▶ Reading for Research

You will need to **read actively** in order to research a topic. You might also need to generate an interesting, relevant, and researchable **question** on your own and locate appropriate print and nonprint information from a wide variety of sources. Then, you will need to **categorize** that information, evaluate it, and **organize** it in a new way in order to produce a research project for a specific audience. Finally, **draw conclusions** about your original research question. These conclusions may lead you to other areas for further inquiry.

Reading Skills Handbook

Locate Appropriate Print and Nonprint Information

In your research, try to use a variety of sources. Because different sources present information in different ways, your research project will be more interesting and balanced when you read a variety of sources.

Literature and Textbooks These texts include any book used as a basis for instruction or a source of information.

Book Indices A book index, or a bibliography, is an alphabetical listing of books. Some book indices list books on specific subjects; others are more general. Other indices list a variety of topics or resources.

Periodicals Magazines and journals are issued at regular intervals, such as weekly or monthly. One way to locate information in magazines is to use the *Readers' Guide to Periodical Literature*. This guide is available in print form in most libraries.

Technical Manuals A manual is a guide or handbook intended to give instruction on how to perform a task or operate something. A vehicle owner's manual might give information on how to operate and service a car.

Reference Books Reference books include encyclopedias and almanacs, and are used to locate specific pieces of information.

Electronic Encyclopedias, Databases, and the Internet There are many ways to locate extensive information using your computer. Infotrac, for instance, acts as an online readers guide. CD encyclopedias can provide easy access to all subjects.

Organize and Convert Information

As you gather information from different sources, taking careful notes, you will need to think about how to **synthesize** the information, that is, convert it into a unified whole, as well as how to change it into a form your audience will easily understand and that will meet your assignment guidelines.

1. First, ask yourself what you want your audience to know.
2. Then, think about a pattern of organization, a structure that will best show your main ideas. You might ask yourself the following questions:
   - When comparing items or ideas, what graphic aids can I use?
   - When showing the reasons something happened and the effects of certain actions, what text structure would be best?
   - How can I briefly and clearly show important information to my audience?
   - Would an illustration or even a cartoon help to make a certain point?

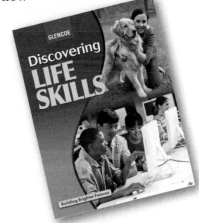

How To Use Technology

Introduction

Computers are a path to the libraries of the world. You can find the answers to many of your questions on the Internet, often as quickly as the click of your mouse. However, they can also be misused. Knowing some simple guidelines will help you use technology in a safe and secure way.

Practice Safe Surfing!

Before you sign on to any site or visit a chat room, there are several things to consider:

◇ **Know to whom you are giving the information.** Check that the URL in your browser matches the domain you intended to visit.

◇ **Never give personal information of any sort** to someone you meet on a Web site or in a chat room, including your name, gender, age, or contact information.

◇ **Think about why you are giving the information.** If a parent orders something online to be delivered, he or she will need to give an address. But you should never give out your social security number, your birth date, or your mother's maiden name without adult consent.

◇ **Check with a parent or other trusted adult** if you are still unsure whether it is safe to give the information.

Tips for Using the Internet for Research

Here are some ways to get better search results:

◇ **Place quotes around your topic,** for example, "sports medicine." This will allow you to find the sites where that exact phrase appears.

◇ **Use NEAR.** Typing "sports NEAR medicine" will return sites that contain both words and have the two words close to each other.

◇ **Exclude unwanted results.** Simply use a minus sign to indicate the words you do not want, for example, "sports medicine" – baseball.

◇ **Watch out for advertisements** Know which links are paid links. They may or may not be worth exploring.

◇ **Check for relevance.** Google displays few lines of text from each page and shows your search phrase in bold. Check to see if it is appropriate for your work.

◇ **Look for news.** After you have entered your search phrase and have looked at the results, click on a *News* link on the page. This will show you recent stories about your topic.

◇ **Try again!** If you have made an extensive search and not found what you want, start a new search with a different set of words.

◇ **Check other sources.** Combine your Internet search with traditional research methods.

How to Evaluate Web Sites

Learning to evaluate Web sites will make you a more savvy surfer and enable you to gather the information you need quickly and easily. When you are trying to decide whether a Web site provides trustworthy information, consider the following:

✧ **First, ask, "Who is the author?"** Do a quick Web search to see what else the author has written. Search online for books he or she has written and consider whether the person is credible.

✧ **Look at the group offering the information.** Be wary if they are trying to sell a product or service. Look for impartial organizations to provide unbiased information.

✧ **Look for Web sites that provide sources for each fact,** just as you do when you write a term paper. Look for clues that the information was written by someone knowledgeable. Spelling and grammatical errors are signs that the information may not be accurate.

✧ **Check for the date the article was written and when it was last updated.** The more recent the article, the more likely it will be accurate.

✧ **Finally, when using information from a Web site, treat it as you would treat print information.** Anyone can post information on a Web site. Never use information that you cannot verify with another source.

Plagiarism

Plagiarism is the act of taking someone else's ideas and passing them off as your own. It does not matter if it is just one or two phrases or an entire paper. Be on guard against falling into the trap of cutting and pasting. This makes plagiarism all too easy. If you quote sources in your work, identify those sources and give them proper credit.

Copyright

A copyright protects someone who creates an original work. This can be a single sentence, a book, a play, a piece of music. If you create it, you are the owner. Copyright protection is provided by the Copyright Act of 1976, a federal statute.

Once a work's copyright has expired, anywhere from 28 to 67 years from the date of creation, it is considered to be in the public domain and anyone can reprint it as he or she pleases. Remember the following tips:

✧ **What is copyrighted?** Original work published after March of 1989 is copyrighted.

✧ **Can I copy from the Internet?** Copying information from the Internet is a serious breach of copyright. Check the site's *Terms of Use* to see what you can and cannot do.

✧ **Can I edit copyrighted work?** You cannot change copyrighted material, that is, make "derivative works" based on existing material.

Student Organizations and FCCLA

What Is a Student Organization?

A student organization is a group or association of students that is formed around activities, such as:

- Family and consumer sciences
- Student government
- Community service
- Social clubs
- Honor societies
- Multicultural alliances
- Technology education
- Artists and performers
- Politics
- Sports teams
- Professional career development

A student organization is usually required to follow a set of rules and regulations that apply equally to all student organizations at a particular school.

Why Should You Get Involved?

Being an active part of a student organization opens a variety of experiences to you. Many student clubs are part of a national network of students and professionals, which provides the chance to connect to a wider variety of students and opportunities.

What's In It for You?

Participation in student organizations can contribute to a more enriching learning experience. Here are some ways you can benefit:

- Gain leadership qualities and skills that make you more marketable to employers and universities.
- Demonstrate the ability to appreciate someone else's point of view.
- Interact with professionals to learn about their different industries.
- Explore your creative interests, share ideas, and collaborate with others.
- Take risks, build confidence, and grow creatively.
- Learn valuable skills while speaking or performing in front of an audience.
- Make a difference in your life and the lives of those around you.
- Learn the importance of civic responsibility and involvement.
- Build relationships with instructors, advisors, students, and other members of the community who share similar backgrounds/world views.

Find and Join a Student Organization!

Take a close look at the organizations offered at your school or within your community. Are there any organizations that interest you? Talk to your teachers, guidance counselors, or a parent or guardian. Usually, posters or flyers for a variety of clubs and groups can be found on your school's Message Board or Web site. Try to locate more information about the organizations that meet your needs. Then, think about how these organizations can help you gain valuable skills you can use at school, at work, and in your community.

What Is FCCLA?

Family, Career and Community Leaders of America (FCCLA) is a national career and technical student organization for students in Family and Consumer Sciences. Involvement in FCCLA offers members the opportunity to expand their leadership potential and explore careers. FCCLA lets you make a difference in your family, your career, and your community. Involvement offers members the opportunity to expand their leadership potential and develop skills for life—planning, goal setting, problem solving, decision making, character development, interpersonal communication, and career development.

STAR Events Program

STAR Events (Students Taking Action with Recognition) are competitive events in which members are recognized for proficiency and achievement in chapter and individual projects, leadership skills, and occupational preparation. FCCLA provides opportunities for you to participate at local, state, and national levels.

What Are the Purposes of FCCLA?

1. Provide opportunities for personal development and preparation for adult life.
2. Strengthen the function of the family as a basic unit of society.
3. Encourage democracy through cooperative action in the home and community.
4. Encourage individual and group involvement in helping achieve global cooperation and harmony.
5. Promote greater understanding between youth and adults.
6. Provide opportunities for making decisions and for assuming responsibilities.
7. Prepare for the multiple roles of men and women in today's society.
8. Promote family and consumer sciences and related occupations.

UNIT 1 Focus On You

Chapter 1
Discover Yourself

Chapter 2
Your Family

Chapter 3
Your Friendships

Unit Preview

This unit is about the factors that make us who we are. In this unit, you will learn about:

● How you will develop your unique personality.

● Why grooming and personal care are important.

● The structure and comfort that families provide.

● The types of changes families might experience.

● How to be a good friend.

● How to recognize positive and negative peer pressure.

Explore the Photo Answer Answers may include family, friends, heredity, environment, peer pressure, experiences, and culture.

Explore the Photo
Everyone develops their own unique personality. *What are some of the factors that affect your personality and help you develop into the person you are?*

Your Role Models

When you are done studying this unit, you will complete a project in which you will:

✓ Take and collect photographs of people you admire.

✓ Interview one of the people in your photographs.

✓ Create and share a collage of the photos and descriptions of your role models with your class.

The prewriting activity below will help you get started.

 My Journal

Prewriting Activity
Make a List

Think about the stories, cartoons, books, and imaginary friends you enjoyed when you were a small child. Create a list of the characters you enjoyed the most. Next to each one, write a brief description about why the character appealed to you.

● What traits do the characters in your list have in common?

● What do these characters have in common with the real people in your life today?

Chapter 1

Discover Yourself

You Are Unique

■ **Main Idea** Many parts of your life come together to make you a unique person.

Explore the Photo Answer Answers may include such personality traits as outgoing, friendly, shy, independent, confident, funny, artistic, or adventurous.

Grooming and Personal Care

■ **Main Idea** To look your best, it is important to practice good grooming skills and present a positive attitude.

Explore the Photo
The way you look and act can tell others about your personality. *What do you think others can tell about you?*

Writing Activity

Freewriting

Dependability Dependable people can be counted on by family and friends. Show that you can be trusted by keeping your word, meeting responsibilities, and being supportive. Freewrite about a time when you, or someone you know, showed dependability.

Writing Tips To freewrite effectively, follow these steps:

1. Let your thoughts run free and simply begin writing whatever comes to mind.
2. Write without stopping to reread, rephrase, or rethink what you are writing.
3. Set a definite time limit.

Writing Activity Answer See page TM65.

5

Section 1.1 You Are Unique

Reading Guide

Before You Read

Preview Read the Key Concepts. Write one or two sentences predicting what the section will be about.

Read to Learn

Key Concepts

✓ **List** factors that influence who you are.

✓ **Name** the qualities that make people unique individuals.

✓ **Analyze** why it is important to understand emotions.

✓ **Describe** the physical changes that happen during adolescence.

Main Idea

Many parts of your life come together to make you a unique person.

Content Vocabulary

○ heredity
○ culture
○ self-concept
○ self-esteem
○ constructive criticism
○ self-actualization
○ adolescence

Academic Vocabulary

■ respect
■ potential

Graphic Organizer

As you read, list the supporting details for the four main topics in this section. Use the graphic organizer like the one shown to help you organize your information.

Heredity and Environment	What Makes Me Unique?	Emotional Changes	Physical Changes

 Graphic Organizer Go to this book's Online Learning Center at glencoe.com to print this graphic organizer.

- - - - - - - - - **Academic Standards** - - - - - - - - -

 English Language Arts

NCTE 4 Use written language to communicate effectively.

 Mathematics

NCTM Problem Solving Solve problems that arise in mathematics and in other contexts.

Social Studies

NCSS IV C Individual Development and Identity Describe the ways family and other group and cultural influences contribute to the development of a sense of self.

NCTE *National Council of Teachers of English*
NCTM *National Council of Teachers of Mathematics*

NSES *National Science Education Standards*
NCSS *National Council for the Social Studies*

Graphic Organizer
Answer Heredity and Environment: family, culture, experiences, roles; What Makes Me Unique: personality traits, self-concept, self-esteem, values, needs, wants; Emotional Changes: moods, self-control, confusion; Physical Changes: height, weight, body shape.

During your teen years, you enter the stage of life when you start to become your own person. As you leave childhood behind, you will begin to discover what makes you unique. Your unique personality will continue to grow and change. You will also experience many emotions and physical changes. You will develop your own value system, and you will start to see how your values fit into the world around you.

Heredity and Environment

No two people act, think, or feel the same way. Everyone comes from a different background and has different experiences. Everything you do, everywhere you go, and everyone you know influence who you are. Your family members and friends probably have the most influence on you. **Figure 1.1** describes some of the major influences on the person you are becoming.

As You Read Answer Answers will vary, but most students will probably say their parents' values helped to shape their personalities.

As You Read

Connect How do you think your parents are responsible for your personality?

Figure **1.1** **You Are One of a Kind**

Unique Qualities Many factors influence who you are. *How have some of these factors affected you?*

Heredity Genetic traits, such as the color of your hair and eyes, come from your parents.

Family Your family is usually your first influence.

Roles You fill many roles: student, daughter, son, brother, sister, or friend.

Environment You learn about your world from the people and conditions that surround you.

Culture Traditions you enjoy may be influenced by your culture.

Experiences Knowledge and skills build over a lifetime to create a unique set of life experiences.

Figure Caption Answer Answers will vary but should reflect an understanding of how each person is different based on the qualities in Figure 1.1.

◆ Vocabulary
You can find definitions in the glossary at the back of this book.

Some of what makes you an individual is a result of heredity. **Heredity** (hə-'re-də-tē) is the passing on of traits, or characteristics and qualities, from parents to their children. Some of these traits are physical, such as your eye color, your facial features, and your body build. Heredity also can play a part in your intelligence.

You have other qualities that make you a unique individual. These traits are a result of your environment. Some of your interests and abilities are learned from the people and things in your environment. Perhaps your sister taught you how to skate. Maybe a friend got you interested in technology.

Family Roles

Your family is one of the strongest influences on the person you are becoming. Are you an only child, the oldest child, the youngest child, or a middle child? What activities do you do with family members? These questions suggest some of the ways you are influenced by your family.

Succeed in School
Use a variety of teaching styles to accommodate the learning styles of your students. Refer to pages TM39–TM41 for more information about differentiated learning.

Positive Focus
Discover Learning Skills Every person has his or her own best way of learning. Some students learn best by listening to their teacher speak. Others learn best by reading. Many students learn well through hands-on projects. Ask your teacher or guidance counselor how to find out which ways of learning are best for you.

The roles you have determine how you relate to other people and how you act in various situations. A role is your position in a group or situation. You have many roles. At home you may be a daughter or a son, a brother or a sister. At school you may be a student, a best friend, and a team member. In the community you may be a volunteer or a member of a club. Your roles vary, depending on the people with whom you interact and the situations involved. You learn your roles by talking to and watching people who are important to you. Role models are people who help you see what is expected of you in certain situations. Role models can be parents, older siblings, relatives, teachers, coaches, or religious leaders. Who are some of your role models?

Culture

Your culture also influences who you are. Ways of thinking, acting, dressing, and speaking shared by a group of people is called **culture**. Cultures may be based on ethnic group, geographic location, or social class. Culture often determines certain traditions people follow. You may not even think about your culture until you meet someone who speaks another language, enjoys different foods, or celebrates different holidays from yours.

Reading Check Answer Culture is the way a group of people think, act, dress, and speak, based on ethnic group, geographic location, or social class.

✔ **Reading Check** ***Define*** *What is culture?*

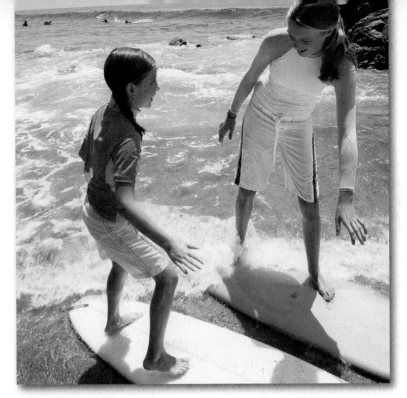

What Makes Me Unique?

Although you share some common qualities with other teens, you are an individual. What qualities do you have that make you different from your friends? Whether you are shy, outgoing, funny, or serious, there is no one else like you. You are unique.

Personality Traits

Personality is the combination of the attitudes, interests, behaviors, emotions, roles, and other traits that make you who you are. Your personality shows in the way you look, the way you communicate, and the way you act. It is the part of you that you show to other people. Your personality continues to change as you experience new things and meet new people. You can become a more interesting person when you develop skills and talents, gain more knowledge, and join in school and community activities.

Everyone's personality is different. Take a look at your personality traits to see how other people relate to you. How dependable are you? Can people count on you to be true to your word? Are you easy to get along with? Can you be trusted? Personality traits such as dependability, cooperation, and honesty help determine the type of relationships you will have with other people. When friends and family members know they can count on you to follow through, you will be trusted to do more on your own. When you learn more about yourself, you can appreciate yourself and other people more.

A Positive Self-Concept

If you have a positive self-concept, you are more likely to succeed in life. A **self-concept** is a mental picture of yourself. Self-concept includes your views about your personality traits and about what activities you perform well. Your self-concept is also influenced by the people around you. It can give you the confidence to try new things. If you have a positive self-concept, you are more willing to make new friends, go to new places, and try new things.

Your self-concept does not always stay the same. It may change as the situation you are in changes. When you help a neighbor, for example, you feel really proud of yourself. On the other hand, if you have an argument with a friend, you may not feel as good about yourself. Even people with a strong self-concept get discouraged when something does not work out as they planned.

It is possible to improve your self-concept. Try to do something each day to help build the qualities you want to improve. Work to achieve your goals and be recognized for your achievements to give your self-concept a boost. In what situations might your self-concept improve?

Here are some qualities that can help you build a positive self-concept:

- **Honesty** Tell the truth and be sincere to show your honesty. Honesty is the quality of communicating truthfully.
- **Thoughtfulness** Think about how your actions affect other people. Help others without being asked. Remember to say "please" and "thank you."
- **Cheerfulness** Being cheerful means being happy, friendly, and seeing the bright side of life. Cheerful people are pleasant and optomistic.
- **Responsibility** Show that you are responsible by doing your homework and chores, and being home on time. It also means being accountable, or accepting the consequences of your actions.
- **Self-Control** Think before you act, and set limits to practice self-control. Use your knowledge of right and wrong to guide your actions.

- **Adaptability** If you are adaptable, you can adjust to different situations at school, at home, or at work.
- **Compassion** Care about others when they are hurting. Let them know that you care to show compassion.
- **Cooperation** Doing what a teacher or parent asks you to do is cooperation.
- **Courtesy** Be considerate and respectful to others.
- **Dependability** Being a person others can count on shows dependability.
- **Enthusiasm** Show that you are willing and eager to do you part at school, at home, and at work.
- **Friendliness** Say hello and smile to show your friendliness to others.
- **Generosity** Be willing to give what you can to others.
- **Sincerity** Always be yourself.

Building Self-Esteem

When you have a positive self-concept, you like yourself. In turn, you will develop self-esteem. **Self-esteem** is a sense of confidence and self-worth. If you have **respect**, or value, for yourself, you can use your own judgment, resist peer pressure, and achieve your goals. Learn to recognize the things you do well. Be realistic about your expectations. No one does everything well. Give yourself credit for your success. Look at your mistakes as opportunities to learn and grow.

How do you feel when someone criticizes you? Do you become defensive? The ability to accept criticism is vital, or very important, to your success in life, at home, at school, at work, and in the community. **Constructive criticism** is helpful advice. It is meant to help you grow and improve and often includes suggestions for solutions. For example, if your music teacher suggests a different song to fit your voice, you could improve your performance by following that advice. Learning to accept constructive criticism is a good way to improve your self-esteem.

Financial Literacy Feature Answer Marco will make $51 less per month if he takes the job that pays $7.15 per hour. (20 x $6.00 x 4 = $480; 15 x $7.15 x 4 = $429; $480-$429 = $51)

Financial Literacy

Calculate Pay

Marco is deciding between two job offers. One pays $6.00 an hour for 20 hours a week. The other job pays $7.15 an hour for 15 hours a week. Marco also needs time for his homework, so he will probably choose the second job. If he does, how much less will he make each month?

Math Concept **Multi-Step Problems** When solving problems with more than one step, think through the steps before you start.

Starting Hint Calculate how much Marco will make in each job per month (4 weeks) before you calculate the difference in pay.

NCTM Problem Solving Solve problems that arise in mathematics and in other contexts.

 For math help, go to the Math Appendix at the back of the book.

Show Responsibility

Each day you make many choices. You are responsible for your own behavior and actions. You can show responsibility by making wise choices. For example, you can take care of your health by choosing to eat healthful foods, to exercise, and to get enough rest. At school you can choose to complete your school-work on time and to try to do your best. The more you show responsibility, the more freedom and trust you may be given in the future. Here are a few ways you can show responsibility:

- **Obey rules.** Families, schools, and communities have rules that help maintain order and keep people safe. You act responsibly when you follow the rules.
- **Help others.** Responsible people look out for their families, friends, and neighbors, not just for themselves. If you see someone in trouble, try to get help.
- **Keep your promises.** If you told a friend that you would help him study for a test, you need to keep that promise. In this way, you will show friends and others that they can count on you.
- **Carry out tasks.** If it is your job to clear the table, do it without being told. When you see other tasks that need to be done, do them. Do not wait to be asked. This shows maturity.

Being responsible is one of the most important qualifications for success in any job. Being responsible means getting to work on time, even when you would rather sleep late or spend time with friends. It means being familiar with the tasks of your job and doing them correctly.

Learning Responsibility

Not everyone has the same responsibilities, and your responsibilities will change over time. Learning responsibility can be hard, but it has many rewards. Other people will respect you and start treating you like an adult. Follow these guidelines for success:

- **Understand expectations.** Find out what is expected of you. Listen carefully. Ask questions if you do not understand.
- **Get advice from role models.** Ask good adult role models to help you learn the right thing to do.
- **Take on new tasks.** You can avoid stress if you take on new tasks gradually and do not take on too much at once.
- **Practice patience.** Be patient with yourself. If you forget to do something or do it wrong, learn from your mistake and try harder the next time.

Certain characteristics go along with being responsible. Which of these characteristics do you have? Responsible people:

- Are reliable.
- Keep their word.
- Show respect for other people and their property.
- Are trustworthy.
- Admit their mistakes and do not blame others.

Your Value System

The way you meet your needs and wants is based on your values. Values are your beliefs about right and wrong and about what is important in life. Most people share some common values, such as a good family life, trust, freedom, and health. Other values are individual, such as being a good student and playing a sport well.

Needs

You have the same basic needs that all people have. Physical needs are basic to your survival and well-being. They include food, clothing, and shelter. You also have emotional needs such as feeling safe and secure. These needs also include a sense of belonging and the need to be loved and accepted by other people. When your emotional needs are met, you feel good about yourself.

Photo Caption Answer Obey rules, help others, keep your promises, and carry out tasks.

Be Responsible Helping others shows responsibility. *What can you do to show that you are a responsible person?*

According to psychologist Abraham Maslow's Hierarchy of Human Needs, you also need self-actualization (see **Figure 1.2**). **Self-actualization** (self-ˌak-ch(ə-w)ə-lə-ˈzā-shən) means to reach your full potential. When you aim to reach your full **potential**, you increase your chances for success. Use your skills, talents, and abilities to achieve your goals in life.

Personal strengths and abilities have a direct impact on the choices you make. For example, a courageous person is more likely to take risks. A creative person is likely to choose a career in the arts. What are your personal strengths and abilities?

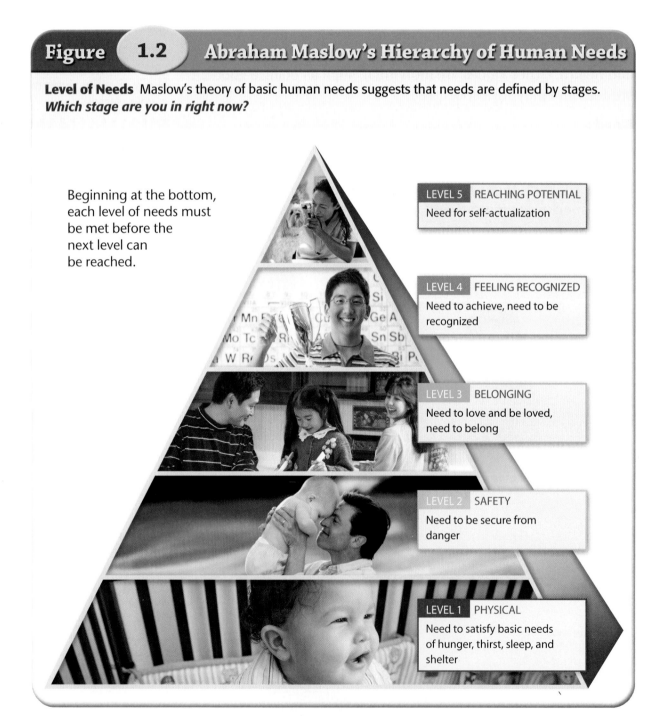

Figure **1.2** **Abraham Maslow's Hierarchy of Human Needs**

Level of Needs Maslow's theory of basic human needs suggests that needs are defined by stages. *Which stage are you in right now?*

Beginning at the bottom, each level of needs must be met before the next level can be reached.

LEVEL 5 REACHING POTENTIAL
Need for self-actualization

LEVEL 4 FEELING RECOGNIZED
Need to achieve, need to be recognized

LEVEL 3 BELONGING
Need to love and be loved, need to belong

LEVEL 2 SAFETY
Need to be secure from danger

LEVEL 1 PHYSICAL
Need to satisfy basic needs of hunger, thirst, sleep, and shelter

Wants

Wants are different from needs. Wants are things that you would like to have, but are not necessary for survival. You may want the latest movie or video game, but you can live without it.

Sometimes people confuse wants and needs. Have you ever wanted something so much that you convinced yourself that you really needed it? Perhaps you felt that you could not live without a new outfit. Did you really need it, or was it something you simply wanted to have?

Values

Like most people, you probably grew up sharing your family's values about tradition, culture, religion, education, and marriage. Your values are the beliefs and principles you choose to live by. Your values define who you are, shape your attitudes and your choices, and help you identify your priorities. Values are usually influenced by family, religious beliefs, teachers, friends, society, and personal experiences. Perhaps your family places a value on how birthdays and holidays are celebrated. A good family life is a common value shared by most people.

People have different values because their interests and experiences are different. People come from a variety of backgrounds. The way you prioritize your values may also be different from the way others prioritize their values. Prioritize means to rank or order things by their importance. For example, some people put a high priority on regular exercise and healthful eating.

You should respect other people's values, even though their values may be different from yours. Other people should also respect your values. Knowing what you value will help you make good decisions. As you develop your value system, you may notice that some of your values are in conflict with each other. For example, you may spend the afternoon finishing a math assignment because you value good grades. What if your friends invite you to the movies that same afternoon? You will have to decide which value is more important. Is it completing your math homework or is it being with your friends? What you value says a lot about you.

Reading Check Answer
Wants are things that you would like to have but can live without, and needs are things you must have in order to survive.

Reading Check *Contrast How are wants different from needs?*

Emotional Changes

An important part of your personality is related to your emotions. An emotion is a strong feeling about someone or something. If you understand your emotions and why they change, you will better understand yourself.

You have many emotions. You may feel pleased and excited when you do something well. You may feel sad or frustrated when things do not go as expected or hoped.

One of the difficult things about emotions is that you may experience more than one at the same time. You may feel both excited and scared about being in a school play. You may feel proud that a college accepted your sister, yet sad that she will be going away. Having two different emotions at the same time can make it hard to sort out your feelings.

Adolescence (a-də-ˈle-sən(t)s) is the period of great growth and change between childhood and adulthood. During adolescence you will be adjusting to many physical and emotional changes. For example, your emotions will seem stronger and harder to control. This is because your body is developing and changing. Your feelings may be hurt more easily. You may also feel ignored or become irritated easily. Sometimes you will feel happy and want to be with your friends. At other times you may want to be alone and not talk to anyone. Adjusting to new emotions can be challenging. When your moods are constantly changing, it may seem as if you lack control over your life. Instead, you can learn to handle your emotions.

Dealing with Your Emotions

Even though these new and changing emotions are difficult to understand, you should not let them rule your life. For example, everyone feels angry at times. However, it is the way you handle your emotions that is most important. Try these healthy ways to deal with your emotions:

- Admit how you feel and why you feel that way.
- Talk about your feelings with a family member, friend, teacher, or counselor.
- Write down your feelings in a journal.
- Work off your feelings by doing something physical, such as taking a walk.
- If you are angry with another person, wait until you have cooled off before speaking to him or her. Tell the person how you feel and what you need or want.

✓ **Reading Check** *Identify What is one healthy way to deal with your emotions?*

Physical Changes

Physical changes in height, weight, and body shape occur during adolescence. You may notice that you or your friends seem to grow inches overnight. Sometimes the different parts of your body do not all grow at the same rate. It can be frustrating when your body is constantly changing and growing. Just when you get used to it one way, it changes again. These rapid changes can make you feel awkward and clumsy. Remember that everyone grows at his or her own rate. Your classmates are growing and changing, too. A positive self-concept can help you adjust to the changes that happen during adolescence.

Photo Caption Answer When you understand your emotions, you can learn to adjust to them and feel more in control of yourself.

 Understand Emotions Two people can have different emotions about the same news. *Why is it important to understand your emotions?*

Section 1.1 After You Read

Review What You Have Learned

1. **Name** two examples of inherited traits.
2. **Explain** how personality is shown.
3. **Describe** ways your emotions are affected during adolescence.
4. **Name** two physical changes that can happen during adolescence.

Practice Academic Skills

 English Language Arts

5. Talk with your family about the traits that you and your family share. Write a list of traits, and next to each trait write whether it is inherited or cultural.

> **NCTE 4** Use written language to communicate effectively.

Social Studies

6. Imagine that you have a younger brother or sister. Write a paragraph to describe what you and your family can do to help the child develop a positive self-concept.

> **NCSS IV C** Describe the ways family and other group and cultural influences contribute to the development of sense and self.

Check Your Answers Check your answers at this book's Online Learning Center at glencoe.com.

Reading Guide

Before You Read

Preview Look at the photos and figures in this section and read their captions. Write one or two sentences predicting what the section will be about.

Read to Learn

Key Concepts

✓ **Describe** the importance of personal grooming.

✓ **Explain** the significance of first impressions.

Main Idea

To look your best, it is important to practice good grooming skills and present a positive attitude.

Content Vocabulary

○ grooming
○ hygiene
○ acne
○ dermatologist
○ cavity

Academic Vocabulary

■ durability
■ opinion

Graphic Organizer

As you read, list the five areas that you should care for when grooming. Use a graphic organizer like the one shown to help you organize your information.

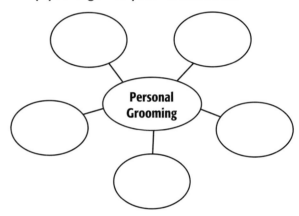

Graphic Organizer Go to this book's Online Learning Center at glencoe.com to print this graphic organizer.

Academic Standards

 English Language Arts
NCTE 3 Apply strategies to interpret texts.

 Social Studies
NCSS I B Culture Predict how data and experiences may be interpreted by people from diverse cultural perspectives and frames of reference.

NCTE *National Council of Teachers of English*
NCTM *National Council of Teachers of Mathematics*

NSES *National Science Education Standards*
NCSS *National Council for the Social Studies*

Graphic Organizer
Answer skin, hair, hands, feet, teeth, clothing

Taking care of your physical appearance affects the way other people see you. It also affects the way you feel about yourself. When you look your best, you feel more self-confident and you are more likely to make a positive impression on people. Grooming and personal care includes caring for your skin, hair, hands, feet, and teeth. Being clean contributes to your health. You will learn how being well-groomed can help you make a good impression when you meet people.

Personal Grooming

How many ads have you seen about grooming aids for teens? **Grooming** includes the things you do to care for your physical appearance. Advertisements may lead you to believe that it takes time, money, and certain products to look good. The fact is that you can look your best by following a basic grooming and hygiene routine every day. **Hygiene** is keeping yourself clean. Take care of your skin, hair, hands, feet, nails, and teeth. Make sure your clothing is neat and clean. Although there are physical features that you cannot change, such as your height, you can still look your best.

Your Skin

During the teen years, the oil glands in your skin begin to work harder. The extra oil can clog your pores and cause skin problems such as acne. **Acne** is a common skin condition that occurs when pores are clogged with oil, dead skin cells, and bacteria. This can cause pimples on the face, back, and chest. Teens with severe acne may need to see a **dermatologist**, a doctor who treats skin disorders. To take good care of your skin, follow these tips:

- Get enough rest and exercise.
- Drink six to eight glasses of water each day.
- Bathe every day.
- Wash your face and neck with mild soap and water at least twice a day.
- Use deodorant or antiperspirant daily.
- Do not pick at or squeeze pimples.
- Choose grooming products that do not irritate your skin. Look for products that are labeled *mild* or *hypoallergenic*.
- Protect your skin from the sun. Use a sunscreen with a sun protection factor (SPF) of at least 15. Reapply the sunscreen after you swim or if you perspire, or sweat.

Your Hair

For many teens, hair is a way to express personality. Whatever hairstyle you prefer, your hair is most attractive when it is clean and healthy. Here are some ways to care for your hair:

- Wash and brush or comb your hair regularly.
- Choose a shampoo made for your type of hair. Is your hair curly, fine, or chemically-treated?
- Shampoo your hair gently. Use your fingertips to work the lather through your hair. Rinse thoroughly.
- When using a conditioner after shampooing, follow the directions on the bottle.

As You Read

Connect How can taking care of yourself now be important to your future?

As You Read Answer If you take care of your health and appearance now, you will feel and look better in the future.

Vocabulary

You can find definitions in the glossary at the back of this book.

Safety Check

Sunscreen
Being outdoors without sunscreen can cause painful sunburn and can lead to skin cancer with continued exposure. Use these tips for applying sunscreen:

- Always use a sun protection factor (SPF) of at least 15.
- Reapply after swimming or other physical activity.

Your Hands and Feet

Good grooming includes taking care of your hands and feet. Keep your nails clean and shaped to help prevent injuries and disease. To care for feet and hands:

- Wash your hands, feet, and nails with soap and water to remove dirt, dead skin, and germs.
- After washing, be sure to dry your feet thoroughly.
- Do not wear wet socks or shoes. This can cause bacteria to grow.
- Moisturize your hands and feet with lotion. Powder your feet to control odor.
- Trim and file your fingernails to shape them. Trim your toenails straight across to keep nails from growing into your skin.

Your Teeth

Your teeth affect not only your appearance but also your health. Your teeth help you chew food. Teeth shape your mouth and your smile. Taking care of your teeth can help prevent cavities and gum disease. A **cavity** is an area of decay in a tooth. The best way to avoid these problems is to keep your teeth clean. Follow these tips for healthy teeth:

- Choose a brush with soft bristles, and use a toothpaste that contains fluoride.
- To brush, use gentle up-and-down strokes to clean between the teeth and massage your gums.
- Floss your teeth once a day. Ask your dentist to show you the proper technique.
- Keep sweets to a minimum, especially between meals.
- Eat a balanced diet with nutritious foods.
- Get regular dental checkups.

Your Clothing

Clothing is form of self-expression. Clothing choices should be based on function, style, and **durability**, or how long it will last. You will learn more about clothing in Chapter 16. Here are some basics:

- Clothing should be clean and changed daily.
- Treat stains as soon as possible.
- Fix any rips or tears before they can get worse.
- Choose the appropriate clothing for each occasion.
- Mix and match separate pieces for new combinations.

Reading Check *Examine* *What should you do in your daily grooming routine to look your best?*

Hands-On LAB

Take Care of Your Nails

In this activity you will work with a partner to give each other a manicure. Before you begin, read through the entire Hands-On Lab assignment. Write down any questions you may have about the activity. Reread the text or ask your teacher for help if you need it.

Supplies
✓ Nail polish remover (optional)
✓ Cotton balls
✓ Hand or cuticle cream
✓ Cuticle stick
✓ Nail clippers
✓ Nail file
✓ Nail buffer
✓ Nail brush

Develop Your Plan
- Gather your supplies and clean them according to your teacher's instructions.
- Partner with someone to give and receive a manicure.
- Review and discuss the steps below to give a manicure.
- Discuss what you and your partner will include in the manicure.

Implement Your Plan
- Remove any nail polish with the nail polish remover and cotton balls.
- Wash hands with a mild hand soap and warm water.
- Gently push back cuticles with a cuticle stick. If the cuticle does not move, soften it with cuticle or hand cream.
- Clip nails if necessary.
- Shape and file nails. File in one direction. Going back and forth can create small tears in the nail that may split.
- Use the nail buffer to buff and shine the nails. Gently rub the buffer back and forth across the top of each nail.
- Wash hands and nails again.

Evaluate Your Results

Describe your manicure experience. How do your nails look? What would you change if you were to do the manicure again? Write a paragraph to explain your answer.

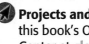 **Projects and Activities** Go to this book's Online Learning Center at **glencoe.com** for more projects and activities.

Evaluate Your Results Answer Students describe how the nails were clipped, filed, and buffed, and the appearance of their nails after the manicure.

First Impressions

All people show certain personality traits, such as polite or rude, accepting or judgmental. Most people show a little bit of all of these traits at one time or another. It is natural to express different traits in different settings. For example, strangers may be more likely to judge each other than they judge friends. How do you want new people to see you? **Figure 1.3** offers tips for how to make a good first impression with a positive attitude.

Figure Caption
Answer Answers will vary but may include: do something nice for yourself; spend time with people who make you feel good about yourself and avoid people who do not; set a new goal for yourself and focus on reaching it.

People form an **opinion**, or judgment, about you the first time they meet you. This instant opinion is called a first impression. It is based on the way you look, dress, talk, and behave. First impressions are important because they help people decide whether they want to know you better. What type of first impression do you make when you are considerate of others? In contrast, what do people think if you use poor table manners?

Figure 1.3 — Make an Impression with Your Attitude

Build a Positive Attitude It is not always easy to think positively, but when you make the effort, the results can be worthwhile. *What can you do to turn your attitude around when you are feeling negative?*

- ■ *Take positive action.* Just taking the first steps toward improving your attitude can make you feel better.
- ■ *Talk positively.* If things do not go as planned, remind yourself that you can learn from the experience. Say to yourself, "What can I do better next time?"
- ■ *Accept yourself.* You have weaknesses as well as strengths. Forgive yourself for mistakes and learn from them. Reward yourself for the things you do well.
- ■ *Stay open to learning.* Learning new skills and knowledge increases your self-esteem.
- ■ *Reach out to others.* Develop good relationships with lots of different people. Seek role models who are positive thinkers. Do not try to be exactly like other people. Instead, adjust your attitude to match their positive qualities.
- ■ *Assert yourself.* You have a right to speak up and act on your beliefs. Maintain a positive environment by saying what you think and feel in ways that are not offensive or hurtful.
- ■ *Accept and respect others as they are.* By treating people with respect, you show that you think of them as worthwhile individuals.

First impressions are not always accurate. When people have a chance to get to know you better, they may change their opinion. Sometimes, however, the first impression is the only chance you have to make a good impression.

Attitude and Your Appearance

Have you ever met an attractive person who became unattractive to you because he or she was mean, had bad manners, or did not treat you well? Perhaps you have met a person you first thought was unattractive, but he or she started to look better to you because of a great personality. This is because your attitude can affect the way you look. If you are often unhappy, angry, or bitter, it can show on your face and it the way you carry yourself. People are not attracted to negativity. On the other hand, if you smile, feel happy, and have a positive self-concept, you will probably find that people are drawn to you because you have traits they admire.

Looking Your Best Practice good grooming to help you make a positive first impression. *What other habits can help you make a good first impression?*

Photo Caption Answer Answers may include: be polite, smile, use good manners, and act and speak with respect.

Section 1.2 After You Read

Review What You Have Learned

1. **List** five things about your personal appearance that require daily care.
2. **Describe** what may be noticed when someone makes a first impression.

Practice Academic Skills

 English Language Arts

3. Create a poster that shows how to care for your skin, hair, hands and feet, or teeth. Use information from your text and pictures clipped from magazines.

> **NCTE 3** Apply strategies to interpret texts.

 Social Studies

4. Write a paragraph about the first impression you had of someone. What did you notice about his or her appearance and personality? What could you tell about his or her culture? What opinions did you form about him or her based on your first impression? Did your opinions change later? If so, why?

> **NCSS I B** Predict how data and experiences may be interpreted by people from diverse cultural perspectives and frames of reference.

Check Your Answers Check your answers at this book's Online Learning Center at glencoe.com.

Discovering Careers

Would you like to help people look and feel their best? Are you comfortable talking with people about medical or psychological issues? If you answered yes to either question, you might want to consider a career in personal health and hygiene. The following chart explores several careers in the personal health and hygiene industry.

Job Title	Job Description
Psychologist	Provides counseling. Assists individuals in achieving personal, social, educational, and vocational adjustments. Collects data through interviews and observation.
Dermatologist	Diagnoses and treats diseases of the skin, hair, and nails. Requires medical degree with specialization.
Dentist	Diagnoses and treats diseases, injuries, and malformations of teeth, gums, and related oral structures. Provides education in oral and dental hygiene.
Theatrical Makeup Artist	Applies makeup to performers to enhance appearance. Consults with photographers and stage and motion picture supervisors.
Cosmetologist	Provides beauty services for customers. Styles hair by cutting, trimming, and tapering. Suggests current styles or listens to customer's instructions.

Career Activities ▼

At School

1 Select three of the careers listed. Research the education, training, and work experience required for each career. Write a summary of your results.

At Home

2 Prepare a pamphlet for your family that explains the importance of properly caring for teeth and gums. Use images from magazines as illustrations. Share the pamphlet with your classmates.

At Work

3 A positive self-concept can help you perform well on the job. How can honesty, thoughtfulness, cheerfulness, responsibility, and self-control benefit you at work? Write one sentence for each quality and discuss them with your classmates.

In the Community

4 Contact and interview someone in your community who works in the personal care industry. Ask this person to describe what his or her typical work day is like. Share what you learned with your class.

Career Activities Answers for these activities can be found on page TM65.

Learn More *Online* glencoe.com

Career Investigations Go to this book's Online Learning Center for activities and worksheets to help you explore careers.

Chapter Summary

Section 1.1 You Are Unique
During your teen years you start to become your own person. You experience emotional and physical changes, and you develop your own values. Family, friends, and culture influence who you are. Your personality shows in your appearance and your actions. A positive self-concept helps you cope with life. You are responsible for your own behavior and actions.

Section 1.2 Grooming and Personal Care
Taking care of your physical appearance contributes to the way other people see you. Grooming and personal care includes caring for your skin, hair, hands, feet, and teeth. When you are clean, you are more likely to be healthy. Being well-groomed can help you make a good impression when you meet people for the first time. A good attitude can affect the impression you make.

Words You Learned

1. Use each of these content vocabulary words and academic vocabulary words in a sentence.

Content Vocabulary
- heredity (p. 8)
- culture (p. 8)
- self-concept (p. 10)
- self-esteem (p. 11)
- constructive criticism (p. 11)
- self-actualization (p. 14)
- adolescence (p. 16)
- grooming (p. 19)
- hygiene (p. 19)
- acne (p. 19)
- dermatologist (p. 19)
- cavity (p. 20)

Academic Vocabulary
- respect (p. 11)
- potential (p. 14)
- durability (p. 20)
- opinion (p. 22)

Review Key Concepts

2. **List** factors that influence who you are.

3. **Name** the qualities that make people unique individuals.

4. **Analyze** why it is important to understand emotions.

5. **Describe** the physical changes that happen during adolescence.

6. **Describe** the importance of personal grooming.

7. **Explain** the significance of first impressions.

Critical Thinking

8. **Describe** how your actions reveal which values are most important to you.

9. **Compare and contrast** needs and wants.

Real-World Skills and Applications

Problem-Solving

10. Choose Hair Care Products Sarah needs to buy products for her hair. She likes the way her friends do their hair, so she asked them what products they like to use. One friend has thick, curly hair, and her other friend's hair is fine and straight. Sarah has curly hair, but she uses a straightener at least once a week. How should Sarah decide what products she should buy for her hair?

Interpersonal and Collaborative

11. Research Adolescence Follow your teacher's instructions to form into teams. Work together to research the physical changes teens experience during adolescence. How do these changes affect relationships with family and friends? How can teens cope with these changes? Present your findings to your class.

Financial Literacy

12. Comparison Shopping There is an almost endless supply of personal care products available. Some are necessary, such as shampoo and toothpaste, and others may not be necessary. Think before you buy. Ask yourself if you really need the product. Maybe you want it because your friends use it or the advertising looks good. Also think about prices and your budget. Visit the hair care section of a supermarket or drugstore. Pick three different shampoos that you would consider using for your hair. Calculate and compare the price per ounce of each product. Which product is the best buy? Why? Share the information with your class.

13. Positive Self-Concept Much of your success depends on developing a positive self-concept. Cut out images from magazines and create a collage that represents the way you see yourself. Include images that show influences on your personality, such as heredity, environment, your experiences, and your culture. Share your collage with your class.

14. Stain Removal To care for your clothing, you may need to treat stains. Think about your daily activities. What kinds of stains might cause problems for you? Pen ink, grass, mud, or salad oil? Make a list of common stains. Then conduct research to find ways to remove stains from clothing. Write a one- or two-page guide that explains how to remove stains. Use graphics or drawings to illustrate your guide.

15. International Cultures Sometimes people do not think about their own culture until they experience other cultures. For example, you may not have tried *kielbasa* (sausage) or *pierogis* (dumplings) unless you have been to a traditional Polish wedding. Conduct research to become familiar with another culture of your choice. Write two or more paragraphs to describe what you learned about the other culture. Include information about traditions, foods, and beliefs.

Academic Skills

 English Language Arts

16. Constructive Criticism Role-Play
Follow your teacher's instructions to form small groups. Work with your group to develop situations in which constructive criticism would be helpful. The situation might be helping a sibling develop a new skill, or helping a friend practice an oral presentation. Each group member should play a part. Write a script and act out the role-play for the rest of the class.

> **NCTE 12** Use language to accomplish individual purposes.

 Science

17. Examine a Problem Taking care of your teeth can help prevent cavities and gum disease.
Procedure Conduct research on the results of poor dental hygiene. Find out about ways to maintain the health of your teeth.
Analysis Make a chart to show what can happen if you do not take proper care of your teeth and gums. Write a list of tips to keep your teeth healthy.

> **NSES A** Develop understandings about scientific inquiry.

 Mathematics

18. Calculate a Budget People who maintain budgets can often avoid money troubles. Imagine that you are living on your own and need to make a personal budget that includes your needs and wants. After making a list of the things you need and the things you want, you determine that your basic needs require 75 percent of your monthly income. Your wants cost 15 percent. If your monthly income is $2,000, how much are you spending on wants?

Math Concept **Multiply Dollars by Percents** A percent is a ratio that compares a number to 100.

Starting Hint To multiply percentages, first rewrite the percent (15%) as a fraction. The numerator is 15 and the denominator is 100. Convert the fraction to a decimal. Multiply this decimal by the number ($2,000). Remember to put the decimal point in the correct place in your answer.

> **NCTM Number and Operations** Understand numbers, ways of representing numbers, relationships among numbers, and number systems.

 Standardized Test Practice ● ● ● ● ● ● ●

Timed Writing
Read and answer the question in five minutes. Use a separate sheet of paper for your answer.

> **Test-Taking Tip** When taking a timed writing, first read the question carefully to see what needs to be included in your response. Then write a quick plan or outline to follow as you write.

19. A person's self-concept includes many qualities. Choose a quality from this chapter that you think is the most important for your own self-concept. Explain why the quality is important to you and give examples of how you show that quality in your own life.

Chapter 2

Your Family

Family Characteristics

■ **Main Idea** Families come in many forms, but each family provides structure, comfort, and a place to learn about the responsibilities of life.

Explore the Photo Answer
Students may describe family as supportive, caring, warm, and loving. Ask volunteers to explain why they chose the word.

Changes in the Family

■ **Main Idea** Families experience different kinds of changes, but they can use positive strategies to adjust.

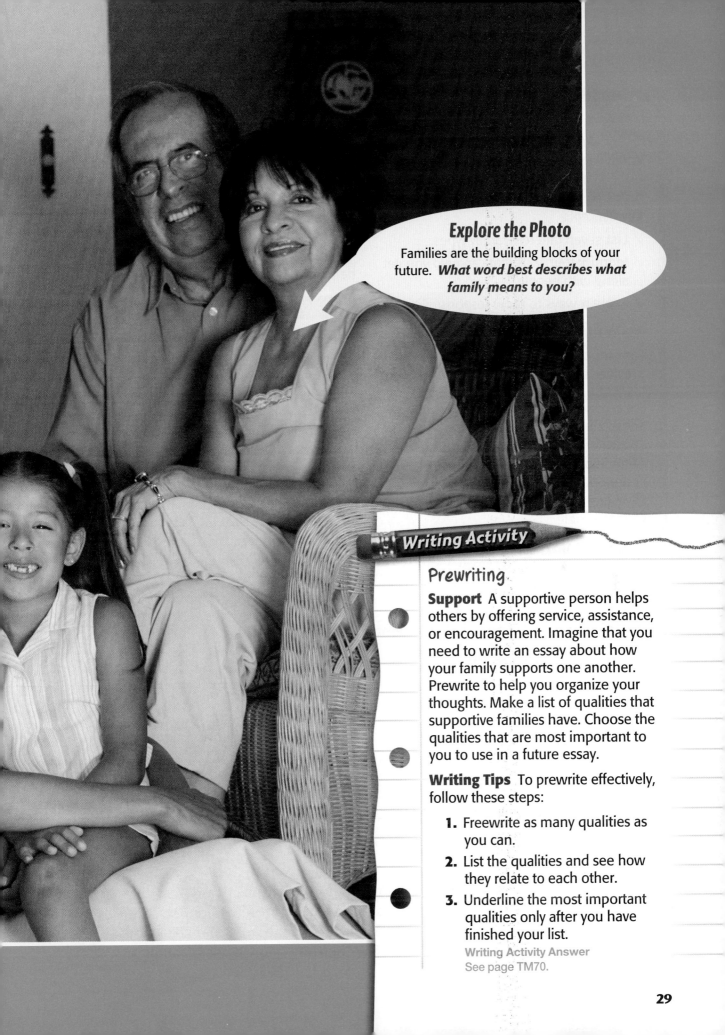

Explore the Photo

Families are the building blocks of your future. *What word best describes what family means to you?*

Writing Activity

Prewriting

Support A supportive person helps others by offering service, assistance, or encouragement. Imagine that you need to write an essay about how your family supports one another. Prewrite to help you organize your thoughts. Make a list of qualities that supportive families have. Choose the qualities that are most important to you to use in a future essay.

Writing Tips To prewrite effectively, follow these steps:

1. Freewrite as many qualities as you can.
2. List the qualities and see how they relate to each other.
3. Underline the most important qualities only after you have finished your list.

Writing Activity Answer
See page TM70.

29

Section 2.1 Family Characteristics

Reading Guide

Before You Read

Preview Choose a Content or Academic Vocabulary word that is new to you. When you find it in the text, write down the definition.

Read to Learn

Key Concepts

✓ **List** seven different family types.

✓ **Identify** four skills that can help you get along with people.

✓ **Explain** ways to show responsibility.

Main Idea

Families come in many forms, but each provides structure, comfort, and a place to learn about the responsibilities of life.

Content Vocabulary

○ environment
○ tradition
○ stereotype
○ sibling
○ responsible

Academic Vocabulary

■ reserved
■ enrich

Graphic Organizer

As you read, list ten ways family relationships can be improved. Use a graphic organizer like the one shown to help you organize your information.

Improve Family Relationships
1. _____
2. _____
3. _____
4. _____
5. _____
6. _____
7. _____
8. _____
9. _____
10. _____

 Graphic Organizer Go to this book's Online Learning Center at **glencoe.com** to print this graphic organizer.

• • • • • • • • • • • • • Academic Standards • • • • • • • • • • • • •

 English Language Arts

NCTE 7 Conduct research and gather, evaluate, and synthesize data to communicate discoveries.

Mathematics

NCTM Problem Solving Solve problems that arise in mathematics and other contexts.

Social Studies

NCSS I E Culture Demonstrate the value of cultural diversity, as well as cohesion, within and across groups.

NCSS V F Individuals, Groups, and Institutions Evaluate the role of institutions in furthering both continuity and change.

NCTE *National Council of Teachers of English*
NCTM *National Council of Teachers of Mathematics*

NSES *National Science Education Standards*
NCSS *National Council for the Social Studies*

Graphic Organizer Answer support each other, laugh and play together, share responsibilities, trust each other, respect each other, attend religious services, create new traditions, plan celebrations, discuss current events, share meals

What comes to mind when you think of family? How do you define family? Is it being together for a holiday? Is it the group of people living next door? Perhaps you think of a large family with lots of children. There are many kinds of families.

Family Structures

The form a family takes is called a structure. The structure can affect the way a family functions. Family structures change over time. Describe each person in your family and his or her relationship to you. Your description will probably match one of the family types in **Figure 2.1.**

The conditions that surround you are your **environment**. No matter what family structure you have, a healthy family environment can be a source of happiness and growth for its members. As you read about families, you will notice that families are as different as the people in them. What really matters is what happens inside the family. Within the family, people gain skills, strength, and knowledge to help them succeed in society.

Healthy families care about each member and work together as a team. Family members work together to:

- Provide food, clothing, and a place to live.
- Create a loving and welcoming environment.
- Encourage independence.
- Teach values and life skills.
- Give friendship, guidance, and support.

As You Read

Connect How does your family structure affect the relationships within your family?

Vocabulary

You can find definitions in the glossary at the back of this book.

As You Read Answer Answers will vary. Students may indicate that they are affected by whether or not they have siblings, if their parents are divorced or remarried, if they live with other relatives.

Figure 2.1 Family Types

Unique Family Structure Families can be as different as the people in them. *What can happen to change a family's structure?*

Nuclear Family	Includes two parents and one or more children.
Single-parent Family	One parent and one or more children.
Blended Family	Formed when two people marry and at least one person has a child or children from a previous marriage.
Adoptive Family	A family with a child or children who are made a permanent part of the family through legal action.
Foster Family	A family that temporarily takes care of a child or children.
Legal Guardian	A person who has financial and legal duties to care for a child or children.
Extended Family	One or two parents and children as well as other relatives, such as grandparents or aunts and uncles.

Figure Caption Answer Answers will vary but may include: divorce; remarriage; the introduction of stepparents, stepbrothers, or stepsisters; the birth or adoption of siblings; older relatives moving in.

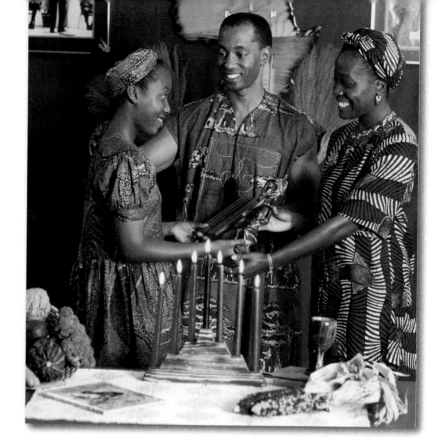

Celebrate Traditions The traditions you follow as a family can strengthen your values and relationships. *What traditions do you enjoy with your family?*

Photo Caption Answer Answers will vary but may include holiday celebrations, special events, eating certain foods, religious practices. The family in this photo is celebrating Kwanzaa, an African American tradition that honors family, community, and culture.

COMMUNITY CONNECTIONS

Family Team Organize a family team to raise money for a community cause. Your family can spend time training and preparing for the event. Working together for a good cause will help your family bond and will help your community as well.

Your Unique Family

The people who make up your family have different skills, talents, and personalities. For example, your father may be an artist. Your sister may play on the soccer team and enjoy reading. Your brother may play in a band and have an outgoing personality. The skills, talents, and personalities of its members make each family unique.

People within families have different ways of expressing, or showing, their emotions. Some show their love for each other openly. They may hug one another and say "I love you" to show affection. Others may be more reserved, or shy. This does not mean that families who do not hug feel less love. They just show it in different ways.

A **tradition** is a custom or belief. Traditions are often passed from previous generations, such as your grandparents and their families. Traditions can influence holiday celebrations, food choices, and religious practices. It is important to understand that customs and traditions can be different without being wrong. An idea about the qualities or behavior of a certain group of people is a **stereotype**. Do not let negative stereotypes keep you from getting to know people and letting them get to know you.

Reading Check Answer
The form a family takes is the family structure.

 Reading Check **Define** *What is a family structure?*

Family Relationships

Families can become closer when family members spend time together. Get involved in each other's daily lives. Share your activities, hobbies, and interests. Characteristics of positive family relationships are easy to spot. Does your family have these positive characteristics?

- Support one another.
- Laugh and play together.
- Share responsibilities.
- Trust one another.
- Respect one another.

Think about the activities you like to share with your parents. Are there things you enjoy doing with your siblings? A **sibling** is a brother or a sister. Share daily events, such as talking about what happened at school, to help strengthen family relationships. Other ways to **enrich**, or improve, family life include:

- Attend religious services.
- Create new traditions.
- Plan special celebrations.
- Discuss books, movies, and current events.
- Sit down together for meals as often as possible.

SUCCEED IN SCHOOL!

Get Feedback
Family Support If you have difficulty in one of your subjects, ask a parent or guardian to help you study.

• • • • • • • • • • • • •

Succeed in School
Encourage your students to get their family members involved in their schoolwork.

Photo Caption Answer
Answers may include sharing games or hobbies, going on family outings, attending religious services, planning special celebrations, discussing books, movies, and current events.

Family Ties Spending time together can bring family members closer. *What are some activities that family members can enjoy together?*

Family members do things to help each other. When her mother had a baby, Maya helped out by making dinner each night. Maya's actions increased the bonds of the family unit. Strong family relationships are especially helpful during difficult times. For example, when a family member becomes ill, it is helpful when the rest of the family pitches in to help and is supportive. It is also important to have fun and enjoy each other's company. **Figure 2.2** illustrates just a few ideas for fun activities families can do at home.

Figure 2.2 Family Activities

Enrich Your Family Life Families can find a variety of ways to spend quality time together at home. *What kinds of activities do you and your family do at home?*

Family Meals It is not unusual in American society to feel too busy for regular sit-down meals with your family. However, it is important to share meals to encourage family closeness.

Movie Night Make popcorn, turn out the lights, and enjoy a movie together at home. Discuss the movie as a family afterwards.

Game Time If weather allows, go outside and play a game. If that is not possible, play cards or a board game inside. You might be pleasantly surprised by how much fun you can have without television or video games.

Getting Along with People

Within your family, you learn and develop the character skills of consideration, cooperation, reliability, and respect. These skills can help you get along with family members. These skills also can help prepare you for relationships with people at school, at work, and in the community.

- **Consideration** Think about other people and their feelings. Treat people the same way you would like to be treated.
- **Cooperation** When you cooperate, you work with others to achieve a common goal. It means doing what is asked of you, and doing what needs to be done to finish a task or a project.
- **Reliability** Do you do what you say you will do? People like to know they can depend on you. Prove to them that you will keep your word. When you are reliable, people will trust you to do what is expected of you.
- **Respect** Think about someone you admire. It may be a friend, a family member, a teacher, a coach, or a community leader. How would you treat such a person? If you have respect for someone, it shows in your behavior. You are kind, you listen to opinions, and you consider the thoughts of feelings of others.

Share Space

How can the character skills listed above help you at home? Whether you are sharing a bedroom, a bathroom, or the kitchen, you must work with other family members to keep shared spaces organized and clean. Sharing space will be easier if you follow these guidelines:

- **Be considerate of others.** Show your consideration by not leaving your belongings in someone else's way. When you finish using the kitchen or the bathroom, be sure to clean up after yourself.
- **Cooperate with family members.** Is there a "morning rush hour" at your house? This can happen when several family members try to get ready for work or school at the same time. The morning will go more smoothly if everyone agrees on a schedule.

Character Counts

Adaptability

Hannah is the youngest of three children. Her two older sisters have left for college and no longer live at home. She finally has her room and her parents all to herself! Then, her parents announce that they are going to have another child. It is a surprise to everyone, but they will all have to adapt. Hannah was expecting to be the center of attention with her sisters being away. Now a baby is on the way, and she feels resentful and angry that the baby will be the new focus of the family.

You Make the Call

Should Hannah keep her feelings to herself? Write a paragraph that explains what you think Hannah should do.

Character Counts Feature Answer Paragraphs will vary. Students may suggest that Hannah tell her parents how she feels. Students might also suggest that Hannah turn the situation into a positive one. She could learn how to take care of the baby's needs, and offer to babysit so her parents can spend time together. She could be a mentor and role model.

MATH YOU CAN USE

Schedule Your Morning

Four people in your home need to be ready for breakfast by 7:30 A.M. Each person needs the bathroom for 15 minutes. Make a schedule for the bathroom so that everyone can be ready in one hour.

Math Concept **Adding Up Time** When you add time, remember that there are 60 minutes in 1 hour.

Starting Hint Start by subtracting 60 minutes, or 1 hour, from 7:30 to determine that the first person would get the bathroom at 6:30.

 For more math help, go to the Math Appendix located at the back of this book.

NCTM Problem Solving Solve problems that arise in mathematics and other contexts.

Math You Can Use
Answer Schedules should show the first bathroom time from 6:30 to 6:45, the second from 6:45 to 7:00, the third from 7:00 to 7:15, and the fourth from 7:15 to 7:30.

- **Show that you are reliable.** As a member of a family, you are expected to participate in the activities that keep a household running smoothly. Family members need to rely on each other to do their share of the work, such as washing dishes, caring for pets, and remembering to turn out the lights.

- **Respect other people's privacy.** If someone's door is closed, knock and wait for a response before entering. Keep your music or television turned low, or use headphones at a safe volume if another person wants to sleep or study. Never read another person's mail or look through someone else's belongings without their permission.

Rights of Family Members

Each family member has the right to expect support, understanding, trust, and respect from other family members. Supportive families make sure each member's rights are respected and expectations are met. When these basic needs are not met, relationships suffer. It is important to support each family member's emotional needs.

Your Parents

As you move toward independence, it helps to understand that your parents are people, too. They, too, are working toward goals. Perhaps they are going back to school, or saving for a family vacation or their retirement. Sometimes parents face work problems, financial difficulties, or health issues. Just like you, they have good days and bad days. It helps to recognize your parents' point of view. If you give your parents love and understanding, family life is more likely to go smoothly.

Communication with your parents is especially important during your teen years. Talk openly to them about your problems, thoughts, and concerns. People who know each other well, such as parents and their children, may believe that they can read each other's minds. This can lead to misunderstandings. Do not try to guess what your parents are thinking. Talk to them and listen to them. Open communication can help both you and your parents understand one another's feelings.

Your Siblings

You love your brothers and sisters. However, there are times when you may not get along. Here are some suggestions to help you get along with your siblings:

- Avoid teasing them.
- Speak kindly.
- Respect their rights as family members.
- Give them compliments and encouragement.
- Share your belongings with them, and ask permission before you use or borrow their belongings.
- Do your share of the chores.

End – 3/22/10

Start here 3/2

Older Relatives

Grandparents and great-grandparents are part of your extended family. They may live with you, nearby, or far away. You can benefit when you interact regularly with your older relatives. Perhaps your grandparents enjoy taking you out to the movies, to sporting events, or on a camping trip. Some grandparents take on a parenting role by caring for grandchildren while parents work.

Whether young or old, everyone can enjoy shared activities such as board games, gardening, or cooking. Take advantage of the time you have with grandparents and older relatives. They can share family stories, traditions, and history. Ask an older relative if they have family photo albums you can look at. When grandparents live far away, letters, phone calls, and e-mails can maintain a long-distance relationship.

✔ Reading Check *Explain How can you respect the space of other family members in your home?*

Reading Check Answer Respect their privacy by knocking before entering. Show consideration by not leaving your belongings out. Cooperate with other family members when you have to be somewhere at the same time. Clean up after yourself.

Photo Caption Answer Answers will vary but may include: look at photo albums together, exchange letters, call them on the phone or send e-mails, ask about your family's history.

⟳ Share Activities
Your grandparents and other older relatives have many experiences and much knowledge to share. *How can you learn about their life experiences?*

SUCCEED IN SCHOOL!

Get Feedback

Guidance Counselors

Guidance counselors are a great source for feedback. They may be able to help you identify options to help improve your academic and career skills.

• • • • • • • • • • • • •

Succeed in School Urge your students to take advantage of the services offered by your school's counseling center.

Family Responsibilities

Society works in many ways to help families with their needs. Society provides resources such as education, health care, and law enforcement to help strengthen and protect families. However, these resources cannot do everything. Families and the individuals within each family need to take active roles as well. Strong families can help society grow stronger. What can you do? Being part of a family means being responsible for yourself and also showing repsonsible behavior to your family. If you are **responsible**, you are dependable and you make wise choices. The values you learn from your family can be applied to your life away from home.

At Home

The people who care for you work hard to provide food, to pay for utilities, and to offer the comforts of home. You can show responsible behavior as well as respect when you take care of the things in your home. There are little things you can do, such as remember to turn off lights and keep your room clean and neat. Regular chores are not punishment. They are part of being in a family, and every member has to do his or her share. Follow your family's rules, and do your chores without being asked and without complaining. These actions can help show your family that you are responsible and on your way toward more independence.

Discover International...
Adoption

Building Your Family

There are many parents in developing nations who do not have the means to support a child. Parents in difficult situations, such as extreme poverty or unfair government practices, may choose to allow a family in another country to adopt their child. For the adopting family, it can be a difficult, emotionally draining, and expensive process. It requires patience and perseverance, and a willingness to accept risks. However, it can be very rewarding. Not only do they have a new family member to love, they also enrich their lives with the culture of the child's native country.

perseverance

['pèr-sə-'vir-ən(t)s] steady and continued course of action or belief over a long period of time, usually accompanied by difficulties, dangers, or setbacks.

NCSS V F Individuals, Groups, and Institutions Evaluate the role of institutions in furthering both continuity and change.

Away from Home

If you learn respect, consideration, cooperation, dependability, and reliability from your family, you are likely to show these qualities away from home, too.

When you are at school, respect your teachers, coaches, and other students. Make smart decisions about avoiding drugs, tobacco, and alcohol. If you are going to be late, call home to let someone know. As you get older and move toward independence, you will probably get a job. The responsibilities you learn at home can help you to be responsible at work.

 Show Responsibility Doing your chores without being asked shows responsibility. *What are some other ways you can show responsibility at home?*

Photo Caption Answer Answers may include: do all of your chores, clean up after yourself, show respect for other people's feelings and space, and follow rules.

Section 2.1 After You Read

Review What You Have Learned

1. **List** two examples of family traditions.
2. **Identify** at least three activities you can do with your family to help you learn and have fun.
3. **Explain** how your family prepares you to deal with responsibilities when you are away from home.

Practice Academic Skills

English Language Arts

4. Interview your parents, grandparents, or other relatives about a tradition in your family. How did the tradition start? Who was there when the tradition began? How does your family continue that tradition today? Write a paragraph about what you learned.

> **NCTE 7** Conduct research and gather, evaluate, and synthesize data to communicate discoveries.

Social Studies

5. Conduct research to learn about the way another culture celebrates the birth of a new family member. How is it similar to the way you and your family celebrate? How is it different? Discuss how learning about other cultures can benefit you.

> **NCSS I E Culture** Demonstrate the value of cultural diversity, as well as cohesion, within and across groups.

Check Your Answers Check your answers at this book's Online Learning Center at .

Section 2.2 Changes in the Family

Reading Guide

Before You Read

What You Want to Know Write a list of what you want to know about adjusting to family changes. As you read, write down the heads in this section that provide that information.

Read to Learn

Key Concepts

✓ **Outline** six changes that can happen in family life.

✓ **Describe** ways to adjust to the changes that can affect families.

Main Idea

Families experience different kinds of changes, and they can adjust through positive strategies.

Content Vocabulary

○ divorce
○ disability

Academic Vocabulary

■ adapt
■ advance

Graphic Organizer

As you read, identify four actions you can take to adjust to changes in your family. Use a graphic organizer like the one shown to help you organize your information.

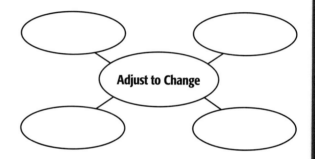

Adjust to Change

Graphic Organizer Go to this book's Online Learning Center at glencoe.com to print this graphic organizer.

Academic Standards

English Language Arts

NCTE 12 Use language to accomplish individual purposes.

Social Studies

NCSS IV B Individual Development and Identity Identify, describe, and express appreciation for the influence of various historical and contemporary cultures on an individual's daily life.

NCTE *National Council of Teachers of English*
NCTM *National Council of Teachers of Mathematics*

NSES *National Science Education Standards*
NCSS *National Council for the Social Studies*

Graphic Organizer
Answer plan ahead, talk, be supportive, look for the positive

Change is a normal part of life. Think of how you have changed since you were a baby. Think of how your family has changed. Some changes are cause for celebration. Other changes may create hardships and challenges. As we grow, we learn to adjust and adapt to all kinds of changes with support from our families.

Changing Family Roles

As each person grows and changes, the rest of the family needs to adapt, or adjust to, the changes. Your roles change as family members grow and change. If your older sister leaves for college, you may find that you have more chores to do at home. You may also find that you have more time to spend with your parents. Sometimes the changes are planned or expected. Other times they come as a surprise. New family members may be born or adopted. Older brothers or sisters may move out of the home, or back home again. A grandparent may move in with your family. **Figure 2.3** describes the four stages of the family life cycle.

Figure Caption Answer Answers may include: newlyweds adjust to living together; parents put the needs of children first; grown children learn to live on their own; seniors adjust to life without children or full-time work.

Figure 2.3 The Family Life Cycle

Families Grow and Change Families experience common stages. *What are the changes that a family might go through at each stage?*

Beginning Stage Newly married couples get to know each other before children are born.

Parenting Stage Couples who choose to have children dedicate the parenting years to meeting the needs of their children.

Launching Stage Children grow older and more independent and leave home.

Senior Stage Parents adjust to being a couple again. People in the senior stage may retire, enjoy more leisure activities, and some may have grandchildren.

Hands-On LAB

Make a Photo Journal

In this activity, you will create a photo journal about a special time you shared with your family. Before you begin, read through the entire Hands-On Lab assignment. Write down any questions that you may have about the activity. Reread the text or ask your teacher for help if you need it.

Supplies

✓ Scrapbook paper (one for each person, and one for the cover)
✓ Photographs and mementos of the special event or vacation
✓ Pens, markers, crayons
✓ Ribbons, yarns, or twine
✓ Glue stick
✓ Scissors or hole punch

Develop Your Plan

- Set a time and place to do the project together.
- Gather your supplies.
- Ask your family to choose a special event or vacation.
- Brainstorm memories about the occasion.

Implement Your Plan

- Give each family member a sheet of scrapbook paper.
- Have each person select 2 or 3 photos and glue them to the paper.
- Add mementos, such as ticket stubs or postcards.
- Have each person write captions for the photos.
- Add bits of ribbon or yarn to decorate the pages.
- Create a cover.
- When everyone is finished, punch holes in the pages and add the cover.
- Thread ribbon or yarn through the holes to tie the journal together.

Evaluate Your Results

Did your family members enjoy making the photo album? Did it turn out as you had planned? Why or why not? Is anything you would change if you did the project again? Write one or more paragraphs to explain your answer.

 Projects and Activities Go to this book's Online Learning Center through **glencoe.com** for more projects and activities.

Evaluate Your Results Answer Answers will vary. Students should include details about the activity, such as whether or not the journal came out as planned, how the other family members reacted to the activity, and what they would do differently.

Divorce

Families must learn to accept changes, even when they are painful. A **divorce** is the legal end to a marriage. When changes are the result of divorce, you may have to deal with one parent moving out. You also may also have to deal with a parent going to work for the first time. You may have to take on more responsibilities. You may feel more alone. Tell both of your parents how you are feeling. They are probably worried about the changes, too. You can reassure each other. Always remember that when parents divorce, it is not the fault of their children.

Remarriage

After a divorce, one or both parents may remarry. This brings more changes. New stepbrothers or stepsisters may join the family. The newly formed couple may decide to have a child together. You are blending a new family and need to share games, space, and parents. You may also have to get used to a visitation schedule, which means going from one parent to the other. This may be difficult, but it will allow you to spend time with both of your parents.

When Justin's father remarried, his stepmother brought her two young children to live with Justin and his father. Now Justin has found himself in a new role as an older brother, and sometimes as a babysitter. What roles do you have within your family? How have your roles changed since you were in grammar school?

Job Loss

A parent may lose a job and the family may have less money to spend. When a parent loses a job, you may fear what will happen to your family. Your routine may be upset and you should discuss your feelings about it. You may not be able to provide money, but you can do your part. Be understanding if you have to cut back on your activities or purchases. Your parents will appreciate your efforts.

Family Roles As family roles change, you may find yourself with different responsibilities. *How might the addition of a younger stepbrother or stepsister change your responsibilities?*

> **▷ Vocabulary**
> You can find definitions in the glossary at the back of this book.

> **Photo Caption Answer** Answers may include help around the house more, help take care of the child, share your space and your belongings with the child.

Disabilities

You may have a sibling or parent with a disability. A **disability** is a permanent or temporary physical, mental, or emotional condition. Your family member may act out in a way that brings attention to your family. Understand that your family member cannot control his or her condition. Be supportive and loving. Look for ways to be helpful. Depending on the person's condition, encourage independence to help boost his or her confidence and self-esteem.

Serious Illness

When a family member is seriously ill, it can be very stressful for the whole family. Perhaps your brother or sister has cancer, or your mother has diabetes, or your father has heart disease. Constant trips to the doctor, reactions to medications, and dealing with constant pain are common.

Confide your fears in someone you trust, such a parent, grandparent, religious leader, teacher, or another responsible adult. Find out what you can do to help. Perhaps you can choose quiet activities when the ill person is sleeping, take on extra chores, or read to the person.

Death

One of the most difficult changes for a family to deal with is the death of a family member. People can find it almost impossible to accept that a part of the family is gone. They sometimes feel guilty about what they did not say or do when the person was alive. These reactions are normal. Everyone in the family can support and comfort one another. Some families seek professional counseling to help them deal with the loss of a family member.

Get Feedback

Ask Your Teacher

Your teacher is most likely the best source to offer feedback on your schoolwork. He or she knows what you do best and how you can improve.

• • • • • • • • • • • • • • •

 Reading Check ***Explain*** *How can you support family members during change?*

Adjusting to Change

Not all changes are negative. Getting your own bedroom or making a new friend are examples of positive changes. No matter what changes occur in your life, you will have to adjust to them. Here are some positive ways to accept change:

- **Plan ahead.** If you know about a change in **advance**, or ahead of time, prepare for it even if you do not want it to happen. For example, if you are going to a new school, visit the school before your first day. You might even make a new friend before school starts.
- **Talk.** Discuss your feelings. Your family and friends can be a great source of strength and encouragement. Teachers, counselors, coaches, religious leaders, and family service workers can also help you understand and handle the change.
- **Be supportive.** When your family faces changes, you can help just by being there. If your brother is nervous about a new job, point out his strengths.
- **Look for the positive.** Remember that changes are a normal part of life. How you deal with changes can help you grow. It does not help to dwell on what is wrong or different. What can you learn from the experience? Every change brings a new experience that can help you prepare for future changes.

Section 2.2 After You Read

Review What You Have Learned

1. **Name** the four stages of the family life cycle.
2. **Explain** how an unexpected change can be positive.

Practice Academic Skills

 English Language Arts

3. Choose a change that your family experienced. Write a journal entry about the change. What was the event? Describe how the event affected you and your family.

> **NCTE 12** Use language to accomplish individual purposes.

 Social Studies

4. Work with family members to collect information about the life experiences of an older relative. Did you learn something about the person that you never knew before? What effect has this person's life had on you? Write a paragraph about what you learned, and attach photos if available.

> **NCSS IV B** Identify, describe, and express appreciation for the influence of various historical and contemporary cultures on an individual's daily life.

 Check Your Answers Check your answers at this book's Online Learning Center at glencoe.com.

Discovering Careers

Would you like to help families build relationships or take care of each other? Do you enjoy organizing activities for people? If you answered yes to either of those questions, you might want to consider a future career in family health. The following chart explores several careers in the family health industry.

Career Activities ▼

At School

1 Select three of the careers listed. Research the education, training, and work experience required for each career. Write a summary of your results.

At Home

2 With the help of a parent, write out the characteristics of a good teacher. Then prioritize the characteristics by what is most important to you.

At Work

3 Confidentiality means to keep personal information private. Write a paragraph that explains why you think confidentiality is important for the careers listed on this page. Share your paragraph with another classmate and discuss your ideas.

In the Community

4 Contact and interview someone in your community who works in the family health industry. Ask this person to describe what his or her typical work day is like. Share what you learned with your class.

Career Activities Answers for these activities can be found on page TM70.

Job Title	Job Description
Family Counselor	Provides individual and family counseling. Helps clients with personal and family problems.
Family Practitioner	Examines patients, orders tests, and diagnoses condition of patient. Advises patients about diet, hygiene, and disease prevention.
Recreation Aide	Assists with recreation activities at community center or other recreation facility. Posts activity schedules and registration requirements.
Elementary School Teacher	Teaches elementary school students. Writes lesson plans. Assigns activities and corrects papers. Works with parents to support children's learning.
Coach	Works with children and/or adults in a specific sport. Encourages teamwork and skill development.
School Guidance Counselor	Provides counseling. Helps with college and career planning for students and parents. Works with teachers and students to achieve academic success.

Learn More *Online* 🔄 glencoe.com

Career Investigations Go to this book's Online Learning Center for activities and worksheets to help you explore careers.

Chapter Summary

Section 2.1 Family Characteristics
A healthy family life can be a source of pleasure and growth for its members. Healthy families care about each other and work together as a team even though they have different skills, talents, and personalities. Families may have various traditions and beliefs handed down from one generation to another. Families can become closer when they spend time together. Within your family, you practice the skills of consideration, cooperation, reliability, and respect.

Section 2.2 Changes in the Family
Families change and adapt for many reasons. Some changes result from divorce. Some divorced parents remarry and new siblings may join the family. Family members may live with a disability or develop a serious illness. Other changes result when a parent loses a job. One of the most difficult changes for a family is death. Not all changes are negative, but whether negative or positive, everyone in the family must learn to adapt. Families can be a source of strength and support during change.

Words You Learned

1. Write each of the vocabulary words below on an index card. Write the definitions on separate index cards. Work in pairs to match each word to its definition.

Content Vocabulary
- environment (p. 31)
- tradition (p. 32)
- stereotype (p. 32)
- sibling (p. 33)
- responsible (p. 38)
- divorce (p. 43)
- disability (p. 44)

Academic Vocabulary
- reserved (p. 32)
- enrich (p. 33)
- adapt (p. 41)
- advance (p. 45)

Review Key Concepts

2. **List** seven different family types.

3. **Identify** four skills that can help you get along with people.

4. **Explain** ways to show responsibility.

5. **Outline** six changes that can happen in family life.

6. **Describe** ways to adjust to the changes that can affect families.

Critical Thinking

7. **Evaluate** why it is important for families to provide more than food, shelter, and clothing.

8. **Explain** how learning about different customs can help you avoid stereotyping people.

9. **Determine** which stage of the family life cycle is the most difficult for people. Why? Which stage do you think is the easiest? Why?

Real-World Skills and Applications

Problem-Solving

10. Obtain Information About a New School Gordon has found out that he and his family are moving this summer. He will attend a new school. Develop a list of resources Gordon could use to gather information about the new school.

Technology Applications

11. Design a Web Page Using information from your text and other resources, design a Web page that includes tips for getting along with your family and other people. Include at least four tips, and provide a real-life example to show how following the tips can help families get along. Come up with a name for your Web site. Use fun language and graphics to communicate the tips.

Financial Literacy

12. Fun for Less Franklin and Norma are looking for activities outside the home that they can share with their four children, ages 14, 12, 8, and 5. They feel that it is important that the family spends quality time together, but they do not have a lot of money to spend on family outings. After researching different types of activities, they have found two that sound promising. Tickets to a local cultural festival are $6.00 for people over age 12, and $3.00 for ages 12 and under. On the same day, the local children's museum, where admission is normally $7.00, is offering 2-for-1 admission. Which activity is less expensive?

13. Create a New Tradition Talk with your family about creating a new tradition that would show who you are as a family. Consider holidays or birthdays as a time to include the new tradition. Discuss with your family how this tradition will be meaningful for your family and when you can first honor it together. Prepare a short presentation to share with your class.

14. Research Your Heritage Talk to your parents, grandparents, and other family members about your heritage, or family history. See how far back you can trace your roots. Prepare a family tree to present to the class. The family tree should include dates and interesting historical details about your family.

15. Genealogy Geneology is information about your ancestors, or the people in your family from previous generations. With permission from your parents or teacher, go online to research your family geneology. Use search words such as your last name, genealogy, or family history. Where did your family name originate? What nationalities and ethnicities are represented in your family? What can you find out about your ancestors? Include this information in your Life Skills binder.

Academic Skills

 ### English Language Arts

16. Persuade A recent article in your local newspaper points out resources, agencies, and support services that can give children what they need for growth and development. "Families are not the most important part of child development," according to the article. Do you think this statement is correct or incorrect? Write a letter to the editor of the newspaper to explain your opinion.

> **NCTE 4** Use written language to communicate effectively.

 ### Social Studies

17. Geography Choose an extended family member who lives some distance away from you. If you do not have a family member who lives far away, choose one of your friends. Use a map to plan a route to get to their home if you went by car. Use the map legend to find out how many miles the trip is.

> **NCSS III B People, Places, and Environments** Create, interpret, use, and synthesize information from various representations of the earth, such as maps, globes, and photographs.

 ### Mathematics

18. Create a Graph Some of your classmates may be the youngest people in their families. One or more may be the oldest child in their household, while others may be only children. Go to ten of your classmates and ask them the ages of each of their brothers and sisters. Write down their responses, and show the number of siblings at each age in a bar graph.

Math Concept **Bar Graphs** A bar graph uses vertical bars to display data. Typically, the vertical axis will indicate quantity, while the horizontal axis can show time periods or other categories.

Starting Hint The horizontal scale in your bar graph should show ages in years (from the lowest age you wrote down to the highest). The vertical scale should show the number of siblings. Draw a bar above each age that indicates how many siblings had that age.

> **NCTM Data Analysis and Probability** Formulate questions that can be addressed with data and collect, organize, and display relevant data to answer them.

Standardized Test Practice

True/False

Carefully read each statement. Decide if each statement is true or false.

> **Test-Taking Tip** For true/false questions, pay attention to key words like *always* or *never*. These mean the statement must be true all of the time or none of the time.

On a separate piece of paper, write T for true statements or F for false statements.

19. Changes in the family always result in negative outcomes.
20. An adopted child is a permanent member of his or her family.
21. Only the parents in a household have rights and responsibilities.

Chapter 3

Your Friendships

Section 3.1

Friends

■ **Main Idea** Friendships grow, develop, and change throughout your life.

Explore the Photo Answer Answers may include: activities are more enjoyable when you are with friends; friends encourage and support you.

Section 3.2

Peer Pressure

■ **Main Idea** Recognizing the difference between positive and negative peer pressure can help you make smart decisions.

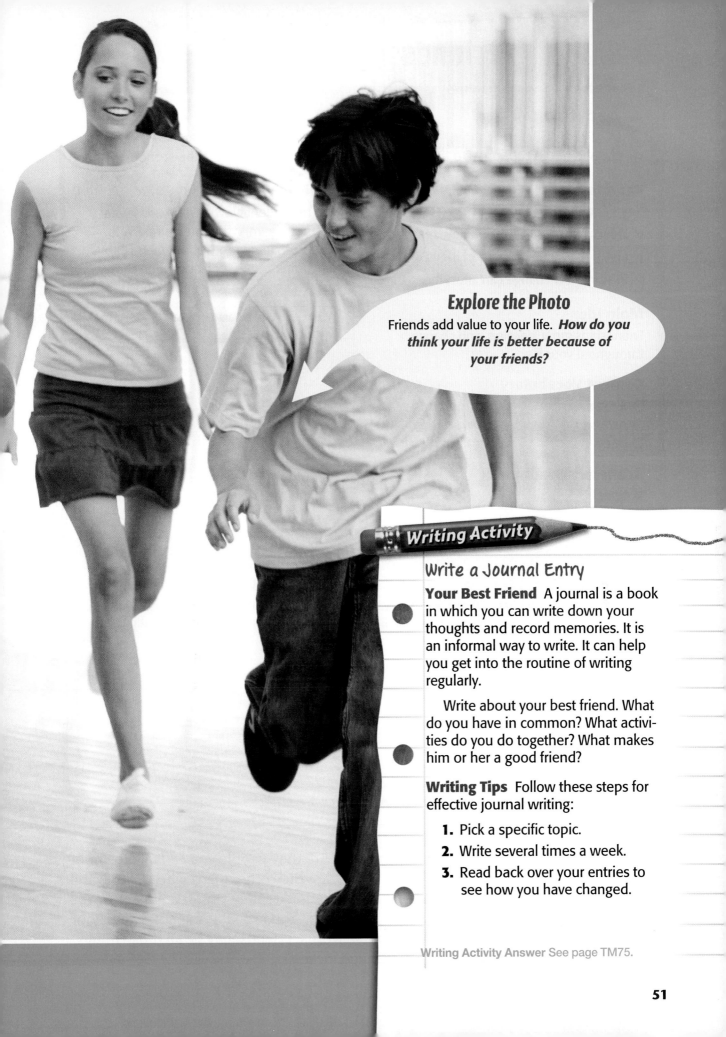

Explore the Photo

Friends add value to your life. *How do you think your life is better because of your friends?*

Writing Activity

Write a Journal Entry

Your Best Friend A journal is a book in which you can write down your thoughts and record memories. It is an informal way to write. It can help you get into the routine of writing regularly.

Write about your best friend. What do you have in common? What activities do you do together? What makes him or her a good friend?

Writing Tips Follow these steps for effective journal writing:

1. Pick a specific topic.
2. Write several times a week.
3. Read back over your entries to see how you have changed.

Writing Activity Answer See page TM75.

Section 3.1 Friends

Reading Guide

Before You Read

Predict Before starting the section, browse the content by reading headings, bold words, and photo captions. Do they help you predict the information in the section?

Read to Learn
Key Concepts
✓ **Describe** ways to make a new friend.
✓ **List** the qualities of a good friend.
✓ **Predict** how change can affect friendship.

Main Idea
Friendships grow, develop, and change throughout your life.

Content Vocabulary
○ acquaintance   ○ compromise
○ diverse   ○ expectation
○ peer   ○ jealousy

Academic Vocabulary
■ benefit
■ confide

Graphic Organizer
As you read, identify what you know, what you want to learn, what you learned, and how you can learn more about friendship. Use a graphic organizer like the one shown to help you organize your information.

What I Know	What I Want to Find Out	What I Learned	How Can I Learn More

 Graphic Organizer Go to this book's Online Learning Center at glencoe.com to print this graphic organizer.

Academic Standards

 English Language Arts
NCTE 7 Conduct research and gather, evaluate, and synthesize date to communicate discoveries.

 Mathematics
NCTM Number and Operations Understand numbers, ways of representing numbers, relationships among numbers, and number systems.

Social Studies
NCSS I E Culture Demonstrate the value of cultural diversity, as well as cohesion, within and across groups.

NCTE *National Council of Teachers of English*
NCTM *National Council of Teachers of Mathematics*
NSES *National Science Education Standards*
NCSS *National Council for the Social Studies*

Graphic Organizer Answer Students should fill in the columns using information from the section and from personal experience.

Who are your friends? Are they people you can talk to about your secrets and goals? Are they other teens who like to watch the movies you like to watch? Are they your teammates or the people in your science club? You probably cannot define your friends in such simple words. Friends may be all those things, but they are also much more.

What Is a Friend?

A friend is someone you like and who likes you. A friend is someone you can talk to. A friend is a person who shares similar interests and goals. For example, you may enjoy going to the mall on a Saturday afternoon with your friends. Perhaps you study with your friends. You and your friends may have similar career goals or college plans. The most important quality that friends have in common is that they care about each other's lives.

How Do Friendships Begin?

Friendships begin and grow when people meet and like each other. You do not instantly have a friend just because you meet someone. Some people are only acquaintances. An **acquaintance** (ə-ˈkwān-tᵊn(t)s) is a person you greet or meet fairly often, but with whom you do not have a close relationship. It may be a classmate, a neighbor, or the librarian at school.

Friendships usually develop from the acquaintances that you have. They are formed with people you are interested in getting to know better. They can grow into lasting friendships as you learn more about each other.

As You Read

Connect When you think of your best friend, what is the first word that comes to your mind?

 Vocabulary

You can find definitions in the glossary at the back of this book.

As You Read Answer Answers will vary. Words may include: loyal, caring, funny, understanding, honest, trustworthy, kind.

Explore the Photo Answer Answers may include at school, in their neighborhood, in a club, on a sports team or other extracurricular activity.

Develop Friendships As you get to know people better, friendships often develop. *How did you meet your friends?*

MATH YOU CAN USE

How to Split a Bill

You and four friends took Sabrina out for her birthday. The bill is $57.00, and you want to include a 15 percent tip. You agree to split the bill and tip equally among you and your four friends so that Sabrina does not have to pay. How much does each person owe?

Math Concept **Find a Percent of a Number** To calculate a certain percentage of a number, change the percent to a decimal by moving the decimal point two places to the left. Then multiply the number by the decimal.

Starting Hint To find 15% of $57.00, multiply 57 by 0.15. Add this number to $57.00 and divide by 5 to determine what each person owes for the birthday dinner.

 For more math help, go to the Math Appendix located at the back of this book.

NCTM Number and Operations Understand numbers, ways of representing numbers, relationships among numbers, and number systems.

Math You Can Use
Answer 57 × .15 = $8.55;
$8.55 + $57.00 = $65.55;
$65.55 ÷ 5 = $13.11 per
person.

Give and Take

A give-and-take relationship means that each person in a friendship **benefits**, or gains something positive, from the other person. Some people are casual friends. You may enjoy their company at school or skating with them in the park. Others may become close friends and with whom you share the details of your life. All friends can learn from each other. They have something to offer each other. Friends can improve your life, and you can improve the lives of your friends. If you ask ten people to describe what they like most about their friends, you will probably get ten different answers. However, certain qualities are basic to all good friendships. Good friends:

- Enjoy each other's company.
- Share good times.
- Support and help each other through difficult times.
- Accept each other as they are.
- Listen when the other needs to talk.
- Are honest with each other.
- Encourage each other to avoid harmful behavior and situations.
- Depend on each other.

Make New Friends

It is not always easy to begin a new friendship. You can be successful if you make an effort. Everyone has to make new friends at times. Old friends may move away, or friendships may change as you grow and develop new interests. For example, you may want a new buddy to go swimming with or to find a person who shares your interest in crafts. Making new friends is a skill that you can learn.

As you go through life, you will have many chances to develop new friendships. Some friendships may begin easily. Others take more effort, and you may need to keep trying. However, not all friendships will work out. The person you thought might make a good friend may be too busy or have different interests. With experience, you can learn to recognize which friendships are worth pursuing, or working for.

Diversity

You live in a diverse society. **Diverse** means made up of many different parts. Most of your friends are probably similar to you in many ways, but different in other ways. You may even have friends who are very different from you. Throughout your life, you will have friendships with a variety of people. Some will be older, and others will be younger. You will have male friends and female friends. You may have friends from different religious or social backgrounds.

Imagine how boring the world would be without diversity. What if everyone had the same hobby or played the same sport? What if all the movies you watched had the same story? What if you never had the chance to learn something new? It would be a very dull world. Differences make life interesting, and differences make people interesting. Do not pass up a possible friendship because someone is a different age, ethnicity, or gender, or has a different cultural background. Diversity can enrich your life. If you establish a relationship with someone different from you, you can learn about new ideas, experience new activities, and become a more interesting person. Developing an appreciation for diversity can help you in school, at work, and in all of the relationships you develop throughout your life.

Reading Check *Recognize* How can friends share and contribute to each others' lives?

Photo Caption Answer Answers may include exposure to different cultures and ideas, new experiences and activities, and knowledge about something they might not know about from their own experiences.

Problem Solving

Buddy Up Learning to solve problems on your own comes with experience. There are some problems, however, that you may be able to solve with the help of a friend. Ask a trusted friend for help when you need it.

Reading Check Answer Answers may include share good times, help each other during bad times, accept each other as they are, depend on each other, listen when the other needs to talk.

Connect with Others These friends have many differences, but they enjoy spending time together. *What qualities can diverse people bring to your friendships?*

start here
3/31

What Makes a Good Friend?

Good friends are supportive, caring, trustworthy, dependable, and reliable. Good friends do not ask or expect you to participate in harmful activities. Good friends accept you as you are. You **confide** in, or tell secrets to, a good friend. It is important that your friends have these qualities. However, it is just as important for you to have these qualities, too. Listen to your friends and offer your help when it is needed. Praise your friends when they do well, and encourage them when things are not going so well.

Being Part of a Group

Adolescence is a time when most teens seek approval from their peers. **Peers** are people the same age as you. Acceptance and recognition from your peers help you develop a sense of belonging. Being accepted by your peers can increase your self-esteem.

Your peer group helps to fill your needs for companionship and support. Within the group, you can learn and practice social skills, such as communication, conflict resolution, and compromise. A **compromise** (ˈkäm-prə-ˌmīz) is an agreement

🔊 **Shared Interests** When you have something in common with someone, you have the start of a possible friendship. *What interests do you share with your friends?*

Photo Caption Answer Answers may include sports, clubs or other extracurricular activities, cultural activities, hobbies, music, movies, books.

in which each person gives up something in order to reach a solution that satisfies everyone. Each person gives a little, and each person takes a little. These skills will be useful throughout your life.

 Reading Check

Analyze How can acceptance and recognition from your peers help you feel a sense of belonging?

Changes in Friendships

Your friendships will probably change over the years. Some of your friends may move away or attend a different school. Some of your friends may have new responsibilities after school. Friendships can also change when you and your friends discover new interests and activities.

Try not to be discouraged when you and a friend grow apart. You will have many chances throughout your life to develop new friends. It is important to remember that changes in friendships can help you grow and learn. You may not choose for these changes to happen, but you can use what you learn from the changes to understand more about yourself and others.

Differences in Expectations

Has there ever been a time when a friend let you down? Some changes in friendships are due to changing expectations. An **expectation** is a person's idea about what should be or should not be.

Reading Check Answer Peers can be supportive, offer encouragement, and accept you for who you are.

Photo Caption Answer Answers may include: changes in interests, expectations, or activities; no longer attending the same school or classes; meeting new people who may have more in common with them; changes in boy/girl relationships.

🔄 **When Friendships Change** Problems can arise when your expectations do not match those of your friends. *What changes in friendships are common during the teen years?*

Character Counts Answer Paragraphs will vary. Sample answer: Jamie could tell Alex that he is still his buddy, but he made a commitment to the team. Jamie could encourage Alex to explore his own interests so he might also be able to make new friends.

A common expectation in friendships is to have and to be a best friend. Best friends expect to trust each other and share common interests. Changes in friendships may occur when someone who was your best friend develops different interests and no longer spends as much time with you. Problems may arise when one friend expects more from the relationship than the other friend wants to give. Changes in best friends are common. You can learn what to expect from your friends and what your friends expect from you.

Expectations between boys and girls also change often during the teen years. Sometimes a boy and girl who were friends develop a boyfriend-girlfriend relationship. This usually means that they have romantic feelings for each other.

Jealousy

Jealousy is when a person feels unhappy about someone else's possessions, accomplishments, or luck. Jealousy can occur when you do not want to share something or someone with another person. It can also happen when someone has something that you want. People often feel jealous when they are unsure of themselves or about their relationship with someone else. When you feel jealous of a friend's achievements, do something that makes you feel good about yourself.

Section 3.1 — After You Read

Review What You Have Learned

1. **Compare and contrast** an acquaintance with a friend.
2. **Explain** why peers are so important to teens.
3. **Describe** the common expectations of a best friend.

Practice Academic Skills

 English Language Arts

4. In small groups, determine what qualities make a good friend. Write a list of questions to ask other classmates about successful friendships. Interview classmates, and present your findings to your class.

> **NCTE 7** Conduct research and gather, evaluate, and synthesize date to communicate discoveries.

 Social Studies

5. Write a list of suggestions to help make a new foreign-exchange student in your school feel welcome.

> **NCSS I E** Demonstrate the value of cultural diversity, as well as cohesion, within and across groups.

Check Your Answers Check your answers at this book's Online Learning Center at **glencoe.com**.

Section 3.2 Peer Pressure

Reading Guide

Before You Read

Use Color As you read, use different colored pens to take notes. This can help you learn new material and study for tests. Try red for vocabulary words, blue for explanations, and green for examples.

Read to Learn

Key Concepts

✓ **Evaluate** how peer pressure can affect the decision-making process.

✓ **Explain** how saying no to high-risk behavior promotes teen safety.

✓ **Describe** how being assertive can help you be more in control of your life.

Main Idea

Recognizing the difference between positive and negative peer pressure can help you make smart decisions.

Content Vocabulary

○ peer pressure
○ refusal skills
○ addiction
○ abstinence
○ assertive
○ bully

Academic Vocabulary

■ acceptance   ■ resist

Graphic Organizer

As you read, list three effects of positive peer pressure and three effects of negative peer pressure. Use a graphic organizer like the one shown to help you organize your information.

Positive Peer Pressure	Negative Peer Pressure

 Graphic Organizer Go to this book's Online Learning Center at glencoe.com to print this graphic organizer.

· · · · · · · · · · · · · **Academic Standards** · · · · · · · · · · · · ·

 English Language Arts

NCTE 8 Use information resources to gather information and create and communicate knowledge.

 Science

NSES F Develop an under-standing of personal and community health.

Social Studies

NCSS V D Individuals, Groups, and Institutions Identify and analyze examples of tensions between expressions of individuality and efforts used to promote social conformity by groups and institutions.

NCTE *National Council of Teachers of English*
NCTM *National Council of Teachers of Mathematics*

NSES *National Science Education Standards*
NCSS *National Council for the Social Studies*

Everyone wants to be accepted and liked by his or her peers. The desire to belong to a peer group can be positive. There are times, however, when peers can have a negative impact on your life. Learn to recognize the differences between positive and negative pressures. It can help you decide if you should go along with the group or act as an individual.

Graphic Organizer Answer Positive peer pressure: encouragement, confidence, acceptance. Negative peer pressure: uncomfortable, unpopular, unwanted.

As You Read

Connect Think about the last time you felt pressured into doing something or not doing something. How did it make you feel?

Peers and Decision Making

The support and confidence peers give you can help your self-confidence and increase your self-esteem. At times, your peers may expect you to join in their actions and activities. **Peer pressure** is the influence you feel to go along with the behavior of your peers. Peer pressure can be negative or positive.

Positive Peer Pressure

Acceptance, or approval, from your peers can help you feel good about yourself. A peer group can give you a sense of belonging and encourage positive behavior. Suppose that you were competing in a tennis match. It would feel good to know that your friends were there to cheer you on. You would feel confident and want to do your best. It can motivate you to try new activities.This type of peer pressure is a positive force.

Negative Peer Pressure

Peer pressure can also be a negative force. Some groups make outsiders feel uncomfortable, unpopular, or unwanted. If one member of a group is critical or has a bad attitude, it may influence the entire group. It may be difficult for you to go against the wishes of your peers. If the group has decided to exclude someone, you may feel pressured to avoid that person even if you like him or her.

Another negative kind of peer pressure is when you feel pushed to participate in activities that go against your values. Maybe someone tried to get you to skip school, smoke, drink alcohol, join a gang, or do something else that you know is dangerous or illegal. Always remember that true friends will not put you in dangerous positions.

As You Read Answer Students may say that if the pressure was negative, they felt annoyed, angry, resentful. If the pressure was positive, they may have felt welcome, accepted, appreciated.

◆ Vocabulary

You can find definitions in the glossary at the back of this book.

Reading Check Answer His or her bad attitude can influence the entire group.

Reading Check

Predict What can happen if one person in a peer group has a bad attitude?

Photo Caption Answer Peers can provide encouragement, give you confidence, give you a sense of belonging and acceptance.

Positive Influence Spending time with your peers can have a positive influence on you. *How can spending time with your peers make you feel good about yourself?*

Handle Peer Pressure

Everyone at one time or another is faced with decisions about following the group or following their own conscience, or sense of right and wrong. When this happens, ask yourself: Are the wishes of a few people more important than what I believe is right? If I do something because of peer pressure, will I be sorry about it later?

Here are some ways to deal with negative peer pressure:

- **Think ahead.** Decide ahead of time what you will do if certain situations come up. You might even practice what you will say and do.
- **Suggest other activities.** Think of things to do that are fun, healthy, safe, and legal. Let your friends know that you would like to be with them, but not if it means doing something wrong, unsafe, or illegal.
- **Choose your friends carefully.** Develop friendships with peers who share your values and interests.
- **Talk to parents and counselors.** Let them know if you are having problems. They can give you the support and encouragement you need to **resist**, or fight against, the pressure.

Practice refusal skills. If your friends ask you to do something that is wrong or against your values, use refusal skills. **Refusal skills** are communication tools that can help you say no when you feel pushed to take part in activities that are unsafe or unhealthful, or that go against your values (see **Figure 3.1**).

COMMUNITY CONNECTIONS

Positive Action To help avoid negative peer pressure, it is important to have alternatives, or other choices. Put together a list of ten positive community activities for teens. Share the list with your class.

Figure Caption Answer Think ahead, practice refusal skills, suggest other activities, choose friends carefully, talk to parents and counselors.

Figure 3.1 Refusal Skills

Peer Pressure Everyone faces negative peer pressure at some point. *What are some ways that you can stand firm against negative peer pressure?*

- State exactly how you feel, directly and honestly.
- Do not apologize for your decisions or for your values.
- Use direct eye contact to show that you mean what you say.
- Use a firm yet friendly tone of voice.
- Use the other person's name.
- Suggest an alternative, or other option.
- Avoid compromise, which can be a slow way to saying yes.

How To...

Say "NO"

You will be faced with many choices and situations. Some are about choosing the way you behave toward others. Some are about reacting to how others behave toward you. Some situations will make you feel uncomfortable or put you in danger. Remember to say "NO" in these situations.

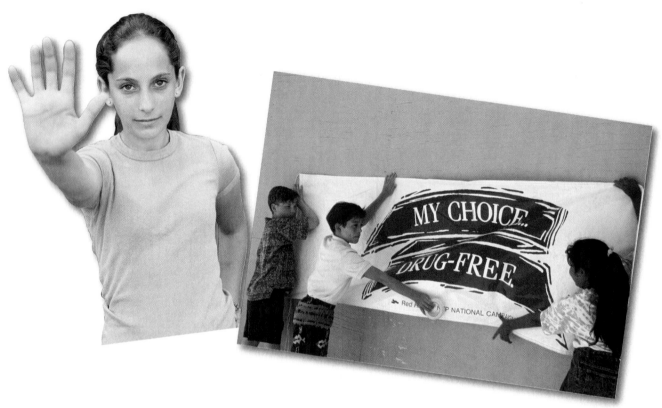

Tobacco, Alcohol, and Other Drugs True friends will not ask their friends to do things they do not want to do. You know what is right and wrong. Do not offer tobacco, alcohol, or drugs to anyone. Refuse any offers of these things from others. Stand up to peer pressure. Say "NO."

Shoplifting Shoplifting is stealing, and the penalties can have a long-term impact on your life.

Gangs Joining a gang can be very dangerous. You may be asked to do illegal things for the sake of other gang members.

Bullying Never try to bully anyone, and do not allow yourself to be bullied. Bullies should not be allowed to hassle anyone. Get an adult to help if you are being bullied or if you see someone else being bullied.

Guns You know that guns are not toys and are dangerous. Never try to bring a gun to school. If someone wants to show you a gun at school, just walk away. Report the situation immediately to an adult.

Avoid Harmful Substances

Everyone wants to be liked and accepted, but some people feel that gaining popularity is more important. Some teens think that they will be popular if they smoke cigarettes, use alcohol or other drugs, or sniff substances. They may do these things to impress friends or because their friends have dared them to do it. It is important to learn to use refusal skills when you feel pressured to join in activities that you believe, or know, are wrong.

If you have ever thought about trying alcohol or other drugs, think again about the reasons why. Carefully consider the long-term effects of such a decision. Using alcohol and other drugs does not make a person popular, build self-confidence, or solve problems. What alcohol and other drugs do is trap a person into a cycle of self-abuse. These harmful substances slow down your ability to act and think normally. They weaken your ability to make wise decisions. If you are faced with negative peer pressure, it is best to say "no" and walk away.

Many people who try tobacco, alcohol, or other drugs soon find themselves addicted. **Addiction** is a person's physical or mental dependence on a drug or other substance. Many people die each year from substance abuse. Excessive use of alcohol, drugs, and even over-the-counter (OTC) medications that you can buy at the supermarket can result in death. In addition, substance abuse often tears families apart and creates problems in the community. Substance abuse often leads to violence, crime, job loss, and suicide. The best way to avoid substance abuse is to never even try to use these substances.

Avoid High-Risk Behaviors

Negative peer pressure can cause more than regrets. Accepting a ride from someone who has been drinking alcohol can result in injury or death from a serious accident. Sexual involvement can result in pregnancy. It can also have harmful, even life-threatening, results in the form of AIDS and other sexually transmitted diseases (STDs).

Responsible people avoid such risks. They know that a healthy future is at stake. **Abstinence** ('ab-stə-nən(t)s) is a decision to avoid high-risk behaviors, including sexual activity and the use of tobacco, alcohol, and other drugs. Abstinence is the only sure way to protect yourself against the potentially dangerous consequences of high-risk behaviors. By saying "no" to behaviors that go against your values, you can feel better about yourself and have more self-respect.

Problem Solving
Ask for Extra Help
If you do not understand an assignment or homework problem, ask your teacher for extra help after school. Most teachers welcome the chance to provide guidance, and they will be glad to see that you are making an effort to solve your problem.
• • • • • • • • • • • • •

Succeed in School Make sure students are aware of the times you are available to help outside of classroom time.

Driving
You may have siblings or friends who drive. Before you ride in a car with someone, it is important to do more than just buckle your safety belt. Remember these tips:

• Never get into a car with someone who has been drinking or using other drugs. Even a small amount can impair one's ability to drive safely.

• Call a parent or trusted adult to pick you up if you do not have a safe ride home.

SCIENCE YOU CAN USE

Second-Hand Smoke

Being around people who smoke is harmful to your health. Second-hand smoke is a combination of a smoker's exhaled smoke, and the smoke from the burning end of a cigarette. Both parts contain chemicals that are harmful to everyone, especially children and teens.

Procedure Conduct research to find out more about the harmful effects of second-hand smoke.

Analysis Write a list of steps a teen can take to reduce his or her exposure to second-hand smoke.

> **NSES F** Develop an understanding of personal and community health.

Think about your values. Doing something that goes against your values is never a good idea. Here are some ways to say "no" to peer pressure:

- This goes against my values.
- I don't want to get hooked on alcohol or drugs.
- I don't smoke.
- I value my life too much to do that.
- I have too much self-respect to take that risk.
- I'm not into that. Go away.
- I'm not ready. I want to wait until I'm married.
- I don't want to get AIDS or an STD.

 Reading Check **Define** What is abstinence?

Assert Yourself

You will be better prepared to handle negative peer pressure if you learn how to use refusal skills and to act assertively. When you are **assertive**, you express your views clearly and respectfully in positive ways. You speak in a confident manner. You do not give in to others when you believe something is wrong. You stand up for what you believe. Assertive teens do not wait for someone else to decide what the group is going to do. They suggest safe, responsible activities. Learn to be assertive to help you feel more in control.

You Have Options Always think about the consequences of high-risk behaviors. It is never worth it, and there are always other choices you can make. *Can you name two situations in which you or someone you know had to say "no" to high-risk behaviors?*

Handle Bullies

A **bully** is a person who physically or verbally abuses some-one to cause injury or discomfort. People may become bullies because of the need for attention, feelings of low self-esteem, abuse in their own lives, or even peer pressure. Help prevent bullying by following these tips:

- Tell your parents, a teacher, counselor, or another trusted adult if someone bullies you or another person.
- Do not get angry and strike back.
- Either respond firmly or walk away.
- Stick up for another person who is being bullied.
- Stay away from bullies and the places they hang out.

When faced with a threatening situation, your brain auto-matically triggers your adrenal glands to release more adrena-line (ə-ˈdre-nə-lən). This will increase your heart rate, pulse, and respiration rate, which causes you to want to fight back or to get away from the threat. The "fight-or-flight response" is your body's physical and mental response to a threat. You have the power to choose between fighting back or getting away. Choose wisely and walk away from bullies.

Section 3.2 After You Read

Review What You Have Learned

1. **Give** an example of positive peer pressure.
2. **Describe** the best way to deal with negative peer pressure.
3. **Identify** the characteristics of a bully.

Practice Academic Skills

English Language Arts

4. Using the tips for handling a bully, create a public service announcement, poster, or skit to present to elementary-age students. Make it fun and educational for this age group.

> **NCTE 8** Use information resources to gather information and create and communicate knowledge.

Social Studies

5. Think about a situation in which you were faced with negative peer pressure. How did you react? How did the pressure affect you? How did the group or individual react to you? After reading this chapter, what could you do differently next time? Write a paragraph to answer these questions.

> **NCSS V D** Identify and analyze examples of tensions between expressions of individuality and efforts used to promote social conformity by groups and institutions.

 Check Your Answers Check your answers at this book's Online Learning Center at glencoe.com.

Discovering Careers

Do you have the desire to help others in unsafe situations? Can you help others make the right decisions? If you answered yes to either of those questions, you might want to consider a future career in public safety. The following chart explores several careers in the public safety industry.

Career Activities ▼

At School

1 Select three of the careers listed. Research the education, training, and work experience required for each career. Write a summary of your results.

At Home

2 Create an escape plan for your family to exit your home in case of an emergency. Use your home's floor plan to show how to exit all areas in the home.

At Work

3 Make a list of at least five things an employee can do to help keep his or her work area safe. Ask a friend or relative who works if you need help with ideas.

In the Community

4 Contact and interview someone in your community who works in the public safety industry. Ask this person to describe what his or her typical work day is like. Share what you learned with your class.

Learn More Online glencoe.com

Career Investigations Go to this book's Online Learning Center for activities and worksheets to help you explore careers.

Job Title	Job Description
Police Officer	Patrols assigned areas. Controls disturbances of the peace, and arrests violators. Reports hazards. Directs traffic around fires or other disruptions.
Postal Clerk	Sells stamps and postage. Registers and insures mail and computes mailing costs. Checks suspicious mail or packages for safety.
Nurse Practitioner	Performs physical examinations and preventative health care within prescribed guidelines. Helps assess patient's clinical problems and health care needs.
Firefighter	Responds to fire alarms and other emergency calls. Administers first aid and artificial respiration to injured persons.
Security Guard	Checks buildings and personnel for any suspicious or dangerous activities. Protect customers in public or commercial buildings.
Airport Security Agent	Checks luggage for suspicious items. Checks passengers for weapons or illegal substances. Helps passengers safely arrive at their gate.

Career Activities Answers for these activities can be found on page TM75.

Chapter 3 Review and Activities

Chapter Summary

Section 3.1 Friends

Friendships begin and develop when people meet and like each other. Good friendships are based on a give-and-take relationship. Friends enjoy good times together, help each other in bad times, accept each other as they are, and encourage and support each other. Good friends are supportive, caring, trustworthy, dependable, and reliable. Your friendships will grow, develop, and change throughout your life.

Section 3.2 Peer Pressure

Positive peer pressure gives you a sense of belonging and encourages positive behavior. Negative peer pressure encourages participation in unsafe or unhealthful behaviors that go against your values. When faced with negative peer pressure, say "no" and walk away. Negative peer pressure can cause more than regrets. You will be better prepared to handle negative peer pressure if you learn how to use refusal skills and to act assertively.

Words You Learned

1. Label each of these content vocabulary words and academic vocabulary words as a noun, verb, or adjective.

Content Vocabulary
- acquaintance (p. 53)
- diverse (p. 55)
- peer (p. 56)
- compromise (p. 56)
- expectation (p. 57)
- jealousy (p. 58)
- peer pressure (p. 60)
- refusal skills (p. 61)
- addiction (p. 63)
- abstinence (p. 63)
- assertive (p. 64)
- bully (p. 65)

Academic Vocabulary
- benefit (p. 54)
- confide (p. 56)
- acceptance (p. 60)
- resist (p. 61)

Review Key Concepts

2. **Describe** ways to make a new friend.

3. **List** the qualities of a good friend.

4. **Predict** how change can affect friendship.

5. **Evaluate** how peer pressure can affect the decision-making process.

6. **Explain** how saying no to high-risk behavior promotes teen safety.

7. **Describe** how being assertive can help you be more in control of your life.

Critical Thinking

8. **Compare and contrast** positive and negative peer pressure.

9. **Explain** how those who abuse drugs and alcohol can be a burden on society.

Real-World Skills and Applications

Problem-Solving

10. Make Decisions about Drinking
Lucas has been asked by one of his acquaintances, Jolie, to go to a party on Friday night. Jolie has a reputation for sneaking alcohol into parties. Develop a plan for Lucas to decide what he should do.

Interpersonal and Collaborative

11. Practice Refusal Skills Follow your teacher's instructions to form teams. With your team, come up with a list of situations in which negative peer pressure can be a factor. Then pick one of the situations and write a script for a realistic scenario. Include planning ahead and using refusal skills. Make sure everyone in the group has a part to play. Perform the scenario in front of the class. After all class members have performed their scenarios, discuss what worked well and what could be improved.

Financial Literacy

12. Calculate an Entertainment Budget Cole makes $150 per month at his after-school job. He would like to set aside 50% of his monthly income in his savings account. He has budgeted another 30% of his income for paying various expenses, such as food and bus fare. The remainder of his income is available to use on entertainment and fun activities. Cole and his friends like to go to movies on weekends. Movies cost $10 per ticket. They also like to go bowling, at $3 per game. Given his budget, how many movies could Cole see in one month? How many games could he bowl in one month? If he bowls three games, how many movie tickets could he then buy in the same month?

13. Friendship T-Shirt To communicate your care for a friend, make a Friendship T-Shirt. Use a clean, light-colored T-shirt, fabric markers, and cardboard. Slip cardboard inside the T-shirt. Use fabric markers to decorate the front and back of the shirt with drawings and words that describe your friend. Give your shirt to a friend when you are finished.

14. Research Friendship Poets and writers have described friendship in a variety of ways throughout history. Choose a historical period, such as the Renaissance, and look up poems or other writings about friendship. How was friendship described or symbolized? What kind of words did they use? Would you use the same words to describe your own friendships today? Why or why not? Prepare a short presentation for your class.

15. Peer Pressure in the Past Under the supervision of a parent or teacher, go online to research movies about life in the 1940s or 1950s. Choose a movie with a theme of friendship. If possible, watch the movie. If you cannot watch the movie, find online summaries of the story. Write a one-page essay that describes the story. Compare the peer pressures faced by teens in the movie to the pressures teens face today. Keep your essay in your Life Skills Binder.

Academic Skills

 English Language Arts

16. Write a Persuasive Letter Imagine that one of your good friends has started hanging out with some teens who use alcohol, drugs, and cigarettes. Write a letter to your friend to convince her to stop hanging out with these teens.

> **NCTE 12** Use language to accomplish individual purposes.

 Science

17. Risks and Benefits An action plan is a step-by-step strategy to identify and achieve your goals. Create an action plan for abstaining from the use of alcohol.

Procedure Conduct research about the consequences of alcohol abuse.

Analysis Make a list of negative consequences of alcohol. Next to each consequence, write a way to say "no" to help you avoid the consequence.

> **NSES F** Develop understanding of personal and community health.

 Mathematics

18. Calculate Interest Your friend Gary wants to borrow $100 from you to buy a new MP3 player. You know that he is responsible, and that he will receive a paycheck from his part-time job in a month. You decide that it will be okay to lend him the money for one month. If you charge 8 percent interest, how much money will Gary owe you when he gets paid?

Math Concept **Simple Interest** To calculate simple interest, multiply the amount borrowed by the interest percentage.

Starting Hint Multiply the amount of the loan ($100) by the interest rate (8%, or 0.08) to calculate the interest amount. Add this number to $100 to come up with the total due at the end of the month.

> **NCTM Problem Solving** Solve problems that arise in mathematics and in other contexts.

Standardized Test Practice

Short Answer

Answer each of the questions in one to three sentences.

Test-Taking Tip When answering a short answer question, it is important to read the question carefully so that you respond with only the information it is asking.

19. Describe what kind of friend you are.
20. How can friendships change during your teen years?
21. How can practicing abstinence keep you healthy?

Your Role Models

Like everyone else, there are people in your life who influence you. Famous people may have achieved goals that you admire. Friends and family members may have values that are important to you. This project will help you explore the traits you wish to develop.

My Journal Complete the journal entry from page 3, and refer to it to complete your list of role models.

Project Assignment ▼

In this project, you will:

- Create a list of people you consider role models.
- Choose, take, or collect photographs of your role models.
- Describe admirable traits that your choices possess.
- Interview one of your role models.
- Create a collage that displays photographs and descriptions of your role models.
- Present your findings to your class.
- Include this project in the first section of your personal Life Skills binder.

Step 1 Make a List of Your Role Models

To figure out the kind of person you hope to become, think about people you already admire. List the names of people in three categories of your life: Family, Friends, and Celebrities. Then describe the traits that you find admirable.

Step 2 Find Photographs of Three Role Models

Find photographs in magazines if you have famous role models. Look through family albums or take your own photographs of friends and family role models. Think about how you will prepare each photo to display

in a collage. Then write two or more paragraphs that answer these questions:

- ✔ What traits do you find admirable about each person?
- ✔ How does their photograph reflect those traits?
- ✔ Why did you choose each specific picture?
- ✔ How do these role models reflect your own values?

Step 3 Interview Someone You Admire

Interview one of your role models. Ask these questions:

- ✔ What do you think makes you unique?
- ✔ What would you consider your most important values?
- ✔ Who are your role models?

Use these interviewing skills when conducting your interview and these writing skills when writing the summary of notes from your interview.

Interviewing Skills
- Record interview responses and take notes.
- Listen attentively.

Writing Skills
- Use complete sentences.
- Use correct spelling and grammar.

Step 4 Create and Present Your Collage

Use the Life Skills Project Checklist on the right to plan and complete your collage and give an oral report on it. Before you speak, ask other students to describe your pictures to see if they accurately depict your role model.

Use these speaking skills when presenting your final report.

Speaking Skills
- Speak clearly and concisely.
- Be sensitive to the needs of your audience.
- Use standard English to communicate.

Step 5 Evaluate Your Presentation

Your project will be evaluated based on:

✔ Completeness and organization of your list of role models.
✔ Your photographs and descriptions that represent your role models' traits.
✔ The creativity of your collage.
✔ The summary written from interview notes.
✔ Grammar and sentence structure.
✔ Presentation to the class.
✔ Creativity and neatness.

⚡ **Evaluation Rubric** Go to this book's Online Learning Center through glencoe.com for a rubric you can use to evaluate your final project.

Life Skills Project Checklist

Research Your Role Models

✅ Create your list of role models.
✅ Collect photos or take photos of your choices.
✅ Interview one of your chosen role models.

Writing Skills

✅ Describe the traits you find admirable.
✅ Describe the role models in your photographs.
✅ Write a summary from your interview with your role model.

Present Your Findings

✅ Prepare a collage and a short presentation to share the photographs of your role models and the descriptions of their traits that you admire.
✅ Invite the students of the class to ask any questions they may have. Answer these questions with responses that respect their perspectives.
✅ Add this project to your Life Skills binder.

Academic Skills

✅ Conduct research to gather information.
✅ Communicate effectively.
✅ Organize your presentation so the audience can follow along easily.
✅ Thoroughly express your ideas.

NCSS IV F Individual Development and Identity Analyze the role of perceptions, attitudes, values, and beliefs in the development of personal identity.

NCTE 8 Use information resources to gather information and create and communicate knowledge.

UNIT 2

Take Charge of Your Life

Chapter 4
Communicate With Others

Chapter 5
Citizenship and Leadership

Chapter 6
Goals and Decision Making

Unit Preview

This unit is about being in control of your own life. In this unit, you will learn about:

- Using verbal and nonverbal skills to communicate efficiently.
- Recognizing the causes of conflict.
- The duties of being a responsible citizen.
- The importance of leadership skills.
- Why setting goals is essential.
- Making smart decisions.

Explore the Photo Answer Answers will vary but may include long-term versus short-term goals or that the goal be realistic, specific, challenging, flexible, active, and well thought-out.

Explore the Photo
Achieving a goal can be a very fulfilling experience. *What are some of the things you should think about when setting goals?*

Your Point of View

When you are done studying this unit, you will complete a project in which you will:

✓ Discover an issue in your community that you care about.

✓ Interview someone who holds an elected office.

✓ Share your opinion on the issue with your class.

The prewriting activity below will help you get started.

 My Journal

Prewriting Activity
Research Newspaper Stories

Find and read stories in your local newspaper about local issues that you care about. Cut out these stories for your journal, and write a summary of the article beside each one.

● What are the facts and issues discussed in each article?

● What are the different opinions about each issue? There are often two sides to an issue. If this is the case, summarize the opinion of each side.

Chapter 4

Communicate with Others

Section 4.1

Explore the Photo Answer Answers may include making eye contact, nodding to show understanding or encouragement, not interrupting.

Listening and Speaking Skills

■ **Main Idea** Communication is more than just talking. Learn to use verbal and nonverbal skills to build better communication.

Section 4.2

Handle Conflict

■ **Main Idea** You can learn to recognize the causes of conflict. There are ways to communicate that can help you prevent, avoid, and resolve conflict.

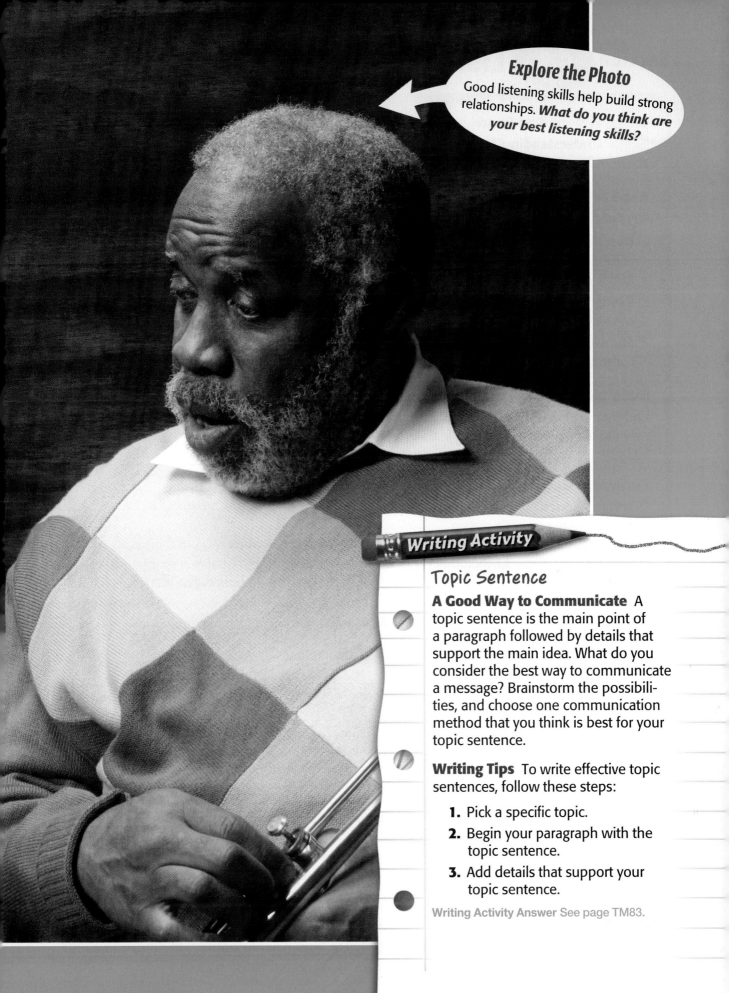

Explore the Photo
Good listening skills help build strong relationships. *What do you think are your best listening skills?*

Writing Activity

Topic Sentence

A Good Way to Communicate A topic sentence is the main point of a paragraph followed by details that support the main idea. What do you consider the best way to communicate a message? Brainstorm the possibilities, and choose one communication method that you think is best for your topic sentence.

Writing Tips To write effective topic sentences, follow these steps:

1. Pick a specific topic.
2. Begin your paragraph with the topic sentence.
3. Add details that support your topic sentence.

Writing Activity Answer See page TM83.

Reading Guide

Before You Read

Understanding Write down questions while you read. Many of them will be answered as you read. If not, you will have a list ready for your teacher.

Read to Learn
Key Concepts

✓ **Describe** how verbal and nonverbal communication can show how you feel about yourself and others.

✓ **Recognize** that listening is as important as speaking.

✓ **Show** how asking questions can improve communication.

Main Idea

Communication is more than just talking. Learn to use verbal and nonverbal skills to build better communication.

Content Vocabulary

○ communication
○ sign language
○ body language
○ gesture
○ perception
○ feedback
○ gossip
○ rumor
○ diplomacy

Academic Vocabulary

■ signal
■ exchange

Graphic Organizer

As you read, look for verbal and nonverbal guidelines for effective communication. Use a web like the one shown to help you organize your information.

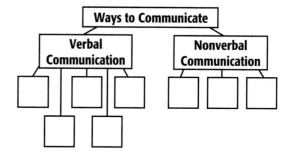

Ways to Communicate
- Verbal Communication
- Nonverbal Communication

 Graphic Organizer Go to this book's Online Learning Center at glencoe.com to print this graphic organizer.

· · · · · · · · · · · · · · · **Academic Standards** · · · · · · · · · · · · · ·

 English Language Arts
NCTE 7 Conduct research and gather, evaluate, and synthesize data to communicate discoveries.

Science
NSES A Develop abilities necessary to do scientific inquiry.

 Mathematics
NCTM Number and Operations Compute fluently and make reasonable estimates.

 Social Studies
NCSS VI G Power, Authority, and Governance Evaluate the role of technology in communications as it contributes to or helps resolve conflicts.

NCTE *National Council of Teachers of English*
NCTM *National Council of Teachers of Mathematics*

NSES *National Science Education Standards*
NCSS *National Council for the Social Studies*

Graphic Organizer Answer
Verbal Communication: speak for yourself, avoid speaking for others, be clear and direct, be aware of your listener, ask questions. Nonverbal Communication: body language, posture, personal space.

Interacting with other people is a part of your daily life. Phone conversations, talking face to face, e-mail, and instant messages are just a few examples of how you communicate. Improve your communication with speaking and listening skills.

Verbal and Nonverbal Communication

Communication is the process of sending and receiving messages about ideas, feelings, and information. Messages are sent with words and without words. We use spoken words, written words, sign language, images, and even our bodies and faces to communicate.

Verbal Communication

Verbal communication can be spoken or written. Carefully select the right words to express yourself. Say what you think and feel, but always be polite. Effective verbal communication guidelines include the following:

- **Speak for yourself.** Share your own experiences and feelings. Do not assume that other people know what you think, how you feel, or what you want.
- **Avoid speaking for others.** Do not assume that you know what other people think, how they feel, or what they want. Ask them. Let them speak for themselves.
- **Be clear and direct.** Tone of voice can reveal your feelings. You can send mixed messages if your tone does not match the words you are using.
- **Be aware of your listener.** Check to see that your listener understands what you are saying.
- **Ask questions.** Ask "who," "what," "when," "where," and "how" questions. These questions help others share their thoughts and feelings.

As You Read

Connect How has technology changed the way people talk to each other?

Vocabulary

You can find definitions in the glossary at the back of this book.

As You Read Answer Answers may include that cell phones, e-mail, text messages, and instant messages have replaced landline telephones, letters, and greeting cards. Some students may say communication is easier; others may say communication is less personal with technology.

Be a Good Listener
Listening is just as important as speaking. *How does it make you feel when someone really seems to listen to what you say?*

Photo Caption Answer Answers may include that it makes you feel like the other person cares about or understands you.

Safety Check

Nonverbal Communication

Nonverbal communication is communication without using words. You may think of sign language when you think of nonverbal communication. **Sign language** is a system of hand signs used by or for people who have a hearing impairment. However, there are many other ways people communicate without words. Think about the common greeting, "It is nice to meet you." Now, think about that greeting spoken with a handshake and a smile. Nonverbal communication can add to verbal communication and make it more effective. **Figure 4.1** describes common nonverbal communication signals. We communicate without words in the following ways:

- **Body Language** You communicate a lot through body language. **Body language** is nonverbal communication through gestures, facial expressions, behaviors, and posture. A **gesture** ('jes-chər) is the use of body movements to communicate meanings or emotions. Sometimes you use body language instead of words without being aware of it.

- **Posture** Your posture can signal, or show, your interest level. Tense posture may indicate that you are nervous, angry, or worried. Folded arms can show that you do not want to listen. If you appear relaxed, people are more likely to open up to you.

- **Personal Space** Some people prefer that others do not stand or sit too close to them. Others are more comfortable with physical closeness. The space in which you feel comfortable is your personal space. The amount of personal space you require can communicate your feelings. For example, if you keep your distance from people, it can show that you are not interested in conversation. If you allow people to be closer to you, you appear open to conversation.

Reading Check Answer
body language, posture, personal space

✔ **Reading Check** **List** *What are three types of nonverbal communication?*

Be an Active Listener

The ability to listen is just as important as the ability to speak. Listening is not the same as hearing. When you hear, you are aware of the words being said. When you listen, you make an effort to understand the message. An active listener restates what the speaker says to make sure he or she understands the message.

You can improve your listening skills by using the following guidelines:

- Give your full attention to the speaker.
- Do not interrupt.
- Concentrate on what the speaker is saying, not on what you will say next.
- Listen for the overall meaning, not just the details.
- Pay attention to nonverbal signs.
- Avoid making quick judgments.
- Try not to become distracted.
- When the other person is finished, ask questions to show that you understand.

Figure 4.1 Nonverbal Signals

Communicate Without Words Watch people when they are not speaking and you can see that they are still communicating. *How can you show a person that you are interested in the conversation without using words?*

Body Signals Folded arms can signal disinterest or anger. Hands on your hips can show impatience. Lean forward and face the speaker to show concern and interest.

Nod or Shake Your Head You can nod your head and smile to show approval or that you agree. You can shake your head to show that you disagree or do not understand.

Eye Contact Look the other person in the eye to show interest and caring. If you do not look at the other person, it could make him or her think you are bored, distracted, or uninterested.

Figure Caption Answer Nod your head, lean forward, make eye contact, smile.

SCIENCE YOU CAN USE

Is Body Language Affected by Gender?

To complete a scientific investigation or experiment, you collect data. Scientists collect data as numbers and descriptions, and then organize the data in different ways. Use your science skills to determine whether or not gender plays a part in body language.

Procedure Choose a locations to observe teens, such as at your school, a community center, or a favorite place to meet your friends. Using the examples in Figure 4.1 as a guide, create a chart to record the types of nonverbal communication used by boys and the types used by girls.

Analysis What body language did you see most often? Did boys make certain gestures more often than girls? Did girls use different kinds of body language from boys? Draw conclusions from the data to share with classmates.

> **NSES A** Develop abilities necessary to do scientific inquiry, understandings about scientific inquiry.

Science You Can Use Answer Answers will vary. Students should present a chart that shows types of body language observed and which gender demonstrated each type the most often. Conclusions drawn will vary depending on students observed.

Reading Check Answer assertive, passive, aggressive

Perception and Communication Styles

How well you listen affects your perception. **Perception** (pər-'sep-shən) is using your senses to get information about what is around you. Perception can be influenced by where you grew up, your education, your values, and your cultural heritage. These factors can affect the way verbal and nonverbal messages are sent and received.

Just as people's perceptions can differ, so can communication styles. Assertive communicators make sure their points get across. Passive communicators often listen more than they speak. Aggressive communicators may offend other people by taking over the conversation. Remember to consider the other person's perception and communication style when listening to what they are saying to you.

 List *What are three styles of communication?*

Conversation

Conversation involves the **exchange**, or sharing, of ideas, thoughts, and feelings. It is a two-way street. You must be willing to express yourself as well as listen to others.

For a conversation to be interesting and effective, it is important for each person to have a chance to talk. A good way to start is to ask the other person about his or her interests. Most people like to talk about their own experiences.

Ask Questions

It is important to give and receive feedback during a conversation. **Feedback** is the response given to a message sent. Ask questions to help you find out about other people's interests. Think about the following example: Rena asks, "Do you like baseball?" Eric answers, "Yes." That is the end of the conversation. This kind of closed-end question means that the answer is either "yes" or "no." There is no room for further discussion. Rena could get a better response if she asks, "What did you think of the game today?" Eric might say, "My favorite player scored three runs!" This is an example of an open-ended question. It leaves the possibility for more to talk about.

Avoid asking "why" questions such as "Why did you change your mind?" This type of question forces the other person to explain or defend his or her actions. You also should avoid questions that lead the other person to answer the way you think he or she should answer. For example, if you ask, "Don't you think vegetarian pizza is the best?" is really a statement of what you think. It is a way to get the other person to agree with you. Instead ask, "What kind of pizza do you like best?"

Avoid Gossip

Do you know people who gossip? **Gossip** is talking to people about someone else's personal life or private business. It is often done in an unkind way and can lead to rumors. A **rumor** is a statement spread from one person to another without knowing whether or not it is true. The information spread through gossip may be hurtful. It can damage friendships and ruin reputations. When you avoid gossip and rumors, you can show that you are a mature, caring, and responsible person.

Financial Literacy

Cell Phone Costs

Anna would like to purchase a cell phone so she can better communicate with friends and family. After doing some research, she finds that the phone will cost $39.45, the prepaid minutes will cost $19.99, the activation fee will be $15.50, and a case to hold the phone will be $16.65. How much will Anna need to buy the phone?

Math Concept **Adding Decimals** To add decimals, list the numbers vertically, being sure to line up the decimal points. Add normally from right to left, carrying when necessary. Be sure to bring the decimal point down into the answer.

Starting Hint: List the numbers ($39.45, $19.99, $15.50, and $16.65) in a vertical line with the decimal points lined up. Then add, starting with the hundredths place. Be sure to place the decimal point correctly in the answer, and label the answer.

NCTM Number and Operations Compute fluently and make reasonable estimates.

 For math help, go to the Math Appendix at the back of the book.

Character Counts

Integrity

Shanda has just moved to a new town and school. She really wants to fit in and get to know people. Two girls in her neighborhood offered to walk to school with her, introduce her to their friends, and show her around. On the first day of school, she walked with her new acquaintances. The girls started gossiping about some other girls that Shanda has not met. Shanda does not know whether or not the things they said are true.

You Make the Call

Should Shanda continue walking with the girls and participate in the gossip? Should she find someone else to walk to school with? Write a paragraph that explains what you think Shanda should do.

Character Counts Feature Answer Answers will vary. Students may suggest that Shanda not confront the girls about the gossip since they are just acquaintances. Shanda should make efforts to meet other people to walk to school with and be friends with.

Be Diplomatic

When you say things in a way that will not embarrass someone or cause hurt feelings, you are being diplomatic. **Diplomacy**, (də-ˈplō-mə-sē) also called tact, is being honest without being hurtful. It is important that negative comments focus on the issue, not the person. For example, imagine if your teacher said, "There is only one day left before the test. What can I do to help you prepare?" How would you react to that question? Most likely, you would feel glad or relieved that your teacher wants to help. Now imagine if the teacher said, "Why aren't you ready for the test yet?" How would you react to that question? You would probably feel defensive or angry and less willing to answer. Think before you speak. Sometimes, the way you say something can be even more important than what you say.

Section 4.1 After You Read

Review What You Have Learned

1. **List** the guidelines for effective verbal communication.
2. **Describe** ways to improve your listening skills.
3. **Explain** why gossip can be destructive to other people.

Practice Academic Skills

 English Language Arts

4. Observe interactions between two of your friends. Then write a paragraph to describe what was said, how it was said, and to evaluate whether or not they effectively used any of the communication skills from this chapter.

> **NCTE 7** Conduct research and gather, evaluate, and synthesize data to communicate discoveries.

 Social Studies

5. How has technology changed the way people talk to each other? Do you think these changes are positive or negative? Explain your answers.

> **NCSS VI G** Evaluate the role of technology in communications, transportation, information-processing, or other areas as it contributes to or helps resolve conflicts.

 Check Your Answers Check your answers at this book's Online Learning Center at glencoe.com.

Section **4.2** Handle Conflict

Reading Guide

Before You Read

Buddy Up for Success One advantage to sharing your notes with a buddy is that you can compare notes before you start quizzing each other.

Read to Learn

Key Concepts
- ✓ **Identify** factors that can cause conflict.
- ✓ **Explain** how you can prevent conflict.
- ✓ **Suggest** ways to resolve conflict.

Main Idea

You can learn to recognize the causes of conflict. There are ways to communicate that can help you prevent, avoid, and resolve conflict.

Content Vocabulary
- ○ conflict
- ○ prejudice
- ○ negotiation
- ○ peer mediation

Academic Vocabulary
- ■ escalate
- ■ neutral

Graphic Organizer

As you read, list five causes of conflict. Next to each cause, write something you can do to prevent the conflict. The first one is completed for you. Use a graphic organizer like the one shown to help you organize your information.

Causes of Conflict	Ways to Prevent the Conflict
1. Misunderstandings	Listen closely. Repeat what the other person said.
2.	
3.	
4.	
5.	

 Graphic Organizer Go to this book's Online Learning Center at glencoe.com to print this graphic organizer.

Academic Standards

English Language Arts

NCTE 5 Use different writing process elements to communicate effectively.

Social Studies

NCSS I B Culture Predict how data and experiences may be interpreted by people from diverse cultural perspectives and frames of reference.

NCTE *National Council of Teachers of English*
NCTM *National Council of Teachers of Mathematics*

NSES *National Science Education Standards*
NCSS *National Council for the Social Studies*

Do you get along with everyone all of the time? If you are like most people, your answer is probably no. In fact, you might even find that lately you get into more arguments than you did when you were younger. That is because you are developing opinions of your own. Learn how to handle and communicate your opinions in positive ways. This is an important part of becoming an adult.

Graphic Organizer Answer
(2) Differing opinions: each person has the right to an opinion; (3) Gossip: suggest other conversation topics; (4) Jealousy: focus on your own accomplishments and goals; (5) Prejudice: being different does not mean bad or wrong.

Face Conflict

A **conflict** is a disagreement or struggle between two or more people. Everyone experiences conflict at one time or another. You have probably had disagreements with both friends and family members.

Causes of Conflict

Think about the last time that you had a disagreement. Can you remember the cause? Conflict with friends and peers is not unusual, especially during the teen years.

- **Misunderstandings** Conflicts often occur when people do not communicate effectively. Take the time to listen closely to what the other person is saying.
- **Differing Opinions** You have your own opinions about a wide range of topics. You might feel a need to defend your opinions. It is important to remember that each person has the right to his or her opinion. Do not let this become a power struggle. Conflicts over control can hurt the people involved.
- **Gossip** If a group of teens started gossiping about your best friend's parents going through a divorce, your friend would probably feel hurt and angry. You might feel angry, too. Suggest other conversation topics to help avoid gossip.
- **Jealousy** If you and a friend both tried out for the lead in the school play and your friend got the part, you might feel jealous. Do not waste your energy being jealous of others. Focus on your own accomplishments and goals instead.
- **Prejudice** Some conflicts are caused by **prejudice** ('pre-jə-dəs), an opinion about people that is formed without facts or knowledge. Prejudice causes people to judge others without taking the time to get to know them. Remember that just because someone is different from you does not mean they are bad or wrong. Get to know people for who they are. Do not allow stereotypes to keep you from forming friendships.

 Reading Check **Define** *What is conflict?*

As You Read

Connect Think about the skills you have or want to learn to help you resolve conflicts.

As You Read Answer Answers may include listening, understanding, showing respect, remaining calm.

Vocabulary

You can find definitions in the glossary at the back of this book.

Photo Caption Answer Answers may include: the relationship could be tense or awkward; anger and resentment could grow; relationships with other family members may be affected; future conflicts will be more likely.

Damage Control Unresolved conflict can damage relationships. *What can happen if you do not resolve a conflict with one of your parents?*

Reading Check Answer A conflict is a disagreement or struggle between two or more people.

Prevent and Avoid Conflict

You can prevent some conflicts by heading off problems before they start. The best way to do this is to pay attention to your own behavior. How do you treat others? Why do you say or do certain things? When you explore your actions, you may find that there are some qualities you can improve in yourself. Try to look at situations from their point of view.

Control Anger

A conflict can escalate, or get worse, if you get angry. Learning to control your anger is an important way to prevent conflicts. When you or another person is angry, it can be easy for things to get out of hand. If you are angry, follow these tips to keep your anger from making a conflict worse:

- **Write in a journal.** Put your feelings on paper in a journal.
- **Listen to or play music.** Music can have a calming effect.
- **Find a creative outlet.** Draw, paint, write songs or poetry, or start a scrapbook project.
- **Exercise.** Use your energy for a long walk or run, or work it off at the gym.
- **Get some rest.** Anger can drain your energy and make you feel tired. Take a break, a nap, or go to bed early. Sleep helps you focus.
- **Talk to someone.** Talk about your feelings with a trusted adult.

Reading Check *Understand* What can you do to help control your anger in conflict situations?

Hands-On LAB

Practice Peer Mediation

In this activity you will practice the steps in peer mediation. If time permits, practice once as a mediator and once as a person with a conflict. Before you begin, read through the entire Hands-On-Lab assignment. Write down any questions that you might have about the activity. Reread the text or ask your teacher for help if you need it.

Supplies
✓ Paper
✓ Pen or pencil

Develop Your Plan
■ Come up with a set of rules for the process. Write them down.
■ Assign two students to be in the conflict and another to be the mediator.
■ Each student should tell his or her side of the story or complaint. If necessary, the mediator can meet with each person separately.
■ Create and discuss possible solutions.
■ Once a solution is reached, both students should sign a "contract" stating that they agree to the solution.

Implementation
■ Each student should listen quietly until the other finishes his or her side of the story.
■ The mediator should ask any questions he or she has.

■ The mediator should paraphrase, or tell the story in his or her own words, what was said to make sure the issues are clear.
■ Each side should offer several solutions to the conflict.
■ The peer mediator should choose the best solution.
■ Both students should sign a contract agreeing to the solution.

Evaluate Your Results
What problems did you have in this exercise? Were you able to work out a solution to which both students agreed? If so, what was the solution? What would you do differently next time? If you are ever in a conflict at school, would you seek out a peer mediator for help? Why or why not? Write one or more paragraphs to explain your answer.

 Projects and Activities Go to this book's Online Learning Center through **glencoe.com** for more projects and activities.

Evaluate Your Results Answer Answers should include details about the problem, the solutions, and what was learned during the mediation process.

Resolve Conflict

People who handle conflict well use good communication skills. You do not have to wait for a conflict to practice these skills. In fact, if you work on these skills every day, you may have fewer conflicts in the first place. However, conflicts can occur in spite of your best efforts. When they do, you and the other person can work out your differences in a way that satisfies both of you. Use the communication skills in **Figure 4.2** on page 88 to help you resolve conflicts.

Compromise and Negotiation

Resolving a conflict often means reaching a compromise. A compromise is an agreement in which each person gives up something in order to reach a solution that satisfies everyone. This is also called a give-and-take solution. Even if you are not involved in a conflict yourself, you can help other people solve conflicts. Instead of taking sides, try to get the people involved to talk to each other about compromise. This kind of support can help them see that they do not have to fight to come to a resolution.

Negotiation is one of the best ways to compromise. **Negotiation** (ni-ˌgō-shē-ˈā-shən) is the process of talking about a conflict and deciding how to reach a compromise. This requires a lot of give-and-take, in which both sides give up some demands and both sides get some of what they want.

For negotiation to work, both sides must be willing to stop asking for certain things or at least change their demands. For example, Rachel gets angry when her younger brother, Mark, borrows her CDs without asking. Mark, however, cannot always ask because Rachel is at basketball practice when he has time to listen to them. Perhaps Rachel could agree to let him borrow certain CDs when she is not home. In return, Mark could let her borrow his handheld electronic game without asking when she wants to play it after he has gone to bed.

- **Follow up.** When you negotiate you must make sure that you can follow through with your promises. If you agree to behave differently, you must actually do so. Otherwise, your agreement is worthless.
- **Get help.** Sometimes compromises can best be reached with the help of a third person who is **neutral**. To be neutral means to not take sides. This person may be a parent, teacher, school counselor, or other trusted adult. Sometimes this third person is a peer.

Seek Encouragement
Your Community
Look for sources of support in your community. The local library and other educational resources may provide tutoring.

• • • • • • • • • • • • • •

Succeed in School
Find out if your local library offers tutoring or other educational resources. Share this information with your students.

Figure 4.2 Skills to Help Resolve Conflict

Conflict Resolution Resolving a conflict with an important person in your life can lead to a stronger relationship. *What are some different ways you have successfully resolved disagreements?*

- **Open communication lines.** Choose a quiet location where there will not be any interruptions or distractions. Be willing to listen to each other and to explain your point of view.

- **Use "I" statements.** When you speak, avoid sentences that start with "you." The other person might feel attacked and stop listening. Start sentences with the word "I" and give a description of how you feel. For example, say "I feel like I am not being respected," instead of "You don't respect me."

- **Listen carefully.** When you speak, you want the other person to listen. You should do the same. Do not interrupt. If you have questions, wait until the other person has finished. It can be helpful if you repeat back the other person's point of view to make sure that you understand it.

- **Control your anger.** Take deep breaths. Count to ten. Do not allow anger to take over. If you feel that you cannot control your anger, excuse yourself and try again when you feel ready.

- **Negotiate a solution.** Each person should decide what is most important about the outcome. Use these priorities to negotiate.

- **Compromise to reach an agreement.** Give-and-take can help you and the other person come to a solution. A compromise helps both people get some of what they want.

Figure Caption Answer Answers will vary but may include talk out the problem; agree on a compromise; apologize and move forward.

start here on Friday 4/9/10

Peer Mediation

Many schools use peer mediation to help resolve conflicts among students. **Peer mediation** is a process in which trained students help other students find a solution to a conflict before it becomes more serious. Students are often successful with peer mediation because the mediators are students themselves. Peer mediators can often see solutions that those involved in the conflict are too angry or emotional to see. An important part of making any kind of mediation successful is confidentiality. This means the people involved can trust that no one else will hear what is said. This helps students feel free to talk openly and honestly.

Walk Away

Suppose that you made every effort to head off problems before they could lead to a conflict. You tried to resolve problems through communication, negotiation, and compromise. Still, a conflict is growing to a dangerous point. You are at school and a classmate is bullying you. What do you do? Sometimes the best response is to walk away. In such situations it is helpful to seek out and talk to an adult at school or at home. You cannot solve every problem alone. What is important is that you do your best to behave in a way that reflects your values.

 Peer Mediator A peer mediator helps his or her peers resolve conflicts. *What personal qualities does a peer mediator need to have?*

Photo Caption Answer Answers may include patience, good listening skills, good speaking skills, empathy, ability to remain neutral.

Section 4.2 After You Read

Review What You Have Learned

1. **Predict** ways gossip can lead to conflict.
2. **Identify** ways to control anger.
3. **Describe** how negotiation can lead to agreement.

Practice Academic Skills

English Language Arts

4. Write an e-mail to a friend with whom you have had a disagreement. Write what you think started the conflict. Suggest ideas for you and your friend to find a resolution.

> **NCTE 5** Use different writing process elements to communicate effectively.

Social Studies

5. Predict what could happen if the new student in your class makes false assumptions about you based on your ethnicity or cultural background.

> **NCSS I B** Predict how data and experiences may be interpreted by people from diverse cultural perspectives and frames of reference.

Check Your Answers Check your answers at this book's Online Learning Center at glencoe.com.

Discovering Careers

Do you like to communicate your message to others? Is it important for you to get the message right? If you answered yes to either of those questions, you might want to consider a future career in communication. The following chart explores several careers in the communication industry.

Job Title	Job Description
Speech Pathologist	Evaluates speech and language skills as related to educational, medical, social, and psychological factors. Plans, directs, or conducts treatment programs.
Newscaster	Broadcasts news items of local, national, and international significance. Prepares or assists in preparation of scripts.
Actor	Plays roles in dramatic productions, commercials, or other media. Interprets or presents characterization to audience.
Public Relations Specialist	Plans and conducts programs designed to create and maintain a favorable public image for employers or clients. Prepares press releases.
Journalist	Gathers and researches information from a variety of sources. Writes articles with accuracy. Uses correct grammar and punctuation
Copy Editor	Edits articles or books for grammar, punctuation, and style. Makes sure written materials communicate clearly and accurately.

Career Activities ▼

At School

1 Select three of the careers listed. Research the education, training, and work experience required for each career. Write a summary of your results.

At Home

2 Put together a list of events and activities that will be happening at home or with your family in the next few days. Use the list to create a newscast. Play the role of newscaster and read your story to your family members.

At Work

3 Make a list of what you think are the three most important qualities in a good journalist. Share your list with your classmates and discuss your choices.

In the Community

4 Contact and interview someone in your community who works in communication. Ask this person to describe what his or her typical work day is like. Share what you learned with your class.

Career Activities Answers for these activities can be found on page TM83.

Learn More Online *Online* glencoe.com

Career Investigations Go to this book's Online Learning Center for activities and worksheets to help you explore careers.

Chapter **4** Review and Activities

Chapter Summary

Section 4.1 Listening and Speaking Skills
Communication is sending and receiving messages about ideas, feelings, and information. Nonverbal communication can show how you feel about yourself and others. Listening is just as important as speaking. People use different styles of communication, sometimes based on their personality or background. Communication through conversation is the sharing of ideas, thoughts, and feelings

Section 4.2 Handle Conflict
Conflicts happen. You can prevent some conflicts by heading off problems before they start. Pay attention to your own behavior. Learn to control your anger. Conflict resolution often means reaching a compromise. Negotiation skills can help you find a compromise. This requires give-and-take, in which both sides give up some demands and both sides get some of what they want.

Words You Learned

1. Write your own definition for each content and academic vocabulary word.

Content Vocabulary
- communication (p. 77)
- sign language (p. 78)
- body language (p. 78)
- gesture (p. 78)
- perception (p. 80)
- feedback (p. 80)
- gossip (p. 81)
- rumor (p. 81)
- diplomacy (p. 82)
- conflict (p. 84)
- prejudice (p. 84)
- negotiation (p. 87)
- peer mediation (p. 88)

Academic Vocabulary
- signal (p. 78)
- exchange (p. 80)
- escalate (p. 85)
- neutral (p. 87)

Review Key Concepts

2. **Describe** how verbal and nonverbal communication can show how you feel about yourself and others.

3. **Recognize** that listening is as important as speaking.

4. **Show** how asking questions can improve communication.

5. **Identify** factors that can cause conflict.

6. **Explain** how you can prevent conflict.

7. **Suggest** ways to resolve conflict.

Critical Thinking

8. **Predict** how you will use communication skills the next time you have a disagreement with a family member.

9. **Analyze** the factors that could cause a small disagreement to become a large conflict.

Real-World Skills and Applications

Problem-Solving

10. **Action Plan** Paul is starting high school next year. He has noticed than in the past six months or so, he has had more arguments with his parents. He also finds that he loses his temper more than he used to with his younger brother. He wants to go into high school with a good attitude, but he is worried that his temper will have a negative effect on him. Develop an action plan for Paul to help him with his attitude. Present you plan to your classmates.

Interpersonal and Collaborative

11. **Evaluate Ways to Communicate** Should you have a conversation or write a letter? Follow your teacher's instructions to team up with another student. Have a face-to-face conversation about your favorite athlete or musical group or another topic of your choice. Then, write a letter to each other on the same topic. Exchange your letters. With your partner, compare your face-to-face conversation to the letters. Which worked better? Explain why.

Financial Literacy

12. **Communicating with Shoppers** Visit a mall shop, a supermarket, a convenience store, or a general merchandise store. How does the store communicate to shoppers about the things they want you to buy? What do you notice when you first enter the store? Is it a selection of new products? Are they having a big sale? Are they offering special promotions, like "buy one, get one free?" Does a salesperson approach you to give you information? Make a list of the forms of communication you notice in the store. Do you think they are effective? Do you think they help you save money or spend more money? Do you think shoppers will buy something they were not planning to buy? Write one or more paragraphs to explain your answer.

13. **Conflict Handbook** Write and illustrate a Conflict Handbook for teens. Develop guidelines for facing, preventing, avoiding, and resolving conflict. Use graphics to illustrate the handbook. Present the Conflict Handbook to your classmates with an eye-catching presentation.

14. **Conflict in History** Pick a well-known historical conflict. It can be a war, a battle, or a court case. What were the circumstances? Who or what was involved? What were the conflicting issues? How was the conflict resolved? Present this information to your classmates.

15. **Give Feedback** Imagine that you worked for two weeks on a history project. You put a lot of hard work into it, and you are eager to find out what your grade is. Now imagine that your teacher accepts your project, but does not offer feedback. How do you know what you did well? How do you know where to improve? With permission from your teacher or parents, go online to learn more about how to provide feedback. Create a list of tips to keep in your Life Skills Binder.

Academic Skills

English Language Arts

16. Teach Imagine that one of your elementary school teachers invites you and a partner to speak to her 4th grade class about communicating without words. You and your partner will have five minutes to teach the younger students about body language, facial expressions, and gestures. Make your presentation fun, engaging, and appropriate for this age group.

> **NCTE 12** Use language to accomplish individual purposes.

Social Studies

17. Research Conduct research to find examples of groups and agencies that help people resolve conflicts. Choose the group you think is the most interesting. What specific conflict resolution strategies does the group use? Do they mention the importance of negotiation, compromise, and mediation? Share what you learned with the class in a one-paragraph summary.

> **NCSS IA Culture** Analyze and explain the ways groups, societies, and cultures address human needs and concerns.

Mathematics

18. The Cost of Compromise Dale suggests playing baseball in Benjamin's backyard after school. Benjamin hits a line drive. Harry does not catch it and the ball smashes a window. The three boys negotiate a compromise to split the $168.21 replacement cost of the window, with Benjamin paying twice as much as Harry, and Harry paying twice as much as Dale. How much will each boy need to pay?

Math Concept **Solving Algebraic Equations** You can write an algebraic equation and find the solution. Use a variable to represent an unknown amount.

Starting Hint Let x stand for Dale's share. Harry's share is $2x$. Since Benjamin owes twice as much as Harry, his share is $2 \times 2x = 4x$. You then know that $x + 2x + 4x = \$168.21$. Solve from there.

> **NCTM Algebra** Represent and analyze mathematical situations and structures using algebraic symbols.

Standardized Test Practice

Multiple Choice

Read the paragraph. Then read the question and the answer choices. Choose the best answer and write it on a separate sheet of paper.

> **Test-Taking Tip** In a multiple-choice test, read the question and try to answer it before you read the answer choices. This way, the answer choices will not confuse you.

19. Jacob came home and found that his brother used his portable music player again without asking. Now the battery needs recharging, and Jacob wants to use it while doing his homework. What should Jacob do?

   a. Wait until he calms down to talk with his brother.

   b. Confront his brother right away since this happens all the time.

   c. Go tell his parents how mad he is at his brother.

   d. Go take something of his brother's to show him what it feels like.

Citizenship and Leadership

Section 5.1

Good Citizenship

■ **Main Idea** Citizenship comes with rights and responsibilities.

Section 5.2

Leadership Skills

■ **Main Idea** Leaders demonstrate leadership skills and motivate team members to work together to achieve goals.

Explore the Photo Answer Answers will vary, but most students will probably agree that good leaders and team players require some of the same qualities, such as technical skill, getting along with others, and being supportive.

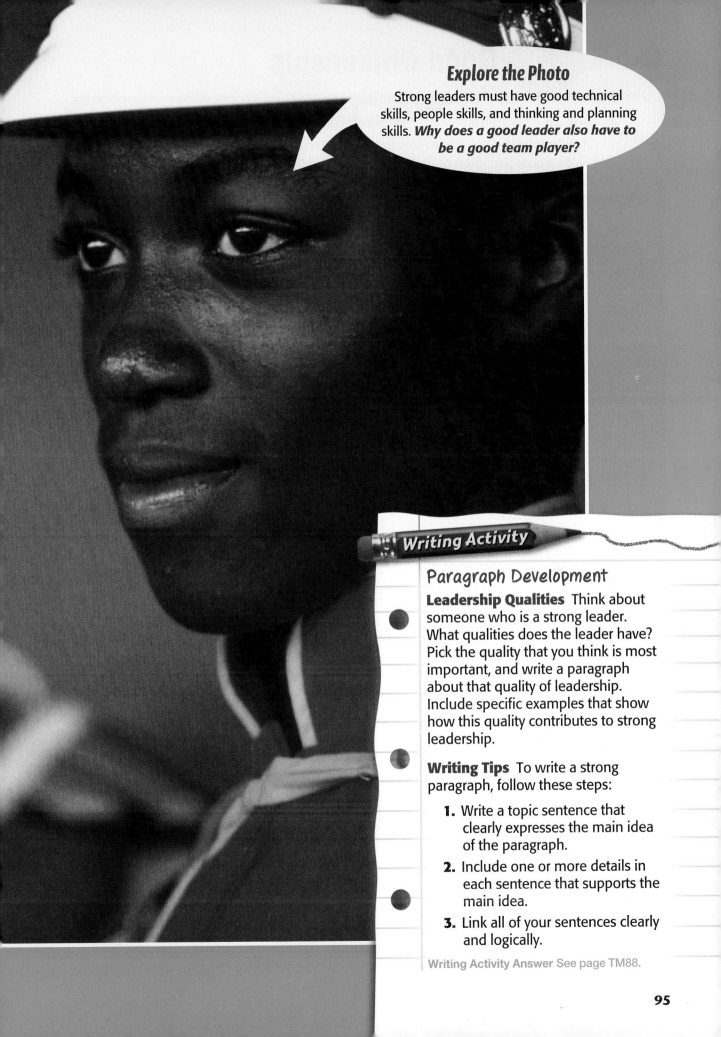

Explore the Photo

Strong leaders must have good technical skills, people skills, and thinking and planning skills. *Why does a good leader also have to be a good team player?*

Writing Activity

Paragraph Development

Leadership Qualities Think about someone who is a strong leader. What qualities does the leader have? Pick the quality that you think is most important, and write a paragraph about that quality of leadership. Include specific examples that show how this quality contributes to strong leadership.

Writing Tips To write a strong paragraph, follow these steps:

1. Write a topic sentence that clearly expresses the main idea of the paragraph.

2. Include one or more details in each sentence that supports the main idea.

3. Link all of your sentences clearly and logically.

Writing Activity Answer See page TM88.

95

Reading Guide

Before You Read

Stay Involved One way to stay involved when reading is to turn each of the headings into a question, then read the section to find the answers. For example, Rewards and Responsibilities of Citizenship might be "What are the rewards and responsibilities of citizenship?"

Read to Learn
Key Concepts
✓ **Name** one responsibility you owe to your community.

✓ **Summarize** the rewards of citizenship.

Main Idea

Citizenship comes with rights and responsibilities.

Content Vocabulary
○ citizen
○ citizenship
○ volunteer

Academic Vocabulary
■ entitled
■ thrive

Graphic Organizer

As you read, identify five ways that you can be responsible in your community. Use a graphic organizer like the one shown to help you organize your information.

Ways to Be Responsible in Your Community

 Graphic Organizer Go to this book's Online Learning Center at glencoe.com to print this graphic organizer.

· · · · · · · · · · · · · · · · · **Academic Standards** · · · · · · · · · · · · · · · ·

 English Language Arts

NCTE 8 Use information resources to gather information and create and communicate knowledge.

 Mathematics

NCTM Measurement Apply appropriate techniques, tools, and formulas to determine measurements.

Social Studies

NCSS X B Civic Ideals and Practices Identify, analyze, interpret, and evaluate sources and examples of citizens' rights and responsibilities.

NCSS I C Culture Apply an understanding of culture as an integrated whole that explains the functions and interactions of language, literature, the arts, traditions, beliefs and values, and behavior patterns.

NCTE *National Council of Teachers of English*
NCTM *National Council of Teachers of Mathematics*

NSES *National Science Education Standards*
NCSS *National Council for the Social Studies*

Graphic Organizer
Answer remember your manners, do your share, show respect for others, help other students, take care of shared property

To be a member of your community, you need to do your share and be responsible. Communities need people who are willing to step up and meet responsibilities such as voting, caring for others, and helping neighbors. When you contribute, or give back, to your community, you can feel a sense of pride and belonging.

Citizenship

The first unit of this book is about discovering who you are, taking care of yourself, and developing your friendships. However, that is just the beginning. Personal growth activities do take up most of your time, but you have another purpose in life. You can make a difference in the lives of others. For example, Sandra and her mom help at the soup kitchen at least once a month. Eric helps his elderly neighbor with her gardening chores.

As an infant, you were completely dependent on others to care for your needs. As a preschooler, you probably were taught to share your toys. Gradually, you learned that what you did or did not do affected others around you. Now you are learning to share your time and talents to improve the lives of others. There are many opportunities for you to make a difference at home, at school, at work, and in your community.

A **citizen** is a member of a community such as a city, state, or country. Citizens are **entitled** to, or allowed to expect, certain rights. For example, the Bill of Rights gives United States citizens the right to:

- Vote for government representatives.
- Express opinions freely and publicly.
- Receive an education.
- Travel freely within the country.
- Receive a fair and speedy trial.
- Enjoy equal protection under the law, regardless of gender, race, or ethnic group.

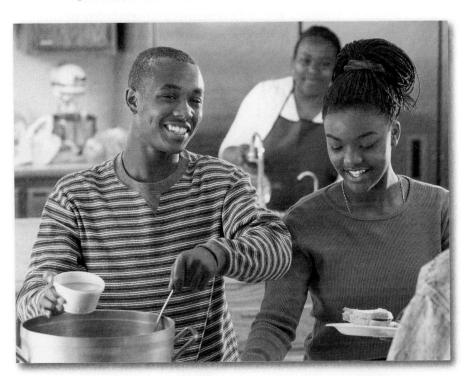

As You Read

Connect What are some ways to participate in your government?

As You Read Answer Answers will vary but may include: vote, volunteer in campaigns, learn about current events.

Vocabulary

You can find definitions in the glossary at the back of this book.

Volunteer Activities Volunteering can improve your self-esteem. *How can volunteering help you feel good about yourself?*

Photo Caption Answer Helping people can make you a more caring person, and it can be very satisfying to know that something you do helps someone else.

MATH YOU CAN USE

Teamwork

Deenie has formed a team with her classmates to design a garden for the school library. They must determine how much fencing they need to enclose the garden. The garden is in the shape of a triangle. The sides measure 6 yards, 8 yards, and 10 yards. How much fencing is needed to enclose the garden?

Math Concept **Finding Perimeter** The perimeter of any polygon (a closed shape with 3 or more sides) is calculated by adding the length of all of the polygon's sides.

Starting Hint The fencing will run along the perimeter of the garden. Calculate the perimeter by adding the 3 side lengths: 6 yards + 8 yards + 10 yards.

 For more math help, go to the Math Appendix located at the back of this book.

NCTM Measurement Apply appropriate techniques, tools, and formulas to determine measurements.

Math You Can Use Feature
Answer The team needs
24 yards of fencing to
enclose the garden.
(6 + 8 + 10 = 24 yards)

In return for the rights you enjoy, you have responsibilities to your community. You are required to obey laws and rules. Communities benefit when everyone plays a positive role.

The way you handle your responsibilities as a citizen is called **citizenship**. One of those responsibilities is to give back to the community. Volunteer work can be a valuable experience. When you **volunteer**, you give your time and energy without pay to help others. Volunteering is a good way to demonstrate your citizenship skills. Working with others who share your concerns can be a good way to make friends. As a volunteer, you may come into contact with people you may not meet otherwise. These people may be hungry, homeless, or lonely. Helping people can make you a more compassionate, or caring, person. It can be very satisfying to know that something you do helps someone else.

There are many ways you can volunteer your talents and skills:

- Read to people in a hospital or nursing home.
- Volunteer for an organization that records reading materials for people with visual impairments.
- Join efforts to clean up parks and recreation areas.
- Offer to take care of pets when your neighbors go on vacation.
- Pick up litter and put it in the proper place.
- Return lost items to the lost-and-found department or to the rightful owner.

Whether you demonstrate your citizenship skills alone or in a group, being a good citizen can give you a sense of belonging. You can also develop work experience and skills that you can apply to future jobs. What other ways can you think of to show your citizenship skills?

Reading Check Answer
A citizen is a member of a
community such as a city,
state, or country.

 Define *What is a citizen?*

Be a Volunteer

In this activity you will research opportunities to volunteer in your community. Then you will volunteer for one of these opportunities based on your interests and availability. Before you begin, read through the entire Hands-On Lab assignment. Write down any questions that you have about the assignment. Reread the text or ask your teacher for help if you need it.

Supplies
✓ Newspapers
✓ Telephone directory
✓ Computer with Internet access (optional)

Develop Your Plan
▪ Make a list of volunteer activities that interest you.
▪ Search newspapers, telephone directories, and the Internet for local volunteering opportunities.
▪ Call your public library and ask about various organizations that meet there.
▪ On a sheet of paper, list several organizations that use volunteers.

Implement Your Plan
▪ Find out what type of help each organization needs from its volunteers.
▪ Make a list of what you find out and compare it with your values.

▪ List the days and times each organization needs volunteers. Are you available? Do you have transportation?
▪ Choose one volunteer opportunity from your list that works with your schedule.
▪ Contact the organizer and make a commitment to volunteer.

Evaluate Your Results
Describe the opportunity for which you volunteered. Why did you choose that opportunity? What did you learn from the volunteer experience? Would you volunteer with the same organization again? Why or why not? Write one or more paragraphs to explain your answers.

Projects and Activities Go to this book's Online Learning Center through glencoe.com for more labs and activities.

Evaluate Your Results Answer Paragraphs will vary but should include details about the volunteer opportunity, why it was chosen, and what the student learned. Students should write about whether or not they would volunteer again and why.

Responsibilities and Rewards of Citizenship

Being responsible to your community can bring rewards for you. The sense of pride you can feel when you help and support others in your community can give you a strong connection to your community. You can feel like you are part of something more than yourself.

Be Responsible in Your Community

A community can be a neighborhood, a workplace, a school, a city, and a state. A community will **thrive**, or survive and improve, only if each person works to make it a better place for everyone. Good citizens look out for other people in the community. Look for ways to care for others and to offer help where it is needed.

Remember Your Manners

When you live and work with other people you need to respect them and yourself. Your home is where you first learn to respect yourself. Your parents probably taught you at an early age to share your toys and say "please" and "thank you." That was just the beginning of good manners. Here are just a few ways to demonstrate your good manners at home, at school, and in your community.

- When you bump into someone, say "Excuse me."
- Do not cut in line. Wait your turn.

Japanese Table Etiquette

In Japan, it is common to share several dishes of food at the table rather than serving each person his or her own meal. Chopsticks may be provided specifically for serving food. If not, it is polite to move some food from the common dishes onto your plate with the opposite end of your own chopsticks. After eating, return all of your dishes to the same position they were in when the meal began. Replace the lids on dishes. Put your chopsticks on the chopstick holder or back into their paper slip.

chopsticks A pair of slender sticks held between the thumb and fingers used primarily in Asian countries or Asian restaurants to lift food to the mouth. Chopsticks can be made of wood, bamboo, metal, bone, and plastic. Chopsticks can be plain and functional, or decorated and engraved as works of art.

NCSS I C Apply an understanding of culture as an integrated whole that explains the functions and interactions of language, literature, the arts, traditions, beliefs and values, and behavior patterns.

- If you knock something over, pick it up. Do not leave the mess for someone else to clean up.
- Apologize when you make a mistake.
- Do not interrupt someone when he or she is speaking. Wait until the person is finished speaking.
- Open doors for other people when you reach the entryway first.
- Whether you win or lose, always be courteous when playing sports or games.
- Practice good table etiquette, or manners. This shows respect for other people seated at the table.

Do Your Share

Offer to pitch in and help. Look for ways that you can lend a hand to family members, neighbors, teachers, and friends. Volunteer to help at school or in your community. Get involved in a community-sponsored event, such as a park clean-up or recycling campaign.

Show Respect for Others

Treat others as you would like to be treated. For example, wait your turn instead of trying to get to the front of a line. Give others in your family a chance to use the computer or telephone. Speak respectfully to adults, including parents, grandparents, teachers, and law enforcement officers. Remember to show respect for everyone, not just people you know well or especially like.

Help Other Students

Make new students feel comfortable, and introduce them to other people. If you meet someone with different values from your own, be willing to listen and understand. When you disagree with someone, give that person a fair chance to explain his or her opinion.

Take Care of Shared Property

Be as careful with library books or park equipment as you would be with your own belongings. Then the next person will be able to use and enjoy them, too. The same is also true for recreation areas, school buildings, and streets and sidewalks.

Photo Caption Answer
Answers will vary but may include that good manners show respect for yourself and for others.

Good Manners Always be considerate and polite when sharing meals with family and friends. *Why is using good manners appropriate in every situation?*

Section 5.1 After You Read

Review What You Have Learned

1. **Name** three rights that a U.S. citizen has.
2. **Suggest** ways you can volunteer in your community.

Practice Academic Skills

 English Language Arts

3. Conduct research to develop a public service announcement (PSA) that tells teens about local volunteer opportunities. Share your PSA with the class.

Social Studies

4. Conduct research to find a copy of the Bill of Rights. Choose one of the ten amendments. What does the amendment mean? Why do you think the amendment is important?

> **NCTE 8** Use information resources to gather information and create and communicate knowledge.

> **NCSS X B** Identify, analyze, interpret, and evaluate sources and examples of citizens' rights and responsibilities..

Check Your Answers Check your answers at this book's Online Learning Center at glencoe.com.

Section 5.2 Leadership Skills

Before You Read

Prior Knowledge Look over the Key Concepts at the beginning of the section. As you read, write down what you already know about each concept, and write down what you want to find out by reading the lesson.

Read to Learn

Key Concepts

✓ **Describe** how a leader can guide a group to accomplish goals.

✓ **Define** two different leadership styles.

✓ **Give** examples of teamwork.

Main Idea

Leaders demonstrate leadership skills and motivate team members to work together to achieve goals.

Content Vocabulary

○ leadership
○ leader
○ motivate
○ autocratic leader
○ democratic leader
○ teamwork

Academic Vocabulary

■ elect   ■ delegate

Graphic Organizer

As you read, identify five qualities that a good leader should have. Use a graphic organizer like the one shown to help you organize your thoughts.

Good Leadership Qualities

 Graphic Organizer Go to this book's Online Learning Center at glencoe.com to print this graphic organizer.

······· **Academic Standards** ·······

 English Language Arts

NCTE 4 Use written language to communicate effectively.

Social Studies

NCSS IX D Global Connections Analyze the causes, consequences, and possible solutions to emerging global issues, such as health and environmental quality.

NCTE *National Council of Teachers of English*
NCTM *National Council of Teachers of Mathematics*

NSES *National Science Education Standards*
NCSS *National Council for the Social Studies*

Have you ever been in a group where no one was in charge? It probably seemed disorganized and confusing. Groups need leadership to direct the way tasks are accomplished. There are skills that help leaders guide groups successfully. When the leader is effective, so is the group.

Graphic Organizer Answer motivate others, encourage others, know when to share responsibilities, maintain positive attitude, make decisions after facts are known

As You Read

Connect How do you practice teamwork at home?

As You Read Answer Students may say they help with chores, help younger siblings with homework or class projects, help in planning family events.

◆ Vocabulary

You can find definitions in the glossary at the back of this book.

Succeed in School Refer students to pages 117–119 for more information about setting and achieving goals.

Success Is What You Make It!

Achieve Your Goals After you determine what success means to you, set goals to achieve your success. Break these goals into steps that will help you keep track of your progress.

• • • • • • • • • • • • • •

Leadership

Leadership is the direction or guidance that helps a group accomplish its goals. Every group needs a **leader**, a person with the ability to guide and motivate others. Leaders can be found in front of the team to show the way, or they may be in the background to encourage others. Leaders must use good communication skills and know how to work with people.

Sometimes people **elect**, or choose, leaders. For example, the captain of your hockey team and the mayor of your community were probably elected. At other times the job of a leader is not a formal job. When you organize a birthday party for a friend or get your siblings to help rake the leaves, you are in a leadership role. You can become a good leader when you motivate and encourage others, share responsibilities and rewards, have a positive attitude, and make smart decisions.

Motivate Others

When you are the leader, you need to help your group members be enthusiastic about the tasks you want to accomplish together. When you **motivate** someone, you make him or her feel enthusiastic, interested, and committed to a project or task. Motivate the group by being upbeat about the tasks and challenges you need to accomplish together. Set a good example. Be the first person to jump in and work on a project.

Encourage Others

It is easy for group members to become discouraged about the task and their part. Encourage others with positive words. Point out what they are contributing to the group. Be specific, "Thanks for jumping in on that task. I appreciate the way you offer your ideas to others." You can always find something nice to say. Listening is also a good way to encourage someone to share his or her ideas.

Share Responsibilities

You do not have to do it all yourself. Know when to **delegate**, or hand over, some of the responsibilities. Let others have a role in the task you are trying to accomplish. The group will feel good about what they accomplish, and you can feel good about teaching them something new. Share the work and the fun. Work cooperatively with others.

Have a Positive Attitude

Group members will look to you to set the tone for your tasks. Have a positive attitude about every task. Your enthusisam can have a positive effect on the other members. A positive attitude can make the difference in how well a job gets done and how well your group works together. Resolve any conflicts in a positive, affirming way.

Make Sound Decisions

Get all of the facts before making a decision. You should never make a snap decision. Investigate the details first. Make sound decisions on behalf of your group to help build your trustworthiness as the leader. Identify clear goals for the group.

Character Counts

Tolerance

Luke is running for the student council where students will work together to lead and accomplish projects for his school. Some of his friends are actively campaigning against Lian, who has been critical of the way the student council has been run in the past. Luke's friends want him to join in the campaign against Lian. He knows that Lian has very different opinions and ideas about the way things should be done on the student council.

You Make the Call

Should Luke campaign against Lian in the student council election? What should Luke tell his friends? Write a paragraph that explains what you think Luke should do.

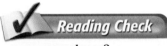

Reading Check *Explain* *How can a leader encourage group members?*

Character Counts Answer Answers will vary. Sample answer: Luke should expect that others have different opinions and ideas. No one will think exactly like he does. He should use the campaign time to promote himself instead of pointing out Lian's flaws. Luke should be tolerant of other opinions and ideas and allow the student body to decide who they want to lead them.

Reading Check Answer Encourage others with positive words, and point out what they are contributing to the group.

Photo Caption Answer Team members would be unsure of what to do or what they were working for.

Work with Your Team When you work together with other people on your team, you set common goals. *How would your team be affected if you did not have goals?*

FCCLA

In this activity, you will explore the benefits of joining FCCLA (Family, Career and Community Leaders of America). Before you begin, read through the entire Hands-On Lab assignment. Write down any questions that you have about the assignment. Reread the text or ask your teacher for help if you need it

The Ultimate Leadership Experience

Supplies
✓ Computer with Internet access
✓ FCCLA Mission Statement

Develop Your Plan

◼ Go to the FCCLA Web site (www.fcclainc.org), and read the benefits of joining FCCLA.

◼ Copy the FCCLA Mission Statement in your notebook.

◼ List the five steps of the FCCLA Planning Process.

◼ Share examples of good leaders and the qualities that you think make them good leaders.

Implement Your Plan

◼ List the leadership qualities that you already have, then list the qualities that you want to develop.

◼ Set a personal leadership goal and write it down in your notebook.

◼ Use the FCCLA Planning Process to create a plan for meeting your personal leadership goal.

◼ In an essay, explain the following:
— How joining FCCLA could help you develop as a leader.
— How being a better leader could help you in your relationships.
— How FCCLA can help you develop character, creative and critical thinking skills, interpersonal communication skills, practical knowledge, and career preparation skills.

Evaluate Your Results

Exchange your FCCLA essay with a classmate and read his or her essay in return. Give each other feedback. Ask your teacher to evaluate your FCCLA plan for your personal leadership goal and provide feedback.

Projects and Activities Go to this book's Online Learning Center through glencoe.com for more projects and activities.

Evaluate Your Results Answer Essays will vary but should demonstrate students' understanding of how FCCLA can help them develop their leadership skills. Essays should include details about how FCCLA can help them with character development, creative and critical thinking skills, interpersonal communication skills, practical knowledge, and career preparation skills.

Leadership Skills and Styles

Leaders need to have certain basic skills to be successful. They must have technical skills, which means they need to have the ability to do specific tasks. For example, knowing how to use a computer application is a technical skill. Leaders need to be willing to learn new skills when technology changes. Leaders must also have good people skills. People will have a variety of opinions and personalities. Leaders need to communicate effectively with all types of people, and to respect the differences among them. A person who can help solve problems makes a good leader. Leaders also need good thinking skills. A good leader thinks critically and creatively, and knows how to make and carry out plans. It is not always easy to learn these skills. It takes practice to become a good leader.

Leaders often have distinctive or unique leadership styles. Think of a leader in a group you were in. What characteristics of his or her leadership did you notice?

COMMUNITY CONNECTIONS

Fundraiser Look for ways to help out with a local fundraiser in your community. You and your family could participate together in a walk-a-thon, relay, or other community project.

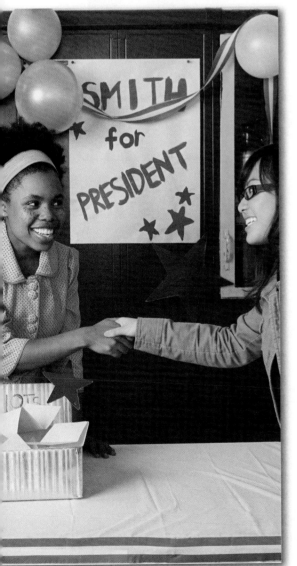

Leaders who dictate are called **autocratic leaders**. This type of leader runs the show, from the smallest details to the big picture. Leaders who involve everyone in the decision-making process are **democratic leaders**. This type of leader helps the group in making decisions. The leader and the group make decisions together. How do you lead? What leadership style do you think works best?

Contrast *How do autocratic leaders and democratic leaders differ?*

Reading Check Answer
Autocratic leaders dictate and make all of the decisions. Democratic leaders make decisions with the group.

Leadership Opportunities A leader motivates others to accomplish goals. *What leadership opportunities does your school offer?*

Photo Caption Answer
Answers may vary but may include student government, sports teams, study groups, scout troops.

Figure (5.1) Effective Interaction

Teamwork When you interact with other people, you will find that they have a variety of personalities, opinions, and ways of doing things. *Why is it beneficial to work in teams?*

Whether you are the leader or a team member:

- Let group members help set goals and make decisions.
- Keep an open mind about the opinions and ideas of others.
- Invite shy team members to get involved.
- Let others make some of the decisions.
- Be enthusiastic and positive.
- Encourage team spirit.
- Ask for everyone's opinion.
- Get everyone involved.
- Be respectful of others.
- Say thank-you.
- Be positive.

- Be considerate of other people's feelings.
- Use effective communication skills.
- Take every opportunity to compliment others.

Figure Caption Answer
Answers may include that working in teams gets the job done faster, teaches you how to work with others, and can prepare you for future jobs.

Teamwork

A group such as a family, a school, or a community needs all of its members to work together. The most effective groups are those that function as teams. When people use **teamwork**, everyone works together to reach a goal. Teamwork means that people in the group help each other and share information. Teams can accomplish more as a group than individual members can accomplish alone. **Figure 5.1** lists several ways you can work effectively with others. Without the cooperation and support of all members, a team cannot operate effectively. For example, you demonstrate teamwork when you:

- Participate in a school fundraiser.
- Play on a sports team.
- Join the student council.
- Pitch in to help your family with yard work.
- Take part in a walk-a-thon.

Be a Strong Team Member

Not everyone can be a leader. In fact, if everyone wanted to be in charge, there would be nothing but conflict. The right combination of team leaders and team members is what makes a team effective.

Help the Team Succeed

A team's success depends on good leadership and good followers. If the followers do not do their share, how can the leaders get anything accomplished? The role of leader requires a lot of time and effort. If the leader has dependable followers, he or she has more time to spend on managing the team's goals. The team is more likely to succeed when the leader has a strong support system.

Do Your Part

If you join a team, be prepared to do your fair share. When everyone does a little work, no one has to do a lot of work. Have fun with your fellow team members, but remember to fulfill your duties as well.

Section 5.2 After You Read

Review What You Have Learned

1. **Explain** why the ability to motivate others is important for good leadership.
2. **Identify** three skills that a good leader should have.
3. **Summarize** the importance of teamwork.

Practice Academic Skills

 English Language Arts

4. Imagine you have been asked to interview a person who is running for president of your school's student council. Write three questions to ask the person that would help you find out about his or her leadership skills.

NCTE 4 Use written language to communicate effectively.

 Social Studies

5. For one day, keep a list of what you put in the trash and what you recycle. List an describe at least two actions you could take that would help you reduce waste on a long-term basis.

NCSS IX D Analyze the causes, consequences, and possible solutions to emerging global issues, such as health and environmental quality.

🚀 **Check Your Answers** Check your answers at this book's Online Learning Center at glencoe.com.

Discovering Careers

Do you find satisfaction in seeing a task accomplished by working together? Do you enjoy seeing people serve their community? If you answered yes to either of those questions, you might want to consider a future career in community service. The following chart explores several careers in the community service field.

Career Activities ▼

At School

1 Select three of the careers listed. Research the education, training, and work experience required for each career. Write a summary of your results.

At Home

2 Plan an informational program about your family's history. Include details about your heritage, places where you have lived, and interesting stories that are unique to your family. Present an outline of the program.

At Work

3 Make a list of the community concerns that a legislator or commissioner might need to address. Prioritize your list based on what is most pressing for your community.

In the Community

4 Contact and interview someone in your community who works in community service. Ask this person to describe what his or her typical work day is like. Share what you learned with your class.

Career Activities Answers for these activities can be found on page TM88.

Job Title	Job Description
State Legislator	Helps establish laws and policies in accordance with the state constitution and by-laws. Addresses the concerns of citizens.
Park Naturalist	Plans, develops, and conducts programs to inform public of historical, natural, or scientific features of parks. Schedules programs.
Election Clerk	Compiles and verifies voter lists from official registration records. Distributes ballots to voters and answers questions about procedures.
Little League Coach	Plans practice and play for young baseball players. Works with parents to organize play. Works with team on skills.
County Commissioner	Works with other commissioners to establish policies within a county. Works with citizens and their concerns.

Learn More *Online* glencoe.com

Career Investigations Go to this book's Online Learning Center for activities and worksheets to help you explore careers.

Chapter 5 Review and Activities

Chapter Summary

Section 5.1 Good Citizenship
A citizen is a member of a community and is entitled to certain rights. In return, citizens have responsibilities to their community, such as obeying the law. A good way to demonstrate citizenship skills is to be responsible to your community. Citizens feel pride when they help and support others in their community, which can lead to a strong connection to the community. Citizens care about what happens to family, neighbors, and their community.

Section 5.2 Leadership Skills
Leadership is the direction that helps a group to accomplish its goals. Every group needs a leader. Good leaders motivate and encourage others, share responsibilities and rewards, have a positive attitude, and make smart decisions. Leaders have different leadership styles, and a successful group needs all of its members to work together. When people use teamwork, everyone works together to reach a goal.

Words You Learned

1. Use each of these content vocabulary words and academic vocabulary words to create a crossword puzzle on graph paper. Use the definitions as clues.

Content Vocabulary
- citizen (p. 97)
- citizenship (p. 98)
- volunteer (p. 98)
- leadership (p. 104)
- leader (p. 104)
- motivate (p. 104)
- autocratic leader (p. 107)
- democratic leader (p. 107)
- teamwork (p. 108)

Academic Vocabulary
- entitled (p. 97)
- thrive (p. 100)
- elect (p. 104)
- delegate (p. 104)

Review Key Concepts

2. **Name** one responsibility citizens owe to their community.

3. **Summarize** the rewards of citizenship.

4. **Describe** how a leader can guide a group to accomplish goals.

5. **Define** two different leadership styles.

6. **Give** examples of teamwork.

Critical Thinking

7. **Analyze** how much of a role popularity plays in leadership.

8. **Describe** who must pay when public property is damaged or destroyed.

9. **Explain** why some people may not want to participate in volunteer activities.

Real-World Skills and Applications

Problem-Solving

10. Which Is Better? Find a time to observe two different teams in your school or community, such as a sporting event, group project, or school assembly. What kind of leadership style do you observe in each group? List the pros and cons of each style you observe. Do you think one group has better leadership than the other? Share your observations with your class.

Interpersonal and Collaborative

11. Work Together to Get Involved Follow your teacher's directions to form groups. Work in groups to come up with a list of community groups for which you could volunteer. How could you make a difference? Put together a list for your class with your recommendations and ways to get involved.

Financial Literacy

12. Compare Nonprofits Like any corporation or organization, charities have expenses that must be paid. Non-profit organizations have administrative expenses, which means paying for employee salaries, office locations, and supplies. They also must spend money on mailings, phone calls, Web sites, and special events in order to raise more money. As a result, when you donate to a charity, only a certain percentage of your donation goes to the actual cause. Select two non-profit organizations you would consider donating money to. Conduct research to find out how each one uses the money it collects. Choose the organization that uses the higher percentage of donations for the cause.

13. Build Awareness Spend a day being more aware of people than you usually are. Introduce yourself to people you do not know. Smile and say hello. Ask questions to learn more about the people around you. Write a report about the reactions you got. Was this an easy or difficult task for you? Explain your answer in your report.

14. Research a Leader Choose a current or historical world leader and conduct research to learn about his or her leadership style. Find two examples of how he or she worked with other countries. Create a presentation for your class that explains whether or not you think the leader's style is or was effective.

15. Famous Quotes With permission from your parents or teacher, go online and choose a search engine. Type in a phrase such as "leadership quotations" or "motivational quotes." For example, you may come across this quote from fomer First Lady Rosalynn Carter: "A leader takes people where they want to go. A great leader takes people where they do not necessarily want to go, but ought to be." She probably means that great leaders have the skill and ability to encourage others to do their very best. Read several more, then list three quotations that you think apply to the types of leadership described in this chapter or in your class.

Academic Skills

 ### English Language Arts

16. Create a Children's Book Partner with a kindergartener, a young neighbor, or younger sibling and read a book together. Then, ask the child to help you come up with an idea for a short children's story. Write the story and draw pictures to go with it. Bind the book with yarn or ribbon. Write a paragraph that describes your experience. Give the book to your partner to enjoy again later.

> **NCTE 12** Use language to accomplish individual purposes.

 ### Social Studies

17. Voting Records Contact a local election office to find out how many registered voters live in your district or precinct. How many of them voted in the last election? What percentage of registered voters actually voted? Do you think this is an acceptable percentage? Why or why not? Write a paragraph to explain the information you find.

> **NCSS X C Civic Ideals and Practices** Locate, access, analyze, organize, synthesize, evaluate, and apply information about selected public issues.

 ### Mathematics

18. Calculate Claire is a supervisor at a non-profit company that raises money to build homes for low-income families. She has taken her employees out for a team-building lunch. During lunch they discussed their goals and the ways they want to work together to meet them. Claire decided to pay the bill herself so that the company can use more of their funds for the home-building efforts. The final bill is $92.50. If Claire leaves $110 including tip, what percentage did she leave as a tip?

Math Concept Finding a Percent
To find what percent a number is of a second number, divide the first number by the second number. Multiply the result by 100 and add the percent symbol.

Starting Hint Figure out the amount of the tip by subtracting $92.50 from $110. Divide this tip amount by the original bill amount ($92.50), and multiply by 100 to get the percent.

> **NCTM Problem Solving** Build new mathematical knowledge through problem solving.

Standardized Test Practice

Essay

Read the paragraph. Write your answer on a separate piece of paper.

 Test-Taking Tip Brainstorm ideas before you begin writing. Use graphic organizers such as a web diagram to put your ideas on paper before you start to organize the essay.

19. You will soon have the opportunity to vote in a presidential campaign. What qualities will you look for when voting for the leadership of our country? Prioritize these qualities and write an essay that describes the kind of leader you would vote for.

Chapter 6

Goals and Decision Making

Section 6.1

Goals

■ **Main Idea** You can accomplish your goals when you are focused and positive. Learn to set short-term and long-term goals to achieve success.

Section 6.2

Explore the Photo Answer Answers may include: get a good grade on a test or paper, win a game, start or finish a school project.

Decisions

■ **Main Idea** You make decisions every day. Decisions can be big or small. Making responsible decisions now can have a positive impact on your future.

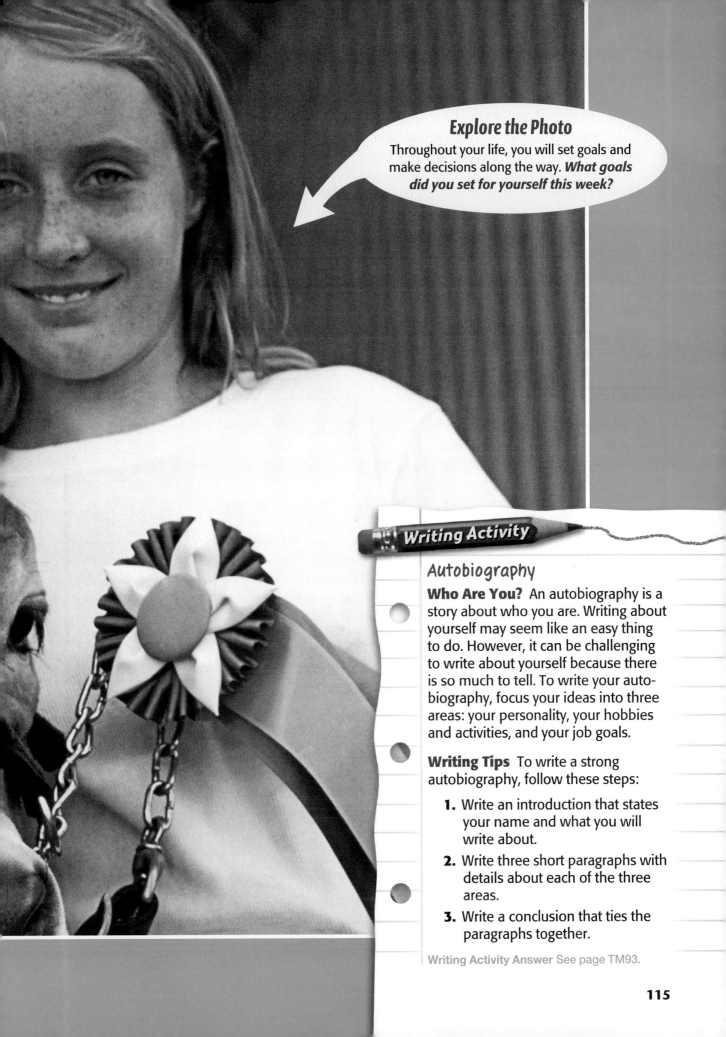

Explore the Photo
Throughout your life, you will set goals and make decisions along the way. *What goals did you set for yourself this week?*

Writing Activity

Autobiography

Who Are You? An autobiography is a story about who you are. Writing about yourself may seem like an easy thing to do. However, it can be challenging to write about yourself because there is so much to tell. To write your autobiography, focus your ideas into three areas: your personality, your hobbies and activities, and your job goals.

Writing Tips To write a strong autobiography, follow these steps:

1. Write an introduction that states your name and what you will write about.
2. Write three short paragraphs with details about each of the three areas.
3. Write a conclusion that ties the paragraphs together.

Writing Activity Answer See page TM93.

Section 6.1 Goals

Before You Read

Predict Before you start the section, browse the content by reading headings, bold terms, and photo captions. Do they help you predict the information in the section?

Read to Learn
Key Concepts
✓ **Differentiate** between long-term and short-term goals.
✓ **Explain** how attitude helps achieve goals.

Main Idea
You can accomplish your goals when you are focused and positive. Learn to set short-term and long-term goals to achieve success.

Content Vocabulary
○ goal
○ long-term goal
○ short-term goal
○ attitude
○ priority
○ trade-off

Academic Vocabulary
■ worth
■ accomplish

Graphic Organizer
As you read, list and explain five qualities of realistic goals. The first one has been done for you. Use a graphic organizer like the one shown to help you organize your information.

Realistic Goals should be…	Why?
Specific	So you can follow your progress and keep yourself on track.

Graphic Organizer Go to this book's Online Learning Center at glencoe.com to print this graphic organizer.

· · · · · · · · · · · · · · · · · · · **Academic Standards** · · · · · · · · · · · · · · · · · ·

 English Language Arts
NCTE 12 Use language to accomplish individual purposes.

 Mathematics
NCTM Number and Operations Understand numbers, ways of representing numbers, relationships among numbers, and number systems.

 Social Studies
NCSS II C Time, Continuity, and Change Identify and describe significant historical periods and patterns of change within and across cultures.

NCTE *National Council of Teachers of English*
NCTM *National Council of Teachers of Mathematics*
NSES *National Science Education Standards*
NCSS *National Council for the Social Studies*

Graphic Organizer Answer
Challenging, so you can push yourself to reach a big goal but be practical; Active, so you do something every day to work toward your goal; Thought-out, so you can plan for possible problems; Flexible, so you can change your plans if you need to.

Having something to aim for can give you purpose and direction in your life. It takes planning and skill to reach goals. You can learn learn these skills with time and practice. If you know what is important to you, it is easier to set goals and make decisions that can help you reach your goals.

Goal Setting

Goals are essential, or necessary, for success in life. A **goal** is something you want to achieve or accomplish. You will have many goals throughout your life. Some goals will be big, such as learn to fly a jet or get a college degree. Other goals will be smaller, such as pass tomorrow's math test or finish one more chapter in the book you are reading. Many other goals will fall somewhere in between. Personal goals can help you do your best and achieve the things you want and need.

Long-Term and Short-Term Goals

You may not think often about setting goals, but it is something you do almost all the time. Some of your goals may take months or even years to reach. This kind of goal is called a **long-term goal**. Your long-term goals may include marriage, owning a car, going to college, or saving enough money to buy a new computer.

A **short-term goal** can be reached quickly, perhaps in a few days or weeks. Your short-term goals might include complete a science project, pass a math test, or make the cheerleading team.

Sometimes short-term goals can help you achieve a long-term goal. Set short-term goals, such as completing a CPR course, to prepare yourself for your long-term goal of becoming an emergency medical technician. What are your short-term goals? What are your long-term goals?

Set Realistic Goals

When you set goals, you need to make sure that they are realistic. If your goals are too hard to reach, you may become discouraged and give up. If they are too easy, you may lose interest in them. Realistic goals are both reachable and challenging. **Figure 6.1** on page 118 offers guidelines for setting realistic goals.

As You Read

Connect What resources might you need to reach your goals?

Vocabulary

You can find definitions in the glossary at the back of this book.

As You Read Answer
time, money, energy, knowledge, skills, family, friends

Photo Caption Answer
Answers will vary but may include marriage and children, job or school plans, buying a car or home, passing a test, finishing a paper, getting on a sports team or into a club. Some students may associate the term with sports. If so, use the opportunity to compare planning and strategy in sports goals to life goals.

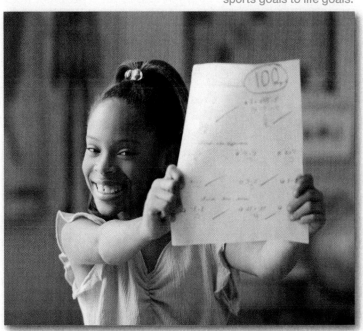

Personal Goals It can be very rewarding to reach a goal. *What do you think of first when you hear the word goal?*

Reduce Stress

Organize Your Schedule Write down assignments and projects with their due dates. Include test dates and set aside time to study. This can help you avoid the last-minute rushing to complete your work.

• • • • • • • • • • • • •

Reading Check
Answer complete a science project, pass a math test, make the cheerleading team

Goal setting requires planning. Identify a long-term goal and make a list of what must be done to reach it. Each step you take toward that long-term goal could become a short-term goal. A plan that includes short-term goals as well as long-term goals can provide you with the guidance you need to be a success. A written plan can help you see progress.

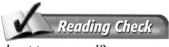 **Reading Check** **List** *What are three examples of a short-term goal?*

Achieve Goals

Achieving your goals is not something that just happens. You need to plan how you can reach each goal. For a good first step, write down the goal. This can help you get a clear picture of what you want to accomplish.

You also need to figure out what resources will be needed to reach your goal. Resources include your time, money, energy, knowledge, and skills. Your family and friends are also resources that are available to you. Use your resources wisely to achieve your goals.

Figure **6.1** **Realistic Goals**

Plan and Prepare The way you plan your goals and prepare to reach them has a lot to do with your success. *How can being prepared for a problem help you reach a goal?*

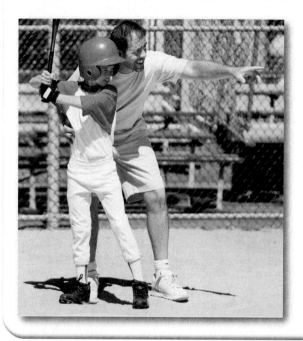

To be realistic, your goals should be:

- **Specific** Give yourself a very clear idea of your goal. That way, you can follow your progress easily and keep yourself on track.
- **Challenging** It is good to push yourself to reach a big goal. However, you should be practical about your abilities.
- **Active** Do something every day to work toward your goal.
- **Thought-out** Try to imagine possible problems. Plan positive, creative ways to deal with them. Being prepared for problems can keep you from being caught off guard if your plan hits a snag.
- **Flexible** Even with planning, the unexpected can happen. Be flexible so you can change your plans if you need to.

Figure Caption Answer If you think ahead for possible problems, you will not be caught off guard if your plan hits a snag.

Goal Setting

In this activity you will use a past goal to learn the process of making short-term and long-term goals. Before you begin, read through the entire Hands-On Lab assignment. Write down any questions that you have about the assignment. Reread the text or ask your teacher for help if you need it

Supplies
✓ 2 sheets of paper
✓ Pen or pencil

Develop Your Plan

■ Fold a sheet of paper in half. On the left side, write down a long-term goal that you have already achieved. Perhaps it was getting a part-time job, earning a place on an athletic team, or joining a club.

■ On the right side of the paper, list what you did to reach that goal. You may not have realized it, but these were your short-term goals.

■ On the back of the paper, write how achieving the goal made you feel. Did you feel proud of yourself? Did you feel inspired to make an even bigger goal next time?

Implement Your Plan

■ Fold a second sheet of paper in half. On the left side, write down a new long-term goal that you want to achieve. For example, you may want to buy a car, get a full-time job, or attend college.

■ On the right side of the paper, list what you will do to reach that goal. For example, if attending college is your long-term goal, you would need to finish high school, research college options, and gather information about requirements. These steps are some of your new short-term goals.

■ On the back of the paper, write how you think you will feel when you reach the goal.

Evaluate Your Results

What did you learn from this exercise? How can you use this process to help you reach your future goals? Write one or more paragraphs to explain your answers.

 Projects and Activities Go to this book's Online Learning Center through **glencoe.com** for more projects and activities.

Evaluate Your Results Answer Answers will vary. Students may write that they understand how goals are set every day without thinking about it. Students should explain that setting short-term goals can help you reach long-term goals by breaking a large goal into smaller steps. This process may help them reach future goals by putting their plans in writing and having something to refer to if they get discouraged.

Financial Literacy

Working to Meet Goals

Toni set a long-term goal for herself to rent an apartment. She is comparing rent costs to help make her decision. She found a one-bedroom apartment downtown that rents for $600. She found a one-bedroom apartment in the suburbs that rents for 75% of the cost of the downtown apartment. What is the rent of the apartment in the suburbs?

Math Concept **Multiplying by Percents** To determine the cost of the apartment in the suburbs, multiply the cost of the apartment in the downtown area by 75%.

Starting Hint: To multiply by a percent, you must change the percent to a decimal. To do this, move the decimal point two places to the left. In this problem, 75% becomes .75, which you will multiply by $600.

NCTM Number and Operation Understand numbers, ways of representing numbers, relationships among numbers, and number systems.

 For math help, go to the Math Appendix at the back of the book.

Financial Literacy Answer
The rent in the suburbs is
$450.00. (.75 x 600 = 450)

COMMUNITY CONNECTIONS

Help Others Set a goal for yourself that can help you as well as help others. Look for volunteer opportunities in your community such runs or walks for charity, tutoring for children, and environmental clean-up efforts.

You may need to plan more than one way to reach your goal in case your first plan does not work. For example, suppose that you want to take up a new sport. If you find that you do not like team sports, you could try an individual sport such as swimming, jogging, or biking.

Attitude Counts

A positive attitude can go a long way toward helping you achieve your goals. Your **attitude** is the way you feel about something. A positive attitude can help you do your best, even if the task is something you may not enjoy. It can inspire you to keep working toward your goal even if you hit snags or make mistakes along the way. A positive attitude can help you tackle a difficult job rather than put it off. It also can help you be flexible when things do not go exactly as you planned.

Set Priorities

Some of your goals will be more important to you than others. You may even find that two or more goals are in conflict with each other. When this happens, you need to set priorities for your goals. A **priority** is something ranked high in importance. Putting tasks in order of importance can allow you to focus on the goals that mean the most to you.

Setting priorities for your goals may involve making trade-offs. A **trade-off** is something that you give up in order to get something more important. For example, if being on the debate team is very important to you, you may need to put off trying out for the band.

Success and Disappointment

As you experience success in reaching your goals, you can feel good about yourself. Successful experiences can help you grow and develop during your teen years and throughout the rest of your life. When you accomplish a goal, it can inspire you to set new goals and to try new things. This can add to your sense of personal worth, or value.

There may be times when you do not achieve a goal you set for yourself. If you fail to reach a goal, try to figure out what went wrong. Was your goal realistic? Did you have a clear picture of what you wanted to **accomplish**, or achieve? Did you use your resources wisely and plan other ways to reach your goal? Did you have a positive attitude? Did you set priorities? You may be disappointed, but if you know what went wrong, you can learn from it and improve your chances for success the next time.

 Learn from Disappointment No one likes to fail, but sometimes it happens. *How can you turn a goal that was not reached into a positive experience?*

Photo Caption Answer If you can figure out what went wrong, you can learn from mistakes and improve your chances for success the next time.

Section 6.1 After You Read

Review What You Have Learned
1. **Identify** the importance of setting a realistic goal.
2. **Explain** how a positive attitude can help you reach your goals.

Practice Academic Skills

English Language Arts

3. Write a paragraph to explain how you can use resources to accomplish a short-term goal. Identify the goal, the resources you would use, and how you would use the resources to reach your goal.

> **NCTE 12** Use language to accomplish individual purposes.

Social Studies

4. Conduct research to learn about a major historical accomplishment, such as the invention of the television or the Internet, that changed the way people lived. Or, choose an event such as the moon landing or the civil rights movement in the United States that changed the way people think. Who was responsible? What kinds of goals do you think the individuals or groups had to reach on their way to achieving the accomplishment?

> **NCSS II C** Identify and describe significant historical periods and patterns of change within and across cultures.

 Check Your Answers Check your answers at this book's Online Learning Center at glencoe.com.

Section 6.2 Decisions

Before You Read

Check for Understanding If you have questions as you are reading, that means you are checking your understanding of the material. To get the most out of the text, try to answer those questions as you read.

Read to Learn

Key Concepts

✓ **Name** the different ways that decisions are made.

✓ **Recognize** how decisions you make now can affect your future.

Main Idea

You make decisions every day. Decisions can be big or small. Making responsible decisions now can have a positive impact on your future.

Content Vocabulary

○ decision
○ alternative
○ proactive
○ consequence

Academic Vocabulary

 outcome
 integrity

Graphic Organizer

As you read, identify six resources you can use when making decisions. Use a graphic organizer like the one shown to help you organize your information.

Decision-Making Resources

Graphic Organizer Go to this book's Online Learning Center at glencoe.com to print this graphic organizer.

· · · · · · · · · · · · · · · **Academic Standards** · · · · · · · · · · · · · · ·

English Language Arts
NCTE 2 Read literature to build an understanding of the human experience.

Social Studies
NCSS II F Time, Continuity, and Change
Apply ideas, theories, and modes of historical inquiry to analyze historical and contemporary developments, and to inform and evaluate actions concerning public policy.

NCTE *National Council of Teachers of English*
NCTM *National Council of Teachers of Mathematics*

NSES *National Science Education Standards*
NCSS *National Council for the Social Studies*

Graphic Organizer Answer information, advice from others, past experiences, time, energy, money

You may find that success in life depends a lot on your ability to make smart decisions. Learning to make responsible decisions now can help you make more complicated or difficult decisions as you get older. The ability to make responsible decisions can give you a sense of pride and help increase your independence.

Decision Making

You will make many decisions in your life. A **decision** is something that you choose or make up your mind about after thinking over all possible choices. Each day you decide what to eat for lunch, what to do with your free time, and how hard to study. Other decisions require much more thought and planning, such as whom to marry, whether or not to have children, or whether or not to attend college. Here are some different types of decisions:

As You Read

Connect What are some of the small decisions you make every day?

- **Everyday Decisions** Some decisions are choices that you make every day. They usually do not require a lot of time or thought. Deciding what clothes to wear is an everyday decision. It may be important to you at the moment, but it does not change your life.

- **Decisions with Long-Term Effects** Decisions that have long-term effects on your life are major decisions. Some of the major decisions you will make as a teen are what courses you choose to take in high school and whether to get a part-time job.

As You Read Answer Answers may include what to wear, what to eat for lunch, which television show to watch, which songs to listen to.

- **Decisions that Become Habits** Some decisions become habits. These are decisions that you repeat without thinking about it. Brushing your teeth and doing your homework are decisions that become habits.

- **Life-Changing Decisions** Some major decisions, such as whether or not to go to college, can be life-changing. They require much time and thought and may be difficult to make. They are decisions that will affect you throughout your life.

Photo Caption Answer Answers will vary. Some students may say that they did not have breakfast. If so, explain that not eating breakfast is a decision, too, just like deciding to eat fruit or cereal.

Daily Decisions Simple things people do every day involve decision making. *What did you decide to eat for breakfast this morning?*

Sometimes you make decisions by responding to something that has happened. For example, you decide to start an exercise program after doing poorly in gym class. You also make decisions that can cause something to happen. For example, you decide to take on more responsibilities at home so that your family will give you more freedom. Sometimes you can choose to not make a decision at all. For example, you can ignore an invitation to a party. However, not making a decision is actually a decision in itself. When you do not make a decision, you leave the outcome, or result, up to chance or, in some cases, up to other people.

Decisions are made in several different ways:

- **Planned Decisions** Weigh all the facts before making a choice.
- **Default Decisions** Let someone else, or the circumstances, make the decision.
- **Impulse Decisions** Take the first choice available.
- **Emotional Decisions** Pick the choice that feels good without thinking it through.
- **Resistance Decisions** Pick the choice that will result in the least amount of conflict.

The outcome from decisions you make now can affect your future choices in positive and negative ways. For example, if you decide now to drop out of school, you will have fewer job options later. On the other hand, if you decide now to stay in school, you increase your chances of finding a good job in the future. An **alternative** is a choice between two or more different things or actions. Why do you think it is good to have several alternatives when making an important decision?

Make Proactive Decisions

You are more likely to make good decisions and choices if you are proactive. **Proactive** people think ahead about possible decisions or problems and take action right away. They do not ignore a problem, hoping that it will go away or resolve itself. They act as soon as they know something needs to be done. For example, Adam heard about a job opening in a sporting goods store near his home. It was so close he could walk to work. He immediately went to the store to fill out an application. By being proactive, he helped himself get the job. If he had put if off for a few days, the job might have gone to someone else.

 Reading Check *Define What is a decision?*

Make Decisions and Solve Problems

The Decision-Making Process To make decisions and solve problems, you need a process to help you make smart and responsible choices. Everyday decisions, such as what to order for dessert or which shoes to wear do not require a process. However, more complicated decisions do need to be thought through with care. Follow the steps below to deal with difficult problems and choices.

1. **Identify the decision or problem.** The first step in making a choice is to identify what needs to be decided. Break big problems or choices into parts. Then you can tackle one part at a time. Start at the beginning and patiently work through the issues.

2. **Consider the alternatives.** Once you have a clear idea about the problem you need to solve, look for ideas about what you can do. The more alternatives you can identify, the better prepared you are to make a choice or solve a problem.

3. **Choose the best alternative.** Think about the advantages and disadvantages of each alternative. Ask yourself, "What would happen if I ...?" Consider your needs, wants, and goals. Thinking through all the possibilities can help you make a better decision. Use your values as guidelines to make your decision.

4. **Act on the decision.** After you have decided what to do, put your decision into action. Keep in mind that it is all right to change your mind if you figure out that you made the wrong choice. Sometimes new information or more thought can lead you in a different direction.

5. **Evaluate the decision.** When you evaluate, you study the results of your actions. Ask yourself these questions: Were my actions effective? Did my decision solve the problem? If not, why? What can I do better next time? Do I feel good about the outcome and the steps I took to reach it? By evaluating, you can improve your decision-making skills for future problems and choices.

Make Responsible Decisions

Learning to make responsible decisions can give you a sense of control over your life. Instead of accepting whatever happens to you, you can help control how things happen.

Here are some suggestions to help you make responsible decisions:

- **Use good timing.** Make your decisions at the right time. Avoid making quick decisions. Give yourself time to consider all the facts. On the other hand, do not put off a decision too long. If you do, you may find that some of your options are no longer available.
- **Consider the consequences.** A **consequence** (ˌkän(t)-sə-ˌkwen(t)s) is a result of your choice. Think about how your decision can affect your life now and in the future. How will your decision affect you, your family members, or your friends?
- **Be willing to make mistakes.** Any time you make a decision, there is a chance that you will make a mistake. Be willing to make mistakes and to learn from them.
- **Seek advice when you need it.** Advice from family members, teachers, and friends can help you make decisions. Sometimes they have had to make similar decisions. Listen to others and use their advice if it is helpful.

Reduce Stress

Ask Your Family
Talk to your family members about any stress you are feeling. Often, all you need to do is tell someone about it to feel better. Someone in your family may have experienced similar feelings and may have advice to offer.

• • • • • • • • • • • • • •

Succeed in School
Encourage students to share their everyday activities with family members. Talking about the little things on a daily basis may make it easier to approach tougher subjects.

- **Accept responsibility for your decisions.** When you make your own decisions, you must accept responsibility for the consequences. You cannot make excuses or blame others when you make a poor decision. To accept responsibility for your decisions and the consequences of those decisions is a sign of maturity.

Photo Caption Answer They may have experienced similar situations or faced difficult choices. They may have advice to offer that could help you decide what to do.

Experience Counts Your parents and teachers have had their share of choices to make. ***How can their experiences help you make decisions?***

Take Responsibility for Decisions

It would be easier to let someone else take the blame when things go wrong. However, you are only responsible for the decisions you make. If your decisions or choices do not turn out well, you show **integrity**, or honor and truthfulness, when you admit that you made a mistake. When decisions turn out well, you feel proud. Take responsibility for your decisions because:

- Making mistakes is part of the process. Use the opportunity to learn from them.
- People do not respect you when you make excuses or blame others.
- People do respect you when you try to fix a mistake.
- When things go well, you get to accept the praise and recognition.

Character Counts

Courtesy

Jane's friend Carrie is getting married in two weeks. Jane was invited to the wedding two months ago. Jane did not respond to the invitation because she was thinking about attending another event that ended up being canceled. Carrie does not know if Jane is coming to the wedding. The reception is being catered, and the caterer needs to know how many guests will attend so he can prepare the right amount of food. Jane wants to go to the wedding, but she thinks it is too late to respond.

You Make the Call

Is it too late for Jane to respond to the invitation? Write a paragraph that explains what you think Jane should do.

Character Counts Feature Answer It was inconsiderate for Jane to wait so long to make a decision, but it is not too late to try to be courteous. She should call Carrie right away and apologize for the delay, and ask Carrie if it is still possible to accept the invitation.

Section 6.2 After You Read

Review What You Have Learned

1. **Explain** what can happen if you choose not to make a decision.
2. **Identify** ways to make responsible decisions.

Practice Academic Skills

 English Language Arts

3. Conduct research to find a literary character who had to make a difficult decision. Was the character's process effective? What was the outcome? What would you have done differently if you were faced with the same decision as the character? Write a paragraph about how the character used the decision-making process.

> **NCTE 2** Read literature to build an understanding of the human experience.

Social Studies

4. Choose a leader in world history. Research information about the person to find an issue he or she had to decide upon. Prepare a presentation that includes the leader you chose, the factors that lead to the decision, and the outcome of the decision.

> **NCSS II F** Apply ideas, theories, and modes of historical inquiry to analyze historical and contemporary developments, and to inform and evaluate actions concerning public policy.

Check Your Answers Check your answers at this book's Online Learning Center at glencoe.com.

Focus on Careers in Emergency Response ▼

Do you work well under pressure? Are you able to make quick decisions? Do you want to help people in crisis? If you answered yes to any of those questions, you might want to consider a future in an emergency response career. The following chart explores several careers in the emergency response field.

Job Title	Job Description
Firefighter	Protect life and property from fires. Often the first emergency responders at traffic accidents. Firefighters are often required to treat injuries as well as fight fires.
Police Officer	Investigates complaints, maintains order, helps individuals, and identifies criminal offenders. Makes quick decisions in emergency situations.
Emergency Room Nurse	Cares for patients in various states of illness or injury. Helps decide which patients are in the most need of immediate care.
9-1-1 Operator	Answers calls from people in distress. Consults detailed manual to provide quick and often life-saving instructions to callers. Coordinates with fire, ambulance, and police services as needed.
Emergency Medical Technician (EMT)	Responds to emergency situations. Makes split-second decisions about patient care. Administers health care for accidents, injuries, and illness.

Career Activities ▼

At School

1 Select three of the careers listed. Research the education, training, and work experience required for each career. Write a summary of your results.

At Home

2 Create an emergency plan with your family in case of fire or other crisis. Make a map of your home with a planned escape route, and agree with you family on a specific place to meet.

At Work

3 Make a list of at least five jobs that require strong decision-making skills. Next to each job listed, write an example of a decision that might need to be made on the job.

In the Community

4 Contact and interview someone in your community who works in an emergency response career. Ask this person to describe what his or her typical work day is like. Share what you learned with your class.

Career Activities Answers for these activities can be found on page TM93.

Learn More *Online* 🔎 glencoe.com

Career Investigations Go to this book's Online Learning Center for activities and worksheets to help you explore careers.

Chapter Summary

Section 6.1 Goals

A goal is something you want to achieve. When you set goals, you need to make sure that they are realistic. Goal setting requires planning and a positive attitude. Some goals will be more important to you than others. As you experience success in reaching your goals, you can feel good about yourself. If you do not achieve a goal, you can learn from the experience and improve your skills for the next goal.

Section 6.2 Decisions

Decision making is an important part of daily life. Sometimes you make decisions by responding to something that has happened. Other times you make decisions based on what you have already planned or considered. The decisions you make now can affect the choices you have in the future. Learning to make responsible decisions can give you a sense of control over your life.

Words You Learned

1. Use each of these content vocabulary words and academic vocabulary words in a sentence.

Content Vocabulary

- goal (p. 117)
- long-term goal (p. 117)
- short-term goal (p. 117)
- attitude (p. 120)
- priority (p. 120)
- trade-off (p. 120)
- decision (p. 123)
- alternative (p. 124)
- proactive (p. 124)
- consequence (p. 126)

Academic Vocabulary

- worth (p. 120)
- accomplish (p. 121)
- outcome (p. 124)
- integrity (p. 127)

Review Key Concepts

2. **Differentiate** between long-term and short-term goals.

3. **Explain** how attitude helps achieve goals.

4. **Name** the different ways that decisions are made.

5. **Recognize** how decisions you make now can affect your future.

Critical Thinking

6. **Assess** Is putting off making a decision always negative? When might it be better to put off making a decision?

7. **Evaluate** Why is it possible for someone who grew up with limited resources still be successful?

8. **List** Write a list of the steps in the decision-making process. Next to each step, write a tip that can help you make your next important decision.

9. **Predict** Why should you be flexible when setting goals for your future career?

Real-World Skills and Applications

Problem-Solving

10. **Prioritize** Jacob wants to play football and be in the band. During the fall, both activities hold their practices at the same time, so he has to choose one of the activities. How should he decide which activity to be involved in? What should Jacob consider as he prioritizes his activities?

Technology Applications

11. **Design a Template** A template is a model or an outline. Use word-processing or spreadsheet software to create a template people can use when they want to achieve a long-term goal. Refer to the steps in the decision-making process. Include helpful tips for each step they should take.

Financial Literacy

12. **Set Career Goals** You may already know what career you wish to have when you are finished with school. Even if you do, you may have the opportunity in the coming years to reconsider your decision. While money is not the only factor that should guide your career decisions, salaries do play a part in goal setting. Identify three jobs that you might like to have when you have completed your education. Conduct research to find out the typical starting salary for each of the three jobs you selected. How might those salaries affect other long-term goals that you may have? What trade-offs might you have to make?

13. **The Impact of Your Choices** Choose five decisions you have made in the last week. For each decision, make a list of all the people affected by your choice, including yourself. Put a plus sign next to each name if your choice had a positive effect on the person, or a minus sign if your choice had a negative effect. Rate yourself on how well you consider the consequences of your choices. Are you satisfied with the results?

14. **Identify and Evaluate Resources** Knowing how to gather information from various resources can help you make decisions and solve problems. Do you plan to attend college? Maybe you want to join a branch of the military, or perhaps you plan to enter the job market right away. List three things you want to do after high school. Then identify sources of information for each. Rank the information sources on your list from most useful to least useful and give reasons for your ranking.

15. **Goal Setting Online** With permission from your parents or teacher, go online to search for information about how to achieve goals. What advice can you find? Are there tips available online that apply to specific goals? Are there any Web sites about goal setting that you would recommend to a friend? If so, explain why you would recommend them. Write down useful goal-setting tips to share with your classmates and to include in your Life Skills Binder.

Academic Skills

English Language Arts

16. Advertise Your student council is launching a campaign to encourage students to make wise decisions by using the decision-making process. Create a pamphlet that that will teach your class-mates how to use the decision-making process. What information will you include? What will the design be?

> **NCTE 8** Use information resources to gather information and create and communicate knowledge.

Science

17. Collect Data An important part of the scientific method is collecting data and studying it to see what it reveals about something. Collect your own data about what people do when they make decisions.

Procedure Choose a place, like a fast food restaurant or movie theater, to record the body language you observe while a person makes a decision.

Analysis Organize your findings in a chart. What conclusions can you draw?

> **NSES A** Develop understandings about scientific inquiry.

Mathematics

18. Calculate Elena is going to give a speech about setting goals at a luncheon for business executives. Her speech will be accompanied by a slide show. The presentation time limit is 15 minutes, and Elena figures she will use 25 slides. What is the average number of seconds she should spend on each slide without going over the time limit?

Math Concept **Performing Calculations with Time** When performing calculations with time, it is helpful to convert all numbers to the same units prior to calculating. Since a minute has 60 seconds, to convert minutes to seconds, multiply by 60. To convert seconds to minutes, divide by 60.

Starting Hint The average is the total time divided by the number of slides. Convert the number of minutes for the speech (15) to seconds by multiplying by 60. Divide the answer by the number of slides (25). Label your final answer with the correct unit of time.

> **NCTM Measurement** Understand measurable attributes of objects and the units, systems, and processes of measurement.

Standardized Test Practice

Reading Comprehension Read the passage, then answer the question.

> **Test-Taking Tip** Read the passage carefully, underlining key statements as you go. Answer the questions based only on what you just read in the passage, not based on your previous knowledge.

English has thousands of words borrowed from French. However, most of our basic English vocabulary is more similar to German. Compare English *house* and German *Haus* or English *finger* and German *Finger.* In fact, English is much more closely related to German than it is to French. English and German are both part of the Germanic language family.

19. According to this passage, why does English have many words that are similar to German?

UNIT 2 Life Skills Project

Your Point of View

Forming your own opinions shows a sense of responsible citizenship. Local newspapers may highlight issues that are important to your community. Your parents and teachers may have opinions on topics that you can consider. This project will help you explore your own point of view.

 My Journal Complete the journal entry from page 73, and refer to it to write your current events summary.

Project Assignment ▼

In this project, you will:

- Clip a news story about an important issue in your community.
- Describe the opposite points of view about the issue.
- Write about your own opinion.
- Interview someone who holds elected office.
- Present a campaign poster and speech about your topic to the class.
- Include this project in the second section of your personal Life Skills binder.

Step 1 Research News Stories of Current Events

Forming your own opinion is easier when you know a lot of information about the issue. Read the local newspaper and clip a story that discusses local topics. Write a summary of the facts of the story and describe the opposing viewpoints.

Step 2 Select an Issue and a Slogan

Choose an issue that interests you. Pick a viewpoint that you agree with. Develop an idea for a poster with a slogan that supports your opinion. Then prepare to write a speech that answers these questions:

✔ What are the facts about your issue?
✔ What do the opponents of your position believe?

✔ What facts can you give to support your opinion?
✔ How would you convince others to agree with you?

Step 3 Interview an Elected Official

Interview someone in your community who was elected to their position. Ask these questions:

✔ What methods did you use to get people to vote for you?
✔ What is your opinion about the issue I am studying?
✔ How do you prepare to give a speech?

Use these interviewing skills when conducting your interview and these writing skills when writing the summary of notes from your interview.

Interviewing Skills
- Record interview responses and take notes.
- Listen attentively.

Writing Skills
- Use complete sentences.
- Use correct spelling and grammar.

Step 4 Create and Present Your Poster and Speech

Use the Life Skills Project Checklist on the right to plan and complete your poster and write and deliver a two-minute speech about your opinion on this issue.

Use these speaking skills when presenting your final report.

Speaking Skills
- Speak clearly and concisely.
- Be sensitive to the needs of your audience.
- Use standard English to communicate.

Step 5 Evaluate Your Presentation

Your project will be evaluated based on:

- ✔ Completeness and organization in the description of your opinion of the issue you chose.
- ✔ The poster that reflects your opinion on an issue.
- ✔ Your speech about your point of view on an issue.
- ✔ The summary written from interview notes.
- ✔ Grammar and sentence structure.
- ✔ Presentation to the class.
- ✔ Creativity and neatness.

🖝 **Evaluation Rubric** Go to this book's Online Learning Center through glencoe.com for a rubric you can use to evaluate your final project.

Life Skills Project Checklist

Research News Stories

- ✅ Read the newspaper and then clip a chosen article.
- ✅ Write down facts and opinions from the article.
- ✅ Create a poster about your topic.
- ✅ Interview an elected official in your community.

Writing Skills

- ✅ Describe the viewpoints and facts in your news story.
- ✅ Write a speech that communicates your point of view.
- ✅ Write a summary from your interview with an elected community member.

Present Your Findings

- ✅ Prepare a short presentation to share your poster and deliver a speech that reflects your point of view.
- ✅ Invite students to ask any questions they may have. Answer these questions with responses that respect their perspectives.
- ✅ Add this project to your Life Skills binder.

Academic Skills

- ✅ Conduct research to gather information.
- ✅ Communicate effectively.
- ✅ Organize your presentation so the audience can follow along easily.
- ✅ Thoroughly express your ideas.

NCSS X D Civic Ideals and Practices Practice forms of civic discussion and participation consistent with the ideals of citizens in a democratic republic.

NCSS VI J Power, Authority, and Governance Prepare a public policy paper and present and defend it before an appropriate forum in school or community.

Chapter 7
Explore Careers

Chapter 8
Enter the Workplace

Unit Preview

This unit is about preparing for a career. In this unit, you will learn about:

- Why it is important to start thinking about your career now.
- The different reasons people work.
- Skills that are important in the workplace.
- Being a responsible worker.

Explore the Photo Answer Answers will vary and students will have different dream careers, but ways to plan for and attain their dream careers may include: get part-time work in the field, volunteer in the field, develop skills necessary for that career, talk to people in the field, and networking.

Explore the Photo
Setting a career goal now can help you attain it later. *What career goals do you have, and what can you do now to help you attain your dream career?*

You in Ten Years

When you are done studying this unit, you will complete a project in which you will:

✓ Explore your skills and talents.

✓ Interview someone who has a job you want to learn about.

✓ Imagine what you will do for a living and describe it to your class.

The prewriting activity below will help you get started.

 My Journal

Prewriting Activity
Prepare an Outline

Are you good at math? Do you love children? Are you very artistic? Maybe your friendly nature is appealing to people. Write an outline about jobs or careers you could be doing in ten years.

● What kind of jobs might be suitable to your personality and talents?

● What would you most like to do for a living?

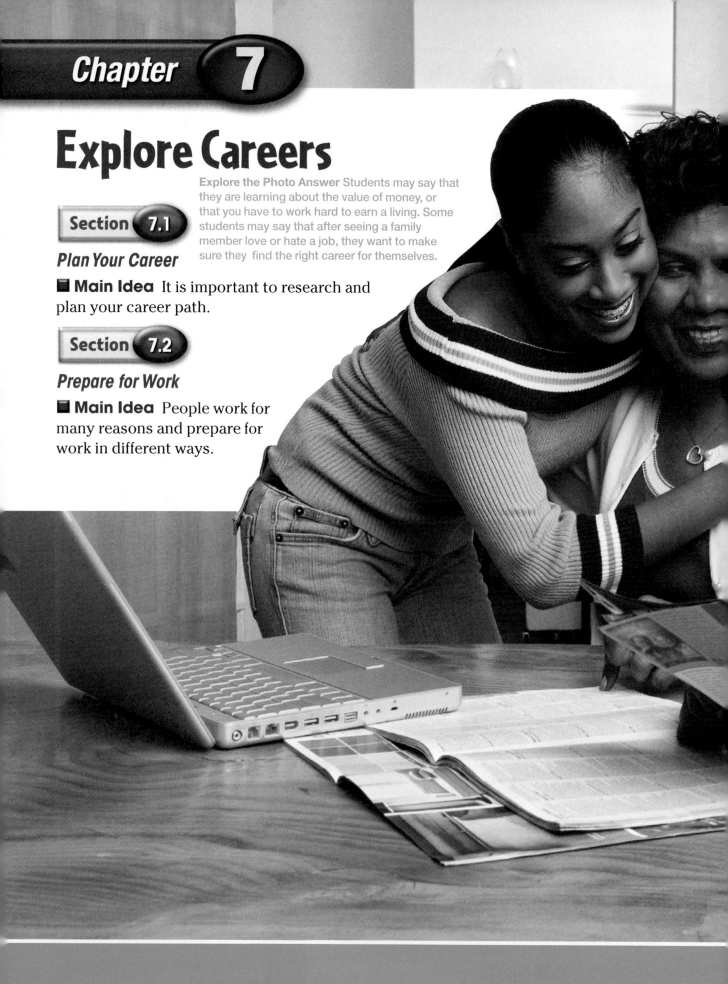

Chapter 7

Explore Careers

Explore the Photo Answer Students may say that they are learning about the value of money, or that you have to work hard to earn a living. Some students may say that after seeing a family member love or hate a job, they want to make sure they find the right career for themselves.

Section 7.1

Plan Your Career

■ **Main Idea** It is important to research and plan your career path.

Section 7.2

Prepare for Work

■ **Main Idea** People work for many reasons and prepare for work in different ways.

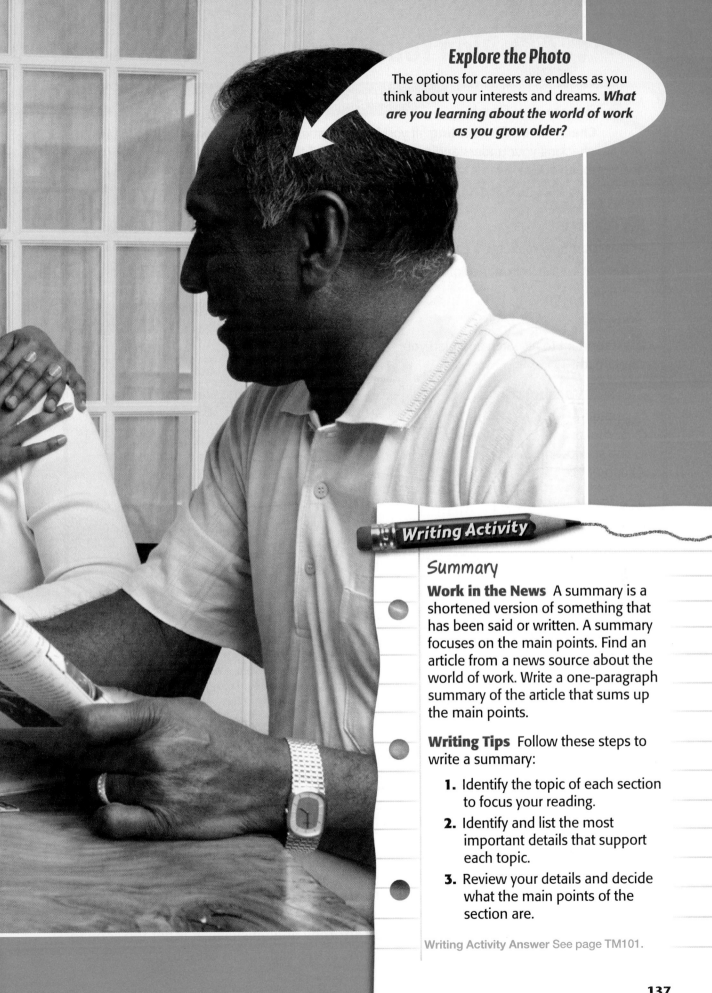

Explore the Photo
The options for careers are endless as you think about your interests and dreams. *What are you learning about the world of work as you grow older?*

Writing Activity

Summary

Work in the News A summary is a shortened version of something that has been said or written. A summary focuses on the main points. Find an article from a news source about the world of work. Write a one-paragraph summary of the article that sums up the main points.

Writing Tips Follow these steps to write a summary:

1. Identify the topic of each section to focus your reading.
2. Identify and list the most important details that support each topic.
3. Review your details and decide what the main points of the section are.

Writing Activity Answer See page TM101.

Reading Guide

Before You Read

Check for Understanding If you have questions as you are reading, that means you are checking your understanding of the material. To get the most out of the text, try to answer those questions.

Read to Learn

Key Concepts

✓ **Describe** how to create a career plan.

✓ **Recognize** the importance of researching careers.

Main Idea

It is important to research and plan your career path.

Content Vocabulary

○ aptitude
○ portfolio
○ job shadowing
○ apprentice
○ networking
○ mentor

Academic Vocabulary

■ modify
■ reveal

Graphic Organizer

As you read, identify six factors to review when researching a career. Use a graphic organizer like the one shown to help you organize your information.

Job Research	
1.	
2.	
3.	
4.	
5.	
6.	

 Graphic Organizer Go to this book's Online Learning Center at glencoe.com to print this graphic organizer.

· · · · · · · · · · · · · · · **Academic Standards** · · · · · · · · · · · · · · ·

 English Language Arts

NCTE 5 Use different writing process elements to communicate effectively.

 Science

NSES G Students should develop understanding of science as a human endeavor.

Social Studies

NCSS V G Individuals, Groups, and Instructions Analyze the extent to which groups and institutions meet individual needs and promote the common good in contemporary and historical settings.

NCTE *National Council of Teachers of English*
NCTM *National Council of Teachers of Mathematics*

NSES *National Science Education Standards*
NCSS *National Council for the Social Studies*

Graphic Organizer Answer educational requirements; job responsibilities; salary potential; promotion opportunities; working conditions; future of field

"What do you want to be when you grow up?" You have probably heard that question before. Have you really thought about your answer? Perhaps you are interested in becoming a gourmet chef or an astronaut. You have many choices. Whether you choose to be an attorney or a musician, it is not too soon to start thinking about the career you might want to have one day.

Explore Your Options

It is a good idea to start exploring career opportunities now. That way you will be better prepared to make a career choice. When you think about your options, consider your strengths, interests, abilities, values, and goals. Decisions based on these factors can lead you to work you enjoy. Ask other people how they got started in a career to get ideas for your own career path.

Career Planning

It is a good idea to begin thinking ahead about some of the specific skills that will help you get a job. What are the careers that interest you? It is important to learn about the kind of education and training you will need for the career you choose. It is also important to collect occupational and labor market information about each career. For example, Marissa loves to draw and paint pictures, but she learned through research that the demand for traditional artists is not as high as it used to be. Marissa decided she would need to learn how to use computer graphics software to become a digital artist.

When considering a career, you should also think about your values and goals. What is important to you? What do you want to do with your life? Do you want to help other people? Consider a career in health services. Do you like to build things? Look into construction or architecture. Knowing your values and goals can help you focus on an area that fits your personality. Review your career plan often and **modify**, or change it, as needed.

As You Read

Connect What skills do you have now that can help you in your future career?

As You Read Answer Answers may include reading, spelling, math, science, listening and speaking, and artistic or creative skills.

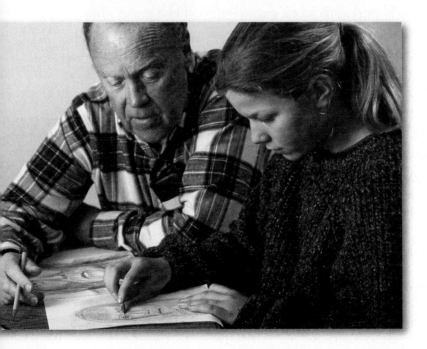

Choose What You Enjoy Have you ever noticed that when you are doing something you enjoy, it does not seem like work? *What activities or hobbies do you enjoy that might lead to a career?*

Photo Caption Answer Answers may include any hobby or activity that students enjoy.

Family and Consumer Sciences Teacher Teaching Family and Consumer Sciences involves much more than cooking and sewing. *What other subject areas are involved?*

Photo Caption Answer Answers may include nutrition, communication skills, fashion design, caring for children, job preparation, and money management.

◆ Vocabulary

You can find definitions in the glossary at the back of this book.

Succeed in School Make sure students know what resources are available to them in your school library, as well as any classroom resources you provide.

School Resources

School Library
Librarians or media center specialists can help you conduct research and find reading materials. They can also help you locate online tutorials and other learning programs.

● ● ● ● ● ● ● ● ● ● ●

If you need help deciding, there are special tests that can help you discover your aptitudes. An **aptitude** is a natural talent or ability for something. You may not even know about it yet. An aptitude test can help predict your ability to learn certain skills. A test of this kind can help **reveal**, or show, your strengths. However, this only one of many things you can do to help you decide. You also need to think about your interests. For example, the field of family and consumer sciences includes a wide variety of career options, such as cooking, nutrition, sewing, job preparation, fashion design, caring for children, and money management.

Career Portfolio

As you study and gain work experience, it is a good idea to create a **portfolio**, which is a neatly organized collection of your skills, experiences, and qualifications. Employers view career portfolios as presentations of your skills and abilities. For example, Martin is interested in a career in photography. He has selected prints of his best photos to put in his career portfolio. He also included certificates he earned from the Digital Photography Club. Later, Martin will add letters of recommendation and a list of the knowledge and skills he has gained. Think of a career portfolio as a way to show off your best efforts. Portfolios can be created online, too. Ask your teacher or school librarian for help if you want to get started on your portfolio.

Reading Check Answer Take an aptitude test and consider your interests.

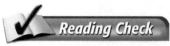

Reading Check *Identify How can you discover your natural abilities, strengths, or talents?*

Research Careers

Talk about career possibilities with your parents, family members, school counselors, and teachers. They can offer you advice and answer questions. Choose a few careers that interest you and do some basic research. **Figure 7.1** lists six important factors to review when researching career possibilities.

Reading about jobs on the Internet and hearing about jobs from others is useful. However, if you want to get a more direct experience, try job shadowing. **Job shadowing** is spending a day or a few hours with someone to observe him or her on the job.

Character Counts

Work Ethic

Clarence works part-time at a local grocery store. He has a variety of responsibilities, from stocking shelves to bagging groceries. His friend Jake drops by almost every day to visit and chat. Often when Jake comes to the store, Clarence finds himself talking with him in the storage room or on an aisle when he is stocking shelves for fifteen or twenty minutes at a time. Clarence knows that he does not get as much done when Jake is there.

You Make the Call

What should Clarence do to use his time at work wisely? Write a paragraph that explains what you think Clarence should do and why.

Character Counts Answer Clarence should talk with Jake and explain that while he enjoys their talks, he needs to focus on his job while he is at work. Clarence could suggest that they meet after work instead.

Figure 7.1 Job Research

Know What to Expect When you know what to expect from a job, it will be easier to decide which ones interest you and match your personality. *Do you think your first job will be in the same field as your career? Why or why not?*

- **Educational Requirements** What education is required for the job? You may need a college degree or certification in the field.

- **Job Responsibilities** What responsibilities or duties are performed on the job? Your work day may include a variety of tasks, or you may do the same tasks every day.

- **Salary Potential** What is the average income of entry-level workers in this position? Know ahead of time what the starting salary is, and what you can expect to earn as you gain more experience.

- **Promotion Opportunities** What opportunities for promotion exist? You may earn a promotion after demonstrating expertise. Some companies require further training to help you move forward.

- **Working Conditions** What are the working conditions? You may be required to attend safety training on the job.

- **Future of Field** Will there be a need for more workers in this field in the future? You may have to upgrade your education or training to keep your job, or find a new job if necessary.

Figure Caption Answer Answers will vary. Most students will probably say that their first job will be something to earn spending money, and that their careers will be in a different field.

SCIENCE YOU CAN USE

Making Connections

Many careers are rooted in some form of science. In farming, you must know about plants and how they grow. In cooking, you have to know about how heat works to cook food.

Procedure Research a career related to science. Explain how this career is related to science, and find out how it could benefit people.

Analysis Prepare a written report indicating how science knowledge is used in this career. Include how the science and the career benefit people. Illustrate your report if possible.

NSES G Develop an understanding of science as a human endeavor.

Apprenticeship Many skilled workers learn their trade in formal apprenticeship programs. *How can both the apprentice and trainer benefit from an apprenticeship?*

If you find a job that you believe would be worth the investment of time and money, an apprenticeship may be a good route to take. An **apprentice** works under the guidance of a skilled professional in order to learn an art, craft, or trade. Once the new skill is mastered, the apprentice may become a professional. Electricians, carpenters, mechanics, sculptors, plumbers, and barbers are just a few professions that may offer apprenticeships.

Networking

If you ever followed up on a job tip you received from a family member or friend, you practiced networking. **Networking** means using your personal connections to help achieve your goals. When you seek job information from people you know, you have a good chance of going into the job application process informed and confident.

Networking is one of the most direct ways to find a job. In addition to networking with your family members you can also network with:

- friends and classmates.
- teachers and mentors.
- employers and coworkers.
- national organizations such as FCCLA (see **Figure 7.2**).
- community organizations.
- recruiters at job fairs.

When you network, be courteous. Do not pressure people for information. If you are given a job lead, follow up in a responsible manner. It is important to follow up when someone passes on information that can help you. Your behavior reflects on you and on the person who recommended you.

Mentor

A **mentor** is someone with experience who supports, advises, and encourages the progress of a less experienced person. To identify a mentor, think about a person you admire and respect who has talents and skills you would like to learn. Then arrange to meet with this person and discuss your goals. Mentors can keep you from getting discouraged. Their experience can help you avoid common mistakes. Your mentor may also be able to help you network.

Professional Organizations

Another source of job postings is professional organizations. These organizations are made up of people already employed in a field. You usually need to pay a membership fee to join professional organizations. The services they offer include employment listings, job placement services, scholarships, and network opportunities.

School Resources
Guidance Counselors
Guidance counselors are excellent resources at your school. They can help you choose classes and plan a career path.

• • • • • • • • • • • • • •

Succeed in School
Tell students that it is not too early to start thinking about possible jobs and careers. Direct them to any career planning resources you may have at your school.

Figure 7.2 FCCLA

The Ultimate Leadership Experience Middle and high school students can develop their leadership skills in many ways. *Why is it important to join a professional organization such as FCCLA?*

Family, Career and Community Leaders of America (FCCLA) is a national organization of middle and high school students enrolled in family and consumer sciences courses. FCCLA activities provide opportunities for leadership development. Student members benefit from programs that include individual projects which strengthen critical thinking and decision-making skills. Members also participate in team projects to improve cooperative learning.

Figure Caption Answer
Answers may include: professional contacts; develop leadership skills; network opportunities; job placement services; employment listings; scholarships.

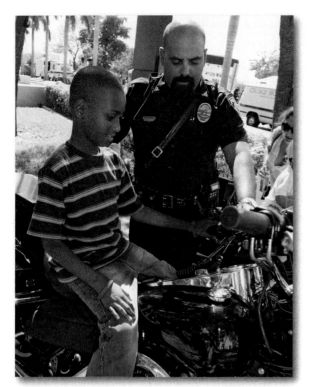

The Internet

You can also learn about careers through the Internet. You can go online to get ideas, find out what jobs are available, and research specific job requirements. When you are ready, you can submit your résumé online. You will learn more about résumés in the next chapter.

Ask your parents, librarian, or teacher to help you:

- Search *The Occupational Outlook Handbook* or the *Dictionary of Occupational Titles.*
- Find job postings and job descriptions.
- Post a résumé.
- Locate professional organizations.
- Register with online employment agencies.

 Find a Mentor Think about a person you admire and respect who has talents and skills you would like to learn. *How can a mentor help you with your career goals?*

Photo Caption Answer Mentors can encourage, support, and advise you. They can share their own experiences to help you learn about what they did to succeed.

Section 7.1 After You Read

Review What You Have Learned
1. **List** the factors you should consider when you think about career options.
2. **Explain** why it is important to network.

Practice Academic Skills

 English Language Arts

3. Should a person ever choose a career that does not match his or her interests? Why or why not? Explain your answer in a short speech.

> **NCTE 5** Use different writing process elements to communicate effectively.

Social Studies

4. Locate professional organizations for a career that you are considering. What kinds of benefits do they offer for their members? Write a summary of how the organization could help you prepare for your career.

> **NCSS V G** Analyze the extent to which groups and institutions meet individual needs and promote the common good in contemporary and historical settings.

Check Your Answers Check your answers at this book's Online Learning Center at glencoe.com.

Section **7.2** Prepare for Work

Reading Guide

Before You Read
Predict Before starting the section, browse the content by reading headings, bold words, and photo captions. Do they help you predict the information in the section?

Read to Learn
Key Concepts
- ✓ **Explain** why people work.
- ✓ **Identify** steps you can take to prepare for work.

Main Idea
People work for many reasons and prepare for work in different ways.

Content Vocabulary
- ○ job satisfaction
- ○ entrepreneur
- ○ franchise

Academic Vocabulary
- ■ technology
- ■ credit

Graphic Organizer
As you read, identify four ways that part-time work can prepare you for full-time work. Use a graphic organizer like the one shown to help you organize your information.

 Graphic Organizer Go to this book's Online Learning Center at glencoe.com to print this graphic organizer.

Academic Standards

English Language Arts
NCTE 8 Use information resources to gather information and create and communicate knowledge.

Mathematics
NCTM Data Analysis and Probability Select and use appropriate statistical methods to analyze data.

Social Studies
NCSS I E Culture Demonstrate the value of cultural diversity, as well as cohesion, within and across groups.

NCSS V D Individuals, Groups, and Institutions Identify and analyze examples of tensions between expression of individuality and efforts used to promote social conformity by groups and institutions.

NCTE *National Council of Teachers of English*
NCTM *National Council of Teachers of Mathematics*
NSES *National Science Education Standards*
NCSS *National Council for the Social Studies*

Just about everyone works. Jobs provide income for homes, cars, food, and other things, like vacations and recreation. Since you are going to spend most of your adult years working, it is important to consider how you can best plan and prepare for the world of work. Take advantage of the many resources available to help you find ideas and opportunities.

Graphic Organizer Answer Learn to get along with supervisors and coworkers; find out if a certain type of work is a good match with your personality; gain helpful experience for applying for a full-time job; understand requirements needed for full-time work.

As You Read

Connect Why is it important to think about your career goals now?

As You Read Answer
If you know what kind training and education is required for your career, you can start taking steps now to prepare.

 Vocabulary

You can find definitions in the glossary at the back of this book.

SUCCEED IN SCHOOL!

School Resources
Ask Your Teacher
If you are having problems in a particular subject, ask your teacher for additional help. He or she may be able to provide after-school tutoring or other activities to help you tackle specific problems.

The World of Work

You will have several jobs during your lifetime. One of the first steps in finding a job that satisfies you is to consider your skills. Do you have special skills that could be useful in a particular type of work? For example, do you love to read? Are you creative? Do you think science is fascinating? Would you volunteer or work part-time to strengthen those skills?

Why People Work

People work for many reasons. The main reason is to earn a living, but there are many other benefits. People take pride in their work and enjoy job satisfaction. **Job satisfaction** is a feeling of accomplishment from a job well done. Every job helps another person in some way. This can help people feel good about themselves and feel satisfied about what they do for others. Work is also a way to meet people and make friends.

Enjoy What You Do

Most people choose jobs based on their interests and skills. Some people enjoy physical tasks, such as installing machinery. Others prefer artistic work, such as digital photography or home design. Still others want jobs in which they can help people, such as responding to medical emergencies, or caring for young children.

Photo Caption Answer High school diploma or a 2-year college degree, formal medical training to get a certificate.

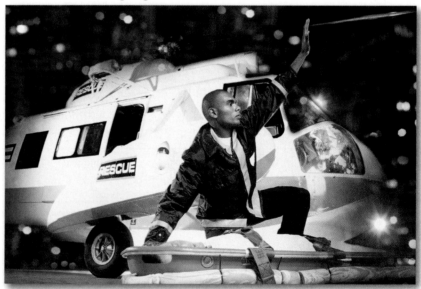

Draw on Your Interests A person who is interested in the medical field and wants to help others may choose a career as an emergency medical technician. *What kind of education or training do you think this person needed?*

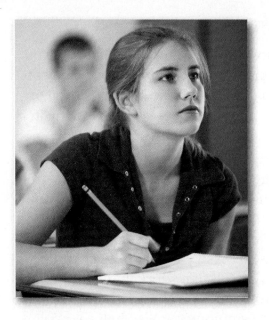

Future Plans Education and training continue beyond high school. *What plans do you have after high school graduation?*

Photo Caption Answer Answers will vary. Students may express interest in college, trade school, the military, or finding work right away.

COMMUNITY CONNECTIONS

Learn through Volunteering
Volunteering in your community is a great way to introduce yourself to particular career field. Find opportunities to help others and explore your interests. For example, if you are interested in the health field, volunteer at a hospital. If you are interested in journalism, volunteer at a newspaper.

Most people spend 40 or more years in the workforce. It is worth the effort to research and learn as much as you can about your work options.

Reading Check *Examine* How do most people make decisions about what job they want to do?

Reading Check Answer Most people choose jobs based on their interests and skills.

Get Ready to Work

Without a high school education, your job opportunities will be limited. Your school counselor will have a lot of information about how you can finish school successfully. There are many ways to continue your education and training after high school. You may choose to:

- **Attend college.** Community colleges, four-year colleges, and universities offer degrees in a wide variety of fields.
- **Enroll at a career and technical center.** A technical training program can train you for specific occupations, such as computer programming, automotive technology, or the culinary arts.
- **Get on-the-job training.** Some companies offer on-the-job training. Others will help you go to school while you are working. Many offer formal apprenticeship programs that require both coursework and work experience.
- **Join a branch of the military.** You can get training in specified fields and save money for college. You may even decide to choose a military career.
- **Volunteer.** Volunteer work is work without pay, but it can provide valuable and rewarding work experience and improve your self-esteem as you help others.

MATH YOU CAN USE

Calculate Average Pay

José enjoys working with people, and is considering going to nursing school to become a nurse. Curious about how much beginning nurses typically make where he lives, he surveys a few local hospitals and doctors' offices. One pays its starting nurses $17.65 per hour, another $18.95 per hour, a third $18.30 per hour, and fourth $17.90 per hour. Based on these figures, what is the average hourly pay for beginning nurses in José's area?

Math Concept **Find the Mean** When you have a series of values, calculate the average (also known as mean) by finding the sum of all of the values, and dividing that sum by the number of values.

Starting Hint Find the average pay rate by adding up all four hourly amounts discovered by José, then divide by the number of values. In this case, the number of values is 4.

 For more math help, go to the Math Appendix located at the back of this book.

> **NCTM Data Analysis and Probability** Select and use appropriate statistical methods to analyze data.

Math You Can Use Answer The average hourly pay is $18.20. ($17.65 + $18.95 + $18.30 + $17.90 = $72.80, and $72.80 ÷ 4 = $18.20.)

Photo Caption Answer Answers may include being a server, host, or cook in a restaurant.

Work Experience Part-time jobs provide valuable work experience. *What kind of part-time work would be useful for someone who wants to own a restaurant?*

Part-Time Work

Before you look for a full-time job, you will probably have part-time jobs. You can get valuable experience by babysitting or delivering newspapers and by working in restaurants, businesses, and stores.

A part-time job can provide you with spending money. However, you might also consider saving a percentage of your money to use toward future education costs. Part-time work plus ongoing education can increase your chances of finding well-paying full-time work in the future. Aside from providing you with an income, part-time employment also helps you:

- **Learn** to get along with your supervisors and coworkers.
- **Find** out if a certain type of work matches you personality.
- **Gain** work experience that will be helpful when you apply for a full-time job.
- **Understand** job requirements and other qualities that you need to have for full-time work.

Be an Entrepreneur

In this activity you will imagine that you are an entrepreneur starting a new business. Before you begin, read through the entire Hands-On Lab assignment. Write down any questions that you have about the assignment. Reread the text or ask your teacher for help if you need it.

Supplies
✓ Calculator
✓ Computer with Internet access (optional)
✓ Paper and colored pens

Develop Your Plan

■ Choose a business such as babysitting, dog walking, or lawn mowing.

■ Find out what other teens would charge for the same jobs, or what clients would be willing to pay.

■ Gather supplies to create flyers, posters, and business cards to advertise your business.

■ If possible, access a computer graphics program to plan an imaginary Web page.

Implement Your Plan

■ Use graphics to create a fun and colorful flyer.

■ Create business cards with your name, contact information, and a brief list of your services.

■ Design an imaginary Web page to advertise your business.

■ Figure out how many hours you can spend on your business and what you will charge for your services.

■ Calculate the costs of maintaining your business, such as additional flyers and business cards, transportation, and Web site maintenance.

■ Multiply the hours you can work by your hourly rate. Subtract the costs to find your profit.

Evaluate Your Results

What did you learn about starting a business? Is there anything you would change if you could do it again? Do you think you would enjoy being your own boss? Write one or more paragraphs to explain your answer.

 Projects and Activities Go to this book's Online Learning Center through glencoe.com for more projects and activities.

Evaluate Your Results Answer Answers will vary. Some students may say that starting a business is more work than they expected. Others may say that starting a business would be fun and challenging.

Summer Abroad

International summer expedition programs for teens are becoming popular. Australia, Costa Rica, Ecuador, France, Peru, South Africa, Spain, Thailand, the United Kingdom, Hawaii, and Vietnam are just a few of the places offering wilderness and nature programs. Tour companies are looking for responsible, enthusiastic leaders to guide tours and teach about the host country. Most wilderness programs require certification in First Aid, CPR, and Wilderness First Responder. Programs involving marine expeditions often require SCUBA or sailing experience. Most programs also require language skills and knowledge of the culture in the host country. Successful applicants usually have prior outdoor leadership experience. Some programs require special training before leaving for the expedition.

expedition |ˌek-spə-'di-shən| a trip made by a group of people for a specific purpose, such as exploring unknown territory, or to do scientific study.

NCSS I E Culture Demonstrate the value of cultural diversity, as well as cohesion, within and across groups.

Effective Use of Technology

At work, you can use technology as effectively as you use any other resource. Depending on your job, this may mean knowing how to operate anything from a copy machine to an electronic ordering system to an aerospace production line. No matter what your job, here are some tips to keep in mind:

- **Do not expect technology to do your job.** Technology can assist you a great deal, but it cannot think or solve problems. Learn the technology that applies to your job, but remember that you are the one who makes decisions about how to use it.

- **Apply your computer skills.** If you know how to work standard computer software, you can adapt your knowledge and skills to a variety of uses. Many software applications offer free online tutorials to help you improve your skills and learn new ones.

- **Use your computer responsibly.** When you are at school or on the job, remember to use technology only for school or work purposes. Personal e-mail, Web surfing, online chatting, and computer games are inappropriate uses of your school's or employer's resources.

Entrepreneurship

For some people, the way to begin a career or to advance is to strike out on their own. An **entrepreneur** (ˌänˈn-trə-p(r)ə-ˈnər) is a person who starts and runs his or her own business. Running your own business has many advantages. You are your own boss. You get credit, or praise and recognition, for all of your successes. Of course, when you are an entrepreneur you are also responsible for every part of the business. If the business does not do well, you could lose a lot of money. This type of work requires a lot of planning and preparation beyond just finding something you enjoy.

Entrepreneurs generally run independent businesses. There are many other types of businesses. A **franchise** (ˈfran-ˌchīz) is an agreement or license to sell a company's products to operate a business that carries that company's name. It is a common form of ownership used by many chain stores and restaurants.

 Be Your Own Boss Some people get a great deal of job satisfaction from owning their own business. *What kind of personality traits and skills would an entrepreneur need to have?*

Photo Caption Answer
Answers may include: outgoing, willing to take risks, confident, good judgment, good decision maker, able to delegate, good communication skills.

Section 7.2 After You Read

Review What You Have Learned
1. **Name** the benefits of working part-time.
2. **Explain** the advantages of running your own business.

Practice Academic Skills

 English Language Arts

3. Gather information about education and training in your area. What colleges and universities are near your home? Are there trade and technical schools nearby? Can you find apprenticeships offered in your area? What are the costs and requirements of each? Write a summary of your findings.

> **NCTE 8** Use information resources to gather information and create and communicate knowledge.

 Social Studies

4. Research a successful entrepreneur who went against the norm to find new a new way to do something, or to create a new product. Prepare a short presentation about how this entrepreneur's success affected his or her society.

> **NCSS V D** Identify and analyze examples of tensions between expression of individuality and efforts used to promote social conformity by groups and institutions.

Check Your Answers Check your answers at this book's Online Learning Center at glencoe.com.

Discovering Careers

Would you like to help other people find what they do best? Do you have an eye for spotting the talents and skills of other people? If you answered yes to either of those questions, you might want to consider a future career in employment services. The following chart explores several careers in the employment services industry.

Career Activities ▼

At School

 Select three of the careers listed. Research the education, training, and work experience required for each career. Write a summary of your results.

At Home

2 Write a job description for the job that one of your family members does at home.

At Work

3 Look through the local classified ads and make a list of jobs that match your career interests.

In the Community

4 Contact and interview someone in your community who works in the employment services industry. Ask this person to describe what his or her typical work day is like. Share what you learned with your class.

Learn More *Online* 🔗 glencoe.com

Career Investigations Go to this book's Online Learning Center for activities and worksheets to help you explore careers.

Job Title	Job Description
Recruiter	Informs individuals of opportunities, incentives, benefits, and advantages of different careers. Interviews people to determine their suitability for positions.
Human Resources Generalist	Within a specific company, works to fill a variety of positions following hiring guidelines. Interviews candidates and recommends possible hires.
Career Counselor	Supports career exploration. Helps individuals sort out appropriate careers for interests and skill set.
Résumé Writer	Create résumés that present an individual's strengths, skills, and experience in the best possible manner.
Creative Agency Executive	Works with a variety of individuals to place them in appropriate projects based on talents, skills, and experience.
Talent Manager	Represents an individual in the music, movie, or television industries. Locates possible roles or opportunities for performance.

Career Activities Answers for these activities can be found on page TM101.

Chapter Summary

Section 7.1 Plan Your Career
When you think about your career options, consider your strengths, interests, abilities, values, and goals. Begin thinking about the specific skills and the education and training you will need for the career you choose. As you study and gain work experience, put together a portfolio of your skills, experiences, and qualifications. Talk about career possibilities with your parents, family members, school counselors, and teachers.

Section 7.2 Prepare for Work
One of the first steps in finding a job is to consider your interests. Most people choose jobs based on their interests and skills. Without a high school education, your job opportunities will be limited. There are many options for education after high school. Part-time employment is part of your preparation for full-time employment. Some people go out on their own as an entrepreneur, starting and running his or her own business.

Words You Learned

1. Use each of these content vocabulary words and academic vocabulary words in a sentence.

Content Vocabulary
- aptitude (p. 140)
- portfolio (p. 140)
- job shadowing (p. 141)
- apprentice (p. 142)
- networking (p. 142)
- mentor (p. 143)
- job satisfaction (p. 146)
- entrepreneur (p. 151)
- franchise (p. 151)

Academic Vocabulary
- modify (p. 139)
- reveal (p. 140)
- technology (p. 150)
- credit (p. 151)

Review Key Concepts

2. **Describe** how to create a career plan.

3. **Recognize** the importance of researching careers.

4. **Explain** why people work.

5. **Identify** steps you can take to prepare for work.

Critical Thinking

6. **Compare and contrast** careers and jobs. Give examples.

7. **Analyze** which is more important: working in a job you love, or working in a job that earns you a lot of money? Why?

8. **Predict** how you will use the Internet to research and find your career.

9. **Assess** the values and interests you might need for a career in middle school counseling. Share your lists with your classmates.

Real-World Skills and Applications

Problem-Solving

10. Take an Aptitude Test Go to your school counselor and ask about aptitude tests that may be available for you to take. Your teacher may direct you to the school counselor, or there may be tests available online. Take at least one test. What were the results? What did you learn about yourself that you did not know before? How can you use the information to plan your career path? Write a summary of your discoveries.

Interpersonal and Collaborative

11. Career Goals Checklist Follow your teacher's directions to form groups. As a group, choose two different careers to research. Create a checklist for each career to show the steps involved in achieving the career goal. Include education, certification, apprenticeships, and special training. Compare the two checklists. Which career would be the most challenging to obtain? Discuss your results with the class.

Financial Literacy

12. Employee Benefits When comparing jobs, it is important to look at the total compensation you will receive for working. Compensation is the salary plus the value of any benefits offered, such as paid vacation, holidays, and sick time. Many positions come with health insurance, while some jobs include additional insurance, and other benefits such as tuition. Determine total compensation by adding the value of each of these benefits to the salary. Gustavo has received a job offer. In addition to his $26,000 per year salary, he will receive a health insurance plan worth $5,000, two weeks of paid vacation, five paid personal days, and five sick days. Assuming that there are 52 weeks in a year, and 5 work days in a week, how much is Gustavo's employment package worth if he accepts this job?

13. Job Application Obtain a job application from a place where you might consider working. Fill out the application. If you do not have experience or job skills yet, fill out the form with what you think would be required for the job. Follow your teacher's instructions to form pairs. Read each other's applications and offer feedback. Use this exercise to help you learn what you need to work on before applying for a job.

14. Military Training Conduct research to find out what the military can offer in terms of job training. Select a branch of the U.S. Armed Forces and create a list of jobs you can pursue with training in the military. How can you use this job training outside of the military?

15. Start Your Portfolio With permission from your parents or teacher, go online to gather information about a career that interests you. Find out the education required for jobs in that field, responsibilities for duties to be expected, working conditions, and the employment outlook. Create a computer-generated career portfolio to include in your Life Skills Binder.

Academic Skills

English Language Arts

16. Conduct an Interview Follow your teacher's instructions to form pairs. With your partner, create a list of interview questions that you might expect during a job interview. Take turns interviewing one another about your aptitudes, abilities, interests, and values. Take notes on your partner's responses. Write a one-paragraph summary describing what you learned about your partner.

> **NCTE 8** Use information resources to gather information and create and communicate knowledge.

Science

17. Describe a Biome Biologists study the features of different areas around the earth called biomes. A biome is an area of the earth that has related geographic features, temperatures, moisture, plants, and animals. **Procedure** Research what kind of plants and animals live in a desert biome. **Analysis** Is it similar to or different from the biome where you live? In which kind of biome would you like to live and work? Explain your answer in a one-page report.

> **NSES G** Students should develop understanding of science as a human endeavor, nature of scientific knowledge, historical perspective.

Mathematics

18. Compare Numbers Volunteer work is important to Sheila. Of the 2,400 hours she works each year, she spends 400 hours doing volunteer work at the animal shelter and at the assisted living facility where her grandmother lives. The rest of her work time is spent doing paid work in a legal office. What is the ratio of Sheila's volunteer work time to her paid work time? What is the ratio of her volunteer time to her total work time?

Math Concept **Ratios** A ratio is a comparison of two numbers, typically written as a fraction (with one number over the other number). Make sure that you write the ratio in the order suggested by the question, and always simplify it to lowest terms.

Starting Hint If Sheila spends 400 hours doing volunteer work, then she spends $2,400 - 400 = 2,000$ hours doing paid work. The first ratio will include the numbers 400 and 2,000. Write it as a fraction, and reduce it to the lowest terms.

> **NCTM Number and Operations** Understand numbers, ways of representing numbers, relationships among numbers, and number systems.

Standardized Test Practice

Multiple-Choice

Choose the phrase that best completes the statement.

> **Test-Taking Tip** In a multiple-choice test, the answers should be specific and precise. Read the questions first, then read all the answer choices. Eliminate answers that you know are incorrect.

19. An employer looks for an employee who has initiative. Initiative means
a. to follow someone else's example.
b. to do what needs to be done without being told.
c. to get going.
d. to prohibit from doing something.

Chapter 8

Enter the Workplace

Section 8.1

Your Job Search

Explore the Photo
Answer Teamwork and following Through with your job responsibilities can help you achieve success and job satisfaction.

■ **Main Idea** Reading, writing, math, science, speaking, listening, and technology skills contribute to success in the workplace.

Section 8.2

On the Job

■ **Main Idea** A successful interview helps you get a job, and being responsible on the job helps you keep your job.

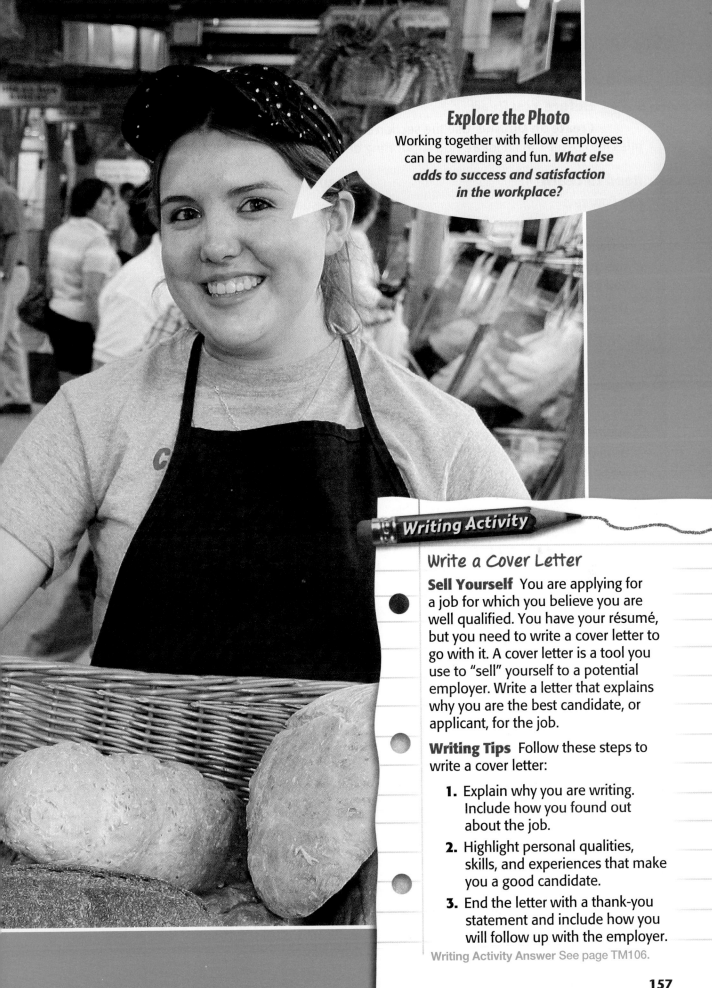

Explore the Photo
Working together with fellow employees can be rewarding and fun. *What else adds to success and satisfaction in the workplace?*

Writing Activity

Write a Cover Letter

Sell Yourself You are applying for a job for which you believe you are well qualified. You have your résumé, but you need to write a cover letter to go with it. A cover letter is a tool you use to "sell" yourself to a potential employer. Write a letter that explains why you are the best candidate, or applicant, for the job.

Writing Tips Follow these steps to write a cover letter:

1. Explain why you are writing. Include how you found out about the job.

2. Highlight personal qualities, skills, and experiences that make you a good candidate.

3. End the letter with a thank-you statement and include how you will follow up with the employer.

Writing Activity Answer See page TM106.

Reading Guide

Before You Read

Create an Outline Use the section's heading titles to create an outline. Make the titles into Level 1 main ideas. Add supporting details to create Level 2, 3, and 4 details.

Read to Learn

Key Concepts

✓ **Examine** the importance of developing basic employability skills.

✓ **Identify** the paperwork you need before you begin a job search.

✓ **Describe** what to do to apply for a job.

Main Idea

Reading, writing, math, science, speaking, listening, and technology skills contribute to success in the workplace.

Content Vocabulary

○ employability skill
○ comprehend
○ reference
○ résumé
○ orientation

Academic Vocabulary

■ persuade   ■ essential

Graphic Organizer

As you read, identify seven employability skills. Use a graphic organizer like the one shown below to help you organize your information.

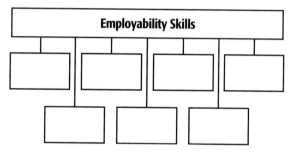

Employability Skills

Graphic Organizer Go to this book's Online Learning Center at glencoe.com to print this graphic organizer.

· · · · · · · · · · · · · · · · · · · **Academic Standards** · · · · · · · · · · · · · · · · ·

 English Language Arts

NCTE 5 Use different writing process elements to communicate effectively.

 Science

NSES B Students should develop an understanding of motions and forces and interactions of energy and matter.

 Social Studies

NCSS IV F Individual Development and Identity Analyze the role of perception, attitudes, values and beliefs in the development of personal identity.

NCTE *National Council of Teachers of English*
NCTM *National Council of Teachers of Mathematics*

NSES *National Science Education Standards*
NCSS *National Council for the Social Studies*

Graphic Organizer
Answer Reading,
Writing, Math, Science,
Speaking, Listening, and
Technology.

To prepare for getting a job, you need to practice your skills and gain experience. Preparation starts at home and at school. Getting a job requires reading, writing, math, science, speaking, and listening skills. You use these basic skills when applying for a job, interviewing with employers, and interacting with customers and coworkers.

Develop Your Skills

The most important key to your success is developing basic employability skills. **Employability skills** help you function in life and at work. Reading, writing, math, science, speaking, listening, and technology are some of the most important skills you can have. Each one is necessary for almost every part of your life.

You need reading and writing skills to fill out a job application. You need speaking and listening skills for your job interview. To understand the information on your paycheck and to budget your money, you will need math skills. Science skills will help you understand how technology affects people and their environment. Listening and speaking skills are necessary to communicate with people at home, school, work, and in the community. Technology skills help you do things efficiently. Using basic employability skills every day is the best way to develop them.

Reading Skills

Reading provides a basis for most of the other employability skills. Without reading skills, you could not write, read directions, understand and solve math problems, or use a computer.

🔊 **Employability Skills** You may not realize that you use basic employability skills every day. *How do use employability skills in your daily activities?*

📖 **As You Read**

Connect What can you do to present your qualifications to a potential employer?

As You Read Answer Send a résumé and cover letter or submit a job application. If you are asked for an interview, you can provide more details about your qualifications in person.

◈ **Vocabulary**

You can find definitions in the glossary at the back of this book.

Photo Caption Answer Answers may include: reading and writing homework assignments, reading recipes to prepare meals, comparing prices, listening to your teacher, talking to your friends, and using computers, cell phones, and media players.

Listening Skills

Pay Attention Give your full attention to your teacher, or to a classmate who is giving a presentation. This helps you focus on what is being said and increases your understanding.

• • • • • • • • • • • •

Succeed in School Make plenty of eye contact with your students as you speak. This will help them focus on what is being taught.

Photo Caption Answer Having someone else look at your work can help you find errors that you can avoid next time.

Build your vocabulary to help develop your reading skills. You can use a dictionary to learn to pronounce words correctly and find out what they mean. You must learn how to follow written directions. The main goal of reading is to comprehend information. When you **comprehend** what you are reading, you understand the words and what they mean. With practice, you can improve your comprehension. **Figure 8.1** explains a reading comprehension technique called SQ3R.

Writing Skills

Writing is a way to express your ideas. When you develop your writing skills, you can feel good about yourself and make a positive impression on others. The ability to express yourself clearly in writing can improve your chances of getting and keeping a job.

You can improve your writing skills by taking time to organize your thoughts. Think about the purpose of what you are going to write. Perhaps you are writing a letter to a potential employer. How can you **persuade**, or convince, the employer to call you in for an interview?

Outline the major points you want to make. Write a rough draft of your letter, and reread it to see if it can be improved. Proofread, or check for errors in your grammar. Use a dictionary to be sure that you use the right words and spell them correctly. Check to be sure that your work is neat and accurate, or correct. You want to make a good first impression with your letter. Ask a parent or guardian to proofread your letter. Having another person look over your work can help you find errors you may have missed. You can avoid making the same errors the next time you write.

Math Skills

You use math and science skills every day in ways you may not realize. For example, you use math and science when you compare prices, prepare a meal, or remove stains from your clothes.

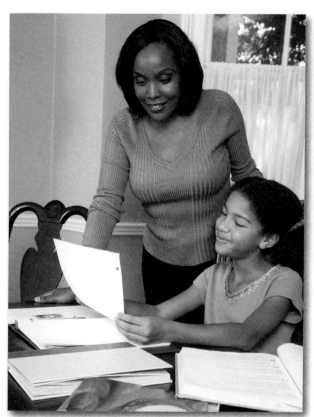

Check Your Work Ask someone to read what you have written. ***How can this help you improve your writing?***

Figure 8.1 SQ3R

Reading Comprehension Like any other skill, reading takes practice. *What techniques do you use to help you better understand what you read?*

- **Survey** Skim the headings and summaries to get an idea of what will be covered.

- **Question** Ask yourself questions about what you are reading.

- **Read** Read to answer your questions.

- **Recite** After reading, recite what you read in your own words.

- **Review** Go back over your reading to make sure all your questions were answered. Ask yourself what you learned.

Figure Caption Answer Answers may include taking notes, highlighting key words and sentences, making outlines, asking questions.

Some of the math skills you must develop are addition, subtraction, multiplication, and division. You also need to master fractions, decimals, and percentages. These math skills will help you figure your weekly earnings. Correct use of a calculator is another necessary math skill. Developing good math skills now can open the door to many opportunities later.

Science Skills

You use science skills every day, too. Knowing how chemical and physical reactions occur is useful in many practical situations. For example, think about what happens when food is cooked or frozen. Science skills can also help you develop an appreciation for your environment. Something as simple as knowing how to select clothing to protect you from the weather is scientific knowledge.

Calculate Speed

Have you ever thought about becoming a pilot and flying faster than the speed of sound? The speed of sound is about 761 miles per hour, or Mach 1. Calculate the speed of a pilot flying at Mach 3.

Procedure Mach is the ratio of an object's speed to the speed of sound. If a jet is going twice the speed of sound then it is moving at Mach 2.

Analysis To figure Mach 3, take the speed of Mach 1 (761 miles per hour) and multiply it by 3.

NSES B Students should develop an understanding of motions and forces and interactions of energy and matter.

Science You Can Use Answer The speed of a jet flying at *Mach 3* would be 2,283 miles per hour.

Speaking Skills

Speaking is just as important in the workplace as reading and writing. Developing the ability to express your thoughts verbally can help you perform well on the job, no matter what career you choose. There are many ways to improve your speaking skills:

- **Think** before you speak in order to organize your ideas.
- **Speak** in a direct and straightforward manner.
- **Pronounce** words clearly and correctly.
- **Make** sure that the other person understands what you are saying.
- **Find** a different way to express your idea if your listener does not understand you.

Listening Skills

To be an effective listener, you need to hear, think about, and respond to what the speaker is saying. On the job, you will need to make a real effort to understand what others say to you. If you do not understand what your employer wants you to do, you may not be able to do your job correctly. Here are several ways to improve your listening skills:

- **Concentrate** on what the other person is saying.
- **Let** the other person know that you are listening.
- **Allow** the other person to finish speaking without interrupting.
- **Listen** even if you do not agree with everything the other person is saying.

 Ask Questions
Do not be afraid to ask questions as you learn about your job duties. *What might happen if you do not ask questions about your job responsibilities?*

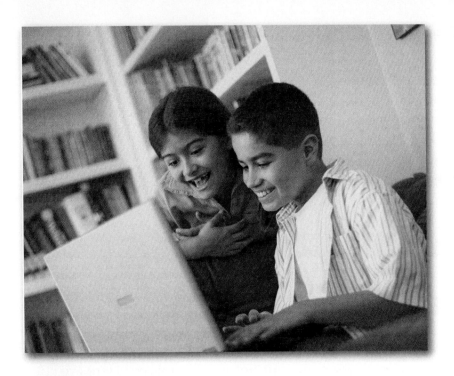

Computer Skills
Technology helps us do our jobs. *How do you think technology will help you at work?*

Photo Caption Answer
Computers save time, make communication easier, help with research, and they do much of the work that people or other equipment (such as calculators) used to do.

Technology Skills

Technology makes life easier. You can stay in touch by using cell phones and e-mail and by accessing the Internet for information and resources. Computers have changed the way we live and work. Knowing how to use a computer is **essential**, or absolutely necessary, in today's work world. If you have not spent much time using a computer, now is a good time to practice your keyboarding, or typing, skills. Most computer software is user-friendly, which means it is created to be easy for beginners to use.

Reading Check *Explain Why is reading such an important skill?*

Reading Check Answer
Reading is the basis for many other skills, including writing, math, science, and technology.

Get Organized

Before you look for a job, you need to get organized. First, decide what kind of job you want. Next, decide when and for how many hours you can work. Now, decide when you should look for a job. If you want a summer job, start looking in the spring.

Labor Laws

The Fair Labor Standards Act (FLSA) sets requirements for wages, hours, and safety for workers under age 18. As a general rule, the FLSA sets 14 as the minimum age for employment, and limits the number of hours that people under 16 can work. Check the U.S. Department of Labor and the laws in your own state for more information.

Legal Documents

If you were born in the United States, your parents may have applied for you to have a social security card shortly after you were born. If you do not have a social security card, you must get one. You will need a copy of your birth certificate or other proof that you are a United States citizen. You may also need a work permit or employment certificate if you are under the age of 16 or 18. Once you have the necessary papers, you are ready to begin your job search.

Reading Check **Recall** *How can you find out more information about labor laws?*

Apply for Jobs

When you find a job opening that interests you, fill out a job application. The way you fill out a job application will make an impression on your potential employer. Here are some guidelines to follow:

- **Read** the application form carefully. Follow the instructions exactly.
- **Print** as neatly as possible, using blue or black ink.
- **Check** that you answered every question. If a question does not apply, write "NA" (not applicable).
- **Be prepared** to describe your education, skills, past work experience, and references, even if you already provided this information on an application.

On an application form you may be asked to list several references. A **reference** is a responsible adult who can tell an employer about your character and quality of work. You might choose teachers, counselors, coaches, previous employers, or religious leaders. Be sure to ask each person for permission before you use his or her name as a reference.

Many employers also require a résumé. A **résumé** ('re-zə-'mā) summarizes your qualifications, work experience, education, and interests. **Figure 8.2** shows a sample of a completed résumé. References may be added to a résumé or listed as "available upon request."

First Impression
Your job application may be the first impression you give to a potential employer. *How can the appearance of a job application affect your chances for consideration for a job?*

The Job Interview

If the employer who reviews your application or résumé thinks that you might be suitable for the job, you will be invited to an interview. A job interview is a meeting between an employer and a job applicant to discuss qualifications. The interviewer will ask many questions. Be prepared to answer such questions as:

Figure 8.2 Your Résumé

All in One Your résumé allows potential employers to view your qualifications, work experience, education, and activities all at once. *What information is included on a résumé?*

ROBIN SANDERS

208 Denver Way
Anytown, CA 55555
(555) 555-4996
robin@555email.net

CAREER OBJECTIVE
· A professional sales position in the foods industry.

SKILLS AND ABILITIES
· Stocked groceries
· Tracked incoming deliveries
· Prepared inventory reports for supervisor
· Assisted customers in finding groceries
· Provided assembly service for bicycles
· Created customer feedback program

WORK EXPERIENCE
· Stock person: Super Discounts, May 20-- to present

EDUCATION
· Currently attending Chandler Junior College
· Graduate, Chandler High School, May 20--

ACTIVITIES
· Served as Student Council Vice President
· Coordinated Student Council car wash
· Coordinated charity fundraiser, which resulted in $21,000 in donations
· Honor Roll student

REFERENCES
· Available upon request.

- "Why do you think you can do this job?"
- "Can you tell me more about your experience?"
- "What do you hope to accomplish in this job?"
- "What are your career goals?"

The interview also gives you a chance to learn more about the job by asking questions of the employer. For example, you might ask what your job duties would be. You should also ask about company benefits, such as vacation, insurance, and pay schedules. You may also want to ask about holidays, overtime, training, and employee assistance programs.

After an interview, you need to follow up. Send a thank-you letter to the employer, even if you decide you are no longer interested in the job. He or she spent time reading your application and speaking to you, so it is professional and courteous to show your appreciation. If you are asked to contact the employer on a specific date, be sure to do so.

Listening Skills
Focus Your Mind
Avoid distractions when you are listening to someone speak. Do not let your mind wander. Concentrate on making eye contact with the speaker to help you focus.

• • • • • • • • • • • • •

Make the Best of Your Interview

To be considered for a position, a potential employer will want to interview you. This is your opportunity to make the best impression possible and to convince the employer to hire you for the position.

Research the Employer Find out as much as you can about the employer. Ask people who work at the business why they like to work there. Check the company Web site for background information and details about the company. Know directions to the company ahead of time so you do not get lost, or make arrangements for transportation.

Make a Good Impression Choose appropriate clothing for the interview. Make sure it is clean and pressed. Keep jewelry to a minimum. Make sure you are clean, your hair is clean, your breath is fresh, and you have clean fingernails. If you do not appear professional, the employer will not take you seriously.

Prepare for the Interview Arrive at least 10 minutes early for the interview. Have some questions prepared to ask the interviewer about the job. For example, you may want to know what days and hours you would be expected to work, and what kind of training is offered. Bring your résumé and any other materials that were requested, such as your portfolio, or a list of references if you have not already provided them.

Be Professional During the Interview Turn off your cell phone or other electronic devices. Think before you answer each question. Smile, speak clearly, and be friendly and enthusiastic. Make eye contact. Practice good posture and good manners. Do not chew gum.

Follow Up after the Interview Send a thank-you letter after the interview. Tell the employer that you appreciate his or her consideration. Ask for feedback on how you did during the interview for future growth and development. If you decide that you do not want the job, it is still important to send a thank-you letter to thank the employer for his or her time.

Job Offers

When you receive a job offer, you have three options:

- **Accept the offer.** The employer will usually set up an **orientation** (ˈor-ən-ˈtā-shən) during which you will be given details about pay, benefits, and job expectations. You may be given a tour as well.
- **Ask for time to consider the offer.** This is the time to bring up any unanswered questions that might affect your decision. With the employer, agree on when you will notify him or her of your decision. Do not put off responding to the employer.
- **Turn down the job offer.** You may decide the job is not right for you. Say, "Thank you for considering me, but I am no longer interested in the job."

The Interview An interview gives you a chance to convince the employer that you are right for the job. *Why should you send a thank-you letter to the employer after the interview?*

Photo Caption Answer You should thank the employer for his or her time and consideration, even if you decide you do not want the job.

Section 8.1 After You Read

Review What You Have Learned

1. **Name** the steps for the SQ3R reading comprehension technique.
2. **Describe** how you use math and science skills everyday.
3. **Identify** ways to improve your listening skills.

Practice Academic Skills

 English Language Arts

4. Think of three questions you expect a job interviewer to ask. Respond to those questions with answers that will persuade the employer to offer you the job.

> **NCTE 5** Use different writing process elements to communicate effectively.

 Social Studies

5. Interview someone you know about how he or she prepared for a job. Ask: How did your family influence your choice? How did your family react to your job? What experience did you have? What is important to you in your job? Summarize their answers, and explain how he or she may influence your ideas about work.

> **NCSS IV F** Analyze the role of perception, attitudes, values and beliefs in the development of personal identity.

Check Your Answers Check your answers at this book's Online Learning Center at glencoe.com.

Section 8.2 On the Job

Reading Guide

Before You Read

Prior Knowledge Look over the Key Concepts at the beginning of the section. Write down what you already know about each concept and what you want to find out by reading the lesson. As you read, find examples for both categories.

Read to Learn

Key Concepts

✓ **List** the responsibilities that you have as an employee.

✓ **Recognize** the importance of leaving a job on a positive note.

Main Idea

A successful interview helps you get a job, and being responsible on the job helps you keep your job.

Content Vocabulary

○ discrimination
○ harassment
○ flexibility
○ work ethic
○ promotion
○ resign

Academic Vocabulary

■ accommodation   ■ notice

Graphic Organizer

As you read, identify four keys to being a responsible employee. Use a graphic organizer like the one shown to help you organize your information.

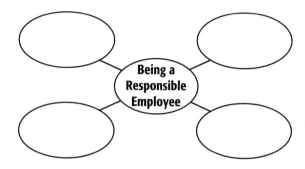

Graphic Organizer Go to this book's Online Learning Center at glencoe.com to print this graphic organizer.

- - - - - - - - - - - - - - **Academic Standards** - - - - - - - - - - - - -

English Language Arts

NCTE 12 Use language to accomplish individual purposes.

Mathematics

NCTM Number and Operations Understand the meanings of operations and how they relate to one another.

Social Studies

NCSS VI A Power, Authority, and Governance Examine persistent issues involving the rights, roles, and status of the individual in relation to the general welfare.

NCTE *National Council of Teachers of English*
NCTM *National Council of Teachers of Mathematics*
NSES *National Science Education Standards*
NCSS *National Council for the Social Studies*

Graphic Organizer
Answer fulfill your responsibilities, accept diversity, avoid harassment, evaluate yourself

How you perform on a job can determine whether you keep or lose the job. It can also affect whether or not you move into a job with more responsibility. Your habits at work determine what you can achieve. Being a responsible and flexible team player can help you succeed on the job. There are several keys to being effective in the workplace.

Be a Responsible Employee

The key to success in any job is to be a responsible employee. Job responsibilities are similar to your responsibilities at school. You need to arrive on time, follow rules, and do your work.

Fulfill Your Responsibilities

Besides general job responsibilities, every job also has specific duties. Your supervisor will explain your specific responsibilities to you. You may be given an employee manual which outlines the rules that employees must follow. In particular, it is important to follow safety rules. These rules help protect employees from workplace hazards and human errors. The key to success is to do your job. This sounds simple, and it is. Arrive on time, ask questions if you do not understand something, and make your job responsibilities your top priority. It is also important to avoid inappropriate conversations at work. For example, Sean ignored customers at the check-out because he was on the phone with his friend. Sean was fired. Conversations at work should be professional and work-related.

As You Read

Connect How can your strengths and weaknesses at school affect the way you may perform on a job?

As You Read Answer Answers will vary. Sample answers: Good English skills can help in a job that requires reading and writing; athletic skills can help in a job that requires physical activity. Poor math skills may affect your ability to deal with money; lack of teamwork skills could make it difficult to work with others on the job.

Vocabulary

You can find definitions in the glossary at the back of this book.

Show Responsibility Working as a team shows responsibility. *How else can you demonstrate that you are responsible?*

Photo Caption Answer Answers may include arriving at work on time, following all of the rules, and completing your assignments.

Safety in the Workplace

It is important to know guidelines and procedures for emergencies at your place of work. Whether it is an accident with equipment or a fire, know how to take care of yourself and your co-workers.

- Always use equipment correctly and wear required safety gear.
- Learn the fire escape route and other disaster procedures.
- Follow all safety guidelines for the work that you perform.

Character Counts Answer
Sam should be flexible and realize that there is more than one way to accomplish a task. He should work on developing a positive attitude, listen attentively to others, and do his share of the work. When the first meeting takes place, he can express his ideas as well as listen to the ideas of the other team members.

Character Counts

Teamwork

Sam is a member of a team at work. They are doing a research project together. He has a good idea about how he thinks the project should be done. There are several meetings planned for the team to make decisions before they begin. Sam thinks that his time could be used for more important things, but his supervisor has directed him and the rest of the team to work together.

You Make the Call

How can Sam be a successful part of the team? Write a paragraph to explain what Sam should do and why.

Accept Diversity

Each workplace is made up of people from diverse cultures and with varying abilities. The Equal Employment Opportunities Act requires businesses to keep discrimination from occurring. **Discrimination** (dis-ˈkri-mə-ˈnā-shən) is the unfair treatment of people based on age, gender, race, or religion. The Americans with Disabilities Act (ADA) ensures that all employees are treated equally, regardless of any disability they may have. The law requires reasonable **accommodations**, or adjustments, be made for people with disabilities, whether they are employees or customers. Working with people who are culturally diverse and who have different abilities makes the workplace more interesting. Together, people can help each other get the job done.

Avoid Harassment

Teasing, intimidation, and threats are all forms of **harassment**. Workplace harassment is offensive and violates people's rights. Any kind of harassment in the workplace is unacceptable. Sexual harassment involves unwelcome behavior of a sexual nature, whether physical or verbal. If you experience or observe any type of harassment, tell the harasser to stop. Report the situation to your supervisor.

Evaluate Yourself

At the end of each workday, you should evaluate your performance on the job. Did you fulfill your responsibilities? How could you have done your job better? Conditions on the job often change, so most work situations require flexibility. **Flexibility** is the ability to adjust to new conditions. For example, technology is constantly changing. Workers must adapt their skills to accomplish tasks.

Teamwork

Relationships are an important part of every job. You have to learn to get along with your employer, supervisor, and coworkers, and perhaps customers or clients. The better your relationships are with the people around you, the more you will enjoy work and experience success.

Teamwork

In this activity, you will work in a team to complete a project of your choice. Before you begin, read through the entire Hands-On Lab assignment. Write down any questions that you have about the assignment. Reread the text or ask your teacher for help if you need it.

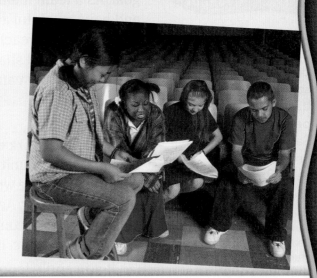

Supplies
✓ White board, chalk board, or newspaper print
✓ Paper or pen

Develop Your Plan
- Make a timeline for what needs to be accomplished by the team.
- Write down the topics you will talk about at your meetings.
- Decide how decisions will be made, such as by majority vote, or when everyone agrees.
- Decide who will lead the group.
- Pick one person to remind other group members of meeting times and places, and to take notes when you meet.

Implement Your Plan
- As a team, choose a project to complete during class.
- Set goals for your team meeting and a time limit for the meeting. Make sure all team members understand the goals.

- Make everyone comfortable by giving each team member a chance to share his or her ideas. When a team member is silent, the leader should ask for his or her input.
- Write down what each person is responsible for along with any special instructions.
- Set a deadline for the project, and work as a team to complete it.

Evaluate Your Results
What did you accomplish at your team meeting? What would you change if you could do it over again? How did team members interact while working on the project? Write one or more paragraphs to explain your answer.

 Projects and Activities Go to this book's Online Learning Center through **glencoe.com** for more projects and activities.

Evaluate Your Results Answer Evaluations will vary but should include a description of what the student teams accomplished, what they would do differently next time, and a summary of how team members interacted while working on the project.

SUCCEED IN SCHOOL!

At work, you become part of a team. A team can be any group of two or more people who work toward a common goal. As a team member, you work with and listen to others and have a helpful attitude. You build teamwork while working together to reach a goal. When coworkers cooperate with one another and share feelings of pride in their work, they get along better and can reach their goals more effectively.

Work Ethic

A positive work ethic can lead to job success. **Work ethic** is a personal commitment to doing your very best. You can develop a positive work ethic by being responsible, flexible, and a team player. Avoid such poor habits such as being tardy, uncooperative, or unreliable. These traits do not contribute to a positive work ethic. In fact, they could cause you to lose a job.

If you apply for a job with a different company, that employer will probably check with your former employer to see how you worked. Work hard and fulfill your responsibilities. This will help you keep a job, and it can help you when it is time to move on to other jobs.

 Reading Check *Describe How can you develop a positive work ethic that leads to job success?*

Changing Jobs

Employees who use their employability skills to do a good job are likely to be promoted. A **promotion** is a move into a job with more responsibility. For example, you might be promoted from stock clerk to assistant manager. A promotion usually includes a raise in salary. Another way to advance, or move ahead, is to accept a job with more responsibilities and higher pay with another company.

Leaving Your Job

The decision to **resign** from a job should be made very carefully. When you decide to leave a job, try to leave on good terms with the employer. Show courtesy, respect, and appreciation to your employer. The following tips can help you leave on a positive note:

Financial Literacy

Spending Your Salary

Monica works 12 hours a week, 3 weeks a month, at a part-time job after school, where she makes $8 an hour. Each month she has expenses of $75 for gas and $100 for food, and she has also set aside $50 a month for clothes and $25 a month toward paying off a new set of skis. How much money does she have left to spend on entertainment?

Math Concept **Net Cash Flow** Your net cash flow, which equals income minus expenses for a given period of time, is one part of your financial health.

Starting Hint Determine Monica's total income for the month (12 hours per week x $8 per hour x 3 weeks), and then subtract her total monthly expenses.

NCTM Number and Operations Understand the meanings of operations and how they relate to one another.

 For math help, go to the Math Appendix at the back of the book.

Financial Literacy Feature Answer Total monthly income = 12 x 8 x 3 = $288. Total monthly expenses = $75 + $100 + $50 + $25 = $250. Her net cash flow is $288 - $250 = $38.

172 Unit 3 Make Your Career Plan

- **Give Notice.** Notice, or an announcment, should be given soon enough for the employer to find a replacement by the time you leave the job. A two-week notice is what most workplaces consider appropriate.
- **Submit a Letter of Resignation.** The letter should be given to your direct supervisor. The letter should state the exact date you expect to be your last day of employment. It should also thank the employer for his or her help during your time with the company. Be sure to give a brief explanation of why you are leaving.

 Job Resignation The decision to leave a job should not be made lightly. *What are two things you should do when you leave a job?*

Photo Caption Answer Give at least a two-week notice and write a letter of resignation.

Section 8.2 After You Read

Review What You Have Learned

1. **Explain** what to do if you experience or observe harassment.
2. **Summarize** what a letter of resignation should include.

Practice Academic Skills

English Language Arts

3. Imagine that you have decided to quit your job. Write a letter of resignation that includes the information recommended in the chapter.

> **NCTE 12** Use language to accomplish individual purposes.

Social Studies

4. Research current guidelines for giving references to former employees. What can a supervisor legally say about a former employee? What are your rights as an employee regarding your personal work record? Share your findings with the class.

> **NCSS VI A** Examine persistent issues involving the rights, roles, and status of the individual in relation to the general welfare.

Check Your Answers Check your answers at this book's Online Learning Center at glencoe.com.

Discovering Careers

Do you like to work behind the scenes? Can you support the work of other fields? If you answered yes to either of those questions, you might want to consider a future career in research and development. The following chart explores several careers in the research and development industry.

Career Activities ▼

At School

1 Select three of the careers listed. Research the education, training, and work experience required for each career. Write a summary of your results.

At Home

2 Virtually every product in your home required work from a team of research and development experts. Choose a product in your home, such as shampoo, a frozen dinner, or a kitchen appliance, and write a paragraph about what kind of research was needed to develop the product.

At Work

3 On a sheet of paper, create one column for each of the seven employability skills discussed in this chapter. Under each heading, list of all the ways you can think of to use these skills in the workplace.

In the Community

4 Contact and interview someone in your community who works in the research and development industry. Ask this person to describe what his or her typical work day is like. Share what you learned with your class.

Career Activities Answers Answers for these activities can be found on page TM106.

Job Title	Job Description
Press-Service Reader	Reads newspapers, magazines, and other articles on specific subjects. Marks items to be clipped for each customer.
Mathematician	Conducts research for science, management, and other fields. Tests hypotheses. Develops ideas for use in a variety of fields.
Scientific Linguist	Studies structure and relationships of languages. Helps develop methods of translation. Prepares teaching materials and handbooks.
Computer Software Engineer	Installs and tests computer software and hardware. Writes computer programs to meet company or client needs.
Quality Assurance Tester	Designs methods, tests, and procedures for use by the development team to ensure company standards are met.

 Learn More *Online* glencoe.com

Career Investigations Go to this book's Online Learning Center for activities and worksheets to help you explore careers.

Chapter Summary

Section 8.1 Your Job Search
The key to your success is developing basic employability skills in reading, writing, math, science, speaking, listening, and technology. When you find a job that interests you, fill out a job application with information about your education, skills, activities, work experience, and references. If the employer thinks that you are suitable, you will be asked for an interview.

Section 8.2 On the Job
An important part of any job is to be a responsible employee. You have to learn to get along with your employer, supervisor, and coworkers, and perhaps customers or clients. At work, you become part of a team working toward a common goal. A positive work ethic can lead to job success. Employees who use their employability skills to do a good job are likely to be promoted.

Words You Learned

Write your own definition for each of these content and academic vocabulary words.

Content Vocabulary
- employability skill (p. 159)
- comprehend (p. 160)
- reference (p. 164)
- résumé (p. 165)
- orientation (p. 167)
- discrimination (p. 169)
- harassment (p. 170)
- flexibility (p. 170)
- work ethic (p. 172)
- promotion (p. 172)
- resign (p. 172)

Academic Vocabulary
- persuade (p. 160)
- essential (p. 163)
- accommodation (p. 170)
- notice (p. 173)

Review Key Concepts

2. **Examine** the importance of developing basic employability skills.

3. **Identify** the paperwork you need before you begin a job search.

4. **Describe** what to do to apply for a job.

5. **List** the responsibilities that you have as an employee.

6. **Recognize** the importance of leaving a job on a positive note.

Critical Thinking

7. **Predict** how your positive work ethic will affect coworkers and supervisors.

8. **Explain** why you should send a thank-you letter when you decide not to accept a job.

9. **Analyze** how you can play up your strengths and abilities in a job interview without sounding like you are bragging.

Real-World Skills and Applications

Problem-Solving

10. Organize Information Use the résumé on page 165 as a model for writing a résumé. Gather your own employment history, skills, and information so that you can create your résumé. If you do not have any work history or job experience yet, ask a parent or family member for help. Together, come up with a fictional background to help you create a résumé. Organize the information for reference.

Interpersonal and Collaborative

11. Teen Jobs Follow your teacher's directions to form teams. Research jobs available in your area that would be suitable for teens. Consider the hours, type of work, skills required, and other factors to present a list of jobs you would recommend for teens. As a team, rank the jobs in order of preference based on your research.

Financial Literacy

12. Overtime Pay Casey, a senior in high school, is planning to go to junior college next year before transferring to a 4-year university. He plans to major in veterinary medicine, so he just accepted a summer job as a tour guide at the zoo. He makes $8.50 per hour at the zoo job, and he hopes to get as much overtime as he can to save for college expenses. His employer pays time-and-a-half overtime for any hours worked over 8 per day. Casey's first week on the job was a busy one, and as a result, he was able to get some overtime hours right away. During that first week, he worked 9 hours on Monday, 10 hours on Wednesday, and 8 hours on Friday. How much money did he make during his first week?

13. Teamwork Poster Conduct research to find information about how to successfully work in teams. Come up with at least five tips. Create a poster with photos, illustrations, or computer graphics to communicate this information. Display the poster in your classroom.

14. Research Job Changes Jobs have changed throughout history based on economic and technological changes. Fifty years ago, there were few jobs in genetic engineering or environmental engineering. Research a job that is growing in demand that did not exist fifty years ago. Include information about the job and its requirements. What happened to create a need for this job? Share what you learned with the class.

15. Job Search With permission from your parents or teachers, go online to search for three jobs that you would be interested in. For each position, research the company's background, and note the qualifications, salaries, benefits, and job requirements. Use this information to create a spreadsheet. Then, using what you learned in the chapter, include information about how you would prepare for each job. Include this information in your Life Skills Binder.

Academic Skills

 ## English Language Arts

16. Speak Up You can use several basic employability skills by preparing a speech. Write a one-minute speech on the importance of employability skills. Make note cards for reference during your speech. Practice your speech in front of the mirror. Present the speech to your classmates. Ask them what they learned from it and how you could make it better.

> **NCTE 8** Use information resources to gather information and create and communicate knowledge.

 ## Social Studies

17. The ADA The Americans with Disabilities Act is law that ensures that all employees are treated equally, regardless of any disability they may have. The law requires reasonable accommodations be made for people with disabilities. Imagine that you visit a place of business and observe that a person in a wheelchair is having difficulty accessing certain areas. Write a letter to the owner or manager of the business. Express your concern, and offer suggestions to help.

> **NCSS I A Culture** Analyze and explain the ways groups, societies, and cultures address human needs and concerns.

 ## Mathematics

18. Prepare a Résumé Tanya would like to send her résumé out to local employers with the hope of finding a summer job. Tanya wants to make a good impression on potential employers so she thinks it would be a good idea to have her résumé printed on high-quality paper. After printing a copy of the résumé, she heads to her local copy shop. Tanya has budgeted $6 for making copies of her résumé. If she selects a paper stock that costs 5 cents a copy, how many can she make? What if she selects one that costs 6 cents per copy?

Math Concept **Dividing Decimals**
When dividing a number by a decimal, multiply the decimal by a power of ten to make it a whole number. Multiply the other number by the same power of ten.

Starting Hint You will need to divide $6.00 by $0.05, and also divide $6.00 by $0.06. To remove the decimals, multiply all numbers by 100, which you can do by moving each decimal point two places to the right.

> **NCTM Number and Operations** Understand meanings of operations and how they relate to one another.

Standardized Test Practice

Multiple-Choice

Read the sentence. Then read the question below the sentence. Read the answer choices and choose the best answer to fill in the blank.

> **Test-Taking Tip** With multiple choice questions that rely on information given, read the paragraph very carefully to make sure you understand what it is about. Read the answer choices. Then read the paragraph again before choosing the answer.

19. Mark and Grace started their new jobs at the restaurant on the same day. Their supervisor took them on a tour of the kitchen and the dining area during a 1-hour *orientation,* which also included a review of the New Hire Handbook.
In this sentence, the word *orientation* means _____ .
a. direction   b. arrangement
c. introduction   d. position

You in Ten Years

What you choose to do for a living is important. Investigating jobs that parents and other adults are doing can help you decide what would be suitable for you. Classified Ads show different skills that employers look for. This project can help you explore your job opportunities.

 My Journal Complete the journal entry from page 135, and refer to it to complete your list of skills and talents.

Project Assignment ▼

In this project, you will:

- Write an outline of your skills and talents.
- Research jobs that are interesting to you.
- Create a PowerPoint presentation about your chosen career.
- Interview someone with a profession you want to learn more about.
- Present your findings to your class.
- Include this project in the third section of your personal Life Skills binder.

Step 1 List Your Skills, Talents, and Abilities

What you do for a living will be more satisfying if it is something you are good at. List your qualifications, and then open the classified section of the newspaper. Circle job listings that match your skills, and make a list of the skills you still need to learn.

Step 2 Choose a Job or Career to Investigate

Choose a job you can imagine doing in ten years. Write down your ideas for a PowerPoint presentation that outlines the education, training, and experience you will need to be qualified for that job. Answer these questions in your PowerPoint:

✔ Does this job require some talents that you already have?
✔ How many years of education or training will you need?
✔ What will you need to wear to work each day?
✔ What rewards do you imagine this job will bring you?

Step 3 Interview Someone with an Appealing Job

Interview someone in your community with the job that you have chosen. Ask these questions:

✔ Why did you choose to do this for a living?
✔ What is the most important skill for this job?
✔ Where did you get your training and education?

Use these interviewing skills when conducting your interview and these writing skills when writing the summary of notes from your interview.

Interviewing Skills
- Record interview responses and take notes.
- Listen attentively.

Writing Skills
- Use complete sentences.
- Use correct spelling and grammar.

Step 4 Create and Present Your PowerPoint Presentation

Use the Life Skills Project Checklist on the right to plan and complete your PowerPoint presentation and give an oral report on it. Present your information as if it were ten years in the future. Imagine you are already working in this job and describing it to students on Career Day.

Use these speaking skills when presenting your final report.

Speaking Skills
- Speak clearly and concisely.
- Be sensitive to the needs of your audience.
- Use standard English to communicate.

Step 5 Evaluate Your Presentation

Your project will be evaluated based on:

✔Completeness and organization of your outline of skills and talents.
✔Your PowerPoint presentation of the steps to qualify for your job.
✔The presentation as if you are doing the job in ten years.
✔The summary written from interview notes.
✔Grammar and sentence structure.
✔Presentation to the class.
✔Creativity and neatness.

🧭 **Evaluation Rubric** Go to this book's Online Learning Center through **glencoe.com** for a rubric you can use to evaluate your final project.

Life Skills Project Checklist

Research Job Skills and Training

- List your skills and talents.
- Circle classified ads of jobs that might suit you.
- Create a PowerPoint presentation of the steps to qualify for your job.
- Interview someone who currently holds that job.

Writing Skills

- Write about skills you need to achieve.
- Write the presentation as if you are doing the job you chose in ten years.
- Write a summary from your interview with a person who does that job.

Present Your Findings

- Prepare a short presentation about what you will be doing in ten years. Wear a uniform or appropriate clothing of your job.
- Invite the students of the class to ask any questions they may have. Answer these questions with responses that respect their perspectives.
- Add this project to your Life Skills binder.

Academic Skills

- Conduct research to gather information.
- Communicate effectively.
- Organize your presentation so the audience can follow along easily.
- Thoroughly express your ideas.

NCTE 4 Use written language to communicate effectively.

NCTE 8 Use information resources to gather information and create and communicate knowledge.

Chapter 9
Caring for Children

Chapter 10
Child Care Basics

Unit Preview

This unit is about child development and caring for children. In this unit, you will learn about:

- Being a successful parent.
- The different stages of childhood.
- Keeping children safe.
- The benefits of being a babysitter.

Explore the Photo Answer Answers may include that babysitting: teaches responsibility; gives teens experience with making, handling, and managing their own money; allows teens to become familiar with caring for and interacting with children.

Explore the Photo
Being a babysitter can help you to develop important skills that can be useful later in life. *What are some skills that babysitting might help you learn?*

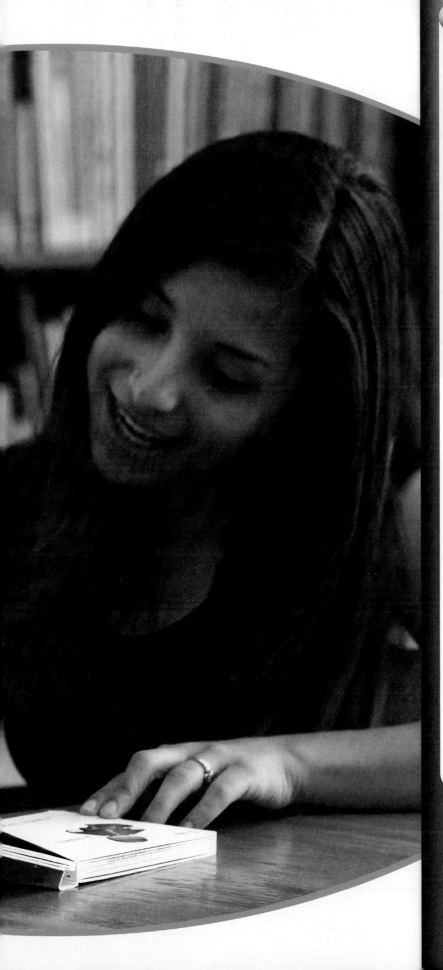

Your Relationship with Children

When you are done studying this unit, you will complete a project in which you will:

✓ Observe and analyze how children play with toys.

✓ Interview someone who cares for young children.

✓ Design a game or toy and share it with the class.

The prewriting activity below will help you get started.

 My Journal

Prewriting Activity
Make a List

Make a list of your five favorite toys or games from when you were young. After each toy or game, write a description that answers these questions:

● What age group was the toy or game designed for?

● Why was the toy or game fun?

● How did the toy or game help you learn?

Chapter 9

Caring for Children

Section 9.1

Responsible Parenting

■ **Main Idea** Strong parenting skills can help you protect children and meet their needs.

Section 9.2

Child Development

■ **Main Idea** Children develop in stages and learn through play and interaction at every stage.

Explore the Photo Answer Answers may include help them ride the school bus, ride bikes in the neighborhood, help with school work, help them tie their shoes.

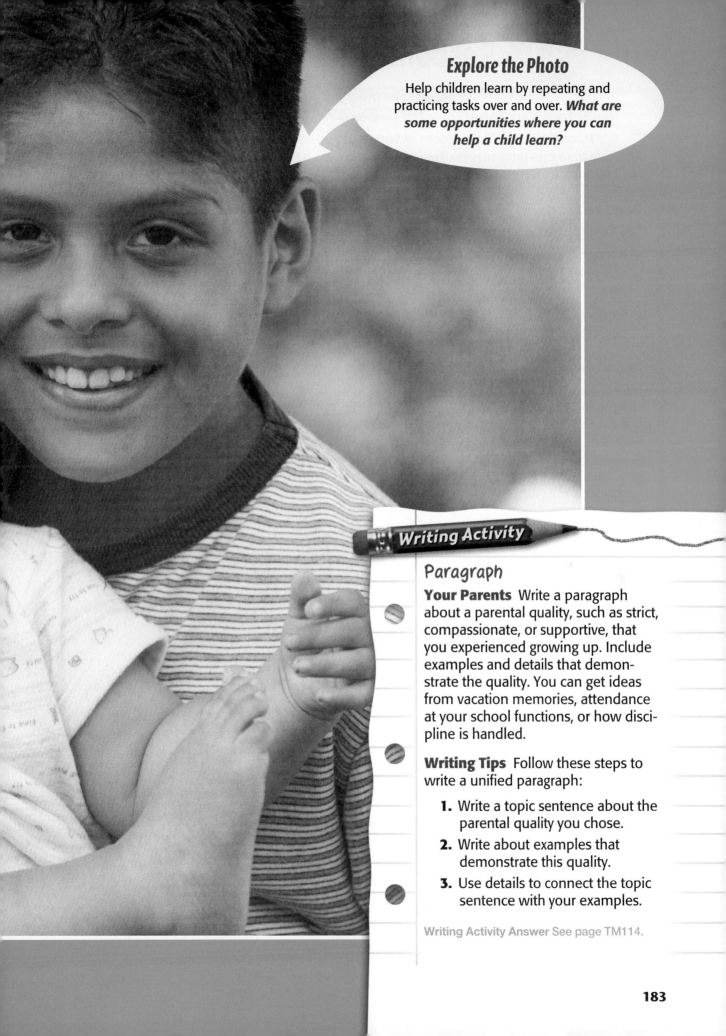

Explore the Photo
Help children learn by repeating and practicing tasks over and over. *What are some opportunities where you can help a child learn?*

Writing Activity

Paragraph

Your Parents Write a paragraph about a parental quality, such as strict, compassionate, or supportive, that you experienced growing up. Include examples and details that demonstrate the quality. You can get ideas from vacation memories, attendance at your school functions, or how discipline is handled.

Writing Tips Follow these steps to write a unified paragraph:

1. Write a topic sentence about the parental quality you chose.

2. Write about examples that demonstrate this quality.

3. Use details to connect the topic sentence with your examples.

Writing Activity Answer See page TM114.

Reading Guide

Before You Read

Pace Yourself Short blocks of concentrated reading repeated frequently are more effective than one long session. Focus on reading for 10 minutes. Take a short break. Then read for another 10 minutes.

Read to Learn
Key Concepts
✓ **Recognize** that parenting is a lifelong commitment to help children grow and learn.
✓ **Explain** the causes of child abuse and neglect how it can be prevented.

Main Idea
Strong parenting skills can help you protect children and meet their needs.

Content Vocabulary
○ parenting
○ guidance
○ discipline
○ child abuse
○ child neglect

Academic Vocabulary
■ commitment
■ consistent

Graphic Organizer
As you read, list examples for each of the three basic needs that must be met for children to develop in healthy ways. Use a graphic organizer like the one shown to help you organize your information.

Children's Basic Needs		
Physical	Intellectual	Emotional/Social

 Graphic Organizer Go to this book's Online Learning Center at glencoe.com to print this graphic organizer.

Academic Standards

 English Language Arts
NCTE 4 Use written language to communicate effectively.

 Mathematics
NCTM Number and Operations Compute fluently and make reasonable estimates.

Social Studies
NCSS IV C Individual Development and Identity Examine factors that contribute to and damage one's mental health and analyze issues related to mental and behavioral disorders in contemporary society.

NCTE *National Council of Teachers of English*
NCTM *National Council of Teachers of Mathematics*
NSES *National Science Education Standards*
NCSS *National Council for the Social Studies*

Graphic Organizer Answer Physical: healthful food, appropriate clothing, rest and sleep, safe environment; Intellectual: books, puzzles, blocks, and toys help develop intellectual abilities; Emotional and Social: speak kindly, and hug, kiss, and hold children so they feel loved.

Do you remember who taught you to ride a bike, tie your shoes, or tell time? Was it your mother, father, grandmother, grandfather, or another adult? You can probably think of many people who have taught you what you know today. These caregivers have had a major influence on your life.

Parenthood

Parents and other caregivers need to use good parenting skills. **Parenting** is the process of caring for children and helping them to grow and learn. This process can be very rewarding, but it also takes a lot of hard work.

Babysitting for younger siblings or other young children can introduce you to the basic skills necessary for good parenting. You can also learn parenting skills from watching your parents and by taking a child development or parenting course. The more you know about children, the more comfortable you will be with them. You will find that the way you handle children affects the way they behave toward you.

Lifelong Commitment

Imagine coming across this job description:

- Work or be on-call 24 hours a day.
- Accept full responsibility for everything that happens.
- Give up a good deal of sleep, personal time, and freedom.
- Promise that you will do this job for a lifetime.
- Benefits may include unconditional love, joy, and a deep feeling of satisfaction.
- Do it all for no paycheck. In fact, this job will cost you money!

Would you apply for this job? These are just a few of the many things that might appear in a job description for parenthood. Parenthood is a major decision and a lifelong **commitment**, or promise. Effective parents must provide love, patience, guidance, and financial resources.

As You Read

Connect In what ways will you still need your parents after you enter adulthood?

As You Read Answer Answers may include: advice, support, help with raising their own children, friendship.

◆ **Vocabulary**

You can find definitions in the glossary at the back of this book.

Photo Caption Answer Answers may include patience, humor, understanding, kindness.

Parenthood Lasts Forever Choosing to be a mother or a father is a lifelong commitment. *What skills do you have that might make you a good parent?*

Discover International...
Languages

Words for "Mom"

What do you call your mother? Is it Mom, mommy, or mama? People who study linguistics know that there are many names for "mother" around the world, and it is interesting to see how much the names are alike. For example, *ma* and *mama* are used in parts of the Middle East and Latin America. In much of North America, she is *mom* or *mommy*. In some parts of the United Kingdom, children call their mothers *mum* or *mummy*, and in other parts she is called *mam* or *mammy*. She may be called *maman* in France, or *maadar* in the Farsi-speaking world.

linguistics |liŋ-ˌgwis-tiks| the study of human language, including the nature, structure, and modification of language. Linguists study the words, the sounds, and the written representations of languages around the world.

NCTE 9 Develop an understanding of diversity in language use across cultures.

Parents are primary caregivers. They are responsible for providing a safe, loving, and educational environment for their children. They must fulfill a child's physical needs as well as provide emotional support.

Many new parents are surprised to find how demanding parenthood can be in terms of time, energy, and money. Parents often have to make adjustments or give up their personal desires in order to provide for their children.

Parenthood can also bring many joys, however. The special relationship that develops between a parent and child is a fulfilling experience. All over the world parents claim that parenthood brings them happiness, love, and pride.

Photo Caption Answer Answers may include read books out loud to the child, play with puzzles and blocks, and let the child experiment with safe toys or other objects.

Intellectual Needs Interacting with children helps improve their intellectual skills. *What are some other ways you can meet a child's intellectual needs?*

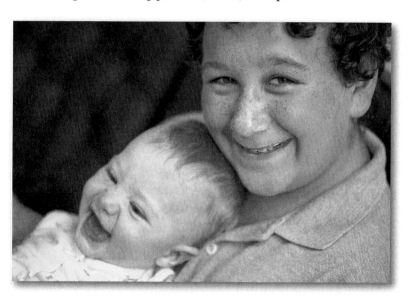

186 Unit 4 Children and Parenting

Children's Needs

Young children have physical, emotional, social, and intellectual needs that must be met. While you care for, play with, and teach children, it is up to you to fulfill these needs.

- **Physical Needs** All children have basic physical needs. They need healthful food, appropriate clothing, rest and sleep, and a safe environment. Infants express their needs by crying. Crying is their way of telling you they are hungry, wet, tired, frightened, ill, or unhappy. As children get older, they are better able to use words and sentences to express their needs.

- **Intellectual Needs** Children have intellectual needs, too. They need a stimulating, or interesting and exciting, environment and opportunities to explore. Read books out loud to children. Help a child play with puzzles and blocks. Offer toys or other safe objects, such as a wooden spoon and a plastic bowl, to experiment with. All of these activities can help children develop intellectual abilities.

- **Emotional and Social Needs** Children need to be held, cuddled, and comforted. Sometimes a kiss, a hug, or a gentle pat is all children need to be reassured that someone cares. Children are very sensitive to your feelings about them. Speak kindly to them. They can tell by the way you touch, hold, and talk to them that they are loved. In turn, children learn how to make friends, how to love, and how to interact with other people.

Character Counts

Resourcefulness

When Danielle and her husband wanted to see a play, they needed a babysitter for their 9-month-old daughter, Amanda. Danielle called her younger brother, Christopher, and he agreed to babysit. When he arrived, the baby was sleeping. When Amanda awoke from her nap after her parents left, she was screaming loudly. Christopher changed her diaper and wrapped her in a warm blanket. He warmed a bottle for her, but she refused to take it and continued to scream. The screaming started to bother Christopher. He did not want to call and interrupt his sister at the play, but he was getting frustrated.

You Make the Call

Christopher is tempted to just leave Amanda alone in her crib and shut the door, but he knows that would be wrong. Write a paragraph that explains what you think Christopher should do.

Character Counts Feature Answer Suggest that the baby may be too warm in the blanket; try burping her; hold her and walk around; rock her and sing to her; try to distract her with a toy or some music; call his own mom or dad for advice. If all else fails, he could call his sister.

Positive Communication

Children, like adults, respond better to positive statements than to negative ones. For example, say "Let's play outside for awhile," instead of "Do not play in the living room." Emphasize what the children are allowed to do rather than what they should not do. You may also need to explain why. "Try to climb on the jungle gym this way, so you will not fall and get hurt."

Praise is another way of focusing on the positive. You might say to a young child, "I think you did a terrific job finding all those marbles that spilled. You have really sharp eyes."

Encourage Independence

Children want to become independent and be able to perform tasks by themselves. As children try to do new tasks on their own, they will make mistakes and make messes. Be patient with children. It takes practice to learn skills such as using a fork, brushing teeth, or tying a shoe. Just like you, they learn from their mistakes.

As children perform more tasks for themselves, they learn to be more independent. Encourage independence:

- A step stool by the sink lets children wash their hands by themselves.
- Child-size toothbrushes, combs, and towels help children learn to groom and clean themselves.
- If children make mistakes, encourage them to keep trying. Praise their efforts, even when the results are not perfect.
- Allow children to decide which story to read or what game to play to make them feel important.

Provide Guidance

Children need guidance to learn appropriate behavior. **Guidance** is the direction caregivers need to give children so they can learn basic rules for behavior. These rules help children stay safe, learn self-control, and learn to get along with others. Guidance can be direct, such as when you remind a child to put her shoes away, or when you make sure she does not touch the hot stove. Guidance can also be indirect. You can show children the proper ways to behave when you set good examples, such as practicing good habits and manners.

With effective guidance, children start to learn to control their emotions and reactions. Guidance gives children security and positive self-esteem. When children are very young, they only understand being praised or being scolded. As they grow older, the guidance from caregivers will help them learn the difference between right and wrong. Children will gradually learn how to act appropriately in new situations.

Quiet-Play Activities

In this activity you will create an activity box of quiet play activities that you can use with small children. Before you begin, read through the entire Hands-On Lab assignment. Write down any questions that you have about the assignment. Reread the text or ask your teacher for help if you need it.

Supplies
- ✓ Paper
- ✓ Child-safe scissors
- ✓ Nontoxic glue sticks
- ✓ Nontoxic crayons
- ✓ Old magazines
- ✓ Modeling clay
- ✓ Storybooks
- ✓ Music CDs
- ✓ Craft box or plastic tub

Develop Your Plan
■ Making up stories, reading books aloud, or listening to music are good activities for infants and toddlers. Drawing with crayons, painting, making collages, and playing with clay are quiet activities for preschoolers.

■ Fill a craft box or plastic tub with paper, children's safety scissors, nontoxic glue sticks, old magazines, crayons and markers, and modeling clay. Add your favorite children's books and CDs of children's music.

Implement Your Plan
■ Take your quiet-play activity box to a babysitting job. Choose one or more age-appropriate activities to use.

■ Watch how the child reacts to each quiet activity. Write down what you learn by watching the child's response to each activity.

■ Make a list of how the child used his or her senses during each activity.

Evaluate Your Results
List the ways that quiet activities differed from active play activities. What conclusions can you draw? What other activities could you add to your activity box? Write one or more paragraphs to explain your answers.

Projects and Activities Go to this book's Online Learning Center through glencoe.com for more projects and activities.

Evaluate Your Results Answer Students should describe how their activites worked with the children. They should discuss how the children responded to the quiet-play activities, make suggestions for other activities that might be appropriate, and the differences between active and quiet activities.

🛑 **Set an Example** You can guide children in the right direction by your own actions and behaviors. ***What can you do to set a good example?***

Community Resources
Public Libraries
Librarians in public
libraries may be able
to help you find online
resources. You may be
able to access these
resources at home or
use them in the library.

• • • • • • • • • • • • • •

Discipline (ˈdi-sə-ˈplən) is the task of teaching a child which behaviors are acceptable and which are not. It is important to be **consistent**, or react the same way to a situation each time it occurs. It also means that you follow through and do what you say you will do. For example, 4-year-old Kyle throws his stuffed bear at his sister. If you tell Kyle that you will take the bear away if he does it again, then you must follow through and take away the bear. If you do not follow through, Kyle will not take you seriously and the negative behavior will continue. When you are consistent, children know what to expect.

In addition to being consistent, avoid making false threats. For example, telling a child that you will leave him or her at home alone if he or she misbehaves is a false threat. You know that it would be unsafe to leave a child at home alone without supervision.

✔ **Reading Check** ***Explain*** *What are some ways to encourage children to be independent?*

Child Abuse and Neglect

Hundreds of thousands of children become the victims of child abuse and neglect each year. **Child abuse** means physical, emotional, or sexual injury to children. **Child neglect** is failure to meet a child's physical and emotional needs. People who leave young children alone or do not provide adequate food or medical attention are guilty of neglect. Many abused and neglected children are the victims of their own parents. Some children suffer from both abuse and neglect.

Abuse and neglect occur in families from all income levels and racial and ethnic groups. Many victims suffer silently. They may have been threatened by their abusers with harm if they tell someone. Victims often feel guilty, even though the abuse was not their fault. Unless help is found, abuse and neglect tend to occur again and again.

Causes of Abuse and Neglect

Why would someone injure a child? Emotional outbursts of anger and frustration are often the cause of child abuse. Adults who lose their tempers can inflict serious, life-threatening injuries on infants and children. The abuser may expect too much of a child. He or she may not be able to cope with personal problems. In some cases, substance abuse is also involved. In others cases, parents or caregivers may incorrectly think they are helping to teach the child right from wrong. Often times the abusers were abused or neglected as children. The emotional and physical damage that was done to them may cause them to do the same thing to their own children. It is never acceptable to hurt a child, no matter what the reason.

When a child does not receive basic food, clothing, shelter, or health care, he or she is the victim of neglect. Families under financial or emotional stress should seek help from agencies, friends, or extended family members.

Prevent Abuse and Neglect

Abuse is very serious. If you ever suspect a child has been abused or neglected, tell a trusted adult. You can even make an anonymous report to a child protective services agency. If you think a child is in immediate danger, call 9-1-1. State child protective agencies require a social caseworker to investigate each report. In addition, early childhood professionals, health care providers, and teachers are required by law to report child abuse and neglect.

Photo Caption Answer Answers may include shelters, the police, abuse hotlines, hospitals, children and family service organizations.

Victim Assistance There are many agencies that provide assistance to families and children in abusive situations. ***What resources are available in your area that might provide assistance to victims of abuse?***

To help prevent abuse, a child should never be left with someone who is not reliable. Relatives, neighbors, and friends can often provide help in times of need. Several helpful groups exist to provide parenting support, including parenting courses. Some communities even have crisis nurseries where parents can leave their children while they cool off. One self-help group found in many cities is Parents Anonymous. While the children are occupied with activities, parents support each other as they learn new parenting skills and attitudes.

Child abuse is illegal and should never be hidden. All types of abuse and neglect have lasting effects on children. The longer abuse continues, the more serious the problem becomes. There is no prescribed treatment for child abusers. Counseling and parenting courses can help abusers face their problems. However, a good support system is always necessary. You can get more information about child abuse and its prevention from groups such as the National Committee for the Prevention of Child Abuse. Lists of agencies, organizations, and laws that provide help for victims of child abuse and neglect in your area can be found in telephone directories and online.

Section 9.1 After You Read

Review What You Have Learned

1. **Explain** why it is important to be consistent in discipline.
2. **Summarize** the reasons for child abuse and child neglect.

Practice Academic Skills

 English Language Arts

3. Create an informational flyer that offers tips to new parents about how to create a loving environment for children. Be sure to include information about providing for basic needs, independence, guidance, discipline, and setting a good example.

> **NCTE 4** Use written language to communicate effectively.

 Social Studies

4. Abuse and neglect have long-term effects. Research the long-term mental effects of child abuse or neglect. Prepare a short presentation for your classmates on how being abused as a child can affect a person as an adult.

> **NCSS IV C** Examine factors that contribute to and damage one's mental health and analyze issues related to mental and behavioral disorders in contemporary society.

 Check Your Answers Check your answers at this book's Online Learning Center at glencoe.com.

Section 9.2 Child Development

Reading Guide

Before You Read

Be Organized A messy environment can be distracting. To lessen distractions, organize an area where you can read this section comfortably.

Read to Learn

Key Concepts

✓ **Name** the developmental stages between birth and 5 years.

✓ **Analyze** the importance of learning through play.

Main Idea

Children develop in stages and learn through play and interaction at every stage.

Content Vocabulary

○ developmental task ○ independent play
○ attention span   ○ cooperative play

Academic Vocabulary

■ sequence
■ coordination

Graphic Organizer

As you read, identify five milestones that usually occur during the preschool years of ages 3 to 5. Use a graphic organizer like the one shown to help you organize your information.

Milestones: The Preschool Years

 Graphic Organizer Go to this book's Online Learning Center at glencoe.com to print this graphic organizer.

Academic Standards

 English Language Arts

NCTE 4 Use written language to communicate effectively.

Science

NSES A Develop understandings about scientific inquiry.

Social Studies

NCSS IV D Individual Development and Identity Apply concepts, methods, and theories about the study of human growth and development, such as physical endowment, learning, motivation, behavior, perception, and personality.

NCTE *National Council of Teachers of English*
NCTM *National Council of Teachers of Mathematics*

NSES *National Science Education Standards*
NCSS *National Council for the Social Studies*

Graphic Organizer Answer Any five of the following: opens doors; dresses self; recognizes colors; rides a tricycle; repeats rhymes, songs; brushes teeth; speaks in sentences; begins cooperative play

As you grow, you change physically, emotionally, and mentally. These changes begin when you are born and continue through childhood. Much growth and development occurs during infancy, the toddler years, and the preschooler years. Play and positive interaction with parents and other caregivers are the major ways that children learn and develop during these rapidly changing years.

As You Read

Connect What did you learn from playing with toys when you were a young child?

As You Read Answer
Answers may include learning about sounds, colors, and shapes; learning the names of common objects and animals.

◆ Vocabulary

You can find definitions in the glossary at the back of this book.

Photo Caption Answer
Answers may include play, interaction, reading, take children to museums or parks, show affection.

Expectations for Children

There are general patterns to how children develop, but each child is unique and will develop in his or her own special way. It is important to treat each child as an individual. Even children who have the same parents experience different growth rates and patterns. After you spend time with children and get to know them, you will have an idea of what you can expect from each child.

The concept of developmental tasks is important to understand when caring for children. A **developmental task** is an achievement, such as walking or talking, that can be expected at specific ages and stages of growth.

The sequence, or order, of developmental tasks follows a pattern. For example, infants crawl before they walk. Some children achieve these milestones faster than others. Janie learned to walk by the age of 12 months, but Marta did not take her first step until 15 months.

Developmental tasks are useful for explaining what the typical child can do by certain ages. Toddlers babble sounds before they learn to say words. They say individual words before they speak in complete sentences. However, each child is a unique individual. Just as children do not grow at the same rate physically, they do not all perform developmental tasks at the same time.

Growth Milestones Children reach different milestones as they grow and develop. *What can you do to encourage development?*

Infants

Katrina, a newborn baby, eats every few hours. She sleeps 16 to 20 hours each day. As she gets older, she will stay awake longer and eat less often. In the first few months, her parents will develop a schedule so that Katrina can learn to have regular times for eating, bathing, sleeping, and playing.

Katrina will have many developmental tasks to learn, such as how to eat, sit alone, pick up objects, and crawl. She will learn how to play with toys and be comfortable with different people and places. Katrina will also need a great deal of love and attention. See **Figure 9.1** for a summary of developmental milestones that Katrina and all children will experience.

Infant Milestones (Birth to 1 year of age)

- Coos and laughs (Birth to 6 months)
- Grasps at rattle (2 months)
- Smiles (2 months)
- Puts objects in mouth (2 months)
- Rolls over (3 to 6 months)
- Sits up alone (4 to 6 months)
- Says single words (6 to 12 months)
- Crawls (7 to 9 months)
- Pulls self up (9 to 12 months)
- Plays peek-a-boo (10 to 12 months)

Toddlers

Toddlers are children who are one to three years old. The name comes from the unsteady way they walk, or toddle. Toddlers are usually full of energy and ideas. At birth, a child's brain is about 25 percent of its approximate adult weight. By age three, a child's brain has reached almost 90 percent of its size.

They are learning to be more independent by doing tasks for themselves and by being less dependent on the people who care for them. As a part of this new independence, they often use the word "no." Toddlers can come to the table for meals when called, eat food without being encouraged, and follow safety rules such as not touching something hot.

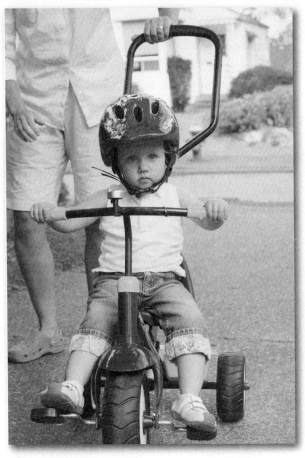

⬆ Everything Is New You have been looking at the world for a long time, but everything is brand new to infants and toddlers. *What are some important things to remember when caring for adventurous toddlers?*

Photo Caption
Answer Students should recognize that this the time when children want to do new things and be more independent. They need to be monitored very carefully so they do not get hurt or lost.

Figure 9.1 Child Development

Growing in Stages Children develop physically, intellectually, emotionally, socially, and morally. *Other than parents, who plays a role in the development of children?*

Physical Development During the first 12 months of life, a child puts on weight, grows longer, and gains the muscle control to hold her head up, sit up, and crawl.

Intellectual Development During the first few years of life, a child develops the ability to think, reason, and solve simple problems. She learns to recognize familiar faces and places, and she learns to talk.

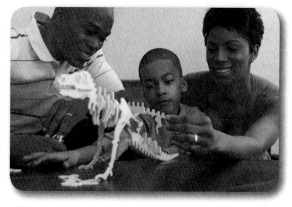

Social Development During the first weeks of life, a child has begun to learn how to relate to others. As a toddler, he learned to play with other children, make friends, and share toys.

Moral Development Parents teach their child a system of rules to guide his behavior. They teach him right from wrong, and they help him learn about the world around him.

Emotional Development As an infant, a child's needs were met as soon as she cried. A child learns to trust her caregivers, which is the first stage of emotional development.

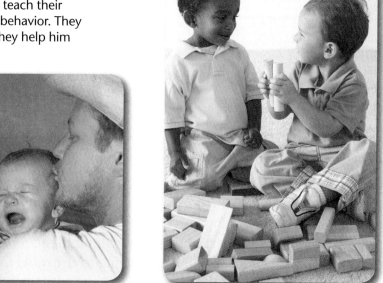

Figure Caption Answer Answers will vary, but may include grandparents, aunts, uncles, stepparents, siblings, teachers, babysitters.

Toddler Milestones (1 to 3 years of age)

- Walks
- Learns the meaning of "No"
- Follows simple instructions
- Feeds self with spoon
- Identifies pictures
- Climbs stairs
- Undresses self
- Plays beside others
- Puts words into sentences
- Begins toilet learning

Preschoolers

Preschoolers are children who are three to five years old. Preschoolers interact more with their playmates and like to play with children of all ages. They like to talk. Preschool children may carry on a conversation with make-believe playmates. They might imitate their heroes or pretend to be superhuman.

Preschooler Milestones (3 to 5 years of age)

- Opens doors
- Dresses self
- Recognizes colors
- Rides a tricycle
- Repeats rhymes and songs
- Brushes teeth
- Speaks in sentences
- Begins cooperative play

Children with Special Needs

Some children have special needs. Jake walks with a leg brace. Peter wears a hearing aid. Joanna has emotional problems. Each of these children has a particular special need, yet what they need most is to learn how to develop their abilities and enjoy life. For example, they need to learn to be as independent as possible, and they need encouragement to develop a positive self-concept. The attitudes of people around them are important in making this possible.

Special Needs Children with special needs learn from caregivers who encourage independence. *How can children with special needs benefit from being independent?*

Photo Caption Answer Like all children, those with special needs can develop a positive self-concept when encouraged to do things for themselves.

 Reading Check *Define* What is a developmental task?

Reading Check Answer A developmental task is an achievement that can be expected at specific ages and stages of growth.

COMMUNITY CONNECTIONS

Child Care There are many opportunities to help parents and children. Find out what organizations in your community could use help providing childcare. Volunteer to provide childcare for the organization during meetings or other events.

Age-Appropriate Toys

In this activity you will learn to choose age-appropriate toys. Before you begin, read through the entire Hands-On Lab assignment. Write down any questions that you have about the activity. Reread the text or ask your teacher for help if you need it.

Supplies
✓ Toy catalogs
✓ Computer with Internet access (optional)

Develop Your Plan

■ Look through toy catalogs or visit Web sites that sell toys, or go to a store with a large selection of toys.

■ Read the descriptions of several toys for different ages. If possible, visit an actual toy store so you can examine the toys.

■ Toy packages are labeled for the appropriate age, usually 0-6 months, 6-12 months, 1-3 years, and 3 years and up. Choose at least two toys from each age group.

■ For each toy, write what you think the child would learn. For example, does the toy teach about shapes and colors, or letters and numbers?

■ Note any dangers, such as choking hazards, that each toy might have if given to a child who is not the appropriate age.

Implement Your Plan

■ Choose a toy to give to a sibling, family friend, or neighbor's child, based on his or her age.

■ Watch how the child plays with the toy. Make a list of all the things he or she learns by using the toy.

■ Compare the list with the one you made while developing your plan, and see how many matches you have.

Evaluate Your Results

What types of toys do you think are the favorites among infants, toddlers, or preschoolers? What did you learn about choosing toys for children? Write one or more paragraphs to explain your answer.

Projects and Activities Go to this book's Online Learning Center at glencoe.com for more projects and activities.

Evaluate Your Results Answer Answers will vary. Sample answer: infants would enjoy anything that they can put in their mouths; toddlers would enjoy toys that make noise; preschoolers would like hands-on activities. Students should learn that safety and age-appropriateness are the determining factors in toy selection.

How Children Learn

Young children learn from exploring their environment through the fives senses of sight, sound, taste, touch, and smell. Children learn something from everyone and everything around them, including toys. Their first toys help develop their **coordination**, or movement. Other toys help children learn shapes, colors, letters, and numbers. As children grow, activities and toys can help them improve their intellectual abilities.

Young children also learn when they practice tasks over and over again. They learn when they observe and imitate others, and explore their environment. Everywhere a child is taken is a learning opportunity. Whether it is an aquarium, zoo, museum, garden, the neighbor's house, or a music festival, all of the senses are affected.

Learning Through Play

Although every child is unique, most children go through a similar pattern of growth and development. As an older brother or sister, or as a babysitter, you can help children learn and discover new things by interacting with them. Show children that you are interested in them and that what they say and do matters to you. Children at every stage of development can benefit from playing with parents, caregivers, siblings, and other children. Playtime helps them develop motor skills, which is the development of their muscles, as well as their emotional, social, and intellectual skills.

The Five Senses Young children learn by using all five senses. *How can you provide hands-on learning experiences?*

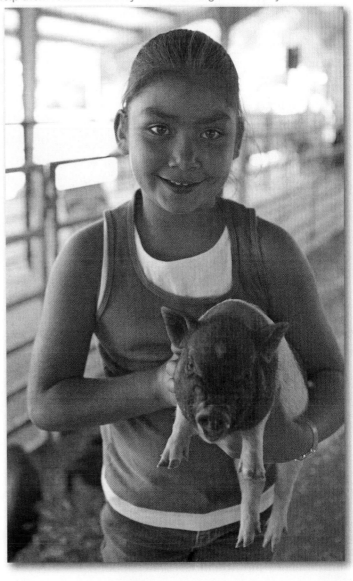

Community Resources
Summer Programs
Some schools and communities offer summer programs that help students improve their academic skills. Check your local newspaper or school bulletin board, or go online to find out what services are available in your area.

Succeed in School Research summer programs in your area and share the information with your students. If your area does not have such programs, offer suggestions to help them retain what they learned during the school year.

Observe Child Behavior

To complete a scientific investigation or experiment, you collect data. Scientists collect data as numbers and descriptions, and then organize the data in different ways. Use your science skills to research the way different children react to the same activity.

Procedure Go to a park or children's play area to observe children at play. Select three individual children of the same age to observe. Record your observations in a chart like the one below. Examples are filled in for you.

Activity	Child 1	Child 2	Child 3
Slide	afraid to use it	used slide over and over	got to the top and changed her mind
Sandbox	played with pail and shovel	not interested	only wanted to use it when he was alone

Analysis What patterns do you notice in the data? What conclusions can you draw about the way children play?

> **NSES A** Develop understandings about scientific inquiry.

Infant Playtime

Four-month-old Nicholas is happy waving his arms and kicking his legs. He likes when someone plays with him. He enjoys being moved from place to place so he can look at new sights. A walk outside or to the grocery store is very interesting to him. Nicholas does not stay with one toy for very long. He, like other infants, has a short **attention span**. This means that toys and other objects hold his interest for only a short amount of time.

When infants discover their hands and can hold a toy, play becomes more important to them. They gradually learn to pick up a toy and hold it. It is natural for infants to play happily, first picking up one toy, then another. Playing with toys is one way babies learn about the world around them.

Infants who play alone and show little interest in interacting with other children are engaging in **independent play**. Infants play with their hands, toes, toys, or other objects. Toys that are easy to pick up and hold with tiny fingers are best for first toys. Infants like toys that are pleasant to touch, see, and chew on. Musical toys, squeeze toys, and stacking and nesting blocks are good toys for infants. Even small kitchen items, such as plastic measuring cups and spoons, or pots and pans, can be entertaining toys.

Toddler Playtime

Toddlers need to play to develop their minds, bodies, and social skills. Toddlers are curious about everything and spend much of their time exploring. They pull out various toys, look them over, and go on to something else. Most toddlers play alone or watch others play. They engage in parallel play, which is play that occurs next to another child instead of with another child. They are just beginning to learn to share toys with others.

Toddlers need toys for both active and quiet play. Their toys should help them develop socially and physically. The toys you choose for toddlers should also help them think and use their imagination. Toddlers like toys that move.

However, save the jack-in-the-box for older children. Toys with too much noise or movement can frighten a toddler. Riding toys and balls help toddlers develop skill and coordination. Toy cars, bulldozers, and airplanes stimulate their imagination.

Preschooler Playtime

Preschoolers play together with one or two other children and share toys. This is called **cooperative play**. As they get older, they enjoy playing with other children, especially those their own age. The benefits of playtime for preschoolers include learning how to take turns, share with others, and get along with a group. These skills will become more important and necessary as children get older.

As children develop, their interests slowly start to change. New toys help keep pace with their natural development. Preschoolers are increasing their motor skills and using their imaginations. Preschoolers enjoy action toys that encourage physical exercise, such as tricycles and climbing equipment. Toys for pretend play include briefcases, dress-up clothes, and nontoxic art materials.

Section 9.2 After You Read

Review What You Have Learned

1. **Explain** why children from the same family have different growth and development patterns.
2. **Describe** ways that children learn.

Practice Academic Skills

English Language Arts

3. Write a one-page "How To" guide for playing and interacting with infants. Include information about activities or toys that support and encourage infant development. Use illustrations to make your guide more interesting.

> **NCTE 4** Use written language to communicate effectively.

Social Studies

4. Abraham Maslow developed a list of the basic human needs (see Chapter 1, page 14). Review Maslow's list of five human needs. Explain how these needs relate to child development. Summarize your findings in a one-page report.

> **NCSS IV D** Apply concepts, methods, and theories about the study of human growth and development, such as physical endowment, learning, motivation, behavior, perception, and personality..

Check Your Answers Check your answers at this book's Online Learning Center at glencoe.com.

Discovering Careers

Focus on Careers in Child Protection and Development ▼

Do you enjoy being around young children? Do you enjoy doing things to help children? If you answered yes to either of those questions, you might want to consider a future career in child protection and development. The following chart explores several careers in the field of child protection and development.

Career Activities ▼

At School

 1 Select three of the careers listed. Research the education, training, and work experience required for each career. Write a summary of your results.

At Home

2 Work with your parents to put together a list of toys you played with as an infant, toddler, and preschooler.

At Work

3 Make a list of subject areas you would need to study in school in order to find a job in the field of child development.

In the Community

4 Contact and interview someone in your community who works in the field of child protection and development. Ask this person to describe what his or her typical work day is like. Share what you learned with your class.

Career Investigations Go to this book's Online Learning Center for activities and worksheets to help you explore careers.

Job Title	Job Description
School Nurse	Provides health care services to students. Plans school health program. Evaluates health of students and establishes policies for health emergencies.
Pediatrician	Plans medical care program for children. Examines patients to determine presence of disease and to establish preventive health. Prescribes medicine.
Clinical Social Worker	Provides mental health services and counseling to children and families in crisis. May work in hospitals, child welfare agencies, schools, or community organizations.
Child Advocate	Works to represent the best interests of neglected, abused, or abandoned children. Provides suggestions in court cases for resolutions that benefit children in custody battles.
Preschool Teacher	Plans age-appropriate curriculum and activities. Interacts positively with children. Provides safe environment for children to learn and develop.

Career Activities Answers for these activities can be found on page TM114.

Chapter Summary

Section 9.1 Responsible Parenting
Parenting is the process of caring for children and helping them to grow and learn. Effective parents must provide love, patience, guidance, and financial resources. Children want to become independent and be able to perform tasks by themselves. Caregivers need to give children guidance, or direction. That is how children learn basic rules for behavior.

Section 9.2 Child Development
Developmental tasks are achievements, such as walking and talking that can be expected at various ages and stages of growth. Developmental tasks are useful for explaining what the typical child can do by certain ages. It is important to treat each child as an individual. Young children learn from exploring their environment. Children learn something from everyone and everything around them.

Words You Learned

1. Use each of these content vocabulary words and academic vocabulary words in a sentence.

Content Vocabulary
- parenting (p. 185)
- guidance (p. 188)
- discipline (p. 190)
- child abuse (p. 190)
- child neglect (p. 190)
- developmental task (p. 194)
- attention span (p. 200)
- independent play (p. 200)
- cooperative play (p. 201)

Academic Vocabulary
- commitment (p. 185)
- consistent (p. 190)
- sequence (p. 194)
- coordination (p. 199)

Review Key Concepts

2. **Recognize** that parenting is a lifelong commitment to help children grow and learn.

3. **Explain** the causes of child abuse and neglect how it can be prevented.

4. **Name** the developmental stages between birth and 5 years.

5. **Analyze** the importance of learning through play.

Critical Thinking

6. **Predict** how parents can raise children to feel good about themselves without making their children self-centered.

7. **Evaluate** how a family who eats meals together can help encourage the physical, intellectual, social, and emotional growth of the child or children in the family.

8. **Analyze** the ways empty threats can result in developmental problems.

9. **Compare and contrast** independent play and cooperative play.

Real-World Skills and Applications

Problem-Solving

10. Communication Skills Dan thinks his wife, Kelly, is too strict with their daughter, Teri. Dan puts up with some of Teri's behaviors that Kelly will not accept. Dan rarely disciplines or punishes Teri. Kelly thinks Dan is making her look like a mean parent. What should Dan and Kelly do? Create a list of suggestions.

Interpersonal and Collaborative

11. Family Dinner Follow your teacher's directions to form groups. In groups, create an imaginary scene in which several children have dinner with their parents, siblings, and extended family members. Demonstrate ways for family members interact positively with the children. When your group is finished, ask others to explain what was successful about the dinner, and what could be improved.

Financial Literacy

12. Planning for College Paying for a private college can be expensive. Most experts predict that college tuition will increase by 7% a year for the foreseeable future. A child born today would head off to college in about 18 years. If tuition continues to rise at the same rate until then, tuition will cost about 340% more in 18 years than it does today. Research the current annual tuition costs of three different types of schools near you: a four-year private university, a four-year public school, and a two-year public school. How much will it cost to send a child to each of those schools in 18 years? Remember to multiply the annual cost by 4 for the four-year schools and by 2 for the two-year schools.

13. Sensory Learning Create musical shakers for children. You will need two sturdy paper plates to make each shaker. Use colored markers to decorate the backside of each paper plate. Fill one plate with dried beans or rice. Use masking tape to attach the two plates together so the food is completely sealed between the two plates. If possible, give your shaker to a child and encourage him or her to use it to keep pace with their favorite music.

14. Kid Show Analysis Watch two different television programs made for young children. What do the programs teach? How does the program deliver its message? Would you want your child to watch these shows? Why or why not? Write an analysis of each program to explain your answers.

15. Research Toys Choose one development stage to focus on: infant, toddler, or preschool. Then, with permission from your teacher or parents, go online to research a variety of children's toys and games. Put together a list of the ten best educational toys and games for the age group you chose. Write a short description of each toy or game. Describe why it is good for learning. Include the list and descriptions in your Life Skills Binder.

Academic Skills

 English Language Arts

16. Interpret Read an article in a parenting magazine about a problem or challenge in raising children. Summarize the problem or challenge in your own words. What advice does the article recommend? Do you think the advice is realistic? Ask your own parents or guardians what they think about the article. Write one or more paragraphs to explain your answers.

> **NCTE 3** Apply strategies to interpret texts.

 Science

17. Video Games Learn about the effects of video game playing on early childhood development.
Procedure Research what can happen to children who spend too much time playing video games.
Analysis Write a paragraph to summarize the results of your research. Using this information, decide how much time you think is acceptable for a child to play video games. How do video games compare with active play?

> **NSES F** Develop an understanding of personal and community health.

Mathematics

18. Make Estimates Rosalind has just given birth to a son, Peter, who weighs 6 pounds, 14 ounces. On average, babies weigh twice their birth weight at 5 months, triple their birth weight at 12 months, and quadruple their birth weight at 2 years. Estimate how much Peter will weigh at 5 months, 12 months, and 2 years.

Math Concept **Using Compatible Numbers** When asked to make an estimate, you can perform calculations quickly without using a calculator by replacing any decimals, fractions, or other difficult numbers with their closest compatible numbers. The compatible number should be easy to work with in your head.

Starting Hint Since Peter's birth weight of 6 pounds, 14 ounces is close to 7 pounds, use 7 pounds as the compatible number. Calculate 7×2, 7×3, and 7×4 to estimate his weight for the different time periods.

> **NCTM Number and Operations** Compute fluently and make reasonable estimates.

Standardized Test Practice ● ● ● ● ● ● ● ● ●

True/False

Read each of the statements and determine whether they are true or false.

> **Test-Taking Tip** In a true/false test, be sure to budget your time. Go through the questions and statements. Answer the ones you know first. As time allows, reread the ones you are unsure of and try to answer them. Many times your first guess is the correct answer.

19. Parenting ends when children turn 18.
20. Learning about children before becoming a parent does not help when you have your own children.
21. Most preschoolers are ready to use tricycles and climbing equipment.

Chapter 10

Child Care Basics

Section 10.1

Child Safety

■ **Main Idea** Keep children safe by childproofing, preventing accidents, and always being aware of where children are.

Section 10.2

Babysitting

■ **Main Idea** Caring for children is a serious and important job. Good babysitters are responsible, reliable, and help children grow and learn.

Explore the Photo
Answer Babysit, take child development or parenting classes, take care of younger siblings.

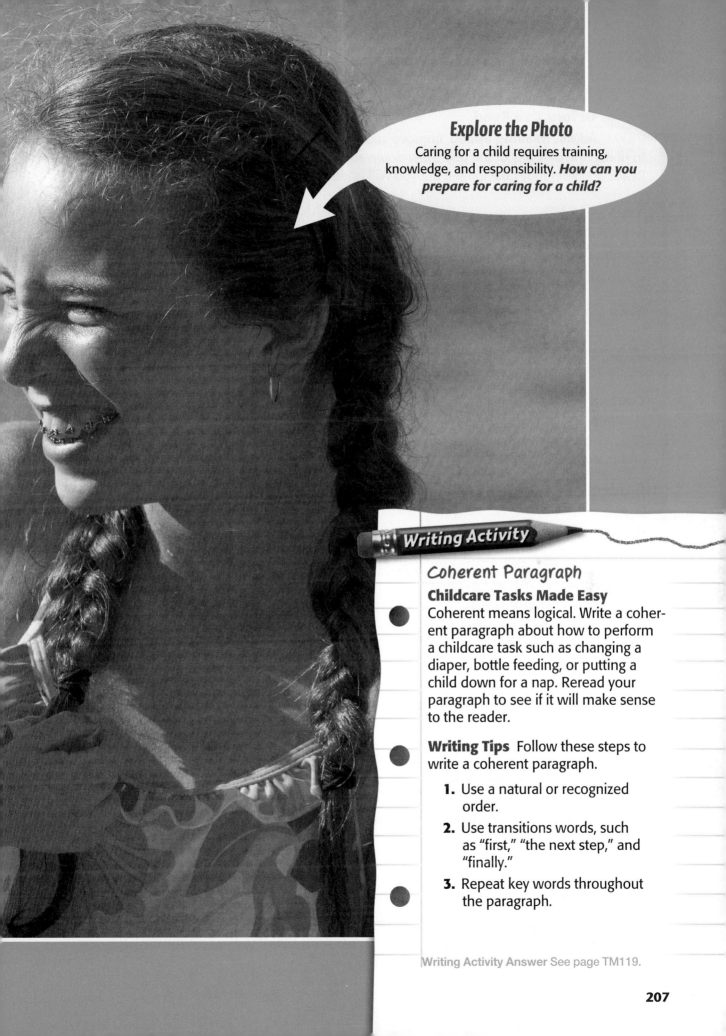

Explore the Photo
Caring for a child requires training, knowledge, and responsibility. *How can you prepare for caring for a child?*

Writing Activity

Coherent Paragraph

Childcare Tasks Made Easy
Coherent means logical. Write a coherent paragraph about how to perform a childcare task such as changing a diaper, bottle feeding, or putting a child down for a nap. Reread your paragraph to see if it will make sense to the reader.

Writing Tips Follow these steps to write a coherent paragraph.

1. Use a natural or recognized order.
2. Use transitions words, such as "first," "the next step," and "finally."
3. Repeat key words throughout the paragraph.

Writing Activity Answer See page TM119.

Section 10.1 Child Safety

Read to Learn

Key Concepts

✓ **Identify** ways to childproof a home.

✓ **Explain** the purpose of learning first aid.

Main Idea

Keep children safe by childproofing, preventing accidents, and always being aware of where children are.

Content Vocabulary

○ childproof
○ monitor
○ intruder

Academic Vocabulary

■ precaution
■ restrict

Graphic Organizer

As you read, identify what you know, what you want to learn, what you learned, and how you can learn more about keeping children safe. Use a graphic organizer like the one shown to help you organize your information.

What I Know	What I Want to Learn	What I Learned	How I Can Learn More

 Graphic Organizer Go to this book's Online Learning Center at glencoe.com to print this graphic organizer.

Academic Standards

 English Language Arts

NCTE 8 Use information resources to gather information and create and communicate knowledge.

 Science

NSES F Develop understanding of personal and community health; natural resources; environmental quality.

Social Studies

NCSS I A Culture Analyze and explain the ways groups, societies, and cultures address human needs and concerns.

NCTE *National Council of Teachers of English*
NCTM *National Council of Teachers of Mathematics*

NSES *National Science Education Standards*
NCSS *National Council for the Social Studies*

Graphic Organizer Answer
Answers will vary depending on students' current knowledge and experience with caring for children.

Caring for children is a big responsibility. The more often you care for children, the more you learn about protecting them and caring for their basic needs. Training and taking safety measures can prepare you to care for children in a variety of situations.

Keep Children Safe

Safety should be a top priority for every person who cares for a child. Accidents and injuries can have tragic results. However, most can be avoided by paying attention and by taking some simple steps to avoid common hazards. Young children do not understand the dangers that surround them. In their eagerness to explore, they can easily hurt themselves by playing with a dangerous object or substance. Families with a child or children need to make their homes childproof. A **childproof** home is a safe environment where children can play and explore. A good way to identify hazards is to explore on your hands and knees. At that level, which is the level of a young child, it is easier to see potential dangers that you might not spot otherwise. **Figure 10.1** lists some **precautions**, or safety measures, caregivers can take to help keep children from getting hurt.

Even if a home has been childproofed, you still need to watch children carefully to make sure that they are safe. Infants will put just about anything in their mouths. It is extremely important that you make sure anything small enough to be swallowed is kept out of reach. If an object can fit in or through a roll that holds paper towels, it is too small for children under four years old.

 As You Read

Connect What can you do in your home to keep visiting children safe?

As You Read Answer
Keep children in view at all times; only let them play in a safe room away from stairs or exits; make sure they do not put anything in their mouths; keep pets away from children.

▷ Vocabulary

You can find definitions in the glossary at the back of this book.

Figure 10.1 Childproofing

Eager to Explore Babies and young children love to explore, which very often includes putting things in their mouths and grasping anything that might look interesting. *What dangers are in your home that would need to be fixed to keep a child safe?*

- Put safety latches on cabinet doors and drawers.
- Use safety gates at the top and bottom of stairs.
- Put safety covers on electrical outlets.
- Move cleaning supplies and other dangerous items out of children's reach.
- Remove poisonous plants.
- Check all toys to be sure they are nontoxic and do not have any small or broken parts.

Figure Caption Answer
Answers may include exposed outlets and electrical cords, furniture edges, household chemicals, small or breakable items within a child's reach, stairways.

Succeed in School
Remind students to ask their families to help them to avoid distractions.

SUCCEED IN SCHOOL!

Study Skills
Avoid Distractions
Study in a quiet place. Turn off the television. If you have a cell phone, let voicemail answer your calls until you are done studying.

• • • • • • • • • • • •

Safety Check

Phone Safety

When you babysit in a home, you may be responsible for answering the telephone. Since you do not know who may be calling, it is important to follow some guidelines for talking with a stranger while babysitting:

• Never tell a caller that you are the babysitter and alone with children.

• Tell the caller that the parents are not available rather than they are not home.

• If you sense trouble, hang up and call a trusted adult for help.

It is very important to monitor young children at all times. **Monitor** means to watch carefully over someone or something. You may be surprised by how quickly toddlers can get themselves into new and sometimes dangerous situations. Toddlers are adventurous. They do not know yet what it means to be careful. It is up to caregivers to keep busy toddlers out of danger. Preschoolers are just starting to learn what it means to be careful. However, they are just as likely as toddlers to get into dangerous situations. Preschoolers need constant reminders to be careful.

Intruders

Keeping children safe involves more than childproofing the child's living areas. It also means protecting children, and yourself, from intruders. An **intruder** is someone who uses force to get into a home. Caregivers need to take the following precautions:

• Make sure that all doors and windows are locked.
• Do not open the door for strangers.
• Do not let callers know that you are alone with the children.
• Call a neighbor, another trusted adult, or dial 9-1-1 if a stranger does not go away.

Reading Check **Predict** *Why is it necessary to watch infants and children who are in childproof areas?*

Safe Toys Infants explore by putting things in their mouths. *How can you help keep an infant from choking?*

Prevent Accidents

When caring for young children, you need to take precautions to prevent accidents. Some common accidents are falls, injuries, fires, and poisoning. It is a very good idea to take a first-aid course. Some parents will only hire caregivers and babysitters who know basic first aid. Small cuts, scrapes, contact with common poisonous plants, and nosebleeds are minor injuries that can be treated with first aid.

If a child gets hurt and requires emergency care, stay calm and call for help. A broken bone, serious bleeding, and burns require emergency care. Insect stings and animal bites can be very dangerous, too. Call the child's parents, a neighbor, or dial 9-1-1 for help.

Falls and Injuries

Falls are the leading cause of accidental deaths in the home in the United States. When caring for children, follow these guidelines to help prevent falls and other common injuries:

- Never leave an infant alone on a changing table, sofa, or bed. The infant may roll over and fall off.
- Make sure all stairways are blocked with safety gates.
- **Restrict**, or limit, crawling infants and toddlers only to places they can explore safely.
- Never leave a child alone in or near a bathtub or pool.
- Keep children away from electrical wires and outlets.
- Remove all breakable or dangerous objects.
- Make sure that toys are age-appropriate and free of loose parts.
- Do not allow plastic bags near children. Plastic bags can cover their mouths or noses and lead to suffocation.
- Keep knives and other sharp objects away from children.
- Always watch children to keep them from running into the street.
- Children should always ride in a properly installed child car seat.
- Never leave children alone in a car or a home.

SCIENCE YOU CAN USE

Disposable vs. Cloth Diapers

Though most parents use disposable diapers for infants, there is also the option of using cloth diapers. Compare the environmental effects of disposable diapers versus cloth diapers and laundering them.

Procedure Interview parents and conduct research to find out how many diapers an infant goes through in his or her first year of life.

Analysis Use this information to determine the environmental effects of both disposable and cloth diapers. Which choice has the least impact on our environment?

NSES F Develop understanding of personal and community health; natural resources; environmental quality.

Science You Can Use **Answer** Many experts agree that there is no difference in the environmental impact of disposable versus cloth diapers because of the laundering of cloth diapers and the resources needed. Students may find varying studies and should be able to cite their sources.

Learn First Aid Basic first aid is a must for caregivers. *What are some minor injuries that do not require emergency care?*

Photo Caption Answer Small cuts, scrapes, contact with common poisonous plants, and nosebleeds.

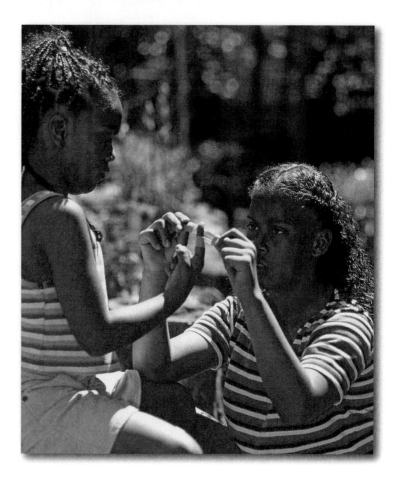

Fires

Fires are the second leading cause of accidental death in the United States. Follow these guidelines to help prevent fires in the home:

- Be sure that there are smoke alarms on every floor of the home.
- Keep all matches and lighters away from children.
- When cooking, avoid wearing clothing with long, full sleeves.
- Turn pot and pan handles away from the edge of the stove, and keep the oven door closed.
- Never allow a child to be alone in the cooking area.

If you smell smoke or see a fire while you are caring for children, get the children out safely first. Then call the fire department (9-1-1) after you are safely away from the fire. Use a cell phone if you have one. If not, ask a neighbor to call. Do not try to put out the fire yourself.

Try not to panic if you are trapped by smoke or fire. Stay close to the floor. If you can, put a wet cloth over your nose and mouth and crawl to safety. If you cannot get out, close the door to the room and stuff wet towels around the cracks in the door. Call for help immediately.

Safety Check

House Fires

According to the National Fire Protection Association (NFPA), it takes less than five minutes for a fire to spread through a house. Follow these tips when you are babysitting:

- Ask the parents for their emergency evacuation plan.
- Be aware of stoves and ovens if you cook while babysitting.
- Supervise children's activities at all times.

Poisonings

Common sense is the best way to keep children away from dangerous household substances. All poisonous items should be kept in locked cabinets. If that is not possible, keep the items on a high shelf, out of the reach of children.

The first step to take if you suspect a child has been poisoned is to call 9-1-1 or the poison control center. Get this number before you start any babysitting job, and keep it near the phone. You can find the number of the nearest poison control center in the telephone book or by calling directory assistance.

Dangerous Products Many common household items are dangerous and even deadly. Keep them out of a child's reach. *What can you do to help prevent poisoning while you are babysitting?*

Photo Caption Answer Make sure all household chemicals and cleaners are in locked rooms or cabinets, or out of the reach of children. Supervise at all times.

Section 10.1 After You Read

Review What You Have Learned
1. **Explain** what precautions a caregiver can take to protect against an intruder.
2. **Name** the two leading causes of accidental deaths in the United States.

Practice Academic Skills

 English Language Arts

3. Write a guide to parents-to-be or new parents to explain how they can childproof their home for an infant. Conduct research to find out what equipment or supplies they might need. You may want to ask your own parents for ideas. If possible, illustrate your guide with graphics or drawings.

> **NCTE 8** Use information resources to gather information and create and communicate knowledge.

Social Studies

4. Interview a person who was raised in a culture different from yours. Name and describe three values about children in his or her culture. Explain how these values affect childcare. Present your findings to the class in an oral report.

> **NCSS I A** Analyze and explain the ways groups, societies, and cultures address human needs and concerns.

Check Your Answers Check your answers at this book's Online Learning Center at glencoe.com.

Reading Guide

Before You Read

Stay Engaged One way to stay engaged when reading is to turn each of the headings into a question, then read the section to find the answers.

Read to Learn
Key Concepts

✓ **List** the information you should find out before accepting a babysitting job.

✓ **Name** four needs that require attention when caring for infants.

✓ **Describe** how to distract a toddler after his or her parents leave.

✓ **Plan** what you should have when caring for preschoolers.

Main Idea

Caring for children is a serious and important job. Good babysitters are responsible, reliable, and help children grow and learn.

Content Vocabulary

○ reliable
○ redirect

Academic Vocabulary

■ appreciate
■ imitate

Graphic Organizer

As you read, identify five ways you can show that you are a reliable babysitter. Use a graphic organizer like the one shown to help you organize your information. The first one is filled in for you.

How I Can Show That I Am Reliable
1. Keep a constant, careful eye on the children.
2.
3.
4.
5.

 Graphic Organizer Go to this book's Online Learning Center at glencoe.com to print this graphic organizer.

Academic Standards

 English Language Arts

NCTE 4 Use written language to communicate effectively.

 Mathematics

NCTM Problem Solving Solve problems that arise in mathematics and other contexts.

Social Studies

NCSS V B Analyze group and institutional influences on people, events, and elements of culture in both historical and contemporary settings.

NCTE *National Council of Teachers of English*
NCTM *National Council of Teachers of Mathematics*

NSES *National Science Education Standards*
NCSS *National Council for the Social Studies*

Graphic Organizer Answer
Ask questions to show I am serious about the job. Leave the home as neat as I found it. Do not allow my friends to visit. Do not open the door for strangers.

Babysitting is often the easiest kind of job for young people to find. It provides good experience. It gives teens an opportunity to interact with children. It also gives teens a chance to learn about responsibility and discipline. The best babysitter is a person parents can rely on to care about their children.

Babysitting Responsibilities

When you babysit, you are totally responsible for the safety and well-being of the children in your care. If you do your job well, you will gain valuable experience and earn money. You will also have an opportunity to play with children and teach them new things.

Before you begin looking for a babysitting job, you should take a course in first aid through a local hospital, a community center, or the American Red Cross. You could also volunteer as a parent's helper. This is someone who cares for an infant or a young child under a parent's supervision. Parents looking for babysitters will **appreciate**, or be thankful for, someone who has taken steps to prepare for the serious job of babysitter.

When parents ask you to babysit, find out the following information before you accept the job:

- the number of children and their ages
- the time you should arrive
- how long the parents plan to be gone
- the rate of pay you will receive

If everything about the job sounds good to you, check with your parents to make sure that the job meets with their approval. After you accept the job, write down the date, time, and place. Give your parents the telephone number at the home where you will be babysitting. If possible, you should also give your parents the cell phone numbers of the parents for whom you are babysitting.

 As You Read

Connect Think about your favorite babysitter. Why was he or she your favorite?

As You Read Answer Answers will vary but may include that the sitter was fun, caring, liked to play, took good care of children.

Succeed in School Tell students that even though it can be tempting to do homework in bed, it can lead to irreglar sleep patterns, which have been linked to academic and behavioral problems.

Study Skills

Be Comfortable Find a good table and chair or desk for studying. If you are comfortable, you are more likely to focus and study longer.

• • • • • • • • • • • • •

Photo Caption Answer You can practice your skills while the parents supervise. They can help you learn, and if you make mistakes they can teach you the correct things to do. You can gain experience without full responsibility for children until you are ready.

Parent's Helper Volunteer to be a parent's helper to gain childcare experience. *How can this prepare you for babysitting jobs?*

Babysitting Resource Binder

In this activity you will create a resource binder for babysitting. Before you begin, read through the entire Hands-On Lab assignment. Write down any questions that you have about the activity. Reread the text or ask your teacher for help if you need it.

Supplies
✓ 3-ring binder
✓ 3 section dividers
✓ Paper and pens

Develop Your Plan

■ Divide your binder into three sections: Families, Emergencies, and Entertainment.

■ Gather information on burns, CPR, choking, poisons, drowning, insect bites, and other injuries.

■ Gather meal and entertainment ideas.

Implement Your Plan

■ In the Families section, write down the names of all the adults for whom you babysit. Include addresses, home, work, and cell phone numbers, e-mail addresses, and children's names.

■ In the Emergencies section, write down telephone numbers for the local fire, police, and rescue units, poison control center, and local hospitals. Include the name and number of each child's doctor.

■ In the Entertainment section, write your ideas for games, toys, and activities. You may also want to include fun meal ideas, such as pancakes with faces made of fruit and yogurt.

■ Take your binder with you on each babysitting job and use it as a reference.

Evaluate Your Results

What other information could you add to your binder? How can having the information in the binder help you on babysitting jobs? Write one or more paragraphs to explain your answer.

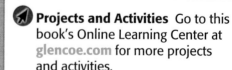

Projects and Activities Go to this book's Online Learning Center at **glencoe.com** for more projects and activities.

Evaluate Your Results Answer Answers will vary. Other information for the binder could include a section for additional notes, and any special instructions for each child, such as allergies, bedtimes, television guidelines, and approved snacks. Having the information can help you feel prepared and confident.

Babysitting Job Tips

The first time you babysit for a family, ask the parents if you can arrive a little early. That way, you have a chance to get to know the children while the parents are still at home. It is a good idea to ask the parents to go over a few of the family rules in front of the children. Be sure to ask about:

- television viewing
- homework
- telephone use
- visits from friends
- snacks
- bedtime

Discuss any rules or limits that might cause problems later. Meet the family pets. Find out if the family has a swimming pool. Take a walk through the house with the parents to become familiar with the layout and emergency exits. Find out if there are any rooms that the children should not enter, such as a room that has not been childproofed.

If you are friendly and caring with children, it can help them feel comfortable with you in charge. Show the children that you enjoy being with them. Let them know you are interested in what they want to do or say. Try to get them involved in something enjoyable so they stay happy and busy. Take time to put the children you are babysitting at ease. **Figure 10.2** on page 218 lists some suggestions you can follow to help children feel comfortable with you.

If the children are comfortable with you, the parents will seek you out again. **Reliable** babysitters can be counted on. Parents need babysitters they can trust with the safety and care of their children. Reliable, trustworthy babysitters are likely to be asked to babysit in the future. They establish good relationships with the parents and children. Parents who are happy with your work may recommend you to their friends who have young children. To show that you are a reliable babysitter:

- Keep a constant, careful eye on the children.
- Ask questions to show you are serious about the job.
- Leave the home as neat as you found it.

Financial Literacy

Babysitting Income

Miya currently makes $7.00 per hour working as a babysitter for her neighbors. She is trying to work extra hours during the summer to save money for school expenses. The family gave her two options. The first option is for her to babysit for 20 hours a week with a 15% raise beginning immediately. The second option is for her to receive a $200 cash bonus at the end of the summer. If the summer is ten weeks long, which option will provide Miya with more pay?

Math Concept **Percent Increase** When a number is increased by a certain percentage, you can determine the amount of increase by multiplying the percent times the original number. Add this amount of increase to the original number to find the new increased number.

Starting Hint Determine Miya's pay rate if she takes the raise by multiplying $7.00 by 0.15, and then adding that amount to $7.00. Multiply this new pay rate by the number of hours per week (20) and by the number of weeks (10) to find her total pay for the summer. For the bonus option, you will need to use her current pay rate ($7.00) and multiply $7.00 × 20 × 10. Add the bonus amount to that total to find her total pay for the summer.

 For math help, go to the Math Appendix at the back of the book.

NCTM Problem Solving Solve problems that arise in mathematics and other contexts.

Financial Literacy Answer
If Miya accepts the raise, she'll make $8.05 per hour, and $8.05 x 20 x 10 = $1,610 over the entire summer. If Miya accepts the bonus, she'll make $7.00 x 20 x 10 = $1,400 + $200 = $1,600 over the entire summer. She should take the raise.

Figure 10.2 Help Children Feel at Ease

Join in the Fun Like you, children are more comfortable when the people around them are enjoying themselves. *What can you do to show a child that you are ready to play?*

- When talking children, sit or kneel so that you are at eye level.
- Ask children how you can join in their play. For example, "Those farm animals look like fun! Can I help you feed the cows?"
- Smile and speak kindly.
- Some children do not like people outside of their family to give them hugs and kisses. Let the child decide if and when affection is appropriate.
- Be patient. Listen to what they say without correcting them or trying to finish their sentences.

Figure Caption Answer Answers may include offering to play games, join in the child's play, find toys and activities to interest the child.

Reading Check Answer Reliable, trustworthy babysitters are likely to be asked to babysit in the future. Parents may recommend you to their friends who have young children.

- Do not allow your friends to visit.
- Do not open the door for strangers.

Being responsible for children is a serious and important task. It can also be a lot of fun. Children of different ages have different needs and require different types of care. Learning how to take care of infants, toddlers, and preschoolers will help you meet their needs and enjoy your time with them.

Reading Check *Predict* *What is likely to happen if you are a reliable babysitter?*

Infant Care

Infants are cute, fun to cuddle, and easy to entertain. Infants cannot do things for themselves. The rely entirely on their caregivers for all of their physical, emotional, and social needs. Infants communicate their needs for sleep, food, comfort, and attention by crying.

When an infant cries, check to see if she has dirty diapers. Offer a bottle to see if she is hungry. She may be too hot or too cold. Maybe something on her clothing is irritating her skin. She may need to be burped. If none of these things calm her, try rocking with her or walking her around the room. Some babies are comforted by riding in their strollers.

If possible, secure the infant in her stroller and take her for a walk. If you cannot go outside, walk her around the house. The movement of going back and forth down a hallway can soothe a cranky baby.

Holding Infants

Infants cannot hold their heads up without help. To support an infant's head, place one hand under his head and the other hand and arm under the lower part of his back. Then you can lift him safely to your shoulder or cradle him in the bend of your arm and elbow area.

Diaper Changes

Ask the parent to show you the diaper changing area and where to put dirty diapers. When you change a diaper, gather everything you need before you begin. Infants can roll off changing tables and beds. Never leave an infant alone or even turn your back to the infant while changing a diaper.

Feeding Time

A young infant drinks mother's milk or formula. Cradle the infant in your arm when you give a bottle. After he stops drinking, hold him over your shoulder, and lightly pat his back until you hear a burp. It may take a few moments for the burp to come. Be patient. Also know that infants do not always burp.

Character Counts

Reliability

Joann is babysitting for a new family. When she first arrived, the parents made it clear that they did not want any other teens in their home while they were gone. After the children went to bed, Joann's friend, Brenda, dropped by with a movie that just came out on DVD that Joann really wanted to see. There is plenty of time to watch the movie before the parents return.

You Make the Call

Is there really anything wrong with watching a movie while the children sleep? Write a paragraph that explains what you think Joann should do.

Character Counts Answer Joann may have enough time to watch the movie before the parents return, but the parents made it clear that they did not want any other teens in their home. Joann should follow the rules the parents set up with her. If she does not follow the rules, she will not be asked to babysit again.

Photo Caption Answer Babies feel warm and secure because you have to hold them close to feed them. They can look into your eyes or listen to your voice and feel a sense of trust and comfort.

◀ More Than Nutrition

Babies rely entirely on their caregivers for all of their physical, emotional, and social needs. *What benefits do infants receive from being fed besides nutrition?*

Diaper a Baby

An infant needs several diapers a day. The most important thing to remember when changing a baby's diaper is safety. Never leave an infant unattended at any time during the process. It takes practice, but by following some basic guidelines, changing a diaper can be a fairly smooth process.

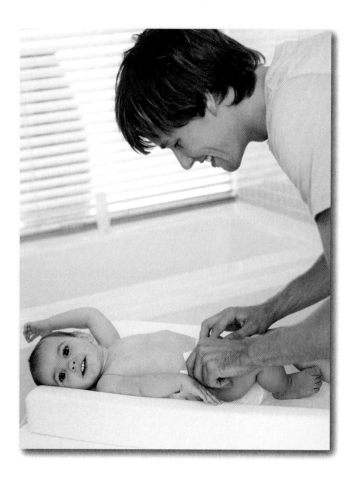

Step 1. Gather the supplies. You will need a diaper, baby wipes or washcloth, and diaper rash ointment (optional). Make sure all your supplies are within reach before setting the baby on the changing surface.

Step 2. Find a safe place for the baby. Most likely, there will be a changing table in the baby's room. If not, you can set a towel or blanket on a bed or even on the floor. Wherever you choose to change the baby, make sure the surface is secure and free of any hazards.

Step 3. Remove the dirty diaper. Lay the baby on his or her back. Unfasten the diaper tabs. Raise the child's bottom off the dirty diaper by gently grasping the ankles and lifting. Use baby wipes or a wet washcloth to clean the baby's bottom, wiping front to back. Remove the diaper from the baby's reach.

Step 4. Put on the clean diaper. Apply diaper rash ointment if needed. Pull the front of the new diaper between the baby's legs. While holding the front of the diaper over the baby's belly, open one side tab and pull it across to the front placement mark. Open the other side tab and pull it into place so the diaper is snug, but not too tight. Redress the baby, then place him or her in a safe place, such as a crib or playpen.

Step 5. Clean up. Dispose of the dirty diaper by wrapping the tabs all the way around it to form a ball. Clean up the changing area and thoroughly wash your hands.

Safe Sleeping

To put an infant to sleep, place her on the side or back, never on the stomach. Be sure to pull up the side of the crib and fasten it securely. When the infant is sleeping, check her often to make sure that everything is all right. Keep toys and other objects out of the crib, and make sure she is not too hot or too cold. Many experts agree that it is best to avoid blankets and pillows in cribs.

Reading Check **List** *What can you check when an infant is crying?*

Toddler Care

Toddlers require a lot of attention. They need help and understanding as they grow and make new discoveries. They also demand a lot of attention because they are busy moving from one thing to another. Toddlers are starting to enjoy the company of others. They will want you to play with them and keep them entertained. However, they may not stay interested in the same activity for very long!

Meal Time

Children between one and three years old are able to eat many of the foods that adults enjoy. However, they are still learning proper way to eat, chew, and swallow. Make sure you only feed the child food that his parents approve. Foods should be soft and cut into small pieces to avoid choking. Never leave a toddler unattended while she is eating. Be patient. Some young children eat very slowly, and they tend to be messy.

Activities and Skills

Coordination and understanding improve a great deal during the toddler years. While toddlers enjoy showing off their growing independence, most will need extra comfort when their parents leave. Ask the parents for a selection of their favorite toys or a beloved blanket. You may need to redirect them with a toy, puzzle, or game. When you **redirect** children, you turn their attention to something else. They will usually get over missing their parents in a few minutes.

Interaction Toddlers enjoy showing their new discoveries to the people around them. *What can you do to encourage a toddler to explore his or her world?*

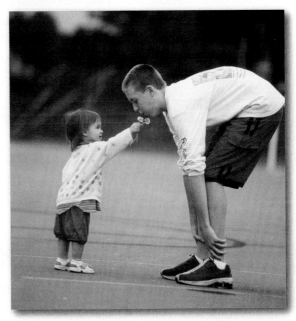

Children at this age like to **imitate**, or copy, what their caregivers do. Fun activities for toddlers include playing with a toy vacuum cleaner, lawn mower, or telephone. They might also enjoy plastic dishes and food, plastic or wooden tools, or a bucket and shovel.

If the toddler has learned to use the toilet, you may have to help him or her in the bathroom. Depending on the child's level of skill, help him or her unfasten clothes and get onto the toilet or potty seat. Afterwards, help the child wash his or her hands. Clean up any accidents, and replace the diaper or underpants if needed.

Reading Check **Explain** *How can you help a toddler use the toilet?*

Reading Check Answer Unfasten clothes, and help him or her get onto the toilet or potty seat, then help the child wash his or her hands.

Preschooler Care

Preschoolers are curious and often look forward to being with caregivers they like. They like to be kept busy, and they want others to interact with them.

Photo Caption Answer Answers will vary, but responses should be for activities that are safe and age-appropriate.

Creative Playtime Involve children in activities while you babysit. *What creative ideas do you have for playtime?*

Meal Time

Preschoolers are often picky eaters. Be sure to follow their parent's list of acceptable foods and snacks. Preschoolers have all of their teeth and are much more experienced with eating. However, they can still be messy. As with toddlers, be patient and keep an eye on the child while he or she is eating.

Activities

Babysitting preschoolers can be exhausting, but it can be a good experience if you plan well. During this period, children's motor skills and imagination improve. Their creativity and curiosity seem endless. Plan to have a list of back-up activities to help keep them entertained. Fun activities for most preschoolers include play dough, puzzles, dolls, construction sets, coloring with crayons, and using paints. Ask the child tell you to draw something, such as a favorite animal or a familiar character. The child will enjoy watching what you create. Then have the child do the same thing. If you can manage to keep an active preschooler busy, you can help him or her be more willing to go to sleep at bedtime.

Section 10.2 After You Read

Review What You Have Learned

1. **Identify** which family rules you should discuss with parents before they leave.
2. **Recall** the instructions for properly holding an infant.
3. **Explain** why it is important to stay with a toddler who is eating a meal.
4. **Describe** what you can do to prepare a busy preschooler for bedtime.

Practice Academic Skills

English Language Arts

5. Create a flyer to advertise the babysitting services of a teen who has had a good deal of babysitting practice. Include his or her experience, special skills, contact information, and the fee charged. Use graphics to make the flyer colorful and interesting.

> **NCTE 4** Use written language to communicate effectively.

Social Studies

6. Write a short essay about the impact of daycare on society. How is daycare used and provided in today's society? How are children affected by daycare?

> **NCSS V B** Analyze group and institutional influences on people, events, and elements of culture in both historical and contemporary settings.

 Check Your Answers Check your answers at this book's Online Learning Center at glencoe.com.

Discovering Careers

Do you enjoy caring for children? Do you seek out opportunities where you can teach or be a role model for children? If you answered yes to either of those questions, you might want to consider a future career in child care. The following chart explores several careers in the child care industry.

Job Title	Job Description
Pediatric Speech Therapist	Develops programs for children with speech and language disorders, hearing disorders, and oral motor disorders.
Child Care Instructor	Organizes and leads activities of preschool children in nursery schools and daycares. Directs snack time, nap time, and toileting.
Special Needs Aide	Attends to personal needs of disabled children. Secures children in medically-required equipment. Helps children perform physical activities.
School Music Director	Plans and develops music education program. Coordinates vocal and instrumental music activities.
T-Ball Coach	Organizes and teaches preschool-age children how to play baseball. Helps develop basic throwing, running, and catching skills for young children.

Career Activities ▼

At School

1 Select three of the careers listed. Research the education, training, and work experience required for each career. Write a summary of your results.

At Home

2 With your parent, put together a list of the regular tasks he or she did for you when you were an infant or toddler. Use the list to come up with the job description of "Parent."

At Work

3 Make a list of five or more jobs aside from those listed on this page for people who want to work with children. Compare your list with those of your classmates.

In the Community

4 Contact and interview someone in your community who works in the child care industry. Ask this person to describe what his or her typical work day is like. Share what you learned with your class.

Career Activities Answers for these activities can be found on page TM119.

Learn More *Online* glencoe.com

Career Investigations Go to this book's Online Learning Center for activities and worksheets to help you explore careers.

Chapter Summary

Section 10.1 Child Safety
Children do not understand the dangers that surround them. Families can child-proof their homes to create a safe environment for children to play and explore. Even if a home has been childproofed, children must be watched carefully to make sure they are safe. To keep children safe, protect them from intruders, take precautions to prevent accidents, learn how to handle emergencies, and keep children away from dangerous household products.

Section 10.2 Babysitting
When you babysit, you are totally responsible for the safety and well-being of the children in your care. Prepare for babysitting by learning first aid and volunteering as a parent's helper. Being responsible for children is a serious and important task. Infants rely on their caregivers for all their needs. Toddlers need help and understanding as they grow and make new discoveries. Preschoolers are curious and often look forward to being with caregivers they like.

Words You Learned

1. Use each of these content vocabulary words and academic vocabulary words in a sentence.

Content Vocabulary
- childproof (p. 209)
- monitor (p. 210)
- intruder (p. 210)
- reliable (p. 217)
- redirect (p. 221)

Academic Vocabulary
- precaution (p. 209)
- restrict (p. 211)
- appreciate (p. 215)
- imitate (p. 222)

Review Key Concepts

2. **Identify** ways to childproof a home.

3. **Explain** the purpose of learning first aid.

4. **List** the information you should find out before accepting a babysitting job.

5. **Name** four needs that require attention when caring for infants.

6. **Describe** how to distract a toddler after his or her parents leave.

7. **Plan** what you should have when caring for preschoolers.

Critical Thinking

8. **Evaluate** whether or not you should allow a well-coordinated 18-month-old child play with a toy that is designed for a 3-year-old child.

9. **Predict** what you would do if a child in your care was exposed to poison ivy.

Real-World Skills and Applications

Problem-Solving

10. Learn What to Expect You have been recommended as a great babysitter. A new family has called you to find out if you are able to babysit this weekend. List five questions to ask the family about what you can expect on your first night of babysitting.

Technology Applications

11. Write an Evaluation Using word processing software, create an evaluation to give to parents after you have completed a babysitting job them. Choose areas for the parents to evaluate that would be helpful for your growth and development in caring for children. Have parents rate each area with a number, for example: 1 = poor, 2 = needs improvement, 3 = fair, 4 = good, and 5 = excellent. Leave space for them to add their own comments.

Financial Literacy

12. Plan Ahead Your school's formal Winter Dance is coming up in just three months, but you are worried about the costs of attending the event. Your parents have agreed to help you by paying half of your expenses, but you still need to come up with your share. You estimate that a new outfit and shoes will cost $350, tickets to the dance will cost $89, and transportation will be another $65. To cover your half of the expenses, you would like to take a babysitting job. If the job pays $7.00 per hour, how many hours will you have to work each week to raise enough money to pay for your share of expenses? Assume there are four weeks in a month.

13. Puppet Play Children love to use their imaginations. A favorite activity for young children is to use puppets for storytelling. Make puppets from socks, yarn, ribbon, buttons, markers, and pieces of scrap fabric. You could also use lunch-size paper bags. Take your puppets to your next babysitting job and let the kids tell stories and play with the puppets. Bring extra supplies to let the children make their own puppets.

14. Babysitting History In the 1900s on the American plains, the care of children was the responsibility of all family members and they were not paid for it. Children were expected to care for themselves and siblings much earlier than they are today. Choose a time in history and find out how children were cared for during that period. Did they call it "babysitting?" Did sitters get paid? If so, how much? Present your findings to the class.

15. Babysitting Training With permission from your parents or teacher, go online to find what kind of training is offered to prepare babysitters for their work. Find out about training for CPR, first-aid techniques, child development, and activities for children. Include this information in your Life Skills Binder.

Academic Skills

English Language Arts

16. Seeking Babysitters Imagine that you are a parent seeking a babysitter for your two children. Use the information from this chapter as well as any personal experience you may have to write an advertisement that would attract qualified babysitters. The ad would appear at local high schools and colleges. Describe the duties you expect to be performed, and list the qualifications you expect from the babysitter.

> **NCTE 4** Use written language to communicate effectively.

Social Studies

17. Car Seats Find information about child safety seats for use in vehicles. How have they changed since they were invented in the 1920s? What are the current standards for car seats? What is the proper use and position of the car seat? How do they help children stay safe? Are there laws in place about using car seats? Explain your answers in a short report.

> **NCSS VIII C Science, Technology, and Society** Analyze how core values, beliefs, and attitudes of society shape scientific and technological change.

Mathematics

18. Comparing Numbers During the summer, LaTisha has been working many evenings as a babysitter for families in her neighborhood. Last week, she worked two nights at the Aquino house, and four nights for the Brooks family. What is the ratio of nights worked at the Aquino house to nights worked at the Brooks house? For the week, what was LaTisha's ratio of nights that she did not work to nights that she did work?

Math Concept **Ratios** A ratio is a comparison of two numbers that can be represented in different forms: as a fraction (for example, ½), with a colon (1:2), or as a phrase ("1 to 2"). Whichever form is used, the ratio should be reduced to the lowest terms.

Starting Hint For each question, write a ratio as a fraction in the lowest terms. Make sure that the two numbers in your ratios are in the same order given by the question.

> **NCTM Number and Operations** Understand numbers, ways of representing numbers, relationships among numbers, and number systems.

Standardized Test Practice

Multiple-Choice

Read the questions, then choose the appropriate answer.

> **Test-Taking Tip** Look for negative words such as *not* and *no* in multiple choice questions. These words can be easily missed but can change the entire meaning of a sentence.

19. Which is not a characteristic of a good babysitter?
 a. Reliable
 b. Social
 c. Caring
 d. Prompt

UNIT 4 Life Skills Project

Your Relationship with Children

Understanding how to take care of children can help you become a good caregiver. Watch a younger relative or friend to see how they play and learn. This project can help you to understand how young children learn through play.

 My Journal Complete the journal entry from page 181, and refer to it to complete your list of favorite toys.

Project Assignment ▼

In this project you will:

- Create a list of your favorite toys or games from when you were young.
- Choose an age group and research its development.
- Design a toy or game for a young child.
- Interview someone who cares for children.
- Present your design to your class.
- Include this project in the fourth section of your personal Life Skills binder.

Step 1 Make a List of Your Favorite Toys and Games

Understanding what children enjoy can be easier if you remember the toys and games you liked when you were younger. Choose your favorite toy, and describe it. Write about why you loved it and what made it fun to play with.

Step 2 Choose a Toy for an Infant, Toddler, or Preschooler

Review Section 9.2 to remind yourself of the developmental milestones of the three age groups. Think about a toy you could design that would help a child develop or practice these skills. Then write two or more paragraphs that answer these questions:

✔What age group are you designing a toy for?
✔Which milestones will your toy help develop or practice?
✔Why do you think children will enjoy your toy?
✔How can you ensure that your toy will be safe?

Step 3 Interview Someone Who is Responsible for Children

Interview someone in your community who takes care of young children. Ask these questions:

✔How old are the children you take care of?
✔What are the children's favorite toys?
✔What skills have they learned from playing with each one?

Use these interviewing skills when conducting your interview and these writing skills when writing the summary of notes from your interview.

Interviewing Skills
- Record interview responses and take notes.
- Listen attentively.

Writing Skills
- Use complete sentences.
- Use correct spelling and grammar.

228   Unit 4   Children and Parenting

Step 4 Create and Present Your Toy or Game

Use the Life Skills Project Checklist on the right to plan and design a toy or game. Draw your design in a diagram or build it out of craft materials to show how it works, and give an oral presentation to the class.

Use these speaking skills when presenting your final report.

Speaking Skills
- Speak clearly and concisely.
- Be sensitive to the needs of your audience.
- Use standard English to communicate.

Step 5 Evaluate Your Presentation

Your project will be evaluated based on:

✔ Completeness and organization of your list of favorite toys and games.
✔ The design of the toy or game for a young child.
✔ The description of how your toy or game is safe and appropriate for its age group.
✔ The summary written from interview notes.
✔ Grammar and sentence structure.
✔ Presentation to the class.
✔ Creativity and neatness.

Evaluation Rubric Go to this book's Online Learning Center through glencoe.com for a rubric you can use to evaluate your final project.

Life Skills Project Checklist

Research Toys and Games

- Create a list of toys and games you enjoyed when you were a child.
- Check the developmental milestones of infants, toddlers, and preschoolers.
- Interview someone in your community who takes care of children.
- Design or build a toy or game.

Writing Skills

- Describe your favorite toy or game from your childhood.
- Explain how your design will be age-appropriate.
- Write a summary from your interview with someone takes care of children.

Present Your Findings

- Prepare a short presentation to share and describe your toy or game design and explain how it is age-appropriate, safe, and fun.
- Invite the students of the class to ask any questions they may have. Answer these questions with responses that respect their perspectives.
- Add this project to your Life Skills binder.

Academic Skills

- Conduct research to gather information.
- Communicate effectively.
- Organize your presentation so the audience can follow along easily.
- Thoroughly express your ideas.

NCTE 4 Use written language to communicate effectively.
NCTE 5 Use different writing process elements to communicate effectively.

Chapter 11
Manage Your Money

Chapter 12
Manage Resources, Time, and Stress

Unit Preview

This unit is about learning how to manage your time, money, and other resources. In this unit, you will learn about:

- Evaluating the purchases you make.
- The importance of managing your money.
- The resources that are available to you and how to manage them.
- Different methods of dealing with stress.

Explore the Photo Answer Answers may include comparison shopping, price, quality, value, return policy, your budget, whether or not you need the product, and the guarantee or warranty.

Explore the Photo
It is very important for you to learn how to manage your resources, including money. *What are some things you should consider when you want to buy something?*

Manage Your Grocery Budget

When you are done studying this unit, you will complete a project in which you will:

✓ Make a list and shop for groceries.

✓ Interview a grocery store worker.

✓ Demonstrate the results of your shopping experience to your class.

The prewriting activity below will help you get started.

 My Journal

Prewriting Activity
Create a Chart

Ask the primary shopper in your family for a receipt from the last time he or she went grocery shopping. Create a chart with two columns. In the first column, list the items your family must have, such as nutritious foods, and label it "Needed Items." In the second column, list the items your family wants but does not necessarily need, such as magazines and snack food, and label it "Wanted Items."

● How much money could your family have saved if the "Wanted Items" had not been purchased?

● How can your family save money on the "Needed Items?"

Chapter 11

Manage Your Money

Explore the Photo Answer Answers may include: look for the best prices; carry only the amount of cash you are able to spend; plan and stick to a budget; keep a record of what you earn and spend.

Be a Smart Consumer

■ **Main Idea** Evaluate advertisements and carefully consider what you want and need from the products you purchase.

 Section 11.2

Spending and Saving Basics

■ **Main Idea** Shopping skills, consumer rights and responsibilities, and money management help you spend and save wisely.

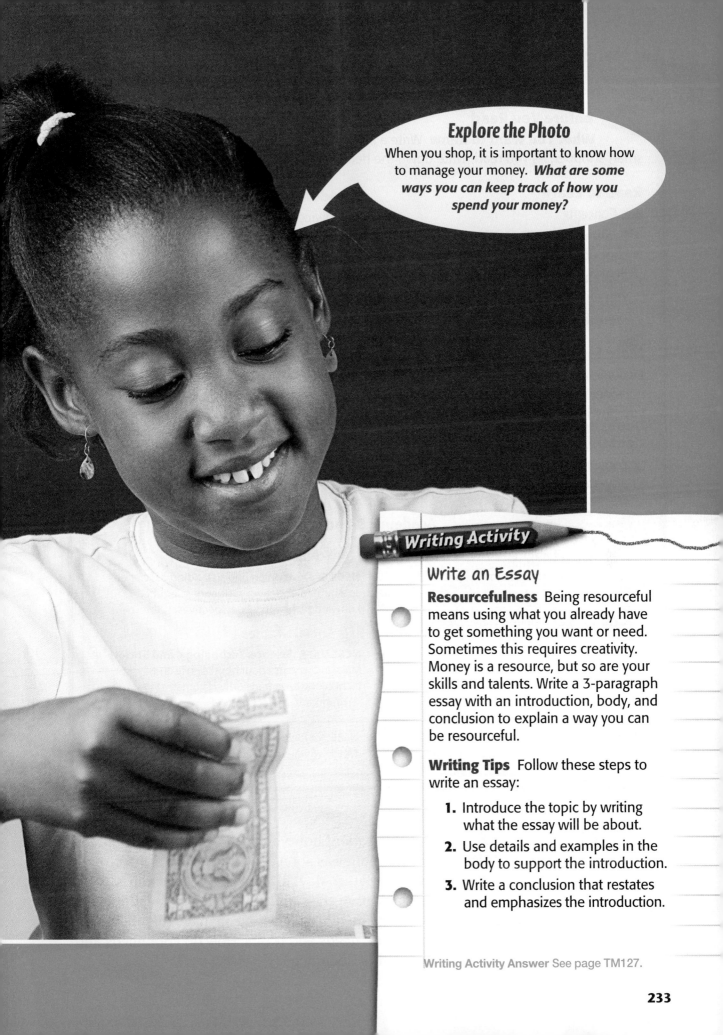

Explore the Photo

When you shop, it is important to know how to manage your money. *What are some ways you can keep track of how you spend your money?*

Writing Activity

Write an Essay

Resourcefulness Being resourceful means using what you already have to get something you want or need. Sometimes this requires creativity. Money is a resource, but so are your skills and talents. Write a 3-paragraph essay with an introduction, body, and conclusion to explain a way you can be resourceful.

Writing Tips Follow these steps to write an essay:

1. Introduce the topic by writing what the essay will be about.
2. Use details and examples in the body to support the introduction.
3. Write a conclusion that restates and emphasizes the introduction.

Writing Activity Answer See page TM127.

Reading Guide

Before You Read

What You Want to Know Write a list of what you want to know about being a smart shopper. As you read, write down the heads that provide that information.

Read to Learn
Key Concepts
✓ **Evaluate** how you can be a smart shopper.
✓ **Explain** how your habits affect the way you decide what to buy.
✓ **Identify** the purpose of advertising.

Main Idea
Evaluate advertisements and carefully consider what you want and need products you purchase.

Content Vocabulary
 consumer   trend
 advertisement   media

Academic Vocabulary
■ service   ■ endorse

Graphic Organizer
As you read, compare and contrast information advertisements and image advertisements. Use a graphic organizer like the one shown to help you organize your information.

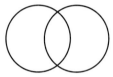
Information Ads   Image Ads

Graphic Organizer Go to this book's Online Learning Center at glencoe.com to print this graphic organizer.

Academic Standards

English Language Arts
NCTE 3 Apply strategies to interpret texts.

Mathematics
NCTM Problem Solving Solve problems that arise in mathematics and in other contexts.

Science
NSES G Develop an understanding of science as a human endeavor, nature of scientific knowledge, historical perspectives.

Social Studies
NCSS VIII B Science, Technology, and Society Make judgments about how science and technology have transformed human-environment interactions.

NCTE *National Council of Teachers of English*
NCTM *National Council of Teachers of Mathematics*

NSES *National Science Education Standards*
NCSS *National Council for the Social Studies*

Graphic Organizer
Answer Information Ads: describe features; list price and quality; product is a good value. Image Ads: connect to a lifestyle; use celebrities; life will be better if consumers use product. Both: catch your attention and convince you to buy; present product in an attractive way.

Do you ever think about how you spend your money? Do you spend all of your money as soon as you receive it, or do you put some away for later? Maybe you want to save money for a friend's birthday gift. At the same time, you may be hoping to buy a new video game. The way people manage their money can depend on their needs and wants. How do your needs and wants influence your spending?

Teens as Consumers

Teens spend their money to buy goods and services. Goods are products made for sale, such as MP3 players, computer games, or jeans. A **service**, or work performed for others, is also something people purchase. Services include the work done to repair your bike, or the time your instructor spends teaching you how to play an instrument. Even if you do not spend a great deal of money, you can be a smart shopper if you know what factors influence your buying decisions. A **consumer** is a person who buys goods and services.

As a consumer, you have many decisions to make. You must decide what to buy, where to buy, and when to buy. You have to decide how to get the best value for your money. By making wise purchases, you will be a satisfied consumer.

 Reading Check *Define* *What is a consumer?*

Reading Check Answer A consumer is a person who buys goods and services.

 As You Read

Connect Think about the last product you bought. What did you consider before you bought it?

 Vocabulary

You can find definitions in the glossary at the back of this book.

As You Read Answer Answers may include price, quality, and whether or not the item was really necessary.

Photo Caption Answer Answers may include comparing products for price and quality, and sticking to a budget.

Spend Wisely As a consumer, you have many choices when it comes to spending your money. *How can you make wise spending choices?*

Buying Decisions

When you bought your last pair of athletic shoes, what influenced your decision? Did your friends convince you that you needed the shoes? Maybe your decision was based on price. Perhaps you saw an athlete you admire **endorse**, or recommend, the shoes in a television advertisement. An **advertisement** is a message that persuades consumers to buy a product or service.

Have you ever tried out a new shampoo because your friend recommended it? Have you ever decided to buy a new backpack because your friend has one? Your friends can have an influence on your buying decisions.

A **trend** is a temporary fashion or product. Can you think of any recent movies that inspired a line of products in toy stores? What celebrities can you think of who start trends with their personal styles? These items may become status symbols, or signs of popularity and importance.

Before you make a purchase, evaluate the product. Give it some thought. Ask yourself, "Do I really need these jeans for $80.00?" or "Is it really necessary for me to wear sunglasses by this designer?" Trends come and go. You may decide that you do not really need the product at all. Do what is best for you, and be proud of your individuality.

MATH YOU CAN USE

Saving Money

When you put money in a savings account, the bank can use that money for other purposes until you withdraw it. The bank pays you a fee, known as interest, for this privilege of being able to use your money. Interest is usually paid at a rate based on an annual percentage of the money you have deposited, known as the principal. The interest is added to your savings account along with the principal. Imagine that Andrew has $550 in his savings account on January 1st. If the account pays 5% simple interest, how much money will be in Andrew's account at the end of the year?

Math Concept **Simple Interest** Calculate simple interest by multiplying the interest rate by the principal.

Starting Hint To calculate the interest Andrew will receive for the year, multiply $550 by 5%, which is the same as multiplying $550 x 0.05. Add this interest amount to the principal (the amount already in the account at the beginning of the year).

 For math help, go to the Math Appendix at the back of the book.

NCTM Problem Solving Solve problems that arise in mathematics and in other contexts.

Buying Habits

As you have probably discovered, many of your buying decisions are influenced by your habits. If you always shop at the same store, you may be passing up good prices offered at another store. Perhaps you feel loyal to certain brands. Loyalty is good, but if you do not take notice of other options, you may be missing out on good products and good deals. Sometimes you need to evaluate your habits to make sure that you are being a careful shopper.

 Reading Check **Assess** *Why should you evaluate a product before you buy it?*

Trends Before you buy something trendy, think about why you want to make the purchase. *Who or what has an influence on what you buy?*

Advertising

Advertising is a major influence on people's buying decisions. Advertising is everywhere you look. **Figure 11.1** on page 238 shows several types of media. **Media** are various forms of communication that advertisers use.

Advertisements, or ads, are designed to catch the attention of consumers and convince them to buy a product or service. Ads influence consumers by presenting goods or services in an attractive way.

Ads introduce new products and point out their benefits. In addition, they let you know about sales. Looking at the weekly advertising circulars you find in newspapers or in your mail is a great way to compare prices.

Some ads deliver a public-service message. They may warn people about the dangers of tobacco, alcohol, and other drugs. Other advertisements ask people to conserve resources or donate money to charitable organizations.

There are some disadvantages to advertising. Some ads persuade people to buy items they may not need, especially if the product is endorsed by an admired celebrity. Ads can also be misleading or make exaggerated or unrealistic claims. If something sounds too good to be true, it probably is not.

Figure 11.1 Types of Advertising

Media Advertisers use different media to tell consumers about their products or services. *Why do you think some are more effective than others?*

Electronic Media

The Internet, radio, and television are examples of electronic media. Internet advertising appears on the computer screen when users are online. The ads that you hear on the radio and see on television are called commercials.

Print Media

Newspapers and magazines are examples of print media. Food and clothing stores often place ads in newspapers to reach their local customers.

Signs and Displays

Signs and displays are two other types of media that you have seen many times. Advertising signs can appear on billboards, buses, taxis, and storefronts. Stores attract buyers with window displays and product displays.

Direct Mail

Mail-order catalogs and coupons are examples of direct mail. Catalog retailers and wholesalers use direct mail. Some companies use only direct mail to advertise their products.

Telemarketing

Telemarketing means calling a person directly to discuss a product or service. Telemarketers use this means to reach people they think will respond to telephone offers.

Figure Caption Answer Answers will vary. Sample answers: Electronic media is more effective because it reaches the most people. Print media is more effective because people tend to change the channel or station, or close pop-up windows.

Succeed in School Ask for volunteers to copy their notes for students who are absent.

SUCCEED IN SCHOOL!

Class Attendance

Get Notes If you know that you are going to be absent, arrange with a classmate to take notes and make a copy for you.

Types of Advertisements

Advertisements generally fall into one of two categories: information ads and image ads. Both are used to grab your attention and sell a product or service, but each type of ad sends a different kind of message.

Information Ads

These ads describe the features of a product or service and give facts about its price and quality. Information ads send the message that an item is a good buy for the price or because of its high quality.

Image Ad

These ads connect a product or service to a lifestyle that consumers would like to have. Image ads often use celebrities to endorse a product. They send the message that consumers will be more attractive or popular, or perhaps smarter or healthier, if they use the product or service. Image ads are often used to promote fashions, cosmetics, and other items that a person may want but does not necessarily need.

Evaluate Advertising

Before you decide to buy a service or product, be sure to analyze the advertising claims. **Figure 11.2** describes common techniques that advertisers use to get your attention and your business. Ask yourself questions like these to help you make wise choices:

- Does the ad suggest that the product will make me healthier, more attractive, or even happier than is realistic?
- Is the celebrity in the commercial an expert in nutrition, medicine, or fashion?
- Does the catchy slogan really mean something, or is it just to make me remember the product's name?

Figure 11.2 Getting Your Attention

Advertising Techniques Advertisers use different techniques to get you to buy their products or services. *Name some ads you have seen on television or online, heard on the radio, or seen in print that use some of these techniques.*

Slogans

Advertisers use slogans and jingles, or catchy songs, to remind people of their products.

Endorsements

Advertisers use famous people, including movie and television celebrities, politicians, athletes, and musicians, to promote their products.

Cartoon Characters

A popular technique is to use animated characters to advertise products.

Emotional Appeals

With this technique, advertisers tell you that you will be happier, healthier, or more popular if you use their products.

Science You Can Use Answer Answers will vary but should include material from the chapter, including creating a budget and sticking to it, organizing receipts, and living within one's means.

Figure Caption Answer Answers may include celebrities who endorse weight loss or personal care products; politicians who endorse themselves; singers who promote their concerts; cartoon animals that sell a variety of products.

Get More Information

Although the federal government requires advertisers to make truthful claims, there are some companies that will exaggerate how good their products are. Product advertisements, whether in print, online, on the radio, or on television, can be misleading. You do not have to depend on advertisements for all of your information about a product or service, however. Other sources of useful information are also available to you.

One of the most reliable sources of information is the people you know. Ask your family and friends what brand of a product they use, whether it works well, and if the item was worth the money they paid. The Consumer Product Safety Commission is a government agency that provides safety information about various products. You can check the Better Business Bureau (BBB) for reputable, or trustworthy, businesses. Another good way to obtain information is from consumer resources in print or online. Consumer organizations test products, survey the customers, and then report their findings. They are independent and are not paid by the advertisers, so they have no reason to make false claims.

Section 11.1 After You Read

Review What You Have Learned

1. **Identify** the decisions that make as a consumer.
2. **Recognize** the influences on your buying decisions.
3. **Name** two types of advertisements.

Practice Academic Skills

 English Language Arts

4. Choose a common product or service such as window cleaner or car insurance. Compare and contrast two types of ads, such as a television commercial and a magazine ad, that promote that type of product or service. Write a short report to present your analysis.

> **NCTE 3** Apply strategies to interpret texts.

 Social Studies

5. Evaluate how Internet advertising affects consumers. How is it different from traditional advertising? Explain your answer in a short oral report.

> **NCSS VIII B** Make judgments about how science and technology have transformed human-environment interactions.

 Check Your Answers Check your answers at this book's Online Learning Center at glencoe.com.

Reading Guide

Before You Read

Preview A cause is an action that makes something happen. An effect is a result of a cause. Ask yourself, "Why does this happen?" to help you recognize cause-and-effect relationships.

Read to Learn

Key Concepts

✓ **List** the different types of stores where you can shop.

✓ **Explain** why consumers need rights and how you can be a responsible consumer.

✓ **Understand** how to manage your money wisely.

Main Idea

Shopping skills, consumer rights and responsibilities, and money management help you spend and save wisely.

Content Vocabulary

- ○ impulse buying
- ○ comparison shopping
- ○ guarantee
- ○ shoplifting
- ○ income
- ○ expenses
- ○ budget
- ○ credit

Academic Vocabulary

- ■ merchandise
- ■ expire

Graphic Organizer

As you read, list four guidelines for exchanging merchandise or asking for a refund. Use a graphic organizer like the one shown to help you organize your information.

Refunds and Exchanges

 Graphic Organizer Go to this book's Online Learning Center at glencoe.com to print this graphic organizer.

- **Academic Standards** -

English Language Arts

NCTE 5 Use different writing process elements to communicate effectively.

Social Studies

NCSS I D Culture Compare and analyze societal patterns for preserving and transmitting culture while adapting to environmental or social change.

NCSS VI A Power, Authority, and Governance Examine persistent issues involving the rights, roles, and status of the individual in relation to the general welfare.

NCTE *National Council of Teachers of English*
NCTM *National Council of Teachers of Mathematics*

NSES *National Science Education Standards*
NCSS *National Council for the Social Studies*

It is easier to spend money than to save it, but managing money so you can do both is important for your long-term financial goals. Shopping for the best buys and knowing your rights and responsibilities as consumers can contribute to successful money management.

Graphic Organizer Answer Know the store's policy; Keep proof of your purchase; Determine if you are entitled to a refund; Be ready to process your claim.

Shopping Skills

As You Read

Connect How can reading the care instructions on a clothing label help you to decide whether or not to buy it?

Skillful shoppers get the best value for their money. As you develop your shopping skills, you will learn how to spot a good value and how to spot an overpriced product. This ability can help you save a great deal of money over the years.

Be an informed shopper. Read labels and compare prices at different stores and among different brands. Look closely at merchandise to judge its quality. Check to see whether the manufacturer will replace or repair the item if it breaks. It is possible to find out some of this information before you even walk into a store. Conduct research, ask friends and family, and read consumer publications to get as much information as possible before you buy.

Impulse buying means making a sudden decision to buy something you did not plan to purchase. Did you ever decide to buy candy or a magazine while you were standing in the checkout line? Stores place items in these locations just for that reason. If you buy something on impulse, you may end up with something you do not need or that is not worth the money. You risk wasting your money and hurting your budget.

Collect information about products from friends and family members and advertisements. Word of mouth is a great way to find out about products and services. Information obtained from people you know and who are not paid to sell products is generally reliable. Ask friends and family such questions as:

- Are you satisfied with the product?
- What do you like or dislike about it?
- Would you buy the product again?

Vocabulary

You can find definitions in the glossary at the back of this book.

As You Read Answer The item may need special care such as dry cleaning, which can be expensive and time consuming. It may also contain a fiber that irritates your skin, shrinks easily, or cannot be machine washed or dried.

Photo Caption Answer Remind yourself that you do not need the item; bring only the amount of cash you can afford to spend; if you shop with friends, ask them to remind you not buy unnecessary items.

Impulse Buying Store managers often stock impulse-buy items, such as magazines and candy, near the checkout counter. *How can you avoid impulse buying?*

Where Should I Shop?

What types of stores are familiar to you? Different kinds of stores carry different selections of **merchandise**, or products available to buy. The best stores for you depend on the particular items you want to buy, the prices you are willing to pay, and the kinds of services you need.

- **Department Stores** Most department stores sell clothing, shoes, household items, and electronic equipment. Prices for the same item often vary among stores. Department stores usually offer many services, such as gift-wrapping and delivery.
- **Specialty Stores** A store that carries only a specific type of merchandise is a specialty store. The prices may be higher than in a department store.
- **Chain Stores** Stores in separate locations that have the same name and carry the same merchandise are called chain stores.
- **Factory Outlets** A factory outlet generally carries only one manufacturer's products. Outlets stock items that are left over from other stores. Some of the products may have slight defects but are still useable. Shopping at factory outlets can be a great way to save money on brand name products.
- **Discount Stores** Discount stores carry a selection of items at low prices. Some discount stores specialize in a particular kind of merchandise. Other stores that sell merchandise at discounted prices include membership warehouses and thrift shops.

Catalogs and the Internet

Besides going to actual stores, you can also buy products from catalogs. Some catalogs are associated with stores and carry merchandise that the stores cannot keep in stock. Other catalog companies do business only by telephone and mail.

Electronic shopping is available on the Internet. Consumers can view pictures and descriptions of the merchandise offered by many different stores and manufacturers. While online, you can place an order that will be processed instantly, then shipped directly to you.

Catalog and online shopping are fast and convenient ways to shop. However, keep in mind that you cannot inspect merchandise before buying. Before you commit to an online or catalog purchase, find out about their return policy. This information should be provided in the catalog or on the Web site.

Safety Check

Credit Card Safety

You may not have a credit card yet, but debit cards and credit cards are virtually unavoidable for today's purchases, especially online. Credit card numbers are personal. Do not share them with anyone. Make sure you are aware of where your credit card is at all times.

- When using a Web site, make sure it is a secure site.
- When paying in a store, watch the clerk as he or she runs you card to make sure that the card is only used for your purchase.
- Keep receipts in a safe place, or destroy them when you are sure you no longer need them.

Comparison Shopping

After you decide where to shop, you need to consider certain factors before making your purchase. **Comparison shopping** is evaluating similar items to check quality and price. Which one is the better value? Also, compare labels and guarantees to help you get the best value for your money.

Some people think that price is a sign of how good a product is. They think that a more expensive product must be superior. That is not always the case. Items that are on sale may be less expensive than regular-priced items, but may not be of the same quality. Stores sometimes sell products that they have bought at special, lower prices. The quality of these items may also be lower than that of their regular merchandise. You need to look carefully at products on sale to see if they really are bargains. Sometimes it is worth extra money to get higher quality.

Higher-priced items may be of good quality, but they may also contain features that you do not need. For example, you may not want to spend the extra money on an MP3 player that holds 20,000 songs when one that holds 500 is all you need. Be practical, especially when deciding on expensive items.

You can often save money by using generic products. Generic products do not have a famous brand name. However, generic products are often made from the same or similar ingredients or materials as the brand-name products. The difference is the amount of money spent on packaging and advertising. The extra cost of brand-name products is passed on to consumers.

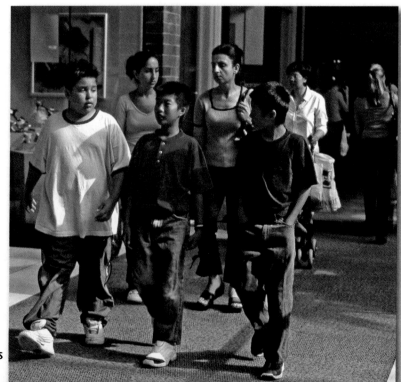

Shopping Options Choosing where to shop can be challenging. *What should you consider when deciding where to shop?*

Photo Caption Answer Price, quality, value, variety, condition of the merchandise, convenience, return policy, services offered.

Guatemalan Quetzal

The quetzal is the currency, or money, of Guatemala. It is named after the national bird of Guatemala, the "Resplendent Quetzal." It is divided into 100 centavos, much like a United States dollar is divided into 100 cents. The Mayans, who are the native people of Guatemala, used the long tail feathers of the male quetzal bird as currency in ancient times. Today, both the United States dollar and the Guatemalan quetzal carry value for making purchases in Guatemala. The image of the quetzal bird appears on Guatemalan paper currency and on some coins, and it carries historical importance for the people of Guatemala.

quetzal |ket-|säl 1. a Central American bird with brilliant green and red feathers. The male quetzal has very long, streaming tail feathers. 2. the main unit of Guatemalan currency.

NCSS I D Culture Compare and analyze societal patterns for preserving and transmitting culture while adapting to environmental or social change.

Guarantees

Many items come with a guarantee, sometimes called a warranty. A **guarantee** (ˈgär-ən-tē) is the manufacturer's written promise to repair or replace a product if it does not work as claimed. Service providers also offer guarantees that they will perform their services as promised. Be sure to read the guarantee or warranty so that you know what is promised. Some warranties apply only to certain parts of the product or only under specific conditions. For example, a product may be guaranteed to work properly for a specific length of time unless it is misused by the consumer.

No matter how you pay for an item, remember to keep the receipt and tags as proof of your purchase. Keep the receipt and the guarantee or warranty in a safe place. If you decide to return the item, you will need the receipt.

 Identify What are the risks of impulse buying?

Reading Check Answer
You may purchase something you do not need or that is not worth the money. You risk wasting your money and hurting your budget.

Your Consumer Rights and Responsibilities

Do you consider yourself a responsible consumer? Be courteous, count your change, handle merchandise carefully, and get the information you need. This is all part of being a responsible consumer.

Consumers have rights that protect them from false advertising and unsafe products. The law requires manufacturers to put labels on food and clothing and to make products that are safe to use. Your rights make it possible for you to make a complaint if you are not satisfied with a product or service. Your consumer rights may have helped you already. If you returned a shirt that did not fit, you exercised some of your rights. **Figure 11.3** explains the rights you have as a consumer.

Be Courteous

When you have to return an item to the store, you should do so in a polite way. Calmly explain what the problem is and how you would like to resolve it. For example, do you want your money back, or do you want to trade the item for another size or color? Remember to bring your receipt with you.

Figure 11.3 Consumer Rights

Exercise Your Rights As a consumer, you have the right to return items that do not fit your needs. Return policies vary by store. *What should you have available if you need to return a product?*

- **The Right to Safety** Products must be well designed and, if used properly, must not cause harm or injury.

- **The Right to Be Informed** Labels give you information about products. Laws protect you from false or misleading advertisements.

- **The Right to Choose** Consumers are entitled to choose from a variety of products. They have the right to select the items that fit their needs.

- **The Right to Be Heard** Consumers can speak out about a product if they are not satisfied with it.

- **The Right to Redress** Action taken to correct a wrong is called redress. Consumers can seek redress if they have a problem with a product.

- **The Right to Consumer Education** Consumers are entitled to learn about their rights. Consumer rights protect you and help you get the best product for your money. However, along with those rights you also have responsibilities.

Behave Responsibly

The manufacturer also has responsibilities. Manufacturers must produce products that are functional, safe, and reasonably priced. As a responsible consumer, you need to read and follow the instructions. Experts who understand the product prepare instructions that provide for your safety and satisfaction. It is important to follow them.

Another way to behave responsibly is to handle merchandise with care. This applies to more than breakable items. Clothing can be damaged while you are trying it on. Remove your shoes before trying on pants. Make sure any jewelry you wear does not snag on fabric. Leave the dressing room neat.

If you get a warranty card with a product, fill it out and send it to the manufacturer. The date on the card lets the manufacturer know when the warranty will **expire**, or come to an end. Keep your warranties together in one place.

Be Honest

When paying cash for your purchases, pay attention to the change you receive. If you receive too much change, return it to the clerk. Otherwise the clerk may be responsible for replacing the money.

Some people do not realize the seriousness of shoplifting. **Shoplifting** is taking items from a store without paying for them. It is stealing and it is punishable by law. Some people look at shoplifting as a prank. Their friends may dare them to do it. Shoplifting is a serious crime for which a person may go to jail and pay a fine. It is a crime that remains on that person's record. All customers have to pay higher prices to make up for the money that stores lose because of shoplifting.

Refunds and Exchanges

Like most people, you have probably purchased a product that did not work properly, did not fit, or was not what you expected. What did you do? Did you ask to exchange the unwanted product for something else? Did you ask for a refund, or return, of your money? Perhaps you accepted store credit.

Character Counts

Truthfulness

Candace's parents bought a cell phone for her birthday. They told her to be very careful with the expensive phone. If she damaged or lost it, she would have to pay to have it replaced. One day Candace and her friends went to the beach. Candace thought it would be a good idea to protect her phone from the sand by storing it in a plastic cup. Unfortunately, the cup was full of water! Her phone was ruined. She would have to pay for a new one. Then a friend suggested that she just tell her parents it was stolen. That way they could not be mad at her and they would have to buy her a new phone.

You Make the Call

Is the friend's suggestion reasonable? Can anyone be harmed when no one actually stole the phone? Write a paragraph that explains what you think Candace should do.

Character Counts Answer If Candace lies, she will risk losing the trust of her parents. That will hurt her relationship with them. Also, her parents would be harmed because they may pay the full price of a new phone based on a lie. Candace should tell her parents what really happened. She was being responsible by trying to protect her phone, so maybe her parents will understand that it was an accident. She could ask her parents if they would be willing to split the cost of the replacement phone.

Before you return a product, follow these guidelines:

- **Know the store's policy.** Every store sets its own return-and-exchange policy. The policy is usually posted where you pay for the item. Read the policy. If you do not understand it, ask the clerk before paying for the purchase. Never assume that you can return an item.
- **Keep proof of your purchase.** The store receipt is proof of the price, date of purchase, and store where you bought an item. Most stores require you to show your receipt in order to receive a refund.
- **Determine whether you are entitled to a refund.** Defective, or broken or flawed, merchandise may be sold "as is." Sale items may be marked "All Sales Final." In these cases you are not entitled to a refund. Certain products such as bathing suits, underwear, and pierced earrings are usually not returnable because of health codes.
- **Be ready to process your claim.** Take your merchandise and sales receipt to the store if you are entitled to a refund. You may be asked to complete a form giving a reason for returning the item. When the item is defective, be sure to provide this information so that the store can notify the manufacturer.

Reading Check **Connect** *What are the long-term consequences of shoplifting for the consumer?*

Reading Check Answer
All customers have to pay higher prices to make up for the money that stores lose because of shoplifting.

Photo Caption Answer Fill out and send in warranty cards, understand your rights as a consumer, be polite when asking for a refund or exchange, handle merchandise with care.

Take Responsibility
As a consumer, it is your responsibility to follow the manufacturer's instructions. *What else can you do to be a responsible consumer?*

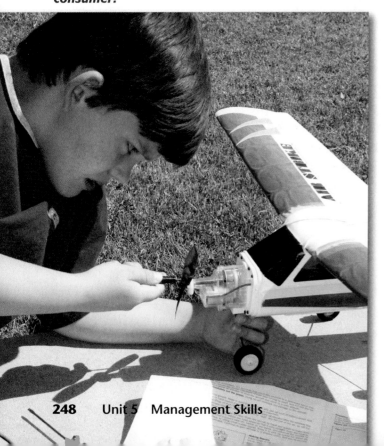

Money Management

You will be earning, spending, and saving money all of your life. The key to managing your money is to remember that the amount you have to spend is less important than how you spend it. Even if you have only a small amount to spend, you can stretch your buying power by learning to buy and save wisely.

To manage your money wisely you will need to:

- Know the source of your income.
- Determine how much money you will have.
- Look at how much money you are spending.
- Evaluate what you are buying.

Create a Budget

In this activity you will create a budget to plan and track your expenses. Before you begin, read through the entire Hands-On Lab assignment. Write down any questions that you have about the activity. Reread the text or ask your teacher for help if you need it

Supplies

✓ Notebook and pen
✓ Spreadsheet software (optional)

Develop Your Plan

■ Figure how much money you make every month from work or allowance. This is your monthly income. If you do not have a monthly income, use imaginary but realistic numbers.

■ Create categories for your regular expenses, such as Food, Entertainment, and School Expenses.

■ Add another category for miscellaneous expenses, such as unexpected purchases or items that do not fit your other categories.

■ Add a final category to your chart so you can label each item as a need or a want. For example, you need food, but you want a new wallet.

Implement Your Plan

■ Create a budget for the next month. If available, use spreadsheet software.

■ Estimate how much of your monthly income you will spend on each category.

■ Write the amounts down, or enter the amounts into your spreadsheet.

■ Record your income and expenses for one month.

■ At the end of the month, add the total spent on needs and the total spent on wants.

Evaluate Your Results

What surprised you about your spending habits? Did you spend more or less that you thought you would? Where did you spend the most? The least? How can you better spend your money next month? Write one or more paragraphs to explain your answer.

 Projects and Activities Go to this book's Online Learning Center through **glencoe.com** for more projects and activities.

Your **income** is the amount of money you earn or receive regularly. Your **expenses** are the goods and services on which you spend your money. If you manage your money well, you will not spend more on expenses than you receive as income. What are your sources of income? What are your expenses?

Plan and Budget

A **budget** is a plan for using your money. You need to examine your goals before you set up a budget. Do you want to save enough money for a new skateboard? Do you want to pay for singing lessons so that you can try out for the musical at school? Are you saving money to buy your parents an anniversary gift?

Your budget should include a savings plan. A savings plan helps you put money aside for unexpected needs and for future use. Many people find it easier to save when they set goals, such as having money for holiday activities. Some teens begin saving for a car or a college education. Unless you plan ahead and save regularly, it will be difficult to achieve your financial goals.

Planning a budget requires an income, a record of your expenses, and a goal. Begin by setting aside enough money to cover your expenses. When your income does not cover your expenses, you will need to make some adjustments. You may choose to cut back on some of your expenses. Another option is to look for new ways to add money to your income, such as babysitting or taking on extra chores for an allowance.

Paying for Purchases

Most people pay for their purchases with cash until they are ready to open a checking account or apply for a credit card. There are a variety of payment options besides cash:

- **Check** A check is a written order directing a bank to pay the person or business named on the check. In order to pay by check, you must open a checking account and deposit enough money to cover the checks you write. A checking account is a convenient way of handling money without keeping cash on hand.
- **Layaway Plan** A layaway plan is a scheduled payment plan in which you put a small amount of money down and make regular payments until you have paid for the item. When the item has been paid for in full, you can take it home.
- **Debit Card** A debit card is used to electronically withdraw money directly from a person's checking account.

Debit cards are considered the same as cash. There must be a balance, or a certain amount of money, in the account in order to use the card. Debit card transactions are an option at most retail establishments.

- **Credit Cards** You can buy now and pay later using a method of payment called **credit**. The seller or a bank issues credit to the buyer. That means that the buyer can use credit to make an immediate purchase. Then he or she must make regular payments to the seller or bank until the item is paid for in full. Credit is often used to buy expensive items such as furniture or large appliances. Be very careful when you use credit cards. It is easy to get caught in the credit trap. Credit cards are easily available, but you will pay a high price if you do not use them wisely. Your unpaid balance rolls over each month and extra fees called finance charges are added. If you only pay the minimum amount due, you will get further into debt because of the finance charges. This can damage your credit rating. A bad credit rating will make it difficult to get an apartment or a loan for a car or home. Do not take on the responsibility of credit card payments until you are fully prepared to pay what you owe.

Section 11.2 After You Read

Review What You Have Learned

1. **Describe** how you can become an informed shopper.
2. **Explain** how to return an item in a courteous way.
3. **Evaluate** how a savings plan can help you meet financial goals.

Practice Academic Skills

 English Language Arts

4. Create a pamphlet that encourages teens to save money for financial goals. Use graphics to make your pamphlet colorful and easy to read. Include steps for how to save, and the benefits of saving money.

> **NCTE 5** Use different writing process elements to communicate effectively.

 Social Studies

5. Research laws about consumer protection and consumer rights in your state. Choose a specific law that you find interesting, and present the information to the class in a short report.

> **NCSS VI A** Examine persistent issues involving the rights, roles, and status of the individual in relation to the general welfare.

Check Your Answers Check your answers at this book's Online Learning Center at glencoe.com.

Discovering Careers

Do you plan carefully before you spend your money? Have you offered advice to others about their finances? If you answered yes to either of those questions, you might want to consider a future career in finance. The following chart explores several careers in the finance field.

Job Title	Job Description
Accountant	Prepares financial reports. Documents business transactions. Prepares balance sheets and profit-and-loss statements.
Bank Teller	Receive, process, deposit, and distribute money for bank and financial institution customers. Cash payroll checks, exchange foreign currency, receive loan payments, issue traveler's checks.
Debt Collector	Collects debts by phone, mail, and in person. Contacts people to set up payment arrangements. Reports delinquent accounts.
Tax Preparer	Prepares federal, state, or local tax returns for individuals, businesses, or organizations. Computes taxes owed according to laws and regulations.
Credit Counselor	Counsels people who have difficulty managing money. Sets up spending plans. Arranges pay plans between creditors and debtors for debt repayment.

Career Activities ▼

At School

1 Select three of the careers listed. Research the education, training, and work experience required for each career. Write a summary of your results.

At Home

2 With help from family members, keep a record of all purchases made by your family in one week. List expenses by category. Other than rent and house payments, where does your family spend the most money?

At Work

3 Make a list of buying decisions that might need to be made in a business office. Compare lists with your classmates.

In the Community

4 Contact and interview someone in your community who works in the finance field. Ask this person to describe what his or her typical work day is like. Share what you learned with your class.

Career Activities Answers for these activities can be found on page TM127.

Learn More *Online* glencoe.com

Career Investigations Go to this book's Online Learning Center for activities and worksheets to help you explore careers.

Chapter Summary

Section 11.1 Be a Smart Consumer
Teens spend their money to buy goods and services. As a consumer, you must decide what to buy, where to buy, and when to buy. An advertisement is a message that persuades consumers to buy a product or service. Family, friends, and the media influence your buying decisions. Before you decide to buy a service or product, analyze the advertising claims and get as much information as possible.

Section 11.2 Spending and Saving Basics
Skillful shoppers get the best value for their money. Today's consumers have many shopping options. Consumers have rights and responsibilities. Be courteous, follow instructions, and get the information you need to be a responsible consumer. The key to managing your money is to save more than you spend. Set up a budget that includes a savings plan.

Words You Learned

1. Write your own definition for each content and academic vocabulary term.

Content Vocabulary
- consumer (p. 235)
- advertisement (p. 236)
- trend (p. 236)
- media (p. 237)
- impulse buying (p. 242)
- comparison shopping (p. 244)
- guarantee (p. 245)
- shoplifting (p. 247)
- income (p. 250)
- expenses (p. 250)
- budget (p. 250)
- credit (p. 251)

Academic Vocabulary
- service (p. 235)
- endorse (p. 236)
- merchandise (p. 243)
- expire (p. 247)

Review Key Concepts

2. **Evaluate** how you can be a smart shopper.

3. **Explain** how your habits affect the way you decide what to buy.

4. **Identify** the purpose of advertising.

5. **List** the different types of stores where you can shop.

6. **Explain** why consumers need rights and how you can be a responsible consumer.

7. **Understand** how to manage your money wisely.

Critical Thinking

8. **Predict** what can happen if you fall into the credit card trap.

9. **Analyze** the way advertising works in your age group. What do advertisers do to appeal to you as a member of the teen audience? In what media forms are you likely to find ads for your age group?

Real-World Skills and Applications

Problem-Solving

10. Shop Around You need a new radio alarm clock to use in your room. You arrive at the electronics department and find that the store carries a large variety of radio alarm clocks, with a wide price range and several brands. What should you do before you make your decision?

Interpersonal and Collaborative

11. The Power of Influence Follow your teacher's directions to form groups. Make a list of at least five items that you purchased recently. Next to each item, identify what influenced your buying decision the most. Was it friends, family, habit, the media, or advertising? Compare your lists, and determine which influence has the most power in your group. What conclusions can you draw from this activity?

Financial Literacy

12. The Rule of 72 In finance, the "Rule of 72" works as a rule of thumb for quickly estimating the number of years it will take for your money to double at a given interest rate. Simply divide 72 by the interest rate percentage to find the number of years until your money doubles. For example, Shannon is a first-year college student who will have loans to pay off when she graduates. She wants to start saving now. If she chooses an account that pays 9% interest, it will take approximately $72 \div 9 = 8$ years to double her money. How many years would it take to double her money at a rate of 4%? If she wanted to double her money in 2 years, what rate would she need?

13. Savings Plans Conduct research to learn about saving money at a bank. Choose three banks. For each bank, create an information card with the bank name and the type or name of the savings account on the front. On the back of each card, list the details of the plan. For example, how much money do you need to open an account? What is the interest rate? When can you access your money? Highlight any unfamiliar terms on your cards to discuss in your class.

14. Advertising Analysis Find five advertisements for products geared toward teen buyers. Using Figure 11.2 on page 239 as a guide, identify the advertising techniques used. Which do you think is the most effective? Which is the least effective? After reading this chapter, do you think you will react to ads in different ways? Why or why not? Explain your answer in a presentation to your class.

15. Start Saving Now You may think it is difficult to save money when you do not make much money in the first place. However, with creative planning you can start your money management strategies now. With permission from your teacher or parents, go online to find information that can help teens save money. Write down or print out the tips and suggestions you find and include them in your Life Skills Binder.

Academic Skills

English Language Arts

16. Create a Brochure Conduct research to learn more about how to manage credit. Use the information to write a brochure that will help teens manage their credit when they are on their own. Provide useful tips from the chapter and other resources. If possible, illustrate your brochure to add color and interest.

> **NCTE 8** Use information resources to gather information and create and communicate knowledge.

Science

17. Research Ingredients To complete a scientific investigation, you collect data. Use this science skill to research the ingredients in brand-name and generic products.

Procedure Record the ingredients of brand-name and generic condiments. Choose your five favorite condiments, and create a chart to collect your data.

Analysis Using your chart, determine whether or not generic products are the same as brand-name products. What conclusions can you draw from the information you found?

> **NCES A** Develop understandings about scientific inquiry.

Mathematics

18. Calculating Insurance Decreases John pays $500 for car insurance a year. When he turns 21, his payments will decrease by 10%. After that, if he takes a safe driving course, he will receive another 2% discount. How much will he pay each year after receiving both reductions?

Math Concept **Calculating Discounted Prices** To calculate a discounted price when you know the percentage of discount, subtract the discount percentage from 100%, and multiply the resulting percentage by the original price. For example, if you receive a 25% discount, then the new price will be 100% - 25% = 75% of the original price.

Starting Hint Subtract the first discount (10%) from 100%. Multiply the new percent by the insurance payment ($500). The result is the price after the 21-and-over discount. Multiply that price by 100% minus 2% to find the price after the safe driving course discount is also added.

> **NCTM Number and Operations** Understand the meanings of operations and how they relate to one another.

Standardized Test Practice

Essay
Write a half-page response to the writing prompt.

> **Test-Taking Tip** When writing an essay test response, it is important to take a few moments to plan. Read the question several times and underline key words or phrases, such as explain, support, details, and examples. Key words or phrases tell you what you have to do.

19. Advertising and other influences bombard students on every front. It can be difficult to know how to make choices about spending and saving money. Write an essay about how to make the best choice when making a major purchase. Explain how you make your choice, the events or people who influence your choice, and the effects of your purchase on your finances. Support your explanation with details and examples.

Chapter 12

Manage Resources, Time, and Stress

Explore the Photo Answer Answers may include: use a planner, set aside specific times for homework and extracurricular activities, work together with family members and friends to plan ahead.

 Section 12.1

Manage Resources

■ **Main Idea** Learn how to use personal resources and how to apply management skills to all areas of your life.

 Section 12.2

Manage Time and Handle Stress

■ **Main Idea** Learn and use time-management skills to have more time for things you want to do, and to help you reduce the stress that can happen when you try to do too much.

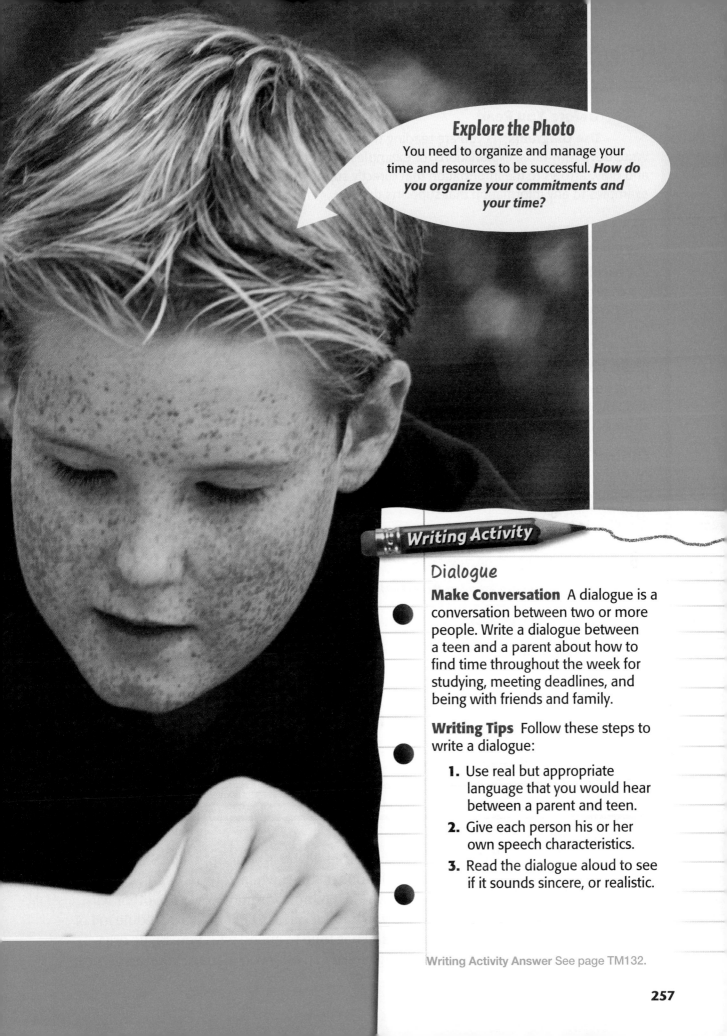

Explore the Photo

You need to organize and manage your time and resources to be successful. *How do you organize your commitments and your time?*

Writing Activity

Dialogue

Make Conversation A dialogue is a conversation between two or more people. Write a dialogue between a teen and a parent about how to find time throughout the week for studying, meeting deadlines, and being with friends and family.

Writing Tips Follow these steps to write a dialogue:

1. Use real but appropriate language that you would hear between a parent and teen.
2. Give each person his or her own speech characteristics.
3. Read the dialogue aloud to see if it sounds sincere, or realistic.

Writing Activity Answer See page TM132.

Reading Guide

Before You Read

Use Diagrams As you are reading through this section, write down the main idea. Write down any facts, explanations, or examples you find in the text. Start at the main idea and draw arrows to the information that directly supports it. Then draw arrows from these examples to any information that supports them.

Read to Learn

Key Concepts

✓ **Describe** each of the four steps you can take to be a good manager.

✓ **Identify** resources that can help you manage your life.

Main Idea

Learn how to use personal resources and how to apply management skills to all areas of your life.

Content Vocabulary

○ management   ○ energy
○ resource

Academic Vocabulary

■ potent   ■ material

Graphic Organizer

As you read, list the four steps you can take to be a good manager. Use a graphic organizer like the one shown to help you organize your information.

Steps to be a Good Manager	
Step 1	
Step 2	
Step 3	
Step 4	

Graphic Organizer Go to this book's Online Learning Center at glencoe.com to print this graphic organizer.

································· **Academic Standards** ·································

English Language Arts

NCTE 5 Use different writing process elements to communicate effectively.

Mathematics

NCTM Number and Operations Understand numbers, ways of representing numbers, relationships among numbers, and number systems.

Social Studies

NCSS I E Culture Demonstrate the value of cultural diversity, as well as cohesion, within and across groups.

NCTE *National Council of Teachers of English*
NCTM *National Council of Teachers of Mathematics*

NSES *National Science Education Standards*
NCSS *National Council for the Social Studies*

Graphic Organizer Answer
(1) Decide on your goal
(2) Make a plan
(3) Put the plan into action
(4) Evaluate the results

You probably have a friend who is your opposite. She always has her homework done on time, while you are often working on yours until the last minute, or maybe it is the other way around. Perhaps you have another friend with a schedule full of activities, but he still has time to spend with you. Being organized and planning ahead can help you manage your resources.

The Management Process

People who manage well accomplish more with greater ease. They use their time and energy wisely. You may hear the word management and think of the workplace. However, you can apply management skills to all areas of your life. **Management** is the skillful use of resources to accomplish a task. Katie and Hassan are good managers. For example, Katie uses the time in her mom's car on the way to school to study. Hassan catches an early bus so he can get to school in time to spend 30 minutes in the computer lab.

You can be a good manager if you learn to follow the steps in the How To feature on page 260. These steps work whether you are writing a report or organizing a fundraiser for the school band. Tasks, assignments, goals, and even unexpected events can be more manageable when you make a plan. Writing out your plan is useful for several reasons. Having a written list gives you a visual reminder of what you need to do. It helps you organize your ideas. The physical act of writing something down can help you remember it better than just thinking about it. What goals do you have for which the four-step management plan would be helpful?

Reading Check *Explain* *How can management skills help you get more accomplished?*

As You Read
Connect Name a goal you achieved recently. What did you do to meet that goal?

Vocabulary

You can find definitions in the glossary at the back of this book.

As You Read Answer Answers will vary. Sample answers: raise a grade by setting aside extra study time; get a part in a play by rehearsing at home; saving enough money from babysitting to buy a new DVD.

Reading Check Answer Practicing management skills helps you learn to use your time and energy wisely.

Photo Caption Answer Write down your goals serves as a visual reminder; it helps you organize the steps to reach your goal, and the act of physically writing something down helps you remember it.

Write It Down
The key to management, whether in class, at home, or at work, is planning. *Why does writing down goals make planning easier?*

Make a Management Plan

It may seem like more work to take the time to write down a plan for your goals. However, if you take that extra time in the beginning, you can save time later. Creating a plan can help you focus and organize your thoughts. Use these four steps to help you map out the path to whatever you want to achieve.

Step 1
Decide on Your Goal Do you need to finish your science project by a certain date? Write down your goal to help you commit to it.

What is Your Goal? Write it down in a notebook or keep a file in you computer.

Step 2
Make a Plan Decide how you want to achieve the goal. Maybe the goal can be broken into smaller, short-term goals that are easier to reach. For example, if you want to finish the project in two weeks, you could work on research this week and a rough draft next week.

Break It Down Break your goal down into smaller, easy-to-manage goals.

Step 3
Put the Plan into Action Begin working on your plan. If you are going to try out for the soccer team, do not just talk about it. Start practicing now!

Just Do It Do not put it off. Get started on your plan today.

Step 4
Evaluate the Results When you evaluate the outcome of your plan, you determine the value of what you accomplished. Are you satisfied with the way your plan worked? If not, what would you do differently the next time?

Evaluate Your Plan Think about what you accomplished and what you would do differently next time.

Resource Management

Management is a word often applied to supervisors and their tasks in a work environment. While this is true, management also applies to just about any task you do. For example, did you know that when you organize your school papers or arrange music on a portable music player, you are using management skills? To be a good manager you must make full use of your resources. A **resource** is something or someone that is a source of help or information. Learn how to manage personal resources, material resources, and community resources to help you reach goals and get things accomplished.

Personal Resources

Personal resources are time, energy, knowledge and education, skills and talents, and people. How well you use your personal resources can make a difference in how much you accomplish.

Time

Everyone has 24 hours each day. Much of this time is spent sleeping, eating, grooming, studying, working, and socializing. Learn to use your time wisely. Section 12.2 will provide more information to help you manage your time effectively.

Energy

Energy is the power or ability to be active. It has to do with the strength of the body and mind to work and to enjoy your free time. You can keep your energy level up when you get enough sleep, eat nutritious foods, and participate in physical activities. Keep a positive attitude toward what has to be done to help improve your energy level.

Knowledge and Education

Knowledge is information and understanding. Education does not stop when you finish school. There will always be something new to learn. Keep yourself open to new ideas and other opinions. Knowledge and education are **potent**, or powerful, personal resources. You can continue to strengthen them for the rest of your life.

Financial Literacy

Pay Yourself First

When you receive your paycheck or allowance, pay yourself first. That means that you should set aside some money for savings before you spend any of it. Imagine that you have a job that pays $860 per month. If you save 2% of each monthly paycheck for one year, how much would you have at the end of the year? What if you saved 5%?

 Math Concept **Find the Percent of a Number**
A percent is a ratio of a number to 100. For example, 27% is the same thing as 27/100, or 27 divided by 100. To find a percent of a number, multiply the number by the percent. Change the percent to a decimal by removing the percent sign and moving the decimal point two places to the left. Multiply this decimal by the number.

Starting Hint At the end of one month, you will have $860 x 2%, or $860 x 0.02 in your savings account. Multiply that monthly amount by 12 to find out your total savings for the full year. Then, do the same calculations using 5% instead of 2%. How much more do you have at the 5% rate?

Math For math help, go to the Math Appendix at the back of the book.

NCTM Number and Operations Understand numbers, ways of representing numbers, relationships among numbers, and number systems.

Financial Literacy Answer You can save an extra $309.60 at the higher percentage. At the 2% rate, you will save 0.02 x $860 x 12 = $206.40 at the end of one year. At the 5% rate, you will save 0.05 x $860 x 12 = $516 at the end of the year. $516 - $206.40 = $309.60.

Commitment

Raquel was just offered a big part in the school's yearly musical production. If she accepts the part, rehearsals will be every Tuesday and Wednesday from 4:00 until 8:30 for the next three months. On Mondays she has her French club meetings after school, and on Thursday evenings she takes a dance class at the recreation center. Every other Friday after school, she works in her dad's office to help him file papers. Raquel decided to start a weekly planner to keep track of her busy schedule. She quickly realized that with the addition of the musical rehearsals, she would not have any free evenings for homework or studying. She also realized that her only free time would be on weekends, and that is when she does her chores and spends time with her friends.

You Make the Call

Raquel has over-committed herself. She wants to do it all, but there just is not enough time. Write a paragraph explaining what you think Raquel should do and why.

Character Counts Answer Raquel should make a priority list to help her decide which activities she can cut out of her schedule. She can rank the musical, French club, and dance class. She should consider what she enjoys the most, what can be postponed until next year, and what she must do versus what she wants to do. Then she can drop whichever activities are not first on her priority list. She can also ask her dad if she can work for him once a month instead of every other week.

Skills and Talents

A skill is an ability that comes from training or practice. You have reading, writing, and computer skills. You may also have other skills, such as the ability to play tennis, which you learned by taking lessons. Talents are different from skills. A talent is a natural ability, such as being able to draw, sing, or dance. Both skills and talents can be improved. What are your talents and skills? It is important to explore these areas to find out what you like to do. Making time for fun actiities is important for relieving stress and enjoying life.

People

People are valuable resources. Strong relationships with family and friends can provide support all your life. The encouragement of family and friends can help you gain confidence and strengthen your self-concept. Take advantage of opportunities to meet new people. Even if you never see someone again, a brief conversation with a person can inspire you or give you an idea. For example, you might go to an art festival and meet someone from another country or culture. Perhaps her artwork inspires you to redecorate your room.

Material Resources

Material resources are possessions, objects, and money. **Material** things are not necessary for survival like food, shelter, and water, but they can make life easier and more enjoyable. Your personal possessions might include a bike, a stereo, or books. Objects might include a refrigerator, a table, or a microwave oven. How do these possessions and objects help you do what you want to do? What role does money play in reaching your goals?

Personal possessions give you enjoyment and satisfaction. Riding your bike and listening to your stereo are two ways that you gain enjoyment from your possessions. Objects make life easier. For example, using a washing machine to wash clothes is easier than washing them by hand. Buying a cake is quicker and easier than baking your own cake.

Community Resources

Every community provides a variety of resources for its citizens to use. These include schools, hospitals, and police and fire departments. Many communities have interesting places to visit, such as museums or important historic buildings. Among other community resources are youth programs, libraries, parks, and recreational facilities.

Communities also provide resources for people who have special kinds of problems. Most communities offer programs for the homeless, the elderly, people with low income, and people who have problems with alcohol and other drugs. There are also programs to protect battered spouses and abused children.

Local Activities Community parks allow you to enjoy many outdoor activities. *What resources are provided by your community?*

Photo Caption Answer Answers will vary depending on your area. Students should recognize a variety of community resources, such as parks, schools, libraries, museums, shelters, youth programs, and human services.

Section 12.1 After You Read

Review What You Have Learned

1. **Define** management.
2. **Identify** what you can gain from material resources.

Practice Academic Skills

 English Language Arts

3. Apply the four-step management plan to a goal that you recently achieved. What was the goal? How did you break it into smaller steps? What was your action plan? What were the results? What would you do differently next time? Share an outline of your achievement and evaluation with your class.

> **NCTE 5** Use different writing process elements to communicate effectively.

Social Studies

4. People can be a valuable resource. Write a scenario in which you meet a teen from another culture who inspires you to do or to think about something new. Explain how this encounter can be beneficial to both of you.

> **NCSS I E** Demonstrate the value of cultural diversity, as well as cohesion, within and across groups.

Check Your Answers Check your answers at this book's Online Learning Center at glencoe.com.

Section 12.2 Manage Time and Handle Stress

Reading Guide

Before You Read

Be Organized A messy environment can be distracting. To lesson distractions, organize an area where you can read this section comfortably.

Read to Learn
Key Concepts
✓ **Explain** the benefits of having good time-management skills.

✓ **Understand** techniques you can use to handle stress.

Main Idea
Learn and use time-management skills to have more time for things you want to do, and to help you reduce the stress that can happen when you try to do too much.

Content Vocabulary
○ time management ○ procrastinate
○ multi-tasking ○ stress

Academic Vocabulary
■ alternate ■ cope

Graphic Organizer
As you read, list five things you can do to make the best use of your study time. Add your own ideas to the list. Use a graphic organizer like the one shown to help you organize your information.

Study Skills
1.
2.
3.
4.
5.
My own ideas:

 Graphic Organizer Go to this book's Online Learning Center at **glencoe.com** to print this graphic organizer.

- - - - - - - - - - - - - - - - - - **Academic Standards** - - - - - - - - - - - - - - - - - -

 English Language Arts
NCTE 4 Use written language to communicate effectively.

 Science
NSES A Develop abilities necessary to do scientific inquiry, understanding about scientific inquiry.

Social Studies
NCSS IV C Individual Development and Identity Describe the ways family, religion, gender, ethnicity, nationality, socio-economic status, and other group and cultural influences contribute to the development of a sense of self.

NCTE *National Council of Teachers of English*
NCTM *National Council of Teachers of Mathematics*

NSES *National Science Education Standards*
NCSS *National Council for the Social Studies*

Graphic Organizer Answer (1) make a to-do list (2) set the time (3) set the atmosphere (4) remove distractions (5) gather supplies. Students own ideas will vary, but should be sensible ideas to help with study time.

Do you sometimes feel that with school responsibilities, homework, extracurricular activities, and family commitments, you do not have time left over for yourself? It is easy to get involved in so many things that you feel like you cannot get anything done. Learn how to manage your time so that you can make the best use of the 24 hours you get every day.

Time Management

Use good time-management skills to help you in all areas of your life. **Time management** is the development of practices and skills that increase how quickly and effectively you can do something. Learn and use these skills so that you will have more time for the things you want to do. You can finish your homework and studying and still have time left for basketball, dance lessons, or for relaxing with a good book. Good time-management skills can help you meet deadlines and stay on schedule. Here are some ways to save time:

- Divide big jobs into small tasks.
- Do more than one task at the same time. This is called **multi-tasking**.
- Try to avoid interruptions.
- Tell your family members about your plans so they know when you are available, and when you need time for yourself.
- Stick with a task until it is done.
- Establish routines for daily tasks.
- Evaluate your activities on a regular basis so that you do not over-commit yourself.

🕐 **To-Do List** Making a to-do list can help you organize and prioritize your goals. *How can you prioritize your study time to make it count?*

As You Read

Connect What can lead to a feeling of not having enough time in the day to finish what you need to do?

As You Read Answer Answers may include making too many commitments, not knowing how to organize or prioritize, having too many people or activities that demand time. Some students may admit to a lack of motivation.

◆ **Vocabulary**

You can find definitions in the glossary at the back of this book.

Photo Caption Answer Write down what you need to do in order of importance, then check off items as they are completed so you can see your progress.

Succeed in School Remind students to update their schedules or planners at the end of class.

Time Management *Update Your Schedule* Look at your schedule each morning. Add any tasks you did not complete the day before, and add new tasks.
● ● ● ● ● ● ● ● ● ● ● ●

Time management also includes dealing with problems that may arise. You may find that two activities occur at the same time. You may have to make a choice between two things you really want to do. Try making a list of pros and cons. Pros are the good things about an activity or event. Cons are the negative things. For example, one of your choices may be going to the movies with your friend. A "pro" would be spending time with your friend. A "con" might be that it will take away from the time you need to practice for your piano recital. When you have a pros and cons list written down for each option, it will probably become clear which choice to make.

Sometimes you have several things you want to accomplish during a day. It may be difficult to know where to begin. When you prioritize, you rank tasks in order of importance. For example, if you use a to-do list, put a *1, 2, 3* and so on next to each task. As you complete each task, cross it off the list. It can motivate you to continue when you see how much you have accomplished.

Another challenge is dealing with unexpected changes. Sometimes schedules and plans do not work out exactly as planned. You may need to rearrange your priority list. A friend may have to cancel a shopping trip to the mall. The rain may prevent you from raking leaves. Whatever the case, stay flexible. Make the most of your time by having ideas for **alternate**, or different, activities.

Photo Caption Answer Do not put things off, plan ahead, multi-task, keep a schedule or planner, get enough rest so you can focus, keep your work area organized and neat.

Organize Supplies Organizing the tools or supplies you need before beginning a task helps you save time. *What are some other ways to save time?*

Make Time Count

Have you ever turned on the television to watch one 30-minute show, and then several hours later you were still watching television? Perhaps you spent a lot of time looking for your math book, only to find that it was on your desk all along, hidden under a pile of papers. Here are some ways to help you avoid wasting time:

- **Do not put things off for later.** If you **procrastinate** (prō-ˈkras-tə-nāt,) by waiting until the last minute to do something, you can waste a lot of time thinking and worrying about the task. Often you will find that the task itself does not take as long as the time you spent worrying about it.
- **Get organized.** Almost any task goes faster when you are organized. Before you begin the task, gather the tools or equipment you need and find out how to do the task. When you are finished, clean up or put things away. It may seem like it takes too much time to tidy up. However, think about the math book example above. Neatness and organization will save you time when you can find your book right away next time you need it.
- **Get Your Sleep.** You may think that you can give yourself more time by sleeping less. It does not work that way. You will accomplish less instead of more, because you are tired and unfocused.
- **Schedule Breaks.** Another mistake people can make is working nonstop on a task. You may think a job will be finished quicker if you plow through it. However, it is better to allow yourself a break or two while you work. A break, even if it is only for 5 or 10 minutes to get a snack or play with a pet, can help refresh your mind and body before getting back to your task.

Study Skills

As a student, you will find that much of your time is spent studying. Effective study skills include reading, note-taking, test-taking, listening, computer skills, and time-management skills. Make sure your study time is well spent by organizing and prioritizing your homework assignments, projects, and test preparation time.

SCIENCE YOU CAN USE

The Buddy System

Studies show that having a support system in place can help ease the stress of certain situations. Support from others can help take the stress out of a situation and have a calming effect on the person or people experiencing stress.

Procedure Study your classmates during a stressful time, such as waiting to be chosen for a team, or during the last few minutes of a ball game. Record the reactions of those who have support from peers and those who do not.

Analysis Using your results, determine whether or not the Buddy System relieves stress.

> **NSES A** Develop abilities necessary to do scientific inquiry, understanding about scientific inquiry.

Science You Can Use Answer Answers will vary. Logical conclusions should be drawn based on the students' data.

Succeed in School Use checklists in your classroom as a model for students to follow.

Time Management
Make a Checklist
Write down all of your assignments and tasks for the next week. Draw a small box next to each item. As you finish each task, put a check in the box. You can see your progress and feel a sense of accomplishment with each check.

• • • • • • • • • • • •

Time Management

Time for Tasks
Estimate how much time each of your assignments will take. Make a daily schedule. Write down due dates and the time you think each assignment will take. This can help you meet deadlines.

• • • • • • • • • • • • • •

Succeed in School
Remind students to check their schedules every day. Ask volunteers to remind the class about important due dates.

Reading Check Answer
Make a list of pros and cons for each option, then make a choice based on the list.

Keep track of the areas where you need to improve your study skills. Ask for help when you need it. Parents, teachers, siblings, and friends are resources you can use for help. Ask a parent to quiz you before a test, or ask your brother to help you with your vocabulary assignment. Teachers can suggest extra resources such as tutoring if you need it. It is important that you continue to improve your study skills. You will use them at home, at school, on the job, and in the community. See **Figure 12.1** for some more suggestions to help improve your study skills.

Reading Check *Evaluate* How can you decide between doing two things that you really want to do?

The Stress Connection

When you try to do too much, you may experience stress. **Stress** is the body's reaction to feeling overwhelmed by responsibilities, demands, or events. Both pleasant and unpleasant events can cause stress. For example, performing a solo in a school concert may be stressful even though you enjoy singing. A fight with your parents causes a different kind of stress. Whatever the situation, remember that stress is a natural part of life. You have the power to learn how to control the way you handle stress. Figure Caption Answer Answers may include: make and use a list, have a set time for studying, get rid of distractions, have all the supplies.

Figure (**12.1**) **Improve Your Study Skills**

Organize and Prioritize Create a plan to organize and arrange your tasks to make the most of your study time. *How do you plan for your study time?*

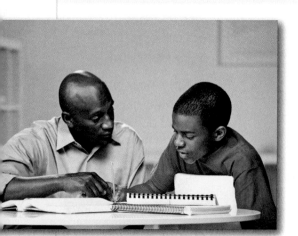

- **Make a to-do list.** Write down what you want to accomplish.
- **Set the time.** Decide how much time you are going to spend studying. Prioritize your tasks to fit that block of time. Try to study at the same time every day.
- **Set the atmosphere.** Choose a quiet place to study. Make sure the space has enough light, and enough space to spread out. If it helps to have music, keep the volume low.
- **Remove distractions.** Turn off the television, and do not use the telephone while you study. If you have a cell phone, let your calls go to voicemail. When using a computer, disable instant messaging. Keep your e-mail closed until you are finished studying.
- **Gather supplies.** Collect all of your pens, pencils, papers, and books before you begin.

How much stress you feel depends on how much is going on in your life and how you react to events. For example, adjusting to a new class and making new friends can be stressful. If you are experiencing another major life change at the same time, such as starting a new job or attending a new school, the stress may be even greater.

Stress and Your Health

Stress can motivate and challenge you. It can help you accomplish your goals. The stress of wanting to make the soccer team, for example, can motivate you to exercise and practice. However, too much stress, especially when it is not managed well, can have a negative impact on your health. Symptoms of too much stress can include headaches, stomachaches, loss of appetite, fatigue, depression, and anxiety. People who are unable to **cope**, or adjust to difficult and stressful situations, may become seriously ill. Sometimes they try to run away from their problems by turning to alcohol or other drugs. When you manage your time and other resources in your life, you will be better equipped to handle stress when it occurs.

Stress and Nutrition

When you get busy with homework, studying, friends, hobbies, sports, and other activities, it is easy to forget about having a balanced diet. You may be tempted to skip meals or eat unhealthful foods out of convenience.

SUCCEED IN SCHOOL!

Time Management
Time for Tasks
Estimate how much time each of your assignments will take. Make a daily schedule. Write down due dates and the time you think each assignment will take. This can help you meet deadlines.

Succeed in School Remind students to check their schedules every day. Ask volunteers to remind the class about important due dates.

Relax Take the time to unwind, relax, and enjoy a few moments alone. *What are some other ways you can cope with stress?*

Photo Caption Answer Participate in physical activities, spend time with people who care about you, do something you enjoy.

Manage Stress

Stress can affect your life in many ways. Symptoms may include changes in appetite, headaches, stomachaches, mood swings, and the inability to concentrate. Use these techniques to help you manage activities and events that can cause stress.

Get Away from the Routine Remove yourself from stressful situations, even if it is just a short break. Take a walk, spend time with a pet, or listen to some music. Do something you enjoy. Deep-breathing exercises can slow a racing heart and help clear your mind.

Set Priorities Decide what tasks or activities are the most important and prioritize them. Make sure your goals are realistic. Plan ahead for events that you know will happen.

Seek Out Your Support System Go to the people in your life who can provide support, encouragement, and advice. Friends and family who care about you can help in times of stress.

Do Something for Others Volunteer to help someone else. When you do something that benefits another person, it can help you feel proud and satisfied, and it can give you a greater sense of self-worth. These feelings can go a long way toward decreasing your own stress level.

Take Care of Yourself Do not let your health suffer when you are feeling stressed. Participate in a physical activity to release endorphins (en-ˈdȯr-fənz), your body's natural stress and pain reliever. Also, get plenty of sleep, eat balanced and nutritious meals, drink water, and take time to relax.

Adjust Your Attitude Be positive about your situation. Remind yourself that stress is a part of life and you can work through it. Do your best to maintain a positive and flexible attitude.

When your body does not get the nutrients it needs, you may end up trying to do more with less energy. This can lead to poor health and add even more stress to your busy life. Here are some easy ways to eat healthfully, even when you think you do not have the time:

Eat breakfast. When you skip breakfast, it is more difficult for your body to maintain stable blood sugar levels and energy during your busy morning. You can easily grab a hard-boiled egg and container of orange juice on your way out the door.

Carry a snack. Keep some protein-rich, healthful snacks in your backpack to help you avoid dips in your blood sugar levels and the mood swings and tiredness that can result. Trail mix, granola bars, and some energy bars all contain good nutrition.

Drink water. You should always have water handy. It is vital to health and proper physical functioning.

Get your family involved. It is easier to avoid sugary, fatty, and otherwise unhealthful foods if they are not in your home. Ask family members to stock the house with healthful foods and snacks, and to keep unhealthful foods to a minimum.

Section 12.2 After You Read

Review What You Have Learned

1. **Explain** how you can prioritize tasks you need to accomplish.
2. **Identify** five tips for managing stress.

Practice Academic Skills

 English Language Arts

3. Write an e-mail to a friend who feels stressed because she cannot seem to find time to do her homework, rehearse for the play, prepare for exams, practice for softball tryouts, and hang out with her friends. Suggest things she can do to manage her time and help reduce her stress.

NCTE 4 Use written language to communicate effectively.

 Social Studies

6. Interview family members about how they manage their time. How is the way you manage time similar or different? What influences do you see on your own time-management skills? Write a paragraph that describes your findings about how you and your family manage time.

NCSS IV C Describe the ways family, religion, gender, ethnicity, nationality, socio-economic status, and other group and cultural influences contribute to the development of a sense of self.

 Check Your Answers Check your answers at this book's Online Learning Center at glencoe.com.

Discovering Careers

Are you a detail-oriented person? Do you like to be in charge of organizing people or events? If you answered yes to either of those questions, you might want to consider a future career in management. The following chart explores several careers in the management field.

Job Title	Job Description
Librarian	Maintains collections of books, magazines, documents, and other materials. Assists individuals in locating and obtaining materials.
Trans- portation Scheduler	Prepares schedules for transportation. Determines number of vehicles and trips. Arranges stops, length of routes, and runs per shift.
Production Manager	Trains and supervises employees in production of radio or television programs. Makes sure the program follows station policies and regulations.
Hotel Manager	Coordinates reservations and room assignments. Trains and directs hotel's front desk staff. Greets guests, resolves complaints and problems, handles special requests from guests.
School Principal	Works with administrators, students, parents, and local representatives to set school policies and goals and to raise funds. Prepares budgets and attendance reports.

Career Activities ▼

At School

1 Select three of the careers listed. Research the education, training, and work experience required for each career. Write a summary of your results.

At Home

2 Develop a master schedule for your family for a week. Use all the activities your family is involved at home, as well as commitments at work or in the community.

At Work

3 Make a list of your computer skills and the software you know how to use. How will these skills help you on the job?

In the Community

4 Contact and interview someone in your community who works in a management position. Ask this person to describe what his or her typical work day is like. Share what you learned with your class.

Career Activities Answers for these activities can be found on page TM132.

Learn More *Online* glencoe.com

Career Investigations Go to this book's Online Learning Center for activities and worksheets to help you explore careers.

Chapter 12 Review and Activities

Chapter Summary

Section 12.1 Manage Resources
Management skills are not just for the workplace. Follow a plan for your goals, and make full use of your resources. Learn how to manage personal resources, material resources, and community resources to help you reach goals and get things accomplished. Personal resources are time, energy, knowledge, skills, and people. Material resources are possessions, objects, and money. Every community provides a variety of resources for its citizens to use.

Section 12.2 Manage Time and Handle Stress
Time management is the development of practices and skills that increase how quickly and effectively you can do something. Learn to organize and prioritize your time. When you try to do too much, you can experience stress. Stress can motivate and challenge you, but too much stress can have a negative effect on you. When you manage your time and other resources in your life, you will be better equipped to handle stress.

Words You Learned

1. Create a fill-in-the-blank sentence for each of these vocabulary words. The sentence should contain enough information to help determine the missing word.

Content Vocabulary
- management (p. 259)
- resource (p. 261)
- energy (p. 261)
- time management (p. 265)
- multi-tasking (p. 265)
- procrastinate (p. 267)
- stress (p. 268)

Academic Vocabulary
- potent (p. 261)
- material (p. 262)
- alternate (p. 267)
- cope (p. 269)

Review Key Concepts

2. **Describe** each of the four steps you can take to be a good manager.

3. **Identify** resources that can help you manage your life.

4. **Explain** the benefits of having good time-management skills.

5. **Understand** techniques you can use to handle stress.

Critical Thinking

6. **Evaluate** how your family manages the tasks and activities of everyday life.

7. **Compare and contrast** material resources and personal resources.

8. **Predict** what could happen if you allow day-to-day stress, such as studying for tests or getting to class on time, to upset you.

9. **Recognize** that stress can be a positive factor in your life.

Real-World Skills and Applications

Problem-Solving

10. Action Plan Your brother needs help managing his busy schedule. He has to find time for homework, studying, hockey practice, family obligations, and his scout troop. Write a list of suggestions to help him manage his time and resources.

Technology Applications

11. Weekly Planner Create a weekly planner using spreadsheet, word processing, or design software. Customize it to your personal schedule. Include school activities, assignments, tests, family activities, chores, special events, and personal time. What do you notice about your week's activities? Are they manageable, or can you make adjustments to better organize your time and resources?

Financial Literacy

12. Financial Document Organization Andre's financial records are out of control. His receipts and bills are scattered all over his room. He does not know what is due, what is late, or how much he has spent. Andre also tends to forget about keeping track of his bank balance, so he never knows how much money he has available. Not only does this lack of organization cause Andre unneeded stress, but he also wastes about 15 minutes a week looking for his bills and paperwork. If Andre spent 20 minutes a month carefully organizing all of his financial documents to eliminate this stress and wasted time, how much time would he save over the course of a 52-week year?

13. Organize Your Study Area Collect an assortment of boxes, cartons, and jars in a variety of sizes. Use your imagination to decorate the containers. For example, cut the top off of a small milk carton and cover it with construction paper or left over gift wrap. Glue beads to the outside of a recycled pickle jar. Use the finished containers as pencil holders, paper trays, and storage for items like paperclips to organize your study area at home.

14. Successful Stress Management Interview someone you know, such as a teacher, a family member, or friend, about how they handle stress at work, at home, or in other areas of their lives. Ask such questions as, "What situations make you feel stressed?" and "What stress relief techniques work for you?" Ask him or her for tips and suggestions that you might be able to apply when you feel stressed. Prepare a list of tips and present them to your class.

15. Learn How to Study With permission from your parents or teacher, go online to search for tips on how to study. It may seem like something you already know how to do, but there are different methods for studying. You may find a method or idea that will help you improve the way you study. Make a list of at least five study tips. Explain how you can apply them to your homework and test preparation. Include the list in your Life Skills Binder.

Academic Skills

English Language Arts

16. Design A Workspace What does your ideal workspace look like? Create a sketch of workspace that would help you organize your personal resources and study tools. Look for ideas in magazines, furniture catalogs, interior decorating books, or online resources. Next to the sketch, list all of the supplies you would like to have in your ideal workspace. Present your sketch and list to the class and explain how your design and supplies will help you manage time and reduce stress.

> **NCTE 12** Use language to accomplish individual purposes.

Science

17. Long-Term Stress Chronic, or long-term, stress can affect physical health. **Procedure** Conduct research to find out what people can do to help prevent long-term stress. What recommendations can you find for managing stress? **Analysis** Prepare a short presentation to share with the class.

> **NSES F** Develop understanding of personal and community health.

Mathematics

18. Evaluate Your Time Chiyoko has decided to evaluate how he uses his time so he can make adjustments that would allow for more study time. When he realized that he spends 3 hours a day watching television, and 45 minutes a day playing video games, he knew it was time for some changes. Figure out what percentage of the day Chiyoko spent watching television. What percentage of the day did he spend playing video games?

Math Concept **Time Calculations** When performing multiplication or division with time, make sure all numbers are in the same units. Since there are 60 minutes in an hour, you can convert hours to minutes by multiplying by 60. Similarly, convert days to hours by multiplying by 24.

Starting Hint To find the TV percentage, divide 3 hours by 24 hours, then write the result as a percentage (multiply by 100 and add the "%" symbol). To find the videogame percentage, first you will need to convert 24 hours into minutes by multiplying 24 by 60.

> **NCTM Number and Operations** Understand the meanings of operations and how they relate to one another.

Standardized Test Practice

Analogies

Select the pair of words that best expresses a relationship similar to that expressed in the capitalized pair.

> **Test-Taking Tip** Analogies are relationships between two words or concepts. Common relationships in analogy questions include cause and effect, part-to-whole, general classification and specific example, and synonym/antonym.

19. NUTRIENTS:HEALTH
a. safety:injury
b. stress:deep breathing
c. sleep:alertness
d. emergency:rescue breathing

Manage Your Grocery Budget

Knowing how to shop is a key life skill. Observing the choices your parents make at the grocery story can be useful. Clip coupons, compare prices in newspapers, buy in bulk, and read labels to help you save money and become a better consumer.

 My Journal Complete the journal entry from page 231, and refer to it to complete your grocery list.

Project Assignment ▼

In this project, you will:

■ Analyze the groceries your family usually buys.

■ Make a grocery list and shop for your family.

■ Describe your shopping experience.

■ Interview someone who works in a grocery store.

■ Create a chart to demonstrate cost-saving techniques.

■ Present your findings to your class.

■ Include this project in the fifth section of your personal Life Skills binder.

 Step 1 Research the Best Buys and Make a List

Creating a shopping list is easier if you know what your family usually buys. While making your list, check newspapers for prices, sales, and coupons. Write a summary of your research, explaining how you plan to save money at the grocery store.

Step 2 Go Shopping

Finalize your grocery list. Go to a grocery store with a parent or trusted adult. Compare products before you buy, use coupons, and search for the best deals. Then write two or more paragraphs that answer these questions:

✔Did you decide to cross any items off of your list?

✔What coupons did you use?

✔What generic items did you buy instead of brand-name products?

✔Did you find items you could buy in bulk?

✔What other ways did you find to save money?

✔How much money did you save?

Step 3 Interview a Grocery Store Worker

Interview a person who works in a store where groceries are sold. Ask these questions:

✔What tips or tricks can you share that would help families save money on groceries?

✔Is there a time of day or week that is better for getting good deals?

✔What are your own strategies for saving money at the market?

Use these interviewing skills when conducting your interview and these writing skills when writing the summary of notes from your interview.

Interviewing Skills
• Record interview responses and take notes.
• Listen attentively.

Writing Skills
• Use complete sentences.
• Use correct spelling and grammar.

Step 4 Create and Present Your Chart

Use the Life Skills Project Checklist on the right to plan and complete your chart. Use information from your observations, your personal shopping experience, and your interview with the grocery store worker to complete your chart and give an oral report on it.

Use these speaking skills when presenting your final report.

Speaking Skills
- Speak clearly and concisely.
- Be sensitive to the needs of your audience.
- Use standard English to communicate.

Step 5 Evaluate Your Presentation

Your project will be evaluated based on:

✔ Completeness and organization of your shopping list.
✔ Your chart of cost-saving techniques.
✔ The description of your shopping experience.
✔ The summary written from interview notes.
✔ Grammar and sentence structure.
✔ Presentation to the class.
✔ Creativity and neatness.

🧭 **Evaluation Rubric** Go to this book's Online Learning Center through glencoe.com for a rubric you can use to evaluate your final project.

Life Skills Project Checklist

Research Research Cost-Saving Techniques

✅ Study your family's grocery receipts for ways to save money.

✅ Collect coupons for products your family would buy.

✅ Read newspapers to search for bargains.

✅ Read labels on products at the market.

✅ Interview a grocery store worker.

✅ Include your cost-saving techniques in a chart.

Writing Skills

✅ Describe some of the groceries your family typically buys.

✅ Describe your shopping experience.

✅ Write a summary from your interview with grocery store worker.

Present Your Findings

✅ Prepare a short presentation to explain what you did to save money.

✅ Invite the students of the class to ask any questions they may have. Answer these questions with responses that respect their perspectives.

✅ Add this project to your Life Skills binder.

Academic Skills

✅ Conduct research to gather information.

✅ Communicate effectively.

✅ Organize your presentation so the audience can follow along easily.

✅ Thoroughly express your ideas.

NCTE 7 Conduct research and gather, evaluate, and synthesize data to communicate discoveries.

NCTM Number and Operations Compute fluently and make reasonable estimates.

Chapter 13
Your Living Space

Chapter 14
Your Environment

Unit Preview

This unit is about the world you live in, both inside and outside of your home. In this unit, you will learn about:

- Making your home safe and comfortable.
- Adding your personal style to your living space.
- The different types of natural resources and how to conserve them.
- What you can do as an individual to protect the environment.

Explore the Photo Answer Answers may include hiking, nature walks, kayaking, swimming, horseback riding, bird watching, surfing, camping.

Explore the Photo
Spending time exploring nature can be enjoyable and relaxing. *What are some of the activities you enjoy doing in nature?*

Improve Your Home

When you are done studying this unit, you will complete a project in which you will:

✓ Evaluate your living space.

✓ Interview a home design or construction professional.

✓ Create and share floor plans to demonstrate your improved arrangements.

The prewriting activity below will help you get started.

 My Journal

Prewriting Activity
Freewrite

Visit three rooms or areas in your home or someone else's home. Describe how each room or area looks and how it is meant to be used.

● Which rooms or areas seem to work well for their purpose?

● Which rooms or areas need to be rearranged to better suit their purpose?

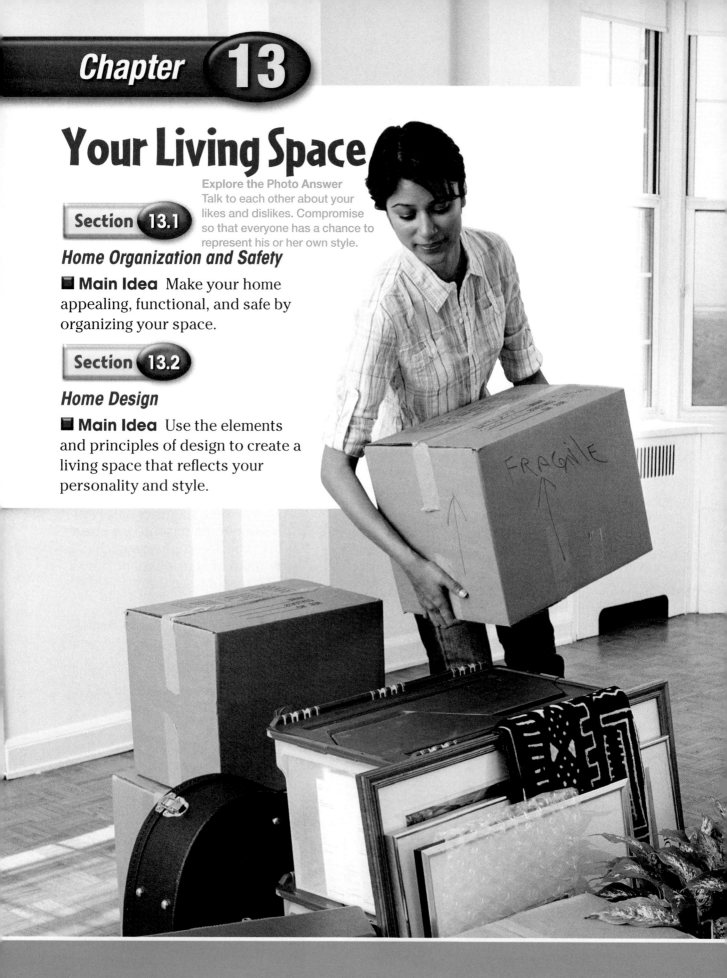

Chapter 13

Your Living Space

Explore the Photo Answer
Talk to each other about your
likes and dislikes. Compromise
so that everyone has a chance to
represent his or her own style.

Section 13.1

Home Organization and Safety

■ **Main Idea** Make your home
appealing, functional, and safe by
organizing your space.

Section 13.2

Home Design

■ **Main Idea** Use the elements
and principles of design to create a
living space that reflects your
personality and style.

Explore the Photo

To design your living space, you will need to work with your roommates. *How can you work with others to create a comfortable home for all involved?*

Writing Activity

Descriptive Paragraph

Describe What would your perfect room be like? Write a paragraph that describes your perfect room and the mood or feel you want it to have. For example, you might want a room that makes you feel like you are in a log cabin. Choose furniture, colors, decorations, and accessories to create the mood or feel you want in your room.

Writing Tips Follow these steps to write a descriptive paragraph:

1. Choose a few words to describe the mood or feel you want and include them in your topic sentence.

2. Describe the furniture, colors, decorations, and accessories that create the mood or feel.

3. Use details and descriptive words to help the reader's imagination.

Writing Activity Answer See page TM140.

Section **13.1** Home Organization and Safety

Reading Guide

Before You Read

How Can You Improve? Before starting the section, think about the last exam you took on material you had to read. What reading strategies helped you on the test? Make a list of ways to improve your strategies in order to succeed on your next exam.

Read to Learn

Key Concepts

✓ **Describe** how a home is more than shelter.

✓ **Explain** the functions of furniture and storage space.

✓ **Identify** reasons for keeping your home clean and neat.

✓ **List** ways to stay safe in and around your home.

Main Idea

Make your home appealing, functional, and safe by organizing your space.

Content Vocabulary

○ shelter
○ floor plan
○ traffic pattern
○ functional

Academic Vocabulary

■ convenient   ■ routine

Graphic Organizer

As you read, write down four things you should consider when organizing your living space. Use a graphic organizer like the one shown to help you organize your information.

Living Space Organization

 Graphic Organizer Go to this book's Online Learning Center at glencoe.com to print this graphic organizer.

········· **Academic Standards** ·········

English Language Arts

NCTE 8 Use information resources to gather information and create and communicate knowledge.

Social Studies

NCSS VIII B Science, Technology, and Society
Make judgments about how science and technology have transformed the physical world and human society and our understanding of time, space, place, and human-environment interactions.

NCTE *National Council of Teachers of English*
NCTM *National Council of Teachers of Mathematics*

NSES *National Science Education Standards*
NCSS *National Council for the Social Studies*

Graphic Organizer
Answer (1) traffic pattern,
(2) space around furniture,
(3) functional arrangements,
(4) related groups

People live in many types of homes. Apartments, manufactured homes, mobile homes, duplexes, town homes, single-family houses, and condominiums all serve the basic human need for shelter. All of these dwellings have one common feature. To the people living inside, each place is called "home." Everyone deserves to live in a comfortable and safe home.

282   Unit 6   Your World

Your Home

Homes satisfy the basic need for shelter. A **shelter** is a structure built to protect people from the weather and extreme temperatures. Homes also provide a place for you to take care of your personal needs. In your home you can bathe, prepare meals, and sleep comfortably. You also have a place to keep your clothes and personal possessions.

You get a sense of well-being and a feeling of security in your home. It is a place to relax and be yourself. Home is a place where you can enjoy listening to music, playing video games, or reading. It is a great place to spend time with family members and friends.

Living Areas

Most homes are divided into living areas in order to meet people's needs and interests. Some areas, such as bedrooms, are designed for sleep and privacy. Other areas, such as family rooms, are used for gathering with family members and entertaining friends. Bathrooms are for bathing and taking care of grooming and personal needs. Dividing space into specific areas makes a home more **convenient**, or easier to manage.

Some areas serve more than one function. When you organize rooms for more than one function, you can make the best use of space, equipment, and furniture. For example, you probably use your bedroom not only for sleeping but also for studying, reading, and listening to music.

Reading Check *Understand* What is the benefit of organizing rooms for more than one function?

Organize Your Space

To organize the space within your home, begin by thinking of the various activities of all your family members. What area would be best for each activity? For example, would exercise equipment be better located in a bedroom, the basement, or the family room? Should the computer be set up in a bedroom or in the den?

How do you and your family use the living space now? Are there improvements that could be made? If a shelving unit or different lighting were added, could the space be expanded to serve an additional function? A **floor plan** is a drawing of a room and how its furniture is arranged. It allows you to see how furniture fits together without actually moving any furniture.

The way you organize your living space depends on the activities in which you and your family participate. Think about the following concepts when arranging your space:

- **Traffic Pattern** Consider the traffic pattern in the room. The **traffic pattern** is the path people take to move around within a room as well as enter and exit the room. Furniture should be placed so it does not get in the way. If you find that you have to constantly walk around a chair, you should try a different arrangement.
- **Space Around Furniture** Leave space around furniture so it can be used comfortably. Drawers and doors require extra space for opening and closing.
- **Functional Arrangements** Place furniture and other items in **functional** groupings so that the arrangement is useful and convenient. Place a small table next to a sofa to keep eyeglasses, the telephone, and remote controls within easy reach.
- **Related Groups** Group related items together. For example, by storing DVDs near the DVD player, your movies are organized and ready to use.

Select Furniture

Furniture is necessary for comfort and convenience, but it is also decorative. Furniture style is a matter of personal taste. You may like furniture with sleek, modern lines. Your sister may prefer country-style furniture. Look in magazines and books to find the furniture styles you like best. Some furniture can serve more than one purpose. A desk that has a large surface area may be used as a computer station or a drawing table. An infant's diaper changing table may be designed to turn into a dresser when the child gets older.

Storage Space

Having enough storage space is important for a room to be functional. Decide what objects should be stored in a given space. For example, paper, pens and pencils, and a dictionary should be stored in a study area. Items that would not be used in this area, such as cleaning supplies, should be stored in another place. Sometimes your storage space might be limited.

When you run out of room, get rid of things you no longer need. See if anyone else in your family could use the items you no longer want. Have a yard sale or donate useable items to charity, and recycle or throw away things that are broken or unusable. Storage containers and crates are available to fit all kinds of spaces, such as your closet floor, under your bed, or in the garage. **Figure 13.1** on page 286 lists several suggestions for how to best use the space in your closet. Shelves can be used for both storing items and for decoration.

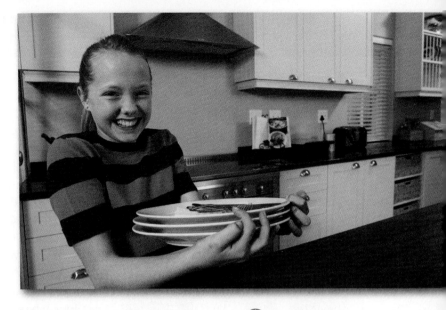

Reading Check *Categorize How can you decide what to store in certain places in your room?*

A Clean and Neat Home

Do you feel proud of your home or your room when it is clean and neat? Do you feel good knowing that your home is safe and secure? Caring for a home means more than just keeping things tidy. It also means keeping things clean and taking safety measures to prevent accidents. Keeping your home clean, neat, safe, and secure is so important because:

A neat home saves time and energy. You waste time and energy when you have to search for items that you need.

Clothes and other possessions last longer. If you take good care of your belongings, they will last longer.

Family members stay healthier in a clean home. A clean home helps family members avoid disease-causing germs.

Most home accidents can be prevented. When everyone in the home takes safety measures, many home accidents and injuries can be avoided.

Security measures can keep a home safe. If a home has good locks, it will be more difficult for intruders to break in.

Organize Cleaning Tasks

Routine, or regular, cleaning tasks are those that must be done every day or every week. These chores include washing dishes, making beds, keeping rooms picked up, and hanging up clothes. Routine tasks keep the home clean and neat so that heavy cleaning is needed less often.

A Place for Everything Smart use of storage space is important for cleanliness and organization. *What can you do when storage space is limited?*

Figure 13.1 Organize Your Closet

Take Advantage of Space Your closet is probably the main storage area in your room. *What can you do to improve the way you use the space in your closet?*

- **Double Your Hanging Space** Add extra rods to the closet for hanging clothes. Double up rods for shirts, vests, and shorter items. Leave one space open to hang longer items such as dresses and dress pants.
- **Add Shelves** Add a shelf along the top of the closet for items you do not use very often. If space allows, build shelves for shoes, accessories, and storage containers.
- **Make Use of Boxes and Baskets** Store loose items like socks and baseball hats in plastic storage boxes, shoeboxes, and baskets.
- **Use Floor Space** Place boots and shoes on the floor of the closet, along with any storage boxes that do not fit on the shelves.
- **Doors** Use the back side of the closet door to hang a mirror or a shoe holder.
- **Install Hooks** You can purchase inexpensive hooks in a variety of sizes to hang belts, ties, and other small accessories.

Figure Caption Answer Answers may include any of the ideas in the figure, or students may have their own suggestions depending on the size and shape of their closets, and on the items they store.

A cleaning plan can help families manage their cleaning tasks. A cleaning plan is a list of daily, weekly, and occasional household jobs, with the name of the person responsible for each job. To make a cleaning plan, decide what jobs need to be done and who will perform each task. Change responsibilities on a regular basis so the work is divided fairly.

Cleaning Shared Space

When each person takes responsibility for keeping his or her personal space in order, much of the housekeeping gets done automatically. To get your share done with ease, you need to establish a routine. For example, hang up your clothes or put them in a hamper. It may seem like tossing them on the floor will take less time, but you will only have to pick them up later.

Bathrooms and the kitchen are used by all family members, so every person in the home must help keep them in order. Rinse the bathtub and sink after each use. Hang towels neatly after each use. Return personal grooming items to their proper place. In the kitchen, wash and dry the dishes, or put them in the dishwasher. Clean up spills right away.

Cleaning Your Room

It will be easier to keep your room clean if you take a little time each day to put it in order. All the tasks do not have to be done at the same time. For instance, make your bed every morning after you brush your teeth. Empty the wastebasket after you finish your homework. Hang up your clothes and straighten your dresser and desk before you go to bed. Throughout the day, put away your belongings as soon as you finish using them. When you do a little bit every day, it makes it easier and quicker to finish your bigger cleaning jobs.

Reading Check **Plan** *What can you do to make heavy cleaning an easier task to handle?*

Safety at Home and in Your Community

Many of the accidents that happen in homes can be prevented or avoided with a little care. Do not let someone in your home get hurt by carelessness. Read the following guidelines and then take the time to make your home safe.

Fire Safety

Protect your home from fire by following these safety rules:

- Have an exit route planned and practice using the exit route on a regular basis.
- Make sure that smoke alarms are installed in the home. Alarms should be installed near the kitchen, outside the bedrooms, and at the top of the stairs. Check smoke alarms once a month to be sure that they are working properly. Change the batteries routinely.
- Keep a fire extinguisher in the home. Learn how to use it properly. Keep the extinguisher properly serviced.
- Make sure that all electrical cords are in good condition. A damaged cord can cause surrounding material to catch fire.

Home Care
When you take care of your home, you also take care of yourself and others who live in the home. *What are some typical cleaning jobs that help keep a home safe?*

Smoke Alarms

Properly installed and maintained smoke alarms provide an early warning and give people inside the home a chance to escape. *What else can you do to prevent fire-related injuries?*

Photo Caption Answer Answers may include: keep curtains and towels away from the stove; keep grease away from the stove area; make sure electrical cords are in good condition; keep a fire extinguisher in the home and know how to use it; use a fireplace screen.

Safety Check

Kitchen Fires

According to the U.S. Fire Administration, cooking is the leading cause of home fires and home fire injuries. To help prevent cooking fires:

- Never leave the stove unattended when cooking.
- Make sure all towels or paper are away from where you are cooking.

- Do not let curtains, towels, or potholders get too close to the stove. If you are cooking, avoid wearing a shirt with loose sleeves that might easily catch fire.
- Keep the area around the stove free of grease. Grease burns easily and can spread a fire.
- If you have a fireplace in your home, make sure that it is used properly. Keep flammable objects away from the fireplace. Use a fireplace screen.

Fall Safety

Protect people from falls in your home by following these safety rules.

- If something is spilled, wipe it up immediately.
- Place nonskid pads under rugs so that they will not slide.
- Be sure to use nonskid strips or mats in bathtubs and showers.
- Make sure that stairs are in good repair, well lit, and free from clutter. Stairs should also have handrails.
- Keep walkways free of clutter.
- Secure windows so children do not climb out.

Hands-On LAB

Plan an Escape Route

In this activity you will plan an escape route for your family. In case of an emergency, it is important for your family to know what to do. Before you begin, read through the entire Hands-On Lab assignment. Write down any questions that you have about the assignment. Reread the text or ask your teacher for help if you need it.

Supplies
✓ Paper and pencil or pen

Develop Your Plan

■ Sit down with all your family members.

■ Make sure everyone in the family knows ways to get out of every room in your home.

■ Teach younger children to crawl on their hands and knees and stay low under smoke.

■ Teach younger children to shout their names out if they are trapped in a smoke-filled room.

■ Plan your escape routes. Choose a place where everyone will meet outside in the event of a fire.

■ Make sure everyone knows that they should never go back into the building after leaving.

■ Use a buddy system to assure everyone gets out safely.

■ Assign someone to call 9-1-1 or the fire department.

■ Assign an adult the responsibility for getting any pets out of the building.

Implement Your Plan

■ Make a drawing of the layout of each floor of your home. Indicate where the windows and doors are. Mark the escape routes from each room.

■ Hold a fire drill once a month.

Evaluate Your Results

How did your family react to creating the escape plan? After your family held a fire drill, did you find anything in the procedure that you wanted to change? If so, what? How will you change it? Write one or more paragraphs to explain your answer.

 Projects and Activities Go to this book's Online Learning Center through **glencoe.com** for more projects and activities.

Evaluate Your Results Answer Answers will vary. Paragraphs should include details about how families reacted to the escape plan. Students should explain what they would change and how. For example, if no one called 9-1-1, they would clarify whose responsibility it is and perhaps assign an alternate.

Neighborhood Safety If you have to walk somewhere, especially at night, walk with a friend and in well-lit areas. *What else can you do to stay safe while walking in or near your neighborhood?*

Photo Caption Answer Answers may include: keep alert, especially at night; pay attention to people and activities; stay away from dangerous areas and dark streets; avoid taking unnecessary risks.

Character Counts Answer There is no right or wrong way to clean a shared space. Yanett and Deenie should try to reach a compromise. For example, since Deenie thinks it looks messy to keep the supplies out, she could put them in a decorative box or basket. That way, they are organized and neat, but Yanett would be able to find them easily when it is her turn to clean.

Character Counts

Compromise

Yanett and Deenie are twins. Each sister has her own bedroom, and they share a bathroom. Both girls are neat and take care of their rooms, but they have different ideas about how to clean and organize the bathroom. Yanett thinks it is faster and easier to clean when the supplies are kept on the counter. If she does not see them, she forgets that she needs to clean. Deenie thinks it looks messy to have the supplies out in the open. To her, leaving supplies out is the same as not making a bed. Though Yanett and Deenie get along most of the time, the bathroom cleaning situation it bothering them, and it is bothering other members of the family who have to listen to them argue.

You Make the Call

Who is right? Who is wrong? Is there only one efficient way to clean a shared space? Write a paragraph explaining what Yanett and Deenie should do before their situation gets worse.

Other Safety Precautions

In addition to fires and falls, there are many other types of accidents that can happen in homes. If there are small children in the home, poisoning is a serious danger. Make sure that all cleaning products and chemicals are kept out of the reach of children. Read the label on every chemical or cleaning product before using it so that you will know how to handle it correctly. If anyone in your family accidentally swallows a poisonous substance, immediately call 9-1-1, a poison control center, or a hospital.

Power tools and sharp knives can also cause injuries if they are not used with care. Knives and other dangerous objects should be kept out of children's reach.

Improper use of electrical appliances is another common cause of accidents. Be sure to connect and disconnect an electrical appliance with dry hands. Do not use any appliance that has a damaged cord. Do not use a hair dryer while in the bathtub or while standing in water.

Community Safety

Have you ever been startled by a loud noise while walking in your neighborhood? Have you ever felt uneasy when you walked home from a friend's house at dusk?

Everyone wants to feel safe in his or her own neighborhood. There are steps you can take to protect yourself. Make sure your home is well lit on the outside. Keep a porch light or yard light on. Solar lights can be placed around the outside of the home and do not require electrical wiring. They absorb light during the day and then glow at night, providing light.

Your family can join or help set up a Neighborhood Watch group. Members of such groups are trained by the police to identify and report suspicious activities. When you walk down the street, keep alert, especially at night. Pay attention to the people around you and to what they are doing. Stay away from dangerous areas and poorly lighted streets. Avoid taking any unnecessary risks.

Get to know your neighbors. If you know who belongs in your neighborhood, it will be easier to spot suspicious activity by strangers. If there is ever an emergency, you will know which neighbors you can call for help. Communities can work together to look after each other.

Safety Check

Social Networking

Most people who join social networking Web sites do not want to hurt anyone. However, just as in the real world, there are people who try to cause harm. Use these tips to help you stay safe online:

- Never reveal personal information.
- Only allow access to people you know in person.
- Never respond to suggestive or threatening messages.
- Never arrange a meeting with a stranger.

Section 13.1 After You Read

Review What You Have Learned

1. **Explain** how to make an area functional.
2. **Define** floor plan and explain how it can help you organize your living space.
3. **List** routine cleaning tasks that should be done every day.
4. **Predict** how knowing your neighbors can help keep you safe.

Practice Academic Skills

 English Language Arts

5. Create a poster to show how to prevent accidents at home. Use guidelines from your text as well as other print or online resources. Use colorful illustrations and large letters to make the information easy to read and understand.

> **NCTE 8** Use information resources to gather information and create and communicate knowledge.

 Social Studies

6. Many "smart" houses have convenient features such as automatic lights and appliances. What do you expect to see in homes of the future? Create a futuristic "home for sale" ad and list the technological features you think it will have.

> **NCSS VIII B** Make judgments about how science and technology have transformed the physical world and human society and our understanding of time, space, place, and human-environment interactions.

 Check Your Answers Check your answers at this book's Online Learning Center at glencoe.com.

Section 13.2 Home Design

Reading Guide

Before You Read

Check for Understanding If you have questions as you read, that means you are checking to see if you understand the material. Try to answer those questions as you read.

Read to Learn

Key Concepts

✓ **Name** the elements and principles of design.

✓ **Understand** how to use decorations and accessories to create your own style.

Main Idea

Use the elements and principles of design to create a living space that reflects your personality and style.

Content Vocabulary

○ design
○ color scheme
○ design principle
○ emphasis
○ proportion
○ accessory

Academic Vocabulary

■ element
■ outline

Graphic Organizer

As you read, identify and describe five design principles that guide how design elements are organized. Use a graphic organizer like the one shown to help you organize your information.

Five Design Principles	Description
1. Balance	items provide equal visual weight or stability
2.	
3.	
4.	
5.	

Graphic Organizer Go to this book's Online Learning Center at glencoe.com to print this graphic organizer.

Academic Standards

 English Language Arts

NCTE 7 Conduct research and gather, evaluate, and synthesize data to communicate discoveries.

 Mathematics

NCTM Measurement Apply appropriate techniques, tools, and formulas to determine measurements.

 Social Studies

NCSS III G People, Places, and Environments Describe and compare how people create places that reflect culture, human needs, and values and ideals as they design and build specialized buildings.

NCSS V B Individuals, Groups, and Institutions Analyze group and institutional influences on people, events, and elements of culture in both historical and contemporary settings.

NCTE *National Council of Teachers of English*
NCTM *National Council of Teachers of Mathematics*

NSES *National Science Education Standards*
NCSS *National Council for the Social Studies*

Graphic Organizer Answer (2) Emphasis: one item serves as the focal point. (3) Proportion: the size of objects in a room as they relate to each other. (4) Rhythm: a visual path through a room through careful placement of elements. (5) Unity: similar elements combined to bring harmony to a room.

You want your home to reflect not only who you are, but also to reflect good design and style. How can you go beyond just organizing? Combine good design with your personal style to help give you the look you want and a place to entertain friends.

Your Room Design

Why do some rooms look more inviting than others? How can a room seem large, even though it is actually small? Different **elements**, or parts, can be combined to create a variety of looks. The way a room appears depends a great deal on how design is used, or not used, to create an overall effect. **Design** is the art of combining elements in a pleasing way. You can use design to create the type of look you want in a room.

Design Elements

The elements of design are space, shape, line, texture, and color. These elements can work alone, or in a variety of combinations. Each contributes its own effect to the final design.

Space Space helps draw attention to objects. For example, a vase on a shelf will stand out and be seen if some space is left on either side of it. On the other hand, too much space between objects can result in a bare, empty look. You can create many looks just by dividing space in various ways.

Shape Shape refers to the **outline**, or form, of solid objects. A bed has a rectangular shape. A table may be rectangular, square, oval, or round. Attractive designs use shape effectively. Too many different shapes in one room can be distracting.

Line Lines are very important to design. Look around a room, and you can see them in the legs of a table, the frame of a door, or the stripes on a curtain. Straight lines make objects seem strong and dignified. Curved lines make objects seem softer and more graceful. Vertical lines go straight up and down and give the appearance of height. They can make objects look taller. Horizontal lines move straight across and make objects appear wider. Lines that are set at a diagonal, or on an angle, suggest action or movement.

As You Read

Connect Think about the last time you visited someone's home. How did the person's personal style show in his or her home?

As You Read Answer Answers may include use of color and fabric, types of furniture, choices in decorations and accessories.

Vocabulary

You can find definitions in the glossary at the back of this book.

Photo Caption Answer The comfortable mood is created by the sofa cushions, the candle, the light coming in, and the casual arrangement of furniture and accessories.

Set the Mood By using different design elements, you can affect the mood of a room. *How do the design elements in this room contribute to the mood?*

Have Fun

Look for Ideas Check your local newspaper's special events section. You may find inexpensive or free activities to enjoy instead of the usual movie or television show.

• • • • • • • • • • • • • •

Succeed in School
Tell students about local events that they might enjoy. Encourage them to look beyond the television or computer for entertainment.

Figure Caption
Answer Answers will vary but students will probably say shades of yellow, orange, red, or pink.

Texture Texture is the way something feels or looks as if it would feel. Texture provides visual interest in a room, and you can add more interest by using a variety of textures. A rug might feel soft and fuzzy. A polished table feels hard and smooth. Textures can also affect the mood of a room. Soft and rounded surfaces make a room look cozy. Angled, hard surfaces create a clean, cool effect.

Color Color probably has the greatest effect on the appearance of a room. Color schemes are used to create style and appeal. A **color scheme** is a system of arranging colors in a pleasing manner. A change of color can make a room look completely different. For example, white or light colors on the walls make a room look larger. Darker colors make a room seem smaller. **Figure 13.2** illustrates cool and warm colors.

Design Principles

A **design principle** is a rule that directs how the elements of design are organized. There are five design principles you can use to when creating your personal living space.

Balance Use two similar items to provide equal visual weight to keep a room or area from looking lopsided. You can balance a room when you place several small items on one side of a fireplace, and a larger object on the other side.

Figure **13.2** **The Color Wheel**

Warm or Cool? The color wheel shows the relationships among colors. *If you want your living area to be warm, comfortable, and welcoming, what colors would you choose?*

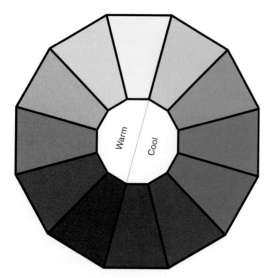

Colors are often described as warm or cool. Pick a few colors from the wheel and imagine how your room would feel if decorated using these colors.

■ **Warm Colors**

Red, yellow, and orange are warm colors. If a room does not get much sunlight or is cold in the winter, warm colors can make the room seem more comfortable.

■ **Cool Colors**

Blue, green, and violet are cool, restful colors. A cool color is a good choice for a room that gets a lot of sunlight. Cool colors are used to set a relaxing mood.

Emphasis Place **emphasis** on an item of special importance if you want it to be noticed. Select one item to serve as the focus of the room. Having a focal point draws the eye directly to the object. For example, a red pillow on a white sofa provides emphasis.

Proportion How one part relates to another is called **proportion**. It is important to keep in mind the sizes of objects in the room as they relate to each other, and to the room as a whole. A large painting with a dark, heavy wood frame would not look well-proportioned in a small room with delicate white furniture.

Rhythm Create a visual path through a room by placing elements carefully. Hang a series of posters on a wall to create a pattern of visual movement, or rhythm.

Unity Combining similar elements brings unity, or harmony, to a room. Arrange several framed photos in an attractive grouping to create unity, or use shades of the same color throughout a room.

 Reading Check *Identify the elements of design.*

Your Own Style

Before you start redesigning your room, you need to think about the look you want for your space. It depends on what you have to work with, but it also depends on your personal taste. Of course, if you share a room you will also need to consider what the other person likes. The elements of design and the design principles can be used in many ways with pleasing results, but not all of them will appeal to you.

First, consider what kind of mood you want to create. What are your interests? Do you want your space to be restful or lively? Are you looking for ways to make the room seem larger? Keep in mind that you will probably have to live with your changes for a long time. Your friend's neon pink and black bedroom might seem like a fun idea, but do you really want to live with those colors for several years? Be sure of your decisions before starting any work on a new look.

 MATH YOU CAN USE

Calculate Square Footage

House, apartment, and room sizes are typically listed in "square feet." One square foot is the area of a rectangle that measures 1 foot by 1 foot. Square feet measurements tell you the area of the living space available inside a home. Derek has measured the inside of his bedroom and determined that it is 12 feet long and 9 feet wide. How many square feet of floor space does Derek have in his room?

Math Concept **Area of a Rectangle**
The area of a geometric shape measures the total size of its surface. For a rectangle, area (A) is given by the formula $A = l \times w$, where l and w are the length and width of the rectangle. If l and w are measured in inches, the area will be in square inches.

Starting Hint Read the problem to determine what numbers to use for l and w, and then use the area formula to determine the area of Derek's room in square feet.

 For math help, go to the Math Appendix at the back of the book.

NCTM Measurement Apply appropriate techniques, tools, and formulas to determine measurements.

Math You Can Use
Answer Derek has 12 feet × 9 feet = 108 square feet of space.

Reading Check
Answer space, shape, line, texture, color

Create a Look

Once you have decided on the mood and style, you can plan how to achieve that look in your room. Make a plan before you start to help your project go smoothly.

Perhaps you would like a new color scheme. What parts of the room will be easiest to change? Walls can be repainted, and you can hang new pictures. Carpet, on the other hand, is difficult and expensive to replace. There a lots of ways to change the look of your room or space. Even small changes can make a big difference.

Accessorize

No room is complete without accessories. An **accessory** is an interesting item added to make a space more personal. You can make your own accessories, such as storage organizers, or buy accessories like lamps and plants. Use accessories to personalize your room. You can add your personal touch with any of these items:

- Curtains
- Handmade items
- Quilts
- Pillows
- Posters and pictures

- Collections and mementos
- Trophies and awards
- Baskets
- Rugs

Decorate

Decorating your room or a personal space in your home is a great way to show off your style and creativity. Get permission from your parents or guardians before putting your creativity to work. Here are some ideas:

Discover International...
Design

Feng Shui

According to Chinese philosophy, all things are composed of five basic elements. Those elements are earth, water, fire, metal, and wood. Many objects in and around a home symbolize these elements. *Feng* means wind and *shui* means water. Feng shui aims to balance and simplify all five of the basic elements in a harmonious design. A design created with the principles of feng shui is meant to provide peace, comfort, balance, and harmony with nature. Feng shui principles can be applied to gardens, homes, and work environments.

feng shui |ˈfən-shwā| the Chinese art of designing gardens, buildings, and interiors to promote harmony between humans and nature.

> **NCSS III G** Describe and compare how people create places that reflect culture, human needs, and values and ideals as they design and build specialized buildings.

- **Walls** Paint can quickly and dramatically change the look of a room. Draw and paint a scene or a geometric pattern on a wall. You can also use an accent color to draw attention to one wall. Hang posters, banners, and bulletin boards to add interest to bare walls.
- **Books** Books are more than just reading material. Put some of your favorites on display in a bookcase or on a shelf.
- **Lampshades** Jazz up an old lampshade. Use hot glue to attach trim or fringe to the upper and lower edges.
- **Pillows** Make or purchase toss pillows for your bed. Choose fabrics to that go with your room colors and stitch them using a pattern that you can find at your local fabric store.
- **Picture Frames** Decorate plain, inexpensive picture frames. Use hot glue to attach buttons, bows, shells, small polished rocks, team pins, or felt or foam shapes in a random pattern around the frame. Showcase your favorite photos inside.

Photo Caption Answer Answers may include: personality traits, hobbies and interests, accomplishments. Some students may acknowledge that the organization or lack of organization reveals a part of their personality.

Express Yourself Your living space, whether it is your bedroom or your own apartment, says a lot about you. *What does your room reveal about you?*

Section 13.2 After You Read

Review What You Have Learned

1. **Describe** how color can affect the mood or feel of a room.
2. **Plan** what you need to do before starting a room design change.

Practice Academic Skills

 English Language Arts

3. Design your ideal living space. Use magazines, photos, and your own drawings to create a collage of furniture, colors, accessories, and fabrics. Sketch a floor plan. Present your collage to the class, and explain how you would put your plan into action.

> NCTE 7 Conduct research and gather, evaluate, and synthesize data to communicate discoveries.

 Social Studies

4. Conduct research to learn how school designs are planned. What factors to designers and builders have to consider? What do you think they considered when your own school was designed? Write a summary of your findings.

> NCSS V B Analyze group and institutional influences on people, events, and elements of culture in both historical and contemporary settings.

Check Your Answers Check your answers at this book's Online Learning Center at glencoe.com.

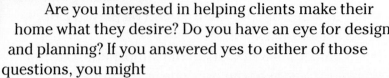
Discovering Careers

Are you interested in helping clients make their home what they desire? Do you have an eye for design and planning? If you answered yes to either of those questions, you might want to consider a future career in home design. The following chart explores several careers in the home design industry.

Career Activities ▼

At School

 Select three of the careers listed. Research the education, training, and work experience required for each career. Write a summary of your results.

At Home

2 What projects in your home could be done by a contractor or design professional?

At Work

3 Describe how the elements and principles of design can be used in an office setting. Share your list with your classmates.

In the Community

4 Contact and interview someone in your community who works in interior or exterior home design. Ask this person to describe what his or her typical work day is like. Share what you learned with your class.

Career Activities Answers for these activities can be found on page TM140.

Job Title	Job Description
Architect	Plans and designs buildings for clients. Uses knowledge of design, construction, zoning and building codes, and building materials. Prepares scale drawings.
Interior Designer	Plans, designs, and furnishes interiors of residential, commercial, and industrial buildings. Determines preferences, purpose, and function of living spaces with client.
Carpet Layer	Lays carpet and rugs. Measures and cuts carpeting to size. Steams sections of carpeting together at seams. Secures carpeting to floor.
Upholstery Cleaner	Cleans upholstered furniture using vacuum cleaner or dry-cleaning fluids. Rubs surfaces with oil and buffs with cloth or hand buffer.
Contractor	Contracts with clients to build new homes or home improvement projects. Works to meet client specifications about projects.

Learn More Online 🧭 glencoe.com

Career Investigations Go to this book's Online Learning Center for activities and worksheets to help you explore careers.

Chapter Summary

Section 13.1 Home Organization and Safety
Homes satisfy the basic need for shelter. You get a sense of well-being, a feeling of security, and self-expression. Most homes are divided into living areas in order to meet people's needs and interests. Keep your home clean, neat, safe, and secure. When each person keeps his or her personal space in order, most housekeeping gets done automatically. Many accidents that happen in homes can be prevented with a little care.

Section 13.2 Home Design
Design is the art of combining elements in a pleasing way. Design elements are space, shape, line, texture, and color. Before you start planning a room makeover, think about the look you want for your space. Be sure of your decisions before starting any work on a new look. Once you have decided, you can plan how to achieve that look in your room. Making a plan before you start will help your project go smoothly.

Words You Learned

1. Create a fill-in-the-blank sentence for each of these vocabulary terms. The sentence should contain enough information to help determine the missing word.

Content Vocabulary
- shelter (p. 283)
- floor plan (p. 284)
- traffic pattern (p. 284)
- functional (p. 284)
- design (p. 293)
- color scheme (p. 294)
- design principle (p. 294)
- emphasis (p. 295)
- proportion (p. 295)
- accessory (p. 296)

Academic Vocabulary
- convenient (p. 283)
- routine (p. 285)
- element (p. 293)
- outline (p. 293)

Review Key Concepts

2. **Describe** how a home is more than shelter.

3. **Explain** the functions of furniture and storage space.

4. **Identify** reasons for keeping your home clean and neat.

5. **List** ways to stay safe in and around your home.

6. **Name** the elements and principles of design.

7. **Understand** how to use decorations and accessories to create your own style.

Critical Thinking

8. **Predict** what might happen if you try to redecorate your room without knowing the principles and elements of design.

9. **Plan** what you can do at home to prepare for a weather or geographical emergency, such as tornadoes or earthquakes, in your area.

Real-World Skills and Applications

Problem-Solving

10. Buying Furniture Imagine that you are moving into your first apartment. You have a limited budget and must decide between buying used furniture and buying inexpensive new furniture. Make a list of pros and cons for each, then decide which would be the best option for your budget and needs.

Interpersonal and Collaborative

11. Share Living Space Follow your teacher's directions to form groups. In your group, discuss problems that might arise when people share a living space. For example, who will clean the bathroom? Who will take care of the plants? Write a list of 5 problems, and then come up with solutions for each.

Financial Literacy

12. Comparison Shopping Choose three accessories, such as a lamp, a collector's item, and a painting, that you would like to have in your room at home. Research the prices for each item from various sources. Consider retail stores, discount stores, garage sales, and online auctions. Determine the best deal for each of the three items. Are there any drawbacks to the least expensive options? Write a brief summary of your findings, including a description or listing of the various shopping locations and their range of prices. Also, determine if the less expensive sources are truly your best options.

13. Herb Garden Create an herb garden display. Choose an attractive assortment of boxes or pots, or make your own. Research which kinds of herbs are suitable for the amount of sunlight that reaches your window. Find out what kind of care is needed for your herb selections. Write a paragraph that explains how an herb garden is both decorative and functional.

14. Caring Communities Neighborhood Watch programs depend on citizens to organize themselves and work with law enforcement to keep an eye and ear on their communities. Neighbors watch out for each other by being alert, observant, and caring. They report suspicious activity or crimes immediately to the police. Research Neighborhood Watch programs to find out what neighbors can do to help each other. Make a list of 5 actions that would benefit your neighborhood.

15. Decorating Styles With permission from your teacher or parents, go online to research decorating styles, such as traditional, modern, or country. Choose your favorite and imagine your room redecorated in that style. How would the room look and feel? How would the style mix with your personal accessories? How do you think visitors would respond? Write one or more paragraphs to answer these questions. Include the information in your Life Skills Binder.

Academic Skills

English Language Arts

16. Internet Safety Pledge Create a list of promises to your family that you will keep to help you stay safe online. For example, your first promise could be "I will ask permission from my parents before downloading anything from the Internet." Show the list to your parents and discuss with them what changes might need to be made. Write your final list in the form of an Internet Safety Pledge and sign it.

> **NCTE 4** Use written language to communicate effectively.

Science

17. Mold Molds are part of the natural environment. Outdoors, molds break down dead organic matter such as fallen leaves. Indoors, mold can cause health problems. **Procedure** Conduct research to learn how mold can contribute to health problems, and how you can prevent mold from growing inside your home. **Analysis** Present a report that summarizes your findings

> **NSES F** Develop an understanding of personal and community health.

Mathematics

18. Painting a Room Amanda wants to paint her bedroom. Her bedroom is 12 feet long and 9 feet wide, and the walls are 10 feet high. If one gallon of paint covers approximately 350 square feet, will one gallon be enough to cover all four of Amanda's walls? If not, how much will she need?

Math Concept **Perimeter** Perimeter is the distance around the edge of a geometric shape. You can calculate perimeter by adding up the lengths of every side, but for some shapes, you can use a shortcut formula. The perimeter (P) of a rectangle is given by the formula $P = 2l + 2w$, where l and w are the length and width of the rectangle.

Starting Hint To find the surface area of all walls in a rectangular room, you can use another shortcut: multiply the perimeter of the room by the height of the walls. Determine the perimeter of Amanda's room, and multiply it by 10 feet. Is the result less than 350?

> **NCTM Problem Solving** Build new mathematical knowledge through problem solving.

Standardized Test Practice

Multiple-Choice

Read the scenario. Determine the meaning of neutral within the context of the scenario, and choose the best answer.

> **Test-Taking Tip** In a multiple-choice test, the answers should be specific and precise. Read the questions first, then read all the answer choices. Eliminate answers that you know are incorrect.

19. Julia's bedroom had not been redecorated since she was a little girl. She decided to change the pink walls to a neutral shade of beige. That way, she could change the look of her room often by simply changing the colors of her pillows, rugs, and other accessories.
In this scenario, the meaning of neutral is
a. not taking sides
b. blends easily with other colors
c. powerful
d. unable to decide

Chapter 14

Your Environment

Section 14.1

Resources and Conservation

■ **Main Idea** It is essential to conserve the natural resources that animals, plants, and humans need for survival.

Section 14.2

Protect the Environment

■ **Main Idea** Individual efforts make a difference when it comes to protecting the environment. Do your part by limiting waste, and use air, water, land, and energy wisely.

Explore the Photo Answer By riding bicycles, they are not contributing to pollution, and they are saving gas and energy by not relying on cars or buses. They are enjoying the environment by being outdoors and getting physical activity.

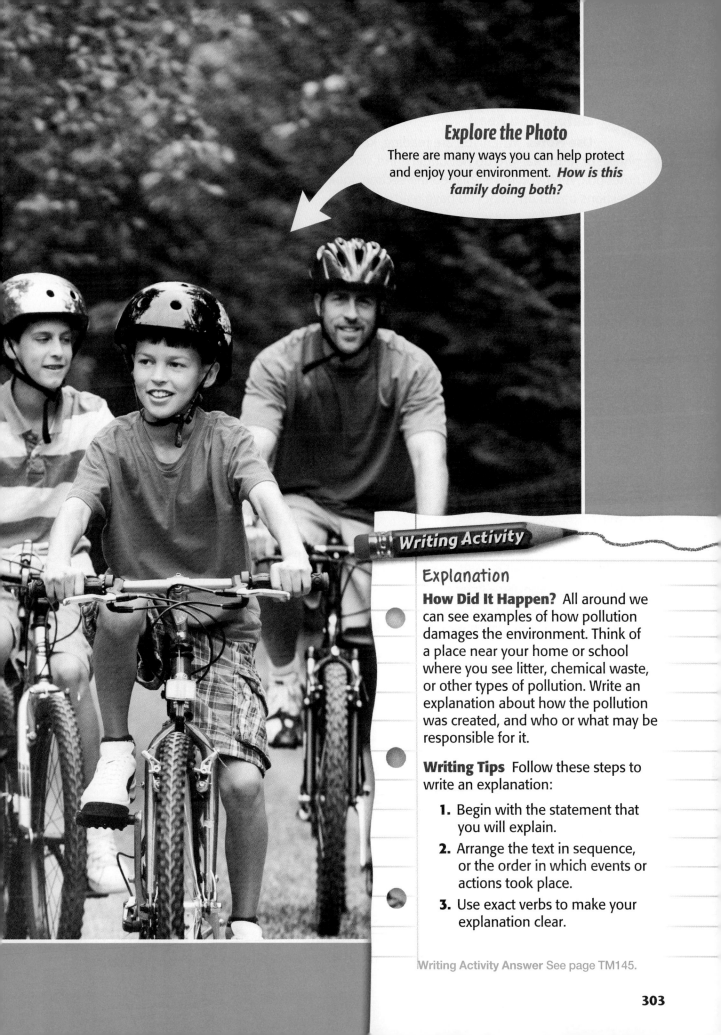

Explore the Photo
There are many ways you can help protect and enjoy your environment. *How is this family doing both?*

Writing Activity

Explanation

How Did It Happen? All around we can see examples of how pollution damages the environment. Think of a place near your home or school where you see litter, chemical waste, or other types of pollution. Write an explanation about how the pollution was created, and who or what may be responsible for it.

Writing Tips Follow these steps to write an explanation:

1. Begin with the statement that you will explain.
2. Arrange the text in sequence, or the order in which events or actions took place.
3. Use exact verbs to make your explanation clear.

Writing Activity Answer See page TM145.

Section 14.1 Resources and Conservation

Reading Guide

Before You Read

Use Notes When you are reading, keep a notebook handy. When you read a phrase or term that you do not understand, write it down in the form of a question in your notebook. After you have finished the section, look up the terms and try to answer your questions based on what you have read.

Read to Learn

Key Concepts

✓ **Identify** the four key natural resources and why we need to protect them.

✓ **Explain** how you can do your part to conserve water and energy.

Main Idea

It is essential to conserve the natural resources that animals, plants, and humans need for survival.

Content Vocabulary

○ natural resource ○ fossil fuel
○ pollution ○ conservation
○ soil

Academic Vocabulary

■ key ■ efficient

Graphic Organizer

As you read, identify the four main natural resources. Use a graphic organizer like the one shown to help you organize your information.

Graphic Organizer Go to this book's Online Learning Center at glencoe.com to print this graphic organizer.

· · · · · · · · · · · · Academic Standards · · · · · · · · · · · ·

English Language Arts

NCTE 7 Conduct research and gather, evaluate, and synthesize data to communicate discoveries.

Science

NSES F Develop an understanding of natural resources; environmental quality; science and technology in local, national, and global challenges.

Social Studies

NCSS V F Individuals, Groups, and Institutions Evaluate the role of institutions in furthering both continuity and change.

NCTE *National Council of Teachers of English*
NCTM *National Council of Teachers of Mathematics*

NSES *National Science Education Standards*
NCSS *National Council for the Social Studies*

Graphic Organizer Answer
Air, Water, Soil, Energy

Do you like to spend time at the beach or in the mountains? Have you ever gone swimming or fishing in a lake or an ocean? Enjoying outdoor activities is one of the greatest pleasures of life. In addition, you could not survive without the elements that nature provides. Taking care of the environment is essential to our survival. This responsiblity belongs to everyone.

Natural Resources

A **natural resource** is a material that is supplied by nature. You might not think about them very often, and you may even take them for granted. For example, you probably take a shower every day without even thinking about where the water comes from, or whether or not it will be there the next day. The health of every human, animal, and plant depends on several **key**, or necessary, natural resources. These include air, water, soil, and the energy that comes from coal, oil, and gas. We must protect these resources for our health and our survival.

At one time it seemed like these resources would last forever. Some, however, are nonrenewable. If they are used up or permanently damaged, they will no longer be available. This damage is often caused by pollution. **Pollution** is the changing of air, water, and land from clean and safe to dirty and unsafe.

Air

Your body uses the oxygen in air to produce energy. Plants use the carbon dioxide in air to produce food and oxygen. Unfortunately, the air you breathe is not completely clean. It may contain dust, smoke, chemical particles, and smog. These substances, which are all forms of air pollution, can be harmful to your health. Some causes of air pollution are:

- **Poisonous gases** such as car exhaust fumes that combine with the atmosphere to create smog when fuels are burned to provide energy.
- **Smoke** from sources such as fireplaces, barbecues, and burning leaves.
- **Chemicals**, including those that kill insects and those used as cooling substances in air conditioners and refrigerators.

Water

Water, like air, is necessary to all living things. In fact, water is your body's most essential nutrient. It is needed for every bodily function. Humans can only survive for a few days without water.

Alternative Energy

Natural resources can provide alternative sources of energy. Alternative energy sources can be used instead of fossil fuels, coal, wood, and uranium. Alternative energy sources must be renewable, nonpolluting, easy to get, and affordable.

Procedure Collect data about alternative power sources. Create a chart that includes the alternative sources of energy and how they are used.

Analysis What alternative energy sources are used most? What do you think could be used more?

NSES F Develop an understanding of natural resources; environmental quality; science and technology in local, national, and global challenges.

⬤ **Clean Food and Water** Animals, plants, and humans all depend on water for survival. *What can happen when animals drink or live in polluted water?*

Photo Caption Answer Animals who drink or live in polluted water can become sick or die.

You may think that there is plenty of water. After all, about 70 percent of the earth's surface is covered by water. Most of it, however, is salt water. Many plants and animals cannot use salt water. Humans cannot drink salt water. Animals and humans need clean, fresh water to survive.

Much of the earth's water is polluted by wastes. Common sources of water pollution are human wastes, detergents, and the chemicals used to kill insects or to fertilize crops. This can cause damage to animals and plants that use the polluted water. Polluted water can cause people and animals to become sick or die.

Soil

The earth's land is made up of soil. **Soil** the loose material in which plants can grow. Soil is made up of mixture of rocks, decayed material, minerals, water, and air. Plants get the nutrients and water they need from the soil. People, in turn, need the nutrients that plants provide in order to live.

Energy

What would happen if we ran out of gasoline for cars, trucks, and buses? How would we heat homes, schools, and office buildings if we ran out of oil and other kinds of fuel? You may think that this could never happen. However, many sources of energy are in limited supply. When oil, natural gas, and coal are used up, they cannot be replaced.

Another form of energy is nuclear energy. Nuclear energy boils water, creates steam, and turns generators to create electricity. Nuclear energy is made partly from uranium, a dense metal found in most rocks. Uranium is more plentiful than **fossil fuels**, which come from the remains of prehistoric plants and animals. Coal, natural gas, and petroleum are examples of fossil fuels.

Succeed in School Most people like to talk about the things they enjoy doing. Ask students to talk about what they enjoy reading.

Reading Skills
Read for Fun Reading is not just for school. Make it a habit to read for pleasure every day. Spend time with an entertaining novel, comic books, magazines, or a graphic novel.

• • • • • • • • • • • • •

Reading Check Answer poisonous gases, smoke, chemicals

 Reading Check *Identify* What can cause air pollution?

Conserve Resources

You may think that pollution and the shrinking supply of natural resources are beyond your control. There are many ways, however, that you can make a difference. One important way is to practice **conservation**, or the saving of resources. The best way to conserve a resource is to use less of it. When you take initiative, you take the first steps toward solving a particular problem. You and your family can work together to conserve natural resources. Some families add more insulation to their homes to save fuel. Insulation is a material installed in a building to keep it cooler in summer and warmer in winter. Families also can help by using extra sweaters and blankets in the winter so the heater does not get overused.

Water

Water is a resource you may often take for granted. All you do is turn on the faucet, and the supply seems limitless. But there is a limit, and you need to conserve the water you have so that there is enough for everyone and for the future. Here are some ways you can conserve water:

- Turn off the water when brushing your teeth.
- Take showers instead of baths.
- Install water-saving showerheads and toilets.
- Repair leaky faucets.
- Run the washing machine only with a full load. Change the level of water in the washing machine according to the amount and type of clothing being washed.

Energy

The **efficient**, or non-wasteful, use of energy is an important way to conserve resources. You can to learn to use energy wisely. Look for appliances that are energy-efficient, or made to use less energy. By using energy efficiently, you not only conserve resources, but you can also save money and help reduce pollution.

➡ **Active Conservation** This teen is conserving water by turning off the faucet while she brushes her teeth. *What can you do to conserve natural resources?*

Safety Check

Cell Phones

The average consumer replaces his or her cell phone every 18 months. Discarded phones fill up landfill space. Many contain toxic chemicals used in manufacturing them, such as arsenic, chemicals used as flame-retardants, and lead. The EPA warns that these substances may be linked to health problems, including cancer. Instead of tossing your old phone, donate it to charity, or contact your service provider about recycling it. You may even get a credit toward a new phone when you turn in your old one for recycling.

Photo Caption Answer
Answers may include ride a bike or walk instead of riding in a car, take showers instead of baths, adjust the water level in washing machines, wear warmer clothes to avoid turning up the heater.

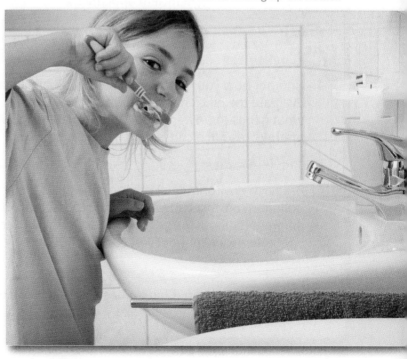

You can save energy at home in many ways. Most of the energy used at home is for heating and cooling, running appliances, and lighting. When your family members buy new appliances, they can look for the most energy-efficient ones by comparing guides that list energy costs per year. Here are some ways to conserve energy at home:

- Use only the amount of hot water you actually need.
- Keep doors to closets and unused rooms closed. There is no need to heat or cool those spaces.
- Whenever possible, use a microwave oven.
- When you use a conventional oven, cook several items at the same time, and avoid opening the oven door while foods are cooking.
- Run the dishwasher only with a full load.
- Avoid leaving the refrigerator door open for too long.
- Use lined drapes to keep the cold out in the winter and the heat out in the summer.
- Seal cracks or gaps around the doors and windows.
- Use energy-saving light bulbs. Many types are available that use less energy and burn longer than standard bulbs.
- Turn the thermostat up in the summer and down in the winter.

Section 14.1 After You Read

Review What You Have Learned

1. **Identify** common sources of water pollution.
2. **Recognize** energy-efficient appliances.

Practice Academic Skills

 English Language Arts

3. Find out how your family uses water and electricity. Then, evaluate the efficiency of your family's use of resources. Record what needs to be improved. Write a plan for your family to improve resource conservation in your home.

> **NCTE 7** Conduct research and gather, evaluate, and synthesize data to communicate discoveries.

 Social Studies

4. Research environmental organizations that focus on ending pollution or conserving natural resources. Write a list of five different issues the organizations address. Next to each issue, suggest an idea for how you can do your part.

> **NCSS V F** Evaluate the role of institutions in furthering both continuity and change.

• •

✈ **Check Your Answers** Check your answers at this book's Online Learning Center at glencoe.com.

Section **14.2** Protect the Environment

Reading Guide

Before You Read

Pace Yourself It can be more effective to focus on reading short sections in 10-minute blocks than trying to read a long section all at once. Read for 10 minutes. Take a short break. Then read for another 10 minutes.

Read to Learn

Key Concepts

✓ **Define** what is meant by "throwaway" society.

✓ **Identify** the negative effects of incineration and landfills.

✓ **Name** the "three Rs."

Main Idea

Individual efforts make a difference when it comes to protecting the environment. Do your part by limiting waste, and use air, water, land, and energy wisely.

Content Vocabulary

○ recycling
○ landfill
○ decompose
○ incineration
○ biodegradable

Academic Vocabulary

■ dispose
■ permanent

Graphic Organizer

As you read, identify and define the "three Rs" for how to limit waste. Use a graphic organizer like the one shown to help you organize your information.

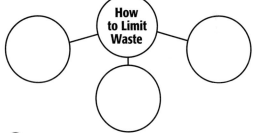

Graphic Organizer Go to this book's Online Learning Center at glencoe.com to print this graphic organizer.

·········· **Academic Standards** ··········

 English Language Arts

NCTE 12 Use language to accomplish individual purposes.

 Mathematics

NCTM Number and Operations Understand numbers, ways of representing numbers, relationships among numbers, and number systems.

 Social Studies

NCSS V G Individuals, Groups, and Institutions Analyze the extent to which groups and institutions meet individual needs and promote the common good in contemporary and historical settings.

NCTE *National Council of Teachers of English*
NCTM *National Council of Teachers of Mathematics*

NSES *National Science Education Standards*
NCSS *National Council for the Social Studies*

Graphic Organizer Answer *Reduce* the amount of waste created; *Reuse* items you might otherwise throw away; *Recycle* to turn waste items into useable products.

How much do you add to the waste that is piling up? Do you know how to limit your use of resources and of the amount of waste you create? By following the "three Rs", you, your family, and your friends can contribute to waste reduction and environmental protection.

As You Read

Connect Why do many people think that they cannot make a difference in their environment?

As You Read Answer
Answers may include: it is too big of a job for one person; there are too many other people who do not seem to care; many people think one person simply cannot do enough to make an impact.

Reading Check Answer
When items are used only once and thrown away, there is too much waste. Currently, there are not enough safe ways to remove waste.

Photo Caption Answer
Answers may include glass or ceramic cups instead of plastic or paper cups; cloth towels at home instead of paper towels; use both sides of paper for notes.

Succeed in School
Have students write down what they already know about recycling.

Reading Skills
What You Know
Before you read, write down what you already know about the subject. You may know more about the subject than you think you do!

Do Your Part

You may think that as long as you do not litter, you are doing your part to keep your community clean. However, there is much more you can do. Since the middle of the 20th century, Americans have lived in a "throwaway" society. Many items are used only once and then thrown away. Think about the bags you use to carry groceries, or the containers used for leftover restaurant meals. As a result, a serious problem exists because there is too much waste. Currently, there are not enough safe ways to remove waste.

Protection of natural resources and the environment begins with people like you. There are many ways for you to make a difference:

- You can use air, water, land, and energy wisely.
- You can make an effort to be energy-efficient at home.
- You can be a concerned citizen who cares about the environment and works with others to keep it clean.

Reading Check **Describe** What problems are created for the environment in a "throwaway" society?

Waste Removal

Billions of tons of waste are created every year in the United States. Where does it all go? Where should it all go? These questions are urgent because the waste continues to grow.

You can work to change the situation. Even though the waste problem is a national issue, the solution depends on individual actions. Your actions can help to make a difference. One way that individuals can help is by recycling. **Recycling** is turning waste items into products that can be used. You will read more about recycling later in this section.

Paper or Plastic?
Neither! Using a cloth grocery bag over and over again is one way an individual can help protect resources and the environment. *What other everyday items can you use over again?*

Composting

In this activity you will learn how to make your own compost for fertilizer. Before you begin, read through the entire Hands-On Lab assignment. Write down any questions that you have about the activity. Reread the text or ask your teacher for help if you need it.

Supplies
✓ Kitchen scraps
✓ Garden clippings
✓ Water
✓ Small shovel
✓ Garden soil

Develop Your Plan

- Compost is a mixture of decayed plants and other organic matter used for enriching soil. Use compost to recycle materials that may otherwise end up in a landfill.

- Find a 3 foot x 3 foot spot outdoors where you can create your compost pile. If this is not possible where you live, ask your teacher for other options.

- Plan a carbon to nitrogen ratio of 20 to 1. For carbon, collect vegetable scraps, fresh lawn and garden clippings, and weeds. For nitrogen, collect dry leaves, sawdust, paper, straw, dry grass, and wood ashes.

Implement Your Plan

- Pile your collect nitrogen and carbon materials into the 3 foot x 3 foot spot to decompose.

- With your shovel, turn the materials every two weeks for 10–12 weeks. Add more materials if they become available, keeping the 20 to 1 carbon to nitrogen ratio.

- Add water regularly so that there is about a 50% moisture content.

- After 10–12 weeks, mix the compost with garden soil.

Evaluate Your Results

How much waste did you save by composting? Where can you use the compost? What was the most difficult part of the process? What would you change if you did this project again? Write one or more paragraphs to explain your answer.

Evaluate Your Results Answer Students' results will vary. Students should list what they used in the compost mixture, and describe how they could use the compost in or around their homes, such as in a flower or vegetable garden, or in potted plants inside the home.

> **Projects and Activities** Go to this book's Online Learning Center through **glencoe.com** for more projects and activities.

Character Counts

Initiative

Noah rides his bike to school every day with a group of his friends. They always take the same route, and Noah has noticed that there is quite a bit of litter along the side of the street. Noah has been studying the environment in one of his classes, and he feels like he and his friends should do something about the litter on their route to school.

You Make the Call

What should Noah do to help solve the litter problem in his neighborhood? Write a paragraph explaining what Noah should do and why.

Character Counts Answer Noah needs to take the initiative to organize his friends to pick up the litter. Noah can also pick trash up himself, but since they all ride the same route, they can work as a team.

◆ Vocabulary

You can find definitions in the glossary at the back of this book.

Reading Check Answer To control the odors, germs, and other unhealthy situations that are created by piles of waste.

Photo Caption Answer The space that can be used for landfills is limited, no one wants to live near a landfill, and landfills may contain materials that will not break down for years.

Landfill Pollution There are thousands of landfills in the United States. *Why do you think landfills will not be a waste-removal option in the future?*

Landfills

About 80 percent of the waste in the United States is sent to landfills. A **landfill** is a huge pit where waste is buried between layers of earth. Most large communities have landfills somewhere on their outskirts, away from homes. These landfills are carefully designed to control the odors, germs, and other unhealthy situations that are created by piles of waste.

Landfills do cause problems, however. Waste buried in landfills is supposed to **decompose** so that it breaks down and becomes part of the soil. However, recent studies have shown that certain kinds of waste, such as plastic foam, do not break down for many years. Landfills take up huge amounts of space, and no one wants to live near a landfill.

Incineration

Another common way to **dispose**, or get rid, of waste in the United States is by incineration. **Incineration** is disposing of waste by burning it. About 10 percent of the waste in the United States is incinerated. When poisonous waste is burned, its smoke is especially dangerous. The air pollution created by burning waste can be so hazardous that it is illegal in many communities to burn waste.

Reading Check *Decide Why is it important to have a carefully designed landfill in a community?*

How To...

Reduce Waste

Every day, Americans throw away thousands of pounds of trash that ends up in landfills. You can make a difference in reducing waste at home, at your school, and in your community.

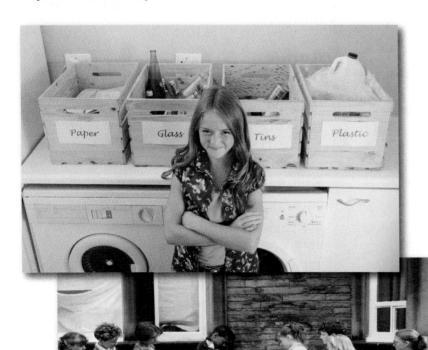

Home Separate plastic, glass, paper, and cardboard from the garbage you collect at home. Manufacturers can process all of these items and use them for new products or packaging.

School If your school participates in a recycling program, you can recycle the paper plates and plastic utensils you use for your lunch. Recycled paper is used to make newspaper and other everyday paper products. If your school does not have a recycling program, ask your teachers to help start one.

Community You can contribute to a recycling program, such as aluminum cans. Recycled aluminum is used every day by manufacturers around the world.

Financial Literacy

Cutting Energy Costs

Using energy efficient appliances, monitoring heating and cooling, and using energy-saving light bulbs can greatly reduce your energy costs. Presently your appliances cost you $850 per year to operate. If you buy energy efficient appliances, you can save 15 percent a year. How much will you save if you use the appliances for ten years?

Math Concept **Percent Calculation** A percent is a ratio that compares a number to 100. To find the percentage of a number, take the percent and convert it a decimal by moving the decimal point two places to the right.

Starting Hint: Take the $850 and multiply by .15 to find the yearly savings. Then multiply this answer by 10 years to get the total savings.

 For math help, go to the Math Appendix at the back of the book.

NCTM Number and Operations Understand numbers, ways of representing numbers, relationships among numbers, and number systems.

Financial Literacy Answer $1275. $850 x .15 = $127.50. $127.50 x 10 = $1275

COMMUNITY CONNECTIONS
Thrift Shops Clean out your closet and recycle! Find charitable organizations in your community that accept used clothing, shoes, and household items to sell in thrift shops or give to needy families.

Limit Waste

Burying waste in landfills and incinerating it both have serious drawbacks. They are both unsafe, and neither choice is a **permanent**, or long-term, solution. What should be done about the problem? The key is to reduce the amount of waste we create. All Americans can do their part by following the "three Rs," which are Reduce, Reuse, Recycle.

Reduce

The first step is to reduce, or lessen, the amount of waste created. To start reducing the amount of waste you create, you can reduce the amount of paper you throw away by using both sides of notebook and printer paper, using only washable cups and plates, and using cloth napkins. Avoid buying disposable products, and pre-cycle, or buy products that use less packaging material than others so there is less to throw away. Use cloth grocery bags instead of paper or plastic ones. Buy products that can be broken down and absorbed by the environment. These types of products are called **biodegradable**.

Reuse

The second of the "three Rs" is reuse. You can limit the amount of waste you create by reusing items you might otherwise throw away. If you use your imagination, you can probably think of many ways to reuse items. Buy products packed in containers that can be refilled or used for something else. Keep boxes, bottles, and cans to use as storage containers. Save and use old towels and clothes as cleaning rags. Think twice before throwing something away. Ask yourself, "What else can I do with this?"

Recycle

Many of the materials we throw away can be easily recycled. Recycling can greatly reduce the amount of waste in our country. For example, newspapers can be turned into pulp to make new paper. Aluminum cans can be melted down and turned into new cans and other products. Plastic can also be recycled. Over half of the waste we create is recyclable.

Photo Caption Answer When you buy and sell used items, it eliminates the need for new items to be created. This helps keep things out of landfills, and reduces the amount of energy required for manufacturing new products.

Recycling also means donating clothes, books, and other items to charities. You also recycle when you give or receive secondhand clothes or exchange magazines with a friend after reading them. These actions may seem small, but each one helps to limit the amount of waste. Imagine how much can be accomplished if every individual makes an effort to use the suggestions in this chapter. By applying the "three Rs," you will do your share to preserve the environment.

Use Your Imagination Find creative ways to reuse items instead of throwing them away. *How can a yard sale or a swap meet help the environment?*

Section 14.2 After You Read

Review What You Have Learned

1. **Identify** three ways you can do your part to protect the environment.
2. **Explain** why incineration is not a safe way to remove waste.
3. **Suggest** three ways for people to reduce waste.

Practice Academic Skills

 English Language Arts

4. Imagine that you have a friend who thinks one person cannot make a difference when it comes to protecting the environment. Write a letter to your friend to convince him or her that individuals really can make a difference.

> **NCTE 12** Use language to accomplish individual purposes.

Social Studies

5. Conduct research to find out about your school's recycling policy. Does your school have a recycling program? Does your school make it easy to recycle? Prepare a short presentation for your class that explains the school's policy, and add your own suggestions for improvement.

> **NCSS V G** Analyze the extent to which groups and institutions meet individual needs and promote the common good in contemporary and historical settings.

 Check Your Answers Check your answers at this book's Online Learning Center at glencoe.com.

Discovering Careers

Do you have a passion for protecting our environment? Do you care about the planet and all of its creatures? If you answered yes to either of those questions, you might want to consider a future career in environmental studies. The following chart explores several careers in the environmental studies field.

Job Title	Job Description
Environmental Analyst	Conducts research studies to develop methods of controlling pollutants. Analyzes sources of pollution to determine their effects.
Ecologist	Researches environmental concerns. Makes studies to determine in what conditions varieties of plants grow and how species resist disease and insects.
Pollution Control Engineer	Plans and conducts engineering studies. Evaluates methods of pollution control to determine contaminants. Performs calculations to determine pollution emissions.
Forester	Manages forests for economic and recreational purposes. Maps forest areas. Estimates the number of trees and future growth. Plans cutting programs.
Wildlife Biologist	Studies habitat, development, growth and influences on wildlife habitat. Make plans for survival and population control of wildlife.

Career Activities ▼

At School

1 Select three of the careers listed. Research the education, training, and work experience required for each career. Write a summary of your results.

At Home

2 Go through your trash at home, and pull items that can be reused recycled. Create a reference list for your family.

At Work

3 List five careers for people who want to protect animals.

In the Community

4 Contact and interview someone in your community who works in environmental studies. Ask this person to describe what his or her typical work day is like. Share what you learned with your class.

Learn More *Online* glencoe.com

Career Investigations Go to this book's Online Learning Center for activities and worksheets to help you explore careers.

Career Activities Answers for these activities can be found on page TM145.

Chapter Summary

Section 14.1 Resources and Conservation
Natural resources are materials that are supplied by nature. Some are nonrenewable and can be damaged by pollution. The air you breathe may contain dust, smoke, chemical particles, and smog. Much of the earth's water is polluted. Energy is in limited supply. You may think that pollution and the shrinking supply of natural resources are beyond your control. However, you can make a difference by conserving resources.

Section 14.2 Protect the Environment
Protection of natural resources and the environment begins with you. Even though the waste problem is a national issue, the solution depends on individual actions. The key is to reduce the amount of waste we create. Do your part by following the "three Rs," which are reduce, reuse, and recycle. Reduce the amount of waste created. Reuse items you might otherwise throw away. Recycle waste items into products that can be used.

Words You Learned

1. Write a sentence using two or more of these content and vocabulary words. The sentence should clearly show how the words are related.

Content Vocabulary
- natural resource (p. 305)
- pollution (p. 305)
- soil (p. 306)
- fossil fuel (p. 306)
- conservation (p. 307)
- recycling (p. 312)
- landfill (p. 312)
- decompose (p. 312)
- incineration (p. 312)
- biodegradable (p. 314)

Academic Vocabulary
- key (p. 305)
- efficient (p. 307)
- dispose (p. 312)
- permanent (p. 314)

Review Key Concepts

2. **Identify** the four key natural resources and why we need to protect them.

3. **Explain** how you can do your part to conserve water and energy.

4. **Define** what is meant by "throwaway" society.

5. **Describe** the negative effects of landfills and incineration.

6. **Name** the "three Rs".

Critical Thinking

7. **Predict** how recycling can make a difference to you personally.

8. **Evaluate** how waste created in the kitchen can be reduced, reused, or recycled.

9. **Compare and contrast** these options for drinking beverages: wash a ceramic cup over and over, and use a new foam cup for every drink. Which do you think is better for the environment?

Real-World Skills and Applications

Problem-Solving

10. Adopt a Mile Many communities provide ways for individuals, organizations, or businesses to help maintain sections of roadside by "adopting" a section of road. Conduct research to find out what these programs do for the environment, and how you can volunteer.

Technology Applications

11. Deforestation Conduct research to find out about deforestation. What does deforestation mean? What causes deforestation? What are the effects of deforestation? Use presentation software to share your findings. Include graphics, photographs, and descriptive text.

Financial Literacy

12. Recycling Pays Research the law in your state to see how much money you can receive for recycling beverage containers. You can usually find this amount printed on the side of bottles and cans. If you recycled all of the glass and aluminum drink containers you use in a week, how much money would you have at the end of a week? A 4-week month? A 52-week year? If your state does not pay for recycling, calculate the numbers using a fee of 5 cents per container.

13. Pressed-Flower Bookmarks Create bookmarks using pressed flowers. Gather small flower blossoms in several colors, paper towels or tissue paper (if you can find tissue paper left over from a gift-wrapping project, reuse it!), a few heavy books, scissors, and clear contact paper. Place the flowers between paper towels or tissue paper and set the heavy books on them overnight. Place the pressed flowers between two sheets of contact paper and gently push out any air bubbles. Cut the bookmarks into strips, about 4 inches long and 1½ inches wide. In what other ways can you used pressed flowers?

14. Research Nuclear Energy Nuclear energy is stored in the nucleus (center) of an atom. Atoms are tiny particles that make up every object in the universe. Conduct research to find out how this energy is released to produce electricity. Why is nuclear energy considered cleaner than traditional forms of energy? Prepare a brief presentation about your findings.

15. Household Hazardous Waste The Environmental Protection Agency (EPA) has given the name "household hazardous waste" to leftover household products that contain poisonous, flammable, or reactive ingredients. With permission from your parents or teacher, go online to learn about the dangers of household hazardous wastes. Create a list of hazardous products that might be found in the typical home. Then write a list of tips to safely store and dispose of household hazardous waste. Keep a copy of the tips in your Life Skills Binder.

Academic Skills

 English Language Arts

16. Write a News Story A technique used by journalists when writing a news story is to ask and answer these six questions: Who? What? When? Where? Why? How? Choose a topic from this chapter, such as pollution, energy use, or wildlife protection. Using the six questions, write an article for your school newspaper that inspires other students to do something positive for the environment.

> **NCTE 4** Use written language to communicate effectively.

 Social Studies

17. Identify Influences Interview your parents, grandparents, or other older relatives about how and why attitudes toward the environment have changed since they were your age. Ask questions about the three Rs, nuclear energy, waste disposal concerns, and other environmental issues. Summarize your findings in a short essay.

> **NCSS IV F Individual Development and Identity** Analyze the role of perceptions, attitudes, values, and beliefs in the development of personal identity.

 Mathematics

18. Save Water Vanessa's kitchen faucet has been dripping for three days at a steady rate of one drip every two seconds (or 30 drips per minute). If it takes 8,000 drips to fill up a two-liter soda bottle, how many two-liter soda bottles could Vanessa fill with all of the water that dripped in three full days?

Math Concept **Multi-Step Problems** When solving problems with more than one step, think through the steps before you start.

Starting Hint Since there are 60 minutes in one hour, and 24 hours in one day, determine the total minutes in three days by multiplying 3 x 24 x 60. Since there are 30 drips per minute, multiply the total minutes by 30 to find the total number of drips. Divide that number by 8,000 to determine how many soda bottles could be filled with those drips.

> **NCTM Number and Operations** Compute fluently and make reasonable estimates.

Standardized Test Practice ● ● ● ● ● ● ● ● ● ●

Open-Ended Response

An open-ended response requires more than a simple yes or no answer. It can usually be answered with one or two sentences.

> **Test-Taking Tip** Open-ended test questions most often require a specific response rather than an opinion. They may include definitions, comparisons, or examples.

Write one or two sentences to answer the questions.

19. Why should you practice conservation?

20. What are biodegradable products?

21. How is an energy-efficient appliance beneficial?

UNIT 6 Life Skills Project

Improve Your Home

You probably spend a lot of time at home, so why not make your living space as attractive and functional as possible? Magazines, home stores, and the homes of your friends can give you ideas. This project can help you learn how to improve the space you live in.

 My Journal Complete the journal entry from page 279, and refer to it to complete your evaluation of the place you live.

Project Assignment ▼

In this project, you will:

- Evaluate your living space for ways it can be improved.
- Draw two floor plans for a room showing how you can change it.
- Describe how you would make the room better.
- Interview someone who designs or builds homes or furnishings for a living.
- Present your findings to your class.
- Include this project in the sixth section of your personal Life Skills binder.

Step 1 Observe How Rooms are Used

Spend a few hours observing the way people use rooms and living spaces. Write a summary of your observations that identifies problems in how the room looks or functions.

Step 2 Draw Two Floor Plans

Choose the room or area you want to redesign and measure it. Create two scale-model floor plans. On the first, draw in the furniture of the room the way it looks now. On the second, lay out your new arrangement. Then write two or more paragraphs that answer these questions:

✔ What problems are you trying to solve?
✔ How does the new plan improve functionality?
✔ Describe the new look of your room.
✔ Does your new room plan allow for wiser energy use and less waste?

Step 3 Interview Someone Who Works in Design or Construction

Interview someone in your community who is a professional builder or designer. Ask these questions:

✔ How would you fix the problems in this room?
✔ What are the most common safety issues you encounter in your work?
✔ What ways do you keep your work environmentally friendly?

Use these interviewing skills when conducting your interview and these writing skills when writing the summary of notes from your interview.

Interviewing Skills
- Record interview responses and take notes.
- Listen attentively.

Writing Skills
- Use complete sentences.
- Use correct spelling and grammar.

Step 4 Create and Present Your Room Improvement Design

Use the Life Skills Project Checklist on the right to plan and complete your floor plans and give an oral report comparing the two plans.

Use these speaking skills when presenting your final report.

Speaking Skills
- Speak clearly and concisely.
- Be sensitive to the needs of your audience.
- Use standard English to communicate.

Step 5 Evaluate Your Presentation

Your project will be evaluated based on:

✔ Organization and attention to detail of your room evaluation.
✔ The accuracy and creativity of your floor plans.
✔ The description of improvements to your room.
✔ The summary written from interview notes.
✔ Grammar and sentence structure.
✔ Presentation to the class.
✔ Creativity and neatness.

Evaluation Rubric Go to this book's Online Learning Center through glencoe.com for a rubric you can use to evaluate your final project.

Life Skills Project Checklist

Research How Rooms Are Used

- Evaluate rooms that could be improved.
- Measure and draw an accurate floor plan of the current room layout.
- Draw a floor plan that shows how you would improve the layout.
- Interview an architect, construction worker, or interior designer in your community.

Writing Skills

- Describe the design problems in the room.
- Describe how your changes improve that room.
- Write a summary from your interview with a person who works in construction or design.

Present Your Findings

- Prepare a short presentation to share your two floor plans and compare the problems in the first to the solutions in the second.
- Invite the students of the class to ask any questions they may have. Answer these questions with responses that respect their perspectives.
- Add this project to your Life Skills binder.

Academic Skills

- Conduct research to gather information.
- Communicate effectively.
- Organize your presentation so the audience can follow along easily.
- Thoroughly express your ideas.

NCTM Measurement Apply appropriate techniques, tools, and formulas to determine measurements.
NCTE 12 Use language to accomplish individual purposes.

Chapter 15
Your Fashion Statement

Chapter 16
Clothing Basics

Unit Preview

This unit is about selecting and caring for clothes. In this unit, you will learn about:

- Your personal style and ways to creatively express it.
- Color, line, and texture in clothing.
- Selecting comfortable and high-quality clothing.
- Clothing care basics.

Explore the Photo Answer Answers may include accessorizing, mixing and matching, resisting fads, discovering what styles flatter you, buying quality clothes, making sure clothes fit you well, thinking of color schemes, learning about different types of fabrics.

Explore the Photo
Today's clothing choices are virtually endless. *What are some ways that you can make smart clothing choices to reflect your personal style?*

Your Personal Style

When you are done studying this unit, you will complete a project in which you will:

✓ Discover your own personal style.

✓ Interview someone whose style you admire.

✓ Share with your class what your project says about you.

The prewriting activity below will help you get started.

 My Journal

Prewriting Activity
Make a Chart

Choose ten items of clothing from your closet. Write each item in one of two columns. Label the first column "Wear a Lot" and label the second column "Wear Rarely".

● What does the clothing in your "Wear a Lot" column have in common?

● What does the clothing in your "Wear Rarely" column have in common?

Chapter 15

Your Fashion Statement

Section 15.1

Explore the Photo Answer Answers will vary. Explain to students that their beliefs about what is important to them contribute to how they choose their clothing.

Selecting Your Clothes

■ **Main Idea** People wear clothes out of necessity and to make a personal statement. You can expand your wardrobe when you add accessories and evaluate what you already have.

Section 15.2

Color, Lines, and Texture

■ **Main Idea** Learn how color, line, and texture can be used to make your wardrobe flattering and flexible.

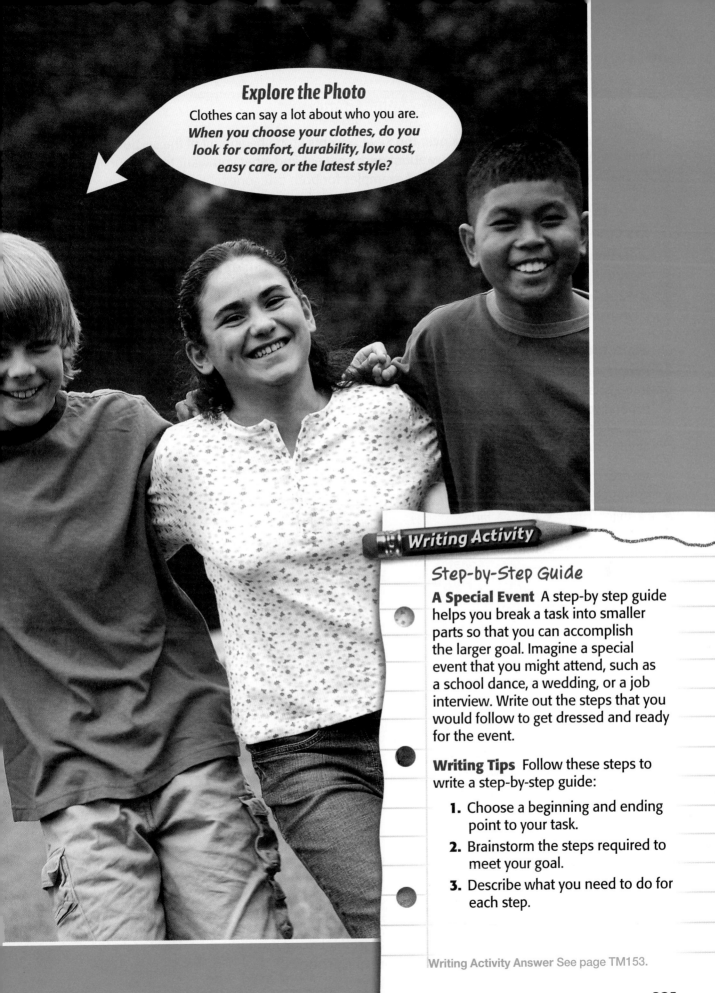

Explore the Photo

Clothes can say a lot about who you are. *When you choose your clothes, do you look for comfort, durability, low cost, easy care, or the latest style?*

Writing Activity

Step-by-Step Guide

A Special Event A step-by step guide helps you break a task into smaller parts so that you can accomplish the larger goal. Imagine a special event that you might attend, such as a school dance, a wedding, or a job interview. Write out the steps that you would follow to get dressed and ready for the event.

Writing Tips Follow these steps to write a step-by-step guide:

1. Choose a beginning and ending point to your task.
2. Brainstorm the steps required to meet your goal.
3. Describe what you need to do for each step.

Writing Activity Answer See page TM153.

Reading Guide

Before You Read

Prior Knowledge Look over the Key Concepts at the beginning of the section. Write down what you already know about each concept and what you want to find out by reading the lesson. As you read, find examples for both categories.

Read to Learn

Key Concepts

✓ **Recognize** the factors that influence your clothing choices.

✓ **Explain** how you can make the most of your wardrobe.

Main Idea

People wear clothes out of necessity and to make a personal statement. You can expand your wardrobe when you add accessories and evaluate what you already have.

Content Vocabulary

○ modesty   ○ alteration
○ style   ○ fad
○ fashion

Academic Vocabulary

■ status   ■ inventory

Graphic Organizer

As you read, identify five reasons for why people wear clothing. Use a graphic organizer like the one shown to help you organize your information.

Clothing Choices

 Graphic Organizer Go to this book's Online Learning Center at glencoe.com to print this graphic organizer.

· · · · · · · · · · · · · · · · · **Academic Standards** · · · · · · · · · · · · · · · · ·

 English Language Arts

NCTE 12 Use language to accomplish individual purposes.

Mathematics

NCTM Number and Operations Understand numbers, ways of representing numbers, relationships among numbers, and number systems.

Social Studies

NCSS IV B Individual Development and Identity Identify, describe, and express appreciation for the influences of various historical and contemporary cultures on an individual's daily life.

NCTE *National Council of Teachers of English*
NCTM *National Council of Teachers of Mathematics*

NSES *National Science Education Standards*
NCSS *National Council for the Social Studies*

Graphic Organizer
Answer Protection,
Adornment, Identification,
Modesty, Status

How do you decide what to wear? Everyone has likes and dislikes. This is why clothes come in so many styles, colors, and fabrics. The clothes you wear are your fashion statement. They send a message about how you see yourself. Clothes and accessories can reflect your individuality. They can also identify you as part of a group.

Clothing Choices

People first wore clothing to protect themselves against the wind, snow, rain, cold, and heat. That first clothing was made from animal skins. As time went on, people decorated their clothes with natural materials, such as earth and clay. Seeds, stones, and shell beads were sometimes added to clothing to show a person's **status**, or position in society.

Today, clothing choices are much more varied, but the purpose of clothing has not changed. Your clothing choices may be influenced by your personal preferences, your family, your friends, and the media. Here are some reasons people wear clothing:

- **Protection** Clothes protect you from the weather and climate. Some occupations require special clothing, such as police uniforms and firefighting gear. Workers in restaurants and hospitals often wear hair coverings and gloves to help protect others.
- **Adornment** Scarves, ties, hats, and vests, can be used as adornment, or decoration. People use such decorations to express creativity and individuality.
- **Identification** You do not always need to announce who you are. Sometimes your clothing can do it for you. For example, uniforms show others that you work at a particular restaurant, play in a school band, or are part of an athletic team.
- **Modesty** The way you wear your clothes and the type of clothing you wear suggest your personal sense of modesty. **Modesty** is a belief about the proper way to cover the body with clothes. The level of modesty can vary with the occasion. For example, it is acceptable to wear a bathing suit to the beach, but not to the office.

As You Read

Connect What does you clothing reveal about your personality?

As You Read Answer Answers may include such personality traits as outgoing, reserved, conservative, traditional, rebellious, sporty.

Vocabulary

You can find definitions in the glossary at the back of this book.

Photo Caption Answer They are participating in the same activity and are wearing the same uniform.

➤ **Uniformity** The teens in this photo share a common interest. *How can you tell?*

- **Status** Some clothes or accessories are worn to show a person's status. Designer labels, logos, and other recognized names and symbols can set certain individuals apart from the group.

Learning what influences your clothing decisions can help you choose clothes that are best for you. Making good clothing choices can help you present the image you want others to see. Your clothing choices say a lot about who you are and what is important to you.

Fashions, Fads, and Styles

The occasion or activity that you are dressing for helps to determine your clothing choices. For instance, you would wear different clothes to a basketball game than to a formal dance. It is important to choose the right outfit for the occasion. When choosing clothes based on your wants instead of your needs, it is important to reflect your personality. Danielle and Brianna shop for clothes together, but they choose different styles. A **style** is the design of a garment. A bomber jacket, a straight skirt, and baggy pants are all types of styles.

Not all styles of clothing are considered fashions. A **fashion** is a style of clothing that is popular at a particular time. Fashions change frequently. Just a slight **alteration** can be made to change the style and give a fashion a fresh, new look. For example, think about how a minor change in skirt length can change the whole look of an outfit. The same can be said for jacket length, collar shape, or the width of pant legs. At any one time, there will be some new fashions coming in, some going out, and other styles that remain popular season after season.

Many fashions become popular very quickly and then lose their appeal. A fashion that is very popular for a short time is called a **fad**. Fad clothing is fun to wear, but often goes out of style as quickly as it came in. Usually, it is not a good idea to spend a lot of money on fad items. It is better to spend most of your clothing budget on classic styles, which are styles that remain in fashion for a long time. Classics include a blazer, crew neck shirt, and cardigan sweater. You can change the look of styles and fashions with accessories such as belts, hats, and jewelry.

✔ **Reading Check** **Explain** *Why is better to spend most of your clothing budget on classic styles?*

Combine Separates

A good way to expand your wardrobe is by combining separates, or single pieces of clothing that can be mixed and matched. Try these ideas for making the most out of your wardrobe.

Mix and Match Lay out all of your clothing pieces and combine them in different ways. When you see everything together instead of hanging in your closet, you may notice possible combinations you might have missed.

Variety Keep your wardrobe versatile, or flexible, with many different colors and styles. Variety can make your outfits more fun and interesting.

Keep it Simple Styles without trim, such as beads and sequins, are more versatile. If you like prints, select prints that include a basic color, such as black or white, so they will go with your more basic items.

Flatter Yourself Make sure you choose styles that flatter your shape, your skin tone, and your personality. Do not waste money on clothes that do not fit or make you look your best.

Quality Invest in good quality. It is better to spend your money on clothes that will last. Choose clothes that are not only classic, but durable as well.

Resist Fads There is nothing wrong with an occasional trendy item just for fun. However, do not waste your money on something that may go out of style in a matter of weeks.

Evaluate Once you have looked over all of your clothing, accessories, and shoes, make a list of other items you can use to add to what you have. As your budget allows, add these items to your wardrobe for even more options.

Comparing Prices

Kim saw a great pair of sandals and a pair of pants at her favorite clothing store, but has been waiting for the price to drop at least 20% before buying them. Last weekend, the sandals were $38, and the pants cost $50. Today, Kim found the sandals marked down to $30, and the pants on sale for $45. Have the prices been discounted enough for Kim to purchase the items?

Math Concept **Percent of Decrease**

Calculate an amount of decrease (or a discount amount) by subtracting the new amount from the original amount. Divide that amount of decrease by the original amount, multiply by 100, and add a percent symbol to find the percent of decrease (discount percentage).

Starting Hint For the sandals, subtract $30 from $38 to find the discount amount, then divide by $38. Multiply this answer by 100 to get the discount percentage. Do similar calculations for the pants.

 For more math help, go to the Math Appendix located at the back of this book.

> **NCTM Number and Operations** Understand numbers, ways of representing numbers, relationships among numbers, and number systems.

➡ **Take Inventory** Before you go on your next shopping trip for clothes, take a look in your closet. *What can you do to help you decide what you really need to buy?*

Make the Most of Your Wardrobe

The first step in deciding what kind of clothes you need is to think about what kind of clothes you wear. Think about your various activities. You need clothes for school, casual clothes for spending time with friends, dressier clothes for special occasions, and clothes for activities such as sports or dance class.

You also need to evaluate your personal style, or the kind of clothes you like best. For example, do you wear a lot of tailored, buttoned shirts, or do you feel more comfortable in T-shirts? The best planning involves thinking about all of your clothes, not just about individual outfits. Keep in mind that shoes and accessories, such as belts, scarves, hats, socks, and jewelry, are part of your clothing wardrobe.

To take a clothing **inventory**, or list, sort your clothing into the following four categories:

- **Clothes that you wear often.**
  Use these clothes to help you evaluate your personal clothing style. What do you like about these clothes? Is it the style, color, or texture?

Photo Caption Answer Check your closet and dresser for clothes that do not fit, or for clothes you may have forgotten about. Make a list of what you already have, and think about items you could buy to update or add to what you already have.

A New Look Imagine this boy's outfit without the tie. ***What does the tie add to the look of his outfit?***

Photo Caption Answer He looks more formal and polished with the tie. The tie makes the outfit dressy instead of casual.

- **Clothes that do not fit.** There is no point in keeping these clothes in your closet. Before you set them aside, however, think about how they might still be used. If the sleeves on a shirt are too short, could they be cut off and hemmed to make a short-sleeved shirt instead? Clothes that are still in good condition but that you are sure you do not want can be donated to charity or given to a younger sibling.

- **Clothes that you never wear.** You may be able to add items to your wardrobe that will make these clothes more useful. Perhaps you bought a great pair of pants, but you do not have a shirt to go with them. If you like the pants, invest in a shirt so you can wear the pants. If not, give them away. As with clothes that do not fit, there is no reason to keep clothes you will never wear in your closet.

- **Clothes in need of repair.** Set these aside and see if they can be fixed. Repair the items you like.

Character Counts Answer Debra should go through all of her clothes and find an outfit she knows looks good on her. She can make it look a little different with shoes, a new hairstyle, and accessories. She should remind herself that her friends may not even notice that she has worn the outfit before, and even if they do, it will not make any difference to a real friend.

Character Counts

Confidence

Debra loves clothes and likes to keep up with the latest fashions. However, she does not have a lot of money to spend on clothes. Next week, she has a special occasion to attend with her friends, and she will have to wear something from her closet. She is afraid that she will not feel good about herself in something that her friends have already seen her wear.

You Make the Call

How can Debra feel confident in an outfit that is not brand new? Write a paragraph explaining what she should do.

Add Accessories

If you are bored with piece of clothing you have had for a long time, try adding a new accessory before discarding the item. A new belt, scarf, tie, or piece of jewelry can create a new look. You can also try changing buttons or adding trim to make a casual garment look dressier. Before you throw away a worn-out garment, check to see if you can save the buttons. Well-chosen accessories can stretch your wardrobe by giving the same outfit an entirely different look.

You can also use accessories to draw attention to your best features and away from features you do not want emphasized, or noticed. For instance, a wide belt can draw attention to a slim waistline. A watchband or bracelet can show off graceful hands. Scarves and neckties can be used to add color or emphasis.

When using accessories, it is best to choose one center of interest, or focal point. Choose a wide belt with a big buckle, for example. Any other accessories should be less noticeable and blend in with the outfit. Too many accessories can create a cluttered look.

Section 15.1 After You Read

Review What You Have Learned

1. **Contrast** style and fashion.
2. **Describe** the four categories you can use to take a clothing inventory.

Practice Academic Skills

English Language Arts

3. Read this statement: It is not important for teens to be concerned about style and fashion. Do you agree or disagree? Prepare a brief oral presentation in which you clearly state your position. Include details to support your statement.

> **NCTE 12** Use language to accomplish individual purposes.

Social Studies

4. Choose a fashion fad that is popular now or was popular in the past. Where did it begin? How did people find out about it? Who was most influenced by the fad? Create a small poster with images or drawings of the fad, and include the information you found in your research.

> **NCSS IV B** Identify, describe, and express appreciation for the influences of various historical and contemporary cultures on an individual's daily life.

 Check Your Answers Check your answers at this book's Online Learning Center at glencoe.com.

Section **15.2** Color, Lines, and Texture

Reading Guide

Before You Read

Two-Column Notes Divide a piece of paper into two columns. In the left column, write down main ideas as you read. In the right column, list supporting details.

Read to Learn
Key Concepts

✓ **Summarize** how color can affect you.

✓ **Describe** how the lines of your clothing can change the way you look.

✓ **Define** texture and list examples.

Main Idea
Learn how color, line, and texture can be used to make your wardrobe flattering and flexible.

Content Vocabulary
○ hue
○ tint
○ shade
○ intensity
○ monochromatic
○ complementary
○ analogous
○ texture

Academic Vocabulary
■ primary   ■ value

Graphic Organizer
As you read, identify what you know, what you want to learn, what you learned, and how you can learn more about color, lines, and texture. Use a graphic organizer like the one shown to help you organize your information.

What I Know	What I Want to Learn	What I Learned	How I Can Learn More

 Graphic Organizer Go to this book's Online Learning Center at glencoe.com to print this graphic organizer.

- - - - - - - - - - - - - - - **Academic Standards** - - - - - - - - - - - - - - -

 English Language Arts

NCTE 5 Use different writing process elements to communicate effectively.

Social Studies

NCSS I D Culture Compare and analyze societal patterns for preserving and transmitting culture while adapting to environmental or social change.

NCSS I B Culture Predict how data and experiences may be interpreted by people from diverse cultural perspectives and frames of reference.

NCTE *National Council of Teachers of English*
NCTM *National Council of Teachers of Mathematics*

NSES *National Science Education Standards*
NCSS *National Council for the Social Studies*

Colors, texture, and lines all add to the way you appear to others. Colors can reflect your moods and also affect your clothing choices. When you are feeling happy, you may choose to wear bright colors. On days when you are feeling thoughtful and quiet, you may select pale or dark colors. You can use clothes to help change your mood or your look.

Graphic Organizer
Answer Answers will vary depending on students' knowledge of color, lines, and texture.

As You Read

Connect What is your favorite color to wear? How do you feel when you wear that color?

As You Read Answer Students may say that a particular color makes them feel confident or stylish.

◆ Vocabulary

You can find definitions in the glossary at the back of this book.

Succeed in School Offer to allow students to practice oral reports with you during office hours. Give them constructive feedback to help them prepare for the presentation.

Presentation Skills

Rehearse Practice your speech before you present it to the class. Practice in front a mirror, or with a friend who will give you constructive feedback.

• • • • • • • • • • • • •

Color

What is the first thing you notice when you see a display of clothing in a store? Like most people, you probably notice the color. As one of several elements of design, color is often noticed first. As you learned in Chapter 13, the other elements of design are line, shape, space, and texture. These are important, but usually do not have as much impact as color.

Learning about color is useful in many ways, especially when making the clothing decisions that build your wardrobe. Why do some colors look better on you than other colors look? If you become familiar with the relationships among colors, you will understand how colors affect your appearance and the way clothes look on you.

Color matters. Colors can affect your mood, energy level, and appetite. For example, red is a powerful color that is full of energy. It stimulates the appetite. Yellow catches the eye better than all other colors. It lifts your mood and brightens rooms. Blue is a soothing color. It can lull you to sleep and suppress the appetite. Green has a calming effect. It is a common color in hospitals, schools, and offices.

When you put clothes together, you can create either single-color outfits or outfits that combine colors. You can learn to combine colors successfully using the color wheel in **Figure 15.1**. A color wheel shows the relationships of colors to each other.

Primary and Secondary Colors

To understand the basic principles of color, you need to know the names of the hues. The three basic **hues** are red, yellow, and blue. These three main colors are called **primary** colors because all other colors can be made from them. Combining equal amounts of red and yellow makes orange. Equal amounts of blue and yellow make green, and combining red and blue makes violet. These are called secondary colors. Intermediate colors are a blend of a primary and secondary color.

Color Values

Another basic element to consider is the **value**, or the lightness and darkness of color. For instance, blue can vary in value from very light blue to navy blue. A light value of a hue is called a **tint**. A dark value of a hue is called a **shade**. The brightness or dullness of a color is called its **intensity**. Bright red is a high-intensity color. Pale pink is a low-intensity color.

Figure (**15.1**) **Color Relationships**

The Color Wheel This color wheel shows how colors are related to one another. *How can you tell which colors are intermediate colors?*

Figure Caption Answer Intermediate colors fall between the primary and secondary colors on the chart.

Colors as Symbols

Not only can colors reveal moods, they can provide information. Imagine a driver coming up on a traffic light and not knowing the meanings of the colors. Anyone who does not understand that green means go and red means stop can get into some serious trouble! Colors can represent groups and countries. The combination of red, white, and blue has very special meaning to Americans. Those same colors are also the colors of France. Think of the flags of Canada and Japan. They are both red and white. What are your school's colors? What are the colors of your favorite athletic team? What are the colors in the flags that represent your heritage? These colors probably mean something to you because you associate them with something that makes you feel proud.

Figure 15.2 Color Schemes

A Plan for Using Color You can use color to decorate a room and to put together an outfit. *Name a color from each color scheme that could be worn with a yellow shirt.*

⬆ **Monochromatic Color Scheme** An outfit made up of one hue, and the tints and shades of that hue, is a monochromatic color scheme.

⬆ **Complementary Color Scheme** This type of color scheme gives great contrast because it combines colors that are opposite each other on the color wheel. Orange and blue used together form a complementary color scheme.

⬆ **Analogous Color Scheme** The colors in an analogous color scheme have one common hue. A combination of yellow and green is an analogous color scheme.

⬆ **Accented Neutral Color Scheme** Wearing a neutral color, such as beige, gray, black, or white, with another color as the accent is an accented neutral color scheme. A combination of black and yellow is an example of this color scheme.

Figure Caption Answer Answers may include green (analogous), purple (complementary), yellow (monochromatic), or black or white (neutral accented).

Color Warmth and Coolness

Colors are considered either warm or cool. Red, yellow, and orange are warm colors. They are bright and cheerful. Blue, green, and violet are cool colors. They can give you a sense of tranquility, or peacefulness.

Selecting Colors

When you try different color combinations, you will discover that some look better on you than others. Flattering colors can make your complexion look healthier and draw attention to your hair and eyes.

Colors affect your appearance in other ways, too. They can highlight certain areas of your body. Light, warm, and bright colors can make you look larger. Dark, cool, and dull colors can make you look smaller. Carl wears one-color **monochromatic** (ˈmä-nə-krō-ˈma-tik) outfits so that he will look taller. Ronda, on the other hand, likes complementary colors. **Complementary** (ˈkäm-plə-ˈmen-t(ə-)rē) means contrasting or opposite, such as purple and yellow, and the effect makes her appear shorter than she is. Joaquin tends to wear **analogous** (ə-ˈna-lə-gəs) colors, which means he likes colors that are next to each other on the color wheel, like green and yellow. Experiment with colors and combinations to see what looks best on you. See **Figure 15.2** for ideas.

Reading Check   *Contrast*   *What is the difference between monochromatic colors and complementary colors?*

Presentation Skills
Learn from Others
You can learn a lot from watching and listening to others when they speak. Pay attention to how speakers use their hands, make eye contact, and vary their speech patterns. All of these things can help make your speech more interesting.

• • • • • • • • • • • •

Succeed in School As you speak to your class, ask students to observe how you use your hands, make eye contact, and vary your speech pattern. Ask how these actions make lectures more interesting.

Reading Check Answer
Monochromatic means one color; complementary means contrasting or opposite colors.

Discover International...
Styles

Kente Cloth
Kente cloth, a hand-woven cloth from Africa, is worn today by people from every social class. In the past, certain designs were meant to be worn only by royalty. In the United States in the 1960s, traditional African garments and home fashions made of kente cloth became popular again in the African-American community. African-Americans began using kente cloth as a symbol of their cultural heritage and as a mark of pride and inspiration.

kente cloth |ˈken-ˌtā| a colorful, patterned, hand-woven cloth from Ghana. The designs in the fabric may reflect cultural beliefs, historical events, social relationships, or political organizations.

NCSS I D Culture Compare and analyze societal patterns for preserving and transmitting culture while adapting to environmental or social change.

Lines and Appearance

The way a garment looks on you is also affected by its lines. Lines form the outer shape, or outline, of a garment. For example, compare straight-leg, tapered, and flared pants. Sometimes lines are formed by the seams and waistlines of a garment. Other lines can be part of the fabric's design, such as stripes or plaids.

Lines can be either straight or curved. Curved lines soften a garment's appearance. Straight lines look strong. When you shop for clothes, learn to look for lines. Try to see vertical, or up-and-down, lines instead of just a row of buttons or a zipper down the front. Look for horizontal lines, or lines that go straight across, instead of seeing only belts, waistlines, or hemlines. See diagonal or curved lines instead of necklines and collars.

You can change the way you look by changing the lines of your clothes:

- Vertical lines can make you look taller and thinner.
- Horizontal lines can make you look shorter and wider.
- Diagonal lines can make you look taller and thinner or shorter and wider, depending on the length and angle of the lines.

Reading Check Answer
horizontal, vertical, diagonal, curved

✓ **Reading Check** **List** *What are four types of lines you should look for when selecting clothes?*

COMMUNITY CONNECTIONS
Dress for Success
There are charitable organizations that specialize in collecting donated business suits to help men and women dress for job interviews. Ask family members if they have such items to donate.

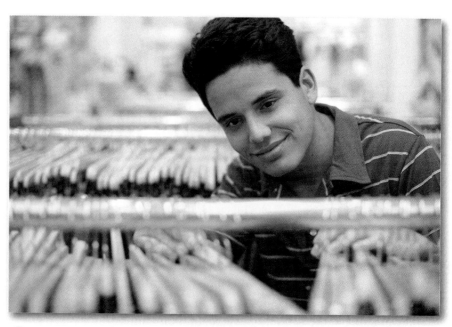

Photo Caption Answer
Curved lines make an outfit appear soft.

🔵 **Look at Lines** When choosing an outfit, look at the direction of the lines. *If you want a soft appearance, what should you look for?*

Clothing Texture

When you choose clothing, you need to consider its texture. **Texture** is the feel and appearance of the fabric's surface. Just as colors and lines create different looks, textures can create different impressions, too. Texture is created by using different yarns and weaves in making fabric. For instance, a wool sweater has a coarse texture that is created in the knitting process. A fabric may be dull like denim or shiny like silk and satin. Nubby fabrics like corduroy and tweed are often used for heavy suit coats. Smooth fabrics like flannel are used for pajamas.

You can use textures to change the way you look. Dull textures can make you look smaller. Nubby or shiny textures add bulk. A tall person can wear a coarse texture, but the same fabric may overpower a small person. To see which textures look best on you, try on clothing with different types of textures.

It All Comes Together Several design elements come together to create a look. Experiment until you find what works best for you. *Discuss this boy's outfit in terms of color, line, and texture.*

Photo Caption Answer Answers may include: the color flatters his skin tone; the heavy texture of his top adds bulk to his shape; the lines in the pants add visual interest.

Section 15.2 After You Read

Review What You Have Learned

1. **List** the primary and secondary colors.
2. **Describe** how lines are formed in clothing.
3. **Explain** how texture is created.

Practice Academic Skills

 English Language Arts

4. Write a description of an outfit that would make a good first impression at a job interview. Use what you have learned about color, lines, and texture to choose the right outfit.

> **NCTE 5** Use different writing process elements to communicate effectively.

Social Studies

5. When you think of a traditional wedding dress worn by a bride in the United States, white is the color that most likely comes to your mind. Conduct research to learn about a culture in which white is not the traditional color choice for weddings. Write a brief paragraph to describe the color scheme and the significance of the color.

> **NCSS I B Culture** Predict how data and experiences may be interpreted by people from diverse cultural perspectives and frames of reference.

Check Your Answers Check your answers at this book's Online Learning Center at glencoe.com.

Discovering Careers

Do you always seem to notice what other people are wearing? Do you think about how you would design a piece of clothing differently? If you answered yes to either of those questions, you might want to consider a future career in fashion. The following chart explores several careers in the fashion industry.

Job Title	Job Description
Fashion Coordinator	Selects garments and accessories for fashion shows. Provides information on current fashions, style trends, and use of accessories.
Fashion Designer	Designs men's, women's, and children's clothing or accessories. Analyzes fashion trends. Uses knowledge to create new styles.
Fabric Designer	Specifies weave patterns, colors, and threads to make new fabrics. Sketches designs and writes instructions to specify fabric details.
Costume Historian	Researches documents and archives of museums, libraries, and historical societies. Describes how the garments people wore reflect history.
Movie Wardrobe Designer	Researches clothing based on movie scripts. Creates authentic designs to fit the period of the movie.

Career Activities ▼

At School

1 Select three of the careers listed. Research the education, training, and work experience required for each career. Write a summary of your results.

At Home

2 Interview a family about the clothing and accessories he or she wears to accomplish tasks in and around the home.

At Work

3 Choose three jobs that you might consider in the future. List the type of clothing that would be appropriate for each job.

In the Community

4 Contact and interview someone in your community who works in the fashion industry. Ask this person to describe what his or her typical work day is like. Share what you learned with your class.

Learn More *Online* 🔁 glencoe.com

Career Investigations Go to this book's Online Learning Center for activities and worksheets to help you explore careers.

Career Activities Answers Answers for these activities can be found on page TM153.

Chapter Summary

Section 15.1 Selecting Your Clothes
Clothing can help you present who you are and what is important to you. The occasion or activity that you are dressing for helps to determine your clothing choices. Think about what kind of clothes you wear. Evaluate your personal style and the clothes you like best.

Section 15.2 Color, Lines, and Texture
Your clothing tells a lot about your personality. Colors can affect your mood, energy level, and appetite. Colors can be either warm or cool. When you try different color combinations, you will discover that some colors look better on you than other colors. The way a garment looks on you is also affected by its lines and texture.

Words You Learned

1. Create a true-false quiz based on the content and academic vocabulary words. Exchange quizzes with a classmate and complete.

Content Vocabulary
- modesty (p. 327)
- style (p. 328)
- fashion (p. 328)
- alteration (p. 328)
- fad (p. 328)
- hue (p. 334)
- tint (p. 334)
- shade (p. 334)
- intensity (p. 334)
- monochromatic (p. 337)
- complementary (p. 337)
- analogous (p. 337)
- texture (p. 339)

Academic Vocabulary
- status (p. 327)
- inventory (p. 330)
- primary (p. 334)
- value (p. 334)

Review Key Concepts

2. **Recognize** the factors that influence your clothing choices.

3. **Explain** how you can make the most of your wardrobe.

4. **Summarize** how color can affect you.

5. **Describe** how the lines of your clothing can change the way you look.

6. **Define** texture and list examples.

Critical Thinking

7. **Decide** whether or not you would you would follow the fashion example set by a celebrity. Explain your answer.

8. **Explain** why some people feel offended when they dress up for dinner at a nice restaurant, and they see that other diners are dressed casually.

9. **Analyze** why neon pink clothes may be "in" one year and "out" the next. Why do you think such color trends occur?

Real-World Skills and Applications

Problem-Solving

10. Fashion Mistakes Imagine that you are invited to the fifteenth birthday of your friend's cousin. You have been to many birthday parties for your friends, and you have always dressed casually. When you arrive at the party in your jeans and casual shirt, you see that the girls are wearing formal dresses and the boys are wearing tuxedos! What should you do? How can you avoid this kind of mistake next time?

Interpersonal and Collaborative

11. Fashion Inspiration Follow your teacher's directions to form small groups. Work with your group to identify how celebrities, athletes, movies, and television shows inspire current fashion. Collect photos and write descriptive captions to create a poster that illustrates this inspiration.

Financial Literacy

12. Investigate Clothing Stocks A share of stock represents partial ownership in a corporation. That means when you own a stock, you actually own part of a company These shares can be bought and sold through what is called a central exchange, such as the New York Stock Exchange. The share prices of each corporation go up and down during each day based on news reports, trends, and other events. Pick three large, clothing-related corporations, such as companies that own the clothing stores where you shop, or that make some of the clothes you own. Research today's stock price for each company.
Find a chart that shows the change in each company's stock price over time. Is the current price higher or lower than it was a year ago?

13. Costume Design Many countries have a national costume or typical style of dress that is instantly recognizable to others. For example, when you see a woman in a kimono, you know that she is wearing clothing from Japan. If you see a man wearing a plaid-patterned kilt, he is likely representing Scotland. The United States has long been called a "melting pot." This means that the people who live in the U.S. come from all over the world to live together in one country. Considering this diversity, design a national costume for America. Share your design with the class, and explain your creation.

14. Color Schemes Identify a color scheme in a room you are familiar with, such as a room in your home, a restaurant, or a classroom. Determine if the room's color scheme is monochromatic, analogous, complementary, or accented neutral. What minor changes could you make to the room to change the color scheme? Present your ideas to the class.

15. Designers Today With permission from your parents or teacher, go online to find information on a current fashion designer of your choice. How did he or she get started in fashion design? What or who were his or her inspirations? What types of designs does he or she create? Who wears the clothes? Summarize your findings and include images. Add the information to your Life Skills Binder.

Academic Skills

English Language Arts

16. Identify Influences List ten different clothing items, outfits, or accessories in your wardrobe. For each item, write down who or what influenced you to buy or wear that item. Are there any items you wish that you had not bought? If so, explain why.

> **NCTE 4** Use written language to communicate effectively.

Social Studies

17. Cultural Values How can clothing reflect a society's values? Conduct research on historical and modern clothing in various cultures. Select three styles or outfits that interest you. For each one, write one or two sentences to describe what you can tell about the culture's values.

> **NCSS I C Culture** Apply an understanding of culture as an integrated whole that explains the functions and interactions of language, literature, the arts, traditions, beliefs and values, and behavior patterns.

Mathematics

18. Calculate Payments Andrea bought some clothing on a department store credit card. Her total came to $250. She qualified for interest-free financing. She made a first payment of $35 and agreed to pay $25 twice a month until the $250 balance was paid. How long will it take for Andrea to pay off her bill?

Math Concept **Operations** To determine the number of payments, subtract the down payment, divide the principal by payment, and divide the number of payments by the frequency of the payment.

Starting Hint Take $35 from $250 and then divide the result by her payments of $25 to see how many payments. Then divide this number by two to figure out how many months it will take.

> **NCTM Number and Operations** Understand numbers, ways of representing numbers, relationships among numbers, and number systems.

Standardized Test Practice ● ● ● ● ● ● ● ● ● ●

Multiple-Choice

Read the sentence. Determine which underlined word contains a spelling error.

> **Test-Taking Tip** As you read, you will often "see" a missing word or letter because you expect to see it. When checking for spelling, slow down your reading speed and carefully look at each letter in the word.

19. Using a <u>monchromatic</u> color scheme, Danetta <u>carefully</u> matched the outfit that she planned to <u>wear</u> for the <u>award</u> ceremony at her school.
   a. monchromatic
   b. carefully
   c. wear
   d. award

Chapter 16

Clothing Basics

Explore the Photo Answer Answers may include check clothing budget or allowance, arrange to meet with friends to shop together, decide what kinds of clothes are needed.

 Section 16.1

Quality Clothing

■ **Main Idea** Learn about fabric, quality, comfort, and planning to help you make smart clothing purchases.

 Section 16.2

Clothing Care Basics

■ **Main Idea** You can stretch your clothing budget and keep your wardrobe looking good when you know how to properly care for and store your clothes.

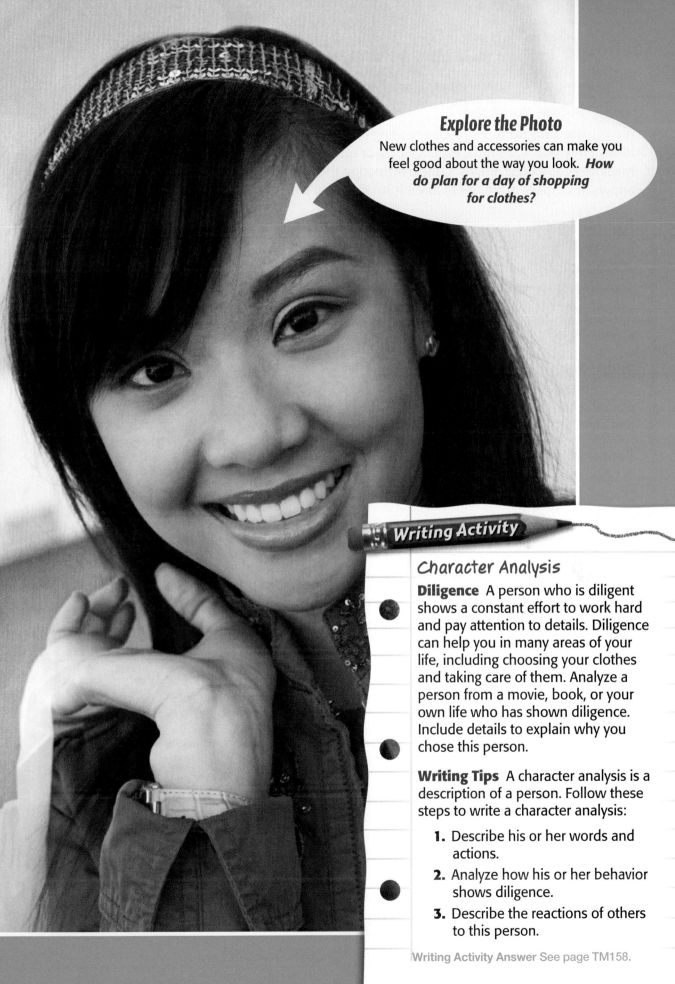

Explore the Photo
New clothes and accessories can make you feel good about the way you look. *How do plan for a day of shopping for clothes?*

Writing Activity

Character Analysis

Diligence A person who is diligent shows a constant effort to work hard and pay attention to details. Diligence can help you in many areas of your life, including choosing your clothes and taking care of them. Analyze a person from a movie, book, or your own life who has shown diligence. Include details to explain why you chose this person.

Writing Tips A character analysis is a description of a person. Follow these steps to write a character analysis:

1. Describe his or her words and actions.
2. Analyze how his or her behavior shows diligence.
3. Describe the reactions of others to this person.

Writing Activity Answer See page TM158.

345

Section 16.1 Quality Clothing

Reading Guide

Before You Read

Use Diagrams As you are reading through this section, write down the main ideas. Write down any facts, explanations, or examples you find in the text. Start at the main ideas and draw arrows to the information that directly supports them. Then draw arrows from these examples to any information that supports them.

Read to Learn

Key Concepts

✓ **Explain** three features of quality fabric.

✓ **Identify** three factors that affect clothing comfort.

✓ **Outline** a shopping plan for clothes.

Main Idea

Learn about fabric, quality, comfort, and planning to help you make smart clothing purchases.

Content Vocabulary

○ fiber
○ natural fiber
○ synthetic fiber
○ blend
○ woven fabric
○ knit fabric
○ grain

Academic Vocabulary

■ slant   ■ strategy

Graphic Organizer

As you read, identify four types of natural fibers and name the plant or animal each fiber comes from. Use a graphic organizer like the one shown to help you organize your information.

Natural Fiber		Comes From
1.	⟶	1.
2.	⟶	2.
3.	⟶	3.
4.	⟶	4.

 Graphic Organizer Go to this book's Online Learning Center at glencoe.com to print this graphic organizer.

- - - - - - - - - - - - - - - - - - **Academic Standards** - - - - - - - - - - - - - - - - - -

 English Language Arts

NCTE 5 Use different writing process elements to communicate effectively.

Social Studies

NCSS I A Culture Analyze and explain the ways groups, societies, and cultures address human needs and concerns.

NCTE *National Council of Teachers of English*
NCTM *National Council of Teachers of Mathematics*

NSES *National Science Education Standards*
NCSS *National Council for the Social Studies*

Graphic Organizer Answer (1) cotton from the seedpod of the cotton plant; (2) linen from the flax plant; (3) silk from silkworm cocoons; (4) wool from sheep fleece.

Visiting clothing stores is a way to discover new styles. Maybe you love to shop, but sometimes you think you do not have enough money for what you want. It is important to know what to look for. It is also important to consider your clothing budget. You can save both time and money by looking for the best values, following care label directions, and storing your clothes properly.

Recognize Quality Fabrics

The best way to learn about fabrics is to take a trip to a fabric store. Check the label on the end of the fabric bolt to see the fiber content. Compare fabrics in different price ranges. Feel various fabrics to see how they handle when stretched or crushed. Quality fabric will spring back. A basic understanding of fabrics can help you make better clothing choices.

Fibers and Fabrics

Most fabrics are made from tiny strands called **fibers**. Fibers can be made from natural or synthetic (sin-,the-tik) materials. **Natural fibers** are made from plant and animal products. Cotton comes from the seedpod of the cotton plant. It is the most widely used fiber in the world. Linen comes from the flax plant. Linen is very absorbent, but wrinkles easily. Silk is generated by silkworms as they spin their cocoons. Silk is strong and resists wrinkling, but it has to be dry-cleaned or hand-washed. Wool is made from the fleece of sheep. It is a durable fiber that traps air, preventing the loss of body heat. Wool is worn in cold weather.

Synthetic fibers are manufactured from substances such as wood pulp and petroleum. Rayon and nylon are both synthetic fibers. Polyester, the most widely used synthetic fiber, is often combined with cotton. When two or more fibers are combined to create a fabric, it is referred to as a **blend**. The clothing label lists the percentage of each type of fiber. For example, a shirt might be a blend of 60% cotton and 40% polyester. Fabrics are made by weaving or knitting fibers together.

Woven Fabrics

When you were a young child, you may have woven strips of paper together to create an art project. This same basic process is used to create **woven fabrics**. They are made by interlacing lengthwise and crosswise yarns, which are several fibers twisted together, on a loom. **Figure 16.1** on the next page illustrates the most common types of woven fabrics.

🔵 **Learn about Fabrics** Fiber content can be found on the fabric bolt. *What else can you learn from a visit to a fabric store?*

Knit Fabrics

Like woven fabrics, **knit fabrics** are made by looping threads together. There are many ways to loop the threads for a variety of textures and patterns. Knit fabrics are made to be stretchy. Knit fabrics move well with the body and are comfortable to wear. Not all knits are heavy like sweaters. Cotton T-shirts are also made of knit fabric.

Fabric Grain

Grain is the direction the threads run in a fabric. Both knit and woven fabrics have a grain, as you can see in Figure 16.1. Well-constructed clothes are cut on grain, with the threads running straight up and down and straight across.

Threads can be pulled off grain when the fabric goes through the finishing process. This makes the grain slant, or set at the wrong angle. If the fabric is off-grain, the garment will appear to pull to one side, especially after a few washings.

Figure Caption Answer
Answers may include: plain weave—shirts, casual clothing, bed sheets, pillowcases; twill weave—jeans, overalls, suits, upholstery; satin weave—formal dresses, blouses, blanket trims.

Figure 16.1 Common Fabric Weaves

Different Weaves Create Different Effects Plain, twill, and satin are the most common weaves. *Can you name something in your wardrobe or home from each of the weave categories?*

Plain Weave The plain weave is the simplest weave. The yarns form an even, balanced weave. Plain weaves are used for shirts, handkerchiefs, and sheets.

Twill Weave Twill weaves create diagonal lines on fabric. Twill weaves are firmer, heavier, and stronger than plain weaves. Denim, used for jeans and jackets, is an example of a twill weave.

Satin Weave The satin weave creates a smooth, shiny surface. Satin fabrics are often used for blouses and formal evening wear.

You can test the fabric grain of a shirt by making sure that the grain runs straight across the back from one underarm seam to the other. Test pants and skirts at the back of the hipline. The grain should be the same on both sides.

Fabric Finishes

Manufacturers often add various finishes to improve the durability of fabrics. Some finishes add body or bulk. Some hold the threads in place so that the fabric will wear well and will not pull out at the seams. Other finishes add softness, luster, strength, or shrinkage control. Finishes can also make caring for fabrics easier.

Clothing labels often tell you what finishes have been added. For instance, a fabric may be treated to be stain-resistant or water-resistant. Washable clothes may have a drip-dry or permanent-press finish, which means that the garment requires little or no ironing.

 Reading Check *Explain How can you test the fabric grain of a shirt?* Reading Check Answer Make sure the grain runs straight across the back from one under arm seam to the other.

Clothing Comfort and Fit

To enjoy wearing your clothes, you must be comfortable in them. Your clothes need to fit correctly. The fabric that a garment is made from and the style of the garment also affect comfort. Knowing how to evaluate these factors can help you select clothes that you will feel comfortable wearing. **Figure 16.2** on page 350 shows what to look for when checking the fit and comfort of clothing.

Selecting Size

Clothing may be sized simply as small, medium, large, or extra-large. Examples of this type of clothing include sweat-shirts, T-shirts, and sweaters. Try on and compare the fit of various styles until you find one that feels comfortable to you. Look in a full-length mirror at the front and back. Sit, bend, walk, and reach while wearing the garment to make sure it feels comfortable as you move around. Since you are still growing, it is a good idea to try clothes on before you buy them, even if you think you are a certain size. Also keep in mind that one manufacturer's "small" may be the same size as another manufacturer's "medium."

Sizes for Girls and Women Female clothing is sold in girls', juniors', misses', women's, and plus sizes. Girls' sizes go up to 14 and are roughly equal to the age of the wearer. Juniors' sizes are designed for a developing figure, but are smaller and shorter-waisted than misses' sizes. Petite sizes are shorter in length, while tall sizes are longer.

Sizes for Boys and Men For males there are three basic size groups: boys', teen boys', and men's. Boys' sizes are designed for small, undeveloped bodies. Teen boys' sizes are for slim teens and young men. Men's sizes are designed for adult bodies. Men's pants are sized by the waist measurement and the inside leg measurement, or inseam. For example, jeans with a 28-inch waist and a 30-inch inseam would be labeled "size 28/30." Dress shirts list two measurements, the collar size and the sleeve length, such as 15/34. Jackets are sold by chest measurement and length, such as 38 short or 38 long.

Figure Caption Answer
The outfit may not fit properly, or it may be made of a scratchy or clingy fabric that does not feel good on your skin. Some outfits may look great on a mannequin or the hanger, but may not be a style that works for you.

Figure 16.2 **Does It Feel as Good as It Looks?**

Comfort Check these features for a comfortable fit. *What can happen if you buy an outfit or garment without trying it on first?*

Neck Opening Is the neck opening comfortable? If it is too large, the front of the garment falls forward and sags. If it is too small, the neck binds and the front rides up.

Shoulder Seams Do the shoulder seams hit you at the shoulder? They should not go over your shoulder unless the garment is designed that way.

Sleeves Do long sleeves cover your wristbone? Can you lift your arms over your head with ease?

Waistband and Hips Does the waistband feel comfortable and fasten easily? Can you sit comfortably in pants or jeans?

Fasteners Do buttonholes, zippers, and other closures lie smoothly?

Hemline Is the hemline even around the bottom? Is the length right for you?

Natural Dyes

In this activity you will experiment with natural dyes. Dyes are used to add color to fabric. Before you begin, read through the entire Hands-On Lab assignment. Write down any questions that you have about the activity. Reread the text or ask your teacher for help if you need it.

Supplies
- ✓ Four 4-inch squares of undyed muslin fabric
- ✓ 2 types of fruit, such as blackberries, blueberries, or raspberries.
- ✓ Carrot juice
- ✓ Tea bag
- ✓ 4 small bowls

Develop Your Plan
- ■ Choose 2 fruits to use as natural dyes.
- ■ Gather the supplies.

Implement Your Plan
- ■ Place a fabric square in each bowl.
- ■ Rub the juice of each fruit on two of the fabric squares.
- ■ Brew a bag of tea. Pour the tea into a bowl with a third fabric square.

- ■ In the last bowl, pour carrot juice over the fabric square.
- ■ Make notes of how the fabric reacted to each natural dye.
- ■ After several minutes, rinse the fabric samples and allow them to dry.

Evaluate Your Results
Which natural dye was the easiest to use? Which made the brightest color? Which dye kept the most color after rinsing and drying? Make a list of items you could dye naturally. Do you think using natural dyes could help the environment? Write one or more paragraphs to explain your answer.

 Projects and Activities Go to this book's Online Learning Center through **glencoe.com** for more projects and activities.

Evaluate Your Results Answer Answers about fabric reactions and dyes will vary depending on individual results. Students may think that natural dyes would help the environment because chemicals would not have to be used; others may say that it might be wasteful to use fruit and vegetables for dyes instead of for food.

Comfort and Style

The fabric that a garment is made from can affect its comfort in many ways. Which fabrics do you think feel pleasant to the touch? Some people dislike the feel of slippery or clingy fabrics. Others find woolen knits rough and scratchy. You will want to buy clothes that suit your own preferences. When you buy clothes, be sure to check the feel of the fabric carefully.

Clothing style also affects its comfort. For example, a full skirt or pants with pleats may provide more room for you to move freely. A scoop neckline or an open collar may feel less restrictive than a turtleneck sweater.

Some styles may also suit your body shape better than others. Trying on a garment is the best way to decide whether a particular style is comfortable and looks good on you.

Comfortable, durable shoes will complete your wardrobe. When shopping for shoes, shop early in the day to get a more accurate fit. Feet tend to get slightly swollen after a day of walking. Try on shoes with the type of socks or hosiery that you would normally wear. Look for shoes that are not too tight or too loose. Be sure that you have room to wiggle your toes. Try on both left and right shoes, and walk around in them. When shopping for shoes to match a certain outfit, wear the outfit or take a sample of the fabric with you.

 Reading Check *Explain* Why should you try on clothes even if you know your size?

⏻ **Evaluate Fit**
Learning how to evaluate fit can help you make wise clothing choices. *Why is it so important to choose clothes according to fit?*

Make a Shopping Plan

A shopping plan is a **strategy**, or way to prepare, for spending the money you have available to buy the clothing you need or want. Before you develop a shopping plan, discuss your ideas with your parents or guardians. They can help you determine how much money should be used to buy the clothes you need, as well as how much money you can spend for items you want.

In addition to your list of clothing needs, your shopping plan should consider these three factors:

- **Clothing Budget** It is a good idea to set up a monthly spending plan. Go over your spending plan with your parents to decide how to make your money go further.
- **Purchase Plan** You learned about several payment methods, including cash, check, credit card, and debit card, in Chapter 11. Can you recall some of the advantages and disadvantages of each payment method?

- **Shopping Options** In most areas, there are several stores to choose from. Specialty stores, discount stores, and department stores are some options. Another choice is to shop for clothes by mail order or on the Internet.

Quality and Cost

It is easy to assume that more expensive clothes are better quality than less expensive clothes. This may be true sometimes, but not always. In addition to looking for details that indicate a well-made garment, you need to evaluate the cost. Consider not only the price tag, but also the cost per wearing. Before you buy a garment, ask yourself these questions:

- How often am I likely to wear it?
- How long is it likely to fit and stay looking nice?
- Is the price appropriate for the level of quality?
- Could I save money by waiting for a sale or buying it somewhere else?
- Could I make it myself for less?
- Is the item worth spending this much of my clothing budget?

Note-Taking Skills
Three-Ring Binder
A three-ring binder with tabs is a great way to keep and organize your notes and handouts. You can add, remove, or rearrange your notes as you need to.

• • • • • • • • • • • • • •

Succeed in School Ask students to share with others in the class how they organize their notes.

Section 16.1 After You Read

Review What You Have Learned

1. **Name** the three most common types of woven fabrics.
2. **Describe** ways to check for fit and comfort while trying clothes on.
3. **Explain** why talking with your parents can help you with shopping.

Practice Academic Skills

 English Language Arts

4. Create an illustration that represents one of your favorite outfits, including shoes. Label each part of the outfit with a suggestion for how to check for fit and comfort.

> **NCTE 5** Use different writing process elements to communicate effectively.

 Social Studies

5. Federal law requires flame-retardant fabrics for children's sleepwear. Conduct research to learn about other kinds of fabric finishes that make life safer or easier. Share your findings with the class.

> **NCSS I A** Analyze and explain the ways groups, societies, and cultures address human needs and concerns.

Check Your Answers Check your answers at this book's Online Learning Center at glencoe.com.

Section 16.2 Clothing Care Basics

Reading Guide

Before You Read

Preview A cause is an event or action that makes something happen. An effect is the result of a cause. Ask yourself, "Why does this happen?" to help you recognize cause-and-effect relationships as you read.

Read to Learn

Key Concepts

✓ **Describe** the information provided on clothing labels.

✓ **Name** six guidelines for stretching your clothing budget.

✓ **List** six steps you can take to properly clean your clothes.

Main Idea

You can stretch your clothing budget and keep your wardrobe looking good when you know how to properly care for and store your clothes.

Content Vocabulary

○ colorfast
○ brand name
○ static cling

Academic Vocabulary

■ coordinate   ■ pressed

Graphic Organizer

As you read, create step-by-step instructions for hand washing a garment. Use a graphic organizer like the one shown to organize your information.

How to Hand Wash a Garment	
Step 1:	Step 4:
Step 2:	Step 5:
Step 3:	Step 6:

Graphic Organizer Go to this book's Online Learning Center at glencoe.com to print this graphic organizer.

Academic Standards

 English Language Arts

NCTE 1 Read texts to acquire new information.

 Mathematics

NCTM Number and Operations Understand the meanings of operations and how they relate to one another.

 Science

NSES E Develop abilities of technological design, understandings about science and technology.

 Social Studies

NCSS IV F Individual Development and Identity Analyze the role of perceptions, attitudes, values, and beliefs in the development of personal identity.

NCTE *National Council of Teachers of English*
NCTM *National Council of Teachers of Mathematics*

NSES *National Science Education Standards*
NCSS *National Council for the Social Studies*

Graphic Organizer **Answer** (1) soak in sudsy water (2) squeeze suds through garment (3) drain sink and refill for rinsing (4) continue rinsing until suds are gone (5) roll garment in a towel (6) hang or lay flat to dry

Clothing can be a significant expense, so you want your clothes to last as long as possible. Imagine that the ketchup stain did not come out of your shirt. Maybe the pants you want to wear have a ripped seam. What if you cannot find your favorite sweater? If any of this sounds familiar, this section can help.

Clothing Labels

You can find a great deal of helpful information by reading clothing labels. Take the time to check the care label before you buy to help you determine the quality, durability, and care of garments. Checking the care labels before you buy clothing can save you time and money. Not following care labels can cause clothing items to shrink, fade, or lose shape.

Every item of clothing must carry a care label that describes its fiber content, where it was made, and how to care for it. This information may be on the same label or on two different labels. Look for this information on labels inside the garment:

- The fiber content is listed on the care label. It also gives the name of the manufacturer and tells where the garment was made.
- The care label will tell you the correct way to clean the garment. Some items must be dry cleaned only.
- A "no bleach" warning on the label means all types of bleach will damage the fabric.
- If the label tells you not to iron the garment, it is because the fabric will be damaged by the heat of the iron.
- If the fabric is colorfast, that fact may be included on the label. A **colorfast** fabric will keep its original color through many washings.

 As You Read

Connect How can you benefit from making clothing care a part of your daily routine?

As You Read Answer
You can easily find what you are looking for; you can iron less; stains will be easier to remove; clothes will last longer.

Photo Caption Answer
Knowing fiber content can help you determine qualities such as durability, wrinkle resistance, and how the item should be washed. Some types of fiber might irritate sensitive skin. You can decide if you want to spend money and time on trips to the dry cleaner.

Vocabulary
You can find definitions in the glossary at the back of this book.

Shop Wisely and Read Labels Manufacturers print fiber content and care instructions on clothing labels. *How can reading care labels help you as a consumer?*

Character Counts Answer Avery already has a jacket that is only a year old. His dad specifically told him not to spend all of his money on one outfit. Avery should show some self-discipline and buy as many separates as he can with the money his father gave him. If he really wants the new jacket, he should save his money and then decide if it is worth it to buy the brand-name jacket.

Reading Check Answer Brand names and designer labels are not necessarily signs of quality.

Brand Name Labels

A **brand name** is a trademark used by a manufacturer to identify its products. Sometimes stores have their own brand names. In addition, clothing labels may identify the designer, which is another kind of brand name. Some people use brand names as a guide in selecting clothing. Brand name items are usually more expensive than those with less well-known names. However, brand names and designer labels are not always signs of quality. Experience will help you decide if brand-name clothing is worth the extra cost.

 Reading Check **Distinguish** *Why is it important to judge clothing on more than just the brand name?*

Your Clothing Budget

When you made your shopping plan, you calculated your clothing budget, or how much money you had to spend. You can make that money go further by understanding and following some simple guidelines:

- **Start with two or three basic outfits.** Choose a few basic colors and classic styles to start your wardrobe. Then you can **coordinate**, or mix and match, additional pieces to go with what you already have.
- **Make the best use of what you have.** Try different combinations and accessories with clothes you own.
- **Take good care of your clothes.** Follow the directions on the care labels to make clothes last longer. Hang up or fold clothes after wearing and washing. Treat stains and wash clothes before putting them away.
- **Compare cost and quality.** No matter what type of fabric your clothing is made from, a quality garment requires good construction. For example, well-made clothes will have straight and smooth seams.
- **Take advantage of sales.** Plan ahead and shop during seasonal sales to get more for your money.
- **Learn to sew.** Save money and express your personality. Knowing how to make simple repairs can help your clothes last longer.

Clothing Care and Saving Money

You can save money when you keep your clothes in good condition. Follow these simple guidelines to take proper care of your clothes:

- Wear clothing that is suitable for the activity. When doing yard work or cleaning out the garage, for example, wear old clothes so that it does not matter if they get dirty.
- Dress and undress carefully to avoid snagging, ripping, or stretching your garments.
- Inspect your clothes carefully after each wearing. Repair any tears or holes before they get worse. If you find stains, treat them immediately and wash the garment as soon as possible.

Reading Check *Predict How can simple sewing skills help you save money?*

Special Care Learn how to take care of special clothing, such as team uniforms and formal wear. *What special care might be necessary for these types of clothing?*

Stains

No matter what you do, you will probably end up with stains on some of your clothes. Water-based stains come from certain foods, grass, perspiration, and washable inks. Oil-based stains come from makeup, ink, and paints.

Procedure Conduct research to find out how to treat common stains, such as ketchup, chewing gum, grass, blood, and paint. Record your findings in a chart.

Analysis Using the information in your chart, what conclusions can you draw about removing stains with the appropriate treatment? Why is it important to treat stains right away?

NSES E Develop abilities of technological design, understandings about science and technology.

Science You Can Use
Answer The treatments provide a chemical reaction that removes the stain. By treating stains as soon as possible, clothing may be protected from permanent damage.

Doing the Laundry

Cleaning clothes properly requires a basic knowledge of fabrics and simple cleaning techniques. Cleaning is just the beginning. You also need to know how to properly dry and iron your clothes. However, these tasks are not difficult if you follow the instructions on clothing care labels and on laundry products and appliances.

Learning the right way to launder, or wash, clothes will help you keep your clothes looking newer longer. Follow these guidelines when washing your clothes:

- **Pretreat stains.** Pretreat means to apply a stain remover before laundering. Besides stains, sleeve cuffs and the fold line on collars often need to be pretreated.
- **Sort clothes.** Check care labels on clothes carefully. Then separate clothes into piles by color: light-colored fabrics, medium-colored fabrics, and dark fabrics.
- **Select the correct water temperature.** Wash your clothes in the water temperature recommended on the care label. Unless otherwise specified, most clothing can be washed in warm water and rinsed in cold.
- **Choose the correct load size.** If you are washing only a few clothes, choose a small-load setting to save water and energy. Never overload the washing machine. Clothes will not get clean if they are packed in too tightly.
- **Use the correct amount of detergent.** Check the detergent label for the correct amount to use. Remember to adjust for the load setting you selected.
- **Use a fabric softener.** If static cling is a problem, liquid fabric softeners can be added to the washer, or dryer sheets can be used in the dryer. **Static cling** happens when electricity builds up in the dryer and causes clothing to stick to itself or to your body. Read product labels carefully to determine which type of softener you are using, and how and when it should be added.

Drying Your Clothes

Generally, clothes can be either line-dried or machine-dried. Line-drying saves energy and money but takes longer. Machine-drying is quick and convenient, but it uses energy and therefore costs more. If you use a dryer, remove clothing as soon as the dryer shuts off. Hang up items such as shirts, pants, and dresses as soon as you take them out of the dryer. This will help reduce wrinkling and make ironing easier. Sort and fold the other items.

Ironing Your Clothes

Some fabrics require that they be **pressed**, or ironed, after each wash. Other items may require some light pressing with a steam iron. The care label gives the proper temperature setting for the fabric. Always match the temperature setting on the iron with the fiber listed on the label. Synthetic fabrics may melt if the iron is too hot. Start by ironing or pressing small areas of the garment, such as the collar, yoke, and sleeves. Then press the larger areas. This way, you can avoid accidentally wrinkling areas you have already ironed.

Laundry Basics
Doing laundry includes cleaning, drying, and ironing clothes. *Why is it important to read all instructions before washing, drying, or pressing your clothes?*

Photo Caption Answer To keep clothing from fading, shrinking, or scorching; to use the correct amount of detergent and fabric softener; and to ensure the safe operation of washing machines, dryers, and irons.

Financial Literacy

Clothing Costs

Daniel went shopping for new clothes for his upcoming job interview. He found the following on sale: a $140 suit at $35 off, a $52 briefcase at 25% off, and two pairs of socks that are $8.00 each. How much did Daniel spend?

Math Concept **Order of Operations** To solve an equation, you must use the correct order of operations. First, simplify within the parentheses. Multiply and divide from left to right, then add and subtract from left to right.

Starting Hint Before solving this problem, write an expression using the correct symbols (remember that 25% off means that he paid 75% (0.75) of the price: $(\$140 - \$35) + (\$52 \times 0.75) + (2 \times \$8)$. Solve using the correct order of operations.

 For math help, go to the Math Appendix at the back of the book.

NCTM Number and Operations Understand the meanings of operations and how they relate to one another.

Financial Literacy Answer
Daniel spent $160:
($140-$35) + ($52 x 0.75) +
(2 x $8) = $105 + $39 + $16
= $160

Hand Washing Your Clothes

Some delicate garments are labeled "hand wash" because machine washing and drying will cause damage to the garment. You might also want to hand wash when you only have one or two garments to wash. To hand wash, start by soaking the item in sudsy water. Then gently squeeze the suds through the garment. Avoid twisting or wringing the garment. Drain the sink or basin and refill it with fresh water to rinse the garment. Repeat the rinse step until there are no more suds in the water. After rinsing, roll the garment in a towel to remove excess water. Then, hang the garment or lay it flat to dry.

Dry Cleaning

Some clothes cannot be washed by a machine or by hand. Rather, they may need to be dry cleaned. The dry cleaning process uses special chemicals instead of water and detergent to get clothes clean. Dry cleaning can be expensive, so choose your clothes wisely to avoid extra costs. You might consider alternatives to taking clothes to a commercial dry cleaner. Some coin-operated laundry facilities have machines for dry cleaning.

Photo Caption Answer
You can avoid snags, wrinkles, and dust, and items will stay cleaner longer.

 Clothing Storage
Store your clothes properly so they will last longer. *What are the advantages of storing your clothes properly?*

You can also buy dry cleaning kits to be used with a dryer. The kits contain specially-treated cloths to place in a bag with your garments. After the garments tumble in the dryer, they must be removed right away. This process works best with wool, rayon, silk, linen, and cotton knits. As with all laundry products, it is important to follow directions carefully.

Storing Your Clothes

Another important part of caring for clothes is storing them properly. When you hang up your clothes, take the time to close zippers and fasten buttons so that the garment will hang straight. Do not overcrowd closets and drawers, or your clothes may wrinkle. Check to be sure that pockets are empty and that garments are clean and repaired before putting them away. Seasonal clothes such as coats, heavy sweaters, and bathing suits, should be washed and dried before storing for the year. Clothes that are worn only for special occasions should be given extra attention, such as covering them with plastic bags to prevent damage and dust build-up. All clothing should be stored in dry areas to prevent mildew damage.

Note-Taking Skills
Use Colored Pens
Try using different colored pens or pencils when taking notes. For example, use red for new words, blue for the main ideas, and green for supporting details.

• • • • • • • • • • • • • •

Succeed in School Tell students that using different colors is a memory aid. Their minds create a relationship between the color and the concept, helping them better understand what they wrote.

Section 16.2 After You Read

Review What You Have Learned

1. **Explain** why you should take time to read labels before you buy your clothes.
2. **Name** three things you can do to keep your clothing in good condition.
3. **Compare and contrast** line-drying and machine-drying.

Practice Academic Skills

 English Language Arts

4. Choose two washable items from your wardrobe, each with different care instructions. For each item, write down the label information. Then describe in detail how you would launder and care for each item. Begin with sorting and end with storage.

> **NCTE 1** Read texts to acquire new information.

 Social Studies

5. Would you rather wear used clothes, hand-me-downs, or vintage clothing? Is there a difference? Why do you think society's attitudes toward wearing used clothing are changing? How do you feel about wearing used clothing? Write one or more paragraphs to express your opinion.

> **NCSS IV F** Analyze the role of perceptions, attitudes, values, and beliefs in the development of personal identity.

• •

Check Your Answers Check your answers at this book's Online Learning Center at glencoe.com.

Discovering Careers

Do you like to shop for clothing? Are you interested in the different kinds of fabric? If you answered yes to either of those questions, you might want to consider a future career in clothing and fabric industry. The following chart explores several careers in the clothing and fabric industry.

Job Title	Job Description
Dry Cleaner	Operates various dry-cleaning machines to clean garments, draperies, and other items as specified by customer.
Fabric Inspector	Inspects fabrics for defective weaving, stitching errors, color variations, and damaged or dirty fabrics. Pulls defective fabrics off the line.
Fabric Store Manager	Supervises and trains staff in customer service, fabric and notion selection, and fabric cutting. Orders supplies and equipment. Builds a team that is enthusiastic about fabric and sewing.
Fabric Designer	Predicts what fibers, textures, and colors will be popular. Designs fabrics.
Fashion Consultant	Help clients understand their wardrobe needs. Show customers ways to maximize their purchases by selecting garments that can be worn in a combination of ways.

Career Activities ▼

At School

1 Select three of the careers listed. Research the education, training, and work experience required for each career. Write a summary of your results.

At Home

2 Sort your family's laundry into piles according to the care instructions. How many piles did you create? What are the different types of cleaning that will need to be done?

At Work

3 Imagine that you work in a juice and smoothie shop. What kinds of stains are you likely to get on your uniform? How can you remove the stains?

In the Community

4 Contact and interview someone in your community who works in the clothing or fabric industry. Ask this person to describe what his or her typical work day is like. Share what you learned with your class.

Career Activities Answers Answers for these activities can be found on page TM158.

Career Investigations Go to this book's Online Learning Center for activities and worksheets to help you explore careers.

Chapter 16 Review and Activities

Chapter Summary

Section 16.1 Quality Clothing
A basic understanding of fabrics can help you make better clothing choices. Fabrics are made from natural or synthetic materials. Fabrics are made by weaving or knitting fibers together. Manufacturers may add finishes to improve the durability and feel of fabrics. When you buy clothes, check the feel of the fabric and check for the correct fit. Use a shopping plan to spend your clothing budget wisely.

Section 16.2 Clothing Care Basics
All clothing must have a care label with fiber content and care instructions. Read labels before you buy to help you determine the quality, durability, and care of garments. Keep clothes in good condition to help save money. Cleaning clothes properly requires a basic knowledge of fabrics and simple cleaning techniques. Your wardrobe will look newer longer when you learn the correct ways to launder and store your clothes.

Words You Learned

1. Arrange the vocabulary words below into groups of related words. Explain why you put the words together.

Content Vocabulary
○ fiber (p. 347)
○ natural fiber (p. 347)
○ synthetic fiber (p. 347)
○ blend (p. 347)
○ woven fabric (p. 347)
○ knit fabric (p. 348)
○ grain (p. 348)
○ colorfast (p. 355)
○ brand name (p. 356)
○ static cling (p. 358)

Academic Vocabulary
■ slant (p. 348)
■ strategy (p. 352)
■ coordinate (p. 356)
■ pressed (p. 359)

Review Key Concepts

2. **Explain** three features of quality fabric.

3. **Identify** three factors that affect clothing comfort.

4. **Outline** a shopping plan for clothes.

5. **Describe** the information provided on clothing labels.

6. **Name** six guidelines for stretching your clothing budget.

7. **List** six steps you can take to properly clean your clothes.

Critical Thinking

8. **Predict** what you would do if you need to clean a garment without a care label.

9. **Analyze** what assumptions consumers might make about high-priced clothing with designer logos.

Real-World Skills and Applications

Problem-Solving

10. **Ask Questions** The eighth-grade graduation party is coming up, and your friend wants to buy a new outfit for the occasion. She found a shirt with a designer logo at a popular mall store. The pants she wants are also in the mall, but at a different store. She found a pair of shoes that cost more than the pants, but she says she can wear them with many different outfits. What questions can you ask your friend to help her decide if buying the outfit is a good idea?

Technology Applications

11. **Clothing Information for Teens** Using presentation software, create a slide show called "A Teen's Guide to Shopping for Clothes." Include tips for choosing fabric, making smart purchases, and caring for clothes. Use illustrations to make your presentation attractive and interesting.

Financial Literacy

12. **Be a Smart Shopper** There are many ways to get more clothes for your money. If you want to shop at brand-name stores at the mall or other locations, it is a good idea to wait for sales. For example, by shopping at the end of a season, you can often find brand names for lower prices. However, brand-name clothing stores are not your only shopping option, and better bargains can often be found elsewhere. Identify five options for buying clothes. Make a table listing the five options, and identify the pros and cons of each one. How many of these options have you already tried? Which options are you likely to choose in the future?

13. **Expand Your Wardrobe** Create a collage with photos of clothing, shoes, and accessories that express your personal style. Look through magazines and cut out pictures of clothing and accessories that you like. Add captions to explain how each item could be used with something you already have in your wardrobe

14. **Synthetic Fibers** There are more than 25 different kinds of synthetic, or man-made, fibers. Find information about five types of synthetic fibers used for clothing. Create a chart that includes what kinds of clothing each type of fiber is suitable for, and what special characteristics the fiber has, such as water resistance or insulation. Also include any drawbacks each fiber may have.

15. **Fabric Development** With permission from your parents or teacher, go online to find information about new types of fabrics. For example, look for fabrics that increase the speed of an athlete, protect against allergies, or fight stains. Create a list of at least five new fabrics. Then choose one that you find especially interesting and write a paragraph about how people can benefit from the new fabric. Include the information in your Life Skills Binder.

Academic Skills

 ### English Language Arts

16. Write a Catalog Description Imagine you are writer for a sportswear company. Describe an outfit for the catalog. Who will wear this outfit? What fabrics and fibers are used? What sizes and colors are available? What are the care instructions? What are the selling points of the outfit? How much do you think this outfit should cost? Use this information to write a catalog ad.

> **NCTE 5** Use different writing process elements to communicate effectively.

 ### Science

17. Environmental Impact As a consumer, it is important to know what you can do to help the environment.

Procedure Locate a detergent designed to be environmentally safe. Look for "green" or "environmentally friendly" on the label. Make a list of the ingredients. Conduct an experiment to compare the cleaning ability of this detergent with a standard brand.

Analysis Is there a difference in cleaning ability, fragrance, or in the feel of the fabric after washing? Summarize your findings.

> **NSES A** Develop abilities necessary to do scientific inquiry, understanding about scientific inquiry.

 ### Mathematics

18. Buy on Layaway Victoria needs a new heavy coat for the winter, but the one she wants is $320, and she has not yet saved up enough money to buy it. The store offers a layaway plan requiring a 25% initial deposit and additional 25% deposits every 30 days until the item is paid in full after 90 days. There is also a $5 service charge per payment after the initial deposit. How much will each payment cost Victoria?

Math Concept **Changing Percents to Fractions.** One way to find the percent of a number is to first convert the percent to a fraction. Since a percent is simply a ratio of a number to 100, write the percent as a fraction with 100 as the denominator, and reduce to lowest terms. Multiply this fraction by the number.

Starting Hint Convert 25% to a fraction by rewriting it as 25/100, and reducing it to lowest terms. Multiply this fraction by $320. Do not forget to add the service charge to the last three payments.

> **NCTM Number and Operations** Understand numbers, ways of representing numbers, relationships among numbers, and number systems.

Standardized Test Practice

True/False

Read the statements and determine if they are true or false.

> **Test-Taking Tip** When answering true/false questions, pay close attention to the wording as you read the questions. Look for words such as *not, nor, any,* or *all.* These words are important in determining the correct answer.

19. Synthetic fibers are not made with plants or animal fleece.
20. All clothing can be hand washed.
21. Creating a shopping plan can help you get the most out of your clothing purchases.

UNIT **7** Life Skills Project

Your Personal Style

Looking your best and showing your own style is important. Magazines may offer ideas on how to be creative with clothes. Craft books may also offer jewelry and other projects that help you express yourself. This project will help you explore your personal style.

 My Journal Complete the journal entry from page 323, and refer to it to complete your design concept.

Project Assignment ▼

In this project, you will:

- Create a list of all the clothes you already own.
- Find examples of clothing that reflect your personal style.
- Describe your personal style.
- Create an illustrated pamphlet to display your personal style.
- Interview someone whose style you admire.
- Present your findings to your class.
- Include this project in the seventh section of your personal Life Skills binder.

Step 1 Create a Clothing Inventory Chart

Analyzing your own personal style is easier if you know what clothing accessories you already have. Create a clothing inventory chart to list and describe the clothing and accessories you own.

Step 2 Find Examples of Clothing That Reflect Your Style

Look through several magazines geared toward teens and preteens. Collect clipped photos to use in a pamphlet that reflects your personal style. Then write two or more paragraphs that answer these questions:

✔ What do these outfits have in common?
✔ How would you describe the colors and styles?
✔ How does your collection of photos reflect your personal style?
✔ How would you describe your personal style?

Step 3 Interview Someone Whose Style You Admire

Interview someone in your community whose fashion style you admire. Ask these questions:

✔ How would you describe your personal style?
✔ Who or what influences your style the most?
✔ How has your style changed over the years?

Use these interviewing skills when conducting your interview and these writing skills when writing the summary of notes from your interview.

Interviewing Skills
- Record interview responses and take notes.
- Listen attentively.

Writing Skills
- Use complete sentences.
- Use correct spelling and grammar.

Step 4 Create and Present Your Personal Style Pamphlet

Use the Life Skills Project Checklist on the right to plan and complete your pamphlet and give an oral report on it.

Use these speaking skills when presenting your final report.

Speaking Skills
- Speak clearly and concisely.
- Be sensitive to the needs of your audience.
- Use standard English to communicate.

Step 5 Evaluate Your Presentation

Your project will be evaluated based on:

✔Completeness and organization of your clothing inventory chart.
✔The collection of photographs that represent your personal style.
✔The description of your personal style.
✔Thoroughness of your personal style pamphlet.
✔The summary written from interview notes.
✔Grammar and sentence structure.
✔Presentation to the class.
✔Creativity and neatness.

Evaluation Rubric Go to this book's Online Learning Center through glencoe.com for a rubric you can use to evaluate your final project.

Life Skills Project Checklist

Research Personal Clothing Styles

- Create your clothing inventory chart.
- Collect photos from magazines that show clothing styles you like.
- Interview someone in your community whose style you admire.
- Include your inventory chart, photos, and descriptions in a pamphlet that displays your personal style.

Writing Skills

- Describe the clothing represented in your pamphlet.
- Describe your own personal style.
- Write a summary from your interview with someone whose style you admire.

Present Your Findings

- Prepare a short presentation to share and describe your pamphlet and explain how it reflects your personal style.
- Invite the students of the class to ask any questions they may have. Answer these questions with responses that respect their perspectives.
- Add this project to your Life Skills binder.

Academic Skills

- Conduct research to gather information.
- Communicate effectively.
- Organize your presentation so the audience can follow along easily.
- Thoroughly express your ideas.

NCTE 5 Use different writing process elements to communicate effectively.

NCTE 7 Conduct research and gather, evaluate, and synthesize date to communicate discovers.

UNIT 8

Prepare to Sew

Chapter 17
Plan Sewing Projects

Chapter 18
Learn How To Sew

Unit Preview

This unit is about the sewing basics. In this unit, you will learn about:

- Using a sewing machine for basic stitches.
- Preparing and planning for sewing projects.
- Selecting and preparing fabrics and patterns.
- Basic sewing and serging skills.

Explore the Photo
Knowing how to sew can be a very valuable skill. *What are some useful things you can do if you know how to sew?*

Explore the Photo Answer Answers may include hem clothing, replace buttons, make your own clothing, resize clothing, repair clothing, make original gifts for people, express your creativity.

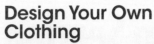
Design Your Own Clothing

When you are done studying this unit, you will complete a project in which you will:

✓ Create a pattern for an article of clothing.

✓ Interview someone who sews as part of his or her job.

✓ Share with your class what your project says about you.

The prewriting activity below will help you get started.

 My Journal

Prewriting Activity
Sketch Ideas

Think of ideas for simple sewing projects that you could wear. Sketch several designs. Below each sketch, describe what fabrics, supplies, tools, and notions you might need to complete it.

● What elements of your designs make them practical, or useful, in regular life?

● What elements of your sketches make your designs stylish?

Chapter 17

Plan Sewing Projects

Section 17.1

Sewing Machine Basics

■ **Main Idea** All sewing machines operate in the same basic way. Use the machine's operating manual to learn the functions of individual machines so you can start learning basic stitches.

Section 17.2

Explore the Photo Answer Answers may include any project suitable for a beginner, such as drawstring pants, handkerchief, pillowcase, simple stuffed toys.

Patterns, Fabrics, and Notions

■ **Main Idea** Before beginning a sewing project, learn about the basics of pattern selection, fabric selection, and choosing notions.

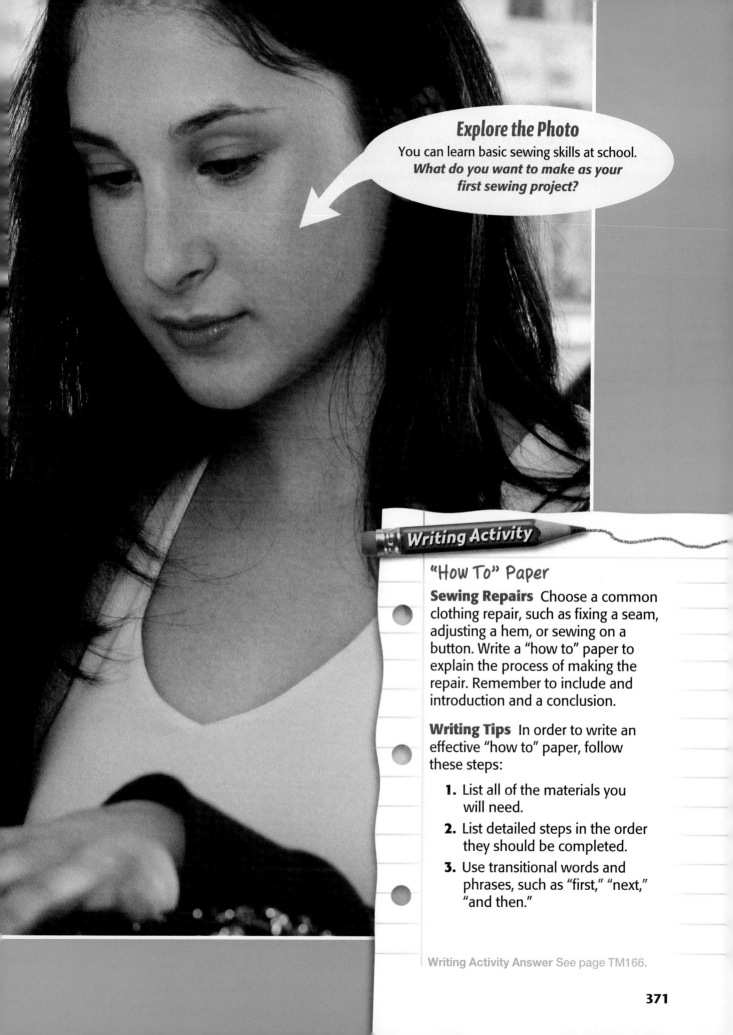

Explore the Photo
You can learn basic sewing skills at school. *What do you want to make as your first sewing project?*

Writing Activity

"How To" Paper

Sewing Repairs Choose a common clothing repair, such as fixing a seam, adjusting a hem, or sewing on a button. Write a "how to" paper to explain the process of making the repair. Remember to include and introduction and a conclusion.

Writing Tips In order to write an effective "how to" paper, follow these steps:

1. List all of the materials you will need.
2. List detailed steps in the order they should be completed.
3. Use transitional words and phrases, such as "first," "next," "and then."

Writing Activity Answer See page TM166.

Reading Guide

Before You Read

Look It Up As you read, use a dictionary in addition to the glossary at the back of the book. If you read a word that you do not know, look it up in the glossary or the dictionary. Before long, this practice will become a habit.

Read to Learn

Key Concepts

✓ **Describe** the main function all sewing machines have in common.

✓ **Explain** how a hem is created.

Main Idea

All sewing machines operate in the same basic way. Use the machine's operating manual to learn the functions of individual machines so you can start learning basic stitches.

Content Vocabulary

○ interlock
○ hem

Academic Vocabulary

■ operate   ■ raw

Graphic Organizer

As you read, list and describe the four basic sewing machine stitches a beginning student can practice. The first one is done for you. Use a graphic organizer like the one shown to help you organize your information.

Sewing Machine Stitch	Description
regular stitch	a medium-length stitch used for sewing most projects

 Graphic Organizer Go to this book's Online Learning Center at glencoe.com to print this graphic organizer.

• • • • • • • • • • • • **Academic Standards** • • • • • • • • • • • •

English Language Arts

NCTE 8 Use information resources to gather information and create and communicate knowledge.

Mathematics

NCTM Measurement Understand measurable attributes of objects and the units, systems, and processes of measurement.

 ### Social Studies

NCSS I A Culture Analyze and explain the ways groups, societies, and cultures address human needs and concerns.

NCTE *National Council of Teachers of English*
NCTM *National Council of Teachers of Mathematics*

NSES *National Science Education Standards*
NCSS *National Council for the Social Studies*

Graphic Organizer Answer bating stitch: a very long stitch used for holding layers of fabric together temporarily; reinforcement stitch: a short stitch used to strengthen a corner or a point; zigzag stitch: a sideways stitch used to make buttonholes, finish seam edges, and sew special seams.

Sewing is a great way to show off your personal style in your wardrobe and in your living space. You can make gifts, personalize your garments, and adjust patterns to make clothes exactly the way you want them. This section introduces you to the sewing machine.

Sewing Machines

Most sewing machines have the same basic parts. Before you use any sewing machine, read the operating manual. You can use it to find the parts on your sewing machine and learn how to use its special features and any accessories. All sewing machines operate, or work, in the same basic way. A needle moves up and down through the fabric, and two sets of threads **interlock** to form closely fitted stitches.

Although sewing machines work the same way, there is a wide range in the number and complexity of functions they can perform. A very basic machine is useful for general sewing projects. Modern sewing machines are computerized and can create detailed embroidery designs for special projects. The more a machine can do, the more it costs. Be sure to use sewing machines carefully and according to the instructions to keep them in good working order. See **Figure 17.1** to familiarize yourself with the parts of a basic sewing machine.

As You Read

Connect What, if any, sewing experience have you had?

◈ Vocabulary

You can find definitions in the glossary at the back of this book.

Figure 17.1   The Sewing Machine

Standard Parts All sewing machines have the same basic parts and functions. *Why do you think sewing machines include different stitch patterns to choose from?*

MATH YOU CAN USE

Converting Measurements

While on vacation in Europe, Grace went into a store that sold sewing patterns. However, when looking for patterns in her size, Grace realized that all of the measurements provided on the envelopes are in the metric system. Grace's measurements are 33 inches (chest), 25 inches (waist), 34 inches (hip), and 16 inches (back-waist). What are her measurements in centimeters? The package tells her that she needs 1.9 meters of fabric. How many yards will she need?

Math Concept **Length Conversions** While the U.S. generally uses the customary system of measurement, most other countries use the metric system. To convert inches to centimeters, multiply by 2.54. To convert yards to meters, multiply by 0.914.

Starting Hint Multiply each inch measurement by 2.54 to convert to centimeters, and round to the nearest centimeter. To convert meters into yards, you will need to divide by 0.914.

 For more math help, go to the Math Appendix located at the back of this book.

NCTM Measurement Understand measurable attributes of objects and the units, systems, and processes of measurement.

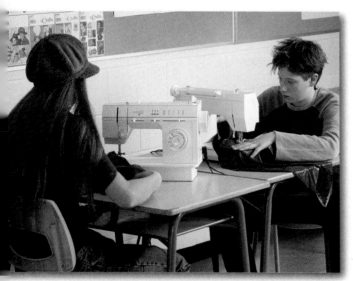

Sewing Lab

Your sewing lab is a great place to learn and practice basic sewing skills. Equipment and supplies are important to understand. However, it is just as important to work cooperatively with others in your sewing class and manage your time wisely. The keys to making the most of your time in the sewing lab are:

- **Organization** Keep your supplies neat and organized so they will be ready to use when you need them.
- **Preparation** Bring in or gather the required supplies. Before you start to sew, read any instructions carefully.
- **Consideration** When you finish using an item, return it to where it belongs.

 Identify What is the term for two sets of threads that form closely fitted stitches?* Reading Check Answer interlock

Hems

A hem finishes the bottom edge of a shirt, jacket, sleeve, skirt, or pants leg. A **hem** is an edge made by folding fabric over and stitching it down. Hems can be sewn by hand or with a sewing machine. Hems are made in ways that depend on the garment's fabric and design. The most common way to make a hem is to turn the **raw**, or unfinished, edge of fabric to the inside of the garment and stitch it in place. A good introduction to using a sewing machine is to practice making hems. The steps on page 376 explain how to make a hem. You will learn much more about other sewing machine functions in the next chapter.

Math Feature Answer Grace's metric measurements are: 33 x 2.54 = 83.82 ≈ 84 cm chest; 25 x 2.54 = 63.5 ≈ 64 cm waist; 34 x 2.54 = 86.36 ≈ 86 cm hip; 16 x 2.54 = 40.64 ≈ 41 cm back-waist. She will need 1.9 ÷ 0.914 = 2.07878 ≈ 2.1 yards of fabric.

Sewing in Class When you are in your sewing class, you need to share equipment and supplies. *Why is it so important to be organized?*

Photo Caption Answer Many people need to use the same supplies, and time in class is limited.

Hands-On LAB

Basic Sewing Machine Stitches

In this activity you will learn to use a sewing machine for four basic stitches. Before you begin, read through the entire Hands-On Lab assignment. Write down any questions that you have about the activity. Reread the text or ask your teacher for help if you need it

Supplies
- ✓ Sewing machine
- ✓ Operating manual
- ✓ Thread
- ✓ Scissors
- ✓ Fabric scraps

Develop Your Plan
- Review the sewing maching operating manual.
- Practice making four basic stitches.

Implement Your Plan
- Follow the instructions in the operating manual to wind your thread from your spool onto the bobbin.
- After you thread the bobbin, insert it in the bobbin case.
- Follow the instructions in the operating manual to thread the machine.

> **Projects and Activities** Go to this book's Online Learning Center through glencoe.com for more projects and activities.

- Use a separate fabric scrap to make each of the four basic stitches:

Regular Stitch A medium-length stitch used for sewing most projects.

Basting Stitch A very long stitch used for holding layers of fabric together temporarily.

Reinforcement Stitch A short stitch used to strengthen a corner or a point.

Zigzag Stitch A sideways stitch used to make buttonholes, finish seam edges, and sew special seams.

Evaluate Your Results

Did you have trouble with any of the stitches? Review the operating manual to find out what you can do to correct any problems you had. Compare your stitch samples with your classmates. How are they the same or different? Write one or more paragraphs to describe your experience.

Evaluate Your Results Answer Answers will vary. Students should explain what difficulties they experienced, and describe how their stitch samples compared with classsmates' samples.

Step 1 Use a seam ripper to remove the thread in the old hem. Press out the hem crease.

Step 2 Put on the garment to determine the new hem length. Place pins every 2 to 4 inches (5–10 cm) around the hemline.

Step 3 Fold the hem to the new length, and pin it in place. Double-check the length to make sure that it is even.

Step 4 Take off the garment. Using a sewing gauge or a ruler, mark the proper length of the finished hem with pins or chalk.

Step 5 Trim away the excess fabric along the markings. Lightly press the fold of the hem.

Step 6 The raw edge can be pinked, zigzag stitched, edge-stitched, or overlapped with hem tape to prevent raveling.

Step 7 Stitch the edge of the hem, making sure the stitches do not show on the outside. Keep the stitches loose so the hemline does not pucker.

Step 8 Carefully press the hem.

Section 17.1 After You Read

Review What You Have Learned

1. **Name** three keys to making the most of the time in your sewing class.
2. **Explain** why you should use loose stitches when sewing a hem.

Practice Academic Skills

 English Language Arts

3. Go to a library or a fabric store, or get permission to go online to find instructions for sewing projects. Find a project designed for beginners and a project designed for people with advanced sewing experience. What conclusions can you draw by comparing instructions from the two projects?

> **NCTE 8** Use information resources to gather information and create and communicate knowledge.

 Social Studies

4. Research the typical clothes of a group of people in American history before 1950, such as a Native American population or an immigrant population. How did families obtain clothing during that time? What materials and techniques were used? Write a summary of your findings in a brief report.

> **NCSS I A** Analyze and explain the ways groups, societies, and cultures address human needs and concerns.

 Check Your Answers Check your answers at this book's Online Learning Center at glencoe.com.

Reading Guide

Before You Read

Prepare with a Partner Work with a partner. Read the heads and ask each other questions about the topics that will be discussed. Write down the questions you both have about each section. As you read, help each other answer those questions.

Read to Learn
Key Concepts

✓ **List** the factors you need to consider before choosing a pattern.

✓ **Explain** how to determine the kind of fabric you need.

✓ **Identify** commonly used notions.

Main Idea

Before beginning a sewing project, learn about the basics of pattern selection, fabric selection, and choosing notions.

Content Vocabulary

○ pattern
○ notions
○ ravel
○ nap
○ interfacing

Academic Vocabulary

■ dart   ■ reinforce

Graphic Organizer

As you read, compare and contrast the ways to take measurement for male and female clothing styles. Use a graphic organizer like the one shown to help you organize your information.

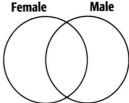

Graphic Organizer Go to this book's Online Learning Center at **glencoe.com** to print this graphic organizer.

 Academic Standards

 English Language Arts

NCTE 7 Conduct research and gather, evaluate, and synthesize data to communicate discoveries.

NCTE 9 Develop an understanding of diversity in language use across cultures.

Science

NSES A Develop abilities necessary to do scientific inquiry, understandings about scientific inquiry.

Social Studies

NCSS I E Culture Demonstrate the value of cultural diversity, as well as cohesion, within and across groups.

NCTE *National Council of Teachers of English*
NCTM *National Council of Teachers of Mathematics*
NSES *National Science Education Standards*
NCSS *National Council for the Social Studies*

Graphic Organizer Answer
Male: neck, chest. Female: bust, back waist length. Both: sleeve, waist, hips.

Wouldn't it be nice to just be able to sit down at the sewing machine and start sewing? Unfortunately, it is not quite that easy. As with almost every project you want to complete, there are steps that need to be taken to get you to the finished product. In addition to learning basic sewing skills, you need to choose the right pattern, the right fabric, and the right tools.

As You Read

Connect Like any project, you need the right tools to get the job done. Other than a sewing machine, what tools do you think you will need to start a sewing project?

As You Read Answer Answers may include scissors, needles, pins, tape measure, thimble.

◀◇ Vocabulary

You can find definitions in the glossary at the back of this book.

Pattern Selection

Most sewing projects call for a pattern. A **pattern** is a plan for making a garment or project. It contains paper shapes of the various pieces and gives the instructions for sewing. Your success in completing your project depends in part on the pattern you choose.

When you choose a pattern, you will want one that matches your abilities and the time you have to complete the project. Before you choose a pattern, consider the following:

- **Purpose** Do you want to make clothing for yourself, something for your room, or a specialty item, such as a backpack or a purse?
- **Sewing Skills and Experience** If you have never worked on a project before, choose a simple pattern. Many patterns are designed especially for beginners.
- **Time** Do you have enough time to complete the project? This is especially important if you are sewing at school and sharing a sewing machine.
- **Cost** How much money are you willing to spend?

These factors can help you choose the best pattern for your needs. When you find a pattern that you like in the fabric store catalog or display, make a note of the brand name and pattern number. Then you can find and read the pattern envelope for more information.

Photo Caption Answer If the pattern is too advanced for your skill level, you may not finish the project. If the pattern is the wrong size, the final product will not fit. If it requires expensive fabric or notions, it may not fit your budget.

Pattern Selection Choose a pattern that matches your skill level, time frame, and budget. *Why is it so important to choose a pattern carefully?*

The Pattern Envelope

The pattern envelope provides you with the information you need to plan a sewing project. The front of the envelope shows a picture of the completed project. Sometimes more than one view is shown. For example, a shirt pattern may show one view with short sleeves and another with long sleeves. On the back of the envelope, you will find the following:

- A drawing showing the pattern pieces and construction features, such as design details, seams, and darts. A **dart** is a tapered, V-shaped seam used to give shape to the garment.
- A chart that tells you how much fabric to buy for the view and size pattern you are using.
- Recommendations for which fabrics to use.
- Additional materials you will need, such as thread and buttons. These are called **notions**.

Pattern Choice

How can you find an appropriate pattern for your first project? Pattern books indicate which patterns are simple to sew and even have special sections for quick and easy projects. In addition, look for these features to help you choose an easy-to-make pattern:

- **Number of Pattern Pieces** Fewer pattern pieces mean fewer pieces of fabric to cut out and stitch.
- **Number of Seams** Seams join two pieces of fabric together. The fewer seams involved, the easier it will be to complete the pattern.
- **Garment Fit** Loose-fitting styles are easier to sew than close-fitting styles.
- **Closures** Elastic waists require less advanced sewing skills than do zippers and buttonholes.

Pattern Size

Patterns, like ready-to-wear clothing, come in different sizes. Pattern sizes are based on five measurements. For females, measure the sleeve, bust, back waist length, waist, and hips.

Clues on the Pattern Envelope The front of the pattern envelope shows you how the finished garment should look. *What information is provided on the front of this envelope?*

Photo Caption Answer
The front of this envelope shows four variations of the skirt, and the sizes that can be made from this pattern.

For males, measure the sleeve, neck, chest, waist, and hips. See **Figure 17.2** to learn how to take these measurements. When taking measurements, be sure that the measuring tape is held parallel to the floor. Never stretch the measuring tape.

Compare your measurements to the measurements on the pattern envelope. Choose the size that has the closest measurements. Use the following guidelines to decide which measurement is most important for a particular type of garment:

- For blouses and tops, fit the bust measurement.
- For shirts, fit the chest and neck measurements.
- For full skirts, fit the waist measurement.
- For pants and semi-fitted skirts, fit the hip measurement.

✓ **Reading Check** **Recall** *What information can you find on the back of a pattern envelope?*

Reading Check Answer
A drawing showing the pattern pieces and construction features; a chart that tells you how much fabric to buy; fabric recommendations; notions you will need.

Figure Caption Answer
Base your choice on the design of the garment. If the design is full or loose-fitting, choose the smaller pattern size. If the garment is closely fitted, choose the larger size.

Figure 17.2 Taking Your Measurements

Accuracy is the Key Choose your pattern size by your actual measurements, not by the size you wear when you buy clothes. *What should you do if your measurements fall between two sizes on the pattern envelope?*

Measurements for Males

Sleeve Bend the arm up, then measure from the base of the neck to the elbow and up over the wrist bone.

Neck Measure around the base of the neck and add ½ inch (1.3 cm).

Chest Measure around the fullest part of the chest.

Waist Measure around the natural waistline over a shirt, but not over pants.

Hips Measure around the fullest part of the hips.

Measurements for Females

Sleeve Measure from the top of the shoulder over the bent elbow to the wrist.

Bust Measure around the fullest part of the bust, continue under the arms and straight across the back.

Back Waist Length Measure from the base of the neck to the waistline.

Waist Measure around the natural waistline.

Hips Measure around the fullest part of the hips.

Build a Sewing Kit

To complete any sewing project successfully, you need the right tools. Experience and the types of projects you choose will determine the exact items you need. The items shown on this page represent some basic tools you will probably use for almost every project. These tools are a good start toward building your sewing kit.

Shears, Scissors, and Pinking Shears Shears are large scissors that often have a raised handle easier cutting. Scissors are used for trimming, clipping, and cutting threads. Pinking shears are scissors that zigzag edge.

Sewing Gauge A sewing gauge ('gāj) is a 6-inch (16-cm) ruler with an adjustable pointer. It is used to measure short spaces, such as hems and seam widths.

Needles and Thread Needles are used for hand sewing. Select thread color that matches your fabric.

Pins and Pincushion Dressmaker pins are slender, sharp-pointed, and rust proof. The pincushion is a convenient holder for pins and needles.

Seam Ripper This pen-shaped tool has a small, hook-like blade at one end for removing stitches.

Tape Measure A flexible tape is used to take body measurements.

Thimble A thimble protects your finger while you are hand sewing. It makes it easier to push the needle through the fabric.

Choosing Fabrics

Fabrics come in many different colors, textures, designs, and finishes. You need to evaluate the fiber content, how the fabric is made, and any finishes that have been added. When choosing a fabric, ask yourself these questions:

How much sewing experience do I have? Select fabrics that are easy to sew for your first few projects.

Who will use the item? When making something for yourself, look for colors that can be mixed and matched with other clothes you own.

When will I use the item? The time of day and the season the item will be used may affect the type of fabric you choose.

How will I use the item? When making a non-clothing item such as a tote bag, a dark-colored fabric that does not show dirt is a good choice.

What type of care is needed? Look for fabrics that are machine washable and that require little or no ironing.

Some fabrics are challenging. Lightweight and extremely soft fabrics can be slippery and hard to sew. Plaids, stripes, and large prints need to be matched at the seams and may require extra fabric. Loosely woven fabrics tend to **ravel**, which is when loose threads pull out of the cut edge. Fabrics such as corduroy have a one-way texture called **nap**. Napped fabrics require special instructions.

Discover International...
Fabric

Indian Textiles

India has a rich and diverse textile tradition. A textile is a cloth or fabric made from raw materials. The origin of Indian textiles can be traced to the people of the Indus valley civilization, where cotton and silk were handwoven for garments. The ancient Indian epic, *Ramayana*, refers to elaborate garments worn by royalty, and simple garments worn by commoners. Indian silk and cotton was traded around the world in ancient times. Fragments of Indian textiles have been found in Rome, Egypt, China, and Indonesia as far back as the 13th century. Muslin, a thin cotton material, and chintz, a shiny cotton cloth often printed with a flower pattern, were especially popular and remain so today.

Muslin [ˈməz-lən] a thin plain-weave cotton cloth, used to make clothing, curtains, and sheets.

NCTE 9 Develop an understanding of diversity in language use across cultures.

Selecting Quality Fabrics

When you shop for fabrics, you will notice that they come in many price categories. How can you tell which ones are high quality? Keep in mind that you do not have to buy the most expensive one to get a good fabric. Quality is not determined by cost alone. Like ready-to-wear clothing, fabrics can be made by brand-name designers and cost more because of the name. When judging quality in fabrics, examine the following:

- **Crosswise Threads** They should be straight and at right angles to the lengthwise threads. This means the fabric is on grain.
- **Pattern** Make sure that a printed pattern runs straight with the grain. If the fabric is not printed properly, the garment will look off-grain.
- **Weave** The weave should be firm and durable.
- **Color** All colors should be consistent.
- **Finish** The finish should feel comfortable and pleasing to the touch.
- **Label** Read the label on the end of the bolt of fabric. It gives facts about fabric width, fiber content, finishes, shrinkage, and care instructions.

Reading Check *Judge* *Should you buy the most expensive fabric for quality? Why or why not?*

Reading Check Answer
No, because quality is not determined by cost alone. Some fabrics cost more because they are made by brand-name designers.

Photo Caption Answer
The finished garment will be easy to maintain.

Care Instructions
When choosing fabrics, check the fiber content and care instructions listed on the end of the fabric bolt. *What is the benefit of choosing fabric with easy care instruction?*

Thread Color One of the most essential notions is thread, which comes in many types and colors. *How would you choose a thread color for a print or plaid fabric?*

Notions

After you have chosen a fabric, refer to the back of the pattern envelope for a list of the type of notions you will need. In addition to sewing tools, you will need notions to complete the project. Notions are the small items that become a permanent part of the finished product. Choose notions carefully, making sure the colors look good with the fabric you will use. Also, choose buttons, tapes, trims, and interfacings that require the same care as the fabric. For example, a cotton shirt cannot be machine washed if its trim can only be dry cleaned. Here are some basic notions necessary for many types of sewing projects:

- **Thread** Choose thread to match your fabric color. Thread should be the same color as the fabric or slightly darker because it will appear lighter when stitched. Fabric type determines the thread you need. You can find this information on the pattern envelope. A good quality thread is strong and smooth, has even thickness, and resists tangling.
- **Fasteners** There are many types of fasteners to choose from. They are used to close a garment. Some are designed to be almost invisible, such as snaps, and zippers that are sewn into a seam. Others can be functional as well as decorative, such as buttons, buckles, and hook-and-eye closures.
- **Tapes and Trims** Like fasteners, tapes and trims can be functional or decorative. Tapes and trims cover fabric edges and **reinforce**, or strengthen seams. They can also be used to create a design on the outside of a garment. They can be woven, knitted, braided, or made of lace. You can match trims to your fabric, or create contrast with a different color or texture.

- **Elastic** Your choice of elastic depends on whether it will be used in a casings, which you will learn about in the next chapter, or stitched directly to the garment. The pattern envelope will describe what kind of elastic may be needed.
- **Linings and Interfacings** Fabrics used on the inside of the garment are linings and interfacings. A lining is fabric used to finish the inside of a jacket, coat, skirt, dress or pants. Linings can be visible, so choose a color to match or contrast with the out fabric. Fabric **interfacing** is placed between two pieces of fabric to prevent stretching around necklines, closures, and buttonholes. Unlike a lining, it will not be visible in the finished garment. Interfacing adds shape to collars, cuffs, pockets, and hems.

Safety Check

Sewing Equipment
Follow these safety rules when learning how to use the supplies and equipment in the sewing lab:

- Keep your fingers away from the path of the needle.
- Do not attempt to use the machine if it is jammed or making an unusual noise.
- Do not hold pins or needles in your mouth. Use a pin cushion.
- Keep scissors closed when not in use.

Section 17.2 After You Read

Review What You Have Learned
1. **Identify** the features that will help you choose an easy-to-make pattern.
2. **List** the most important qualities to consider when choosing fabric.
3. **Describe** a good quality thread.

Practice Academic Skills

 English Language Arts

4. Imagine that you will soon attend a wedding or a family reunion, or go on a vacation. What special outfit would you like to make? Using information from pattern catalogs, pattern envelopes, and this book, make a list of the fabric, equipment, tools, and notions you would need to complete your special outfit. Present your list in the form of a "how to" report.

> **NCTE 7** Conduct research and gather, evaluate, and synthesize data to communicate discoveries.

Social Studies

5. Cultural heritage can be displayed in fabrics. Some fabric designs and weaves are unique to certain cultures, such as Navajo rugs and blankets. Gather three or more samples of cultural fabrics. Use actual fabric if possible. If not, find images you can copy or print. Create a poster with the samples, and include information about the country of origin and the uses for the fabric.

> **NCSS I E** Demonstrate the value of cultural diversity, as well as cohesion, within and across groups.

Check Your Answers Check your answers at this book's Online Learning Center at glencoe.com.

Discovering Careers

Do you like to work with your hands? Do you have an eye for fabric and for creating actual clothes? If you answered yes to either of those questions, you might want to consider a future career in sewing. The following chart explores several careers in the sewing industry.

Job Title	Job Description
Alterations Specialist	Alters clothing to fit individual customers. Repairs garments as requested by customers. Remakes old garments into new styles.
Machine Operator	Creates fibers, yarns, and fabrics by spinning, weaving, knitting, printing, and dyeing. Oversees multiple machines that treat tanks, dye jigs, and vats.
Pattern-maker	Translates sample garments into paper patterns. Increases and decreases the size of all pattern pieces to correspond to garment sizes.
Apparel Stylist	Creates adaptations of designer originals. Produces fashionable, yet affordable clothing. Makes garments that fit the image of a company or clothing line.
Sewing Instructor	Teach basic sewing techniques. Help those who need advanced help with special projects. Motivate students with the possibilities of sewing.

Career Activities ▼

At School

1 Select three of the careers listed. Research the education, training, and work experience required for each career. Write a summary of your results.

At Home

2 Go through your closet to find clothing that needs repairs. Ask your family members if they have clothing that needs repairs. Make a list of the repairs and explain how you would make the repairs.

At Work

3 List five examples of how fabrics are used in a workplace. Compare lists with your classmates.

In the Community

4 Contact and interview someone in your community who works in the sewing industry. Ask this person to describe what his or her typical work day is like. Share what you learned with your class.

Learn More *Online* ⓐ glencoe.com

Career Investigations Go to this book's Online Learning Center for activities and worksheets to help you explore careers.

Career Activities Answers for these activities can be found on page TM166.

Chapter 17 Review and Activities

Chapter Summary

Section 17.1 Sewing Machine Basics
The keys to making the most of your time in the sewing classroom are organization, preparation, and consideration. Sewing machines all operate in the same way. A needle moves up and down through the fabric, and two sets of threads interlock to form stitches. A good introduction to using a sewing machine is to practice making hems. A hem finishes the bottom edges of sewn projects. Hems can be sewn by hand or with a sewing machine.

Section 17.2 Patterns, Fabrics, and Notions
Patterns, fabrics, and notions are essential for getting started on sewing projects. Choose a pattern to match your abilities and the time you have to complete the project. Quality fabric does not have to be expensive. When selecting fabric, use the information on your pattern envelope to find out what kind and how much fabric you will need. After you have chosen a fabric, refer to the back of the pattern envelope for a list of the type of notions you will need.

Words You Learned

1. Create multiple–choice test questions for each content and academic vocabulary word.

Content Vocabulary
- interlock (p. 373)
- hem (p. 374)
- pattern (p. 378)
- notions (p. 379)
- ravel (p. 382)
- nap (p. 382)
- interfacing (p. 385)

Academic Vocabulary
- operate (p. 373)
- raw (p. 374)
- dart (p. 379)
- reinforce (p. 384)

Review Key Concepts

2. **Describe** the main function all sewing machines have in common.

3. **Explain** how a hem is created.

4. **List** the factors you need to consider before choosing a pattern.

5. **Explain** how to determine the kind of fabric you need.

6. **Identify** commonly used notions.

Critical Thinking

7. **Analyze** this scenario. Christa says to you, "There is no reason I should learn how to sew." Why do you think she would say this? How would you respond?

8. **Predict** what might happen if a beginning sewing student ignores the recommendation on a pattern envelope to use knit fabric.

9. **Describe** how you could alter a garment in your closet to change its look.

Chapter 17 Review and Activities

Real-World Skills and Applications

Problem-Solving

10. Help for Beginners Sewing can be an intimidating task for someone who has never sewn before. Look through a pattern catalogs and select patterns that beginners might use. Identify which features make patterns easy to follow.

Interpersonal and Collaborative

11. Project Management Follow your teacher's directions to form small groups. Work with your group to write a timeline for a long-term project you might work on in class. When will you work on the project? What tasks can you realistically accomplish each time you meet? Who will be responsible for each task? What will you do if someone misses a class? What supplies and resources will you need? Present your information to the class.

Financial Literacy

12. Estimate Costs Imagine that you are going to make two shirts from the same pattern. Research the prices of the pattern, fabric, notions, and any other supplies and materials you will need to complete the project. Using spreadsheet software or a worksheet, make a table presenting these costs. Label four columns with the names *Item, Price, Quantity,* and *Cost.* List one item per row, such as buttons in the first row, thread in the next row, and so on. Show a grand total of all the costs at the bottom of the table. Compare your results to the cost of buying two similar shirts at a clothing store. Which is the better value for your and money? Present your information along with a summary to explain the better value.

13. Fabric Guide Cut out small samples of different types of fabrics. Arrange the fabric samples in a scrapbook or photo album and add descriptive captions. Organize the fabric in a way that is meaningful for you. For example, arrange by texture, color, cultural significance, or type of weave. Add more samples as you discover new fabrics you like to use when sewing.

14. Home Decorating Visit a fabric store and select a pattern for a home furnishings project. Note the recommended fabrics listed on the pattern envelope. Look around the store for fabrics suitable for home decorating. What types of fibers, fabrics, and trims are most common? How are they different from fabrics used for clothing? Summarize your findings a report to present to your class.

15. Sewing Ideas With permission from your parents or teacher, go online to search for information that can help you learn about different ways to apply sewing techniques, such how to customize a pattern, how to make stuffed animals, or how to alter something you already own. Choose a project that you find especially interesting. Make a list of the supplies you would need to complete it, and a list of the skills you would need to learn. Include the information in your Life Skills Binder.

Academic Skills

 ## English Language Arts

16. Personal Style When you know how to sew your own clothes, you have freedom to experiment with colors and fabric. Write a one-page journal entry to describe your personal clothing style. Include descriptions of the projects you would like to make that reflect your style.

> **NCTE 12** Use language to accomplish individual purposes.

 ## Science

17. Modern Technology The first sewing machines were operated by a hand-crank. Today, sewing machines are run by computers that do much of the work for you.
Procedure Consider how the modern sewing machine compares to the earliest sewing machines.
Analysis Choose one function of a modern sewing machine, and use these questions to evaluate the function: 1. Is the function necessary? 2. Does it make me less creative? 3. Does it help me make higher quality projects?

> **NSES E** Develop understandings about science and technology.

 ## Mathematics

18. Estimate Jackson is taking a summer class in clothing construction, and he is planning to make a shirt for his first project. He found a good pattern for $6.98. The project requires 2½ yards of fabric that will cost $10.90. The matching thread costs $2.95, and the buttons he picked out are $8.10. He also needs to add interfacing for $2.60. Use this information to estimate the total amount Jackson needs to make the shirt.

Math Concept **Estimation Using Compatible Numbers** You can perform calculations quickly without using a calculator by replacing decimals with their closest compatible numbers.

Starting Hint Round each dollar amount to the nearest whole dollar by dropping the decimal portion. If the number to the right of the decimal point is 5 or greater, add 1 to the dollar amount.

> **NCTM Number and Operations** Compute fluently and make reasonable estimates.

Standardized Test Practice

Multiple-Choice

Read the sentence. Then read the question below the sentence. Read the answer choices below each question and choose the best answer to fill in the blank.

> **Test-Taking Tip** In a multiple choice test, read the question before you read the answer choices. Try to answer the question before you read the answer choices. This way, the answer choices will not confuse you.

19. By returning the scissors to the teacher's desk, John showed consideration for his classmates. In this sentence, the word consideration means _____.
a. thoughtfulness
b. sympathy
c. disrespect
d. attention

Chapter 18

Learn How to Sew

Explore the Photo Answer
Answers should include choosing a pattern in the correct size, buying fabric, and gathering all of the notions that you need.

Section 18.1

Fabric and Pattern Preparation

■ **Main Idea** A successful sewing project includes planning and preparation.

Section 18.2

Sewing and Serging Basics

■ **Main Idea** Sewing and serging skills allow you to achieve a professional quality in your sewing projects.

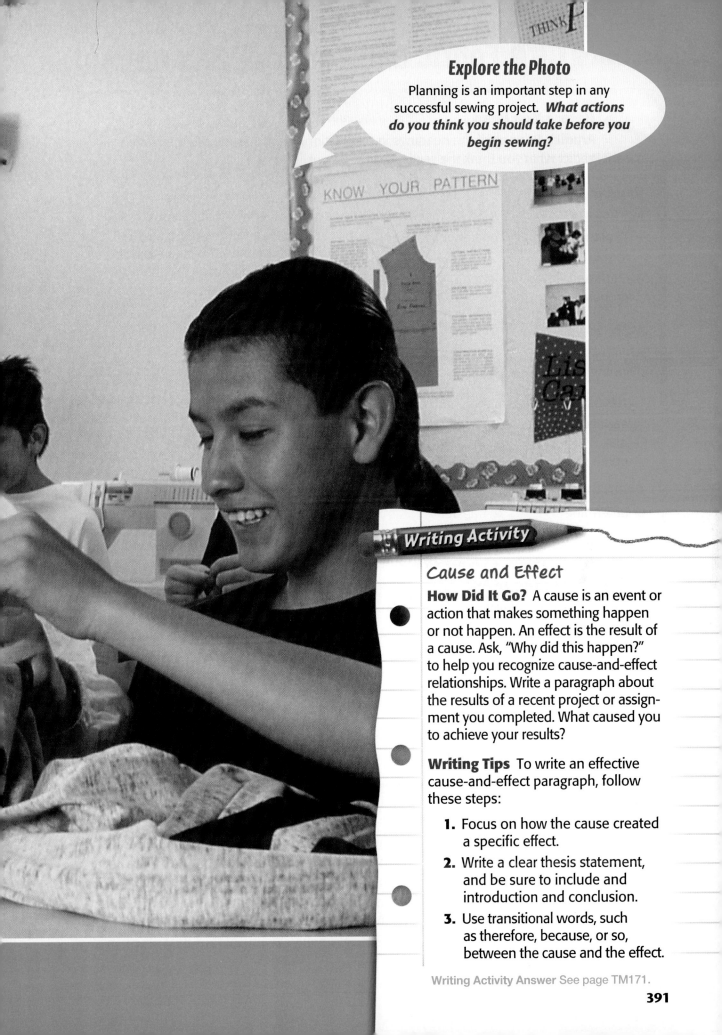

Explore the Photo

Planning is an important step in any successful sewing project. *What actions do you think you should take before you begin sewing?*

KNOW YOUR PATTERN

Writing Activity

Cause and Effect

How Did It Go? A cause is an event or action that makes something happen or not happen. An effect is the result of a cause. Ask, "Why did this happen?" to help you recognize cause-and-effect relationships. Write a paragraph about the results of a recent project or assignment you completed. What caused you to achieve your results?

Writing Tips To write an effective cause-and-effect paragraph, follow these steps:

1. Focus on how the cause created a specific effect.

2. Write a clear thesis statement, and be sure to include and introduction and conclusion.

3. Use transitional words, such as therefore, because, or so, between the cause and the effect.

Writing Activity Answer See page TM171.

Reading Guide

Before You Read

Predict Read all of the headings in this section. Think about what the headings mean. Predict what you think the section will be about.

Read to Learn

Key Concepts

✓ **Explain** why fabric preparation is important.

✓ **Outline** the steps in pattern preparation.

Main Idea

A successful sewing project includes planning and preparation.

Content Vocabulary

○ selvage
○ bias
○ guide sheet
○ layout
○ marking
○ ease

Academic Vocabulary

■ determine
■ transfer

Graphic Organizer

As you read, identify five steps you would take in preparing to sew. Use a graphic organizer like the one shown to help you organize your information.

Preparing to Sew
1.
2.
3.
4.
5.

Graphic Organizer Go to this book's Online Learning Center at glencoe.com to print this graphic organizer.

- - - - - - - - - - - - - - - - - **Academic Standards** - - - - - - - - - - - - - - - - -

 English Language Arts

NCTE 4 Use written language to communicate effectively.

 Mathematics

NCTM Problem Solving Understand the meanings of operations and how they relate to one another.

 Social Studies

NCSS I A Culture Analyze and explain the ways groups, societies, and cultures address human needs and concerns.

NCTE *National Council of Teachers of English*
NCTM *National Council of Teachers of Mathematics*

NSES *National Science Education Standards*
NCSS *National Council for the Social Studies*

Reading Strategy Answer
(1) wash and press fabric
(2) gather notions (3) read the pattern guidesheet
(4) cut out and press pattern pieces (5) check fabric bias

Many people enjoy sewing. Sewing gives you the chance to use patterns and your own creativity to create your own clothing and home fashions. If you have not sewn before, the information in this section can help make your sewing projects successful. You will learn how to prepare your fabric and pattern for sewing. These are important first steps in any sewing project.

Fabric Preparation

It is important to take the time to preshrink your fabric. Some fabrics will not shrink, while others may. Launder the fabric as directed. Cleaning instructions are located on the end of the bolt of fabric. Once the fabric is preshrunk, press it to get rid of wrinkles.

Check the Grain

After you have preshrunk the fabric, you need to check the fabric grain. The fabric grain is the direction that the yarns run in woven fabric. **Figure 18.1** shows where to find the selvages, grains, and bias on a piece of fabric and explains how to check the grain. The **selvage** is the tightly woven edge of the fabric that has no visible loose threads. Raw edges are the unfinished edges of the fabric. You can straighten the fabric by folding it on the true **bias**, or diagonal.

 Reading Check *Explain* *Why should you prepare fabric before sewing?*

Reading Check Answer So the garment will fit properly.

Figure 18.1 Finding the Grain

Take Time It is important for the lengthwise and crosswise threads in fabrics to meet at right angles when you sew. *What might happen if you forget to align the fabric grain before you sew?*

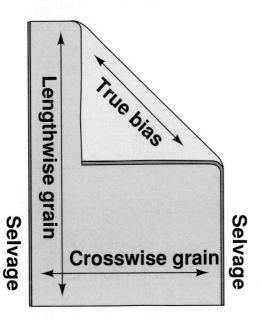

To test the grain, fold the fabric lengthwise so that the selvages are on top of one another. If the raw edges do not line up, do the following:

■ For woven fabrics, clip the selvage and pull a crosswise thread. Cut along the line made by the pulled thread.

■ For knitted fabrics, cut along one crosswise row of loops to straighten the edges.

Test the grain again by folding your fabric and matching selvages.

■ If the crosswise ends match exactly and are at right angles to the selvage, the fabric is straight. The fold will be smooth and unwrinkled.

■ If the edges do not match, the fabric is not straight. If cut that way, the finished garment will twist or hang crooked.

Figure Caption Answer Answers may include: the project will be the correct size; the material will not twist; the garment will not hang crooked.

Pattern Preparation

Study the guide sheet inside your pattern envelope before you begin sewing. A **guide sheet** is a set of step-by-step instructions for sewing a pattern. The guide sheet, as shown in the photo, contains information on how to use the pattern, a diagram of the pattern pieces, an explanation of the pattern markings, and layouts. **Layouts** are diagrams of how the pattern pieces should be placed on the fabric.

After you have read through the guide sheet, you are ready to prepare the pattern pieces. **Figure 18.2** shows how to prepare pattern pieces and understand markings. **Markings** are symbols located on the pattern pieces.

Pattern Guide Sheets

Follow these steps to use a pattern guide sheet:

- Study the diagram of the pattern pieces.
- Circle the letters of the pieces needed for the garment that you plan to make.
- Circle the layout diagram that you will use for your size and style.
- Read through all of the pattern directions before you start to work.

To prepare your pattern pieces, cut apart the pieces you will use, but do not trim them. You will cut off the margins later, when you cut the fabric. Study each pattern piece, and refer to the guide sheet to find out what each marking means. If the pattern pieces are wrinkled, press them with a warm, dry iron.

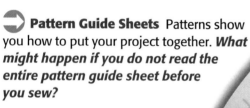

Pattern Guide Sheets Patterns show you how to put your project together. *What might happen if you do not read the entire pattern guide sheet before you sew?*

Photo Caption Answer
Answers may include: fabric may be cut incorrectly, you might run out of fabric, patterns at the seams may not match.

Figure (18.2) Pattern Markings

Marked Guides Pattern markings guide you throughout a sewing project. *What might happen if you did not follow the pattern markings?*

Dots are points matched for accuracy. If a shirt pattern shows a dot at the center of the back and a dot at the center of the collar pieces, match these dots to make the collar fit correctly.

Notches are v-shaped markings on cutting lines that show which seams are matched and stitched together to join seams evenly.

Place on folds are thin single lines on straight edges that mean to place the pattern on fabric fold. Do not cut on the fold line.

Adjustment lines are parallel lines that show where patterns can be lengthened or shortened.

Grain lines are double-pointed arrows that show pattern placement on the straight grain of the fabric.

Cutting lines are heavy lines, scissors symbols, or double lines along the pattern edge that show where to cut.

Stitching lines are broken or dotted lines that indicate stitching lines. These are usually 5/8 inches (1.5 cm) inside the cutting lines and are often marked by a presser foot symbol or by arrows. These symbols show the direction to stitch fabric.

Darts are broken lines that indicate stitching lines. Solid lines show where to fold.

Figure Caption Answer Answers may include: the garment may not fit correctly, the fabric patterns may not match, the seams do not match properly.

Check Pattern Measurements

Before you place the pattern pieces on the fabric, you need to make sure that the pattern you selected fits your body. To do that, compare your measurements with the body measurements listed on the pattern envelope. If you need to make any alterations, or changes to the pattern to make the garment fit, do it before you cut the fabric.

Length Adjustments

Use the two parallel lines labeled lengthen or shorten. Your teacher can show you how to do this. Be sure to make the same changes on both the front and back pieces of the pattern.

Width Adjustments

Determine, or figure out, how much ease is included in the pattern. **Ease** is the amount of fullness added for movement and comfort. The amount of ease depends on the stress that will be put on that part of the garment when it is worn. Your teacher can show you how to adjust the amount of ease.

 Reading Check *Explain Why are pattern changes sometimes needed?*

Pin the Pattern

Look at the layout on the guide sheet to see how to fold your fabric. Most layouts show the right sides of the fabric folded together. Lay the pattern pieces on top of the fabric. The lengthwise grain markings must be parallel to the selvage. Check them with a ruler as you pin. Do not cut out any pieces until they have all been pinned in place. Follow these steps to pin your pattern:

Step 1 Pin the large pattern pieces that belong on the fold.

Step 2 Pin the pattern pieces that have a grain-line arrow. To check the grain line, place a pin at one end of the grain-line arrow. Measure from the arrow to the selvage of the fabric edge. Position the pattern so that the other end of the arrow is exactly the same distance from the edge. Then pin the piece in place.

Step 3 Place the pins diagonally inside the cutting line. This keeps the fabric flat and makes it easier to cut.

Step 4 Place pins about 2 inches (5 cm) apart.

Step 5 Double-check your pinned layout against the layout on the pattern guide sheet.

Cut Out the Pattern

It will be easier to sew straight seams if you cut the edges of the fabric evenly. Follow these steps to cut out your pinned pattern:

Step 1   Place the fabric flat on the table. Use one hand to hold the fabric in place and the other hand to cut.

Step 2   Cut with long, even strokes.

Step 3   Cut in the direction of the arrows printed on the pattern's seamline. In this way, you will be cutting with the fabric grain, and you will not stretch the fabric.

Step 4   Cut around the outside of each notch. Cut double and triple notches together with one long edge across the top.

Step 5   Leave the pattern pieces pinned to the fabric until you are ready to stitch that piece.

MATH YOU CAN USE

Calculate Measurement

You need to increase the waistline of your pattern by 4 inches. How much should you increase the measurement for each seam allowance?

Math Concept Multiply Fractions To multiply fractions, multiply the numerators and multiply the denominators. Mixed numbers must first be changed to improper fractions.

Starting Hint Rewrite the whole number representing the increase as a fraction. Then multiply that fraction by $1/a$, with a representing the number of seam allowances. To increase a waistline by two inches, the formula would be $2/1 \times 1/4 = 2/4$. Then $2/4$ would be reduced to $= 1/2$.

  For more math help, go to the Math Appendix located at the back of this book.

NCTM Problem Solving Understand the meanings of operations and how they relate to one another.

Math You Can Use Answer
$4/1 \times 1/4 = 4/4 = 1$"

 Cutting Patterns
Before you cut out your project, practice cutting fabric scraps. *Why are clean edges on the fabric pieces important?*

Photo Caption Answer To keep the fabric from raveling and to match the seams correctly.

Character Counts

Honesty

Susan is working on the final semester project for her sewing lab. The project is 20% of the final class grade. Susan needs to score at least 93% on her project to pass the class. Susan's best friend, Megan, who attends a different school, earned an A on her final sewing project. Megan offers to let Susan use her own completed project for the class. Susan has delayed in starting her project, and is now almost out of time to turn in her best quality work.

You Make the Call

Should Susan use Megan's sewing project and say that it is her own? Write a paragraph that explains what you think Susan should do.

Character Counts
Answer Paragraphs should include the student's position and should explain the reasoning behind his or her advice to Susan.

Transfer Markings

After you cut out your pattern, transfer, or move, the markings from the pattern to the fabric. Markings must be visible as you sew, but they should never show on the outside of a finished garment. The lines and symbols on pattern pieces are important guides during construction. Markings include darts, pleats, tucks, dots, fold lines, and buttonholes. Hemlines need not be marked. Different marking methods may be used for different fabrics and types of marks. These include tailor's chalk, tracing paper, air-soluble pens, and water-soluble marking pens. When transferring markings:

- Always test your marking device on a fabric scrap to make sure the marks come out of the fabric completely.
- When using a tracing wheel and paper, choose a color of tracing paper that will show up on the fabric.
- Mark dots with an X.
- Mark the ends of darts with a short line.
- Mark each seamline so that you will know exactly where to stitch.

Section 18.1 After You Read

Review What You Have Learned

1. **Identify** reasons why pattern preparation is important.
2. **Name** five steps you would take in planning to sew.

Practice Academic Skills

 English Language Arts

3. Write a detailed paragraph that discusses why fabric preparation is important.

> **NCTE 4** Use written language to communicate effectively.

 Social Studies

4. Many fleece and wool garments are made in Peru because of the animals in the region, such as sheep, llamas, and alpacas. Conduct research to find three other types of contemporary or historical fabrics. List the geographic region and the types of garments or objects made from the fabric.

> **NCSS I A** Analyze and explain the ways groups, societies, and cultures address human needs and concerns.

Check Your Answers Check your answers at this book's Online Learning Center at glencoe.com.

Reading Guide

Before You Read

Preview Choose a content or academic vocabulary word that is new to you. When you find it in the text, write down the definition.

Read to Learn

Key Concepts

✓ **List** ten basic sewing techniques.

✓ **Describe** what a serger does.

Main Idea

Sewing and serging skills allow you to achieve a professional quality in your sewing projects.

Content Vocabulary

○ staystitch
○ feed dog
○ casing
○ sew-through button
○ shank button
○ cone
○ looper
○ tail chain

Academic Vocabulary

■ result
■ product

Graphic Organizer

As you read, list the ten basic sewing techniques described in this section. Use a chart like the one shown below to help organize your information.

Sewing Techniques

 Graphic Organizer Go to this book's Online Learning Center at glencoe.com to print this graphic organizer.

· · · · · · · · · · · · · · · · · **Academic Standards** · · · · · · · · · · · · · · · · · ·

 English Language Arts

NCTE 4 Use written language to communicate effectively.

 Mathematics

NCTM Number and Operations Compute fluently and make reasonable estimates.

Social Studies

NCSS I D Culture Compare and analyze societal patterns for preserving and transmitting culture while adapting to environmental or social change.

NCTE *National Council of Teachers of English*
NCTM *National Council of Teachers of Mathematics*

NSES *National Science Education Standards*
NCSS *National Council for the Social Studies*

Reading Strategy Answer Stitch straight seams, stitch curved seams, turn corners, add seam finishes, make darts, gather fabric, ease fabric, make casings, make facings, sew on buttons and snaps.

Sewing machines have come a long way since they were first introduced for home use in the late 19th century. Today's sewing machines are computerized. They can do all the traditional stitches, and some models can even embroider your own design onto a garment. This section will introduce you to basic sewing machine techniques, and you will become familiar with the parts and functions of an overlock machine, also called a serger.

Beginning to Sew

When you make a garment, the first step is to staystitch the seams. A **staystitch** is a row of stitching made very near the seamline within the seam allowance. Staystitching, as shown in **Figure 18.3**, prevents stretching and helps in turning under edges of hems and bands.

Stitch Straight Seams

You will sew most projects together by stitching straight seams. To sew a seam, place two pieces of fabric right sides together. Line up the edges so that they are even. Match all markings and notches, and pin the two pieces together. The heads of the pins should be near the outside edges of the fabric. For most sewing, pins should be placed about 2 inches (5 cm) apart. Now look at the throat plate on your sewing machine. The line markings show how far the needle is from the seam edge. Most seams are 5/8 inch (1.5 cm) wide. Find the line on the machine that is 5/8 inch (1.5 cm) from the needle. Keep the fabric edge against this mark as you sew and your seam will be straight. As you stitch, guide the fabric with both hands, but do not push it. The feed dog will move the fabric as you sew. The **feed dogs** are the parts of the machine that position the fabric for the next stitch. Operate the machine at a slow, even speed. Backstitch 2–3 stitches at the beginning and end of the seam.

Figure 18.3 Prepare Seams

Prevent Stretching Before you begin sewing seams, always staystitch near the seams to prevent the seam edges from stretching and raveling. *What might happen to a garment if the seams are not staystitched?*

STAYSTITCHING
SEAMLINE

How To...

Sew by Hand

Some sewing must be done by hand. Hand sewing gives you more control than you have using a sewing machine or serger. Try these basic stitches.

Basting Stitch The basting stitch is a temporary stitch used to hold fabrics together for fittings and for matching plaids and seams. To baste, pin fabric layers together and use even stitches.

Slipstitch The slipstitch provides an almost invisible finish. Slipstitching is used on patch pockets, hems, linings, and trims. Slide the needle in one folded edge and out, picking up a thread of the under layer.

Hem Stitch This stitch finishes different hems, especially those with seam binding or a folded edge. A hem stitch is made by taking a tiny stitch in the garment, then bringing the needle diagonally through the hem edge.

Blanket Stitch The blanket stitch can be used as a decorative edge finish and as thread loops, eyes, belt carriers, bar tacks, and French tacks. Stick the threaded needle through the right side of the fabric and pull it out at the edge. Keep the thread from the previous stitch under the needle point, pulling the needle and thread through and over the edge.

Backstitch As one of the strongest stitches, backstitches repair machine-stitched seams and fasten thread ends securely. The backstitch is made by carrying the thread back half the length of the preceding stitch. Bring the needle through to the underside of the fabric. Insert the needle back at the beginning of the first stitch, and bring it out again one stitch length in front of the thread.

Stitch Curved Seams

With curved seams, you must guide the fabric with your hands so that the curves are smooth. You also need to keep the stitching an even distance from the edge of the fabric. The best way to learn how to sew curved seams is to practice. Start by stitching curves on a piece of paper. Then practice on scraps of fabric.

Turn Corners

Learning how to turn corners, or pivot, is another skill that takes practice. When turning a corner, follow these steps:

Step 1 Slow down the sewing machine when you come to a corner.

Step 2 Lift the presser foot. Turn the fabric, with the needle still in it. Put the presser foot back down again and stitch the next side. This keeps the sewing line straight and the corner sharp.

Add Seam Finishes

After stitching your project, you may need to add a seam finish. Seam finishes are treatments used on the seam edges to prevent fabric from raveling. The most effective seam finish depends on the type of fabric being used. If the fabric ravels only slightly, pink the edges with pinking shears. For greater protection against raveling, stitch ¼ inch (6 mm) from each edge before pinking. If your fabric ravels easily, use a zigzag finish. Some fabrics do not ravel and do not need seam finishes.

COMMUNITY CONNECTIONS

Sew for a Cause Conduct research on ways that you can use your sewing skills to help others in your community. Identify one organization in which you can use your sewing skills to assist people in need.

Community Connections Feature Answer Answers may include the local social services department, clothing banks, neonatal care units, and homeless shelters.

Fabric Placement Keep the fabric edge against the mark on the needle plate as you stitch. *Why should you practice stitches on fabric scraps before you begin sewing?*

Photo Caption Answer So that you can practice sewing speeds, sew straight lines, and sew using different types of fabrics.

Straight Stitch Stitching a straight line takes practice. *Why should you leave the needle in the fabric before lifting the presser foot?*

Photo Caption Answer This makes the sewing line straight and the corner sharp.

Make Darts

Darts are used to help shape fabric to the curves of the body. They are usually found at the bustline, waistline, elbow, or back of the shoulder. For darts to create the right effect, they must have the correct width and shape. Make sure that they are accurately marked, folded, and pinned before you stitch them.

Gather Fabric

When you need to fit a longer piece of fabric to a shorter one, you can gather the longer piece of fabric. For example, you might use gathering at the tops of sleeves or at the waist of a full skirt.

Ease Fabric

When one piece of fabric is only slightly longer than the piece that it will join, easing is used. Easing creates a slight fullness. To ease fabric, you need to pin it before you stitch the seam. Place the fabric right sides together, matching the notches and ends. Pin every ½ inch (1.3 cm). When you stitch, place the longer piece of fabric on top and gently ease in the extra fullness. An eased seam should look smooth, without puckering.

Make Casings

You may need to sew casings if your garment has a pull-on waistband or sleeve band. **Casings** are fabric tunnels made to enclose elastic or drawstrings. When you draw up the elastic or drawstring, a gathered appearance is created.

Types of Casings

When you sew a casing, make sure that it is ¼ to ½ in. (6 mm–1.3 cm) wider than the elastic or drawstring it will enclose. This will allow the elastic or drawstring to move freely through the fabric tunnel. The two types of casings are fold-down and applied. A fold-down casing is often used for pull-on pants and skirts. An applied casing is often used at the waistline. To make an applied casing, you need to stitch a separate strip of fabric or bias tape to the garment.

⬆ **Gathering** Two pieces of fabric can be fitted by gathering. *Where would you gather fabric in a garment?* Photo Caption Answer Waistline or sleeves.

Make Facings

Facings are used to finish the raw edges of a garment. Facings are sewn around the edges of necklines, armholes, and some waistlines. You stitch facings to the right side of the garment and then turn them to the inside. To achieve a smooth appearance, trim and grade the seam allowance to reduce bulk. **Figure 18.4** shows you how to do this.

Figure 18.4 **Adjusting Seams**

Reducing Bulk There are four ways to reduce bulk in seams. *Can you identify when you would use each of the four ways of reducing bulk in seams?*

Trimming A seam is trimmed by cutting the seam allowance to 3/8 or ¼ inch (9 or 6 mm). This reduces the bulk of the seam. This is usually done when the seam is enclosed in a collar, cuff, facing, waistband, or set-in sleeve.

Clipping Curved seams are clipped so that they will lie flat. Slits are cut into the trimmed seam allowance about every ¼ inch to ½ inch (6 mm–1.3 cm). Clip only to within 1/8 inch (3 mm) of the seamline, being careful not to cut through the stitching.

Grading A seam is graded by trimming the seam allowances to different widths. Trim the seam allowance toward the inside of the garment narrower than the outside one. This further reduces the bulk. Grading is often done on seams for facings.

Notching Some curved seams that have too much fabric in the seam allowance may need to be notched. Little Vs or triangles are cut out of the trimmed seam allowance.

Figure Caption Answer Notching when you have too much fabric; clipping to make seams lie flat; trimming to reduce bulk in collars, waistband or sleeves; and grading when facings are used.

Make Drawstring or Pull-On Pants

In this activity you will sew a basic pair of drawstring or pull-on pants using the skills you have learned in this chapter. Before you begin, read through the entire Life Skills Lab assignment. Write down any questions that you may have about the assignment. Reread the text or ask your teacher for help if you need it.

Supplies

✓ Pants pattern of your choice
✓ Cotton fabric such as flannel
✓ Elastic
✓ Thread

Develop Your Plan

■ Choose a basic pants pattern in your size.

■ Acquire the amount of fabric yardage and thread needed.

■ Gather the notions you will need to construct the pants, including scissors, pins, and tape measure.

■ Read through the pattern guide sheet to become familiar with the instructions.

Implement Your Plan

■ Pre-wash, dry, and press your cotton fabric.

■ Circle the correct pattern layout on the pattern guide sheet.

■ Cut out the pattern pieces for your size.

■ Pin the pattern pieces to your fabric according to the pattern layout.

■ Cut out the pattern pieces from your fabric.

■ Transfer markings onto your fabric from the pattern pieces.

■ Wind the bobbin and insert it in the sewing machine. Thread your machine needle.

■ Follow the instructions on the pattern guide sheet to sew your pants.

Evaluate Your Results

What did you learn about pattern layout? Is there anything you would change the next time you make a pair of pants? Write one or more paragraphs to explain your answer.

 Projects and Activities Go to this book's Online Learning Center through glencoe.com for more projects and activities.

Sew on Buttons and Snaps

There are two types of buttons: sew-through and shank. A **sew-through button** has two or four holes through it and no loop on the back. It is used when materials joined need to lie flat. A **shank button** has a stem on the back. Shanks are used with thick fabrics. When you attach a sew-through button, you will need to add a thread shank. **Figure 18.5** shows you how to sew on both types of buttons.

Snaps are used to hold together overlapping edges. The two parts of a snap are the ball half and the socket half. Follow these guidelines when replacing a snap:

- Place the ball half of the snap on the underside of the overlap, far enough from the edge so that it will not show. Sew five or six stitches in each hole. Carry the thread under the snap from hole to hole.
- Mark the position of the socket half. Stitch it in place. Secure the thread and knot it.

Reading Check *Analyze* Why do garments have different types of closures?

Reading Check
Answer Different weights of fabric require different closures, and various closures serve specific purposes.

Figure Caption
Answer Shank buttons are needed when material is thick, and sew-through buttons are used when two pieces of fabric need to lie flat.

Figure 18.5 Sewing on Buttons

Repair Skills Learning to sew on buttons is an essential clothing repair skill. *Where would you use each of the button types on a garment?*

Sew-Through Buttons

Step 1 Start on the underside of the fabric, and bring the needle and thread to the right side.

Step 2 Stick the needle and thread through one hole in the button. Place a toothpick across the top of or underneath the button to allow for a thread shank. Stitch in and out several times through the fabric and buttonholes and over the toothpick. Finish stitching so that your needle and thread are under the button.

Step 3 Remove the toothpick. Pull the button to the top of the thread loop. Wind the thread several times around the stitches under the button to make a thread shank.

Step 4 Bring the needle back to the wrong side of the fabric.

Step 5 Secure the thread by taking several small stitches in the fabric and knot it.

Shank Buttons

Step 1 Sew a shank button in place using five or six small stitches through the shank and into the fabric.

Step 2 Fasten the thread securely.

Step 3 Insert an eye fastener and sew the eye in place first.

Serging Basics

A serger is a machine that sews, trims, and finishes a seam in one step. A serger can save time and handle a variety of fabrics, from slippery silks to stretchy knits. A serger keeps the edges from raveling on all fabrics. On stretchy fabric, serging also allows for movement of the fabric.

How Sergers Work

A serger feeds several strands of thread through guides that are placed above the machine. **Cones** are the large cylinders used to hold large spools of thread. Sergers use cones instead of spools because sergers use more thread than sewing machines do. A cone can hold up to five times more thread than a spool can hold.

Sergers are known as two-thread, three-thread, four-thread, or five-thread, depending on the number of threads used to make the stitch. Each thread passes through its own tension dial. Sergers do not have bobbins. Instead, they have **loopers**, which are rounded parts that hold the thread inside a serger. The looper threads loop around each other and are interlocked with the needle thread or threads. Depending on the model, sergers may have one or two needles. The remaining threads are wrapped by the loopers. **Figure 18.6** on page 408 shows the basic parts of a serger.

Small knife blades are located inside the serger. These knives trim the fabric as it passes through the machine. The result, or outcome, is a seam allowance that is exactly the width of the serger's stitch. As you serge, the entire seam allowance is wrapped inside the serge stitch.

A serger does not replace a sewing machine because it cannot sew a single line of locked stitches, create buttonholes, or insert zippers. It allows you to use a greater variety of fabrics, including stretchy knits and sheers. Sergers are most commonly used to sew knits and stitch stretch fabrics. Sergers can also be used to sew conventional skirt or pant hems or narrow, rolled hems, such as those on scarves safely.

Financial Literacy Answer $9.00 + $7.00 + $2.00 + $1.00 = $19.00. Yes, Katie has enough money.

Safety Check

Serging Without Pins

Serging with pins in place can cause safety concerns for you and others around you. Doing this can also cause serious damage to the serger's knife blades. Use these tips to use a serger

- Instead of pinning the fabric into position, baste the fabric, or tack it with glue.
- Be sure to check each pattern piece for pins before sewing.

Financial Literacy

Sewing Costs

Katie needs to buy materials for a sewing project, but she does not have a calculator. She has $25.00 to spend. Does she have enough money? Use rounding to determine the total cost of the following items.

Fabric....... $8.99	Thread....... 2.15
Pattern....... 6.50	Pins.............. .99

Math Concept **Cost Estimation** To estimate the sum of a set of numbers, round the amounts to the same place-value position and add. When rounding, look at the first digit to the right of the decimal point. If the first digit to the right of the decimal point is 5 or greater, round up to the nearest dollar. If the digit is less than 5, round down.

Starting Hint: To round $8.99 to the nearest dollar, look at the number to the right of the decimal. Since 9 is more than 5, you would round $8.99 up to $9.00.

NCTM Number and Operations Compute fluently and make reasonable estimates.

Math For math help, go to the Math Appendix at the back of the book.

Figure 18.6 Basic Serger Parts

High-Speed Machine A serger has many working parts. *Find the loopers in this diagram and explain their function.*

Thread guide keeps threads separate.

Pressure control regulator changes pressure on presser foot.

Tension dial applies pressure to the thread and alters the pattern of the stitch.

Side cover protects the gears and sewing mechanism.

Spool pin keeps thread cones in place.

Thread guide pole holds threads above serger to prevent tangling.

Thread cone holds up to 1,000 yards of thread.

Spool base supports thread cones.

Hand wheel lowers and raises needle.

Power switch turns the serger on and off.

Front cover protects the loopers.

Upper looper helps form the overlock stitch by carrying thread to the top of the fabric.

Lower looper helps form the overlock stitch by carrying thread to the bottom of the fabric.

Movable upper knife cuts the fabric.

Needle creates stitch, along with loopers.

Stationary lower knife trims fabric as it goes under the needle.

Stitch finger determines the stitch width.

Feed dog feeds the fabric under the needle.

Figure Caption Answer Loopers are the rounded parts that hold the thread inside the serger. Threads loop around each other and are interlocked with the needle thread.

Using a Serger

When you are ready to begin a project, set the stitch-length and tension dials on the serger to the desired settings. Use fabric scraps to test how the serged stitch will look on the final **product**, or result, either with or against the grain. Keep adjusting the stitch length and tension until you achieve the result that you want.

When you have tested the serge stitch on fabric scraps and basted your fabric, you are ready to serge. Position the fabric for feeding through the machine. Unless the fabric is unusually thick, you should not need to lift the presser foot. The fabric is moved along by the feed dogs. You should begin and end each seam with a **tail chain**, a length of thread shaped like a chain. A tail chain is made by pressing on the presser foot without placing fabric under the needle. It keeps the fabric from raveling and eliminates the need to tie off the threads of the seam.

⬆ **Difficult Fabrics** Hard-to-handle fabrics, such as stretchy knits, are easier to handle on a serger than on a regular sewing machine. *Which garments in your wardrobe have "serged" seams?*

Photo Caption Answer
T-shirts, sweaters, pants, and skirts.

Section 18.2 After You Read

Review What You Have Learned
1. **Identify** the two types of casings and how each is used.
2. **Identify** the advantages of using a serger.

Practice Academic Skills

 English Language Arts

3. Choose three items of clothing from your closet. Determine if the stitching was done by a sewing machine, a serger, or both. Explain how you can tell.

> **NCTE 4** Use written language to communicate effectively.

 Social Studies

4. The art of quilt making is experiencing a revival. Quilts are works of art in museums, and can be seen on display at fairs and festivals. Write a paragraph to explain how a quilt can serve as a historical record.

> **NCSS I A** Compare and analyze societal patterns for preserving and transmitting culture while adapting to environmental or social change.

🖱 **Check Your Answers** Check your answers at this book's Online Learning Center at **glencoe.com**.

Discovering Careers

Would you like to help people plan their wardrobes or design clothing for them to wear? Are you creative and have a knack for putting outfits together? If you answered yes to either of those questions, you might want to consider a future career in fashion or design. The following chart explores several careers in the fashion industry.

Job Title	Job Description
Clothier	Designs original garments, sews from existing patterns, and does alterations and repairs.
Clothing Inspector	Checks finished garments for stitching, colors, and sizes. Corrects errors in partially completed garments or returns garments for repairs.
Clothing Clerk	Helps customers find clothing. Checks sizes and makes recommendations to the customer. Organizes and stocks clothing racks.
FACS Teacher	Teaches Family and Consumer Sciences courses in middle or high schools.
Personal Shopper	Assesses clients' styles, needs, wardrobes, and purchases items for clients.
Wardrobe Consultant	Assembles wardrobes to project a desired image. Teaches basic clothes-buying strategies such as mixing, matching, and accessorizing.

Career Activities ▼

At School

❶ Select three of the careers listed. Research the education, training, and work experience required for each career. Write a summary of your results.

At Home

❷ Role-play with a family member the role of wardrobe consultant. Let your family member be your client. Determine the image he or she wants to project. Compile a wardrobe from magazine photos or online to show your client.

At Work

❸ Like all clothing, uniforms require a design and someone to make them. List at least five jobs you can identify by the uniform.

In the Community

❹ Contact and interview someone in your community who works in the fashion industry. Ask this person to describe what his or her typical work day is like. Share what you learned with your class.

Career Activities Answers for these activities can be found on page TM171.

Learn More *Online* 🔎 glencoe.com

Career Investigations Go to this book's Online Learning Center for activities and worksheets to help you explore careers.

Chapter Summary

Section 18.1 Fabric and Pattern Preparation
To prepare fabric for sewing, preshrink it and check the grain. Then read the pattern guide sheet. This will allow you to understand the overall project, and will help you avoid making mistakes. Check the pattern pieces and compare the measurements to those on the pattern envelope and make changes as needed.

Section 18.2 Sewing and Serging Basics
Sewing is an enjoyable creative activity that can help you expand your wardrobe by adding new garments and repairing older garments. There are ten basic sewing techniques. A serger sews, trims, and finishes an edge in one step. Serging allows you to use a variety of fabrics and to give your projects a professional look.

Words You Learned

1. Use each of these content vocabulary words and academic vocabulary words in a sentence.

Content Vocabulary
- selvage (p. 393)
- bias (p. 393)
- guide sheet (p. 394)
- layout (p. 394)
- marking (p. 394)
- ease (p. 396)
- staystitch (p. 400)
- feed dog (p. 400)
- casing (p. 403)
- sew-through button (p. 406)
- shank button (p. 406)
- cone (p. 407)
- looper (p. 407)
- tail chain (p. 409)

Academic Vocabulary
- determine (p. 396)
- transfer (p. 398)
- result (p. 407)
- product (p. 409)

Review Key Concepts

2. **Explain** why fabric preparation is important.

3. **Outline** the steps in fabric preparation.

4. **List** ten basic sewing techniques.

5. **Describe** what a serger does.

Critical Thinking

6. **Explain** why various fabrics might need to be prepared for sewing differently.

7. **Describe** problems that might occur if you do not prepare your pattern before beginning

8. **Compare and contrast** the uses of a serger versus the uses of a regular sewing machine.

9. **Analyze** which sewing project would be more challenging: a skirt with a fold-down casing or a round pillow with a ruffle. Explain your answer.

Real-World Skills and Applications

Problem-Solving

10. Making Decisions Evan bought a pattern, some fabric, and notions. He plans to start sewing immediately. Is he leaving out a step? Develop a plan of action for Evan that includes the steps that you recommend he take before he begins sewing.

Interpersonal and Collaborative

11. Sewing Machine Timeline Follow your teacher's instructions to form into teams. Work in teams to research and prepare a timeline display showing the history of the sewing machine. When and where was the first sewing machine developed? Who invented it? Was it first used in private homes or by clothing manufacturers? Present your findings to your class.

Financial Literacy

12. Comparison Shopping Think of two items of clothing you would like to buy. Comparison shop for the items of clothing by locating them in different places. You may find the items of clothing in local stores, magazines, and by searching the Internet. Write down where you found the items and how much they cost. Compare the price of the items to determine which store or other source offers the best buy. If you find the items of clothing on the Internet, be sure to add handling and shipping costs to the total cost of the items. Shipping costs may vary based on the type of shipping you choose and by the ship to location.

13. Sewing Lab. Make a personalized pillowcase. Cut a rectangle of fabric 42½ inches × 35½ inches. Serge around the edges ofw the rectangle. Fold the fabric right sides together, and stitch along one long and one short edge. Turn up a 3-inch hem along the remaining short end, facing the wrong side. Stitch in place. Turn the pillowcase right side out.

14. Research Clothing History Clothing styles have changed throughout history. Certain features of clothing, such as colors and fabrics, often represented the status and wealth of the wearer. Choose a historical period and find examples of the clothing worn by both men and women of the period. Did different social groups wear different types of clothing? Prepare a short presentation for your class on what you have found.

15. Clothing Today With permission from your parents or teacher, go online to research teen clothing styles today. How have they changed since a decade ago? One hundred years ago? Find examples of teen clothing styles from past decades and of today's teen styles to include in your Life Skills binder.

Academic Skills

English Language Arts

16. Advertise Imagine that your school is creating a Sewing Club. You have been asked to create a flyer to hand out to your classmates encouraging them to join. Develop a flyer that would encourage both boys and girls to join the club. What information should you include in the flyer? What type of artwork? Describe the advantages of being a member of the club

> **NCTE 5** Use different writing process elements to communicate effectively.

Science

17. Form a Hypothesis The scientific method is a way to answer questions.
Procedure Collect information, form a hypothesis, study the results, and draw conclusions that can be tested by others. One hypothesis might read: It is more expensive to buy clothes in a store than it is to make them.
Analysis Form your own hypothesis about clothing costs and write a list of facts that support your hypothesis.

> **NSES A** Develop abilities necessary to do scientific inquiry, understandings about scientific inquiry.

Mathematics

18. Calculate Average Project Time Nelly, Shar, and Keisha spend a total of 12 hours working together on an assigned sewing project. Each must keep track of the time he or she spends on the project. What is the average number of minutes each of them spends working on the project?

Math Concept **Use Variables and Operations** Translating words into algebraic expressions requires knowledge of the meaning of the verbal descriptions. In algebra, a variable is a symbol used to represent a number. Arithmetic operations include addition, subtraction, multiplication, and division.

Starting Hint Since you are solving for the answer in minutes, first convert the hours into minutes. If x = the average number of hours each worker spends on the project, the algebraic expression for the problem is $3x = (12 \times 60)$. Solve for x.

> **NCTM Algebra** Represent and analyze mathematical situations and structures using algebraic symbols.

Standardized Test Practice

Multiple-Choice

Read the paragraph. Then read the question and the answer choices. Choose the best answer and write it on a separate sheet of paper.

> **Test-Taking Tip** In a multiple-choice test, read the question before you read the answer choices. Try to answer the question before you read the answer choices. This way, the answer choices will not confuse you.

19. Justin is working on a sewing project for his life skills class. He reads the guide sheet included in the pattern he has chosen. The guide sheet says to be sure to check the *bias*. In this sentence, what does the word *bias* mean?

a. a distortion of a set of statistical data

b. voltage applied across an electronic device

c. running diagonally across the weave of a fabric

d. having a preference

Design Your Own Clothing

Knowing how to sew can help you create unique clothing designs. You can learn about designs from studying pattern booklets in sewing stores. Reading fashion magazines may give you ideas for stylish projects. This project will help you design your own clothing.

 My Journal Complete the journal entry from page 369, and refer to it to complete your design concept.

Project Assignment ▼

In this project, you will:

- Sketch ideas for a clothing design.
- Create a sewing pattern for your clothing design.
- Describe your design's practicality and style.
- Interview someone who sews professionally.
- Present your clothing design to your class.
- Include this project in the eighth section of your personal Life Skills binder.

Step 1 Develop Your Unique Design Concept

Pick a sketch that you believe you could successfully design. Color and add detail to the sketch. List the materials someone might need to sew your design and begin to write step-by-step instructions they must follow.

Step 2 Create a Pattern for Your Design

Review pattern markings on page 395 (Figure 18.2). Draw a pattern for your clothing design using the proper markings. Use these questions to write step-by-step instructions to go with your pattern:

✔ What supplies must be on hand before staring the project?
✔ Will a sewing machine be necessary, or can it be sewn by hand?
✔ Does the design call for particular types of stitches?
✔ What is the concept for the final project?

Step 3 Interview Someone Who Uses Sewing in their Work

Interview a seamstress, tailor, clothing designer, or anyone who sews professionally. Ask these questions:

✔ Do you think my pattern would work? Why or why not?
✔ What potential problems do you see in my design?
✔ What could I do to improve my design?

Use these interviewing skills when conducting your interview and these writing skills when writing the summary of notes from your interview.

Interviewing Skills
- Record interview responses and take notes.
- Listen attentively.

Writing Skills
- Use complete sentences.
- Use correct spelling and grammar.

Step 4 Create and Present Your Pattern

Use the Life Skills Project Checklist on the right to plan and complete your sketch and sewing pattern. Give an oral report on the project.

Use these speaking skills when presenting your final report.

Speaking Skills
- Speak clearly and concisely.
- Be sensitive to the needs of your audience.
- Use standard English to communicate.

Step 5 Evaluate Your Presentation

Your project will be evaluated based on:

- ✔ Your sketched design concepts.
- ✔ The sewing pattern of your clothing design.
- ✔ The step-by-step written instructions.
- ✔ The summary written from interview notes.
- ✔ Grammar and sentence structure.
- ✔ Presentation to the class.
- ✔ Creativity and neatness.

Evaluation Rubric Go to this book's Online Learning Center through glencoe.com for a rubric you can use to evaluate your final project.

NCTE 3 Apply strategies to interpret texts.
NCTM Geometry Use visualization, spatial reasoning, and geometric modeling to solve problems.

Life Skills Project Checklist

Research Clothing Design

✅ Sketch designs for a sewing project.

✅ Read sewing pattern booklets for ideas.

✅ Design a sewing pattern for something to wear.

✅ Interview someone who uses sewing skills as part of his or her job.

Writing Skills

✅ Write step-by-step instructions explaining how to use your pattern.

✅ Describe the style and purpose of your design.

✅ Write a summary from your interview with someone who sews professionally.

Present Your Findings

✅ Prepare a short presentation to show your clothing pattern, and explain how to sew your design.

✅ Invite the students of the class to ask any questions they may have. Answer these questions with responses that respect their perspectives.

✅ Add this project to your Life Skills binder.

Academic Skills

✅ Conduct research to gather information.

✅ Communicate effectively.

✅ Organize your presentation so the audience can follow along easily.

✅ Thoroughly express your ideas.

Chapter 19

Nutrition and Wellness

Chapter 20

Health and Fitness

Unit Preview

This unit is about how to stay healthy by managing your nutrition and physical activity. In this unit, you will learn about:

- Eating healthful meals that include all the food groups.

- Using the Dietary Guidelines and MyPyramid.

- The importance of fitness to your physical and mental health.

- The roles exercise and nutrition play in maintaining a healthy weight.

Explore the Photo Answer Answers may include raw vegetables, hummus, fresh fruit, grilled chicken, vegetables, nuts, whole grain bread, salad.

Explore the Photo
Eating healthful foods is essential if you want to maintain your mental and physical health. *What are some healthful foods that you already eat and enjoy?*

Play with Your Food!

When you are done studying this unit, you will complete a project in which you will:

✓ Write a play about good nutrition and fitness.

✓ Interview an expert on diet and exercise.

✓ Perform your play in front of your class.

The prewriting activity below will help you get started.

 My Journal

Prewriting Activity
Take a Poll

Ask your classmates and friends what they think the most important health topics are for your age group. Suggest topics you may have read about such as junk food, diets, trans fat, and working out.

● What health topics are students interested in learning about?

● What health topics are most important to you? Why?

Chapter 19

Nutrition and Wellness

 Section 19.1

Nutrients for Health

■ **Main Idea** Eat healthful and balanced meals with nutrients to help regulate your body functions.

 Section 19.2

Healthful Eating

■ **Main Idea** Use the Dietary Guidelines from MyPyramid to promote a balanced diet.

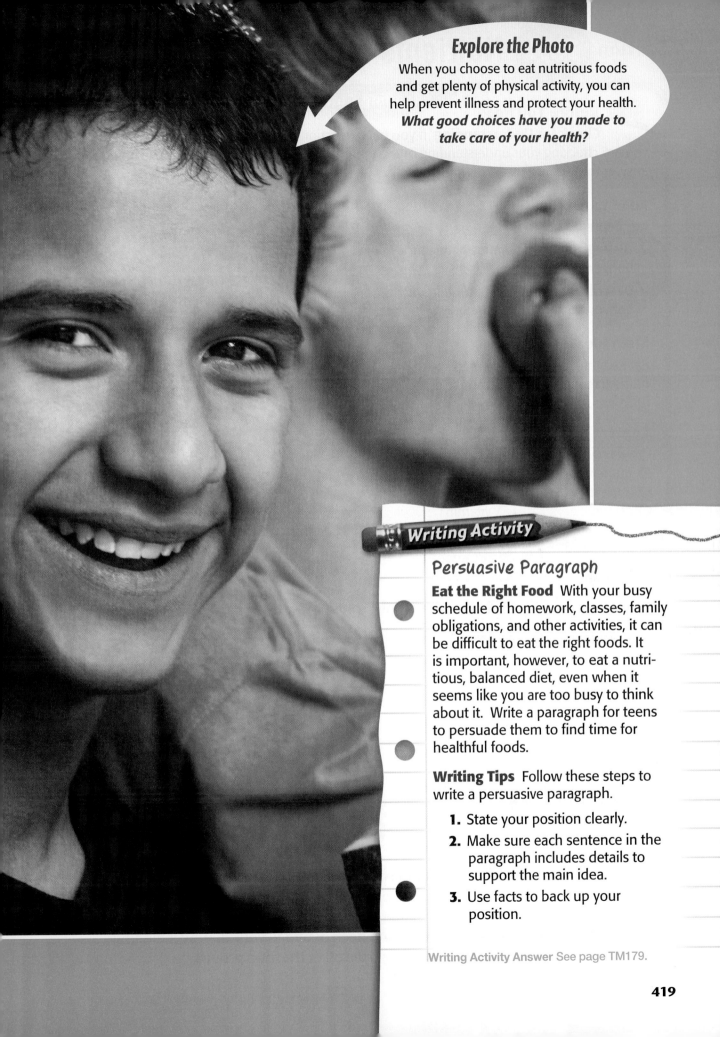

Explore the Photo
When you choose to eat nutritious foods and get plenty of physical activity, you can help prevent illness and protect your health. *What good choices have you made to take care of your health?*

Writing Activity

Persuasive Paragraph

Eat the Right Food With your busy schedule of homework, classes, family obligations, and other activities, it can be difficult to eat the right foods. It is important, however, to eat a nutritious, balanced diet, even when it seems like you are too busy to think about it. Write a paragraph for teens to persuade them to find time for healthful foods.

Writing Tips Follow these steps to write a persuasive paragraph.

1. State your position clearly.
2. Make sure each sentence in the paragraph includes details to support the main idea.
3. Use facts to back up your position.

Writing Activity Answer See page TM179.

Section 19.1 Nutrients for Health

Reading Guide

Before You Read

Check for Understanding If you have questions as you are reading, that means you are checking your understanding of the material. To get the most out of the text, try to answer those questions.

Read to Learn

Key Concepts

✓ **Distinguish** the difference between hunger and appetite.

✓ **Describe** the functions of proteins, carbohydrates, and fats in the human body.

Main Idea

Eat healthful and balanced meals with nutrients to help regulate your body functions.

Content Vocabulary

 wellness
 nutrient
○ appetite
○ calorie
○ protein
○ amino acid
○ carbohydrate

○ fiber
○ whole grain
○ cholesterol
○ vitamin
○ mineral
○ osteoporosis

Academic Vocabulary

■ adequate   ■ brittle

Graphic Organizer

As you read, write down the six nutrients found in food. Use a graphic organizer like the one shown to help you organize your information.

Nutrients

 Graphic Organizer Go to this book's Online Learning Center at glencoe.com to print this graphic organizer.

Academic Standards

English Language Arts

NCTE 8 Use information resources to gather information and create and communicate knowledge.

Mathematics

NCTM Number and Operations Understand numbers, ways of representing numbers, relationships among numbers, and number systems.

Social Studies

NCSS I C Culture Apply an understanding of culture as an integrated whole that explains the functions and interactions of language, literature, the arts, traditions, beliefs and values, and behavior patterns.

NCTE *National Council of Teachers of English*
NCTM *National Council of Teachers of Mathematics*

NSES *National Science Education Standards*
NCSS *National Council for the Social Studies*

Graphic Organizer Answer
proteins, carbohydrates, fats, vitamins, minerals, water

What is your favorite food? Is it pizza, or hamburgers, or maybe yogurt? Perhaps you are a vegetarian and you love vegetable lasagna. Eat a variety of foods to supply your body with the energy you need. Balance your diet by including appropriate foods from all of the food groups.

Look and Feel Good

Your diet affects the way you look and feel. Eating healthful foods can help you look your best. Reaching for your best level of health is called **wellness**. Exercise, adequate rest, and personal hygiene also contribute to your personal health and wellness.

Feeling good and being healthy go hand in hand. Along with exercise and rest, food affects how you feel, no matter what your age. Food is your source of energy for physical and mental activities. You need energy to perform well in school and in all your activities. Without adequate, or enough, nutrients, you may tire easily and feel less alert. A **nutrient** (ˈnoo-trē-ənt) is a substance in food that is important for the body's growth and maintenance. Proper nutrition has a direct effect on achievement. When you eat right, you are more likely to have the energy needed to perform mental and physical activities well. Eating right can help you look, feel, think, and act your best.

Nutrition Value Getting the right nutrients from the foods you eat is very important to your health. *What are some of the body processes which are affected by the nutrients you eat?*

As You Read

Connect Food tastes good, and eating the right foods can keep you healthy. What healthful foods have you eaten today?

Vocabulary

You can find definitions in the glossary at the back of this book.

As You Read Answer Answers may include fruits and vegetables, lean meat, fish, whole grain foods, low-fat milk.

Photo Caption Answer Nutrients affect body processes such as your heartbeat, blood flow, and breathing.

Succeed in School Studies show that students who eat breakfast every day perform better in school and have a longer attention span during class. Tell students to enjoy a healthful meal 1–2 hours after waking up.

SUCCEED IN SCHOOL!

Physical Health
Eat Nutritious Foods
Eating well-balanced meals can help you function at your best in school. When you have the right nutrients in your meals, it can help you focus on your school work and provide energy for other activities.

A healthful eating style helps protect you from illness. When you get the nutrients you need, your body is better able to fight infections, heal wounds, and recover quickly when you do get sick.

Satisfying Your Hunger

When your stomach growls, you are experiencing a sign of hunger. Hunger is the physical need to eat. Hunger tells you that your body needs food, but it does not tell you what to eat. It is up to you to learn to select healthful foods and decide how much to eat.

Appetite is different from hunger. **Appetite** is the desire to eat. When you smell fresh strawberries or a chocolate cake, you might experience an appetite for those foods without necessarily being hungry.

When your hunger is satisfied, it is time to stop eating. Some people still have an appetite, however, so they continue to eat. If people eat too much food, or food that is too high in calories, they may gain weight. A **calorie** is a unit that measures the energy used by the body and the energy that food supplies to the body. However, that energy is stored as fat if you eat food that has more calories than your body uses.

 Reading Check *Explain How can proper nutrition benefit achievement?*

Figure 19.1 What Do Nutrients Do?

Meet the Nutrients There are six kinds of nutrients and each one has an important function. *How do nutrients help the functions of the body?*

- **Proteins** help the body to build, repair, and maintain cells and tissue.
- **Carbohydrates** provide energy and fiber.
- **Fats** provide energy and supply essential fatty acids for normal growth and healthy skin.
- **Vitamins** help your body use other nutrients, store and use energy, and fight infection.
- **Minerals** help build sturdy bones and teeth, maintain healthy blood, and aid in the regular elimination of body wastes.
- **Water** carries nutrients to body cells, aids in digestion, removes wastes, and helps control your body temperature.

Nutrient Functions

Nutrients in food keep you healthy, help you grow, and give you energy. Nutrition is the study of nutrients and how the body uses them. Nutrients are released from food during digestion. Digestion is the process of breaking down food into a form the body can use. Nutrients are then absorbed into the bloodstream and carried to cells where they perform different, important functions. **Figure 19.1** describes the functions of the six kinds of nutrients.

Nutrients affect body processes such as your heartbeat, blood flow, and breathing. These processes, in turn, affect the way you feel and how much energy you have. They also affect the quality of your skin, hair, and nails. To keep your body functioning properly, you must choose foods that supply enough of each nutrient. Lack of nutrients can cause health problems.

Proteins

A **protein** is a type of nutrient that is needed to build, repair, and maintain body cells and tissues. Your skin, hair, blood, muscles, and vital organs are all made of proteins. During the teen years, you need proteins to help your body grow and develop to its adult size.

MATH YOU CAN USE

+ − × ÷ ENTER

Count Calories

Tony is trying to eat 2,700 calories per day, and would like to consume ⅓ of those calories at each meal. For lunch, he eats a large bag of potato chips (380 calories), a cheeseburger with mustard and ketchup (545 calories), and a can of soda (155 calories). What fraction of his total daily calories did Tony consume for lunch? Was this more or less than ⅓?

Math Concept **Comparing Fractions** To compare two fractions with different denominators, rewrite each one as an equivalent fraction with a common denominator. For example, to compare ⅚ and ¾, you would rewrite them as ¹⁰/₁₂ and ⁹/₁₂.

Starting Hint Add up the calories for the chips, cheeseburger, and soda. Write this total as the numerator of a fraction, with 2,700 as the denominator. Reduce to lowest terms. Then, compare that fraction to ⅓ by rewriting each fraction with common denominators.

 For more math help, go to the Math Appendix located at the back of this book.

NCTM Number and Operations Understand numbers, ways of representing numbers, relationships among numbers, and number systems.

Math You Can Use Answer Total calories consumed = 380 + 545 + 155 = 1,080. Lunch consisted of ¹,⁰⁸⁰/₂,₇₀₀, or ⅖ of his daily total. To compare ⅖ to ⅓, rewrite the fractions as ⁶/₁₅ and ⁵/₁₅. Since ⁶/₁₅ > ⁵/₁₅, Tony consumed more than ⅓ of his daily calories at lunch.

Photo Caption Answer Amino acids build proteins that are needed to build, repair, and maintain body cells and tissues.

Combine Proteins Combining proteins will provide the essential amino acids your body needs. ***Why are amino acids important to your health?***

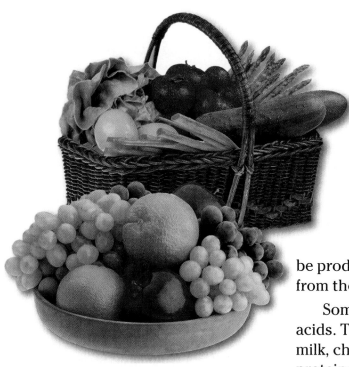

Fiber Source Fruits and vegetables are good sources of fiber. *Why is eating enough fiber important?*

Photo Caption Answer Fiber helps move food through the digestive system and eliminate waste from your body. Fiber may also reduce the risk for certain diseases, such as colon cancer.

Even after you stop growing, you still need proteins to help your body repair itself. Billions of worn-out body cells are replaced every day, and proteins are used to make those new cells.

Each protein is a different combination of amino acids. **Amino acids** are the building blocks that make up proteins. Your body manufactures some amino acids. Others, called essential amino acids, cannot be produced by your body. They must come from the food you eat.

Some foods contain all the essential amino acids. These foods, such as meat, fish, poultry, milk, cheese, and eggs, are called complete proteins. Other foods are good sources of protein, but they lack one or more of the essential amino acids. These foods, called incomplete proteins, come from plants and include dry beans, nuts, and grains.

By combining proteins from grains with proteins from dry beans or nuts, you can get all the essential amino acids that your body needs.

Carbohydrates, Fiber, and Whole Grains

Carbohydrates (ˌkär-bō-ˈhī-ˌdrāts) are the starches and sugars that give the body most of its energy. Starches are found in grains, such as oats, rice, and wheat. Foods made from grain, including bread, tortillas, pasta, and cereals, also provide starch. Potatoes, corn, dry beans, and nuts are additional sources of starch.

Natural sugars are found in fruits and milk, which are also high in other nutrients. Candy, cake, and soft drinks also contain sugar, but they are high in calories and low in other nutrients. They should be eaten less often than fruits and milk.

Almost all carbohydrates come from plant sources, which also provide fiber. **Fiber** is plant material that your body cannot digest. Although fiber is not a nutrient, eating the right amount of fiber-rich foods helps the body function normally. Fiber provides bulk, which helps move food through your digestive system. It also helps your body eliminate waste. A diet rich in high-fiber foods can reduce the risk for certain diseases, such as colon cancer.

Good sources of fiber include foods made from whole grains. **Whole grains** are foods that contain the entire edible grain. Whole wheat breads, whole wheat cereals, and popcorn are whole grain foods. Fruits and vegetables, especially those with edible skins, stems, and seeds, also contain fiber.

Fats

Like carbohydrates, fats are an important source of energy. Fats contain twice as many calories as carbohydrates. There are 9 calories in 1 gram of fat. Saturated fats are the least healthful type of fat. Read labels to find out how much fat is in the foods you eat.

Your body relies on fat cells to store energy and to help regulate body temperature. Your skin needs fats to stay smooth, and your nervous system needs them to work properly. Fats also carry several vitamins needed by the body.

Saturated fats are found in food from animal sources, such as meats, egg yolks, cheese, and butter. Saturated animal fats contain a waxy substance called **cholesterol** (kə-'les-tə-,rōl). Your body produces all the cholesterol it needs, so you do not need to add cholesterol to your diet. In fact, diets high in cholesterol have been linked to an increased risk of heart disease. Unsaturated fats come from plants. These fats are found mainly in vegetable oils, such as olive, corn, or canola oil. No more than 30 percent of the calories you consume should come from fat, with the majority being unsaturated fats.

Vitamins

A **vitamin** is a substance that is needed in small quantities to help regulate body functions. **Figure 19.2** on page 427 lists different vitamins and describes the ways in which these vitamins benefit your body.

The essential vitamins include A, B-complex, C, D, and E. Your body cannot make most vitamins, so you must get them from the foods you eat. These nutrients can easily be obtained from a variety of delicious foods.

Vitamin A Have you ever walked into a dark room after being in the bright sunlight? Vitamin A helps your eyes to adjust to the dark. It also helps keep your skin healthy and helps your body resist infection. Dark green, leafy vegetables, deep yellow vegetables, and dairy products are good sources of vitamin A.

Vitamin Source Dark green, leafy vegetables contain vitamin A. *Why is important to eat foods containing vitamin A?*

B-Complex Vitamins: Thiamine, Niacin, and Riboflavin
B-complex vitamins give you energy by helping your body use calories from carbohydrates, fats, and proteins. Riboflavin, found in dairy products, helps keep your eyes and skin healthy. Thiamine and niacin, found in meat, dry beans, and grain products, promote a healthy nervous system. B-complex vitamins come from many different foods. When selecting grain products, such as flour and bread, try to choose whole-grain or enriched foods.

Vitamin C Ascorbic acid, also called vitamin C, helps your body fight infection and helps wounds heal. It also helps to keep your gums healthy. Good sources of vitamin C include oranges, melons, berries, and dark green, leafy vegetables, such as spinach and broccoli.

Vitamin D Vitamin D helps your body absorb and use minerals, such as calcium and phosphorus. It is essential for normal bone and tooth development. Your body can make its own vitamin D when your skin is exposed to sunlight. Foods that provide vitamin D include fortified milk, fish oils, beef, butter, and egg yolks.

Vitamin E To keep red blood cells healthy, your body needs vitamin E. You can find it in vegetable oils, yellow vegetables, grains, nuts, and green leafy vegetables.

Minerals

Food also contains **minerals**, which are elements needed in small amounts for strong bones and teeth, healthy blood, and regular elimination of body wastes. Like vitamins, minerals are essential to good health.

Every day your body uses minerals. Minerals such as iron, zinc, and iodine, are needed only in small amounts. Calcium, phosphorus, and magnesium are needed in greater amounts. **Figure 19.2** describes the minerals your body needs and the various foods in which they can be found.

Calcium Young people need calcium to develop strong teeth and bones. Calcium is also necessary throughout life to reduce the risk of **osteoporosis** (ˌäs-tē-ō-pə-'rō-səs), a condition in which bones gradually lose their mineral content. Bones can become weak and brittle, or easy to break. Calcium also helps your muscles move and your heart beat.

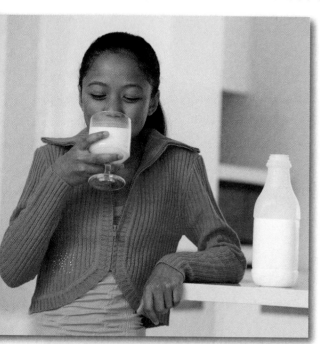

Milk and Calcium Milk is a good source of calcium. *What are some other sources of calcium?*

Figure 19.2 Vitamins and Minerals

Give Your Body What it Needs Vitamins and minerals are essential to good health. *Why is it better to get vitamins and minerals from healthful foods than to replace foods with vitamin and mineral supplements?*

Vitamins	Function and Benefits	Food Sources
Vitamin A	Promotes healthy skin, eyes, nose, mouth, throat	Dark green vegetables, deep yellow vegetables, fruits, eggs, dairy products
B-Complex Vitamins	Help carbohydrates, fats, and proteins produce energy	Whole-grain foods, pork, organ meats, dry beans, peas
■ **Thiamine**	Promotes healthy growth, appetite, digestion, nervous system	Whole-grain foods, pork, organ meats, dry beans, peas
■ **Riboflavin**	Promotes healthy skin, eyes	Milk, cheese, yogurt, eggs, organ meats, poultry, fish, enriched breads, cereals
■ **Niacin**	Promotes healthy digestive tract, nervous system, skin	Whole-grain foods, liver, meat, fish, poultry, nuts
Vitamin C (also called ascorbic acid)	Helps the body fight infection and heal wounds; promotes healthy gums	citrus fruits, berries, melon, broccoli, spinach, potatoes, tomatoes, green pepper, cabbage
Vitamin D	Works with calcium to build strong bones and teeth	Fortified milk, fish liver oil
Vitamin E	Keeps oxygen from destroying other nutrients and cell membranes	Vegetable oil, salad dressing, margarine, grains, fruits, some vegetables
Vitamin K	Helps blood clot	Green leafy vegetables, egg yolks

Minerals	Function and Benefits	Food Sources
Calcium	Promotes healthy teeth, bones, heart function, muscles, soft tissue, nerves, blood clotting	Milk, cheese, yogurt, green leafy vegetables, fish with edible bones
Fluoride	Helps make teeth strong	Drinking water
Iodine	Helps the thyroid gland work properly	Saltwater fish, iodized salt
Iron	Aids in the body's use of oxygen	Meat, liver, eggs, dry beans, dried fruits, whole-grain foods, spinach
Magnesium	Promotes and regulates many body functions and produces energy	Nuts, peanut butter, seeds, dry beans and peas, whole-grain foods, milk, fish, green leafy vegetables, bananas
Phosphorous	Promotes healthy bones and teeth; helps the body produce energy	Milk, yogurt, cheese, egg yolk, meat, fish, poultry
Potassium	Helps regulate body fluids and heart function	Orange juice, bananas, meat, nuts, dried fruits
Zinc	Promotes wound healing; affects growth, taste, appetite, smell	Meat, organ meats, eggs, poultry, seafood, cheese, milk
Sodium	Helps regulate body fluids and muscle function	Table salt, cured meats, pickles, many processed foods

Figure Caption Answer Supplements can be beneficial, but if nutrient-rich foods are available, it is better to eat the foods because they contain other nutrients necessary for good health.

When you bleed, calcium aids vitamin K in helping your blood clot. Calcium also helps keep your nerves and soft tissues healthy. The best sources of calcium are dairy products and dark green, leafy vegetables.

Iron Like calcium, iron is one of the most important nutrients. Iron is an essential component of blood. It helps carry oxygen to your brain, your muscles, and all of your body's cells. Oxygen helps your body produce energy for physical activity. Females need about twice as much iron as males. The best sources of iron are meat, poultry, dry beans, dried fruits, and dark green, leafy vegetables.

Water

Water helps regulate your body functions and carries nutrients to body cells. It aids in digestion, removes wastes, and helps control your body temperature. Water is lost through perspiration and urine, so you must replace it. You should drink at least eight glasses of water each day. When you play basketball, tennis, or engage in other physical activities, your body produces sweat, and you need even more water.

Section 19.1 After You Read

Review What You Have Learned

1. **Explain** how you can achieve a high level of wellness.
2. **Identify** good sources of Vitamin A.

Practice Academic Skills

 English Language Arts

3. Create an informative pamphlet that communicates the importance of minerals in a healthful meal plan. Use information from the chapter for your pamphlet. Find clip art, graphics, or photos to make your pamphlet attractive, informative, and easy to read.

> **NCTE 8** Use information resources to gather information and create and communicate knowledge.

 Social Studies

4. Think about how food plays a part in tradition and culture. Name one of your family's traditions which includes food. Does the food serve a purpose other than nutrition? Be prepared to share your findings and conclusions with the class.

> **NCSS I C** Apply an understanding of culture as an integrated whole that explains the functions and interactions of language, literature, the arts, traditions, beliefs and values, and behavior patterns.

Check Your Answers Check your answers at this book's Online Learning Center at glencoe.com.

Section 19.2 Healthful Eating

Reading Guide

Before You Read

Use Notes When you come across an unfamiliar section or term, write down the word or a question. After you finish the section, look up the terms or try to answer your questions based on what you have read.

Read to Learn

Key Concepts

✓ **Explain** how MyPyramid can help you have a healthy lifestyle.

✓ **Name** the consequences of being overweight.

✓ **Identify** examples of healthful snacks.

✓ **Describe** how to choose your meals when dining out.

Main Idea

Use the Dietary Guidelines from MyPyramid to promote a balanced diet.

Content Vocabulary

○ MyPyramid   ○ diabetes
○ portion   ○ sodium

Academic Vocabulary

■ component   ■ refined

Graphic Organizer

As you read, write down eight topics from the Dietary Guidelines. Use a graphic organizer like the one shown to help you organize your information.

Dietary Guidelines	
1.	5.
2.	6.
3.	7.
4.	8.

Graphic Organizer Go to this book's Online Learning Center at glencoe.com to print this graphic organizer.

Academic Standards

 English Language Arts

NCTE 8 Use information resources to gather information and create and communicate knowledge.

 Science

NSES A Students should develop abilities necessary to do scientific inquiry.

 Social Studies

NCSS III J People, Places, and Environments Analyze and evaluate social and economic effects of environmental changes and crises resulting from phenomena such as floods, storms, and drought.

NCTE *National Council of Teachers of English*
NCTM *National Council of Teachers of Mathematics*

NSES *National Science Education Standards*
NCSS *National Council for the Social Studies*

With so many food options, it is easy to see how it is sometimes difficult to choose the right foods to eat. Tempting advertisements for fast food and soda are often directed at young people. However, you can use the MyPyramid as a guideline for eating right. By following its suggestions, you can live a healthy lifestyle.

Graphic Organizer
Answer get enough nutrients, manage your weight, be physically active, eat key foods, limit fats, choose carbohydrates carefully, reduce sodium (salt) and increase potassium, handle food safely

As You Read

Connect Think about your weight. What are some of the influences that affect the way you see yourself?

As You Read Answer Answers may include self-perceptions, media, friends, family.

Vocabulary

You can find definitions in the glossary at the back of this book.

MyPyramid and the Dietary Guidelines

MyPyramid is a colorful representation of how to make healthful food choices and increase physical activity. Each colored band represents a food group. The width of each band is a guide to portion size. **Portion** is an appropriate amount of food for one person. The smallest band, the yellow one, represents oils and is not considered a food group. The person climbing the side of MyPyramid represents the physical fitness **component**, or part. Your level of physical activity varies depending on your age and also affects how you eat. People who are physically active need to eat more than less active people. Also, as you can see in **Figure 19.3**, nutrition requirements change depending on your age and what stage of life you are in. The important point to remember is that you need to eat foods from all the food groups to get the nutrients you need.

Caption Answer Answers may include eating more fruits and vegetables, eating fewer foods containing fats and added sugars, and balancing meals to make sure they contain appropriate amounts from all of the food groups.

MyPyramid
STEPS TO A HEALTHIER YOU

| GRAINS | VEGETABLES | FRUITS | MILK | PROTEINS |
| Make half your grains whole | Vary your veggies | Focus on fruits | Get your calcium-rich foods | Go lean with protein |

MyPyramid The keys to a healthy lifestyle are being aware of what you eat and following dietary guidelines. *What steps can you take to eat more healthfully?*

Figure 19.3 Nutrition Across the Life Span

Nutrition Stages There are different nutrition requirements for every age. *What are the nutrition requirements for your age group?*

Life Span Period	Nutrition Requirements
Pregnancy (includes nursing mothers)	Approximately 300 additional calories are required each day for increased energy needs.
Infancy (Birth-1 year)	Most of the infant's nutritional needs during the first year are met through human milk or infant formula.
Early Childhood (2-5 years)	Breakfast is especially important, and nutritious snacks help meet the child's daily nutrient needs.
Middle Childhood (6-11 years)	Snack foods may need to be monitored because consumption of sugary foods and empty calorie foods increases during this stage.
Adolescence (12-19 years)	An increased need for calcium occurs due to rapid bone growth. Teens need to increase their intake of foods from the milk group.
Young Adulthood (19-39 years)	Eating a well-balanced diet and exercising on a regular basis are good beginnings for young adults. Iron and calcium intakes are very important.
Middle Adulthood (40-65)	Eat a variety of foods, maintain desirable weight, avoid too much fat and cholesterol, increase fiber intake, avoid too much sugar and sodium, exercise regularly, refrain from smoking, and limit stress.
Older Adulthood (over 65 years)	A healthy diet can help reduce some of the effects of aging. Vitamins B_6, B_{12}, C, D, E, and thiamin, calcium, iron, and zinc are important. Regular exercise is needed.

Figure Caption Answer Adolescents (ages 12-19) tend to increase their intake of foods from the milk group because they require extra calcium due to rapid bone growth.

How can you make sure that your diet contributes to your wellness? **Figure 19.4** on page 432 describes the Dietary Guidelines, which take into account the important effect diet has on your health.

By following the Dietary Guidelines, you can ensure that you are eating the right types of foods. You can also reduce your chances of developing certain health problems. Of course, food alone cannot make you healthy. Good health also depends on your heredity and environment. Your exercise habits also play an important role in your health. Following the Dietary Guidelines can help keep you healthy, and perhaps even help improve your health.

Reading Check Answer The Dietary Guidelines help ensure that you are eating the right types of foods and reducing your chances of developing certain health problems.

✔ **Reading Check** *Explain* What are the benefits to following the Dietary Guidelines?

Figure 19.4 Dietary Guidelines

Improve Your Health To ensure you are eating the right types of foods, follow these Dietary Guidelines. *What else can you do to maintain and improve your health?*

- **Get enough nutrients within your calorie needs.** Choose a variety of nutritious foods and beverages from the basic food groups.

- **Maintain a healthy weight.** To maintain body weight in a healthy range, balance your intake of calories from food and beverages with the calories you burn in physical activities.

- **Be physically active every day.** Regular physical activity promotes health, well-being, and a healthy body weight. Teens should be physically active for at least 60 minutes every day.

- **Choose whole grains, fruits, vegetables, and milk.** Choose a healthy eating plan that emphasizes fruits, vegetables, whole grains, and fat-free or low-fat milk and milk products.

- **Limit fats and cholesterol.** For teens, total fat intake should only be 25 to 35 percent of the total calorie intake. Most fats should come from sources such as fish, nuts, and vegetable oils.

- **Be choosy about carbohydrate foods.** Choose fiber-rich fruits, vegetables, and whole grains often. Look for foods and beverages low in added sugars.

- **Reduce sodium (salt) and increase potassium.** Choose and prepare foods with less salt. Eat plenty of potassium-rich foods, such as fruits and vegetables.

- **Keep food safe.** Know how to prepare, handle, and store food safely to keep you and your family safe.

Figure Caption Answer Get enough rest and physical activity.

Maintain a Healthy Weight

A person who is at a healthy weight is not overweight or too thin. Being overweight is linked with illnesses such as high blood pressure, heart disease, stroke, cancer, and diabetes. **Diabetes** is a condition in which the body cannot control blood sugar properly. Although being too thin is less common, it is also linked with disease and a greater risk of early death.

How can you know if your weight is "healthy"? You should not compare your weight with that of your friends. There are differences among people of the same age and even the same height. For example, people with a large body frame usually weigh more than people of the same height with a smaller body frame. Also, people with a lot of muscle may also weigh more than people of the same height with less muscle. There are many different healthy weights for people of the same height. At this time in your life, growing and gaining weight are normal. To determine if your weight is right for you, consult your doctor. He or she can consider all the factors that contribute to a healthy weight for you.

Reading Check Answer You should not compare your body to others. You need to consult your doctor who will consider all the factors that contribute to a healthy weight for you.

 Reading Check *Examine How can you determine if your weight is right for you?*

How To...

Measure Food Portions

Actual portion sizes can be deceiving. When you fill your bowl with ice cream, you actually may be eating several helpings. Follow these guidelines to judge the right portion when a measuring cup is not handy.

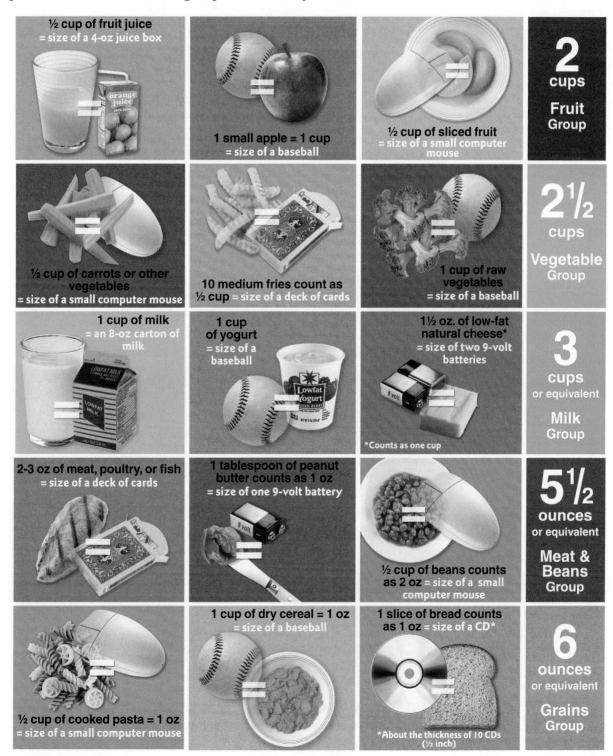

½ cup of fruit juice = size of a 4-oz juice box

1 small apple = 1 cup = size of a baseball

½ cup of sliced fruit = size of a small computer mouse

2 cups Fruit Group

½ cup of carrots or other vegetables = size of a small computer mouse

10 medium fries count as ½ cup = size of a deck of cards

1 cup of raw vegetables = size of a baseball

2½ cups Vegetable Group

1 cup of milk = an 8-oz carton of milk

1 cup of yogurt = size of a baseball

1½ oz. of low-fat natural cheese* = size of two 9-volt batteries

*Counts as one cup

3 cups or equivalent Milk Group

2-3 oz of meat, poultry, or fish = size of a deck of cards

1 tablespoon of peanut butter counts as 1 oz = size of one 9-volt battery

½ cup of beans counts as 2 oz = size of a small computer mouse

5½ ounces or equivalent Meat & Beans Group

½ cup of cooked pasta = 1 oz = size of a small computer mouse

1 cup of dry cereal = 1 oz = size of a baseball

1 slice of bread counts as 1 oz = size of a CD*

*About the thickness of 10 CDs (½ inch)

6 ounces or equivalent Grains Group

Eat Right

Eating the right foods can help you live a long and healthy life. It is important to check the labels of foods before you buy them. Not all foods labeled low fat or sugar-free are healthful. For instance, cereals made with whole grains may also be higher in fat than another cereal, but can still be very healthful. Compare several brands of an item to see which one is really most healthful.

Fats and Cholesterol

Fat is an important nutrient that provides energy. However, health experts recommend a diet that is low in fat and cholesterol. The amount of fat in your diet depends on what you eat over several days, not in one meal or type of food. For example, if you like a small amount of butter on your baked potato, you will not be getting too much fat as long as you limit the amount of other fats you eat. Some foods that contain fats and cholesterol, such as meats, milk, cheese, and eggs, also contain high-quality protein and important vitamins and minerals. Choose low-fat versions of these foods such as non-fat or low-fat milk and cheese. Eating meals and snacks low in fat and cholesterol can help lower your risk of obesity and heart disease.

Healthy Weight Different body types have different healthy weights. *What are some of the factors that affect what a person's healthy weight is?*

Cholesterol is carried through your bloodstream by lipoproteins. Two of the main kinds are high-density lipoprotein (HDL) and low-density lipoprotein (LDL). The cholesterol carried by HDL is sometimes called "good" cholesterol. That is because HDL helps remove cholesterol from the blood and may reduce the risk of heart disease. The "bad" LDL cholesterol builds up in the arteries and may increase the risk of heart disease.

Vegetables, Fruits, and Grains

These foods are an essential part of a varied and healthful diet. They contain complex carbohydrates, fiber, and other nutrients that contribute to good health. In addition, these foods are usually low in fats. If you eat the suggested amounts of these foods, you are also likely to decrease the fat that you are eating and get more fiber. Fiber is found naturally in whole-grain breads and cereals, dry beans and peas, vegetables, and fruits.

Sugar

Sugar is a type of carbohydrate that is found in many foods. Sugar provides calories, and most people like the way it tastes. Eating too much sugar is not healthful, but it is not necessary to avoid sugar entirely. Fruit contains natural sugar. Many foods such as cookies, some cereals, and soft drinks, contain **refined**, or chemically processed, sugar. Natural sugar is preferable to refined sugar so try to make most of your sugar intake natural sugar.

Salt and Sodium

Salt contains **sodium**, a mineral that helps regulate the amount of fluid in our bodies. You need some sodium to stay healthy. However, most Americans take in more sodium than they need. Too much sodium can lead to high blood pressure, heart attack, and stroke. These risks increase as you get older. To reduce the amount of sodium you eat, flavor your food with herbs and spices instead of salt. Avoid salty snacks, and choose processed food made with less sodium.

SCIENCE YOU CAN USE

Hidden Sodium

Salt may be hidden in foods that do not taste salty, such as cake or bread. Many cereal manufacturers add salt to cereal to bring out the taste of the sugar.

Procedure Survey your own cupboard. Choose one type of food, such as canned soup or cereal. Scan the ingredient lists for salt. The closer to the beginning of the list of ingredients, the more salt there is in the food product. Read the nutrition label to find out how much salt is in each serving.

Analysis Write down your findings. Note the amount of sodium (salt) listed on the nutrition label per serving. Indicate where in the ingredients list salt is listed.

NSES A Develop abilities necessary to do scientific inquiry.

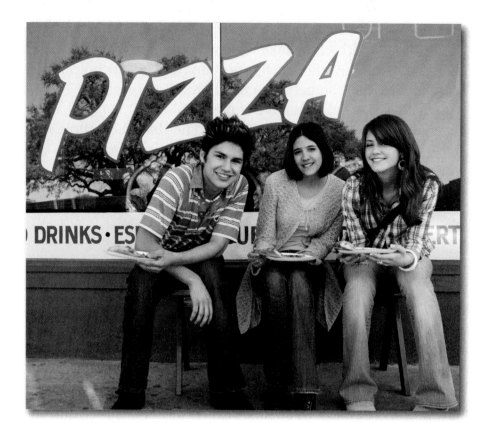

Snacks

Consume empty-calorie snacks in very limited amounts. Empty-calorie foods are foods that are high in calories but low in nutrients. Potato chips, candy, and soft drinks are examples of empty-calorie foods. They often contain large amounts of sugar, salt, and fat, but little nutrition. Select whole-grain items from the bread group. A wide variety of nutrient-dense snacks can be found in the fruit group and vegetable group. For example, blend orange juice and a banana with non-fat yogurt and ice cubes to make a healthful fruit smoothie. Mix nuts, raisins, pretzels, and dry cereal to form a healthful grab-and-go snack.

Reading Check *Identify What are some examples of foods that are high in calories but low in nutrients?*

Dining Out

Do you enjoy dining out? Maybe you like getting together with friends over a meal. Perhaps your family enjoys eating at a restaurant to try new foods. When you dine out, remember to choose your meals with the same attention to nutrition as when you eat at home.

As you look at a menu, the most important point to remember is to choose foods from all of the food groups. Here are some tips for ordering when you dine out:

- Eat only until you feel satisfied. Overeating is more common when dining out.
- Most portion sizes are larger than a serving. Bring left-overs home.
- Select dishes that are low in fat, sugar, salt, and calories. For example, baked potatoes have much less fat than French fries.
- Choose nutrient-dense dishes. For example, order whole-wheat or vegetable pasta. Instead of soft drinks or milk shakes, order juice or milk.
- Remember that sauces and salad dressings add calories. Choose sauces made with tomatoes, rather than sauces made with butter and cream. Ask for dressing on the side of your salad, so you can control the amount.
- Limit desserts. Consider sharing one dessert with your dining companions.

Section 19.2 After You Read

Review What You Have Learned

1. **Explain** what the person climbing the side of MyPyramid represents.
2. **Determine** the best way to know if your weight is right for you.
3. **Identify** the effect of too much sodium in your diet.
4. **Describe** tips for ordering when you are dining out.

Practice Academic Skills

 English Language Arts

5. Prepare a presentation for younger children about how to use MyPyramid. Use information from the chapter and other resources to best communicate how younger children can make good choices for eating. Be ready to share your presentation with elementary students.

> **NCTE 8** Use information resources to gather information and create and communicate knowledge.

 Social Studies

6. Conduct research to learn about environmental factors that can affect food production. Is there any way we can anticipate these and plan for them? If an environmental event negatively affects food production, is there anything we can do to improve the situation? Write a summary of your discoveries.

> **NCSS III J** Analyze and evaluate social and economic effects of environmental changes and crises resulting from phenomena such as floods, storms, and drought.

Check Your Answers Check your answers at this book's Online Learning Center at glencoe.com.

Discovering Careers

Do you like to cook? Are you interested in nutrients and how to eat well? Do you want to help people learn how to make their own healthful food choices? If you answered yes to any of those questions, you might want to consider a future career in the nutrition field. The following chart explores several careers in nutrition.

Career Activities ▼

At School

1 Select three of the careers listed. Research the education, training, and work experience required for each career. Write a summary of your results.

At Home

2 Prepare a dinner menu for your family using MyPyramid as your guideline.

At Work

3 Name five ways you can practice good nutrition and wellness in the workplace. Share your findings with your classmates.

In the Community

4 Contact and interview someone in your community who works in nutrition. Ask this person to describe what his or her typical work day is like. Share what you learned with your class.

Job Title	Job Description
Nutritionist	Develops nutrition education materials and classes. Teaches nutrition education courses. Counsels pregnant women on proper nutrition.
Dietitian	Plans therapeutic diets. Oversees preparation and service of meals. Consults with health care personnel to determine nutritional needs and diet restrictions.
Food and Drug Inspector	Inspects establishments where foods, drugs, and cosmetics are manufactured. Investigates handling of consumer products. Enforces legal standards of sanitation.
Hospital Chef	Oversees food preparation for hospital patients. Trains and supervises kitchen staff. Uses safe food-handling procedures. Develops menus for the special requirements of patients.

Learn More Online glencoe.com

Career Investigations Go to this book's Online Learning Center for activities and worksheets to help you explore careers.

Career Activities Answer Answers for these activities can be found on page TM179.

Chapter Summary

Section 19.1 Nutrients for Health
You can have an appetite without being hungry. Eating a diet low in fat and cholesterol can lower your risk for obesity and heart disease. Proteins are needed to build, maintain, and repair your body. Carbohydrates provide energy. Fats provide energy, keep skin smooth, and help your nervous system work. Vitamins, minerals, and water help regulate your body functions. All contribute to your good health.

Section 19.2 Healthful Eating
MyPyramid and the Dietary Guidelines help promote a balanced diet. A person who is at a healthy weight is not overweight or underweight. Eating the right foods can help you live a long and healthy life. Vegetables, fruits, and grains are an essential part of a varied and healthful diet. Empty-calorie snacks and desserts should be limited. When you dine out, choose your meals carefully.

Words You Learned

1. Use each of these content and academic vocabulary words in a sentence.

Content Vocabulary
- ○ wellness (p. 421)
- ○ nutrient (p. 421)
- ○ appetite (p. 422)
- ○ calorie (p. 422)
- ○ protein (p. 423)
- ○ amino acid (p. 423)
- ○ carbohydrate (p. 424)
- ○ fiber (p. 424)
- ○ whole grain (p. 425)
- ○ cholesterol (p. 425)
- ○ vitamin (p. 425)
- ○ mineral (p. 426)
- ○ osteoporosis (p. 426)
- ○ MyPyramid (p. 430)
- ○ portion (p. 430)
- ○ diabetes (p. 432)
- ○ sodium (p. 435)

Academic Vocabulary
- ■ adequate (p. 421)
- ■ brittle (p. 426)
- ■ component (p. 430)
- ■ refined (p. 435)

Review Key Concepts

2. **Distinguish** the difference between hunger and appetite.

3. **Describe** the functions of proteins, carbohydrates, and fats in the human body.

4. **Explain** how MyPyramid can help you have a healthy lifestyle.

5. **Name** the consequences of being overweight.

6. **Identify** examples of healthful snacks.

7. **Describe** how to choose your meals when dining out.

Critical Thinking

8. **Determine** if there are any fast-foods or beverages that you enjoy that are healthful.

9. **Evaluate** your diet for a week based on MyPyramid and the Dietary Guidelines.

Real-World Skills and Applications

Problem-Solving

10. Choosing Restaurants Compile nutrition information from three different restaurants in your area. Using information from MyPyramid and the Dietary Guidelines, make a list of the top three main dishes from each restaurant. Suggest healthful appetizers, side dishes, beverages, and dessert options.

Technology Applications

11. Create a Spreadsheet Using spreadsheet software, create a spreadsheet to keep track of the fruits and vegetables you eat. Record the number of servings of each fruit and vegetable you eat every day for one week. At the end of the week, show the varieties and your total servings. Review your results, then decide if you are eating enough fruits and vegetables, or if you need to add more to your meals and snacks.

Financial Literacy

12. Comparison Shopping Packaging and processing makes food items more expensive. You may be surprised to find what the cost of processed snacks and foods is. With your family, write out a shopping list for one week of meals at your home. Make your usual list, and then create another list that includes only foods that meet MyPyramid and the Dietary Guidelines. Choose healthful foods and snacks such as fruits and vegetables instead of processed or sugar-filled snacks. Take both lists to the grocery store and track the cost for each list. What is the difference in cost? Which list is the most expensive? What changes could you and your family make based on the results of your findings? How can you live a healthier lifestyle?

13. State of Nutrition Draw or print out a map that shows the outlines of a region in the United States, such as the Southwest, the Pacific Northwest, or the Eastern Seaboard. For each state in your selected region, find out what foods are produced there. For example, Wisconsin is known for its cheese products. Draw a picture of the food product in the outline of the state that produces it.

14. Wellness Organizations Conduct research to find out about government and community organizations that help people with nutrition and wellness issues. Make a list of low-cost or no-cost organizations that provide people with information about such topics as prenatal care, nutrition assistance, or food delivery for individuals who cannot leave their homes. Prepare a brief presentation on your findings to the class.

15. Organic Foods With permission from your parents or teacher, go online to find information about organic foods. What does organic mean? What kinds of organic food products can you find in grocery stores? How much do they cost in comparison to non-organic foods? Include your list in your Life Skills Binder.

Academic Skills

 English Language Arts

16. Write an Advertisement You have been asked to create a full-page advertisement for your local newspaper that shows how to apply the guidelines from MyPyramid into daily eating habits. The advertisement needs to appeal to a variety of readers with colorful graphics, catchy phrases, and photos. Use poster board to create the advertisement and share with your class.

> **NCTE 8** Use information resources to gather information and create and communicate knowledge.

 Social Studies

17. Research Family Food Choose a cultural background from your own family history. Research the kinds of food that the culture has eaten historically. How has the diet of this particular culture affected its health and life span? How do you incorporate this lifestyle and diet into your family today? Write an overview of what you have found.

> **NCSS I C Culture** Apply an understanding of culture as an integrated whole that explains the functions and interactions of language, literature, the arts, traditions, beliefs and values, and behavior patterns.

 Mathematics

18. Limiting Fat Jennifer's health class inspired her to start a more healthful eating plan. Her doctor recommended that she consume 2,200 calories a day. Yesterday, she calculated that she consumed 110 grams of fat during the day. What percent of Jennifer's total calories came from fat? If she wishes to reduce her fat intake to 30% of her daily calories, how many grams of fat should she have per day?

Math Concept **Calculating Percents**
To find what percent a number is of another number, divide the first number by the second number, multiply by 100, and add the % symbol.

Starting Hint There are 9 calories in one gram of fat. Jennifer's total fat calories equal 110×9. Divide that total by 2,200 and multiply by 100 to find her current fat percentage. Reverse the process using the 30% amount to determine her optimal fat intake in grams.

> **NCTM Problem Solving** Apply and adapt a variety of appropriate strategies to solve problems.

Standardized Test Practice

Essay

Read the writing prompt and write an essay using details and examples to illustrate your points.

> **Test-Taking Tip** Plan out your essay before you begin writing. Jot down the main points or details you want to focus on in the margins of your test. Refer to these points frequently as you write. This will help you remain focused.

19. Living a healthy lifestyle is a goal we should all have. Write an essay describing a person you know who is living a healthy lifestyle. Specifically describe the choices that person makes and how he or she lives a healthy lifestyle. Your essay should inspire readers to make their lifestyle healthier.

Chapter **20**

Health and Fitness

Section 20.1

Physical Activity

■ **Main Idea** Choosing to include physical activity in your daily routine can improve your overall state of wellness.

Explore the Photo Answer Physical activity promotes health, helps control weight, makes you stronger, helps reduce stress, and it can be a lot of fun, especially when you join in activities with others.

Section 20.2

Body Weight and Health

■ **Main Idea** The best way to maintain a healthy body weight is to balance nutritous meals with physical activity.

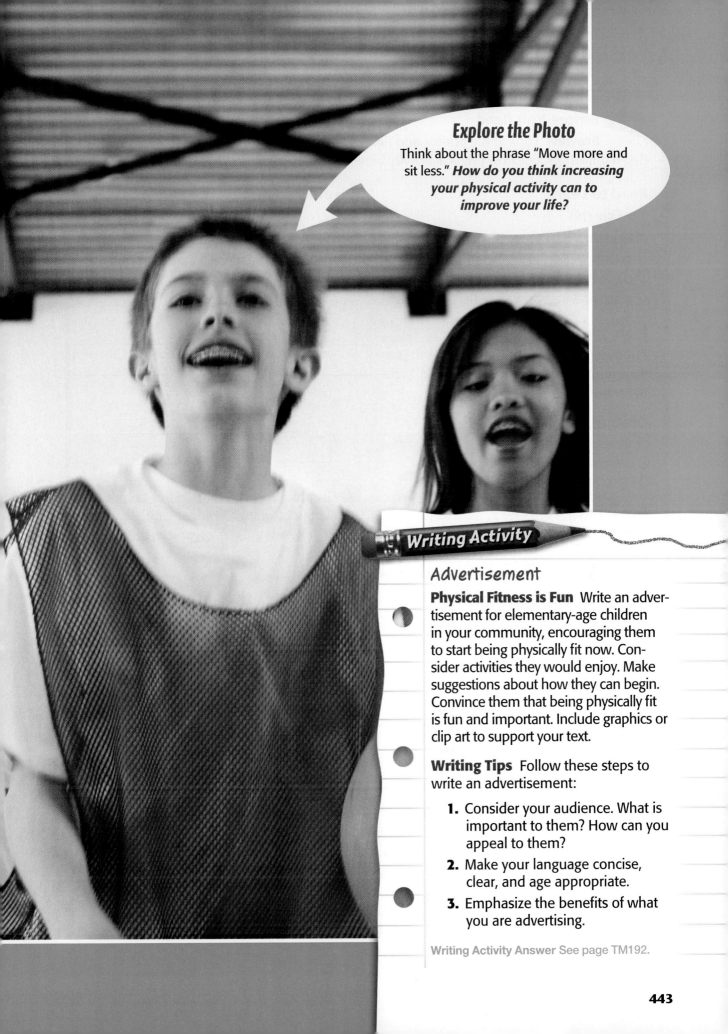

Explore the Photo
Think about the phrase "Move more and sit less." *How do you think increasing your physical activity can to improve your life?*

Writing Activity

Advertisement

Physical Fitness is Fun Write an advertisement for elementary-age children in your community, encouraging them to start being physically fit now. Consider activities they would enjoy. Make suggestions about how they can begin. Convince them that being physically fit is fun and important. Include graphics or clip art to support your text.

Writing Tips Follow these steps to write an advertisement:

1. Consider your audience. What is important to them? How can you appeal to them?
2. Make your language concise, clear, and age appropriate.
3. Emphasize the benefits of what you are advertising.

Writing Activity Answer See page TM192.

Section **20.1** Physical Activity

Graphic Organizer Answer
(1) burns calories, (2) helps heart and lungs work better, (3) tones muscles and skin, (4) controls appetite, (5) relieves tension.

Schoolwork takes up much of Aaron's time. He has chores to do at home, and he has an after-shool job delivering fliers for local restaurants. Aaron also spends time with friends. Even though Aaron is busy, he still finds time to be physically active and to eat well. He stays fit by riding his bike, skating, and swimming at the community pool. What do you do to stay healthy and fit?

Wellness, Fitness, and Your Health

Wellness is taking positive steps toward your overall good health. Wellness has two main goals. One is to keep you healthy, and the other is to help you prevent disease and illness. When you choose wellness, you choose to take care of yourself. It is important that you make the effort now to become informed and to make smart choices that can help protect you for the rest of your life.

When you are physically fit, you look and feel your best. A healthy, fit body means you take care of yourself. **Fitness** is the ability to handle daily events in a healthy way. Fitness means that you:

- Have the energy to do your schoolwork and chores, with enough leftover to have fun too.
- Are confident about your abilities.
- Make physical activity and exercise a part of your life every day.
- Keep your weight at the right level for you.
- Can better deal with stress and the ups and downs of life.

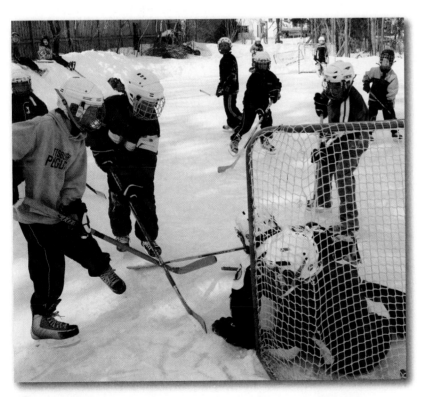

🔊 **Get Outdoors** Outdoor sports are ways to have fun while staying healthy and fit. *What types of outdoor physical activity do you enjoy?*

Photo Caption Answer Answers may include any outdoor team sports (volleyball, soccer, or baseball), or bicycling, hiking, surfing, or going for walks.

 As You Read

Connect Think about the physical activities you enjoy most. How can you make them part of your fitness routine?

As You Read Answer Answers may include anything from finding time on a weekly basis to play basketball or volleyball with friends, to riding a bicycle or walking to school or work when possible.

◼️ **Vocabulary**

You can find definitions in the glossary at the back of this book.

Succeed in School Take opportunities to have students work in pairs, especially with students who do not know each other well. Remind students that all good friends started out as strangers to each other.

 SUCCEED IN SCHOOL!

Build Self-Esteem
Make Friends Make an effort to develop close friendships. These friends will offer support when you need it. It is important to have good friends and also to be a good friend.

● ● ● ● ● ● ● ● ● ● ● ●

Hands-On LAB

Walking as Exercise

In this activity you will learn how to incorporate walking into your regular activities. A brisk walk can burn up to 300 calories an hour. Before you begin, read through the entire Hands-On Lab assignment. Write down any questions that you have about the activity. Reread the text or ask your teacher for help if you need it.

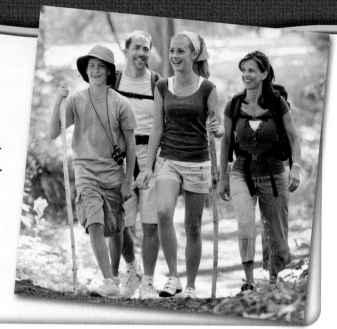

Supplies

✓ Comfortable clothes
✓ Shoes designed for walking
✓ Notebook
✓ Digital step counter (optional)

Develop Your Plan

- Decide how far you want to walk.
- Consider the weather conditions.
- Find routes outdoors and indoors, such as a shopping mall.
- Determine where you can walk safely.

Implement Your Plan

- Dress in comfortable clothes appropriate for weather conditions.
- Wear comfortable walking shoes.
- Walk the route or routes you chose.
- If possible, walk with a friend, family member, or pet.
- Walk at least once a week to start.

- Increase your frequency and distance each week for a month.
- Keep a log of your distance and time walked.
- Record any changes you notice in your physical fitness.

Evaluate Your Results

How did you decide where to you walk? How far and for how long did you walk the first time? How much distance and time did you add to your walks? What differences did you notice in your physical fitness? Write one or more paragraphs to explain your answers.

 Projects and Activities Go to this book's Online Learning Center through glencoe.com for more labs and activities.

Evaluate Your Results Answer Answers will vary. Students should indicate where they walked (mall, hiking trail, neighborhood), and how they made their choices (weather conditions, safety). Students should keep a log of time, distance, and physical changes. Possible physical effects may include: walking up stairs with greater ease, more stamina, more energetic, motivated to exercise more.

You cannot be fit unless you are physically active. By exercising regularly you will enjoy all the benefits of fitness:

- You can feel more positive about yourself. Knowing you are taking care of your body is good for your self-esteem.
- You can look your best. Physical activity helps you control weight and gives you a healthy appearance.
- Day-to-day tasks may seem easier because your energy level may improve.
- Relax and sleep more easily.
- Your physical and mental stamina may increase. **Stamina** is the ability to focus on or perform a single activity for a long time. For example, you may be able to dance without getting too tired, and you may be able to pay more attention in class and learn more.

There are plenty of enjoyable, inexpensive ways to exercise. What is important is that you make physical activity a regular part of your life. For example, Jennifer walks to school instead of taking the bus. Her friend Nick plays on a softball team and enjoys getting together with friends to play volleyball on weekends.

 Reading Check *Name What are the two main goals of wellness?*

Financial Literacy

Exercise Classes

Lucy has recently signed up for a membership at her local gym. She enjoys using the gym's strength and cardio equipment, but she is also interested in the classes the gym offers, such as aerobics, yoga, and kickboxing. However, the classes are not included in Lucy's regular membership. She has the option of paying $2.50 for each class she takes. Another option is to upgrade her membership and take an unlimited number of classes for an extra $15 each month. How many classes would she need to take each month to make the $15 per month upgrade plan the less expensive option?

Math Concept **Solving Algebraic Equations**
Use a variable such as x to represent an unknown quantity. Rearrange the equation step by step so that the variable is on one side of the equals sign, and all other numbers are on the other.

Starting Hint Let x stand for the number of classes. To find the number of classes where the prices of both options are the same, write an equation: $2.50x = 15$. Solve for x by dividing both sides by $2.50.

NCTM Algebra Solve problems that arise in mathematics and in other contexts.

 For math help, go to the Math Appendix at the back of the book.

Financial Literacy Answer If x stands for the number of classes, then both options will be equal if $2.50x = 15$, or $x = 15 \div 2.50 = 6$. Thus, if she takes more than 6 classes each month, the $15 per month option will be less expensive. If she takes fewer than 6 classes, the $2.50-per-class option will be less expensive. If she takes exactly 6 classes, both options are equal.

Reading Check Answer Promote health and prevent disease.

Exercise and Physical Activity

Physical activity is essential if you want to **obtain**, or reach, and maintain a healthy body weight. Whether you want to lose weight, gain weight, or maintain your weight, physical activity has many benefits.

Calories Physical activity burns calories. During physical activity, your body burns up calories from the food you eat. A calorie is a unit of energy. By using calories for energy, your body will store fewer calories as body fat. **Figure 20.1** shows how activities you may be doing can help you burn calories.

There is no way to burn fat in a specific area of the body. Physical activity burns calories and fat from all parts of the body. That is why a variety of physical activity helps your overall appearance.

Heart and Lungs Staying physically active helps your heart and lungs work at peak function. **Aerobic** (ˌer-ˈō-bik) activities are continuous, rhythmic activities that improve the efficiency of your heart and lungs. Aerobic activities such as running, bicycling, and swimming increase your intake of oxygen and help improve circulation.

Flexibility Being flexible allows you to kneel, bend, turn, and throw. It also helps reduce your risk of injury. You can improve your flexibility by doing activities that involve stretching and bending.

Appetite Control Physical activity can help relieve stress and tension, which can trigger a desire to eat more or less than you normally would.

Figure Caption Answer
Answers may include skating, basketball, gymnastics, dancing, or walking a dog.

Figure 20.1 Calories and Physical Activity

What Can You Do in 30 Minutes? Look at how many calories you can burn in 30 minutes by doing a variety of activities. *What other activities can you think of that are fun and burn calories at the same time?*

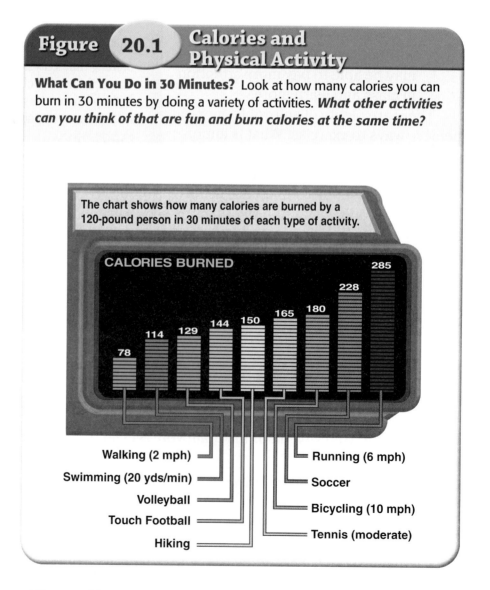

The chart shows how many calories are burned by a 120-pound person in 30 minutes of each type of activity.

CALORIES BURNED

78	Walking (2 mph)
114	Swimming (20 yds/min)
129	Volleyball
144	Touch Football
150	Hiking
165	Running (6 mph)
180	Soccer
228	Bicycling (10 mph)
285	Tennis (moderate)

Choose an Exercise Routine

To exercise regularly, you need to find an exercise routine that suits you and that you enjoy. From walking to dancing to team sports, the options are endless.

Organized Exercise Volleyball, baseball, basketball, and soccer are just a few types of organized ways to participate in physical activity. Sign up to be a part of a team, or organize your friends for a regular game.

Indoor Exercise You can lift small hand weights or work out on larger machines to build muscle and bone density. You can also use cardio machines indoors such as a treadmill, elliptical, or stationary bike.

Outdoor Exercise Walking, running, swimming, biking, and skating are activities you can enjoy outdoors. Being out in the fresh air and sunshine can be very motivating. Find an outdoor activity that you look forward to.

Exercise Anywhere Sit-ups, push-ups, jumping rope, martial arts, and yoga are examples of physical activities you can do anywhere, both indoors or outdoors. These types of activities are often easy to incorporate into your lifestyle since you can do them anywhere, and they require little or no special equipment.

Character Counts

Independence

Janet wants to run in a10k race for a local charity, but she needs to get in shape. It is hard for Janet to train because her friends are not interested in training, and her family is too busy to train with her. The race is two months away, and Janet believes she needs to run four times a week for at least an hour, building up to more time as the run draws near.

You Make the Call

How can Janet get her training done without the support of her friends and family? How can she benefit by training on her own? Write a paragraph explaining what Janet should do and why.

Character Counts Answer Since this is something Janet really wants to do, she can show her independence by creating her own training schedule and working it into her daily routine. This can help her build self-esteem by doing something on her own, and it will also benefit the charity.

Be More Active

There are many ways to put more movement into your life. You do not have to be an athlete to be active. Aim for at least 60 minutes of physical activity every day. You can do it all at once, or spread it out in 15- or 20-minute periods. Try these ideas:

Use your feet. When possible, walk instead of getting a ride.

Use your wheels. Skating and biking are great ways to get moving.

Take the stairs. Avoid elevators and escalators. Get your energy up by using the stairs.

Let music get you moving. Dance alone or with friends.

Do chores. Many chores, such as dusting, raking leaves, and taking out the trash can get you moving.

Help others. See if you have neighbors who need help with chores, pet walking, or yard work.

Play and have fun! Do what you enjoy, as long as it involves movement.

Section 20.1 After You Read

Review What You Have Learned

1. **Explain** the positive ways fitness helps you handle daily events.
2. **Identify** the benefits of exercise.

Practice Academic Skills

 English Language Arts

3. Write an essay that encourages teens to be fit. Include benefits of fitness with specific examples of how fitness helps you look and feel your best.

> **NCTE 4** Use written language to communicate effectively.

 Social Studies

4. Research the benefits of organized exercise versus more individual exercise. How can each aid in the development of not only a person's fitness and lifelong commitment to exercise but also other important characteristics. Be prepared to share you findings with you classmates.

> **NCSS IV D** Apply concepts, methods, and theories about the study of human growth and development, such as physical endowment, learning motivation, behavior, perception, and personality.

 Check Your Answers Check your answers at this book's Online Learning Center at glencoe.com.

Section 20.2 Body Weight and Health

Reading Guide

Before You Read

How Can You Improve? What reading strategies helped you on the last test you took? Make a list of ways to improve your strategies in order to succeed on your next exam.

Read to Learn

Key Concepts

✓ **List** the risks associated with obesity.

✓ **Explain** the most healthful way to lose excess weight.

✓ **Identify** how eating disorders can destroy your health.

✓ **Recognize** the causes of eating disorders.

Main Idea

The best way to maintain a healthy body weight is to balance nutritious meals with physial activity.

Content Vocabulary

○ obesity
○ fad diet
○ eating disorder
○ anorexia nervosa
○ bulimia nervosa
○ binge eating

Academic Vocabulary

■ expend   ■ fast

Graphic Organizer

As you read, identify the three most common eating disorders. Use a graphic organizer like the one shown to help you organize your information.

Eating Disorders

 Graphic Organizer Go to this book's Online Learning Center at glencoe.com to print this graphic organizer.

Academic Standards

 English Language Arts

NCTE 5 Use different writing process elements to communicate effectively.

 Science

NSES F Develop understanding of personal and community health.

Social Studies

NCSS IV J Individual Development and Identity Examine factors that contribute to and damage one's mental health and analyze issues related to mental health and behavioral disorders in contemporary society.

NCSS I A Culture Analyze and explain the ways groups, societies, and cultures address human needs and concerns.

NCTE *National Council of Teachers of English*
NCTM *National Council of Teachers of Mathematics*
NSES *National Science Education Standards*
NCSS *National Council for the Social Studies*

Graphic Organizer Answer
anorexia nervosa, bulimia nervosa, binge eating

Knowing what is healthful for you and your body is a life-long commitment. Though some teens may use celebrities or sports figures as models for the perfect body, it is important for everyone to accept the body they have and work to make it the best it can be. The best way to keep your body healthy is to eat well and exercise regularly.

◇ Vocabulary

You can find definitions in the glossary at the back of this book.

As You Read Answer Students should consider how they perceive their body: by their own standard of fitness or by someone else's level (for example, comparing themselves to movie stars, fashion models, or professional athletes, which is not a healthy way to perceive one's body).

Succeed in School Ask students if they feel pleased when someone offers help or a friendly gesture. Tell them it works both ways: the person offering the help feels pleased, too, because helping others is a way to feel good about yourself.

SUCCEED IN SCHOOL!

Build Self-Esteem

Help Others Part of developing self-esteem is knowing that you can help others. You feel good about yourself when you offer support to your family or friends, or when you take part in community activities such as visiting the elderly or working with children.

Healthy Body Weight

Are you happy with your weight? Do you think that you are too heavy or too thin? People who maintain a healthy body weight are neither overweight nor underweight. Being overweight can lead to obesity. **Obesity** is a condition in which a person's weight is 20 percent or more above his or her healthy weight. Obese people are at greater risk for such illnesses as diabetes and heart disease.

Being underweight is unhealthy, too. People who are underweight often are not eating enough or properly. This means that they are not getting the nutrients they need.

✔ **Reading Check** **Distinguish** *How is being underweight considered unhealthy?*

Reading Check Answer An underweight person is not eating enough of the right foods and to get the necessary nutrients.

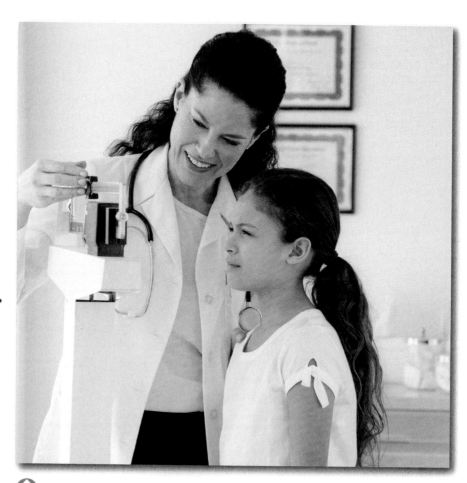

🔘 **Healthy Weight** Your healthy body weight depends on your height and body type. ***How does being overweight or underweight affect your health?***

Photo Caption Answer There is a greater risk for illnesses, such as diabetes and heart disease. You may not be getting the nutrients you need. Also, it can lead to low self-esteem and body image issues.

Healthy and Unhealthy Weight Loss

Think of controlling your weight as a balancing act. You have to balance the calories you get from the foods you eat with the calories you **expend**, or use, for energy. You gain weight when you consume more calories than your body uses. You lose weight when your body uses more calories than you consume. To maintain your weight, you must make sure that the calories you eat equal those you burn as energy.

Many teens think that they need to lose or gain weight. They believe that they have to eat or avoid certain foods or skip meals. It is important to eat a balanced diet. Include foods you enjoy, but limit the amount of fats, oils, and sweets. The most healthful way to lose excess weight is to take in fewer calories and participate in more physical activities.

Fad Diets

Achieving a healthy body weight through physical activity and a well-balanced diet takes time. Only a balanced meal plan combined with physical activity will work for healthy weight loss or maintenance, and long-term success. If you are overweight or obese, you might be tempted to lose weight quickly by going on a fad diet. A **fad diet** promises quick weight loss through unrealistic or unhealthful means.

COMMUNITY CONNECTIONS

Be a Role Model
Volunteer with a youth agency that coordinates physical activities for younger children. Be a trail guide, a coach, or a role model for children to be fit and healthy.

Discover International... Fitness

Yoga
The word yoga means union in Sanskrit, the language of ancient India where yoga began. The union is the relationship between the mind, body, and spirit. In the western world, yoga is most commonly understood as physical exercises and stretching. However, yoga is more than just stretching. It is about creating balance in the body through developing both strength and flexibility. This is done through the performance of poses or postures, each of which has specific physical benefits.

Yoga [ˌyō-gə] a system of exercises, breathing, and meditation for achieving bodily or mental control and well-being.

NCSS I A Culture Analyze and explain the ways groups, societies, and cultures address human needs and concerns.

Balance Calories You can still eat your favorite foods, such as ice cream or potato chips, if you balance physical activity, healthful foods, and calories. *How does exercising affect the amount of calories you can consume?*

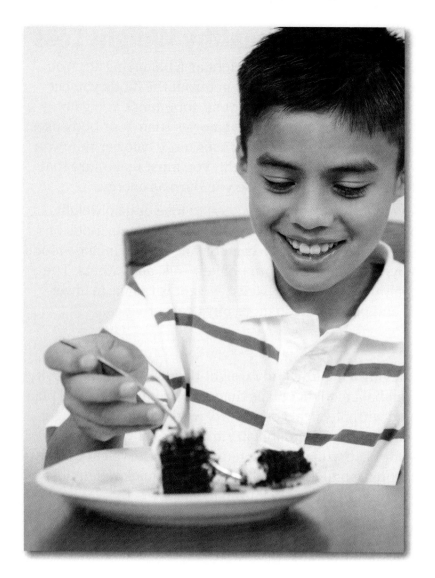

Avoid any diet that encourages:

- **Consuming only liquids.** A low-calorie, all-liquid diet does not offer the food energy, fiber, or nutrients that you need.
- **Fasting.** If you *fast*, or stop eating, even for a short period, your body will not get the nutrients and energy needed to function properly. When you starve yourself, your body will use protein for fat instead of muscle, which is dangerous to your heath.
- **The use of diet pills.** Diet pills contain drugs that can temporarily suppress, or hold back, your desire to eat. However, the drugs can cause harmful side effects like a rapid heart rate, anxiety, and addiction.

Fad diets are rarely successful in controlling weight. Most people who lose weight on a fad diet gain the weight back and sometimes more. Fad diets are often unbalanced, which means that they do not provide all of the nutrients you need. Some may even cause physical harm.

Steroids

Steroids are prescription drugs used for specific medical conditions. Steroids should not be used as bodybuilding supplements. Steroids can damage your skin and even cause a heart attack or stroke. Also, steroids can make you irritable and restless.

The most sensible and healthy way to control your weight is to combine a nutritious and balanced meal plan with physical activity. In the long run, you will be more likely to maintain a healthy weight.

✔ **Reading Check** **Predict** *What are some of the dangers of diet pills?*

Eating Disorders

Some people can develop an **eating disorder**, which is an extreme eating behavior that can lead to depression, anxiety, and even death. Eating disorders are psychological problems that are related to food. Both males and females can suffer from eating disorders. Teens with eating disorders often try to hide them. If left untreated, eating disorders will damage your body.

Anorexia Nervosa

Anorexia nervosa (ˌa-nə-ˌrek-sē-ə (ˌ)nər-ˈvō-sə) is an eating disorder in which a person feels an extreme fear of gaining weight. A person suffering from anorexia nervosa severely limits eating in an attempt to either lose weight or keep from gaining weight. No matter how thin the person becomes, he or she still feels overweight. Dieting turns into self-starvation. Someone suffering from anorexia nervosa may cut food into tiny pieces, chew food for a long time, or constantly rearrange food. An anorexic person also may exercise for dangerously long periods of time. He or she may also spend less time with friends. Anorexia can cause heart disease, stunted growth, brain damage, and even death.

SCIENCE YOU CAN USE

Target Heart Rate

When exercising, it is important to know how hard you may be working or how much harder you can work safely. Knowing your target heart rate zone is a good way to measure this. By measuring your heart rate during exercise, you can work to keep your heart rate in the correct zone.

Procedure During exercise, take your heart rate by putting your index finger to your neck or wrist. Count the beats for 15 seconds. Multiple that number of beats by 4.

Analysis Note your level of exertion. Now, try different types of exercise for different lengths of time (for example, walk quickly up a flight of stairs, run for 5 minutes, run for 2 minutes, walk for 10 minutes, do 50 jumping jacks). Find your heart rate during at least five different types of physical activity and then compare them. Is there consistency with your heart rate and how tired you are? If you exercised longer or harder, did your heart rate increase? What is your heart rate range?

NSES F Develop understanding of personal and community health.

Bulimia Nervosa

Bulimia nervosa (bü-ˈlē-mē-ə (ˌ)nər-ˈvō-sə) is an eating disorder in which a person eats very large amounts of food, then vomits or uses laxatives to get rid of the eaten food. Bulimia patients often suffer from depression and often become dependent on drugs. Bulimia is a secret ritual and can be hard to recognize. Bulimics usually weigh within 15 pounds of a healthy weight. A bulimic person often has stained teeth and swollen cheeks due to damage to the teeth, gums, and esophagus. Without help to control the disorder, bulimea can lead to kidney problems, heart failure, and even death.

Binge Eating

Binge eating is an eating disorder in which a person eats large quantities of food at one time. A binge eater has a lack of control over his or her eating habits and cannot stop eating. Binge eaters do not exercise excessively. People with a binge eating disorder may be overweight or they may gain and lose weight frequently. Binging often results in weight gain, high blood pressure, heart disease, and diabetes.

✔ **Reading Check** **Connect** *What health problems can be caused by eating disorders or extreme eating behaviors?*

🛈 **Self-Concept and Fitness** You are much more than the size or shape of your body. *What can you do every day to keep feeling good about yourself?*

Take Care of Yourself

Eating disorders can be caused by low self-esteem, depression, troubled relationships, poor body image, and chemical imbalances in the brain. If you think you or someone you know has an eating disorder, talk to a parent, teacher, or counselor. It almost always takes medical, nutritional, and psychological counseling to defeat an eating disorder. A key part of preventing eating disorders is educating yourself. You need be aware of the symptoms and be informed about where you can get help. It is also important to remember that your worth as a person is much deeper than your body size.

Remember that you are unique. Do not compare your body type to anyone else. Resist media images of "perfect" body types, such as those of supermodels, movie stars, and professional athletes. There is no such thing as a "perfect" body. Work to maintain a positive attitude about yourself and your life. Be the very best you can be by following a healthy meal plan and enjoying lots of physical activity.

Section 20.2 After You Read

Review What You Have Learned

1. **Define** obesity.
2. **Summarize** the relationship between the amount of calories you consume and the amount of physical activity you get.
3. **Name** the three most common eating disorders.
4. **Explain** what you should do if you think someone has an eating disorder.

Practice Academic Skills

 English Language Arts

5. Write a letter to a friend whom you think may have an eating disorder. Explain what the signs are and what the long-term effects could be. Encourage him or her to find support and help in dealing with the problem.

NCTE 5 Use different writing process elements to communicate effectively.

 Social Studies

6. Choose one of the common eating disorders mentioned in the chapter and research about how it develops, what contributes to its development, and how it is treated. Write an overview of what you discover about the disorder.

NCSS IV I Examine factors that contribute to and damage one's mental health and analyze issues related to mental health and behavioral disorders in contemporary society.

Check Your Answers Check your answers at this book's Online Learning Center at glencoe.com.

Discovering Careers

Do you like to help other people be fit and eat well? Have you spent time exploring your own health and fitness? If you answered yes to either of those questions, you might want to consider a future career in health and fitness. The following chart explores several careers in the health and fitness industry.

Career Activities ▼

At School

1 Select three of the careers listed. Research the education, training, and work experience required for each career. Write a summary of your results.

At Home

2 Create a log of your family's physical activity for a week. Then talk about how you and your family could improve your health and fitness.

At Work

3 Name three ways healthy employees benefit the workplace. Share your findings with your classmates.

In the Community

4 Contact and interview someone in your community who works in health and fitness. Ask this person to describe what his or her typical work day is like. Share what you learned with your class.

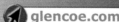

Learn More *Online* 🔍 glencoe.com

Career Investigations Go to this book's Online Learning Center for activities and worksheets to help you explore careers.

Job Title	Job Description
Weight-Loss Counselor	Assists people in devising and carrying out a weight-loss plan. Discusses eating habits that encourage good nutrition.
Sports Trainer	Works with athletes and sports teams to support injuries and training challenges for individuals. Creates plans for training to avoid injury.
Exercise Physiologist	Develops exercise programs. Promotes physical fitness. Records patient's heart activity during exercise under physician's supervision. Checks physical condition of client.
Personal Trainer	Develops personalized training programs based on client's goals and aspirations. Works out with clients on regular basis.
Eating Disorders Therapist	Provides individual, group, and family therapy. Treads physical symptoms, psychological issues, social concerns, and nutritional problems. Works with dietitians and medical professionals to develop meal plans and food shoping strategies

Career Activities Answers for these activities can be found on page TM192.

Chapter 20 · Review and Activities

Chapter Summary

Section 20.1 Physical Activity
Wellness is taking positive steps toward your good health, including physical activity. When you are physically fit, you look and feel your best. A healthy, fit body means you take care of yourself. Fitness is the ability to handle daily events in a healthy way. By exercising regularly you can enjoy all the benefits of fitness. Physical activity is necessary if you want to reach and maintain a healthy body weight. There are many activities you can add to your daily routine to get more movement.

Section 20.2 Body Weight and Health
People who maintain a healthy body weight are neither overweight nor underweight. You have to balance the calories you eat with the calories you use for energy. The most sensible and healthy way to control your weight is to combine a nutritious and balanced meal plan with physical activity. Some people develop eating disorders, or extreme eating behaviors, that can lead to depression, anxiety, disease, and even death. Work to maintain a positive attitude about yourself and your life.

Words You Learned

1. Create a fill-in-the-blank sentence for each of these vocabulary terms. The sentence should contain enough information to help determine the missing word.

Content Vocabulary
- fitness (p. 445)
- stamina (p. 447)
- aerobic (p. 448)
- obesity (p. 452)
- fad diet (p. 453)
- eating disorder (p. 455)
- anorexia nervosa (p. 455)
- bulimia nervosa (p. 456)
- binge eating (p. 456)

Academic Vocabulary
- obtain (p. 447)
- flexible (p. 448)
- expend (p. 453)
- fast (p. 454)

Review Key Concepts

2. **Explain** how fitness affects your daily activities.
3. **Describe** what is needed to reach and maintain a healthy body weight.
4. **List** the risks associated with obesity.
5. **Explain** the most healthful way to lose excess weight.
6. **Identify** how eating disorders can destroy your health.
7. **Recognize** the causes of eating disorders.

Critical Thinking

8. **Compare and contrast** how being overweight and underweight affects the body.
9. **Propose** your own plan for balancing diet and exercise.

Real-World Skills and Applications

Problem-Solving

10. Prioritize For some people, it is often difficult to carve out time for exercise, yet it is something you need to do in order be healthy. Look at your own daily schedule for a week. Make exercise a priority. Come up with a schedule where exercise is a high priority.

Interpersonal and Collaborative

11. Healthful Alternatives Follow your teacher's directions to form groups. In your group, cut out advertisements for junk food. Then create your own advertisement for a healthful alternative made with fruits or vegetables. Cut out pictures or draw your own. Write your own advertisement to convince people to buy your product. Use descriptive language to explain the benefits, including taste and nutrition. Share your advertisements with the other groups.

Financial Literacy

12. Exercise More, Spend Less Many people decide that the best way to commit to working out on a regular basis is signing up for a gym membership. Health clubs have many advantages: they offer a wide array of exercise classes and state-of-the-art fitness equipment. Many people also like working out in a group setting, and the opportunity to work with personal trainers. However, a gym membership can be very expensive. Think about some of the ways you can get some of the same benefits without purchasing a health club membership. Make a list of five low-cost (or no-cost) ways you can get strength training, cardiovascular training, and/or other fitness activities (like those offered in exercise classes) without signing up at a health club.

13. Fitness Picnic Take a group of friends to the park. Fly kites, play baseball, toss a football, run laps, do sit-ups and push-ups, or other simple physical activities. Picnic on delicious yet healthful snacks, such as fresh fruits and vegetables, breads, and cheeses after you have had a good workout. How did you feel after the fitness picnic? How was it better for you than other activities? Share the benefits of the picnic with your class.

14. Research a Fruit or Vegetable Choose a fruit or vegetable that you may not know much about. Research its history, how and where it is grown, who eats it, and the ways it can be prepared. Prepare a brief presentation on what you find to the class. Can you find an unusual recipe that incorporates your fruit or vegetable?

15. Calorie Burning With permission from your teacher or parents, go online and search for a calorie-burning calculator. Calculate how many calories you can burn doing different types of exercise. Record your findings in your Life Skills Binder and refer to them when you exercise.

Academic Skills

 English Language Arts

16. Other Benefits Physical activity is great for the body, but it also benefits your mental health. It can help improve your perspective, or the way you look at life. Write a short essay to explain the ways physical fitness and good nutrition can improve more than just you physical health.

> **NCTE 4** Use written language to communicate effectively.

 Science

17. Cross Training Cross training is important aspect of exercising. Using the same muscles over and over again makes your body accustomed to the activity and can leave you open to injury. It is important to do different types of exercise which use different muscle groups in different ways.
Procedure List different physical activities and how they work your body's muscles. Consider how you could add variety to your workouts.
Analysis Plan a physical fitness program that includes a variety of physical activities for cross training.

> **NSES G** Students should develop understanding of science as a human endeavor.

Mathematics

18. Fitness Goal Sheldon is planning to try out for his school's swim team. He does not have a pool at home, and the community pool is closed for repairs. Since jogging is easy and free, he decided to improve his health and stamina by setting a goal of jogging 20 minutes a day. Sheldon has most of the summer to get ready for the tryouts, so he plans to jog every weekday until school starts. If he jogs for 16 minutes on Monday, 30 minutes on Tuesday, 20 minutes on Wednesday, and 14 minutes on Thursday, how long should he jog on Friday to reach his average?

Math Concept **Calculating Mean** When you have a series of values, calculate the mean, or average, by finding the sum of all of the values, and dividing that sum by the number of values.

Starting Hint The sum of five values, divided by 5, equals 20. Write an algebraic equation to find the missing value: $(16 + 30 + 20 + 14 + x) \div 5 = 20$. Solve for x.

> **NCTM Algebra** Represent and analyze mathematical situations and structures using algebraic symbols.

Standardized Test Practice

Multiple Choice
Choose the letter of the best answer.

> **Test-Taking Tip** Eat well before taking a test. Have a good breakfast or lunch and avoid junk food. Studies show that you need good nutrition to concentrate and perform your best.

19. If I spend 6% of my time doing physical activity over 4000 hours, how much time have I spent?
a. 240 hours
b. 600 hours
c. 24 hours
d. 200 hours

UNIT 9 Life Skills Project

Play with Your Food!

Eating well and exercising are good ways to keep healthy. Your doctor can give you advice to follow for your age and size. Participating in sports and walking are ways to keep active. This project will help you explore ways to stay healthy.

 My Journal Complete the journal entry from page 417, and refer to it to select and research your play's topic.

Project Assignment ▼

In this project, you will:

- List topics about health issues in your age group.
- Research facts about a health topic of your choice.
- Write a short play about nutrition and exercise.
- Interview an expert on physical fitness.
- Act out your play for your class.
- Include this project in the ninth section of your personal Life Skills binder.

Step 1 Select and Research Your Topic

Choose a health issue related to nutrition and fitness. Use the textbook to start your research. Look for more information from magazine articles, health books, or Web sites. Write a summary of your research.

Step 2 Write a Play About Taking Care of Your Body

Invent two characters and imagine a scene in which they talk about your topic. Write a dialogue that uses the facts you have researched to make a point. The play should last about two minutes. Use these questions to help you write the dialogue:

✔ Are your characters explaining the facts we need to know?
✔ Have you picked a situation for the characters that best illustrates the issue?
✔ Is the dialogue natural and understandable?
✔ Does the ending make a strong point?

Step 3 Interview An Expert on Nutrition and Fitness

Read your play to a health expert like a doctor, nurse, nutritionist, or personal trainer. Then ask these questions:

✔ Please give an example of how you handle my topic in your job.
✔ How effective is the play I wrote?
✔ What changes can I make so that I make my point clearly?

Use these interviewing skills when conducting your interview and these writing skills when writing the summary of notes from your interview.

Interviewing Skills
- Record interview responses and take notes.
- Listen attentively.

Writing Skills
- Use complete sentences.
- Use correct spelling and grammar.

Step 4 Perform Your Play for Your Class

Use the Life Skills Project Checklist on the right to plan, memorize your lines, and perform your play for the class.

Use these speaking skills when presenting your final report.

Speaking Skills
- Speak clearly and concisely.
- Be sensitive to the needs of your audience.
- Use standard English to communicate.

Step 5 Evaluate Your Presentation

Your project will be evaluated based on:

✔The detail and organization of your research on the health issue you chose.
✔The written dialogue of the play.
✔The impact of your performance and memorization of lines.
✔The summary written from interview notes.
✔Grammar and sentence structure.
✔Presentation to the class.
✔Creativity and neatness.

Evaluation Rubric Go to this book's Online Learning Center at glencoe.com for a rubric you can use to evaluate your final project.

Life Skills Project Checklist

Research Nutrition and Fitness

✅ Gather facts about your chosen topic.

✅ Imagine a scene that would demonstrate the important ideas and facts of your topic.

✅ Interview a doctor, nutritionist, or other health professional.

Writing Skills

✅ List the facts about your chosen topic.

✅ Write the facts into the dialogue of a play.

✅ Write a summary from your interview with a health professional.

Present Your Findings

✅ Memorize the lines of your play, and partner with another classmate to perform it.

✅ Invite the students of the class to ask any questions they may have. Answer these questions with responses that respect their perspectives.

✅ Add this project to your Life Skills binder.

Academic Skills

✅ Conduct research to gather information.

✅ Communicate effectively.

✅ Organize your presentation so the audience can follow along easily.

✅ Thoroughly express your ideas.

NCTE 4 Use written language to communicate effectively.
NCTE 12 Use language to accomplish individual purposes.

Chapter 21
Working in the Kitchen

Chapter 22
Prepare to Cook

Chapter 23
Cooking Basics

Unit Preview

This unit is about kitchen safety and cooking basics. In this unit, you will learn about:

- Safe kitchen and food-handling practices.
- Preventing accidents in the kitchen.
- Meal preparation and food shopping.
- Reading and following recipes.
- Choosing the best ingredients.
- A variety of cooking techniques.

Explore the Photo Answer Answers may include simple dishes, dishes that students prepare with their parents, family recipes, a dish that the student specializes in making.

Explore the Photo
Cooking can be a fun and delicious experience which allows you to be creative. *What dishes or favorite meals do you know how to cook?*

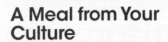

A Meal from Your Culture

When you are done studying this unit, you will complete a project in which you will:

✓ Prepare a dish that reflects your heritage.

✓ Interview a member of your cultural community about the recipe.

✓ Share your meal with the class, explaining why it is important to your family or culture.

The prewriting activity below will help you get started.

 My Journal

Prewriting Activity
Locate Information

Conduct research to find recipes for meals or foods that reflect your cultural heritage. Choose two or three dishes that you enjoy with your family, or meals that have special memories for you. Add recipes for these dishes to your journal and include answers to these questions:

● Besides being tasty, what makes these meals or foods important to you?

● What makes these meals or foods unique to your family or culture?

● What memories are associated with these meals or foods?

Chapter 21

Working in the Kitchen

Section 21.1

Food Safety

■ Main Idea Food contamination occurs when food is handled improperly. Learn techniques to keep your kitchen and food clean and safe.

Section 21.2

Kitchen Essentials

■ Main Idea Most common kitchen accidents can be prevented. You can help avoid them by practicing safe work habits.

Explore the Photo Answer If you do not pay attention, you could: cut yourself with a sharp utensil, get shocked by electrical equipment, slip on a spill, use the wrong ingredients, burn yourself, and risk using spoiled or contaminated food.

Explore the Photo
There are many things you need to keep in mind in order to stay safe in the kitchen. *What can happen if you do not pay attention to what you are doing while you cook or prepare a meal?*

Writing Activity

Write a Personal Narrative

Remember When Choose a vivid memory from your childhood about an event or situation that happened in the kitchen. Narrate the events related to this memory so that your readers will understand why the event was important and memorable.

Writing Tips Follow these steps to write a personal narrative:

1. Use a strong point of view. The reader should be able to imagine what you are describing.
2. Begin with your thesis statement that communicates your memory, the point you want to make, and why the event was so memorable.
3. Tell a story.

Writing Activity Answer See page TM192.

Section **21.1** Food Safety

Reading Guide

Before You Read

Use Color As you read this section, try using different colored pens to take notes, using a different color for each different type of information. This is a visual trick that can help you learn new material and study for tests. For example, you could use red for vocabulary words, blue for explanations, and green for examples.

Read to Learn

Key Concepts

✓ **Name** two types of bacteria that cause food poisoning.

✓ **Explain** how to keep leftovers from spoiling.

Main Idea

Food contamination occurs when food is handled improperly. Learn techniques to keep your kitchen and food clean and safe.

Content Vocabulary

○ foodborne illness   ○ salmonella
○ contamination   ○ perishable
○ E. coli

Academic Vocabulary

■ minimize   ■ promptly

Graphic Organizer

As you read, write down three ways to help prevent food contamination. Use a graphic organizer like the one shown to help you organize your information.

Prevent Food Contamination
1.
2.
3.

 Graphic Organizer Go to this book's Online Learning Center at glencoe.com to print this graphic organizer.

Academic Standards

 English Language Arts

NCTE 5 Use different writing process elements to communicate effectively.

 Mathematics

NCTM Measurement Understand measurable attributes of objects and the units, systems, and processes of measurement.

Social Studies

NCSS V G Individuals, Groups, and Institutions Analyze the extent to which groups and institutions meet individual needs and promote the common good in contemporary and historical settings.

NCTE *National Council of Teachers of English*
NCTM *National Council of Teachers of Mathematics*
NSES *National Science Education Standards*
NCSS *National Council for the Social Studies*

Graphic Organizer Answer
(1) keep your kitchen and utensils clean, (2) prepare food properly, (3) serve and store food safely

When you get home from school, do you remember to wash your hands before eating? Sometimes you may be in a hurry and grab a snack without thinking about washing your hands. Eating unsafe food can make you very sick. Do you practice food and kitchen safety?

Foodborne Illness

Foodborne illness, also called food poisoning, is an illness caused by unsafe food. Food can become unsafe because of bacteria, parasites, fungi, viruses, or harmful chemicals. The symptoms of foodborne illnesses can sometimes feel like a mild flu. Symptoms such as diarrhea, nausea, stomach pain, headache, muscle pain, and fatigue usually appear within four to forty-eight hours after eating unsafe food. Get rest and drink plenty of fluids. If you have symptoms for more than one or two days, call a doctor. The safe handling of food and utensils can prevent most foodborne illnesses.

 Reading Check *Identify* *What are the symptoms of foodborne illnesses?*

Keep Food Safe

Contamination, occurs when food becomes infected with harmful bacteria. If you follow some simple procedures when you handle and prepare food, you can **minimize**, or decrease, the risk of food contamination. In mild cases, people who eat contaminated food may experience headaches, stomach cramps, and fever. In more severe cases, however, medical attention may be necessary.

A few types of bacteria cause most food poisoning. **E. coli** is the most deadly form of food poisoning. E. coli bacteria are found in contaminated water, raw or rare ground beef, and unpasteurized milk. For this reason, you should only eat hamburgers that have been fully cooked. Another common type of food poisoning is caused by salmonella bacteria. **Salmonella** (ˌsal-mə-ˈne-lə) bacteria are often found in raw or undercooked foods, such as meat, eggs, fish, and poultry. Salmonella grow quickly at room temperature and can be spread by hands and cooking utensils. Thoroughly cook all meat, poultry, fish, and eggs. Wash your hands, knife, and cutting board with soap and hot water whenever you cut raw meat, fish, or poultry.

You should always clean up the kitchen as you cook. Wipe up spills immediately and clean off the countertops. As you finish using pots, pans, and cooking utensils, wash them in hot, soapy water. By keeping the kitchen clean, it will be a more healthful and pleasant place to work.

As You Read

Connect Think about the foods and beverages in your refrigerator. Is there anything that should be thrown out?

Vocabulary

You can find definitions in the glossary at the back of this book.

As You Read Answer Answers may include food that has been forgotten, moldy fruits and vegetables, spoiled milk, anything that is past its expiration date, food that no one is ever going to eat.

Reading Check Answer Foodborne illness can feel like a mild flu. Diarrhea, nausea, stomach pain, headache, muscle pain, and fatigue may appear four to forty-eight hours after eating unsafe food.

Succeed in School Keep your classes lively, and provide plenty of opportunities for students to participate. This may help eliminate the temptation for students to daydream.

SUCCEED IN SCHOOL!

Stay Alert
Snooze or Lose
If you are too tired, you will not be able to concentrate well in class. Not getting enough can lead for poor school performance. Balance your time in order to get enough sleep.

Defrosting

After you defrost food, it is important to use it right away. Waiting until later to cook food allows harmful bacteria to grow.

• Defrost food in the refrigerator.

• Do not let it sit out overnight.

Math You Can Use Answer 20 lbs √ 5 lbs = 4. Four days are needed, so move the turkey from the freezer to the refrigerator by Sunday morning.

Handling Food

Another way to reduce the risk of food poisoning is to handle perishable foods carefully. Foods that are **perishable** are likely to spoil quickly. Perishable foods include meat, poultry, fish, eggs, fresh fruits and vegetables, leftovers, and dairy products. Hot foods such as hamburgers should be kept hot, and cold foods such as yogurt should be kept cold until they are eaten. Keep hot foods at 140°F (60°C) or above, and cold foods at 40°F (4°C) or below. Otherwise bacteria might grow.

Foods that have been cooked should not stand at room temperature for more than two hours. For a packed lunch or picnic, use cold packs and a cooler to keep the cold foods cold.

Storing Leftovers

To keep leftovers from spoiling, refrigerate or freeze them **promptly**, or immediately after the meal. Put leftovers in a tightly covered shallow container, and store them in the refrigerator. Many leftovers can also be frozen for use at a later date. When freezing leftovers, pack them in an airtight container, and label them with the name of the food and the date. Freezing food keeps bacteria from growing until the food is thawed. Most foods can be stored in the freezer for several months.

Freezer Storage

You can keep packaged frozen foods, meat, poultry, fish, bread, and home-prepared mixed dishes fresh and appealing by properly freezing them. Some foods do not freeze well, such as cooked egg whites, lettuce, and foods with mayonnaise or salad dressing.

Here are some storage guidelines:

• Store frozen foods in their original packages.

• Wrap foods properly so they do not spoil or get freezer burn. Freezer burn is harmless, but it causes unappealing, dried-up white areas on food. To prevent freezer burn, keep foods airtight in freezer paper, heavy-duty foil, freezer-quality plastic bags, or plastic freezer containers.

• Label frozen foods with the name, date frozen, and serving amount.

MATH YOU CAN USE

Thaw a Turkey

The safest way to thaw a frozen turkey is in the refrigerator. Allow 24 hours of thawing time for every 5 pounds (2 kg) of turkey. On what day do you need to start defrosting a 20-pound (9 kg) turkey for Thanksgiving, which falls on a Thursday?

Math Concept **Selecting Units of Measure** Converting measurements into more manageable equivalents makes problem solving easier. For example, 24 hours = 1 day.

Starting Hint First, determine the number of days needed to defrost the turkey. Then, count backward from Thursday. Remember: the turkey will need to be cooked starting Thanksgiving morning!

 For more math help, go to the Math Appendix located at the back of this book.

NCTM Measurement Understand measurable attributes of objects and the units, systems, and processes of measurement.

How To...

Prevent Food Contamination

To avoid getting sick from the foods you eat, you need to follow some basic guidelines for handling food. These guidelines will help you care for your health and the health of others.

Keep Your Kitchen and Utensils Clean Keep hands, counters, and utensils clean. If you spill something on the floor, wipe it up immediately with a paper towel, cloth, or mop. Wash cutting boards, utensils, and hands after handling raw meat, poultry, or seafood. Use separate towels for drying hands and drying dishes.

Prepare Food Properly When you are ill, it is best not to prepare food for others. Thaw frozen foods in the refrigerator or microwave oven. Keep raw meat, poultry, and seafood separate from other foods. Wash raw foods thoroughly. Keep your hair out of the food.

Serve and Store Food Safely Keep hot foods hot and cold foods cold. Serve cold and cooked food immediately. Refrigerate leftovers immediately. Use a separate spoon for tasting food. After you have used it for tasting, wash the spoon.

Food Safety and Shopping When shopping for food, put raw meat, poultry, and fish in plastic bags so they will not drip on other food. Check package labels for "use by" dates and directions for storage and cooking. Choose chilled, high-quality fresh produce. Refrigerated foods should feel cold and frozen foods should be solid. Avoid discolored or mushy frozen packages. Ice crystals signal thawed, refrozen food. Shop for refrigerated, frozen, and deli foods last. They will have less time to warm up. Avoid food packages with holes, tears, or broken safety seals. Pick canned goods without dents, bulges, rust, or leaks. Bulging cans signal that a food has been contaminated with dangerous organisms. Take groceries home right away. If getting groceries home takes more than 30 minutes, bring an insulated cooler for perishable foods.

Photo Caption Answer It is important to store leftovers properly to prevent them from spoiling and becoming unsafe to eat.

 Store Leftovers Put away leftovers without delay. *Why is it important to store leftovers properly?*

Character Counts Answer Answers may include approaching Jaden in a kind way about her practices in the kitchen and showing her how to keep her kitchen safe. Sawyer could also offer to help with preparation and clean-up so he can act as a role model.

Refrigerator Storage

A refrigerator keeps perishable foods fresh for one day to several weeks. Even properly stored foods will not keep forever. Keep your refrigerator as cold as possible without freezing foods. Safe temperatures range from 32°F to 40°F (0°C to 4°C). Inside shelves and drawers stay colder than door shelves. Refrigerator storage guidelines include:

- Use foil, plastic wrap, zippered plastic bags, or airtight containers to cover and protect food.
- Put meat, poultry, fish, milk, and eggs on inside shelves. Use door shelves for most condiments, such as ketchup, mustard, and relish.
- Place raw meat, poultry, and fish on a plate or in a plastic bag, on the bottom shelf so they do not drip onto other foods.
- Leave space for cold air to circulate around food.
- Wipe spills immediately. Sanitize drawers. Throw away spoiled foods.

Character Counts

Confrontation

Jaden likes to cook for family and friends, but when her friend Sawyer comes for dinner, he finds that he is afraid to eat Jaden's cooking because of her practices in the kitchen. He sees that she does not wash her hands between handling meat and vegetables, and the counters are never wiped off.

You Make the Call

What should Sawyer do about eating dinner with Jaden? Write a paragraph explaining what course of action Sawyer should choose and why.

Dry Storage

Keep nonperishable foods in a cabinet or pantry. This includes grains such as rice, cereal, flour, and crackers. Oils, dry herbs, and unopened cans and jars can alos be stored safely in a cabinet or pantry. Dry storage areas should be clean, dry, dark, and cool (below 85°F or 29°C). Tips for dry storage include:

- Do not store foods above the refrigerator or stove, or near a furnace outlet.
- Do not keep food under a sink. Openings around pipes cannot be sealed. Pests and moisture from pipes can spoil food.
- Do not store cleaning products or trash near food. Cleaners, detergents, and other household chemicals can contaminate food.
- Read the labels on food packaging. Some foods need refrigeration after being opened.

Section 21.1 After You Read

Review What You Have Learned

1. **Identify** places where E. coli bacteria can develop.
2. **Describe** freezer burn and how to prevent it.

Practice Academic Skills

 English Language Arts

3. Write a step-by-step kitchen safety guide for someone who is just starting out in the kitchen. Provide guidelines for keeping the kitchen and food safe. Be sure to include what tools or supplies they will need.

> **NCTE 5** Use different writing process elements to communicate effectively.

 Social Studies

4. Research food safety regulations for restaurants in your community. What are the guidelines for clean kitchens and cooking? How often are restaurants checked for following guidelines? How do the guidelines contribute to public safety? Write a short overview of what you discover.

> **NCSS V G** Analyze the extent to which groups and institutions meet individual needs and promote the common good in contemporary and historical settings.

Check Your Answers Check your answers at this book's Online Learning Center at **glencoe.com**.

Reading Guide

Before You Read

Take Guilt-Free Days of Rest The brain has a hard time absorbing new data when it is stressed. Your reading skills will be much more effective if you are relaxed and ready to learn.

Read to Learn

Key Concepts

✓ **Identify** the five most common kitchen accidents.

✓ **Describe** the benefit of having basic tools and cookware.

✓ **List** five examples of large kitchen appliances.

Main Idea

Most common kitchen accidents can be prevented. You can help avoid them by practicing safe work habits.

Content Vocabulary

○ flammable   ○ convection oven
○ utensil

Academic Vocabulary

■ hazard   ■ conduct

Graphic Organizer

As you read, write down five things you can do to help prevent burns in the kitchen. Use a graphic organizer like the one shown to help you organize your information.

Prevent Burns

 Graphic Organizer Go to this book's Online Learning Center at glencoe.com to print this graphic organizer.

• **Academic Standards** •

 English Language Arts

NCTE 8 Use information resources to gather information and create and communicate knowledge.

 Science

NSES B Develop an understanding of the structure and properties of matter.

Social Studies

NCSS VIII A Science, Technology, and Society Identify and describe both current and historical examples of the interaction and interdependence of science, technology, and society in a variety of cultural settings.

NCTE *National Council of Teachers of English*
NCTM *National Council of Teachers of Mathematics*

NSES *National Science Education Standards*
NCSS *National Council for the Social Studies*

Graphic Organizer Answer use potholders, turn pan handles toward the center, tilt pan lids away from you, use lower temperatures to cook fried foods, clean appliances after they cool

Your home may seem like a safe place to be. However, if you do not take precautions to avoid accidents, your home can become very dangerous. The kitchen is a common place for accidents. How do you keep yourself safe when you cook or help others in the kitchen?

Kitchen Safety

The most common kitchen accidents include falls, burns, fires, cuts, and electric shocks. These types of accidents are usually preventable if you develop good, safe work habits. In general, keep hair, loose clothing, jewelry, and apron strings out of the way. They could catch fire or become tangled in appliances. Always pay attention to your tasks, and use the right tools for each job.

Falls

To prevent falls, follow these guidelines:

- Stand on a short stepladder or a sturdy step stool with a waist-high hand bar to get at high or hard-to-reach items. Do not use chairs because they tip over too easily.
- Turn pot and pan handles toward the center of the stove or counter so that the pots or pans will not get knocked over.
- Clean up spilled foods or liquids immediately.
- Keep cupboard doors and drawers closed when not in use.
- Choose kitchen rugs with a nonskid backing.
- Never walk on a wet floor. Clear away floor clutter.
- Store heavy items within easy reach.

Avoid Kitchen Falls Clean up spilled food and liquids right away to avoid slips and falls. *What else can you do to avoid falls in the kitchen?*

As You Read

Connect Being in the kitchen can be dangerous. What are the potential dangers in you family's kitchen?

As You Read Answer Answers may include spills, breakable items, spoiled foods.

Photo Caption Answer Keep cupboard doors and drawers closed when not in use; make sure the floor is clear of objects and cords use a stepladder or sturdy step stool instead of a chair to reach high places.

Succeed in School If any students in your class appear preoccupied, make sure they know about the value of talking about their problems with a trusted adult or friend.

Stay Alert
Talk It Through
Being stressed can be a distraction. If you are worried about something, you might have trouble focusing on your schoolwork. If something is really bothering you, find someone to talk to about it, like a friend, parent, teacher, or counselor.

SCIENCE YOU CAN USE

Kitchen Fires

Fire requires three ingredients. It needs heat, fuel, and oxygen. When you add an ignition source, you have a fire! The ignition is the mechanism that ignites the fuel. To ignite means to cause to start burning.

Procedure Choose one type of kitchen fire to analyze. Conduct research to identify what might cause this type of fire. Also, find out about safe ways to put out this type of fire.

Analysis Write a report on your findings. In your report, describe the type of fire, typical causes, and safe ways to put out that type of fire.

> **NSES B** Develop an understanding of the structure and properties of matter.

 Vocabulary

You can find definitions in the glossary at the back of this book.

Burns

Several kitchen **hazards**, or dangers, can burn you. You can prevent most burns in the kitchen by following these safety precautions:

- Use dry potholders when cooking hot foods and liquids or removing them from the stove, oven, or microwave.
- Turn pot and pan handles toward the center of the range. This helps keep someone from bumping a hot pan off the range.
- When cooking, remove pan lids by tilting them away from you. This allows steam to escape safely at the back of the pot, away from your hands and face.
- Use medium or low temperatures to cook greasy foods, such as French fries or fried chicken, to avoid splattering hot oil.
- Wait until appliances cool down before cleaning them.

Fires

Fires can happen easily in the kitchen. Follow these safety precautions, or actions taken in advance:

- Keep a fire extinguisher in the kitchen where you can reach it quickly and safely. Be sure that you know how to use it properly.
- Do not wear clothing with long, loose-fitting sleeves when cooking. The sleeves can easily catch fire.
- If your hair is long, tie it back.
- Keep all flammable objects, such as paper bags, potholders, kitchen towels, curtains, and plastic containers, away from the stove. **Flammable** means capable of burning easily.
- Do not leave the kitchen while food is cooking. Fire can spread in seconds.
- If a grease fire starts, turn off the heat and smother the fire with a tight-fitting lid. Never use water. Water causes a grease fire to spread.
- Keep aerosol cans away from heat. They can explode if heated. Also, the spray from aerosol cans may be flammable.

Cuts

Kitchen knives have specific purposes, from trimming and peeling fruits and vegetables to slicing meat.

To prevent cuts from knives and other hazards, observe the following safety rules:

- Keep knives sharp. Sharp knives are often safer than dull ones, since a dull knife will force you to use more force, which can lead to the knife slipping and cutting you.
- Cut food away from your body. Use a cutting board for all cutting jobs, even if it is only a single apple. Do not hold food in your hand to cut.
- Wash knives and sharp objects separately from other utensils.
- Store knives in a special compartment in the drawer or in a knife holder. Put them away immediately after cleaning them.
- If you drop a knife, let it fall. Do not try to catch it.
- Never pick up broken glass with bare hands. Sweep it into a dustpan immediately. Then wipe the floor with several thicknesses of damp paper towels, put the broken pieces into a paper bag, and place the bag in a trash can.
- Throw away chipped or cracked plates and glasses.

Safety Check

Fire Extinguishers
Every kitchen should be equipped with a fire extinguisher. To use one, follow these steps:

- Pull the ring and stand back several feet from the fire. Aim the nozzle at the base of the flames.
- Squeeze the handle.
- Spray back and forth across the base of the fire.

Photo Caption Answer wash knives separately from other dishes, cut food away from your body, use a cutting board for all cutting jobs, do not try to catch a falling knife

Knife Safety To cut safely, use the right knife for the job. Hold your hand so your fingertips are under your knuckles, and be careful of the thumb holding the food. *What else can you do to avoid accidental cuts?*

Electric Shocks

Electrical appliances make kitchen tasks easier, but they can also cause electric shocks. To prevent shocks, take the following precautions:

- Avoid using any appliance with a frayed, or worn, cord.
- Dry your hands before using electrical equipment.
- Disconnect appliances by pulling out the plug directly, not by tugging on the cord.
- Keep portable appliances unplugged when not in use.
- Always unplug a toaster before trying to pry food from it. Forks, knives, or other metal utensils can **conduct**, or carry, electricity and cause an electrical shock.

 List *What are some flammable kitchen items?* Reading Check Answer paper bags, potholders, towels, curtains, plastic containers

Small Equipment

Not all kitchen tools and cookware are essential. For example, you do not have to have a vegetable peeler to peel a carrot. You can also do the job with a paring knife. However, a kitchen equipped with basic tools and cookware makes food preparation much easier.

Photo Caption Answer Having the basic tools and cookware can help you save time, and it makes food preparation much easier.

Kitchen Equipment Tools and small equipment for the kitchen are designed for specific purposes. *Why is it important to have basic tools and cookware in the kitchen?*

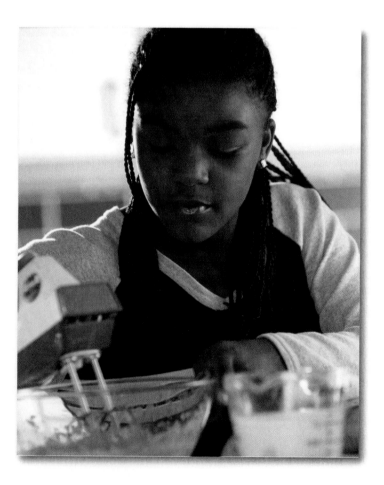

Figure 21.1 Kitchen Tools and Cookware

The Right Tool for the Right Job Having the right tools is an important part of being a successful cook. *Which of these tools would you use to turn chicken on a grill?*

Figure Caption Answer Tongs or a kitchen fork.

Rubber Scraper

Vegetable Peeler

Rotary Beater

Wire Whisk

Tongs

Paring Knife

Chef's Knife

Bread Knife

Metal Spatula

Kitchen Fork

Large Spoon

Tube Pan

Casseroles

Grater

Mixing Bowls

Colander

Sifter

Loaf Pan

Muffin Pan

Cookie Sheet

Saucepan

Pie Pan

Square Cake Pan

Cake Pan

Double Boiler

Roasting Pan

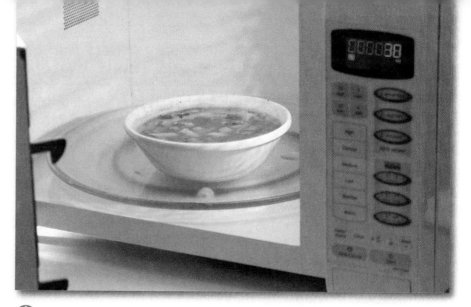

🔊 **Microwave Oven** Convenience and speed are the advantages of microwave cooking. *What kinds of foods would not cook well in a microwave?*

Many types of utensils and cookware are available. A **utensil** is a tool or container used in the kitchen. **Figure 21.1** illustrates many common kitchen items. You can cook just about anything if you have basic kitchen utensils, cookware, and appliances and know how to use them. Preparing food will be easier, more enjoyable, and safer when you select the right tools for the job. The most commonly used utensils include those for cooking, mixing, and slicing or cutting. Commonly used small appliances include toasters, hand mixers, food processors, and blenders. The best cookware to use depends on the type of food you are cooking and where you are cooking it. For instance, you could use a metal cake pan to bake cookies in a conventional oven, but not in a microwave oven. You should never put metal in a microwave oven. Metal in a microwave creates sparks which could result in a fire.

✓ **Reading Check** *Recall* Can you use a metal cake pan to bake cookies in a microwave oven? Why or why not?

Large Equipment

Large kitchen appliances, such as stoves, refrigerators, convection ovens, microwave ovens, and dishwashers, add convenience, speed, and ease to the kitchen. Compare appliances before you buy them. Check the prices, features, and energy efficiency of different models so you can get the best value for your money. Read the owner's manual to learn how to safely used and care for appliances. You can also learn about how each feature works, and what to do if the appliance stops working. Keep the owner's manuals for reference.

The cost of large kitchen equipment varies, depending on extra features they may include. For example:

- **Refrigerators** may have the freezer on the side, on the top, or on the bottom. Some are self-defrosting and have extra features, such as additional freezer space, ice makers, or ice cube and water dispensers.
- **Dishwashers** vary in the number and depth of racks they contain. Quiet-running and energy-efficient models tend to be more expensive.
- **Stoves or ranges** usually come with conventional ovens. Some stoves also include microwave ovens, while others include convection ovens.
- **Convection ovens** use a high-speed fan to circulate hot air throughout the oven, evenly and continuously, which speeds up the cooking. Conventional ovens may be self-cleaning or continuous cleaning. An automatic timer that can turn the oven on or off is another possible feature.
- **Microwave ovens** are fast, convenient, and easy to use. They come in a variety of sizes and have a range of power settings.

Section 21.2 After You Read

Review What You Have Learned

1. **Describe** ways to avoid falls in the kitchen.
2. **Name** some commonly used small appliances.
3. **Explain** why you should keep the owner's manuals that come with appliances.

Practice Academic Skills

 English Language Arts

4. Choose one of the most common kitchen accidents, and create a poster that communicates how to avoid that type of accident. Use photos, clip art, graphics, and attention-grabbing text to show how to avoid this type of accident in the kitchen.

NCTE 8 Use information resources to gather information and create and communicate knowledge.

 Social Studies

5. Choose a small appliance that is used in the kitchen. Research the history of the appliance, including who created it and how it has changed and developed over the years. Be prepared to give a short presentation to your classmates.

NCSS VIII A Identify and describe both current and historical examples of the interaction and interdependence of science, technology, and society in a variety of cultural settings.

Check Your Answers Check your answers at this book's Online Learning Center at glencoe.com.

Discovering Careers

Do you have a keen sense for the taste of food? Do you like to cook or bake for the enjoyment of others? If you answered yes to either of those questions, you might want to consider a future career in food inspection or serving. The following chart explores several careers in food service.

Job Title	Job Description
Flavorist	Identifies the chemical compounds in food flavors. Conducts experiments to test different flavors. Blends and creates flavors.
Head Server	Supervises and trains wait staff to take guests' orders, clear tables, and present checks. Suggests menu items and answers questions regarding foods.
Caterer	Provides food for parties, special dinners, and receptions. Meets with clients to discuss menus. Delivers and serves food.
Cake Decorator	Designs cakes and pastries for sale. Creates decorations on specialty cakes, birthday cakes, and wedding cakes.
Restaurant Kitchen Manager	Organizes procedures for cooking and cleaning. Schedules employees for work. Makes sure policies regarding safe cooking are followed.

Career Activities ▼

At School

1 Select two of the careers listed. Research the education, training, and work experience required for each career. Write a summary of your results.

At Home

2 With a parent, write out the procedures that you and your family follow when cooking. How safe is your home kitchen?

At Work

3 Can you think of all the different types of jobs there are, working in a restaurant? Do some research if necessary.

In the Community

4 Contact and interview someone in your community who works in food service. Ask this person to describe what his or her typical work day is like. Share what you learned with your class.

Learn More *Online* **glencoe.com**

Career Investigations Go to this book's Online Learning Center for activities and worksheets to help you explore careers.

Career Activities Answers for these activities can be found on page TM192.

Chapter Summary

Section 21.1 Food Safety
Foodborne illness, also called food poisoning, is an illness caused by unsafe food. Food can become unsafe because of bacteria, parasites, fungi, viruses, and harmful chemicals. Keeping food safe can prevent food becoming infected with harmful bacteria. By following some simple procedures when handling and preparing food, you can reduce the risk of food contamination. Store food properly and quickly after you are finished eating, and cook meat fully before serving.

Section 21.2 Kitchen Essentials
The most common kitchen accidents include falls, burns, fires, cuts, and electric shocks. These types of accidents are usually preventable if you develop good, safe work habits. For your kitchen, many types of utensils and cookware are available. The best cookware to use depends on the type of food you are cooking and where you are cooking it. Large kitchen equipment such as stoves, convection ovens, microwave ovens, refrigerators, and dishwashers, can also make food preparation easier.

Words You Learned

1. Use at least six of these content and academic vocabulary words in a short essay about food and kitchen safety.

Content Vocabulary
- foodborne illness (p. 469)
- contamination (p. 469)
- E. coli (p. 469)
- salmonella (p. 469)
- perishable (p. 470)
- flammable (p. 476)
- utensil (p. 480)
- convection oven (p. 481)

Academic Vocabulary
- minimize (p. 469)
- promptly (p. 470)
- hazard (p. 476)
- conduct (p. 478)

Review Key Concepts

2. **Name** two types of bacteria that cause food poisoning.

3. **Explain** how to keep leftovers from spoiling.

4. **Identify** the five most common kitchen accidents.

5. **Describe** the benefit of having basic tools and cookware.

6. **List** five examples of large kitchen appliances.

Critical Thinking

7. **Formulate** a plan for keeping food safe in your home.

8. **Evaluate** the safety of your kitchen at home. If there are safety issues, suggest how these can be fixed

9. **Compare and contrast** conventional ovens with convection ovens.

Real-World Skills and Applications

Problem-Solving

10. **First Aid in the Kitchen** You and your older sister prepared a meal for your parents' 15th wedding anniversary. Everything was going well until your sister accidentally knocked over a pan on the stove. The liquid in the pan caused a minor burn on the top of her foot. Write a paragraph to explain the proper first-aid procedure, and include the list of supplies you would need.

Interpersonal and Collaborative

11. **Kitchen Safety Guidelines** Follow your teacher's directions to form groups. Design a brochure about kitchen safety. The brochure should include illustrations and written safety guidelines. Post your team's brochure in the classroom. Remember to share them with family members at home.

Financial Literacy

12. **Appliances and Energy Use** When comparing costs for large kitchen and household appliances, you should consider both the purchase price and the ongoing electricity costs of operating the appliance. The government requires most major new appliances to have a yellow EnergyGuide sticker that shows typical energy usage and costs for that model, and how it compares to other models. Imagine that you are comparing two similar refrigerators. Model A costs $595, and uses $58 worth of electricity a year. Model B costs $715, but uses $35 in electricity a year. If a refrigerator lasts 15 years, which model will end up being the least expensive?

13. **Design a Kitchen** With all the options these days for a kitchen, you can have any type of kitchen you want. Design a kitchen that is safe, convenient, and well-equipped. Begin with a list of what you would want in your kitchen. Then design your kitchen for the most efficient use. Create a diagram of your kitchen that shows where appliances will be placed and where utensils will be found for your perfect kitchen. Include where the cupboards, counters, sink, dishwasher and refrigerator will be. Share your diagram with the class.

14. **Research Disease** Choose either E.coli or salmonella, and research to find additional, in-depth information on one of these illnesses. Find out how it is caused, the symptoms, and ways to prevent it. Prepare a brief presentation on what you find to the class.

15. **Set the Table** With permission from your teacher or a parent, go online to search for information on proper table settings. On plain paper, illustrate different ideas and save them for reference. Label according to the appropriate kind of function, for example, picnic, holiday, or family meal. Compile the different table settings to include in your Life Skills Binder.

Academic Skills

 English Language Arts

16. Establish Safety Procedures Imagine that your class is having a dinner party for the parents. Your job is to make sure that the food served is safe to eat. Write down all the procedures you would follow to make the food safe. Present the procedures in an easy-to-follow list of steps.

> **NCTE 5** Use different writing process elements to communicate effectively.

 Social Studies

17. Research Food Safety Food safety has changed and developed throughout history. Choose a historical period and find examples of how safety was addressed in the kitchen. Did different social groups follow different procedures for food safety? Were men and women involved in food preparation? What were the biggest risks that people of this period had to address? Present your findings to the class.

> **NCSS IV B Individual Development and Identity** Identify, describe, and express appreciation for the influence of various historical and contemporary cultures on an individual's daily life.

 Mathematics

18. Storing Food Marco has just finished cooking 2 quarts (115.5 cubic inches) of vegetable soup that he would like to store in the freezer for later use. He is trying to decide if all of that soup will fit inside one resealable container. The container he would like to use is cylindrical, and measures 8 inches wide and 4 inches tall. Can Marco fit 2 quarts of soup in the container?

Math Concept **Volume of a Cylinder**
A cylinder is a solid with a circular base and top. Calculate the volume (V) of a cylinder as $V = \pi r^2 h$, where r is the radius of the circular base, and h is the cylinder's height. Use 3.14 for π.

Starting Hint The height (h) of the container is 8 inches. Since a circle's radius equals ½ of its diameter, the radius (r) of the top and bottom of the container is ½ x 4 inches = 2 inches. Plug these numbers into the volume formula to find the volume in cubic inches.

> **NCTM Geometry** Use visualization, spatial reasoning, and geometric modeling to solve problems.

Standardized Test Practice ● ● ● ● ● ● ● ●

Mathematics

Choose the letter of the best answer. Write the letter for the answer on a separate sheet of paper.

> **Test-Taking Tip** Study for tests over a few days or weeks, and continually review class material. Do not wait until the night before to try and learn everything.

19. If the formula for converting from Celsius to Fahrenheit is F = 9/5C + 32, what is the formula for converting from Fahrenheit to Celsius?
a. C = 5/9(F − 32)
b. C = 5/9(F − 32)
c. C = 32 − 9/5F
d. C = 9/5(F − 32)

Chapter 22

Prepare to Cook

Section 22.1

Meal Preparation

■ **Main Idea** Plan your meals ahead of time, before you shop for food or begin preparing the meal.

Explore the Photo Answer Answers may include price, personal preferences, items listed in the recipe, store displays and special offers, and money and time available.

Section 22.2

Recipe Basics

■ **Main Idea** Good cooking begins with learning different recipe formats and the meanings of recipe terms and abbreviations.

Lem
5/5

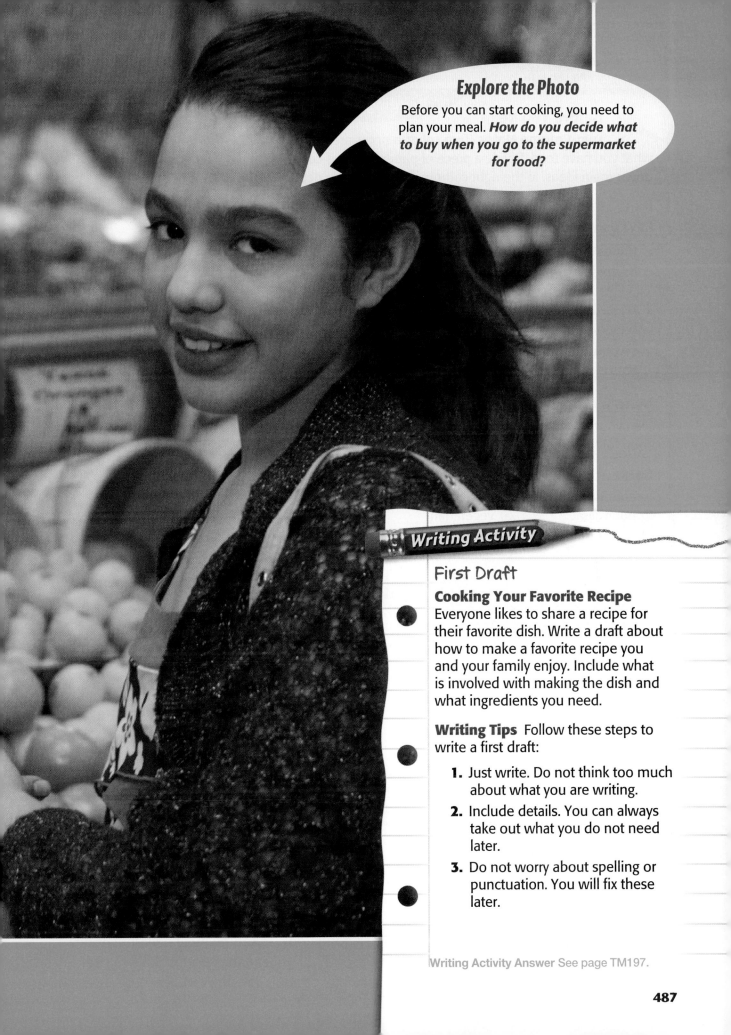

Explore the Photo
Before you can start cooking, you need to plan your meal. *How do you decide what to buy when you go to the supermarket for food?*

Writing Activity

First Draft

Cooking Your Favorite Recipe
Everyone likes to share a recipe for their favorite dish. Write a draft about how to make a favorite recipe you and your family enjoy. Include what is involved with making the dish and what ingredients you need.

Writing Tips Follow these steps to write a first draft:

1. Just write. Do not think too much about what you are writing.
2. Include details. You can always take out what you do not need later.
3. Do not worry about spelling or punctuation. You will fix these later.

Writing Activity Answer See page TM197.

Section 22.1 Meal Preparation

Reading Guide

Before You Read

Two-Column Notes Two column notes are a useful way to study and organize what you have read. Divide a piece of paper into two columns. In the left column, write down main ideas. In the right column, list supporting details.

Read to Learn

Key Concepts

✓ **Identify** the food groups you should include when planning nutritious meals.

✓ **Describe** the information you can find on food labels.

✓ **List** the elements that can destroy nutrients in foods.

Main Idea

Plan your meals ahead of time, before you shop for food or begin preparing the meal.

Content Vocabulary

○ appetizer
○ equivalent
○ meal patterns
○ garnish
○ texture
○ vegetarian
○ unit pricing
○ grade labeling

Academic Vocabulary

■ complement
■ economize

Graphic Organizer

As you read, write down descriptions for national brand, store brand, and generic brand. Use a graphic organizer like the one shown to help you organize your information.

Type of Brand	Description
National Brand	
Store Brand	
Generic Brand	

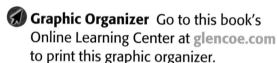 **Graphic Organizer** Go to this book's Online Learning Center at glencoe.com to print this graphic organizer.

- - - - - - - - - - - - - - - - - - - **Academic Standards** - - - - - - - - - - - - - - - - - - -

 English Language Arts

NCTE 5 Use different writing process elements to communicate effectively.

 Science

NSES A Develop abilities necessary to do scientific inquiry, understanding about scientific inquiry.

 Social Studies

NCSS IV B Individual Development and Identity Identify, describe, and express appreciation for the influences of various historical and contemporary cultures on an individual's daily life.

NCTE *National Council of Teachers of English*
NCTM *National Council of Teachers of Mathematics*

NSES *National Science Education Standards*
NCSS *National Council for the Social Studies*

Graphic Organizer Answer
National Brand: advertised in various media; usually the most expensive due to advertising costs. Store Brand: store's name on the label; costs less because there is little or no advertising cost. Generic Brand: lists only the product name and nutritional information; usually the least expensive.

Whether you are throwing a birthday party for a friend or cooking a meal for your family, it is best to start by making a plan. Serving tasty, attractive, and nutritious meals requires more than just being a good cook. Planning meals, reading recipes, and shopping for food put your management skills to use.

Meal Planning

As you plan, think of meals that are simple and nutritious. Include a variety of foods, and consider your skills, time, and money. For good nutrition, plan meals that include foods from each food group from MyPyramid.

The Proteins Group includes all meats, poultry, fish, legumes, eggs, nuts, and seeds. Growing teens need approximately 5½ ounces every day. Foods from this group are usually served as the main dish in a meal.

The Grain Group includes cereal, rice, pasta, breads, and grits. You need 6 ounces every day. Some foods in this group, such as brown rice, whole-wheat bread, and oatmeal are whole grains. You should try to eat at least 3 ounces of whole grains every day.

The Vegetable Group includes broccoli, carrots, spinach, lettuce, asparagus, and green beans. Teens need 2½ cups every day. Raw vegetables can be eaten in salads, as a snack, or as an **appetizer**, a dish served before the main meal. Raw or cooked vegetables can also be served as a side dish.

The Fruit Group includes apples, oranges, tomatoes, avocados, blueberries, plums, and grapes. You need 2 cups of fruit every day. These may include fresh, frozen, dried, and canned fruit as well as fruit juice. Fruit can be part of any meal.

As You Read

Connect When was the last nice dinner party you were invited to? What did you notice about the dinner that made it special?

As You Read Answer Answers may include the variety of food, the color and presentation of food, the way the table was set, seating arrangements, decorations.

Vocabulary

You can find definitions in the glossary at the back of this book.

Photo Caption Answer It is important to have a variety of foods in your diet to promote good health, to maintain proper body weight, and to prevent diseases.

Meal Plan Plan meals by using a variety of nutritious foods. *Why is using a variety of food in your diet important?*

Trans Fat

Trans fat has been connected to increasing LDL cholesterol (the "bad" cholesterol) and lowering HDL cholesterol (the "good" cholesterol). It is important to read labels to know what is in the food you eat. Take a trip to your local grocery store to find what foods have trans fat.

Procedure Use a spreadsheet to track the foods that contain trans fat. Write down the name of the product and the amount of trans fat contained in it.

Analysis What foods did you find that most often had trans fat? Did any of these foods surprise you? What amounts of trans fat did these foods contain? Do you see a pattern in the types of food? What alternatives are there?

> **NSES A** Develop abilities necessary to do scientific inquiry, understanding about scientific inquiry.

The Milk Group includes milk, yogurt, and cheese. As a growing teen, you need 3 cups, or the equivalent of 3 cups, every day. **Equivalent** refers to a food that has equal value, such as consuming a cup of yogurt in place of a cup of milk. Foods from this group can be served with any meal.

Oils Healthful oils are not a food group, but many foods from the five food groups contain healthful oils. Healthful oils include fish oil, vegetable oil, and olive oil.

Meal Pattern

Most people follow **meal patterns**, which are habits that determine when and what they eat each day. They usually select similar types of foods each day for breakfast, lunch, dinner, and snacks. For example, your meal pattern for one day might be:

- **Breakfast** Cereal with fruit and nuts, juice, milk
- **Lunch** Sandwich, fruit or vegetable, dessert, milk
- **Dinner** Meat or poultry, vegetable, rice or pasta, milk
- **Snack** Fresh fruit

Meal planning is easy when you are aware of your meal patterns and choose nutritious foods. Simply choose a combination of foods from the food groups that fit your meal pattern. To plan a lunch for the meal pattern above, you might choose a tuna salad sandwich, carrot sticks, oatmeal cookies, and milk.

Meal patterns should be flexible. You may be trying to gain or lose weight. You may be invited to eat at a friend's home. There may be a special occasion that requires specific food, such as birthday cake, or you may go to a restaurant which limits options.

Variety

Including a variety of foods in each meal makes eating more interesting. Eating many different foods from all of the food groups also makes it easier to get all the nutrients you need. Meals planned with variety in mind look and taste better.

One way to add variety is to vary the way foods are prepared. Another way is to choose foods that provide different colors, sizes and shapes, textures, flavors, and temperatures.

- **Color** Choosing foods of different colors will make the meal look more interesting. For instance, have a salad with tomatoes and carrots to add color to your meal. Add a garnish to provide more color. A **garnish** is a small amount of a food or seasoning to decorate the meal. Parsley, lemon wedges, orange slices, and paprika are examples of garnishes.
- **Size and Shape** Varying the sizes and shapes of foods will give you a much more appealing meal.
- **Texture** Foods with different textures add variety to a meal. **Texture** is the way something feels when touched. For example, raw vegetables are usually crisp, while pudding tends to feel smooth. One way to vary the textures of foods is by preparing them in different ways. For example, think of the difference in texture between raw carrots and cooked carrots.
- **Flavor** Combine flavors that complement each other. Steak, mushrooms, broccoli, and cheese are some flavors that go well together.
- **Temperature** Vary the temperatures of food in a meal. Plan some hot food items and some cold food items.

Gather Your Resources

As you plan your meals, take time to read through the recipes carefully and make sure that you have all of the resources you will need.

- **Skills** If you are a beginning cook, you may want to avoid complicated recipes. Could you choose convenience foods for part of the meal? For instance, you might make a dessert from a mix rather than make it from scratch.
- **Equipment** Some recipes will require a specific utensil. Make sure that you have all of the necessary tools and equipment before you start cooking.
- **Ingredients** Make sure you have all the ingredients the recipe calls for before you start cooking.
- **Money** Do the ingredients fit your food budget? Can you economize, or save money, with coupons or use foods that are less expensive because they are in season?
- **Time** When you know that you will be working within a time frame, such as having only one hour to cook dinner, choose foods that can be prepared within the time allowed.

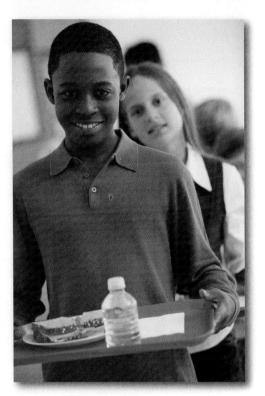

Meal Pattern Knowing your meal patterns can help you plan meals. *What can you do to add variety to your regular meals?*

Photo Caption Answer
Answers my include: use a different type of bread for sandwiches; try new condiments; drink milk or juice instead of soda; try a new fruit; eat crackers instead of chips.

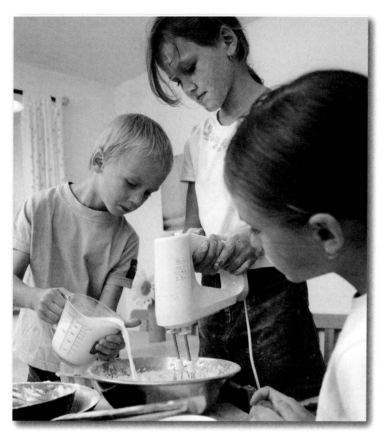

Packaged Mixes Using packaged mixes is a good way to learn the basics of cooking. *What are the benefits of using packaged mixes?*
Photo Caption Answer Packaged mixes can help save you time and simplify meal preparation.

It is also important to make sure that all foods are ready to serve at the right time. Some dishes take longer than others to prepare, and some foods take longer than others to cook. For this reason, you must know what to do first and when to do it. See **Figure 22.1** for a sample time schedule.

Special Dietary Needs

You may need to take into account special diet considerations for a family member, friend, or even yourself. When cooking for guests, ask in advance if anyone has any special diet needs. For example, someone with high blood pressure would need to limit salt and sodium intake. It is also possible that someone could be a **vegetarian** who eats only vegetables, fruits, grains, nuts, and sometimes eggs or dairy products. Many cookbooks are available with special diet recipes. You can also find recipes online.

 Reading Check *Plan* *What preparation should you do before you plan a meal?* Reading Check Answer Read the recipes carefully and gather your resources. Create a schedule to plan out meal preparation time.

Smart Shopping

Learning how to find the best buys is an important part of being a smart shopper. Some brands are better buys than others. Store brands and generic brands are usually less expensive than national brands.

- **National Brands** Products that you see advertised on television or in newspapers or magazines are known as national brands. These products often cost more than others because the manufacturer spends a great deal of money on packaging and advertising. These costs are added to the price of the product.

Balance Your Life

Think Ahead Plan out your week. Studies show that if you schedule your time in advance, you will be able to accomplish more. Writing down what you hope to accomplish in a week can allow you to be realistic about how much you can get done, and find the time to do it.

Figure 22.1 Set a Time Schedule

Make Your Meal a Success Using a time schedule can help you organize your meal so that all the foods are ready to serve at the same time. *What might happen if you do not use a schedule when preparing a meal?*

Sample Time Schedule

- 4:30 Start preparing chicken.
  4:45 Turn on oven.
- 5:00 Place chicken in oven.
  5:15 Wash and chop broccoli.
- 5:30 Begin cooking rice.
- 5:40 Set table.
  5:50 Steam broccoli in microwave.
  5:55 Remove broccoli, rice, and chicken.
- 6:00 Serve the meal.
- 6:45 Wash dishes and clean up kitchen.

Step 1–First list the job that will take longest to do. Then list in order the other jobs to be done until you have listed them all.

Step 2–Some foods take longer to cook than others, so you must plan what to do first and when to do it.

Step 3–Besides cooking time, consider that some dishes take longer to prepare than others.

Step 4–Do not forget to allow time for setting the table, serving the food, and cleaning up.

Step 5–Plan a time schedule backward, from the end to the beginning. First decide at what time you will serve the meal. Then figure out how much time you will need to prepare each of the different foods.

Figure Caption
Answer You might leave out a step; foods may be ready too soon or too late; you could run out of time.

- **Store Brands** Products that have the store's name or another name used only by that store on the label are called store brands. They usually cost less because there is little or no advertising cost. They often have the same ingredients and nutrients as national brands.
- **Generic Brands** Products with labels listing only the product name and nutritional information are generic brands. These often cost even less than store brand products.

Products will vary in price, quality, and taste. Price alone is not an indicator of quality or taste. You will want to compare national brands, store brands, and generic brands to see which ones you prefer.

Character Counts

Respect

Jennifer is preparing a meal for several friends. One of her friends has an allergy to dairy products. Jennifer is planning to serve Mexican food, including quesadillas, tacos, beans, and rice. It will take extra time to prepare something different for her friend, and she is running out of time.

You Make the Call

What should Jennifer so that her friend has something dairy-free to eat? Write a paragraph explaining what course of action Jennifer should choose and why.

Read Food Labels

Food labels give you valuable nutrition information and shopping information. See **Figure 22.2** for explanations of the items listed on food labels. By law, food labels must provide the following information:

- The name of the food.
- The name and address of the roduct's manufacturer.
- The nutritional content, including serving size, calories, and nutrient amounts per serving.
- A list of ingredients in order of amount. For example, a box of dry cereal might list oat flour first, then sugar, followed by other ingredients, to show that oat flour is the main ingredient, then sugar, and then the rest of the ingredients, in order.
- The total weight. For example, which is a better value: a 1-lb. (500-gram) bag of tortilla chips for $1.99 or an 11-oz. (300-gram) bag for $1.49?
- The trans fat amounts.

Unit Pricing

Unit pricing means showing the cost of the product per unit. Examples of units include ounces, pounds, grams, liters, and gallons. Look for the unit pricing label on the edge of the store shelf. It will give you the product name, the size, and the price per unit. You can easily decide which size is the best buy.

Grade Labeling

Understanding and using grade labeling can also help you when you shop. **Grade labeling** is a measurement of food quality using standards set by the government. Many food items including eggs, poultry, and meat are graded. The highest grade is the highest in quality. For example, Grade AA eggs are of higher quality than Grade A eggs.

 Define What are unit pricing and grade labeling?

Figure 22.2 Nutrition Facts

Food Labels Nutrition Facts on food labels can help you decide whether or not you want to purchase the item based on nutrients and ingredients. *There are 2 servings in this can. How many calories does the entire can contain?*

Figure Caption Answer 500 (the can contains 250 calories per serving).

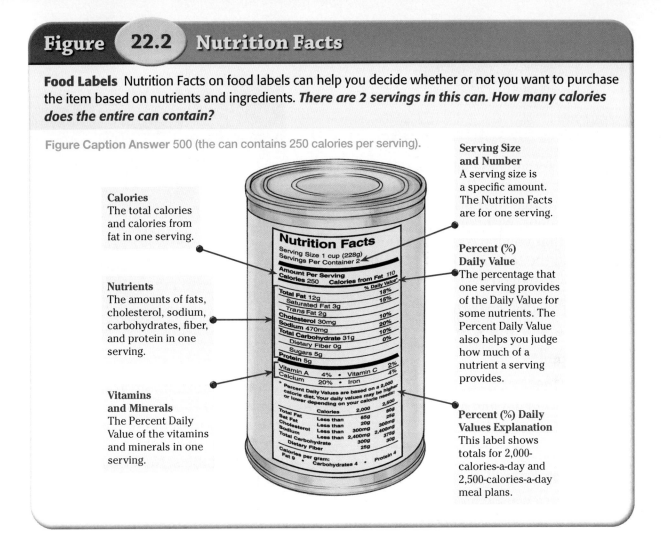

Calories
The total calories and calories from fat in one serving.

Nutrients
The amounts of fats, cholesterol, sodium, carbohydrates, fiber, and protein in one serving.

Vitamins and Minerals
The Percent Daily Value of the vitamins and minerals in one serving.

Serving Size and Number
A serving size is a specific amount. The Nutrition Facts are for one serving.

Percent (%) Daily Value
The percentage that one serving provides of the Daily Value for some nutrients. The Percent Daily Value also helps you judge how much of a nutrient a serving provides.

Percent (%) Daily Values Explanation
This label shows totals for 2,000-calories-a-day and 2,500-calories-a-day meal plans.

Food Storage

When you get home from the supermarket, you will need to store the food you bought. Heat, light, time, and moisture destroy nutrients. They can also affect the flavor and spoil foods. Storing foods properly helps them maintain their freshness and flavor.

Many food items need special treatment to stay fresh. Items you cannot use before the expiration date can be saved by freezing. Here are a few food storage tips:

- Keep butter and margarine covered in the refrigerator, so they do not absorb odors.
- Keep baking powder tightly covered, so it will not lose its strength.
- Slice and freeze fruits and vegetables that you will not iuse right away.
- Green bananas will ripen at room temperature within a couple of days. After that they can be stored in the refrigerator for three to five days.

Hands-On LAB

Plan a Shopping Trip

In this activity you will plan a shopping trip for groceries. Before you begin, read through the entire Hands-On Lab assignment. Write down any questions that you have about the activity. Reread the text or ask your teacher for help if you need it.

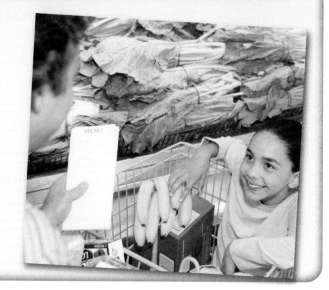

Supplies
✓ Shopping List
✓ Coupons and newspaper
✓ Calculator

Develop Your Plan

■ Make a weekly meal plan and list the grocery items needed.

■ Review your shopping list for staple foods such as milk, eggs, bread, and salt.

■ Clip coupons, and check your local newspaper for sale items.

Implement Your Plan

■ Review the recipes in your meal plan to see what ingredients you need.

■ Make a shopping list. Identify items that are less important in case you exceed your budget. You can put these items back.

■ Discuss the budget with your parent or another adult, and take a calculator with you so you can keep track of what you are spending.

■ Use the information on product labels and unit pricing to help you select items.

■ Look for meat, poultry, and fish that are wrapped in undamaged packaging material to ensure freshness. Look for fresh fruits and vegetables. Never buy dented or bulging cans because the food may be spoiled. Keep raw foods away from cooked and ready-to-eat foods. Choose frozen and refrigerated foods last.

Evaluate Your Results

Did you forget any items on your shopping list? What did you learn about food shopping and your food budget? How would you make your next shopping trip different? Write one or more paragraphs to explain your answer.

 Projects and Activities Go to this book's Online Learning Center through **glencoe.com** for more projects and activities.

Evaluate Your Results Answer Students should explain what, if any, items they forgot, and why. Students may indicate that they learned to save money with coupons, sale items, or generic brands. They should include details about what they learned from the shopping trip, and what they would do differently next time.

- Store onions and potatoes separately. Potatoes will spoil faster when stored near onions.
- Store a container of ice cream inside a heavy, brown bag to prevent freezer burn.
- Freeze leftover broth in ice cube trays. Pop out the broth cubes and store them in a freezer bag for later use.
- Cook fresh meat and freeze it for use at a later meal.

Handle Leftovers Properly

Just like fresh foods, you must also store leftover foods properly to keep them safe. Follow these rules for keeping leftovers:

- Throw away food that has been kept out too long.
- Refrigerate or freeze leftovers as soon as the meal is done.
- Eat refrigerated leftovers within three to four days.
- Reheat leftover solid foods to 165°F (74°C).
- Boil leftover soups, sauces, and gravies before eating.

When you practice food safety procedures, you will help yourself and those in your home stay healthier, enjoy food more, and even save money.

Section 22.1 After You Read

Review What You Have Learned

1. **Describe** ways to add variety to your food.
2. **List** ways to save money when you shop.
3. **Identify** the benefit of proper food storage.

Practice Academic Skills

 English Language Arts

4. Imagine you are going to have a dinner party for close friends and family. Create a formal invitation that includes what you will serve, what time your guests need to arrive, attire to wear, and the place. Use graphics and attention-grabbing text to make your invitation exciting. Clearly communicate the theme you have chosen. Share your invitation with your classmates.

> **NCTE 5** Use different writing process elements to communicate effectively..

 Social Studies

5. What are some meals and foods that are unique to your family? Talk with family members to find out the story behind the foods that you and your family eat that is unique. Bring in a sample menu and recipe. Explain the origin of the food your family enjoys with the class.

> **NCSS IV B** Identify, describe, and express appreciation for the influences of various historical and contemporary cultures on an individual's daily life.

 Check Your Answers Check your answers at this book's Online Learning Center at glencoe.com.

Section 22.2 Recipe Basics

Reading Guide

Before You Read

Study with a Buddy It can be difficult to review your own notes and quiz yourself on what you have just read. Studying with a partner, even for just a short period of time, can help you study better.

Read to Learn

Key Concepts

✓ **Explain** the importance of following recipes.

✓ **Identify** the different ways to mix food.

✓ **Suggest** additions to a recipe's ingredients for better nutrition.

Main Idea

Good cooking begins with learning different recipe formats and the meanings of recipe terms and abbreviations.

Content Vocabulary

○ recipe ○ ingredient

Academic Vocabulary

■ assemble ■ abbreviation

Graphic Organizer

As you read, identify three guidelines for following recipes. Use a graphic organizer like the one shown to help you organize your information.

Recipe Guidelines
1.
2.
3.

Graphic Organizer Go to this book's Online Learning Center at glencoe.com to print this graphic organizer.

•••••••••••••••••••• **Academic Standards** ••••••••••••••••••••

 English Language Arts

NCTE 4 Use written language to communicate effectively.

NCTE 9 Develop an understanding of diversity in language across cultures.

 Mathematics

NCTM Number and Operations Understand numbers, ways of representing numbers, relationships among numbers, and number systems.

Social Studies

NCSS IV B Individual Development and Identity Identify, describe, and express appreciation for the influences of various historical and contemporary cultures on an individual's daily life.

NCTE *National Council of Teachers of English*
NCTM *National Council of Teachers of Mathematics*
NSES *National Science Education Standards*
NCSS *National Council for the Social Studies*

Graphic Organizer Answer Read through the recipe to make sure you understand all the terms and abbreviations; assemble all the ingredients and equipment; do any necessary preparation, such as preheating the oven or greasing a pan.

There will always occasions to cook for other people. To make the best impression, you want the food to be delicious and come out the way you planned. In order for this to happen, you need to know how to follow a recipe that includes specific cooking terms. The more you cook, the better you will become. You will learn something new with every recipe you try, and you may find that friends and family are lining up to eat your food!

Recipes

Almost all cooks use recipes. A **recipe** is a list of directions for preparing a specific food. If you know how to read and follow recipes, you will greatly increase your chances of success in the kitchen.

Some recipes are easier to follow than others. Look at **Figure 22.3** to see which type of recipe format works better for you. While you are learning to cook, look for easy-to-read recipes that do the following:

- State the amount of each or component or part. These are the **ingredients**.
- Provide step-by-step instructions on how to combine the ingredients.
- Mention the sizes of pans that will be needed.
- Specify the cooking time and temperature.
- Estimate the number of servings the recipe should produce.

In whatever format a recipe appears, the procedure for following the recipe remains the same. Some general guidelines for using recipes are on the next page.

As You Read

Connect Think of a recipe you used or saw recently. Was the recipe easy to use? If so, what about the recipe made it easy to use for you?

Vocabulary

You can find definitions in the glossary at the back of this book.

As You Read
Answer Answers will vary, but if the recipe was easy to use, answers may include that the recipe provided step-by-step instructions, specific cooking time, serving suggestions, and utensils needed.

Figure 22.3 Recipe Formats

Reading Recipes Recipes are written in different formats, or styles. *Which do you like better? Why?*

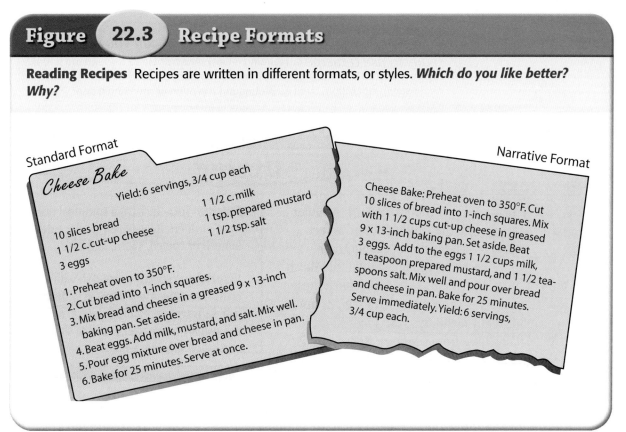

Standard Format

Cheese Bake

Yield: 6 servings, 3/4 cup each

10 slices bread
1 1/2 c. cut-up cheese
3 eggs

1 1/2 c. milk
1 tsp. prepared mustard
1 1/2 tsp. salt

1. Preheat oven to 350°F.
2. Cut bread into 1-inch squares.
3. Mix bread and cheese in a greased 9 x 13-inch baking pan. Set aside.
4. Beat eggs. Add milk, mustard, and salt. Mix well.
5. Pour egg mixture over bread and cheese in pan.
6. Bake for 25 minutes. Serve at once.

Narrative Format

Cheese Bake: Preheat oven to 350°F. Cut 10 slices of bread into 1-inch squares. Mix with 1 1/2 cups cut-up cheese in greased 9 x 13-inch baking pan. Set aside. Beat 3 eggs. Add to the eggs 1 1/2 cups milk, 1 teaspoon prepared mustard, and 1 1/2 teaspoons salt. Mix well and pour over bread and cheese in pan. Bake for 25 minutes. Serve immediately. Yield: 6 servings, 3/4 cup each.

Figure Caption Answer Answers will vary, but most students will probably prefer the step-by-step format of the standard recipe because it is easier to read and follow.

- Read through the entire recipe. Make sure that you understand all the terms and abbreviations.
- **Assemble**, or bring together, all the ingredients and equipment before you start.
- Do any necessary preparation, such as preheating the oven or greasing a pan.

Recipe Abbreviations

Recipes often show measurements in shortened form to save space. To follow the recipe, it is essential to understand what each **abbreviation**, or shortened word, means. Can you imagine how your vegetable soup would taste if you added two tablespoons of salt instead of two teaspoons?

Here are some of the most common abbreviations used in recipes:

t. or tsp.	teaspoon	**lb.**	pound
T. or Tbsp.	tablespoon	**°F**	degrees Fahrenheit
oz.	ounce	**°C**	degrees Celsius
c.	cup	**mL**	milliliter
pt.	pint	**L**	liter
qt.	quart	**g**	gram
gal.	gallon		

✔ **Reading Check** ***Prepare*** *What can you do to get ready to use a recipe?* Reading Check Answer Read through the entire recipe. Assemble all the ingredients and equipment before you start. Do any necessary preparation, such as preheating the oven or greasing a pan.

Discover International... Dining

Italy

Many Italian foods are popular in the United States. In fact, when you eat spaghetti or pizza, you may forget that these foods are not American! Italians generally make these foods in a simpler style. Olive oil, tomato sauces, and vegetables make many Mediterranean foods heart-healthy, especially those from southern Italy. Pasta is usually the first dish in a meal, followed by meat, fish, or a vegetable dish. Traditional foods in northern Italy use more butter and creamy sauces. Polenta, risotto, and hearty bean soups are popular in Italy.

Polenta [pō-'len-tə] a cornmeal dish from northern Italy, which can be eaten as a mush or cooled, sliced, and fried.

Risotto [ri-'sò-tō] a rice dish with a creamy texture, often flavored with chicken, fish, sausage, vegetables, cheese, or wine. It is usually made with a special short-grain rice called Arborio rice.

NCTE 9 Develop an understanding of diversity in language use across cultures.

Cooking and Mixing Terms

Every recipe for hot food has some type of cooking instructions. To follow the recipe, you need to become familiar with some common cooking terms and know what they mean. Here are some cooking terms you are most likely to read:

Bake Cook in the oven without a cover.

Boil Cook in liquid hot enough to bubble rapidly.

Braise Simmer gently in a small amount of liquid in a covered pan. The food may be browned first.

Broil Cook under direct heat.

Brown Cook in a small amount of fat over high heat to brown the surface.

Chill Put in the refrigerator until cold.

Cook Prepare food by dry heat or moist heat.

Cook By Dry Heat Cook food uncovered without adding any liquid.

Cook By Moist Heat Cook in a covered pan with liquid added.

Deep-Fat Fry Cook in hot fat deep enough to cover the food.

Fry Cook in hot fat.

Roast Cook in the oven in dry heat.

Sauté Fry in a small amount of fat until done.

Scald Heat milk until it steams and just begins to bubble around the edge of the pan.

Simmer Cook to just below the boiling point so the liquid barely bubbles.

Steam Cook over boiling water.

Stew Cook slowly in liquid.

Stir fry Cook quickly in a small amount of fat at high heat.

Preheat Heat the oven to the right temperature before putting in the food.

➔ **Steamed Foods** A steamer holds food above boiling water for moist cooking. *What types of food might you steam?* Photo Caption Answer Examples include, vegetables, tamales, rice, fish, chicken.

Financial Literacy

Find the Best Buy

Emily drinks an 8-ounce glass of orange juice every morning. She can buy a 64-fluid-ounce carton of orange juice at the grocery store for $3.75, or a 16-fluid-ounce bottle of fresh-squeezed orange juice for $1.99. She can also buy a 12-ounce can of frozen orange juice concentrate for $2.15. If a can of orange juice concentrate makes 48 fl. oz. of juice, which type of juice is cheapest per ounce?

Math Concept **Calculate Unit Price** The unit price of an item indicates the cost for every 1 unit of measurement. Calculate unit price by dividing the price of an item by the quantity. Round your answer to the nearest cent.

Starting Hint: Calculate the unit price (price per ounce) of the three containers of orange juice by dividing price by the number of ounces of juice that come from the container.

> **NCTM Number and Operations** Understand numbers, ways of representing numbers, relationships among numbers, and number systems.

 For math help, go to the Math Appendix at the back of the book.

Financial Literacy Answer The carton costs $3.75 ÷ 64 ≈ $0.06 per fl. oz. The bottle costs $1.99 ÷ 16 ≈ $0.12 per fl. oz. The frozen concentrate is the cheapest, at $2.15 ÷ 48 ≈ $0.04 per fl. oz.

Figure (22.4) Mixing Terms and Techniques

Mix It Up You can mix food in a variety of ways. *What is the difference between blending and creaming?*

Whip Beat fast with an electric mixer, rotary beater, or wire whip to add enough air to make the mixture fluffy.

Blend Stir until the ingredients are completely mixed.

Cream Blend until smooth and fluffy.

Stir Move the ingredients in a circular motion to mix or to prevent burning.

Beat Mix or stir quickly, bringing the contents of the bowl to the top and down again.

Toss Tumble ingredients lightly with a spoon and fork.

Combine Mix two or more ingredients together.

Figure Caption Answer Blending is stirring until the ingredients are completely mixed. With creaming, you want the result to go beyond being mixed to being smooth and fluffy.

It is equally important to understand mixing terms. For example, do you know how to blend pudding? **Figure 22.4** illustrates basic mixing terms and techniques.

Adjust Recipes for Nutrition and Flavor

Nutrition and flavor are linked. Use proper techniques for preparing food to help keep nutrients and flavor. Nutrients can be lost during preparation. Some are destroyed by heat or by oxygen in the air. You can modify many dishes for nutrition without giving up flavor. Some recipes can be adjusted to lower the calories or fat, or increase the fiber, calcium, iron, and other nutrients. Follow these guidelines to make common recipes more nutritious and to retain nutrients:

- **Add More Vegetables** Add more cut-up vegetables to casseroles, pasta dishes, and other mixed dishes. Pare or trim as little from fruits and vegetables as possible.

- **Increase Calcium** Add calcium-fortified tofu to salads and stir-fries.
- **Reduce Fat** Use less of high-fat ingredients such as butter, margarine, salad dressing, and peanut butter.
- **Add More Fiber** Add fiber-rich dry beans and peas to soups and mixed dishes.
- **Reduce Added Sugar** Use vanilla, cinnamon, and other spices to bring out food's natural sweetness instead of using sugar.
- **Reduce Sodium** Cut down on the salt. Use herbs, spices, and citrus to enhance flavor.
- **Keep Foods Whole** Use whole or large pieces when possible.
- **Use the Correct Temperature** Cook food for the right length of time and serve it at the right temperature
- **Use the Microwave** By microwaving foods, in little or no liquid, you keep more vitamins in the food.

Balance Your Life
Look Ahead Preparation is important. If you have a big paper due at the end of a semester, it is better to work on it a little at a time than to try to cram it all into a week or a few days. If you have a school break coming up, do some extra work ahead of time so you can be carefree and relaxed during your break.

● ● ● ● ● ● ● ● ● ● ● ● ● ● ● ●

Succeed in School Help students plan ahead by reminding them often about deadlines for big projects.

Section **22.2** After You Read

Review What You Have Learned
1. **Explain** what can greatly increase your success in the kitchen.
2. **List** five common cooking terms.
3. **Summarize** ways to save nutrients and enhance flavor.

Practice Academic Skills

 English Language Arts

4. Write a letter to a good friend who has requested a recipe from you. Explain how to make the dish that she or he is requesting in a step-by-step way. Include ingredients, instructions, baking time, servings, and any other information about the recipe. You might want to explain why this recipe is special to you.

> **NCTE 4** Use written language to communicate effectively.

 Social Studies

5. Think about dishes that your grandparents or family members may fix on a regular basis without using an actual recipe. Watch them cook the dish, and ask for the ingredients and instructions. Write them down on recipe cards for other members of your family, including yourself. Consider this to be a part of your family history.

> **NCSS IV B** Identify, describe, and express appreciation for the influences of various historical and contemporary cultures on an individual's daily life.

● ●

 Check Your Answers Check your answers at this book's Online Learning Center at glencoe.com.

Discovering Careers

Are you concerned with the quality of the food that you eat? Do you love to bake? If you answered yes to either of those questions, you might want to consider a future career in Food Preparation. The following chart explores several careers in the food science industry.

Career Activities ▼

At School

1 Select two of the careers listed. Research the education, training, and work experience required for each career. Write a summary of your results.

At Home

2 Look through two or three different brands of the same type of food at your home. How are the ingredients the same? How are they different?

At Work

3 Give three examples of how technology has changed the food prepared and served in the workplace. Compare findings with your classmates.

In the Community

4 Contact and interview someone in your community who works food science industry. Ask this person to describe what his or her typical work day is like. Share what you learned with your class.

Career Investigations Go to this book's Online Learning Center for activities and worksheets to help you explore careers.

Job Title	Job Description
Agricultural Engineer	Applies engineering technology and knowledge of biological sciences to agricultural problems. Concerned with machinery, structures, conservation, and agricultural products' processing.
Agronomist	Studies on crop production and soil and plant sciences. Develops new methods of growing crops for more efficient production, higher yield, and improved quality.
Health Inspector	Visits food service locations to document health conditions. Evaluates areas for food safety hazards. Recommends safe food-handling practices to restaurant managers.
Food Technologist	Conducts new product research for the development of foods. Involved in the quality control, packaging, processing, and use of foods.
Food Tester	Performs tests to determine physical or chemical properties of food or beverage products. Ensures compliance with quality and safety standards.

Career Activities Answers for these activities can be found on page TM197.

Chapter **22** Review and Activities

Chapter Summary

Section 22.1 Meal Preparation

As you plan a meal, think of options that are simple and nutritious. Consider your skills, time needed, ingredients and supplies, and money when choosing your meals. Including a variety of foods in each meal makes eating more interesting and also makes it easier to get the nutrients you need. Learning how to find the best buys is an important part of being a smart shopper. Food labels give you valuable nutrition and shopping information.

Section 22.2 Recipe Basics

A recipe is a list of directions for preparing a specific food. Read through the entire recipe before you begin. Make sure that you understand all the terms and abbreviations. Assemble all the ingredients and equipment. Do any necessary preparation. To be able to follow the recipe, you need to become familiar with some common cooking and mixing terms and abbreviations. Many recipes can be modified to improve nutritional value.

Words You Learned

1. Label each of these content and vocabulary terms as a noun, verb, or adjective.

Content Vocabulary
- appetizer (p. 489)
- equivalent (p. 490)
- meal patterns (p. 490)
- garnish (p. 491)
- texture (p. 492)
- vegetarian (p. 492)
- unit pricing (p. 494)
- grade labeling (p. 490)
- recipe (p. 499)
- ingredient (p. 499)

Academic Vocabulary
- complement (p. 491)
- economize (p. 491)
- assemble (p. 500)
- abbreviation (p. 500)

Review Key Concepts

2. **Identify** the food groups you should include when planning nutritious meals.

3. **Describe** the information you can find on food labels.

4. **List** the elements that can destroy nutrients in foods.

5. **Explain** the importance of following recipes.

6. **Identify** the different ways to mix food.

7. **Suggest** additions to a recipe's ingredients for better nutrition.

Critical Thinking

8. **Analyze** a cookbook recipe. Highlight food preparation terms in the recipe. What will you need to follow this recipe? What do you need to do before you start preparing this recipe?

9. **Evaluate** the variety of foods you ate yesterday. Write down everything you ate, and assess if you are eating balanced meals from each of the food groups.

Real-World Skills and Applications

Problem-Solving

10. Obtain Information Look through your cabinets and pantry at home to find five foods that you regularly eat. Read the labels on the products and write down information about serving size, nutritional content, calories, and the list of ingredients. Are these healthful foods? How can you tell? For the items that are not healthful, what alternatives could you add to your next shopping trip?

Interpersonal and Collaborative

11. Host a Potluck Do you know what a potluck is? A potluck is a meal to which each person brings one dish that is shared by everyone. Follow your teacher's directions to form groups. Plan a potluck. Choose recipes that you and your group can prepare for a meal. Come up with a plan for each person to contribute a dish for your meal. Bring your food to school and eat lunch together, sharing your recipe and the steps you took to prepare the dish.

Financial Literacy

12. Saving at the Supermarket There are many ways to save money on groceries, including using coupons, looking for sales, buying items in larger quantities, and switching to store or generic brands. Michael needs to make sandwiches for a picnic he is planning to attend with his basketball team. The coach gave him a budget for buying ingredients. Michael found good deals and bread and jam, but he is having a difficult time deciding which peanut butter is the best value. He can buy a 28-ounce jar for $4.89, or a 40-ounce jar for $5.99. The 17-ounce jars are normally $3.50 each, but as part of an in-store sale, he can buy two of them for $5.00. He has a coupon that will let him save 50 cents on any size jar, but he cannot use the coupon on sale items. If 1 ounce of peanut butter constitutes one serving, how can Michael get the lowest cost per serving?

13. Recipe Round Up It is fun to share what we like to cook or eat. Create a class cookbook by having everyone contribute a favorite recipe. Make sure that all the recipes are in a step-by-step format and use the correct abbreviations. Collect the recipes in a binder and create a decorative cover.

14. Research Recipes Choose a food that is somewhat common such as bread, pasta, rice, or beef. Research the origin of the food. Find recipes from the past that include that food. How have the food and its preparation evolved? Prepare a brief presentation on what you find to the class.

15. Find an Appetizer Snacks and appetizers are very popular, especially before dinner, at parties, or while watching sports or movies. With permission from a teacher or parent, go online to search for healthful appetizer ideas. Compile what you find and include your list in your Life Skills Binder.

Academic Skills

 English Language Arts

16. Dining Together Write a letter to the local newspaper in your community about the importance of families eating meals together at home on a regular basis. Include examples of what families gain by eating together.

> **NCTE 12** Use language to accomplish individual purposes.

 Science

17. Chemical Reactions For bread to rise and bake into a loaf, there are ingredients that are needed for the chemical reaction that allows the bread to rise. Find recipes for differnet types of bread that require yeast.

Procedure Determine what ingredients are needed for the chemical reaction that makes a loaf of bread.

Analysis What is the list of ingredients that are needed for the chemical reaction? How do they work together to create bread?

> **NSES B** Develop an understanding of the structure of atoms, structure and properties of matter, chemical reactions, motions and forces, conservation of energy and increase in disorder, and interactions of matter and energy.

 Mathematics

18. Changing RecipeYield Daphne would like to prepare homemade granola using a recipe that calls for 4 cups of rolled oats, 1 ½ cups of wheat germ, ½ cup of almonds, ½ cup of coconut, ½ cup of raisins, 1 cup of honey, and ¼ cup of oil. The recipe makes 8 cups of granola, but that is too much for Daphne. Rewrite the recipe so that it yields 6 cups instead.

Math Concept **Multiplying Fractions** To multiply fractions, first convert any mixed or whole numbers to improper fractions. Then multiply all numerators to get the new numerator, and multiply the denominators to get the new denominator. Reduce to lowest terms.

Starting Hint The new recipe yields ⁶⁄₈, or ¾, of the original recipe. To reduce each ingredient by the same proportion, multiply each ingredient amount by ¾.

> **NCTM Number and Operations** Compute fluently and make reasonable estimates.

Standardized Test Practice

Short Answer

Write two or three sentences to answer each question.

> **Test-Taking Tip** Put as much information into your answer as possible. Use easy-to-read, short sentences that define key words. Also give an example that explains your answer.

19. Why do you need to learn how to read a recipe?

20. What is the advantage of planning meals for a whole week in advance?

Chapter 23

Cooking Basics

Choose Your Ingredients

■ **Main Idea** Herbs, spices, fruit, and vegetables all contribute to preparing delicious meals.

Cooking Techniques

■ **Main Idea** Grains, fruits, vegetables, and meats come in endless varieties. All of these foods can be cooked to serve as main dishes, side dishes, or snacks.

Explore the Photo Answer Recipes explain how to put the right amounts of food and seasonings together in just the right way. Recipes have been tried, adjusted, tested and improved, so you know your food has a good chance of coming out right if you follow a recipe.

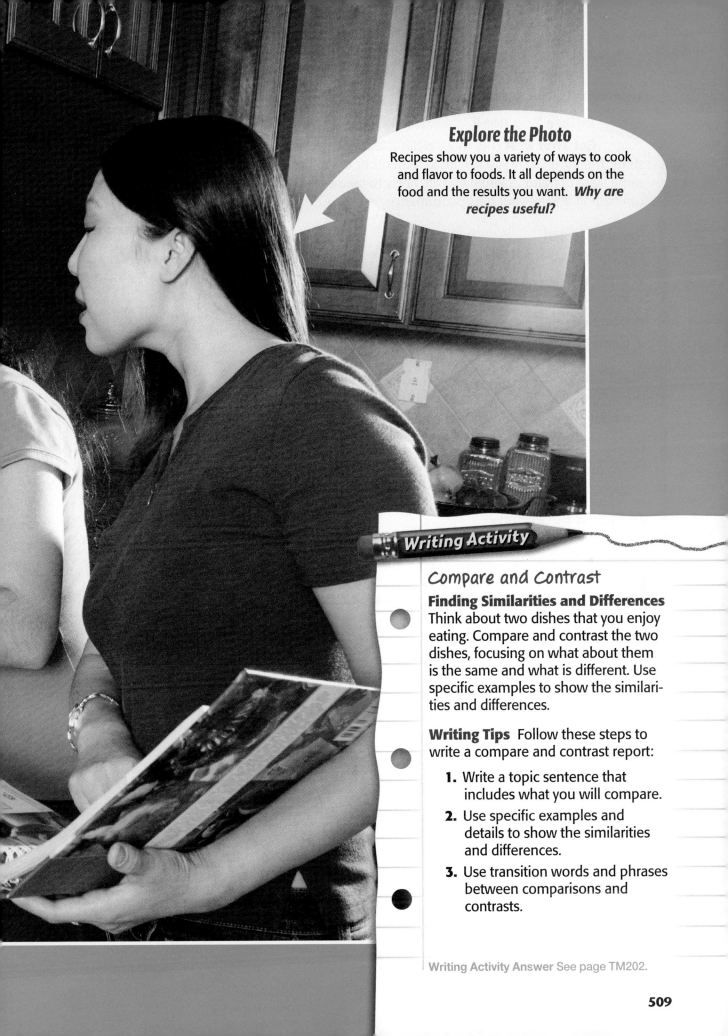

Explore the Photo
Recipes show you a variety of ways to cook and flavor to foods. It all depends on the food and the results you want. *Why are recipes useful?*

Writing Activity

Compare and Contrast

Finding Similarities and Differences
Think about two dishes that you enjoy eating. Compare and contrast the two dishes, focusing on what about them is the same and what is different. Use specific examples to show the similarities and differences.

Writing Tips Follow these steps to write a compare and contrast report:

1. Write a topic sentence that includes what you will compare.
2. Use specific examples and details to show the similarities and differences.
3. Use transition words and phrases between comparisons and contrasts.

Writing Activity Answer See page TM202.

Section 23.1 Choose Your Ingredients

Reading Guide

Before You Read

Get Your Rest The more well-rested and alert you are when you sit down to study, the more likely you will be to remember the information later. Studying in the same state of mind as when you are likely to take a test, fully rested and mentally sharp, can help to ensure your best performance.

Read to Learn

Key Concepts

✓ **Explain** Why herbs and spices are important.

✓ **Describe** how fruit may be processed.

✓ **Name** a benefit of convenience foods.

Main Idea

Herbs, spices, fruit, and vegetables all contribute to preparing delicious meals.

Content Vocabulary

 produce   antioxidant
 processed   ○ convenience food

Academic Vocabulary

■ crucial
■ seasonal

Graphic Organizer

Vegetables come from many different parts of plants. As you read, name eight plant parts that produce the vegetables you eat. Use a graphic organizer like the one shown to help you organize your information.

Vegetable Plant Parts

Graphic Organizer Go to this book's Online Learning Center at glencoe.com to print this graphic organizer.

Academic Standards

English Language Arts

NCTE 5 Use different writing process elements to communicate effectively.

Mathematics

NCTM Data Analysis and Probability Understand and apply basic concepts of probability.

Social Studies

NCSS III B People, Places, and Environments Create, use, and synthesize information from various representations of the earth, such as maps, globes, and photographs.

NCTE *National Council of Teachers of English*
NCTM *National Council of Teachers of Mathematics*

NSES *National Science Education Standards*
NCSS *National Council for the Social Studies*

Graphic Organizer Answer
fruits, flowers, stems, roots, tubers, bulbs, leaves, seeds

Just about everyone knows how to cook something. Maybe you are a whiz at scrambled eggs or pancakes. Perhaps you are already in charge of preparing entire meals for your family. Whatever level of experience you have in the kitchen, you can improve your cooking skills with a few tips and guidelines.

Basic Ingredients

When cooking, the success of your dish depends in part on following step-by-step instructions. As you learn to cook, you will notice that some common ingredients are found in many recipes. Some of these basic ingredients are flour, sugar, shortening or butter, milk, eggs, and spices. Each ingredient in a recipe is used for a specific purpose.

Herbs and Spices

Herbs and spices are the special ingredients that separate average cooks from great cooks. Herbs and spices add taste, color and aroma, or scent, to foods. They are the special ingredients that make some recipes better than others. Herbs and spices are **crucial**, or very important, to the flavor of a dish. There are many varieties of herbs and spices. Learning which herbs and spices to use, and how much to use, is based on experience. Here are some common herbs and spices:

- **Basil** This popular herb has a mild flavor. It is often used in soups, salads, and pizzas.
- **Parsley** Often used as a garnish, this herb is also found in green sauces, such as pesto. It has a soothing effect on your taste buds.
- **Chives** This herb has a mild onion flavor. It is often used as a garnish or to add flavor to soups and dips.
- **Cilantro** This herb has a unique flavor and aroma. It is often used in salsas, Mexican dishes, and dips.
- **Dill Weed** This herb has a delicate flavor. It is often used in dips and fish dishes.
- **Cinnamon** This spice comes from the bark of the laurel tree. Ground cinnamon is common in cakes, cookies, and specialty drinks.
- **Nutmeg** This spice comes from the fruit of the nutmeg tree. It has a nutty, mild flavor. It is used often in pies and puddings.
- **Cumin** Commonly found ground or as a whole seed, this spice is somewhat hot. It is often used in marinades and sauces.
- **Saffron** This yellow spice comes from the crocus plant. It is used to give its yellow color and flavor to foods.
- **Garlic** This strong spice is a dried root from the lily family. It grows in a bulb that is then minced or chopped.

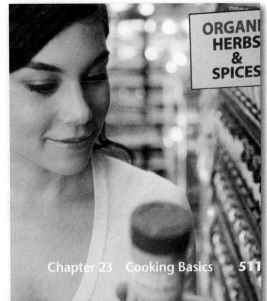

ORGANI HERBS & SPICES

Figure 23.1 Measurement Equivalents

Accurate Measuring It is important to measure accurately when preparing meals. *What would happen if you used 2 cups of milk instead of 1 cup for your mashed potatoes?*

Customary	Customary Equivalent	Approximate Metric Equivalent
1 teaspoon	*none*	5 milliliters (mL)
1 tablespoon	3 teaspoons	15 milliliters
½ cup	8 tablespoons	125 milliliters
1 cup	16 tablespoons 8 fluid ounces	250 milliliters
2 cups	1 pint	500 milliliters
4 cups	1 quart	1000 milliliters or 1 liter (L)
1 pound	16 ounces	500 grams (g)

Measure Ingredients

By measuring accurately, using the proper measuring tools, and following directions, you will ensure that your recipes are consistent and turn out the same way every time you use them.

When you cook, you will probably use customary measurements such as cups for volume and pounds for weight. The customary measurement system is the measurement system commonly used in the United States. However, the metric system can also appear in recipes, so you may need to know how to convert between the two systems. The metric system is a system of weights and measures based on multiples of ten and is used in most other countries. See **Figure 23.1** for measurement equivalents.

Cooking Temperature

The customary system measures temperature in degrees Fahrenheit (°F). The metric system measures in degrees Celsius (°C). Many thermometers show both. Recipes sometimes include length measurements, such as the length and width of a pan or the size of a vegetable. The customary system measures length in inches (in.), while metrics uses millimeters (mm) or centimeters (cm).

Reading Check **Confirm** *How can you make sure that your recipe will come out the way you want?*

Fruits and Vegetables

Fruits and vegetables, also called **produce**, are full of essential nutrients. Vegetables can fit into your eating plan in many ways. Serve them as side dishes, main dishes, salads, and garnishes. Like vegetables, fruits are easy to include in your eating plan. Fruits come in a variety of forms, such as fresh, frozen, canned, dried, and as a juice. Many fruits have skins you can eat, such as apples and pears, which can add fiber to your snacks.

Fruits

Besides tasting great, fruit provides important vitamins and minerals, carbohydrates, and fiber. It is easy to get the recommended number of daily servings because fruits go well with any meal and make great snacks. Try adding dried fruit, such as apples or apricots, on your breakfast cereal. Freeze grapes or berries and use them in place of ice cubes in juices and teas.

Some produce, like strawberries, is **seasonal**, or readily available at certain times of the year. Seasonal food is less expensive than food that is not in season. When you buy produce in-season, you get the best possible quality and also save money. Out-of-season produce may be less nutritious because it is often artificially ripened, or shipped a long distance. If fresh fruits are not available, you might choose processed fruits. **Processed** means that a food is changed from its raw form before being sold. Fruits that are frozen, canned, or dried are considered processed.

Vegetables

Vegetables are a delicious part of a well-balanced diet. They are also valuable sources of carbohydrates, fiber, and important vitamins and minerals. New varieties are developed each year. Like fruits, vegetables are most nutritious when they are fresh. Vegetables are seasonal, but most are available year-round. You can choose frozen, canned, dried, or fresh vegetables.

COMMUNITY CONNECTIONS
Soup Kitchens Volunteer at a soup kitchen where they use the food that is donated. Use your skills at planning menus and using different spices, herbs, fruits, and vegetables to create meals.

MATH YOU CAN USE

Probability

Juanita has baked three dozen cupcakes for a party. Fifteen of the cupcakes have a fresh strawberry filling, another twelve are vanilla, and the remaining 9 are banana. However, Juanita covered each cupcake with the same white vanilla frosting, and now she cannot tell them apart. If she selects one at random, what is the probability it will be strawberry? Vanilla? Banana?

Math Concept **Finding Theoretical Probability** Mathematical probability is a number between 0 and 1 that measures the likelihood of an event occurring. The higher the number, the more likely the event will occur. To find an event's probability, write a fraction (in lowest terms) with the number of ways the event can occur as the numerator and the total number of possible outcomes as the denominator.

Starting Hint Since there are 36 total cupcakes, there are 36 possible outcomes when Juanita goes to pick one cupcake, so use 36 as the denominator of each fraction.

NCTM Data Analysis and Probability Understand and apply basic concepts of probability.

 For more math help, go to the Math Appendix located at the back of this book.

Math You Can Use Answer Strawberry: $15/36 = 5/12$. Vanilla: $12/36 = 1/3$. Banana: $9/36 = 1/4$.

Hands-On LAB

Measuring Correctly

In this activity you will use tools to measure different ingredients accurately. Before you begin, read through the entire Hands-On Lab assignment. Write down any questions that you have about the activity. Reread the text or ask your teacher for help if you need it.

Supplies
- ✓ Flour sifter
- ✓ Dry and liquid measuring cups and spoons
- ✓ Metal spatula
- ✓ Rubber scraper
- ✓ Flour
- ✓ Shortening
- ✓ Oil
- ✓ Baking soda

Develop Your Plan
- Gather measuring utensils.
- Gather ingredients.
- Measure ingredients.

Implement Your Plan
- Gather your measuring utensils and ingredients.
- Sift and measure 1 cup of flour.
- Press shortening into a dry measuring cup, making sure there are no air pockets. Level it with a metal spatula. Remove shortening with a rubber scraper.
- Place the liquid measuring cup on a flat surface. Pour oil up to the ½ cup line. Check it at eye level.
- Pour ¼ teaspoon of baking soda into the measuring spoon. Level the top with a metal spatula.

Evaluate Your Results

Why must you measure ingredients exactly? What could happen if you do not measure ingredients correctly? Write down three tips that you learned from this experience. Write one or more paragraphs to explain your answer.

 Projects and Activities Go to this book's Online Learning Center through **glencoe.com** for more projects and activities.

Evaluate Your Results Answer You must measure ingredients exactly so your recipes are consistent. Failing to measure ingredients correctly can result in your recipe not turning out correctly. Tips could include: sift flower before measuring; when measuring solid ingredients such as shortening, make sure there are no air pockets; use a spatula to scrape excess solid or powdered ingredients from the top of the measuring cup or spoon; when measuring liquids, place the measuring cup on a flat surface.

Vegetables actually come from many different parts of plants. Vegetables can be:

- Fruits, such as tomatoes, eggplants, and peppers.
- Flowers, such as broccoli and cauliflower.
- Stems, such as asparagus and celery.
- Roots, such as beets, carrots, and turnips.
- Tubers (underground stems), such as potatoes.
- Bulbs, such as onions and garlic.
- Leaves, such as cabbage, greens, kale, and spinach.
- Seeds, such as beans, corn, and peas.

Fresh vegetables need to be refrigerated until you are ready to use them. For best results, they should be used within a few days after you buy them. Before serving fresh vegetables, wash them carefully under cold running water. If you plan to eat them raw, you may want to peel the vegetables and blot them dry. To keep raw vegetables crisp, do not wash them too far in advance of serving time. Raw vegetables can be enjoyed alone, or you can try dipping carrots, cauliflower, or broccoli in low-fat ranch dressing for a refreshing and healthful snack.

Many vegetables contain antioxidants. An **antioxidant** ('an-tē-'äk-sə-dənt) is a substance that protects cells from oxidation, a chemical reaction that causes cell damage. Antioxidants may help prevent heart disease, cancer, and other ailments. Antioxidants include vitamins C and E, beta-carotene, and the mineral selenium.

 Reading Check *Identify* *What is an antioxidant?*

Fresh Fruit Choose the freshest fruit you can in order to get the best flavor and highest nutritional value. *How much fruit should you eat every day?*

Photo Caption Answer MyPyramid encourages people to eat 2 cups from the Fruit Group every day.

Convenience Foods

There may be occasions when you will want to prepare meals in a hurry. **Convenience foods** are already prepared or partially prepared to save you time. For instance, you might buy a bag of tossed salad instead of purchasing all the ingredients and cutting them up yourself. A common type of convenience food is a mix such as cake and muffin mixes. Other convenience foods include frozen pizza, canned chili, and soup. Be careful when you use convenience foods as they tend to cost more than fresh foods. Additionally, they may not taste as fresh. They may contain preservatives, which are chemicals added to make foods last longer. However, once in a while it may be worth the extra cost to save time and avoid wasting food.

Always follow the directions given on the package. Make sure in advance that you have all the ingredients and utensils you will need and that you understand all the instructions. When using a general-purpose baking mix, use only the recipes provided on the box. Do not try to substitute the mix for ingredients in another recipe.

Section 23.1 After You Read

Review What You Have Learned

1. **List** the common, basic ingredients found in many recipes.
2. **Name** ways to use vegetables in your food.
3. **Explain** a drawback of using convenience foods.

Practice Academic Skills

 English Language Arts

4. Use clip art, illustrations or pictures from magazines to create a pamphlet encouraging people to buy spices. Discuss the benefits of spices, using specific examples of spices and the dishes in which they can be used. Share your pamphlet with the class.

> **NCTE 5** Use different writing process elements to communicate effectively.

Social Studies

5. Use poster board to create a map that shows where fruits and vegetables are most commonly grown in the United States. Use graphics, clip art, or your own drawings to show the region and the produce grown there.

> **NCSS III B** Create, use, and synthesize information from various representations of the earth, such as maps, globes, and photographs.

Check Your Answers Check your answers at this book's Online Learning Center at glencoe.com.

Section **23.2** Cooking Techniques

Before You Read

Stay Engaged One way to stay engaged when reading is to turn each of the headings into a question, and then read the section to find the answers

Read to Learn

Key Concepts

✓ **Name** two types of breads.

✓ **Explain** how fruits and vegetables are a part of a well-balanced diet.

✓ **Describe** ways to use milk products in cooking.

✓ **Identify** two basic methods of cooking meat, poultry, or fish.

Main Idea

Grains, fruits, vegetables, and meats come in endless varieties. All of these foods can be cooked to serve as main dishes, side dishes, or snacks.

Content Vocabulary

○ quick bread
○ batter
○ yeast bread
○ legume
○ quiche
○ casserole
○ scald
○ curdle
○ omelet

Academic Vocabulary

■ tender   ■ retain

Graphic Organizer

As you read, list the four main types of food discussed in the section. Use a graphic organizer like the one shown to help you organize your information.

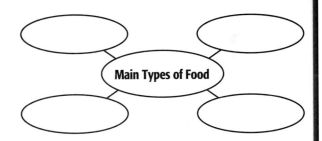

Main Types of Food

Graphic Organizer Go to this book's Online Learning Center at glencoe.com to print this graphic organizer.

---------------------- **Academic Standards** ----------------------

 English Language Arts

NCTE 12 Use language to accomplish individual purposes.

 Social Studies

NCSS VIII A Science, Technology, and Society Identify and describe both current and historical examples of the interaction and interdependence of science, technology, and society in a variety of cultural settings.

NCTE *National Council of Teachers of English*
NCTM *National Council of Teachers of Mathematics*

NSES *National Science Education Standards*
NCSS *National Council for the Social Studies*

Graphic Organizer
Answer Grains; Fruits
and Vegetables; Milk
Products; Meat, Poultry,
and Fish.

There are many different ways to prepare food. To get what you want from your meals, it is important to know how to cook bread and grains, fruits and vegetables, milk products, and meat, poultry, and fish.

As You Read

Connect Think about a recent meal you cooked for yourself, or a meal that was cooked for you. How was each item cooked or prepared?

◆ Vocabulary

You can find definitions in the glossary at the back of this book.

As You Read Answer
Answers may include steaming vegetables, moist heat for meat, or baking a particular kind of bread.

Cooking Grains

Grains include cereal, rice, pasta, and bread. These go well with vegetables, fruits, cheese, meat, chicken, fish, and beans.

Breads

Breads are made from whole wheat, rye, white, or corn flour. Other ingredients are added to give each type of bread a particular flavor, texture, and appearance.

Quick Breads and Yeast Breads

Quick breads are breads in which the leavening agent is baking powder or baking soda. Baking powder and baking soda cause the air bubbles to form, making the bread rise quickly as it bakes. It is important to mix the **batter**, a liquid or semiliquid mixture, usually containing flour, milk, and eggs, just long enough to blend the ingredients. Too much mixing makes quick breads flat and heavy. Air bubbles, which form during baking, make quick breads light and fluffy.

Yeast breads are breads in which the leavening agent is yeast. They take longer to prepare than quick breads. Most sandwich breads, French and Italian breads, and hamburger buns are yeast breads.

A dough made with yeast must rise twice. First, you must let it rise in a warm place outside the oven for an hour or more. Then you punch it down, shape it, and let it rise in the pan before baking. You can also buy frozen yeast dough. Let the dough warm to room temperature and rise until it is ready to be baked.

➜ International
Sandwiches Sandwiches are more than just slices of ham on wheat bread. Greek gyros, and the Asian spring rolls in this photo are also types of sandwiches. *What other types of sandwiches do you enjoy?*

Photo Caption
Answer Answers may include pitas, burritos, wraps, calzones, or empanadas.

Sandwiches

A sandwich is any filling put in or on bread or another edible wrapper. You can use any type of bread or a wrap, such as pita or a tortilla. Then add a spread, such as mustard, mayonnaise, honey, pesto, butter, or margarine. Fillings can include peanut butter, fruit preserves, tuna, chicken salad, meat or cheese. Finally, use lettuce, spinach, avocado, relish, sprouts, tomatoes, peppers, and olives for extra flavor. Try a tuna melt by putting tuna and cheese on a bagel or bread and melting the cheese. Peanut butter with banana slices on oatmeal bread provides foods from three of the five food groups.

Cereal, Rice and Pasta

Some breakfast cereals, rice, and pasta must be cooked before you eat them. Some of the cooking techniques are similar because they all contain corn starch.

Cereal can be enjoyed with cold milk or cooked and eaten hot such as instant oatmeal, grits, and wheat cereals. They can be cooked with water or milk on top of the stove or in a microwave oven. Try adding raisins or sliced bananas to hot cereal to add texture, flavor, and sweetness.

Rice is a grain that must be cooked. Rice should be simmered in water, not boiled. When cooked properly, rice is light and fluffy, not heavy or gummy. Do not rinse rice, because rinsing removes nutrients. Use a little oil in the cooking water to help the grains separate and to prevent foaming. Keep the lid on while cooking and do not drain. Fluff the rice with a fork before serving. Before you cook rice, read the directions on the package.

Pasta is made from wheat flour, water, and sometimes eggs and other flavorings. It comes in many shapes and sizes, from long strands to corkscrews to shells. Pasta is another grain that must be cooked before it is eaten. To make your pasta slippery and not sticky, use plenty of water, about 4 quarts (4L) of water per pound of pasta. Heat the water to a boil before adding the pasta. Keep it boiling during the cooking time. Do not cover the pot. Stir the pasta occasionally to prevent clumping. Cook the pasta just long enough so that it is **tender**, or easily chewed or cut, but slightly firm. Use the package instructions to guide cooking times. Drain the pasta carefully by pouring the pasta into a colander placed in the sink.

 Reading Check *Follow Directions What are some tips for cooking rice?*

Reading Check Answer Do not rinse rice. Use a little oil in the cooking water. Do not remove the lid while the rice is cooking. Do not drain the rice. Fluff the rice with a fork before serving.

Cooking Fruits and Vegetables

When you think of the kinds of fruit you enjoy, you probably think of eating raw fruit, such as apples, grapes, and bananas. However, fruits are used in many cooked dishes, too. Like fruit, vegetables can be enjoyed raw or cooked. Some vegetables, such as potatoes, winter squash, and artichokes, must be cooked before you eat them.

Baked fruit can be used for desserts such as baked apples and baked pears. Recipes include fruit, butter, sugar, cream, and spices such as cinnamon or nutmeg. Fruits can be baked in a conventional oven or a microwave oven or cooked in a pan on the stove.

Fruits taste and look best when they are cooked properly. During cooking, small amounts of some vitamins are lost. Some dissolve in water and some are destroyed by heat and air. To minimize nutrient loss, use low heat and as little water as possible.

Like fruits, vegetables can **retain**, or keep, their nutrients and keep their texture and flavor if they are cooked properly. Cook vegetables until they are tender and crisp, not soft. To prevent vitamin and mineral loss during cooking, add as little water as possible, use a lid to speed cooking time and avoid overcooking. Vegetables that are cooked properly have a somewhat brighter color than raw ones. For example, green beans are bright green when they are done, and olive green when they have cooked too long.

Vegetables can be cooked and served as a side dish or added to other ingredients to make a casserole. A **casserole** is a one-dish meal that is baked and often reheated after cooking. The most common ways to cook vegetables are:

- **Simmering** Cook vegetables in a small amount of liquid, just below the boiling point. Cover the pan with a tight-fitting lid.
- **Steaming** Place vegetables inside a steamer over simmering water inside a covered pan. The vegetables should not touch the water.
- **Baking** Vegetables, such as potatoes, are baked in their skins. Before baking, pierce the skins several times so they do not burst.
- **Stir-frying** Cook vegetables quickly over high heat while stirring them in a small amount of oil.

✓ **Reading Check** **Explain** *How can you prevent vitamin and mineral loss when cooking vegetables.*

Cooking with Milk Products

Milk or cream can be used to make soups, sauces, puddings, and custards. Milk and buttermilk are often used in cakes, pies, breads, and muffins.

Thick, creamy sauces add flavor to many dishes. A basic white sauce made with milk can be served over vegetables or noodles. For extra flavor, add cheese or herbs to the sauce.

When cooking with milk products, it is important to be especially careful. Milk burns, or scorches, easily if the temperature is too high or if it is cooked too long. To cook milk you need to **scald** it, or bring it slowly to a temperature just below the boiling point. Never let milk boil. Heat only until little bubbles begin to appear around the edge of the pan.

Milk may curdle if you do not handle it properly. When milk **curdles**, it separates into little particles or curds. Adding tomatoes or fruit juices to milk may cause curdling, as they contain acid. To avoid this, add ingredients very slowly and stir the milk constantly.

Cheese is an important ingredient in many recipes. Cheese is supposed to melt, not cook, so heating cheese too long or at high temperatures may cause it to burn or become rubbery or stringy. When cooking with cheese, use low to medium heat. Grate or shred hard cheeses, such as cheddar, before adding them to other ingredients. The cheese will blend faster and more evenly. Add cheese at the end of the cooking time so that the cheese will not become overcooked.

Try sprinkling grated cheese on soups, chili, baked potatoes, or burritos. For an easy snack, eat cheese with crackers, crusty bread, or fresh fruit.

Reading Check *Describe* *What can you do to keep cheese from burning or becoming rubbery or stringy when you cook with it?*

Macaroni and Cheese A popular favorite among children is macaroni and cheese. *What ingredients could you add to this dish to make it appealing to adults?*

Cooking Meat, Poultry, and Fish

Protein-rich foods such as meat, poultry, and fish are popular main dishes. They can be prepared in a variety of ways. When cooking meat, poultry, or fish, the two basic methods you will use are moist heat and dry heat (See **Figure 23.2**). The method you choose depends on the recipe you are following and the tenderness of the meat or poultry.

Moist Heat

When you boil, stew, braise, or simmer meat, you are using moist heat. Moist-heat cooking is cooking food slowly in a covered container, usually with water, broth, or a sauce. When cooked, some of the meat juices will flow into the cooking liquid. Moist-heat cooking methods are good choices to use with less expensive, tougher cuts of meat. When cooked slowly in liquid, meats become more tender and flavorful. Use moist heat to cook chuck roast, corned beef, pork blade steak, pot roast, poultry, round steak, spareribs, and stew meat.

Dry Heat

Dry-heat cooking is cooking without liquid. Broiling, charbroiling, roasting, baking, pan frying, and deep frying are dry heat cooking methods. This method is used for tender cuts of meat such as beef rib roast, fish, ground beef, pork, turkey, ham, lamb, pork chops, poultry and sirloin steak.

Figure Caption Answer Moist-heat cooking would help tougher cuts of meat, such as chuck roast, corned beef, pork blade steak, pot roast, poultry, round steak, spareribs, and stew meat, become more tender and flavorful.

Reading Check **List** *What are some dry-heat cooking* methods?

Reading Check Answer Broiling, charbroiling, roasting, baking, pan frying or deep frying

---

Figure 23.2 Cooking Methods for Meat

Dry Heat or Moist Heat? Dry-heat cooking is used for tender pieces of meat, while moist-heat cooking is used to help make tough cuts more tender. *What types of meat would benefit from moist-heat cooking?*

Dry Heat Methods

Frying

Roasting and Baking

Broiling

Moist Heat Methods

Stewing

Braising

Other Proteins

Other high-protein foods can be used as the main dish instead of meat, poultry, or fish. Beans and eggs are two good substitutes. They are high in protein, vitamins, and minerals and low in cost. They are two of the most nutritious foods you can cook. They are also both vegetarian options.

Legumes are dry beans and peas which come in a variety of tastes and textures. Red kidney beans, black beans, white beans, lentils, lima beans, split peas, and black-eyed peas offer healthful alternatives to meat, poultry, and fish dishes. You can make baked beans or roll them in tortillas with rice and cheese to make burritos.

Eggs can also be a main dish. Eggs can be hard-boiled, scrambled, fried, or used in quiches and omelets. A **quiche** ('kēsh) is a main-dish pie filled with eggs, cheese, and other ingredients such as ham, spinach, and mushrooms. An **omelet** is a well-beaten egg that is first cooked in a frying pan without stirring. Then it is filled with other ingredients, such as mushrooms, peppers, and cheese.

Section 23.2 After You Read

Review What You Have Learned

1. **Describe** the process for making yeast bread.
2. **Name** the most common ways to cook vegetables.
3. **Explain** the best ways to cook with cheese.
4. **Identify** two sources of protein other than meat.

Practice Academic Skills

 English Language Arts

5. Write a letter to someone who is trying to cut back on sugar intake. Tell him or her that fruit is an easy, healthful, convenient, and delicious substitute for candy or cookies. Use information from this chapter, but write in your own words.

> **NCTE 12** Use language to accomplish individual purposes.

 Social Studies

6. Choose a historical period and research a cooking technique addressed in the section. Compare and contrast the cooking technique with what we do today. How was cooking different? How have techniques changed? Has the technique improved? Share your information with the class.

> **NCSS VIII A** Identify and describe both current and historical examples of the interaction and interdependence of science, technology, and society in a variety of cultural settings.

Check Your Answers Check your answers at this book's Online Learning Center at glencoe.com.

Discovering Careers

Do you like to try new cooking techniques? Are you interested in how food is prepared before it arrives in markets or restaurants? If you answered yes to either of those questions, you might want to consider a future career in food preparation. The following chart explores several careers in the food industry.

Job Title	Job Description
Menu Planner	Works closely with executive chef to select menu items. Participates in cost control, ordering of supplies, and some food preparation.
Pastry Chef	Prepares a wide variety of pastries and desserts. Supervises pastry cooks. Plans work schedules. Orders supplies.
Farmer	Raises both crops and livestock. Determines crops to be grown and livestock to be bred. Monitors market conditions and weather.
Baker	Uses raw ingredients to bake breads and pastries for sale. Offers specialty breads for a variety of events.
Food Critic	Evaluates restaurants based on standards for cooking techniques, flavor, and service. Writes column or blog with recommendations.

Career Activities ▼

At School

1 Select three of the careers listed. Research the education, training, and work experience required for each career. Write a summary of your results.

At Home

2 Plan a dinner with your family. Each of you should take responsibility for one portion of the meal (for example, main dish, side dish, desert, appetizer, sauce). What techniques did each of you use to cook you part of the meal?

At Work

3 Plan three nutritious brown-bag lunches that you could take to work. Compare your examples with those of your classmates.

In the Community

4 Contact and interview someone in your community who works in the food industry. Ask this person to describe what his or her typical work day is like. Share what you learned with your class.

Career Activities Answers for these activities can be found on page TM202.

Learn More *Online* glencoe.com

Career Investigations Go to this book's Online Learning Center for activities and worksheets to help you explore careers.

Chapter 23 · Review and Activities

Chapter Summary

Section 23.1 Choose Your Ingredients
The success of your dish depends in part on following step-by-step instructions. By measuring accurately, using the proper measuring tools and following directions, you ensure that your recipes turn out the same every time. Herbs and spices add taste, color, and aroma to foods. Fruits and vegetables are a delicious part of a well-balanced meal plan. Convenience foods can save you time.

Section 23.2 Cooking Techniques
There are many techniques for cooking food. Grain products like rice, pasta, and oatmeal are cooked in water. Some foods made from grains must be cooked before you eat them. Like fruit, vegetables can be enjoyed raw or cooked. Vegetables retain their nutrients and keep their texture and flavor when cooked properly. When cooking meat, poultry, or fish, you can use moist heat or dry heat.

Words You Learned

1. Create a fill-in-the-blank sentence for each of these vocabulary terms. The sentence should contain enough information to help determine the missing word.

Content Vocabulary
- produce (p. 513)
- processed (p. 513)
- antioxidant (p. 515)
- convenience food (p. 516)
- quick bread (p. 518)
- batter (p. 518)
- yeast bread (p. 518)
- casserole (p. 520)
- scald (p. 521)
- curdle (p. 521)
- legume (p. 523)
- quiche (p. 523)
- omelet (p. 523)

Academic Vocabulary
- crucial (p. 511)
- seasonal (p. 513)
- tender (p. 519)
- retain (p. 520)

Review Key Concepts

2. **Explain** why herbs and spices are important.
3. **Describe** how fruit may be processed.
4. **Name** a benefit of convenience foods.
5. **Name** two types of breads.
6. **Explain** how fruits and vegetables are a part of a well-balanced diet.
7. **Describe** ways to use milk products in cooking.
8. **Identify** two basic methods of cooking meat, poultry, or fish.

Critical Thinking

9. **Explain** how you can retain the nutrients in vegetables when you cook them.

Real-World Skills and Applications

Problem-Solving

10. Quick and Nutritious Meal You have 30 minutes to prepare a nutritious dinner for you and your family. You have chicken breasts as the main ingredient. What cooking methods could you use to prepare dinner? What could you add to the meal to increase its nutritional value?

Technology Applications

11. Herb and Spice Guide Use a spreadsheet or word-processing software to make a reference guide for cooking with herbs and spices. With permission from a teacher or parent, go online to search for information to add to what you learned in this chapter. Include information about how herbs and spices work together. Also look for examples of foods that work best with specific herbs and spices.

Financial Literacy

12. Buying Convenience Foods As their name implies, convenience foods can save busy home cooks a great deal of shopping and cooking time versus preparing meals and baked goods from scratch. However, convenience foods can be less nutritious than home-cooked foods, and you can pay a lot for all that convenience. Find a simple cake recipe. Determine the cost of all the ingredients you would need to purchase to make that cake from scratch. Then, determine the cost of making a similar cake using a cake mix. Finally, determine the cost of purchasing a finished cake from a bakery or grocery store. How do the prices compare? What are the pros and cons of each type of cake?

13. A Nutritious Gift Snack and fruit baskets are so popular that there are stores and Web sites devoted to creating and selling them as gifts. Create a snack or fruit basket to give to a friend, teacher, or family member as a gift. Include an attractive collection of fruits and tasty, nutritious snacks. Also, find a few recipes for healthful treats. Compile them into a small booklet and create a cover for it, and include the booklet in the basket.

14. Spice Origins What is your favorite spice? Is it sweet like cinnamon or hot like curry? Conduct research to learn where your favorite spice originated. What is the spice made from? What was it originally used for? How is it used today? Can the spice be used for something other than adding flavor to food? Present your information in a brief report.

15. Cancer-fighting Foods According to the National Cancer Institute, antioxidants are plentiful in fruits and vegetables, as well as in other foods such as nuts, grains and some meats, poultry, and fish. Researchers continue to study the effect of antioxidants on cancer prevention. With permission from your parents or teacher, go online to search for foods that may help prevent cancer. Make a list of at least 10 foods and explain how you can add them to your meals. Include this information in your Life Skills Binder.

Academic Skills

English Language Arts

16. Cooking Vegetables Creative preparation can make it easier and more enjoyable to add vegetables to your meals. Having many different options for cooking them will give you more variety in your meals. Create a poster that explains six possible ways to cook vegetables. Include graphics, photos, and clear instructions for each cooking technique. Display your posters in your classroom.

> **NCTE 8** Use information resources to gather information and create and communicate knowledge.

Social Studies

17. Research a Family Recipe Families often have a recipe that has been handed down from one generation to another. Often the recipe has not been written down but is communicated orally from mother or father to daughter or son. Choose a family recipe that has been handed down, and research to find out its origins, the ingredients, and its importance to you family heritage and culture. Write an overview of what you find.

> **NCSS I D Culture** Compare and analyze societal patterns for preserving and transmitting culture while adapting to environmental or social change.

Mathematics

18. Slicing Bread Katherine needs to slice two loaves of fresh-baked bread. The sourdough loaf is 12 in. long, and she would like each slice to be ¾ in. thick. A rye loaf is 13 ½ in. long, and she would like each slice to be ½ in. thick. How many slices will she get out of each loaf?

Math Concept **Dividing with Fractions**
To divide when a fraction is involved, first convert any mixed or whole numbers to improper fractions. Multiply the first fraction by the reciprocal of the second fraction. Reduce your answer to lowest terms.

Starting Hint For the sourdough, you will need to divide 12 by ¾, which requires you to multiply 12/1 by the reciprocal of ¾, or 4/3. For the rye loaf, first convert 13 ½ into an improper fraction by multiplying 13×2 and adding that number to 1 to get the new numerator.

> **NCTM Number and Operations** Understand meanings of operations and how they relate to one another.

Standardized Test Practice ● ● ● ● ● ● ●

Math Word Problem

Read the word problem and possible answers. Then choose the correct answer.

> **Test-Taking Tip** Solve a word problem in two steps. First, translate the words into an equation of numbers and variables. Then solve each equation in order to get the correct answer.

19. You are getting ready to check out of the grocery store. The store is offering a 22% discount for students shopping for their parents. Your total amount is $112.53. After you deduct the discount, what will your amount be?
a. $22.51
b. $90.02
c. $101.00
d. $165.04

UNIT 10 Life Skills Project

A Meal from Your Culture

Preparing food from your own culture is a way to explore your identity. Your family may have favorite dishes that they make on holidays and special occasions. Recipe books are often specific to a culture, nationality, or heritage. This project will help you explore food from your background.

 My Journal Complete the journal entry from page 465, and refer to it to complete your recipe collection.

Project Assignment ▼

In this project, you will:

- Gather recipes of dishes common to your background.
- Write about a recipe that means something to your family.
- Prepare a dish that reflects your culture.
- Interview someone who shares your heritage.
- Present your findings to your class.
- Include this project in the tenth section of your personal Life Skills binder.

Step 1 Gather Recipes from Your Culture

Ask family members or friends if they have recipes that reflect your heritage. Read cookbooks to find more ideas. Compile the recipes you gather, and write a summary of your research that identifies common ingredients and preparation methods.

Step 2 Choose a Recipe and Prepare a Dish

Pick a recipe you can make. Gather the ingredients, and follow instructions carefully. If you need help, ask a parent or friend. Then write two or more paragraphs that answer these questions:

✔ What were the key ingredients?

✔ What was the most challenging part of the preparation process?
✔ Is there any method you use today that an ancestor might have done differently, for example, using a microwave instead of an open fire?
✔ What is the traditional way to serve this dish?

Step 3 Interview a Member of Your Culture

Interview someone in your community who is familiar with the traditions of your culture. Ask these questions:

✔ What does this dish mean to you?
✔ What is the history of this recipe?
✔ Tell me a story about a memorable meal that included this dish.

Use these interviewing skills when conducting your interview and these writing skills when writing the summary of notes from your interview.

Interviewing Skills
- Record interview responses and take notes.
- Listen attentively.

Writing Skills
- Use complete sentences.
- Use correct spelling and grammar.

Step 4 Serve and Present Your Cultural Dish

Use the Life Skills Project Checklist on the right to plan and serve your dish to the class and give an oral report on it.

Use these speaking skills when presenting your final report.

Speaking Skills
- Speak clearly and concisely.
- Be sensitive to the needs of your audience.
- Use standard English to communicate.

Step 5 Evaluate Your Presentation

Your project will be evaluated based on:

✔ Organization and cultural relevance of your collected recipes.
✔ The dish you prepared for the class.
✔ Description of your food preparation experience.
✔ The summary written from interview notes.
✔ Grammar and sentence structure.
✔ Presentation to the class.
✔ Creativity and neatness.

Evaluation Rubric Go to this book's Online Learning Center at **glencoe.com** for a rubric you can use to evaluate your final project.

NCTE 9 Develop an understanding of diversity in language use across cultures.

NCTM Measurement Understand measurable attributes of objects and the units, systems, and processes of measurement.

Life Skills Project Checklist

Research Cultural Recipes

- Collect traditional recipes from your family or friends.
- Read cookbooks about food from your background.
- Prepare a recipe from your heritage.
- Interview someone who is familiar with your culture.

Writing Skills

- Describe common ingredients and preparation methods of your culture.
- Describe your own food preparation experience.
- Write a summary from your interview with someone who shares your background.

Present Your Findings

- Prepare a short presentation to give before serving your dish to the class. Describe how your dish is important to your culture.
- Invite the students of the class to ask any questions they may have. Answer these questions with responses that respect their perspectives.
- Add this project to your Life Skills binder.

Academic Skills

- Conduct research to gather information.
- Communicate effectively.
- Organize your presentation so the audience can follow along easily.
- Thoroughly express your ideas.

Math Appendix

Number and Operations

▶ *Understand numbers, ways of representing numbers, relationships among numbers, and number systems*

Fraction, Decimal, and Percent

A percent is a ratio that compares a number to 100. To write a percent as a fraction, drop the percent sign, and use the number as the numerator in a fraction with a denominator of 100. Simplify, if possible. For example, $76\% = \frac{76}{100}$, or $\frac{19}{25}$. To write a fraction as a percent, convert it to an equivalent fraction with a denominator of 100. For example, $\frac{3}{4} = \frac{75}{100}$, or 75%. A fraction can be expressed as a percent by first converting the fraction to a decimal (divide the numerator by the denominator) and then converting the decimal to a percent by moving the decimal point two places to the right.

Comparing Numbers on a Number Line

In order to compare and understand the relationship between real numbers in various forms, it is helpful to use a number line. The zero point on a number line is called the origin; the points to the left of the origin are negative, and those to the right are positive. The number line below shows how numbers in fraction, decimal, percent, and integer form can be compared.

Percents Greater Than 100 and Less Than 1

Percents greater than 100% represent values greater than 1. For example, if the weight of an object is 250% of another, it is 2.5, or $2\frac{1}{2}$, times the weight.

Percents less than 1 represent values less than $\frac{1}{100}$. In other words, 0.1% is one tenth of one percent, which can also be represented in decimal form as 0.001, or in fraction form as $\frac{1}{1,000}$. Similarly, 0.01% is one hundredth of one percent or 0.0001 or $\frac{1}{10,000}$.

Ratio, Rate, and Proportion

A ratio is a comparison of two numbers using division. If a basketball player makes 8 out of 10 free throws, the ratio is written as 8 to 10, 8:10, or $\frac{8}{10}$. Ratios are usually written in simplest form. In simplest form, the ratio "8 out of 10" is 4 to 5, 4:5, or $\frac{4}{5}$. A rate is a ratio of two measurements having different kinds of units—cups per gallon, or miles per hour, for example. When a rate is simplified so that it has a denominator of 1, it is called a unit rate. An example of a unit rate is 9 miles per hour. A proportion is an equation stating that two ratios are equal. $\frac{3}{18} = \frac{13}{78}$ is an example of a proportion. The cross products of a proportion are also equal. $\frac{3}{18} = \frac{13}{78}$ and $3 \times 78 = 18 \times 13$.

Representing Large and Small Numbers

In order to represent large and small numbers, it is important to understand the number system. Our number system is based on 10, and the value of each place is 10 times the value of the place to its right.

The value of a digit is the product of a digit and its place value. For instance, in the number 6,400, the 6 has a value of six thousands and the 4 has a value of four hundreds. A place value chart can help you read numbers. In the chart, each group of three digits is called a period. Commas separate the periods: the ones period, the thousands period, the millions period, and so on. Values to the right of the ones period are decimals. By understanding place value you can write very large numbers like 5 billion and more, and very small numbers that are less than 1, like one-tenth.

Scientific Notation

When dealing with very large numbers like 1,500,000, or very small numbers like 0.000015, it is helpful to keep track of their value by writing the numbers in scientific notation. Powers of 10 with positive exponents are used with a decimal between 1 and 10 to express large numbers. The exponent represents the number of places the decimal point is moved to the right. So, 528,000 is written in scientific notation as 5.28×10^5. Powers of 10 with negative exponents are used with a decimal between 1 and 10 to express small numbers. The exponent represents the number of places the decimal point is moved to the left. The number 0.00047 is expressed as 4.7×10^{-4}.

Factor, Multiple, and Prime Factorization

Two or more numbers that are multiplied to form a product are called factors. Divisibility rules can be used to determine whether 2, 3, 4, 5, 6, 8, 9, or 10 are factors of a given number. Multiples are the products of a given number and various integers.

For example, 8 is a multiple of 4 because $4 \times 2 = 8$. A prime number is a whole number that has exactly two factors: 1 and itself. A composite number is a whole number that has more than two factors. Zero and 1 are neither prime nor composite. A composite number can be expressed as the product of its prime factors. The prime factorization of 40 is $2 \times 2 \times 2 \times 5$, or $2^3 \times 5$. The numbers 2 and 5 are prime numbers.

Integers

A negative number is a number less than zero. Negative numbers like −8, positive numbers like +6, and zero are members of the set of integers. Integers can be represented as points on a number line. A set of integers can be written {…, −3, −2, −1, 0, 1, 2, 3, …} where … means "continues indefinitely."

Real, Rational, and Irrational Numbers

The real number system is made up of the sets of rational and irrational numbers. Rational numbers are numbers that can be written in the form a/b where a and b are integers and $b \neq 0$. Examples are 0.45, $\frac{1}{2}$, and $\sqrt{36}$. Irrational numbers are non-repeating, non-terminating decimals. Examples are $\sqrt{71}$, π, and 0.020020002….

Complex and Imaginary Numbers

A complex number is a mathematical expression with a real number element and an imaginary number element. Imaginary numbers are multiples of i, the "imaginary" square root of −1. Complex numbers are represented by $a + bi$, where a and b are real numbers and i represents the imaginary element. When a quadratic equation does not have a real number solution, the solution can be represented by a complex number. Like real numbers, complex numbers can be added, subtracted, multiplied, and divided.

Vectors and Matrices
A matrix is a set of numbers or elements arranged in rows and columns to form a rectangle. The number of rows is represented by m and the number of columns is represented by n. To describe the number of rows and columns in a matrix, list the number of rows first using the format $m \times n$. Matrix A below is a 3×3 matrix because it has 3 rows and 3 columns. To name an element of a matrix, the letter i is used to denote the row and j is used to denote the column, and the element is labeled in the form $a_{i,j}$. In matrix A below, $a_{3,2}$ is 4.

$$\text{Matrix A} = \begin{pmatrix} 1 & 3 & 5 \\ 0 & 6 & 8 \\ 3 & 4 & 5 \end{pmatrix}$$

A vector is a matrix with only one column or row of elements. A transposed column vector, or a column vector turned on its side, is a row vector. In the example below, row vector b' is the transpose of column vector b.

$$b = \begin{pmatrix} 1 \\ 2 \\ 3 \\ 4 \end{pmatrix}$$

$$b' = (1 \quad 2 \quad 3 \quad 4)$$

► Understand meanings of operations and how they relate to one another

Properties of Addition and Multiplication
Properties are statements that are true for any numbers. For example, $3 + 8$ is the same as $8 + 3$ because each expression equals 11. This illustrates the Commutative Property of Addition. Likewise, $3 \times 8 = 8 \times 3$ illustrates the Commutative Property of Multiplication.

When evaluating expressions, it is often helpful to group or associate the numbers. The Associative Property says that the way in which numbers are grouped when added or multiplied does not change the sum or product. The following properties are also true:

- **Additive Identity Property:** When 0 is added to any number, the sum is the number.

- **Multiplicative Identity Property:** When any number is multiplied by 1, the product is the number.

- **Multiplicative Property of Zero:** When any number is multiplied by 0, the product is 0.

Rational Numbers
A number that can be written as a fraction is called a rational number. Terminating and repeating decimals are rational numbers because both can be written as fractions.

Decimals that are neither terminating nor repeating are called irrational numbers because they cannot be written as fractions. Terminating decimals can be converted to fractions by placing the number (without the decimal point) in the numerator. Count the number of places to the right of the decimal point, and in the denominator, place a 1 followed by a number of zeros equal to the number of places that you counted. The fraction can then be reduced to its simplest form.

Writing a Fraction as a Decimal

Any fraction $\frac{a}{b}$, where $b \neq 0$, can be written as a decimal by dividing the numerator by the denominator. So, $\frac{a}{b} = a \div b$. If the division ends, or terminates, when the remainder is zero, the decimal is a terminating decimal. Not all fractions can be written as terminating decimals. Some have a repeating decimal. A bar indicates that the decimal repeats forever. For example, the fraction $\frac{4}{9}$ can be converted to a repeating decimal, $0.\overline{4}$

Adding and Subtracting Like Fractions

Fractions with the same denominator are called like fractions. To add like fractions, add the numerators and write the sum over the denominator. To add mixed numbers with like fractions, add the whole numbers and fractions separately, adding the numerators of the fractions, then simplifying if necessary. The rule for subtracting fractions with like denominators is similar to the rule

for adding. The numerators can be subtracted and the difference written over the denominator. Mixed numbers are written as improper fractions before subtracting. These same rules apply to adding or subtracting like algebraic fractions. An algebraic fraction is a fraction that contains one or more variables in the numerator or denominator.

Adding and Subtracting Unlike Fractions

Fractions with different denominators are called unlike fractions. The least common multiple of the denominators is used to rename the fractions with a common denominator. After a common denominator is found, the numerators can then be added or subtracted. To add mixed numbers with unlike fractions, rename the mixed numbers as improper fractions. Then find a common denominator, add the numerators, and simplify the answer.

Multiplying Rational Numbers

To multiply fractions, multiply the numerators and multiply the denominators. If the numerators and denominators have common factors, they can be simplified before multiplication. If the fractions have different signs, then the product will be negative. Mixed numbers can be multiplied in the same manner, after first renaming them as improper fractions. Algebraic fractions may be multiplied using the same method described above.

Math Appendix

Dividing Rational Numbers

To divide a number by a rational number (a fraction, for example), multiply the first number by the multiplicative inverse of the second. Two numbers whose product is 1 are called multiplicative inverses, or reciprocals. $\frac{7}{4} \times \frac{4}{7} = 1$. When dividing by a mixed number, first rename it as an improper fraction, and then multiply by its multiplicative inverse. This process of multiplying by a number's reciprocal can also be used when dividing algebraic fractions.

Adding Integers

To add integers with the same sign, add their absolute values. The sum takes the same sign as the addends. An addend is a number that is added to another number (the augend). The equation $-5 + (-2) = -7$ is an example of adding two integers with the same sign. To add integers with different signs, subtract their absolute values. The sum takes the same sign as the addend with the greater absolute value.

Subtracting Integers

The rules for adding integers are extended to the subtraction of integers. To subtract an integer, add its additive inverse. For example, to find the difference $2 - 5$, add the additive inverse of 5 to 2: $2 + (-5) = -3$. The rule for subtracting integers can be used to solve real-world problems and to evaluate algebraic expressions.

Additive Inverse Property

Two numbers with the same absolute value but different signs are called opposites. For example, -4 and 4 are opposites. An integer and its opposite are also called additive inverses. The Additive Inverse Property says that the sum of any number and its additive inverse is zero. The Commutative, Associative, and Identity Properties also apply to integers. These properties help when adding more than two integers.

Absolute Value

In mathematics, when two integers on a number line are on opposite sides of zero, and they are the same distance from zero, they have the same absolute value. The symbol for absolute value is two vertical bars on either side of the number. For example, $|-5| = 5$.

Multiplying Integers

Since multiplication is repeated addition, $3(-7)$ means that -7 is used as an addend 3 times. By the Commutative Property of Multiplication, $3(-7) = -7(3)$. The product of two integers with different signs is always negative. The product of two integers with the same sign is always positive.

Dividing Integers

The quotient of two integers can be found by dividing the numbers using their absolute values. The quotient of two integers with the same sign is positive, and the quotient of two integers with a different sign is negative. $-12 \div (-4) = 3$ and $12 \div (-4) = -3$. The division of integers is used in statistics to find the average, or mean, of a set of data. When finding the mean of a set of numbers, find the sum of the numbers, and then divide by the number in the set.

Adding and Multiplying Vectors and Matrices

In order to add two matrices together, they must have the same number of rows and columns. In matrix addition, the corresponding elements are added to each other. In other words $(a + b)_{ij} = a_{ij} + b_{ij}$. For example,

$$\begin{pmatrix} 1 & 2 \\ 2 & 1 \end{pmatrix} + \begin{pmatrix} 3 & 6 \\ 0 & 1 \end{pmatrix} = \begin{pmatrix} 1+3 & 2+6 \\ 2+0 & 1+1 \end{pmatrix} = \begin{pmatrix} 4 & 8 \\ 2 & 2 \end{pmatrix}$$

Matrix multiplication requires that the number of elements in each row in the first matrix is equal to the number of elements in each column in the second. The elements of the first row of the first matrix are multiplied by the corresponding elements of the first column of the second matrix and then added together to get the first element of the product matrix. To get the second element, the elements in the first row of the first matrix are multiplied by the corresponding elements in the second column of the second matrix then added, and so on, until every row of the first matrix is multiplied by every column of the second. See the example below.

$$\begin{pmatrix} 1 & 2 \\ 3 & 4 \end{pmatrix} \times \begin{pmatrix} 3 & 6 \\ 0 & 1 \end{pmatrix} = \begin{pmatrix} (1\times3)+(2\times0) & (1\times6)+(2\times1) \\ (3\times3)+(4\times0) & (3\times6)+(4\times1) \end{pmatrix} = \begin{pmatrix} 3 & 8 \\ 9 & 22 \end{pmatrix}$$

Vector addition and multiplication are performed in the same way, but there is only one column and one row.

Permutations and Combinations

Permutations and combinations are used to determine the number of possible outcomes in different situations. An arrangement, listing, or pattern in which order is important is called a permutation. The symbol P(6, 3) represents the number of permutations of 6 things taken 3 at a time. For P(6, 3), there are $6 \times 5 \times 4$ or 120 possible outcomes. An arrangement or listing where order is not important is called a combination. The symbol C(10, 5) represents the number of combinations of 10 things taken 5 at a time. For C(10, 5), there are $(10 \times 9 \times 8 \times 7 \times 6) \div (5 \times 4 \times 3 \times 2 \times 1)$ or 252 possible outcomes.

Powers and Exponents

An expression such as $3 \times 3 \times 3 \times 3$ can be written as a power. A power has two parts, a base and an exponent. $3 \times 3 \times 3 \times 3 = 3^4$. The base is the number that is multiplied (3). The exponent tells how many times the base is used as a factor (4 times). Numbers and variables can be written using exponents. For example, $8 \times 8 \times 8 \times m \times m \times m \times m \times m$ can be expressed $8^3 m^5$. Exponents also can be used with place value to express numbers in expanded form. Using this method, 1,462 can be written as $(1 \times 10^3) + (4 \times 10^2) + (6 \times 10^1) + (2 \times 10^0)$.

Squares and Square Roots

The square root of a number is one of two equal factors of a number. Every positive number has both a positive and a negative square root. For example, since $8 \times 8 = 64$, 8 is a square root of 64. Since $(-8) \times (-8) = 64$, -8 is also a square root of 64. The notation $\sqrt{}$ indicates the positive square root, $-\sqrt{}$ indicates the negative square root, and $\pm\sqrt{}$ indicates both square roots. For example, $\sqrt{81} = 9$, $-\sqrt{49} = -7$, and $\pm\sqrt{4} = \pm2$. The square root of a negative number is an imaginary number because any two factors of a negative number must have different signs, and are therefore not equivalent.

Math Appendix

Logarithm

A logarithm is the inverse of exponentiation. The logarithm of a number x in base b is equal to the number n. Therefore, $b^n = x$ and $\log_b x = n$. For example, $\log_4(64) = 3$ because $4^3 = 64$. The most commonly used bases for logarithms are 10, the common logarithm; 2, the binary logarithm; and the constant e, the natural logarithm (also called $ln(x)$ instead of $\log_e(x)$). Below is a list of some of the rules of logarithms that are important to understand if you are going to use them.

$$\log_b(xy) = \log_b(x) + \log_b(y)$$
$$\log_b(x/y) = \log_b(x) - \log_b(y)$$
$$\log_b(1/x) = -\log_b(x)$$
$$\log_b(x)y = y\log_b(x)$$

▶ Compute fluently and make reasonable estimates

Estimation by Rounding

When rounding numbers, look at the digit to the right of the place to which you are rounding. If the digit is 5 or greater, round up. If it is less than 5, round down. For example, to round 65,137 to the nearest hundred, look at the number in the tens place. Since 3 is less than 5, round down to 65,100. To round the same number to the nearest ten thousandth, look at the number in the thousandths place. Since it is 5, round up to 70,000.

Finding Equivalent Ratios

Equivalent ratios have the same meaning. Just like finding equivalent fractions, to find an equivalent ratio, multiply or divide both sides by the same number. For example, you can multiply 7 by both sides of the ratio 6:8 to get 42:56. Instead, you can also divide both sides of the same ratio by 2 to get 3:4. Find the simplest form of a ratio by dividing to find equivalent ratios until you can't go any further without going into decimals. So, 160:240 in simplest form is 2:3. To write a ratio in the form *1:n*, divide both sides by the left-hand number. In other words, to change 8:20 to *1:n*, divide both sides by 8 to get 1:2.5.

Front-End Estimation

Front-end estimation can be used to quickly estimate sums and differences before adding or subtracting. To use this technique, add or subtract just the digits of the two highest place values, and replace the other place values with zero. This will give you an estimation of the solution of a problem. For example, 93,471 − 22,825 can be changed to 93,000 − 22,000 or 71,000. This estimate can be compared to your final answer to judge its correctness.

Judging Reasonableness

When solving an equation, it is important to check your work by considering how reasonable your answer is. For example, consider the equation $9\frac{3}{4} \times 4\frac{1}{3}$. Since $9\frac{3}{4}$ is between 9 and 10 and $4\frac{1}{3}$ is between 4 and 5, only values that are between 9×4 or 36 and 10×5 or 50 will be reasonable. You can also use front-end estimation, or you can round and estimate a reasonable answer. In the equation 73×25, you can round and solve to estimate a reasonable answer to be near 70×30 or 2,100.

Algebra

▶ Understand patterns, relations, and functions

Relation

A relation is a generalization comparing sets of ordered pairs for an equation or inequality such as $x = y + 1$ or $x > y$. The first element in each pair, the x values, forms the domain. The second element in each pair, the y values, forms the range.

Function

A function is a special relation in which each member of the domain is paired with exactly one member in the range. Functions may be represented using ordered pairs, tables, or graphs. One way to determine whether a relation is a function is to use the vertical line test. Using an object to represent a vertical line, move the object from left to right across the graph. If, for each value of x in the domain, the object passes through no more than one point on the graph, then the graph represents a function.

Linear and Nonlinear Functions

Linear functions have graphs that are straight lines. These graphs represent constant rates of change. In other words, the slope between any two pairs of points on the graph is the same. Nonlinear functions do not have constant rates of change. The slope changes along these graphs. Therefore, the graphs of nonlinear functions are *not* straight lines. Graphs of curves represent nonlinear functions. The equation for a linear function can be written in the form $y = mx + b$, where m represents the constant rate of change, or the slope. Therefore, you can determine whether a function is linear by looking at the equation. For example, the equation $y = \frac{3}{x}$ is nonlinear because x is in the denominator and the equation cannot be written in the form $y = mx + b$. A nonlinear function does not increase or decrease at a constant rate. You can check this by using a table and finding the increase or decrease in y for each regular increase in x. For example, if for each increase in x by 2, y does not increase or decrease the same amount each time, the function is nonlinear.

Linear Equations in Two Variables

In a linear equation with two variables, such as $y = x - 3$, the variables appear in separate terms and neither variable contains an exponent other than 1. The graphs of all linear equations are straight lines. All points on a line are solutions of the equation that is graphed.

Quadratic and Cubic Functions

A quadratic function is a polynomial equation of the second degree, generally expressed as $ax^2 + bx + c = 0$, where a, b, and c are real numbers and a is not equal to zero. Similarly, a cubic function is a polynomial equation of the third degree, usually expressed as $ax^3 + bx^2 + cx + d = 0$. Quadratic functions can be graphed using an equation or a table of values. For example, to graph $y = 3x^2 + 1$, substitute the values −1, −0.5, 0, 0.5, and 1 for x to yield the point coordinates (−1, 4), (−0.5, 1.75), (0, 1), (0.5, 1.75), and (1, 4).

Math Appendix

Plot these points on a coordinate grid and connect the points in the form of a parabola. Cubic functions also can be graphed by making a table of values. The points of a cubic function from a curve. There is one point at which the curve changes from opening upward to opening downward, or vice versa, called the point of inflection.

Slope
Slope is the ratio of the rise, or vertical change, to the run, or horizontal change of a line: slope = rise/run. Slope (m) is the same for any two points on a straight line and can be found by using the coordinates of any two points on the line:

$$m = \frac{y_2 - y_1}{x_2 - x_1}, \text{ where } x_2 \neq x_1$$

Asymptotes
An asymptote is a straight line that a curve approaches but never actually meets or crosses. Theoretically, the asymptote meets the curve at infinity. For example, in the function $f(x) = \frac{1}{x}$, two asymptotes are being approached: the line $y = 0$ and $x = 0$. See the graph of the function below.

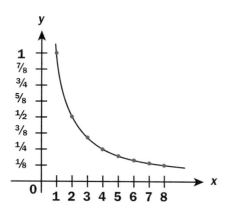

Represent and analyze mathematical situations and structures using algebraic symbols

Variables and Expressions
Algebra is a language of symbols. A variable is a placeholder for a changing value. Any letter, such as x, can be used as a variable. Expressions such as $x + 2$ and $4x$ are algebraic expressions because they represent sums and/or products of variables and numbers. Usually, mathematicians avoid the use of i and e for variables because they have other mathematical meanings ($i = \sqrt{-1}$ and e is used with natural logarithms). To evaluate an algebraic expression, replace the variable or variables with known values, and then solve using order of operations. Translate verbal phrases into algebraic expressions by first defining a variable: Choose a variable and a quantity for the variable to represent. In this way, algebraic expressions can be used to represent real-world situations.

Constant and Coefficient
A constant is a fixed value unlike a variable, which can change. Constants are usually represented by numbers, but they can also be represented by symbols. For example, π is a symbolic representation of the value 3.1415.… A coefficient is a constant by which a variable or other object is multiplied. For example, in the expression $7x^2 + 5x + 9$, the coefficient of x^2 is 7 and the coefficient of x is 5. The number 9 is a constant and not a coefficient.

Monomial and Polynomial
A monomial is a number, a variable, or a product of numbers and/or variables such as 3×4. An algebraic expression that

contains one or more monomials is called a polynomial. In a polynomial, there are no terms with variables in the denominator and no terms with variables under a radical sign. Polynomials can be classified by the number of terms contained in the expression. Therefore, a polynomial with two terms is called a binomial $(z^2 - 1)$, and a polynomial with three terms is called a trinomial $(2y^3 + 4y^2 - y)$. Polynomials also can be classified by their degrees. The degree of a monomial is the sum of the exponents of its variables. The degree of a nonzero constant such as 6 or 10 is 0. The constant 0 has no degree. For example, the monomial $4b^5c^2$ had a degree of 7. The degree of a polynomial is the same as that of the term with the greatest degree. For example, the polynomial $3x^4 - 2y^3 + 4y^2 - y$ has a degree of 4.

Equation

An equation is a mathematical sentence that states that two expressions are equal. The two expressions in an equation are always separated by an equal sign. When solving for a variable in an equation, you must perform the same operations on both sides of the equation in order for the mathematical sentence to remain true.

Solving Equations with Variables

To solve equations with variables on both sides, use the Addition or Subtraction Property of Equality to write an equivalent equation with the variables on the same side. For example, to solve $5x - 8 = 3x$, subtract $3x$ from each side to get $2x - 8 = 0$. Then add 8 to each side to get $2x = 8$. Finally, divide each side by 2 to find that $x = 4$.

Solving Equations with Grouping Symbols

Equations often contain grouping symbols such as parentheses or brackets. The first step in solving these equations is to use the Distributive Property to remove the grouping symbols. For example $5(x + 2) = 25$ can be changed to $5x + 10 = 25$, and then solved to find that $x = 3$.

Some equations have no solution. That is, there is no value of the variable that results in a true sentence. For such an equation, the solution set is called the null or empty set, and is represented by the symbol $\varnothing$ or {}. Other equations may have every number as the solution. An equation that is true for every value of the variable is called the identity.

Inequality

A mathematical sentence that contains the symbols $<$ (less than), $>$ (greater than), $\leq$ (less than or equal to), or $\geq$ (greater than or equal to) is called an inequality. For example, the statement that it is legal to drive 55 miles per hour or slower on a stretch of the highway can be shown by the sentence $s \leq 55$. Inequalities with variables are called open sentences. When a variable is replaced with a number, the inequality may be true or false.

Solving Inequalities

Solving an inequality means finding values for the variable that make the inequality true. Just as with equations, when you add or subtract the same number from each side of an inequality, the inequality remains true. For example, if you add 5 to each side of the inequality $3x < 6$, the resulting inequality $3x + 5 < 11$ is also true. Adding or subtracting the same number from each side of an inequality does not affect the inequality sign. When multiplying or dividing each side of an inequality by the same positive number, the inequality remains true. In such cases, the inequality symbol does not change. When multiplying or dividing each side of an inequality by a negative number, the inequality symbol must be reversed. For example, when dividing each side of the inequality $-4x \geq -8$ by -2, the inequality sign must be changed to $\leq$ for the resulting inequality, $2x \leq 4$, to be true. Since the solutions to an inequality include all rational numbers satisfying it, inequalities have an infinite number of solutions.

Representing Inequalities on a Number Line

The solutions of inequalities can be graphed on a number line. For example, if the solution of an inequality is $x < 5$, start an arrow at 5 on the number line, and continue the arrow to the left to show all values less than 5 as the solution. Put an open circle at 5 to show that the point 5 is *not* included in the graph. Use a closed circle when graphing solutions that are greater than or equal to, or less than or equal to, a number.

Order of Operations

Solving a problem may involve using more than one operation. The answer can depend on the order in which you do the operations. To make sure that there is just one answer to a series of computations, mathematicians have agreed upon an order in which to do the operations. First simplify within the parentheses, often called graphing symbols, and then evaluate any exponents. Then multiply and divide from left to

right, and finally add and subtract from left to right.

Parametric Equations

Given an equation with more than one unknown, a statistician can draw conclusions about those unknown quantities through the use of parameters, independent variables that the statistician already knows something about. For example, you can find the velocity of an object if you make some assumptions about distance and time parameters.

Recursive Equations

In recursive equations, every value is determined by the previous value. You must first plug an initial value into the equation to get the first value, and then you can use the first value to determine the next one, and so on. For example, in order to determine what the population of pigeons will be in New York City in three years, you can use an equation with the birth, death, immigration, and emigration rates of the birds. Input the current population size into the equation to determine next year's population size, then repeat until you have calculated the value for which you are looking.

▶ *Use mathematical models to represent and understand quantitative relationships*

Solving Systems of Equations

Two or more equations together are called a system of equations. A system of equations can have one solution, no solution, or infinitely many solutions. One method for solving a system of equations is to graph the equations on the same coordinate plane. The coordinates of the point where the graphs intersect is the solution. In other words, the solution of a system is the ordered pair that is a solution of all equations. A more accurate way to solve a system of two equations is by using a method called substitution. Write both equations in terms of y. Replace y in the first equation with the right side of the second equation. Check the solution by graphing. You can solve a system of three equations using matrix algebra.

Graphing Inequalities

To graph an inequality, first graph the related equation, which is the boundary. All points in the shaded region are solutions of the inequality. If an inequality contains the symbol $\leq$ or $\geq$, then use a solid line to indicate that the boundary is included in the graph. If an inequality contains the symbol $<$ or $>$, then use a dashed line to indicate that the boundary is not included in the graph.

▶ Analyze change in various contexts

Rate of Change

A change in one quantity with respect to another quantity is called the rate of change. Rates of change can be described using slope:

$$\text{slope} = \frac{\text{change in } y}{\text{change in } x}$$

You can find rates of change from an equation, a table, or a graph. A special type of linear equation that describes rate of change is called a direct variation. The graph of a direct variation always passes through the origin and represents a proportional situation. In the equation $y = kx$, k is called the constant of variation. It is the slope, or rate of change. As x increases in value, y increases or decreases at a constant rate k, or y varies directly with x. Another way to say this is that y is directly proportional to x. The direct variation $y = kx$ also can be written as $k = \frac{y}{x}$. In this form, you can see that the ratio of y to x is the same for any corresponding values of y and x.

Slope-Intercept Form

Equations written as $y = mx + b$, where m is the slope and b is the y-intercept, are linear equations in slope-intercept form. For example, the graph of $y = 5x - 6$ is a line that has a slope of 5 and crosses the y-axis at $(0, -6)$. Sometimes you must first write an equation in slope-intercept form before finding the slope and y-intercept. For example, the equation $2x + 3y = 15$ can be expressed in slope-intercept form by subtracting $2x$ from each side and then dividing by 3: $y = -\frac{2}{3}x + 5$, revealing a slope of $-\frac{2}{3}$ and a y-intercept of 5. You can use the slope-intercept form of an equation to graph a line easily. Graph the y-intercept and use the slope to find another point on the line, then connect the two points with a line.

Math Appendix

Geometry

▶ *Analyze characteristics and properties of two- and three-dimensional geometric shapes and develop mathematical arguments about geometric relationships*

Angles

Two rays that have the same endpoint form an angle. The common endpoint is called the vertex, and the two rays that make up the angle are called the sides of the angle. The most common unit of measure for angles is the degree. Protractors can be used to measure angles or to draw an angle of a given measure. Angles can be classified by their degree measure. Acute angles have measures less than 90° but greater than 0°. Obtuse angles have measures greater than 90° but less than 180°. Right angles have measures of 90°.

Triangles

A triangle is a figure formed by three line segments that intersect only at their endpoints. The sum of the measures of the angles of a triangle is 180°. Triangles can be classified by their angles. An acute triangle contains all acute angles. An obtuse triangle has one obtuse angle. A right triangle has one right angle. Triangles can also be classified by their sides. A scalene triangle has no congruent sides. An isosceles triangle has at least two congruent sides. In an equilateral triangle all sides are congruent.

Quadrilaterals

A quadrilateral is a closed figure with four sides and four vertices. The segments of a quadrilateral intersect only at their endpoints. Quadrilaterals can be separated into two triangles. Since the sum of the interior angles of all triangles totals 180°, the measures of the interior angles of a quadrilateral equal 360°. Quadrilaterals are classified according to their characteristics, and include trapezoids, parallelograms, rectangles, squares, and rhombuses.

Two-Dimensional Figures

A two-dimensional figure exists within a plane and has only the dimensions of length and width. Examples of two-dimensional figures include circles and polygons. Polygons are figures that have three or more angles, including triangles, quadrilaterals, pentagons, hexagons, and many more. The sum of the angles of any polygon totals at least 180° (triangle), and each additional side adds 180° to the measure of the first three angles. The sum of the angles of a quadrilateral, for example, is 360°. The sum of the angles of a pentagon is 540°.

Three-Dimensional Figures

A plane is a two-dimensional flat surface that extends in all directions. Intersecting planes can form the edges and vertices of three-dimensional figures or solids. A polyhedron is a solid with flat surfaces that are polygons.

Polyhedrons are composed of faces, edges, and vertices and are differentiated by their shape and by their number of bases. Skew lines are lines that lie in different planes. They are neither intersecting nor parallel.

Congruence

Figures that have the same size and shape are congruent. The parts of congruent triangles that match are called corresponding parts. Congruence statements are used to identify corresponding parts of congruent triangles. When writing a congruence statement, the letters must be written so that corresponding vertices appear in the same order. Corresponding parts can be used to find the measures of angles and sides in a figure that is congruent to a figure with known measures.

Similarity

If two figures have the same shape but not the same size they are called similar figures. For example, the triangles below are similar, so angles A, B, and C have the same measurements as angles D, E, and F, respectively. However, segments AB, BC, and CA do not have the same measurements as segments DE, EF, and FD, but the measures of the sides are proportional.

For example, $\dfrac{\overline{AB}}{\overline{DE}} = \dfrac{\overline{BC}}{\overline{EF}} = \dfrac{\overline{CA}}{\overline{FD}}$.

Solid figures are considered to be similar if they have the same shape and their corresponding linear measures are proportional. As with two-dimensional figures, they can be tested for similarity by comparing corresponding measures. If the compared ratios are proportional, then the figures are similar solids. Missing measures of similar solids can also be determined by using proportions.

The Pythagorean Theorem

The sides that are adjacent to a right angle are called legs. The side opposite the right angle is the hypotenuse.

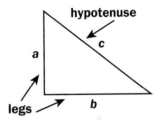

The Pythagorean Theorem describes the relationship between the lengths of the legs a and b and the hypotenuse c. It states that if a triangle is a right triangle, then the square of the length of the hypotenuse is equal to the sum of the squares of the lengths of the legs. In symbols, $c^2 = a^2 + b^2$.

Sine, Cosine, and Tangent Ratios

Trigonometry is the study of the properties of triangles. A trigonometric ratio is a ratio of the lengths of two sides of a right triangle. The most common trigonometric ratios are the sine, cosine, and tangent

Math Appendix

ratios. These ratios are abbreviated as *sin*, *cos*, and *tan*, respectively.

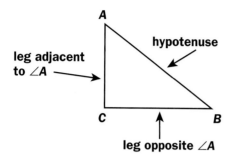

If ∠*A* is an acute angle of a right triangle, then

$$\sin \angle A = \frac{\text{measure of leg opposite } \angle A}{\text{measure of hypotenuse}},$$

$$\cos \angle A = \frac{\text{measure of leg adjacent to } \angle A}{\text{measure of hypotenuse}}, \text{ and}$$

$$\tan \angle A = \frac{\text{measure of leg opposite } \angle A}{\text{measure of leg adjacent to } \angle A}.$$

▶ *Specify locations and describe spatial relationships using coordinate geometry and other representational systems*

Polygons

A polygon is a simple, closed figure formed by three or more line segments. The line segments meet only at their endpoints. The points of intersection are called vertices, and the line segments are called sides. Polygons are classified by the number if sides they have. The diagonals of a polygon divide the polygon into triangles. The number of triangles formed is two less than the number of sides. To find the sum of the measures of the interior angles of any polygon, multiply the number of triangles within the polygon by 180. That is, if *n* equals the number of

sides, then (*n* − 2) 180 gives the sum of the measures of the polygon's interior angles.

Cartesian Coordinates

In the Cartesian coordinate system, the *y*-axis extends above and below the origin and the *x*-axis extends to the right and left of the origin, which is the point at which the *x*- and *y*-axes intersect. Numbers below and to the left of the origin are negative. A point graphed on the coordinate grid is said to have an *x*-coordinate and a *y*-coordinate. For example, the point (1,−2) has as its *x*-coordinate the number 1, and has as its *y*-coordinate the number −2. This point is graphed by locating the position on the grid that is 1 unit to the right of the origin and 2 units below the origin.

The *x*-axis and the *y*-axis separate the coordinate plane into four regions, called quadrants. The axes and points located on the axes themselves are not located in any of the quadrants. The quadrants are labeled I to IV, starting in the upper right and proceeding counterclockwise. In quadrant I, both coordinates are positive. In quadrant II, the *x*-coordinate is negative and the *y*-coordinate is positive. In quadrant III, both coordinates are negative. In quadrant IV, the *x*-coordinate is positive and the *y*-coordinate is negative. A coordinate graph can be used to show algebraic relationships among numbers.

▶ *Apply transformations and use symmetry to analyze mathematical situations*

Similar Triangles and Indirect Measurement

Triangles that have the same shape but not necessarily the same dimensions are called similar triangles. Similar triangles have corresponding angles and corresponding sides. Arcs are used to show congruent angles. If two triangles are similar, then the corresponding angles have the same measure, and the corresponding sides are proportional. Therefore, to determine the measures of the sides of similar triangles when some measures are known, proportions can be used.

Transformations

A transformation is a movement of a geometric figure. There are several types of transformations. In a translation, also called a slide, a figure is slid from one position to another without turning it. Every point of the original figure is moved the same distance and in the same direction. In a reflection, also called a flip, a figure is flipped over a line to form a mirror image. Every point of the original figure has a corresponding point on the other side of the line of symmetry. In a rotation, also called a turn, a figure is turned around a fixed point. A figure can be rotated 0°–360° clockwise or counterclockwise. A dilation transforms each line to a parallel line whose length is a fixed multiple of the length of the original line to create a similar figure that will be either larger or smaller.

▶ *Use visualizations, spatial reasoning, and geometric modeling to solve problems*

Two-Dimensional Representations of Three-Dimensional Objects

Three-dimensional objects can be represented in a two-dimensional drawing in order to more easily determine properties such as surface area and volume. When you look at the triangular prism, you can see the orientation of its three dimensions, length, width, and height. Using the drawing and the formulas for surface area and volume, you can easily calculate these properties.

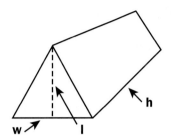

Another way to represent a three-dimensional object in a two-dimensional plane is by using a net, which is the unfolded representation. Imagine cutting the vertices of a box until it is flat then drawing an outline of it. That's a net. Most objects have more than one net, but any one can be measured to determine surface area. Below is a cube and one of its nets.

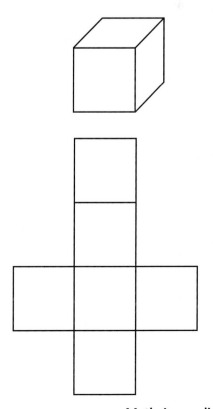

Math Appendix

Measurement

▶ *Understand measurable attributes of objects and the units, systems, and processes of measurement*

Customary System
The customary system is the system of weights and measures used in the United States. The main units of weight are ounces, pounds (1 equal to 16 ounces), and tons (1 equal to 2,000 pounds). Length is typically measured in inches, feet (1 equal to 12 inches), yards (1 equal to 3 feet), and miles (1 equal to 5,280 feet), while area is measured in square feet and acres (1 equal to 43,560 square feet). Liquid is measured in cups, pints (1 equal to 2 cups), quarts (1 equal to 2 pints), and gallons (1 equal to 4 quarts). Finally, temperature is measured in degrees Fahrenheit.

Metric System
The metric system is a decimal system of weights and measurements in which the prefixes of the words for the units of measure indicate the relationships between the different measurements. In this system, the main units of weight, or mass, are grams and kilograms. Length is measured in millimeters, centimeters, meters, and kilometers, and the units of area are square millimeters, centimeters, meters, and kilometers. Liquid is typically measured in milliliters and liters, while temperature is in degrees Celsius.

Selecting Units of Measure
When measuring something, it is important to select the appropriate type and size of unit. For example, in the United States it would be appropriate when describing someone's height to use feet and inches. These units of height or length are good to use because they are in the customary system, and they are of appropriate size. In the customary system, use inches, feet, and miles for lengths and perimeters; square inches, feet, and miles for area and surface area; and cups, pints, quarts, gallons or cubic inches and feet (and less commonly miles) for volume. In the metric system use millimeters, centimeters, meters, and kilometers for lengths and perimeters; square units millimeters, centimeters, meters, and kilometers for area and surface area; and milliliters and liters for volume. Finally, always use degrees to measure angles.

▶ *Apply appropriate techniques, tools, and formulas to determine measurements*

Precision and Significant Digits
The precision of measurement is the exactness to which a measurement is made. Precision depends on the smallest unit of measure being used, or the precision unit. One way to record a measure is to estimate to the nearest precision unit. A more precise method is to include all of the digits that are actually measured, plus one estimated digit. The digits recorded, called significant digits, indicate the precision of the measurement. There are special rules for determining significant digits. If a number contains a decimal point, the number of significant digits is found by counting from left to right, starting with the first nonzero digit.

If the number does not contain a decimal point, the number of significant digits is found by counting the digits from left to right, starting with the first digit and ending with the last nonzero digit.

Surface Area

The amount of material needed to cover the surface of a figure is called the surface area. It can be calculated by finding the area of each face and adding them together. To find the surface area of a rectangular prism, for example, the formula $S = 2lw + 2lh + 2wh$ applies. A cylinder, on the other hand, may be unrolled to reveal two circles and a rectangle. Its surface area can be determined by finding the area of the two circles, $2\pi r^2$, and adding it to the area of the rectangle, $2\pi rh$ (the length of the rectangle is the circumference of one of the circles), or $S = 2\pi r^2 + 2\pi rh$. The surface area of a pyramid is measured in a slightly different way because the sides of a pyramid are triangles that intersect at the vertex. These sides are called lateral faces and the height of each is called the slant height. The sum of their areas is the lateral area of a pyramid. The surface area of a square pyramid is the lateral area $\frac{1}{2}bh$ (area of a lateral face) times 4 (number of lateral faces), plus the area of the base. The surface area of a cone is the area of its circular base (πr^2) plus its lateral area (πrl, where l is the slant height).

Volume

Volume is the measure of space occupied by a solid region. To find the volume of a prism, the area of the base is multiplied by the measure of the height, $V = Bh$. A solid containing several prisms can be broken down into its component prisms. Then the volume of each component can be found and the volumes added. The volume of a cylinder can be determined by finding the area of its circular base, πr^2, and then multiplying by the height of the cylinder. A pyramid has one-third the volume of a prism with the same base and height. To find the volume of a pyramid, multiply the area of the base by the pyramid's height, and then divide by 3. Simply stated, the formula for the volume of a pyramid is $V = \frac{1}{3}bh$. A cone is a three-dimensional figure with one circular base and a curved surface connecting the base and the vertex. The volume of a cone is one-third the volume of a cylinder with the same base area and height. Like a pyramid, the formula for the volume of a cone is $V = \frac{1}{3}bh$. More specifically, the formula is $V = \frac{1}{3}\pi r^2 h$.

Upper and Lower Bounds

Upper and lower bounds have to do with the accuracy of a measurement. When a measurement is given, the degree of accuracy is also stated to tell you what the upper and lower bounds of the measurement are. The upper bound is the largest possible value that a measurement could have had before being rounded down, and the lower bound is the lowest possible value it could have had before being rounded up.

Data Analysis and Probability

▶ *Formulate questions that can be addressed with data and collect, organize, and display relevant data to answer them*

Histograms

A histogram displays numerical data that have been organized into equal intervals using bars that have the same width and no space between them. While a histogram does not give exact data points, its shape shows the distribution of the data. Histograms also can be used to compare data.

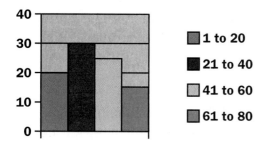

Box-and-Whisker Plot

A box-and-whisker plot displays the measures of central tendency and variation. A box is drawn around the quartile values, and whiskers extend from each quartile to the extreme data points. To make a box plot for a set of data, draw a number line that covers the range of data. Find the median, the extremes, and the upper and lower quartiles. Mark these points on the number line with bullets, then draw a box and the whiskers. The length of a whisker or box shows whether the values of the data in that part are concentrated or spread out.

Scatter Plots

A scatter plot is a graph that shows the relationship between two sets of data. In a scatter plot, two sets of data are graphed as ordered pairs on a coordinate system. Two sets of data can have a positive correlation (as x increases, y increases), a negative correlation (as x increases, y decreases), or no correlation (no obvious pattern is shown). Scatter plots can be used to spot trends, draw conclusions, and make predictions about data.

Randomization

The idea of randomization is a very important principle of statistics and the design of experiments. Data must be selected randomly to prevent bias from influencing the results. For example, you want to know the average income of people in your town but you can only use a sample of 100 individuals to make determinations about everyone. If you select 100 individuals who are all doctors, you will have a biased sample. However, if you chose a random sample of 100 people out of the phone book, you are much more likely to accurately represent average income in the town.

Statistics and Parameters

Statistics is a science that involves collecting, analyzing, and presenting data. The data can be collected in various ways—for example through a census or by making physical measurements. The data can then be analyzed by creating summary statistics, which have to do with the distribution of the data sample, including the mean, range, and standard error. They can also be illustrated in tables and graphs, like box-plots, scatter plots, and histograms. The presentation of the data typically involves describing the strength or validity of the data and what they show. For example, an analysis of ancestry of people in a city might tell you something about immigration patterns, unless the data set is very small or biased in some way, in which case it is not likely to be very accurate or useful.

Categorical and Measurement Data

When analyzing data, it is important to understand if the data is qualitative or quantitative. Categorical data is qualitative and measurement, or numerical, data is quantitative. Categorical data describes a quality of something and can be placed into different categories. For example, if you are analyzing the number of students in different grades in a school, each grade is a category. On the other hand, measurement data is continuous, like height, weight, or any other measurable variable. Measurement data can be converted into categorical data if you decide to group the data. Using height as an example, you can group the continuous data set into categories like under 5 feet, 5 feet to 5 feet 5 inches, over 5 feet five inches to 6 feet, and so on.

Univariate and Bivariate Data

In data analysis, a researcher can analyze one variable at a time or look at how multiple variables behave together. Univariate data involves only one variable, for example height in humans. You can measure the height in a population of people then plot the results in a histogram to look at how height is distributed in humans. To summarize univariate data, you can use statistics like the mean, mode, median, range, and standard deviation, which is a measure of variation. When looking at more than one variable at once, you use multivariate data. Bivariate data involves two variables. For example, you can look at height and age in humans together by gathering information on both variables from individuals in a population. You can then plot both variables in a scatter plot, look at how the variables behave in relation to each other, and create an equation that represents the relationship, also called a regression. These equations could help answer questions such as, for example, does height increase with age in humans?

▶ Select and use appropriate statistical methods to analyze data

Measures of Central Tendency

When you have a list of numerical data, it is often helpful to use one or more numbers to represent the whole set. These numbers are called measures of central tendency. Three measures of central tendency are mean, median, and mode. The mean is the sum of the data divided by the number of items in the data set. The median is the middle number of the ordered data (or the mean of the two middle numbers). The mode is the number or numbers that occur most often. These measures of central tendency allow data to be analyzed and better understood.

Measures of Spread
In statistics, measures of spread or variation are used to describe how data are distributed. The range of a set of data is the difference between the greatest and the least values of the data set. The quartiles are the values that divide the data into four equal parts. The median of data separates the set in half. Similarly, the median of the lower half of a set of data is the lower quartile. The median of the upper half of a set of data is the upper quartile. The interquartile range is the difference between the upper quartile and the lower quartile.

Line of Best Fit
When real-life data are collected, the points graphed usually do not form a straight line, but they may approximate a linear relationship. A line of best fit is a line that lies very close to most of the data points. It can be used to predict data. You also can use the equation of the best-fit line to make predictions.

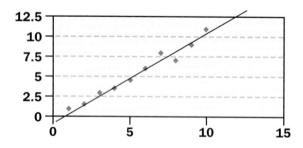

Stem and Leaf Plots
In a stem and leaf plot, numerical data are listed in ascending or descending order. The greatest place value of the data is used for the stems. The next greatest place value forms the leaves. For example, if the least number in a

set of data is 8 and the greatest number is 95, draw a vertical line and write the stems from 0 to 9 to the left of the line. Write the leaves from to the right of the line, with the corresponding stem. Next, rearrange the leaves so they are ordered from least to greatest. Then include a key or explanation, such as 1|3 = 13. Notice that the stem-and-leaf plot below is like a histogram turned on its side.

```
0|8
1|3 6
2|5 6 9
3|0 2 7 8
4|0 1 4 7 9
5|1 4 5 8
6|1 3 7
7|5 8
8|2 6
9|5
```
Key: **1|3 = 13**

▶ *Develop and evaluate inferences and predictions that are based on data*

Sampling Distribution
The sampling distribution of a population is the distribution that would result if you could take an infinite number of samples from the population, average each, and then average the averages. The more normal the distribution of the population, that is, how closely the distribution follows a bell curve, the more likely the sampling distribution will also follow a normal distribution. Furthermore, the larger the sample, the more likely it will accurately represent the entire population. For instance, you are more likely to gain more representative results from a population of 1,000 with a sample of 100 than with a sample of 2.

Validity

In statistics, validity refers to acquiring results that accurately reflect that which is being measured. In other words, it is important when performing statistical analyses, to ensure that the data are valid in that the sample being analyzed represents the population to the best extent possible. Randomization of data and using appropriate sample sizes are two important aspects of making valid inferences about a population.

▶ Understand and apply basic concepts of probability

Complementary, Mutually Exclusive Events

To understand probability theory, it is important to know if two events are mutually exclusive, or complementary: the occurrence of one event automatically implies the non-occurrence of the other. That is, two complementary events cannot both occur. If you roll a pair of dice, the event of rolling 6 and rolling doubles have an outcome in common (3, 3), so they are not mutually exclusive. If you roll (3, 3), you also roll doubles. However, the events of rolling a 9 and rolling doubles are mutually exclusive because they have no outcomes in common. If you roll a 9, you will not also roll doubles.

Independent and Dependent Events

Determining the probability of a series of events requires that you know whether the events are independent or dependent. An independent event has no influence on the occurrence of subsequent events, whereas, a dependent event does influence subsequent events. The chances that a woman's first child will be a girl are $\frac{1}{2}$,
and the chances that her second child will be a girl are also $\frac{1}{2}$ because the two events are independent of each other. However, if there are 7 red marbles in a bag of 15 marbles, the chances that the first marble you pick will be red are $\frac{7}{15}$ and if you indeed pick a red marble and remove it, you have reduced the chances of picking another red marble to $\frac{6}{14}$.

Sample Space

The sample space is the group of all possible outcomes for an event. For example, if you are tossing a single six-sided die, the sample space is {1, 2, 3, 4, 5, 6}. Similarly, you can determine the sample space for the possible outcomes of two events. If you are going to toss a coin twice, the sample space is {(heads, heads), (heads, tails), (tails, heads), (tails, tails)}.

Computing the Probability of a Compound Event

If two events are independent, the outcome of one event does not influence the outcome of the second. For example, if a bag contains 2 blue and 3 red marbles, then the probability of selecting a blue marble, replacing it, and then selecting a red marble is $P(A) \times P(B) = \frac{2}{5} \times \frac{3}{5}$ or $\frac{6}{25}$.

If two events are dependent, the outcome of one event affects the outcome of the second. For example, if a bag contains 2 blue and 3 red marbles, then the probability of selecting a blue and then a red marble without replacing the first marble is $P(A) \times P(B$ following $A) = \frac{2}{5} \times \frac{3}{4}$ or $\frac{3}{10}$. Two events that cannot happen at the same time are mutually exclusive. For example, when you roll two number cubes, you cannot roll a sum that is both 5 and even. So, $P(A$ or $B) = \frac{4}{36} + \frac{18}{36}$ or $\frac{11}{18}$.

Career Appendix

MAKING CAREER CHOICES

A career differs from a job in that it is a series of progressively more responsible jobs in one field or a related field. You will need to learn some special skills to choose a career and to help you in your job search. Choosing a career and identifying career opportunities require careful thought and preparation. To aid you in making important career choices, follow these steps:

STEPS TO MAKING A CAREER DECISION

1. Conduct a self-assessment to determine your:
   - values
   - lifestyle goals
   - interests
   - skills and aptitudes
   - personality
   - work environment preferences
   - relationship preferences
2. Identify possible career choices based on your self-assessment.
3. Gather information on each choice, including future trends.
4. Evaluate your choices based on your self-assessment.
5. Make your decision.

After you make your decision, plan how you will reach your goal. It is best to have short-term, medium-term, and long-term goals. In making your choices, explore the future opportunities in this field or fields over the next several years. What impact will new technology and automation have on job opportunities in the next few years? Remember, if you plan, you make your own career opportunities.

PERSONAL CAREER PORTFOLIO

You will want to create and maintain a personal career portfolio. In it you will keep all the documents you create and receive in your job search:

- Contact list
- Résumé
- Letters of recommendation
- Employer evaluations
- Awards
- Evidence of participation in school, community, and volunteer activities
- Notes about your job search
- Notes made after your interviews

CAREER RESEARCH RESOURCES

In order to gather information on various career opportunities, there are a variety of sources to research:

- **Libraries.** Your school or public library offers good career information resources. Here you will find books, magazines, pamphlets, films, videos, and special reference materials on careers.

In particular, the U.S. Department of Labor publishes three reference books that are especially helpful: the *Dictionary of Occupational Titles (DOT)*, which describes about 20,000 jobs and their relationships with data, people, and things; the *Occupational Outlook Handbook (OOH)*, with information on more than 200 occupations; and the *Guide for Occupational Exploration (GOE)*, a reference that organizes the world of work into 12 interest areas that are subdivided into work groups and subgroups.

- **The Internet.** The Internet is becoming a primary source of research on any topic. It is especially helpful in researching careers.

- **Career Consultations.** Career consultation, an informational interview with a professional who works in a career that interests you, provides an opportunity to learn about the day-to-day realities of a career.

- **On-the-Job Experience.** On-the-job experience can be valuable in learning firsthand about a job or career. You can find out if your school has a work-experience program, or look into a company or organization's internship opportunities. Interning gives you direct work experience and often allows you to make valuable contacts for future full-time employment.

THE JOB SEARCH

To aid you in your actual job search, there are various sources to explore. You should contact and research all the sources that might produce a job lead, or information about a job. Keep a contact list as you proceed with your search. Some of these resources include:

- **Networking with family, friends, and acquaintances.** This means contacting people you know personally, including school counselors, former employers, and professional people.

- **Cooperative education and work-experience programs.** Many schools have such programs in which students work part-time on a job related to one of their classes. Many also offer work-experience programs that are not limited to just one career area, such as marketing.

- **Newspaper ads.** Reading the Help Wanted advertisements in your local papers will provide a source of job leads, as well as teach you about the local job market.

- **Employment agencies.** Most cities have two types of employment agencies, public and private. These employment agencies match workers with jobs. Some private agencies may charge a fee, so be sure to know who is expected to pay the fee and what the fee is.

- **Company personnel offices.** Large and medium-sized companies have personnel offices to handle employment matters, including the hiring of new workers. You can check on job openings by contacting the office by telephone or by scheduling a personal visit.

- **Searching the Internet.** Cyberspace offers multiple opportunities for your job search. Web sites, such as Hotjobs.com or Monster.com, provide lists of companies offering employment. There are tens of thousands of career-related Web sites, so the challenge is finding those that have jobs that interest you and that are up-to-date in their listings. Companies that interest you may have a Web site, which will provide valuable information on their benefits and opportunities for employment.

APPLYING FOR A JOB

When you have contacted the sources of job leads and found some jobs that interest you, the next step is to apply for them. You will need to complete application forms, write letters of application, and prepare your own résumé. Before you apply for a job, you will need to have a work permit if you are under the age of 18 in most states. Some state and federal labor laws designate certain jobs as too dangerous for young workers. Laws also limit the number of hours of work allowed during a day, a week, or the school year. You will also need to have proper documentation, such as a green card if you are not a U.S. citizen.

JOB APPLICATION

You can obtain the job application form directly at the place of business, by requesting it in writing, or over the Internet. It is best if you can fill the form out at home, but some businesses require that you fill it out at the place of work.

Fill out the job application forms neatly and accurately, using standard English, the formal style of speaking and writing you learned in school. You must be truthful and pay attention to detail in filling out the form.

PERSONAL FACT SHEET

To be sure that the answers you write on a job application form are accurate, make a personal fact sheet before filling out the application:

- Your name, home address, and phone number
- Your Social Security number
- The job you are applying for
- The date you can begin work
- The days and hours you can work
- The pay you want
- Whether or not you have been convicted of a crime
- Your education
- Your previous work experience
- Your birth date
- Your driver's license number if you have one
- Your interests and hobbies, and awards you have won
- Your previous work experience, including dates
- Schools you have attended
- Places you have lived
- Accommodations you may need from the employer
- A list of references—people who will tell an employer that you will do a good job, such as relatives, students, former employers, and the like

LETTERS OF RECOMMENDATION

Letters of recommendation are helpful. You can request teachers, counselors, relatives, and other acquaintances who know you well to write these letters. They should be short, to the point, and give a brief overview of your assets. A brief description of any of your important accomplishments or projects should follow. The letter should end with a brief description of your character and work ethic.

LETTER OF APPLICATION

Some employees prefer a letter of application, rather than an application form. This letter is like writing a sales pitch about yourself. You need to tell why you are the best person for the job, what special qualifications you have, and include all the information usually found on an application form. Write the letter in standard English, making certain that it is neat, accurate, and correct.

RÉSUMÉ

The purpose of a résumé is to make an employer want to interview you. A résumé tells prospective employers what you are like and what you can do for them. A good résumé summarizes you at your best in a one- or two-page outline. It should include the following information:

1. **Identification.** Include your name, address, telephone number, and e-mail address.

2. **Objective.** Indicate the type of job you are looking for.

3. **Experience.** List experience related to the specific job for which you are applying. List other work if you have not worked in a related field.

4. **Education.** Include schools attended from high school on, the dates of attendance, and diplomas or degrees earned. You may also include courses related to the job you are applying for.

5. **References.** Include up to three references or indicate that they are available. Always ask people ahead of time if they are willing to be listed as references for you.

A résumé that you put online or send by e-mail is called an *electronic résumé*. Some Web sites allow you to post them on their sites without charge. Employers access these sites to find new employees. Your electronic résumé should follow the guidelines for a regular one. It needs to be accurate. Stress your skills and sell yourself to prospective employers.

COVER LETTER

If you are going to get the job you want, you need to write a great cover letter to accompany your résumé. Think of a cover letter as an introduction: a piece of paper that conveys a smile, a confident hello, and a nice, firm handshake. The cover letter is the first thing a potential employer sees, and it can make a powerful impression. The following are some tips for creating a cover letter that is professional and gets the attention you want:

- **Keep it short.** Your cover letter should be one page, no more.
- **Make it look professional.** These days, you need to type your letter on a computer and print it on a laser printer. Do not use an inkjet printer unless it produces extremely crisp type. Use white or buff-colored paper; anything else will draw the wrong kind of attention. Type your name, address, phone number, and e-mail address at the top of the page.
- **Explain why you are writing.** Start your letter with one sentence describing where you heard of the opening. "Joan Wright suggested I contact you regarding a position in your marketing department," or "I am writing to apply for the position you advertised in the Sun City Journal."
- **Introduce yourself.** Give a short description of your professional abilities and background. Refer to your attached résumé: "As you will see in the attached résumé, I am an experienced editor with a background in newspapers, magazines, and textbooks." Then highlight one or two specific accomplishments.
- **Sell yourself.** Your cover letter should leave the reader thinking, "This person is exactly what we are looking for." Focus on what you can do for the company. Relate your skills to the skills and responsibilities mentioned in the job listing. If the ad mentions solving problems, relate a problem you solved at school or work. If the ad mentions specific skills or knowledge required, mention your mastery of these in your letter. (Also be sure these skills are included on your résumé.)
- **Provide all requested information.** If the Help Wanted ad asked for "salary requirements" or "salary history," include this information in your cover letter. However, you do not have to give specific numbers. It is okay to say, "My wage is in the range of $10 to $15 per hour." If the employer does not ask for salary information, do not offer any.

- **Ask for an interview.** You have sold yourself, now wrap it up. Be confident, but not pushy. "If you agree that I would be an asset to your company, please call me at [insert your phone number]. I am available for an interview at your convenience." Finally, thank the person. "Thank you for your consideration. I look forward to hearing from you soon." Always close with a "Sincerely," followed by your full name and signature.

- **Check for errors.** Read and re-read your letter to make sure each sentence is correctly worded and there are no errors in spelling, punctuation, or grammar. Do not rely on your computer's spell checker or grammar checker. A spell check will not detect if you typed "tot he" instead of "to the." It is a good idea to have someone else read your letter, too. He or she might notice an error you overlooked.

 ## INTERVIEW

Understanding how to best prepare for and follow up on interviews is critical to your career success. At different times in your life, you may interview with a teacher or professor, a prospective employer, a supervisor, or a promotion or tenure committee. Just as having an excellent résumé is vital for opening the door, interview skills are critical for putting your best foot forward and seizing the opportunity to clearly articulate why you are the best person for the job.

RESEARCH THE COMPANY

Your ability to convince an employer that you understand and are interested in the field you are interviewing to enter is important. Show that you have knowledge about the company and the industry. What products or services does the company offer? How is it doing? What is the competition? Use your research to demonstrate your understanding of the company.

PREPARE QUESTIONS FOR THE INTERVIEWER

Prepare interview questions to ask the interviewer. Some examples include:

- "What would my responsibilities be?"
- "Could you describe my work environment?"
- "What are the chances to move up in the company?"
- "Do you offer training?"
- "What can you tell me about the people who work here?"

DRESS APPROPRIATELY

You will never get a second chance to make a good first impression. Nonverbal communication is 90 percent of communication, so dressing appropriately is of the utmost importance. Every job is different, and you should wear clothing that is appropriate for the job for which you are applying. In most situations, you will be safe if you wear clean, pressed, conservative business clothes in neutral colors. Pay special attention to grooming. Keep makeup light and wear very little jewelry. Make certain your nails and hair are clean, trimmed, and neat. Do not carry a large purse, backpack, books, or coat. Simply carry a pad of paper, a pen, and extra copies of your résumé and letters of reference in a small folder.

EXHIBIT GOOD BEHAVIOR

Conduct yourself properly during an interview. Go alone; be courteous and polite to everyone you meet. Relax and focus on your purpose: to make the best possible impression.

- Be on time.
- Be poised and relaxed.
- Avoid nervous habits.
- Avoid littering your speech with verbal clutter such as "you know," "um," and "like."
- Look your interviewer in the eye and speak with confidence.
- Use nonverbal techniques to reinforce your confidence, such as a firm handshake and poised demeanor.
- Convey maturity by exhibiting the ability to tolerate differences of opinion.
- Never call anyone by a first name unless you are asked to do so.
- Know the name, title, and the pronunciation of the interviewer's name.
- Do not sit down until the interviewer does.
- Do not talk too much about your personal life.
- Never bad-mouth your former employers.

BE PREPARED FOR COMMON INTERVIEW QUESTIONS

You can never be sure exactly what will happen at an interview, but you can be prepared for common interview questions. There are some interview questions that are illegal. Interviewers should not ask you about your age, gender, color, race, or religion. Employers should not ask whether you are married or pregnant, or question your health or disabilities.

Take time to think about your answers now. You might even write them down to clarify your thinking. The key to all interview questions is to be honest, and to be positive. Focus your answers on skills and abilities that apply to the job you are seeking. Practice answering the following questions with a friend:

- "Tell me about yourself."
- "Why do you want to work at this company?"
- "What did you like/dislike about your last job?"
- "What is your biggest accomplishment?"
- "What is your greatest strength?"
- "What is your greatest weakness?"
- "Do you prefer to work with others or on your own?"
- "What are your career goals?" or "Where do you see yourself in five years?"
- "Tell me about a time that you had a lot of work to do in a short time. How did you manage the situation?"
- "Have you ever had to work closely with a person you didn't get along with? How did you handle the situation?"

AFTER THE INTERVIEW

Be sure to thank the interviewer after the interview for his or her time and effort. Do not forget to follow up after the interview. Ask, "What is the next step?" If you are told to call in a few days, wait two or three days before calling back.

If the interview went well, the employer may call you to offer you the job. Find out the terms of the job offer, including job title and pay. Decide whether you want the job. If you decide not to accept the job, write a letter of rejection. Be courteous and thank the person for the opportunity and the offer. You may wish to give a brief general reason for not accepting the job. Leave the door open for possible employment in the future.

FOLLOW UP WITH A LETTER

Write a thank-you letter as soon as the interview is over. This shows your good manners, interest, and enthusiasm for the job. It also shows that you are organized. Make the letter neat and courteous. Thank the interviewer. Sell yourself again.

ACCEPTING A NEW JOB

If you decide to take the job, write a letter of acceptance. The letter should include some words of appreciation for the opportunity, written acceptance of the job offer, the terms of employment (salary, hours, benefits), and the starting date. Make sure the letter is neat and correct.

STARTING A NEW JOB

Your first day of work will be busy. Determine what the dress code is and dress appropriately. Learn to do each task assigned properly. Ask for help when you need it. Learn the rules and regulations of the workplace.

You will do some paperwork on your first day. Bring your personal fact sheet with you. You will need to fill out some forms. Form W-4 tells your employer how much money to withhold for taxes. You may also need to fill out Form I-9. This shows that you are allowed to work in the United States. You will need your Social Security number and proof that you are allowed to work in the United States. You can bring your U.S. passport, your Certificate of Naturalization, or your Certificate of U.S. Citizenship. If you are not a permanent resident of the United States, bring your green card. If you are a resident of the United States, you will need to bring your work permit on your first day. If you are under the age of 16 in some states, you need a different kind of work permit.

You might be requested to take a drug test as a requirement for employment in some states. This could be for the safety of you and your coworkers, especially when working with machinery or other equipment.

IMPORTANT SKILLS AND QUALITIES

You will not work alone on a job. You will need to learn skills for getting along and being a team player. There are many good qualities necessary to get along in the workplace. They include being positive, showing sympathy, taking an interest in others, tolerating differences, laughing a little, and showing respect. Your employer may promote you or give you a raise if you show good employability skills.

There are several qualities necessary to be a good employee and get ahead in your job:

- be cooperative
- possess good character
- be responsible
- finish what you start
- work fast but do a good job

- have a strong work ethic
- work well without supervision
- work well with others
- possess initiative
- show enthusiasm for what you do
- be on time
- make the best of your time
- obey company laws and rules
- be honest
- be loyal
- exhibit good health habits

LEAVING A JOB

If you are considering leaving your job or are being laid off, you are facing one of the most difficult aspects in your career. The first step in resigning is to prepare a short resignation letter to offer your supervisor at the conclusion of the meeting you set up with him or her. Keep the letter short and to the point. Express your appreciation for the opportunity you had with the company. Do not try to list all that was wrong with the job.

You want to leave on good terms. Do not forget to ask for a reference. Do not talk about your employer or any of your coworkers. Do not talk negatively about your employer when you apply for a new job.

If you are being laid off or face downsizing, it can make you feel angry or depressed. Try to view it as a career-change opportunity. If possible, negotiate a good severance package. Find out about any benefits you may be entitled to. Perhaps the company will offer job-search services or consultation for finding new employment.

⬤ TAKE ACTION!

It is time for action. Remember the networking and contact lists you created when you searched for this job. Reach out for support from friends, family, and other acquaintances. Consider joining a job-search club. Assess your skills. Upgrade them if necessary. Examine your attitude and your vocational choices. Decide the direction you wish to take and move on!

Glossary

How to Use This Glossary

- Content vocabulary terms in this glossary are words that relate to this book's content. They are **highlighted yellow** in your text.

- Words in this glossary that have an asterisk (*) are academic vocabulary terms. They help you understand your school subjects and are used on tests. They are **boldfaced blue** in your text.

- Some of the vocabulary words in this book include pronunciation symbols to help you sound out the words. Use the pronunciation key to help you pronounce the words.

Pronunciation Key

a . . . . at	ô . . . . fork, all	th . . . thin
ā . . . . ape	oo . . . wood, put	th . . . this
ä . . . . father	ōō . . . fool	zh . . . treasure
e . . . . end	oi . . . oil	ə . . . . ago, taken, pencil, lemon, circus
ē . . . . me	ou . . . out	' . . . . indicates primary stress
i . . . . it	u . . . . up	(symbol in front of and *above* letter)
ī . . . . ice	ū . . . . use	ˌ . . . . indicates secondary stress
o . . . . hot	ü . . . . rule	(symbol in front of and *below* letter)
ō . . . . hope	u . . . . pull	
ȯ . . . . saw	ŋ . . . . sing	

A

*abbreviation A shortened form of a written word or phrase used in place of the whole. (p. 501)

abstinence ('ab-stə-nən(t)s) The decision to avoid high-risk behaviors, including sexual activity and the use of tobacco, alcohol, and other drugs. (p. 63)

*acceptance To acknowledge as satisfactory; to approve. (p. 60)

accessory An interesting item added to make a space or outfit more personal. (p. 297)

*accommodation The providing of what is needed or desired for convenience; adaptation; adjustment. (p. 170)

*accomplish To bring about a result by effort; to succeed in reaching; to achieve. (p. 121)

acne A common skin condition that occurs when pores are clogged with oil, dead skin cells, and bacteria. (p. 19)

acquaintance (ə-kwān-tᵊn(t)s) A person one greets or meets fairly often, but with whom one does not have a close relationship. (p. 53)

*adapt To change; to modify; to adjust. (p. 41)

addiction A person's physical or mental dependence on a drug or other substance. (p. 63)

*adequate Enough to meet a need or to qualify for something. (p. 421)

adolescence (a-də-'le-sᵊn(t)s) The period of great growth and change between childhood and adulthood. (p. 16)

*advance Before a deadline or an anticipated event; ahead of time. (p. 45)

Glossary

advertisement A message that persuades consumers to buy a product or service. (p. 236)

aerobic (ˌer-ˈō-bik) Continuous, rhythmic activities that improve heart and lung efficiency. (p. 447)

alteration A change made to clothing, often to modify the style and give it a fresh, new look. (p. 328)

*alternate Not the same as; distinct; different. (p. 267)

alternative A choice between two or more different things or actions. (p. 124)

amino acid The building block that makes up proteins. (p. 423)

analogous (ə-ˈna-lə-gəs) Alike; comparable; equivalent; similar. (p. 337)

anorexia nervosa (ˌa-nə-ˌrek-sē-ə (ˌ) nər-ˈvō-sə) An eating disorder in which a person feels an extreme fear of gaining weight and severely limits eating. (p. 455)

antioxidant (ˌan-tē-ˈäk-sə-dənt) A substance that protect cells and the immune system from damage by harmful chemicals. (p. 515)

appetite The desire to eat. (p. 422)

appetizer A dish served before a meal. (p. 489)

*appreciate To value or admire highly; to be thankful for. (p. 215)

apprentice Someone who works under the guidance of a skilled professional in order to learn an art, craft, or trade. (p. 142)

aptitude A natural talent or ability for something. (p. 140)

*assemble To bring together; to convene. (p. 500)

assertive Able to express one's views clearly and respectfully in a positive way. (p. 64)

attention span The length of time during which one is able to concentrate or remain interested. (p. 200)

attitude The way one feels about something. (p. 120)

autocratic leader Leader who takes complete control of projects, activities, and decisions. (p. 107)

B

batter A liquid or semiliquid mixture, usually containing flour, milk, and eggs. (p. 518)

benefit Help; useful aid; advantage. (p. 54)

bias A line diagonal to the grain of a fabric. (p. 393)

binge eating An eating disorder in which a person eats large quantities of food at one time. (p. 456)

biodegradable Able to be broken down and absorbed by the environment. (p. 314)

blend Two or more fibers combined to create a fabric. (p. 347)

body language Nonverbal communication through gestures, facial expressions, behaviors, and posture. (p. 78)

brand name A trademark used by a manufacturer to identify its products. (p. 356)

*brittle Easy to break; fragile; weak. (p. 428)

budget The amount of money that is available for or assigned to a particular purpose; a plan for using one's money. (p. 250)

bulimia nervosa (bü-ˈlē-mē-ə (ˌ) nər-ˈvō-sə) An eating disorder in which a person eats very large amounts of food and then vomits or uses laxatives to get rid of the eaten food. (p. 456)

bully A person who physically or verbally abuses someone with the intent to cause injury or discomfort. (p. 65)

C

calorie A unit that measures the energy used by the body and the energy that food supplies to the body. (p. 422)

carbohydrate (ˌkär-bō-ˈhī-ˌdrāt) Any starch or sugar that provides the body with energy. (p. 424)

casing A fabric tunnel made to enclose elastic or a drawstring. (p. 403)

Glossary

casserole A mix of food cooked and served in a covered pot or dish. (p. 520)

cavity An area of decay in a tooth. (p. 20)

child abuse Physical, emotional, or sexual injury to children. (p. 190)

child neglect Failure to meet a child's physical and emotional needs. (p. 190)

childproof Made safe for children to play and explore. (p. 209)

cholesterol (kə-'les-tə-ˌrōl) The waxy substance contained in saturated animal fats. (p. 425)

citizen A member of a community such as a city, state, or country. (p. 97)

citizenship The way one handles one's responsibilities as a citizen. (p. 98)

color scheme A system of arranging colors in a pleasing manner. (p. 294)

colorfast Able to keep its original color through many washings. (p. 355)

*commitment An agreement or pledge to do something in the future; a promise. (p. 185)

communication The process of sending and receiving messages about ideas, feelings, and information. (p. 77)

comparison shopping Evaluating similar items to check quality and price. (p. 244)

*complement To complete or go well with something else. (p.491)

complementary (ˌkäm-plə-'men-t(ə-)rē) Contrasting or opposite colors. (p. 337)

*component Ingredient; element; part. (p. 430)

comprehend To grasp the nature, significance, or meaning of; to understand. (p.160)

compromise ('käm-prə-ˌmīz) An agreement in which each person gives up something in order to reach a solution that satisfies everyone. (p. 56)

*conduct The act, manner, or process of carrying on. (p. 478)

cone A cylinder used to hold large spools of thread. (p. 407)

*confide To tell secrets to; to trust. (p. 56)

conflict A disagreement or struggle between two or more people. (p. 84)

consequence (ˌkän(t)-sə-ˈkwen(t)s) The result of a choice. (p. 126)

conservation The saving of resources. (p. 307)

*consistent Reacting the same way to a situation each time it occurs; free from variation; regular; steady. (p. 190)

constructive criticism Helpful advice meant to help one grow and improve. (p. 11)

consumer A person who buys goods and services. (p. 235)

contamination Becoming infected with harmful bacteria. (p. 469)

convection oven An oven having a fan that circulates hot air evenly and continuously around food. (p. 481)

convenience food Food already prepared or partially prepared to save time. (p. 516)

*convenient Suited to personal comfort or to efficient performance; easier to manage. (p. 283)

cooperative play Playing together with one or two other children and sharing toys. (p. 201)

*coordinate To make suitable for fitting together; to mix and match; to harmonize. (p. 360)

*coordination The harmonious functioning of parts for effective results; movement. (p. 199)

*cope To adjust to difficult and stressful situations. (p. 269)

*credit Honor; praise or recognition; acknowledgment. (p. 151)

credit A method of payment allowing one to buy now and pay later. (p. 251)

*crucial Very important; significant; essential. (p. 511)

culture Ways of thinking, acting, dressing, and speaking shared by a group of people. (p. 8)

curdle To separate into little particles or curds. (p. 521)

D

*dart A tapered, V-shaped seam used to give shape to a garment. (p. 379)

decision Something that one chooses or makes up one's mind about after thinking over all possible choices. (p. 123)

decompose To break down and become part of the soil. (p. 312)

*delegate To assign responsibility or authority; to hand over. (p. 104)

democratic leader A leader who involves everyone in the decision-making process. (p. 107)

dermatologist A doctor who treats skin disorders. (p. 19)

design principle A rule that directs how the elements of design are organized. (p. 295)

design The art of combining elements in a pleasing way. (p. 293)

*determine To come to a decision by investigation, reasoning, or calculation; to figure out. (p. 396)

developmental task An achievement expected at specific ages and stages of growth. (p. 194)

diabetes A condition in which the body cannot control blood sugar properly. (p. 434)

diplomacy (də-'plō-mə-sē) The ability to be honest without being hurtful; tact. (p. 82)

disability A permanent or temporary physical, mental, or emotional condition. (p. 44)

discipline ('di-sə-'plən) The task of teaching a child which behaviors are acceptable and which are not. (p. 190)

discrimination (dis-,kri-mə-'nā-shən) The unfair treatment of people based on age, gender, race, or religion. (p. 169)

*dispose To throw away; to get rid of. (p. 312)

diverse Made up of many different parts. (p. 55)

divorce The legal end to a marriage. (p. 43)

*durability Ability to exist for a long time without significant damage or wear. (p. 20)

E

E. coli The most deadly form of food poisoning, found in contaminated water, raw or rare ground beef, and unpasteurized milk. (p. 469)

ease The amount of fullness added to clothing for movement and comfort. (p. 396)

eating disorders An extreme eating behavior that can lead to depression, anxiety, and even death. (p. 455)

*economize To save money. (p. 491)

*efficient Productive without waste; effective. (p. 308)

*elect To select by vote for an office, position, or membership; to choose. (p. 104)

*element Portion; aspect; part. (p. 293)

emphasis Special weight placed upon something considered important; stress; accent. (p. 295)

employability skill A skill which helps one function in life and at work. (p. 159)

*endorse To approve openly; to recommend. (p. 236)

energy The power or ability to be active. (p. 261)

*enrich To make better by the addition of some desirable quality or ingredient; to improve. (p. 33)

*entitled Having a right or claim to something; allowed to expect. (p. 97)

entrepreneur (,äⁿn-trə-p(r)ə-'nər) A person who starts and runs his or her own business. (p. 151)

environment The conditions by which one is surrounded. (p. 31)

equivalent Something which has equal value as something else. (p. 490)

*escalate To increase in number, amount, or intensity; to get worse. (p. 85)

Glossary

*essential Of the utmost importance; absolutely necessary; fundamental; vital. (p. 163)

*exchange The act of giving or taking one thing in return for another; a trade; sharing. (p. 80)

expectation A person's idea about what should be or should not be. (p. 57)

*expend To make use of for a specific purpose; utilize. (p. 453)

expenses The goods and services on which one spends one's money. (p. 250)

*expire To come to an end; to conclude. (p. 247)

F

fad A fashion that is very popular for a short time. (p. 328)

fad diet A diet which promises quick weight loss through unrealistic or unhealthful means. (p. 453)

fashion A style of clothing that is popular at a particular time. (p. 328)

*fast To stop eating. (p. 454)

feed dog The part of the sewing machine that positions the fabric for the next stitch. (p. 400)

feedback Evaluative or corrective information about an action, event, or process; a response. (p. 80)

fiber (1) A tiny strand or thread, many of which combine to make fabric; (2) Plant material that one's body cannot digest. (pp. 347, 424)

fitness The ability to handle daily events in a healthy way. (p. 445)

flammable Capable of burning easily. (p. 476)

*flexible The body's ability to kneel, bend, turn, and throw. (p.447)

flexibility The ability to adjust to new conditions. (p. 170)

floor plan A drawing of a room and how its furniture is arranged. (p. 284)

foodborne illness An illness caused by unsafe food; food poisoning. (p. 469)

fossil fuel A fuel, such as coal, oil, or natural gas, which comes from the remains of prehistoric plants and animals. (p. 306)

franchise ('fran-ˌchīz) An agreement or license to sell a company's products or to operate a business that carries that company's name. (p. 151)

functional Useful and convenient. (p. 284)

G

garnish A small amount of a food or seasoning, such as parsley, lemon wedges, orange slices, or paprika, used to decorate food. (p. 491)

gesture ('jes-chər) The use of body movements to communicate meaning or emotion. (p. 78)

goal Something one wants to achieve or accomplish. (p. 117)

gossip To talk to people about someone else's personal life or private business. (p. 81)

grade labeling A measurement of food quality using standards set by the government. (p. 494)

grain The direction the threads run in a fabric. (p. 347)

grooming The things one does to care for one's physical appearance. (p. 19)

guarantee ('gär-ən-tē) A manufacturer's written promise to repair or replace a product if it does not work as claimed. (p. 245)

guidance Direction caregivers need to give children so they can learn basic rules for behavior. (p. 188)

guide sheet A set of step-by-step instructions for sewing a pattern. (p. 394)

H

harassment Offensive behavior which violates people's rights; uninvited and unwelcome verbal or physical behavior. (p. 170)

*hazard Something that is potentially dangerous. (p.476)

hem An edge made by folding fabric over and stitching it down. (p. 374)

heredity (hə-'re-də-tē) The passing on of traits, or characteristics and qualities, from parents to their children. (p. 8)

hue Colors, the three basic of which are red, yellow, and blue. (p. 334)

hygiene Keeping oneself clean. (p. 19)

I

*imitate To follow as a pattern, model, or example; to copy. (p. 222)

impulse buying Making a sudden decision to buy something one did not plan to purchase. (p. 242)

incineration The disposal of waste by burning. (p. 312)

income The amount of money one earns or receives regularly. (p. 250)

independent play Playing alone and showing little interest in interacting with others. (p. 200)

ingredient A part of a combination or mixture; a recipe component. (p.499)

*integrity Sticking to a code of moral values; honor and truthfulness. (p. 127)

intensity The brightness or dullness of a color. (p. 334)

interfacing Fabric sewn between two layers of a garment for strength or to prevent stretching around necklines, closures, and buttonholes. (p. 384)

interlock To lock together; to form closely fitted stitches. (p. 272)

intruder Someone who uses force to get into a home. (p. 210)

*inventory An itemized list; a summary. (p. 330)

J

jealousy When a person feels unhappy about someone else's possessions, accomplishments, or luck. (p. 58)

job satisfaction A feeling of accomplishment from a job well done. (p. 146)

job shadowing Spending time with someone to observe him or her on the job. (p. 141)

K

*key Important; fundamental; necessary. (p. 305)

knit fabric Stretchy fabric made by looping threads together. (p. 347)

L

landfill A large pit where waste is buried between layers of earth. (p. 312)

layout A diagram of how pattern pieces should be placed on fabric. (p. 394)

leader A person with the ability to guide and motivate others. (p. 104)

leadership The direction or guidance that helps a group accomplish its goals. (p. 104)

legume The fruit or seed of plants, such as peas or beans, used for food. (p. 523)

long-term goal A goal that may take months or even years to reach. (p. 117)

looper The rounded part that holds the thread inside a serger. (p. 407)

M

management The skillful use of resources to accomplish a task. (p. 259)

marking Symbols located on pattern pieces. (p. 394)

*material Things which are not necessary for survival like food, shelter, and water, but which can make life easier and more enjoyable. (p. 262)

meal patterns Habits that determine when and what people eat each day. (p. 490)

media A form of conveyance or expression; communication that advertisers use. (p. 237)

mentor Someone with experience who supports, advises, and encourages the progress of a less experienced person. (p. 143)

*merchandise Products available to buy. (p. 243)

mineral An element needed in small amounts for sturdy bones and teeth, healthy blood, and regular elimination of body wastes. (p. 428)

Glossary

*minimize To reduce; to decrease. (p. 469)

modesty The belief about the proper way to cover the body with clothes. (p. 327)

*modify To make different; to change; to alter. (p. 139)

monitor To watch carefully over someone or something. (p. 210)

monochromatic (mä-nə-krō-'ma-tik) Having or consisting of one color or hue. (p. 337)

motivate To make someone feel enthusiastic, interested, and committed to a project or task. (p. 104)

multi-tasking Doing more than one job at the same time. (p. 265)

MyPyramid A colorful representation of how to make healthful food choices and increase physical activity. (p. 430)

N

nap A fabric with a one-way texture, such as corduroy. (p. 382)

natural fiber Fibers, such as cotton, linen, silk, and wool, which are made from plant and animal products. (p. 347)

natural resource A material that is supplied by nature. (p. 305)

negotiation (ni-,go-shē-'a-shən) The process of talking about a conflict and deciding how to reach a compromise. (p. 87)

networking Using personal connections to help achieve one's goals. (p. 142)

*neutral Not engaged on either side; indifferent. (p. 87)

*notice Warning of something; an announcement. (p. 173)

notions Additional materials needed to complete a sewing project, such as thread and buttons. (p. 379)

nutrient ('nü-trē-ənt) A substance in food that is important for the body's growth and maintenance. (p. 421)

O

obesity A condition in which a person's weight is 20 percent or more above his or her healthy weight. (p. 452)

*obtain To gain or attain usually by planned action or effort; to reach. (p. 447)

omelet A well-beaten egg that is first cooked in a frying pan without stirring, then topped with other ingredients, such as mushrooms, peppers, and cheese, and finally folded over. (p. 523)

*operate To perform a function; to work. (p. 373)

*opinion A view or judgment formed in the mind about a particular matter. (p. 22)

orientation (,ȯr-ē-ən-'tā-shən) A meeting during which an employee is given details about pay, benefits, and job expectations, and is often given a tour as well. (p. 167)

osteoporosis (,as-tē-ō-pə-'ro-səs) A condition in which bones gradually lose their mineral content and become weak. (p. 426)

*outcome Something that follows as a result or consequence. (p. 124)

*outline A line that marks the outer limits of an object or figure; boundary; shape; form. (p. 293)

P

parenting The process of caring for children and helping them to grow and learn. (p. 185)

pattern A plan for making a garment or project. (p. 378)

peer A person of the same age. (p. 56)

peer mediation A process in which peers help other students find a solution to a conflict before it becomes more serious. (p. 88)

peer pressure The influence one feels to go along with the behavior of one's peers. (p. 60)

perception (pər-'sep-shən) Using one's senses to get information about one's environment. (p. 80)

perishable Likely to spoil quickly. (p. 470)

***permanent** Continuing without change; lasting; long-term. (p. 314)

***persuade** To move by argument to a belief, position, or course of action; to convince. (p. 160)

pollution The changing of air, water, and land from clean and safe to dirty and unsafe. (p. 305)

portfolio A neatly organized collection of one's skills, experiences, and qualifications. (p. 140)

portion An appropriate amount of food for one person. (p. 430)

***potent** Having force, authority, or influence; powerful. (p. 261)

***potential** Best chance for success; existing in possibility; capable of development into actuality. (p. 14)

***precaution** A measure taken beforehand to prevent harm or secure good; safety measure. (p. 209)

prejudice ('pre-jə-dəs) An opinion about people that is formed without facts or knowledge. (p. 84)

***pressed** Smoothed; ironed. (p. 359)

***primary** Basic; fundamental. (p. 334)

priority Something ranked high in importance. (p. 120)

proactive Thinking ahead about possible decisions or problems and taking action right away. (p. 124)

processed Changed from raw form before being sold; subjected to a special treatment. (p. 513)

procrastinate (prə-ˌkras-tə-ˌnāt) To wait until the last minute to do something; to put off. (p. 267)

produce Fruits and vegetables. (p. 513)

***product** The result of something; item; merchandise; output. (p. 409)

promotion A move into a job with more responsibility. (p. 172)

***promptly** Readily; quickly; immediately. (p. 470)

proportion The relation of one part to another. (p. 295)

protein A type of nutrient that is needed to build, repair, and maintain body cells and tissues. (p. 423)

Q

quiche (ˌkēsh) A main-dish pie filled with eggs, cheese, and other ingredients such as ham, spinach, and mushrooms. (p. 523)

quick bread Bread in which the leavening agent is baking powder or baking soda. (p. 518)

R

ravel When loose threads pull out of the cut edge of fabric. (p. 382)

***raw** Not being in a polished or processed form; unfinished. (p. 374)

recipe A list of directions for preparing a specific food. (p. 499)

recycling Turning waste items into products that can be used. (p. 312)

redirect To change the course or direction of; to turn attention to something else. (p. 222)

reference A responsible adult who can tell an employer about one's character and quality of work. (p. 164)

***refined** Chemically processed to remove impurities. (p. 435)

refusal skills Communication tools that can help one say no when one feels pushed to take part in activities that are unsafe, unhealthful, or that go against one's values. (p. 61)

***reinforce** To strengthen by additional assistance, material, or support. (p. 384)

reliable Able to be counted on; dependable. (p. 217)

***reserved** Restrained in words and actions; shy; less expressive. (p. 32)

resign To decide to leave a job; to give up one's position; to quit. (p. 172)

***resist** To place opposite or against something; to fight; to oppose. (p. 61)

Glossary

resource • strategy

resource Something or someone that is a source of help or information. (p. 261)

*respect Value; high or special regard. (p. 11)

responsible Dependable; making wise choices. (p. 38)

*restrict To confine within boundaries; to restrain; to limit. (p. 211)

*result Consequence; end product; outcome; conclusion; effect. (p. 407)

résumé ('re-zə-‚mā) A document which summarizes one's qualifications, work experience, education, and interests. (p. 165)

*retain To hold secure or intact; to keep. (p. 520)

*reveal To open up to view; to display; to show. (p. 140)

*routine Habitual; mechanical; established; regular. (p. 286)

rumor A statement spread from one person to another without knowing whether or not it is true. (p. 81)

S

salmonella (‚sal-mə-'ne-lə) Bacteria often found in raw or undercooked foods, such as meat, eggs, fish, and poultry. (p. 469)

scald To bring slowly to a temperature just below boiling point. (p. 521)

*seasonal Foods more readily available and less expensive at certain times of the year. (p. 513)

self-actualization (self-‚ak-ch(ə-w)ə-lə-'zā-shən) Reaching one's full potential. (p. 14)

self-concept A mental picture of oneself. (p. 10)

self-esteem A sense of confidence and self-worth. (p. 11)

selvage The tightly woven edge of the fabric that has no visible loose threads. (p. 393)

*sequence Order of succession; continuity of progression; order. (p. 194)

*service Work performed for others. (p. 235)

sew-through button A button, used when the joined materials need to lie flat, which has two or four holes through it and no loop on the back. (p. 406)

shade The dark value of a hue. (p. 334)

shank button A button, used with thick fabrics, which has a stem on the back. (p. 406)

shelter A structure built to protect people from weather and extreme temperatures. (p. 283)

shoplifting Taking items from a store without paying for them. (p. 247)

short-term goal A goal that can be reached quickly, perhaps in a few days or weeks. (p. 117)

sibling A brother or a sister. (p. 33)

sign language A system of hand signs used by or for people who have hearing impairments. (p. 78)

*signal To show, communicate, or indicate. (p. 78)

*slant To take a diagonal course; to slope; to angle. (p. 347)

sodium A mineral that helps regulate the amount of fluid in our bodies. (p. 436)

soil The loose material in which plants grow. (p. 306)

stamina The ability to focus on or perform a single activity for a long time. (p. 447)

static cling When electricity builds up in the dryer and causes clothing to stick to itself or to one's body. (p. 358)

*status Rank in relation to others; position in society. (p. 327)

staystitch A row of stitching made very near the seamline within the seam allowance. (p. 400)

stereotype An idea about the qualities or behavior of a certain group. (p. 32)

*strategy A careful plan or method; a way to prepare. (p. 353)

stress The body's reaction to changes around it. (p. 268)

style The distinctive quality or form of something; the design of a garment. (p. 328)

synthetic fiber Fibers, such as rayon, nylon, and polyester, which are made from manufactured substances. (p. 347)

T

tail chain A length of thread shaped like a chain, made by pressing on the presser foot without placing fabric under the needle. (p. 409)

teamwork When a group works together to reach a goal. (p. 108)

*technology A manner of accomplishing a task using specialized processes, methods, or knowledge; equipment and machinery. (p. 150)

*tender Easily crushed, chewed, or cut; fragile. (p. 519)

texture (1) The feel and appearance of a fabric's surface; (2) The way something feels when touched or tasted. (pp. 339, 491)

*thrive To survive and improve; to prosper; to flourish. (p. 100)

time management The development of practices and skills that increase how quickly and effectively one can do something. (p. 265)

tint The light value of a hue. (p. 334)

trade-off Something that one gives up in order to get something else. (p. 120)

tradition A custom or belief. (p. 32)

traffic pattern The path people take to move around within a room as well as enter and exit the room. (p. 284)

*transfer To move to a different place; to shift; to convey. (p. 398)

trend A temporary fashion or product; a current style or preference. (p. 236)

U

unit pricing The cost of a product per unit. (p. 494)

utensil A tool or container used in a household, especially a kitchen; cookware. (p. 480)

V

*value Relative lightness or darkness of a color; luminosity. (p. 334)

vegetarian A person who does not eat meat; one whose diet consisting wholly of vegetables, fruits, grains, nuts, and sometimes eggs or dairy products. (p. 492)

vitamin A substance that is needed in small quantities to help regulate body functions. (p. 425)

volunteer To give one's time and energy without pay to help others. (p. 98)

W

wellness One's best level of health; the quality or state of being in good health. (p. 421)

whole grain Foods that contain the entire edible grain (p. 424)

work ethic A personal commitment to doing one's very best. (p. 172)

*worth The value of something measured by its qualities. (p. 120)

woven fabric Fabric made by interlacing lengthwise and crosswise yarns, which are several fibers twisted together, on a loom. (p. 348)

Y

yeast bread Bread in which the leavening agent is yeast. (p. 518)

Index

Index

E

E. coli, 469
Early childhood, nutrition requirements for, 431
Ease (sewing), 396, 403
Eating. *See* Diet
Eating disorders, 455–457
Eating disorders therapist, 458
Eating out, 436–437
Ecologist, 316
Education, as personal resource, 261
Eggs, 523
Elastic, 384–385
Election clerk, 110
Electric shocks, 478
Electrical appliance safety, 290
Electronic media, for advertising, 238
Elementary school teacher, 46
Emergency medical technician (EMT), 128
Emergency room nurse, 128
Emotion(s), 16
Emotional changes, 16
Emotional decisions, 124
Emotional development, 196
Emotional needs, 187
Emphasis, in design, 295
Employability skills, 159–163
Employment service careers, 152
EMT (emergency medical technician), 128
Encouragement, 104
Energy
  and clothes drying, 359
  conservation, 307–308
  as personal resource, 261
  as resource, 306
Enthusiasm, 11
Entrepreneur, 149, 151
Environment (home)
  and family, 31
  and personal development, 7-8
Environment (natural), 304–317
  careers in, 316
  conservation, 307–308
  natural resources, 305–306
  protecting, 309–315
  waste management, 312–315
Environmental analyst, 316
Environmental studies careers, 316
Equivalent foods, 490
Escape route, 289
Etiquette, 100–101
Exchanges, of merchandise, 247–248
Exercise, 444–450
  for anger control, 85
  choosing a routine, 449

and physical activity, 447–450
  walking as, 446
Exercise physiologist, 458
Expectations
  for children, 194
  differences in, 57–58
  and job research, 141
Expenses, 250
Experiences, and personal development, 7
Extended family, 31
Eye contact, 79

F

Fabric
  careers in, 362
  finishes, 349
  grain, 348–349, 393
  Kente cloth, 337
  muslin, 382
  preparation for sewing, 393
  recognizing quality in, 347–349
  selection of, 382–383
  weaves, 348
Fabric designer, 362
Fabric grain, 393
Fabric inspector, 362
Fabric store manager, 362
Fabric weaves, 348
Facings, 404
FACS (Family and Consumer Sciences) teacher, 410
Factory outlets, 243
Fad diets, 453–454
Fads, 328
Failure, 121
Fair Labor Standards Act (FLSA), 163
Falls
  child safety, 211
  in kitchen, 475
  safety rules at home, 288
Family(-ies), 30–47
  activities, 34
  changes in, 40–41, 43–45
  changing roles within, 41, 43–44
  characteristics of, 30–39
  death in, 44
  disability, 44
  divorce, 43
  getting along with, 35
  illness, 44
  job loss, 44
  life cycle of, 41
  older relatives, 37
  parents, 36
  and personal development, 7, 8

as personal resource, 262
  relationships within, 33–37
  remarriage, 43
  responsibilities within, 38–39
  rights of members, 36
  sharing space, 35–36
  siblings, 37
  structures of, 31
  uniqueness of each, 32
Family and Consumer Sciences (FACS) teacher, 410
Family, Career and Community Leaders of America. *See* FCCLA
Family counselor, 46
Family health careers, 46
Family practitioner, 46
Farmer, 524
Fashion, 328. *See also* Clothing
Fashion careers, 340, 410
Fashion coordinator, 340
Fashion designer, 340
Fasteners, for sewing, 384
Fasting, 454
Fats, 424, 434
FCCLA (Family, Career and Community Leaders of America), 106, 143
Feed dog, 400, 408
Feedback, 80
Feng shui, 296
Fiber
  cloth, 347
  dietary, 424
Finance careers, 252
Finances. *See* Money management
Financial Literacy
  appliances and energy use, 484
  babysitting income, 217
  best buys, 501
  career goals, 130
  cell phone costs, 81
  clothing costs, 360
  clothing stocks, 342
  college costs, 204
  communication with shoppers, 92
  comparing nonprofits, 112
  comparison shopping, 26, 300, 412, 440
  cutting energy costs, 314
  employee benefits, 154
  entertainment budget, 68
  estimation of costs, 388
  exercise class costs, 447
  exercising inexpensively, 460
  family entertainment costs, 48
  financial document organization, 274
  fun for less, 48
  overtime pay, 176

Index

Index

Index

Credits